THE CLUBS

Wul gori-yi-mar – football for all Aboriginal people 1996
Ginger Riley

THE CLUBS

THE COMPLETE HISTORY OF EVERY CLUB IN THE VFL/AFL

VIKING

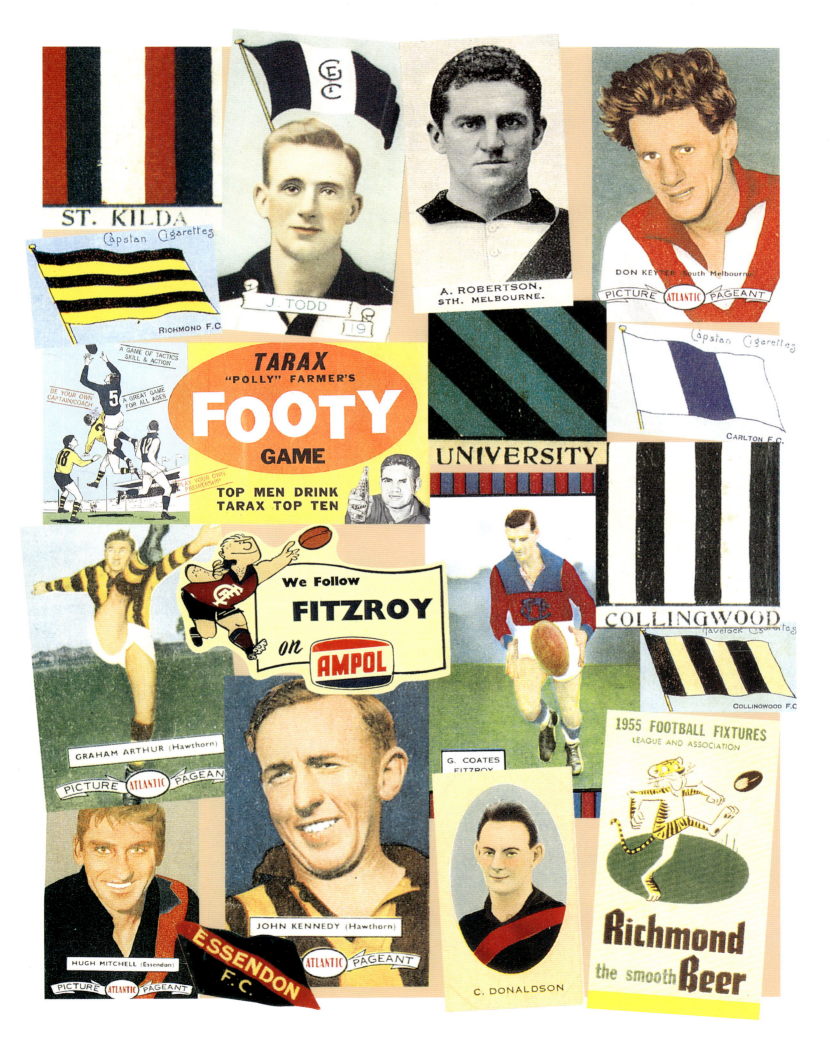

Viking
Penguin Books Australia Ltd
487 Maroondah Highway, PO Box 257
Ringwood, Victoria 3134, Australia
Penguin Books Ltd
Harmondsworth, Middlesex, England
Viking Penguin, A Division of Penguin Books USA Inc.
375 Hudson Street, New York, New York 10014, USA
Penguin Books Canada Limited
10 Alcorn Avenue, Toronto, Ontario, Canada M4V 3B2
Penguin Books (N.Z.) Ltd
Cnr Rosedale and Airborne Roads, Albany, Auckland, New Zealand

First published by Penguin Books Australia Ltd, 1998

10 9 8 7 6 5 4 3 2 1

Copyright © Penguin Books Australia Ltd, 1998

All rights reserved. Without limiting the rights under copyright reserved above, no part of this publication may be reproduced, stored in or introduced into a retrieval system, or transmitted, in any form or by any means (electronic, mechanical, photocopying, recording or otherwise), without the prior written permission of both the copyright owner and the above publisher of this book.

Cover design by George Dale, Penguin Design Studio
Design by Phil Campbell Design
Typeset in Bembo 10 point
Printed by South China Printing Co Ltd, Hong Kong

National Library of Australia
Cataloguing-in-Publication data:

The Clubs: the complete history of every club in the VFL/AFL

Includes index.
ISBN 0 670 87858 8

1. Victorian Football League - History. 2. Australian Football League - History. 3. Australian football teams - History. 3. Australian football teams - History. I. Ross, John, 1938–. II Hutchinson, Garrie, 1949–

796.3360994

FOREWORD

We can argue that Australian football is the greatest spectator sport in the world, and we are entitled to be passionate about the game and to put its greatest exponents – past and present – among the nation's sporting heroes.

Clubs, however, are the foundation of the whole game, the tribal bases which attract our heartfelt allegiance and support. Most of the millions of supporters who go to matches, watch them on TV or listen on the radio each week, are caught up in the emotional business of barracking for a club, wearing the colours, roaring their support and following the team's fortunes week by week.

There have never been any barriers in football, and it is a part of the easygoing and democratic Australian scene. It is a game that puts everybody – battlers and millionaires; men, women and children; old Australians and people from different national backgrounds – on the same footing. If their clubs win, they have that warm feeling of success. If they lose, they are downcast – until next time.

Similarly, the expanded and hugely popular AFL season has a basis of equality. The days of the 'chopping block' teams are over, thanks to the draft system, and a team that languished at the bottom last season might be vying for the Premiership the next. St Kilda and the Western Bulldogs showed this in season 1997, and who knows which clubs will be at the top in 1998? The new equality of clubs has added to the excitement of our game in the increasing number of close finishes in matches, as against the all too regular 'boilovers' of the 70s and 80s.

Despite the heartaches of club dislocation, the AFL has succeeded in expanding the game throughout Australia and making it our premier sport. It has ensured its future as a game of national and increasingly global significance, rather than one in danger of retreating into the southern corners of the southern continent. The establishment of AFL clubs in five States has brought new excitement to the game, spicing the passions of club loyalty with interstate rivalry and introducing a host of new supporters to the game. Clubs need no extra incentive to succeed – the whole ethos of every club is built around growth and success – but if any were needed it would be the desire to keep the Premiership Flag inside State borders.

Seasons 1998 and beyond carry several certainties – that the clubs will be forever trying for victory, for a place in the Eight and a run at the Premiership, that the supporters will remain as fiercely loyal and as vocal as ever (one hopes with the sporting instincts that are a part of the game) and that the game will continue to grow and be enjoyed by millions.

WAYNE JACKSON
CHIEF EXECUTIVE OFFICER
AUSTRALIAN FOOTBALL LEAGUE

The Clubs

was produced by Ross, Hutchinson and Associates for Penguin Books Australia Limited.

Managing Editors: Garrie Hutchinson and John Ross

Deputy Editor: Margaret Geddes

Production Editor: Peter Ascot

Editor: Vanessa Richards

Editorial assistance: Patrick Witton, Alex Hutchinson, Sarah Ross

Index: Fay Donlevy

Editorial services: Donlevy and associates

Photography: Sporting Pix

Design: Phil Campbell

Writers: David Allen, Darren Arthur, David Austin, Peter Blucher, Damien Cash, Rohan Connolly, Gerald Dowling, Les Everitt, Margaret Geddes, Bob Gordon, Russell Holmesby, Col Hutchinson, Garrie Hutchinson, Rick Lang, Ashley Porter, Michael Roberts, John Ross, Ray Stevens, Gary Stocks, Kevin Taylor

Acknowledgements:

Ross, Hutchinson and Associates, and the club writers, wish to thank the following people and organisations for their assistance with the project: Bette Hughson, Dave Scott, Graeme Atkinson, Fitzroy Historical Association, David Gale (Fitzroy), Kerri Cuman, Lynda Carroll, Craig Cameron (Melbourne), Bruce Kennedy, Stephen Rodgers, Col Hutchinson (Sydney, South Melbourne), Bruce Postle (photography), Katherine Ryan and Paul Rovere (the Age Pictorial Library), David Studham (The MCC Library); Gregor McCaskie, (The Australian Gallery of Sport) ; The MCC Museum (Kristin Thornton, Graeme Atkinson), Stephen Gough, Lisa King and Grant Shallard (Carlton), Tony Feder, Kerryn Feder, Stuart Milligan (Sporting Pix), City of Boroondara Library, Peter Habey, Professor James Griffin, Philip, Geraldine and James Mustey (Hawthorn); Scharlaine Cairns (Footscray), Bob Gordon (West Coast and Fremantle) Bill Meaklim, Ron Reiffel, Ian Wilson, staff and contributors of 'The Fighting Tiger' (Richmond), John Sincock (Port Adelaide historian), Ron Lockyer, Nicki Leppitsch (Brisbane), Valeriou Campan and Kate Clarke (St Kilda).

Every endeavour has been made to trace and acknowledge copyright holders of illustrations. The publishers apologise for any accidental infringement and welcome information that would rectify any error or omission in subsequent editions.

Contents

Foreword	7
Adelaide	10
Brisbane	28
Carlton	44
Collingwood	72
Essendon	100
Fitzroy	128
Footscray	140
Fremantle	164
Geelong	176
Hawthorn	204
Melbourne	232
North Melbourne	260
Port Adelaide	284
Richmond	296
St Kilda	318
South Melbourne	344
Sydney	354
University	370
West Coast	372
Index	388

ADELAIDE

MY CLUB
by Ashley Porter

It was absolutely stupid, of course, but as a 10-year-old I dashed from the College of Delinquency every winter Tuesday and Thursday afternoons and caught the train to Alberton. In those days you paid your shilling when you got off the train, so it seemed a good idea to save money by jumping off before the train hit the platform.

Finally the ever-angry old stationmaster realised the schedule and one night had a patrol car waiting. With teary eyes I explained to the officers I was going to watch Port Adelaide train, and surprisingly they took me there and were most impressed by my heroes – including John Cahill, Ian Hannaford, Rex Johns, Ron Elleway, Steve Traynor, Paul Marrett and Geof Motley – who knew me from my regular attendance. Later the officers took me home where I had the daylights beaten out of me.

Much later in life I promised my sweetheart – God help her, a Glenelg supporter – we'd get married if her team won a Flag. I looked safe … Glenelg had won only two Premierships, in 1934 and '73, but when her Tigers finally won another in 1985, the promise was kept. At least she married me in the same old black and white hooped socks that I wore to all formal occasions.

With this in mind – risking my life and then donating it to marital bliss – it might surprise some to learn that I'm a Crows fan, and I didn't switch to the Power when it joined the AFL. Port fans usually remain loyal forever, but this was a different team.

The loyalty really lay with South Australian League football, the competition that had provided me with so much pleasure as a fan and a sportswriter, and the magnificent people involved at every club level. Collectively they were the heart of the Adelaide Football Club when it was formed, and while deep down you can't take the black and white spirit out of the boy, you also can't take the boy out of the game.

Being a Crows fan from the start made you feel a part of history. It was also a new experience quietly supporting a team that wasn't expected to win. You had two choices – become engulfed in the euphoria which had gripped this State, or be an anti-Crow. Given duties from the daily newspaper editor, like monitoring when a Crow suffered from flatulence, made it difficult not to feel some degree of camaraderie with those associated with the team and want to share in their success.

The Crows were being ridiculed by the Victorian scribes and being a South Australian, it was intolerable. Adelaide copped heaps when it lost, and when triumphant the focus was on the opposition losing. Totally unfair, of course, and it made you want to stick up for your own side. Hey, this was a South Australian team.

For the first six years it was never easy

ADELAIDE	
Joined AFL	1991
Home Ground	Football Park
Premierships	1997
Brownlow Medals	nil
Record home crowd	48,522 v Collingwood, 1993
Most games	Nigel Smart, 120
Most goals	Tony Modra, 337
Notable supporters	Greg Champion, Wolf Blass, Sir Jeffrey Archer, Gary Sweet, Glenn Ridge, Greg Blewett, Alexander Downer, Sir James Hardy

being a Crows fan. They would start the season well, and then after all the hype or expectation they would fade dismally game by game. They rarely gained respect, and if you were introduced to someone interstate as a Crows fan they'd look at you with pity.

But come 27 September 1997, everything changed. It could have been pay-back time for all those jibes, a chance to crow. Yet the Premiership was more about experiencing an incredible sense of pride that a South Australian team had won, rather than attempting to reverse the torment. And St Kilda fans had always seemed an honest, rational breed, so only the cruel would rub it in.

The AFL is about clubs, and as difficult as it might seem for Victorians to understand, when you only had one team from your State in the competition it was seen as a representative side, no matter how the publicists tried to promote it otherwise. When the Power emerged there was intra-state rivalry, yet somehow most South Australians hoped both won every week.

But deep down you can only follow one side, and I've always despised turncoats. It's still the Magpies in the SANFL, but the Crows in the AFL. I grew up and learned to pay for the ride, but nothing else will change.

The domes shine, but the Premiership Cup shines brighter.

Above: Something to cheer about: the mighty Adelaide Crows. Right: McLeod chalks one up.

ADELAIDE

Decades of influence

In another 10 decades historians, perhaps our great-grandchildren, will reflect on the current-day players, coaches and administrators and judge those who had a strong influence on this marvellous game.

The name Max Basheer will undoubtedly figure prominently. For more than a record-breaking 20 years as president of the South Australian National Football League he has made an invaluable, and indeed astonishing contribution to South Australian League football, including administering the establishment of Football Park, securing the financial viability of the League and its clubs following some concerning years, and leading SA into the Australian Football League with the Adelaide Football Club in 1991 and Port Adelaide in 1997.

Like Basheer's achievements that have a physical presence around us today, are the works carved in the walls of history by football's pioneers.

The first-recorded etching is that of the merchant John Acraman, who is regarded as the father of South Australian football. In 1854 he had five round footballs sent out from England and erected the first set of goalposts, and we are led to believe he introduced a variation of Gaelic Football.

Slowly in time the rules established by the Victorian founders, Henry Harrison and Tom Wills, were adopted, and after 20 years of confusion and disarray, with the occasional bolting of horses through the fields interrupting play, football became more organised on Monday, 30 April 1877, with the formation of the SA Football Association. This was the foundation for football, more as we know it today, and in 1897 the current body, the SANFL, was formed.

Max Basheer: a football father figure.

Goalkicking sensation

In the history of Australian football at League level, never has anyone recorded such incredible goalkicking achievements as Ken Farmer.

Victorians, quite rightly, live in awe of Collingwood's legendary Gordon Coventry, who kicked 1299 goals for a game average of 4.25, but remarkably they don't quite compare with Farmer's records.

From 1929–41 Farmer played 224 senior games for North Adelaide and represented South Australia 17 times. Since 1981 a medal has been awarded in his honour to the SANFL's leading goalkicker in the home-and-away series.

Here is a breakdown of his amazing feats:
- Kicked 1419 goals for an average of 6.3.
- During his career kicked 42 per cent of North Adelaide's goals.
- Kicked 10 goals or more in a match on 37 occasions.
- Kicked an SANFL-record 23 goals against West Torrens at Prospect Oval in 1940. His quarter-by-quarter scores were 4.0, 5.2, 5.1 and 9.3 for a total of 23.6 out of North's winning score of 26.11.

Ken Farmer: his records still stand.

- Was the first South Australian to kick 100 goals in a season.
- Kicked 100 goals or more for 11 consecutive seasons.
- Set an SANFL record of 134 goals in a season (played 19 matches for an average of 7.0), which was unbeaten until 1969 when Fred Phillis kicked 137 for Glenelg.
- Won North's goalkicking award for 13 consecutive seasons, and was the SANFL leading goalkicker for 11 consecutive seasons.
- There was only one occasion when he was held goalless – and that was when he went off injured after 10 minutes.

Farmer is also one of a select few to coach a side, North, to a Premiership in his first year as a League coach, in 1949. He was also SA State coach in 1954.

Remarkable achievements, indeed. And the best he ever finished in a Magarey Medal count was fourth. What does one have to do?

SANFL NEWS to 1970

SA's first football association was formed in 1877, and two of the eight clubs were Adelaide and, believe it or not, Victoria. The administrators conveniently gathered in the Prince Alfred Hotel, part of the Adelaide Town Hall.

The first game of night football was played under electric light in 1885 at Adelaide Oval. It took six years, a Royal Commission and a change of government to erect lights at Football Park.

A visiting Melbourne Football Club team was arrested in 1892 for 'displaying unprecedented hooliganism in an orgy of destruction' in an inner-city Adelaide hotel. The lads pleaded guilty before a magistrate, but there were no apologies. In fact, upon their return home Melbourne's disciplinary committee not only exonerated their players – suggesting the hotel's landlord was at fault because he was a foreigner and was therefore unsympathetic towards jollity – they offered the team 'three cheers'.

At its inception, the South Australian National Football League comprised seven teams, and progressed to eight with Glenelg in 1921, to 10 with Central District and Woodville in 1964, and back to nine with the amalgamation of Woodville and West Torrens at the end of the 1990 season, coinciding with the new Adelaide Football Club in the AFL.

Frank Golding guided SA to an 11-point win over Victoria in 1926 on a rain-sodden MCG – at that time only

SANFL TO 1970

Jim Deane: Magarey Medallist.

Neil Kerley (left) and Fos Williams: legends as players and as coaches.

Barrie Barbary: Magarey Medallist.

The early champions

In the two decades to follow from 1897 South Australia had on-field marvels like 'Bunny' Daly, Jack 'Dinnie' Reedman, Tom Mackenzie, Jack Tredrea, Tom Leahy, Harold Oliver, Dan Moriarty and 'Wacka' Scott. Later, Ken Farmer emerged with his incredible goalkicking feats, which remain unsurpassed, and the heroics of Bob Quinn, who won a Magarey Medal, went to the Second World War and won a Military Medal, and returned to win another Magarey, brought a wave of great Aussie pride and emotion.

The fifties saw other greats like Jim Deane, Len Fitzgerald and Lindsay Head emerge, and born was the legend of Fos Williams. From 1954–59 Port Adelaide equalled Norwood's amazing Australian record of six consecutive Premierships set in 1883, and the story of the inspirational Neil Kerley began to unfold.

From those embryonic years of the Acraman style, South Australian League football was well and truly coming of age, and those who created the decades of influence became immortalised in the halls of fame.

Harry Kernahan: father of Stephen.

its sixth victory in 28 games there – and the Croweaters thought footy was easy. They didn't beat Victoria again in Melbourne for 37 years.

In July 1963 SA beat Victoria again on its hallowed MCG, 12.8 (80) to 10.13 (73). SA's coach was Fos Williams, and Barrie Barbary was rated as SA's best player. The 21-man SA squad was: Brian Sawley, Geof Motley, Jeff Bray, Don Lindner, John Cahill, Robert Day, Jeff Potter, Neil Hawke, Harry Kernahan, Bill Wedding, Fred Bills, Ian Hannaford, Bob Hammond, Ken Eustice, Ron Benton, Bob Shearman (captain), Neil Kerley, John Halbert, Lindsay Head, Barrie Barbary and Robert Oatey.

After causing a huge upset by beating the Vics the jubilant SA team later surrounded a pub owned by media jester Lou Richards, and gave him heaps. 'We want Lou-Lou; we want Lou-Lou', the lads chanted. Lou bit his famous lip, and responded: 'You boys from Disneyland can have a drink on me.' And not a chair was broken.

Glenelg officials endeavoured to use a yellow ball for the first time ever in 1968. North Adelaide's chairman of selectors Jack Sutter went on to the ground and kicked the yellow ball into the crowd, only to be tackled by Glenelg doorkeeper George Brown.

Against Sturt in 1968, Glenelg's Doug Long kicked a 'goal' but it was signalled a behind. The goal umpire said he was unsighted when clobbered by a paper-bag filled with sand. Sturt won the game by a point.

ADELAIDE

John Platten: 1984 Magarey Medallist.

Stephen Kernahan playing for Glenelg.

Graham Cornes: future Crows coach.

Ray Huppatz: played for SA and Vics.

Craig Bradley in his Port days.

Above left: Glenelg's Peter Carey lines up.
Above right: Central District's Sony Morey.

Golden greats

The era is 1970–1990 … two memorable decades of South Australian League football. A time when Football Park was developed, all-time legends graced the field, records were broken, and the game entered the modern, professional arena. In the end League football, as South Australia had known it for more than a century, changed dramatically with the decision in October 1990 to enter a team in the AFL. With mixed public emotions SANFL club football was changed forever. SA had the Best of the Best. 1970–90 was the Golden Era.

Here is an attempt to place the greats of this time in one side. Numerous champions missed out. Some players like John Cahill, Peter Darley, Brenton Adcock, Rick Schoff and Bob Shearman were towards the end of their careers, and this team is based purely on SANFL performances between 1970–90.

F: Graham Cornes, Tim Evans, Chris McDermott
HF: Andrew Jarman, Malcolm Blight, Michael Graham
C: Craig Bradley, Russell Ebert, Michael Aish
HB: Peter Marker, Greg Phillips, John Riley
B: Michael Taylor, Bruce Winter, Paul Bagshaw
1R: Rick Davies, Barrie Robran, John Platten
Int: Garry McIntosh, Peter Carey, Neil Craig

SANFL NEWS 1970–1990

The development of Football Park was without doubt the decision or event that had the greatest impact on SA League football. The idea evolved from a huge confrontation over members' rights and gate receipts between the SANFL and the SA Cricket Association (silently, it still simmers) and the first game at the SANFL's new headquarters at West Lakes – which was transformed from a swamp – was played on 4 May 1974, between Central District and North Adelaide.
Glenelg kicked a record SANFL score of 49.23 (317) against Central District at Glenelg Oval on 23 August 1975. The Tigers also recorded their biggest winning margin in that game – a whopping 238 points.
In May 1977, Norwood became the first club to win a night competition involving interstate clubs, the Ardath Cup, beating East Perth by eight points at Norwood Oval.
Port Adelaide's Tim Evans kicked a club-record 16 goals in a match against West Adelaide at Alberton in 1980.
The SANFL failed to convince their Victorian counterparts in April 1981 that it should have a Norwood–Port Adelaide combined side in an expanded VFL competition.
Central District full-forward Greg Edwards, who became the first Bulldog to kick 100 goals in a season in 1982, was accidentally punched in the eye while contesting a mark in a pack in February 1983 during a pre-season trial

1970-1990

The magic of Robran

Robran's first coach, Port Adelaide's 1964 Magarey Medallist Geof Motley, once said: 'There are great players and then there is Barrie Robran.' Another coach and former Victorian champion Mike Patterson said: 'He's incredible … name any Victorian and Barrie can match him in any phase. I've seen him do things that the best players over there have been unable to accomplish.'

Robran really was that good, and there is no doubt in the minds of those privileged to have seen him at his best that he would have won a fourth Magarey Medal had he not suffered a serious knee injury in 1974 during an interstate match against Victoria at the SCG.

Robran excelled in most positions, particularly at centre and on the ball, and among his numerous memorable performances was the Champions of Australia Premiers match against Carlton at Adelaide Oval in 1972. At one stage he had the ball with three Carlton players, including the brilliant Alex Jesaulenko, charging towards him. Robran ran backwards, and skilfully handballed over them to set up a goal. Jesaulenko stopped and applauded Robran. It was a great moment in sportsmanship; so typical of the champion's finesse.

Barrie Robran: 'There are great players – and then there's Barrie Robran.'

Robran: three-time Magarey Medallist.

Oatey, the legendary coach

There will never be another coach like Jack Oatey; his record will last as long as Australian football exists. He first coached in 1945, and while this chapter relates to a golden era, 1970-90, and the pinnacle of his success was a string of five Premierships from 1966, he can be the only choice as the Best Coach because his Australian record extended to 1982.

Oatey, AM, the Master, coached an Australian-record 778 League games, including 63 major-round games of which he won an Australian-record 33. Overall, he won 513, lost 260 and drew five, and competed in 30 finals series in his 37 years as a League coach at Norwood from 1945–56, West Adelaide 1957-60, and Sturt 1962-82. He won 10 Premierships – with Norwood (1946, '48, '50) and Sturt (1966-70, '74 and '76).

Also an outstanding player for Norwood, South Melbourne, and the State, Oatey gave an unrelenting, immense contribution to SA League football, and his own style was partly seen in others. Those to be coached by the great man, and to go on to coach a SA League side, were Neil Kerley, John Halbert, Daryl Hicks, Mike Nunan, Neil Craig, Rick Davies and Bruce Winter.

Oatey died in February, 1994, aged 73. His record will live forever.

Jack Oatey: master coach.

and became blind in one eye. He never played League football again.

Sturt's Rick Davies booted a club-record 15 goals in a match against West Adelaide on 21 May 1983 at Football Park – all against the same opponent. West coach Neil Kerley thought it would be a good lesson for the lad rather than moving someone else on to Davies.

In 1983, West Adelaide won its first Premiership since 1962, and hasn't won one since. Roger Luders became the first West player to kick 100 goals in a season, and still remains as the only one to achieve this feat.

Former Hawthorn champion Don Scott created a dubious League record on 12 May 1985 when he quit after coaching South Adelaide for only six games – for six losses.

In 1987 the West Australian Football League went back on its word to remain steadfast alongside the SANFL to gain far better terms and conditions of entry to a near-national competition.

7 October 1989 is a day North Adelaide wants to forget. It kicked 1.8 in the Grand Final against Port Adelaide, equalling the same record-low Grand Final score it kicked against Port in 1914.

Woodville and West Torrens played their last game against each other on 8 September 1990, before merging. The Eagles' Ian 'Scruff' Hanna, who had broken his neck in a pool accident, was sent on with a few minutes to go and Woodville, which had the game won, 'allowed' him to kick a goal.

ADELAIDE

Here we go ...

Neil Armstrong could have gone back to the moon to retrieve his golf ball and not have captured bigger headlines in South Australia than the Crows' first match, against Hawthorn on Friday, 22 March 1991. Crowmania had struck the City of Churches and an AFL-starved State moved into an exciting new era, in line with most of Australia.

It was an astonishing achievement to put together a club, a team and the trimmings – all in just 187 days – and the Crows' first coach, Graham Cornes, did an exceptional job in their first year.

After disappointments in 1992, the Crows reached the finals the following year – seven goals up against Essendon in a Preliminary Final and they lost ... oh so close to contesting their first Grand Final.

In the Crows' first three years they used 63 players, and remarkably only one – Stuart Wigney – had not originally come through the SANFL ranks.

The Crows were projected as a State side and along with it the fierce rivalry with the Victorians developed beyond the wildest imagination. In difficult times, they were seen as the only thing positive in the State and outside expectations ran high.

It was ridiculous, of course, and these hidden, one-team-town pressures burdened the Crows, and many of the on-field heroes became affected by the Hollywood-style star status bestowed upon them by the media.

Fortunately as time progressed – the reality of losing is a great leveller – the Crows, their fans and indeed the city matured.

Interstate rivalry livens up as fierce Crows fans take on the Vics.

The Crows savour victory after defeating Hawthorn in their first AFL game.

The Crows hit the park

First team:
B: Scott Lee, Nigel Smart, Rodney Maynard.
HB: Bruce Lindsay, Tom Warhurst, Robbie Thompson.
C: Simon Tregenza, Andrew Jarman, David Marshall.
HF: Darren Smith, John Klug, Grantley Fielke.
F: Bruce Lindner, Peter McIntyre, Darel Hart.
R: Romano Negri, Chris McDermott, Tony McGuinness.
Inter: Eddie Hocking, Rod Jameson.
Coach: Graham Cornes.

CLUB NEWS 1991–1993

Coach Graham Cornes took control of the Crows' first squad of 66 for the first time on 25 October 1990.

A 'scratch match' was held at Football Park on 12 January 1991. A thousand people watched their new team.

The Crows went on show for the very first time against opposition in a trial game against Essendon at Football Park on 31 January 1991. Nearly 50,000 fans were there to see the Crows win by 27 points.

The local Sunday tabloid produced an eight-page wraparound when the Crows defeated Essendon in the pre-season trial game, and the Lord Mayor declared the Town Hall would be floodlit in the Crows' red, blue and gold colours every time they won.

The Crows won their first game interstate, Round 3 against Sydney at the SCG, 19.18 (132) to 15.18 (108) on 7 April 1991.

Down nine points against Fitzroy at Football Park on 12 June 1991 with 67 seconds to go, the Crows received two free kicks. David Marshall goaled and then Rod Jameson goaled after the siren, to win by three points. Later that night he celebrated his 21st birthday.

Mark Mickan created a unique record. He captained Brisbane in its first-ever game in 1987, and in October 1991 became the first-ever Adelaide club champion.

The Crows produced their best showing of true grit when, in wet, slippery conditions at Waverley Park on 8 June

1991 – 1993

Fighting with fire

One of the most amazing chapters in the Crows' brief history – in football, actually – was the night coach Graham Cornes organised his players to walk over coals.

No football team had tried this ... and no wonder. It happened pre-season 1992 at the Crows' camp at Rapid Bay.

The instigator of this stunt was Nigel Smart, who had read about it in an in-flight magazine. He presented the idea to Cornes, who was convinced that if his players could psych themselves up enough to walk over red-hot 400°C coals, then they would possess the mental toughness to cope with any of the pressures that may arise in a match.

While the players – and Cornes, who was prepared to walk the coals too – went through three hours of intensive lecturing and training, quarry workers organised a bonfire to create the coals. The trouble was, they thought, gee, this is for the Crows so let's build the biggest and the best. Instead of having to walk over a short stretch, the players were confronting a glowing cricket pitch from hell.

Smart asked to be the first to walk over the coals. Despite his admirable self-motivation, self-belief and courage, things didn't go as planned. He seemed to lose concentration towards the end of the strip and blistered his feet. Cornes swiftly ordered an end to the proceedings.

Even though Smart was able to play in the pre-season trial a week later, blisters and all, he and his coach will never be allowed to forget this sensational stunt.

The Crows carried the hopes and dreams of South Australia at Football Park.

Mark Mickan: first Best and Fairest.

Time of firsts

In their early days, everything seemed to be a 'first', and here we capture these slices of history.

First coach: Graham Cornes.
First captain: Chris McDermott.
First game: Football Park, Friday, 22 March 1991.
Adelaide   6.2   11.6   17.10   24.11 (155)
Hawthorn 2.0   3.3   6.8   9.15 (69)
Best: Adelaide: Marshall, Jarman, McGuinness, Negri, Klug, Smart, Tregenza, Lee. Hawthorn: Anderson, Allan, Wittman, Pritchard, Ayres.
Goals: Adelaide: Lindner, Klug, McIntyre 4; Maynard, McGuinness 3; Smith, Marshall 2; Hart, Jarman. Hawthorn: Dunstall, Jarman, Morrissey, 2; Anderson, P. Dear, Wittman.
Umpires: Peter Cameron, Hayden Kennedy.
CROWD – 44,902
First kick: Simon Tregenza
First goal: Tony McGuinness
First club champion: Mark Mickan
First club leading goalkicker: Rod Jameson (49)
First final: 5 September 1993, 1st Elimination Final, Adelaide 16.14 (110) defeated Hawthorn 13.17 (95)

1991 – 1993 HONOUR ROLL

Year	Pos	Leading Goalkicker	No.	Best & Fairest	Captain	Coach
1991	9th	Rod Jameson	49	Mark Mickan	Chris McDermott	Graham Cornes
1992	9th	Scott Hodges	48	Chris McDermott	Chris McDermott	Graham Cornes
1993	3rd	Tony Modra	129	Tony McGuinnness	Chris McDermott	Graham Cornes

1992, they overcame a nine-point deficit at three-quarter time to beat Hawthorn by a point. The Crows hit the front for the first time with only two minutes to go and Darel Hart kicking the winning goal with only seconds remaining.

After the Crows beat North Melbourne on 24 February 1993 by an incredible 147 points in the Foster's Cup series, 27.21 (183) to 5.6 (36) the 'Roos sacked their coach Wayne Schimmelbusch.

The Crows started the 1993 season with a bang, thrashing Richmond 28.10 (178) to 12.12 (84) in their opening game at the MCG.

The Crows' 1993 dominance over Richmond continued when Tony Modra kicked a club-record 13 goals against them at Football Park on 16 July 1993. He also kicked 13 against Carlton there on 27 March 1994.

The Crows had to beat Collingwood on 29 August 1993 to play in the finals for the first time ever. Before a record crowd of 48,522 at Football Park they trailed 6.1 to 1.5 at quarter time, but produced a stunning second half and won 19.21 (135) to 17.9 (111).

The Crows defeated Hawthorn 16.14 (110) to 13.17 (95) in the 1993 First Elimination Final with Smart, Liptak and McGuinness among their best players.

Tony McGuinness was named Crows' Club Champion for 1993. The accolade was sweet for McGuinness after coming runner-up for the award in 1991 and 1992 at Adelaide, and in 1990 at his former club, Footscray.

ADELAIDE

Tony Modra demonstrates just why the supporters call him Godra.

Irrepressible Mods

There's a touch of Hollywood about Tony Modra. He's got the movie star looks with his styled blond hair and strong physique, he's mobbed by adoring young female fans as he walks the streets and he's the most recognisable person in South Australia, probably ever. He lives in the fast lane, drives a flashy sports car and frequents the night clubs. Most of all, he's a terrific footballer who, with his fantastic aerial leaps, can pluck the seemingly impossible marks and send a throng of 45,000 fans at Football Park into a frenzy. They call him Godra and his fans like to believe there is something sacrosanct about him.

This is all part of the Modra phenomenon, an experience people interstate would have difficulty in comprehending. His achievements include 129 goals in 1993 (which made him only the 25th footballer in VFL or AFL history to kick a century or more goals in a season) and his John Coleman Medal in 1997 with 81 goals.

A lot has been written or said about this enigmatic AFL star – not all flattering – but no one can deny his immense value to the Crows. More than any other player, he can generate an immeasurable degree of excitement when he plays, especially when he takes those exceptional high-flying marks and kicks those magical goals.

Unfortunately, Modra required a knee reconstruction during the 1997 Finals series, and the Crows and his fans were left anxiously awaiting his return.

Exit Graham Cornes

Emotions can run high in sport, but Adelaide Football Club officials put their feelings aside on 14 September 1994 when they sacked coach Graham Cornes. Within a fortnight the Crows appointed Robert Shaw, a decision they were later to regret.

Under Cornes the Crows had finished ninth in 1991 with 10 wins and 12 losses; ninth in 1992 (11–11); third in 1993 (13–10) and 11th in 1994 (9–12 and one draw).

He drew a significant amount of flak from his critics, who were often remiss in forgetting the fact the club was established in such a hurry and was hampered by a lack of concessions when it joined the competition – and that Cornes lacked the raw material of established AFL footballers to work with.

Cornes developed a typical South Australian League style of play in the Crows – free flowing, plenty of handball and running.

The Crows started season 1994 on a bright note, winning four of their first six games including two away matches – at the SCG and the Gabba – but from there it was inconsistent and suffered some heavy losses interstate.

A huge factor was the incredible number of injuries. The Crows were forced to use 37 of their 42 players, a total of 193 games were missed through injuries, and 25 players were hospitalised during the year.

Graham Cornes: a sad exit.

Ultimately, the undoing of Cornes developed from a lack of unity among the players toward him. The board was seen to back the players rather than the coach.

CLUB NEWS 1994

Adelaide and Brisbane played a pre-season trial game at the Village Green at the Hyatt Regency, Coolum on February 5. In very wet and humid conditions, the Crows won by 16 points in front of 4000 fans.
Adelaide beat the West Coast Eagles by 28 points in a trial game at Football Park on February 12, the first time the three field umpire system was used in South Australia. The umpires were Kevin Chambers (SA), Trevor Garrett and Greg Scroop (WA).
The Crows played in their first-ever Night Grand Final in the Foster's Cup on March 19. After earning their spot by defeating West Coast, Fitzroy and Collingwood, they lost to Essendon, 15.12 (102) to 9.14 (68) before 43,925 fans at Waverley Park.
Goals rained at the SCG on April 10 when the Crows kicked 24.10 (154) against Sydney – their highest score against the Swans – while Sydney kicked 21.9 (135), its highest score against Adelaide.
Talk about a turnaround. A charge against Mark Ricciuto on May 15 by the emergency umpire for striking Essendon's David Calthorpe was not sustained, but then Calthorpe was reported under the trial by video system for striking Ricciuto and he copped two games.
Crows captain Chris McDermott questioned the team's effort after the massive 97-point defeat by Hawthorn at Football Park in Round 8. At the early

1994

Good for some

Despite a disappointing club performance in 1994 the Crows managed to have Shaun Rehn and Mark Ricciuto named in the AFL's All-Australian Team of the Year.

Rehn also won the club champion award ahead of Tony McGuinness, while Ricciuto finished third but won the Crows' best team-man award.

Sadly for Rehn the next two years were horrendous. He played only three games in 1995 after requiring a left knee reconstruction, and again played only three games in 1996 after requiring another reconstruction on the same knee.

As for Ricciuto, season 1994 proved a powerful launching pad to a magnificent AFL career. He is now a major playmaker for the Crows.

Mark Ricciuto: Crows' best team-man.

Andrew McLeod: a new boy.

Departure lounge

Season 1994 proved to be the wrong time to start an AFL career with the Crows.

They blooded eight new players – Brett Chalmers, Matthew Kluzek, Martin McKinnon, Josh Mail, Nick Pesch, Shane Tongerie, Peter Turner and Sean Wellman – as well as recruiting Tony Hall from Hawthorn. Not one of them is still playing with the club, although Hall is a selector after retiring from playing AFL football.

And at the end of the 1994 season four others departed – Randall Bone, Chris Groom, Stephen Schwerdt and Stuart Wigney.

Picked up at the 1994 national draft were Matthew Collins, Brett Higgins, Toby Kennett, Jason McCartney and Allen Nash, who are also no longer at the club. But there were two positives from this draft – Matthew Connell, who won the club champion award in 1995, and the biggest prize of all (through a trade with Fremantle), Andrew McLeod.

Add these significant changes to the Crows' make-up with the end-of-season departure of Cornes, plus the poor season, and you could definitely say 1994 wasn't a happy time for many. But for others, they had a good time in London on an end-of-season trip.

Shaun Rehn goes for the knock-out.

1994 HONOUR ROLL

Year	Pos	Leading Goalkicker	No.	Best & Fairest	Captain	Coach
1994	11th	Tony Modra	70	Shaun Rehn	Chris McDermott	Graham Cornes

morning training practice the following day he called their performance 'unacceptable' and declared it humiliating and embarrassing.
North Melbourne managed to kick 23 behinds when it defeated the Crows by 80 points at Optus Oval in Round 11.
Adelaide was involved in its first – and to date only – draw, with St Kilda at Waverley Park on June 25: Adelaide 11.13 (79), St Kilda 12.7 (79).
From July 31 to September 3, the Crows kicked their lowest scores against Geelong (5.8), Footscray (4.10) and Brisbane (12.14) in successive weeks for a combined loss of 140 points. The next week the Crows kicked their highest score against Essendon (17.13) following that up with its lowest against Hawthorn (6.11).

It was a bad year for injuries. Incredibly, 2582 treatments were given to injured players, an average of 63 per player.
Scott Hodges, de-listed by the Crows at the end of the 1993 season, finished with 114 goals for season '94 for Port Adelaide in the SANFL to win his second Ken Farmer Medal. He also played in Port's Premiership side.

Tony Modra suffered the celebrity treatment with the press keen to capture his every move. Wild rumours circulated about his private life and the full-forward just about broke under the pressure of being a superstar and publicly considered quitting football. He was persuaded to stay and South Australia in general (teenage girls in particular) breathed a sigh of relief.

ADELAIDE

The Crows: the team was unsettled under their new coach Robert Shaw.

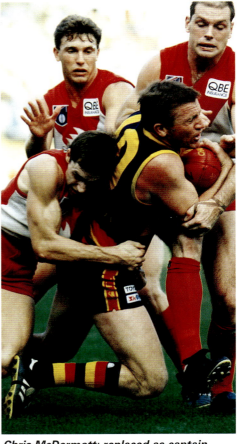

Chris McDermott: replaced as captain.

Enter Robert Shaw

Pressured to arrest an alarming trend after making the finals and then collapsing, Adelaide disposed of Graham Cornes as coach and brought in Robert Shaw. In hindsight, it was a bad move as things got worse.

Shaw certainly didn't endear himself to the Crows' fans, particularly when not that long after his arrival from Fitzroy he made a comment to the effect the fans 'need educating'. However, his reasoning was misinterpreted as he was basically saying that South Australians needed a more Victorian approach by becoming less fickle as supporters. In many ways he was right.

Much later, Shaw was to cop huge flak for suggesting the Crows weren't fit enough, and it was a reason for their dismal fade-outs and regular poor performances, especially interstate. In time, with the appointment of Malcolm Blight as coach and Neil Craig as fitness coach, he was proven right again.

It seemed that no matter what Shaw said or did, especially in his first year at the club, he didn't have total support among his players and especially the general football public, and

Robert Shaw: got off to a bad start.

there is no doubt this had an adverse affect on his performance as a coach. He appeared to be treated as an 'outsider', the old South Australian thing about 'we don't need the Vics', and he sorely lacked confidence.

Shaw's coaching ability, indeed some of his game tactics and approach to his players, were increasingly questioned among his growing list of critics, creating an unprecedented level of disharmony. Overall, it was reflected on the scoreboard.

Not helping matters was the fact that Tony Modra, who had kicked 129 and 70 goals the previous two seasons, managed to amass only 42. This led to the 'superstar' being dropped to West Adelaide in the SANFL for a few matches.

There were claims that he was unpopular among his team-mates and they deliberately ignored him when attacking for goal, and again Robert Shaw copped much of the blame.

No, season 1995 wasn't a happy one, but little did anyone, especially Shaw, realise that it was to get worse in 1996.

CLUB NEWS 1995

After beating Geelong, West Coast Eagles and Sydney, the Crows entered their second successive Ansett Cup Grand Final on March 25, but lost again, this time to North Melbourne by 30 points. Then they had to play North Melbourne in the first home-and-away round the next week, and lost again, by three points.

On April 16, the Crows held St Kilda to 3.8 – a record low score by any club against Adelaide – and won by 11 goals, but there was a huge price – Shaun Rehn suffered the first of his two knee injuries.

The Crows led Sydney by 17 points at three-quarter time at the SCG on April 30, but then disaster. In the Crows' worst-ever last quarter, the Swans booted 11.9 to a solitary point to win by 57 points – an incredible turnaround.

Andrew McLeod played his first game for the Crows on May 5, against Melbourne at Football Park. At the end of the season he won the club's 'emerging talent' award.

Fitzroy won only two games in 1995, and the first was on May 20 against the Crows by 33 points at Football Park. It was the most embarrassing loss in the Crows' history.

Tony Modra left the ground with a knee injury in the game against Geelong at Kardinia Park in Round 10, and the Crows went down by 25 points.

Adelaide played its 100th game in the AFL on June 10, beating Footscray

1995

Ton up victory

Round 11, 1995 saw the Crows play their 100th game, and they didn't spoil the occasion, beating Footscray by 44 points, 12.18 (90) to 6.10 (46). In four and a half seasons they had used 67 players.

Adelaide had won 48, lost 51 and drawn one of its 100 games, and it was reflected on the Premiership tables by regularly finishing mid-field. Only Brisbane was yet to beat Adelaide, while statistically the Crows' toughest opponent was Collingwood.

The Crows' biggest win was against Richmond by 139 points at Football Park in 1993, and their biggest loss was against St Kilda by 131 points at Moorabbin.

The club celebrated the century-game occasion with a $100 per ticket gala ball at the Hyatt Regency, while across town Port Adelaide celebrated its 125 years in the SANFL with a free fish'n'chips night on the Port River docks. The contrast did nothing to help the Crows rid themselves of the 'chardonnay set' tag, which touches the sensitive nerves of their administrators.

Concerned Crows take in the coach's words at three-quarter time.

McGuinness: unlucky century captain.

McChanges

Robert Shaw wasn't coach for long before he made a controversial move. He axed Chris McDermott, who had played all 22 games in 1994, as the captain and replaced him with his long-time mate Tony McGuinness.

It was seen as a huge knock-back for McDermott, the club's first captain who had guided the side in exemplary fashion, always leading by example. As it turned out, the change didn't work out that year as unfortunately McGuinness was plagued by a knee injury and played only half the season, leaving much of the on-field leadership problems to vice-captain Mark Bickley. Meanwhile, McDermott played 20 games in his typical workmanlike and courageous fashion.

At the end of the 1995 season there were further significant changes. Michael Taylor resigned as the assistant coach to coach West Adelaide in the SANFL, and was replaced by former Crow and North Adelaide coach Darel Hart, while John Reid was appointed to a new role as football operations manager.

Player-wise, there was a huge shake-up at the end of the season with the departures of Tony Hall, Scott Hodges (later returned), Scott Lee, Toby Kennett, Brett Higgins, Anthony Ingerson, Martin McKinnon, Alan Nash, Simon Pedler, Paul Rouvray, Stephen Rowe and Sean Wellman. This was partly seen as a reaction to another bitterly disappointing season, finishing 11th with only nine wins.

Matt Connell joined a select few to win a club's Best and Fairest award in his first season at a new club, beating Andrew Jarman by one vote. In the Brownlow Medal count Jarman clearly led Adelaide's voting with 13 votes while Connell picked up just one.

Anthony Ingerson: last year with Crows.

1995 HONOUR ROLL

Year	Pos	Leading Goalkicker	No.	Best & Fairest	Captain	Coach
1995	11th	Tony Modra	42	Matthew Connell	Tony McGuinness	Robert Shaw

by 44 points at Football Park. It was also Mark Ricciuto's 50th game for the club.
Adelaide and Fremantle clashed for the first time, at Football Park on June 24, and the Crows won by 21 points.
Round 13 and things were not looking too good. Captain Tony McGuinness and Tony Modra returned to the team after injuries but still the Crows lost – to Collingwood, by 96 points.

Chris McDermott became the first to play 100 AFL games for the Crows on July 8, and Tony McGuinness played his 200th AFL game. But it was a dismal day – Essendon hammered the Crows by 122 points.
The Crows broke the drought when they finally defeated a Melbourne team in Melbourne. They beat St Kilda at Waverley Park in Round 18 – their first win in Melbourne since the 1993 Qualifying Final in which they beat Hawthorn.
Tony Hall played his 114th and last AFL game on September 2 – 102 with Hawthorn and 12 for the Crows. It was a great achievement after having both knees reconstructed.
Matt Connell, who was recruited from the West Coast Eagles, achieved a rarity in football (excluding newly formed clubs) by winning his club's Best and Fairest award in his first year at his new club.
Andrew Jarman polled the most Crows votes in the Brownlow Medal with 13. His brother Darren, still at Hawthorn at the time, received 18 votes to come second to the winner, Paul Kelly.

ADELAIDE

The 1996 Crows team with captain Mark Bickley (fifth from the left): a season dogged by injury and disquiet.

All-time low

Season 1996 rates as the worst year in the history of the Adelaide Football Club. There were internal problems, and on the field the Crows won only eight matches and lost 14 to finish 12th – their worst performance.

It came as no surprise at the end of the season when the board sacked Robert Shaw, and replaced him with Malcolm Blight. Effectively, this meant Adelaide had three coaches within a two-year period, starting with Graham Cornes.

Shaw wasn't the only end-of-season casualty … Adelaide's inaugural captain Chris McDermott was dumped, so too was the 1996 captain and another club champion Tony McGuinness, and a real character and previously brilliant player, Andrew Jarman.

After a disappointing 1995 season there were high expectations with the recruiting of Darren Jarman, Kym Koster, Troy Bond, Shane Ellen and Peter Caven, plus the continued development of some outstanding youngsters.

And the early signs were promising when the Crows won their opening four games in magnificent fashion … arguably the best football they had ever played.

However, the rot really set in when the injury list to key players mounted, none more significant than when Shaun Rehn required another knee reconstruction almost 12 months to the day after his first.

Matthew Robran: another Robran shines.

The Crows played most of the season without passion, confidence and flair. The squad was unsettled, and there were signs of a lack of harmony among the players, especially toward Tony Modra.

Overall, the Crows played well below themselves, and with a lot of players privately expressing their lack of support for Shaw – as they did with Cornes – it came as no surprise when Shaw departed. It was also felt that the board didn't take enough of the blame for Adelaide's poor efforts.

Greg Anderson: played his last AFL game.

1996 HONOUR ROLL

Year	Pos	Leading Goalkicker	No.	Best & Fairest	Captain	Coach
1996	12th	Tony Modra	75	Matthew Liptak	Tony McGuinness	Robert Shaw

CLUB NEWS 1996

The Crows used their new multi-million dollar training facilities on Friday, February 23 for the first time after a trial game against Melbourne.

One game into the season and things were looking good. A crowd of 40,665 saw the Crows thrash Sydney by 90 points. At half-time the score was 12.6 to 1.0.

Nigel Smart played his 100th game when Adelaide defeated Fitzroy at the Western Oval. Smart, who has been with the Crows since the beginning, and former captain Chris McDermott are the only playing Crows to have reached 100 games. McDermott played his 110th.

The Crows defeated Geelong at Football Park in Round 3. It was the fourth time in a row the Cats had failed to win in Adelaide under lights.

Adelaide's Andrew and Darren Jarman, Rod Jameson and Nigel Smart were fined a total of $16,000 on April 12 for taking part in a melee with six Geelong players. The Crows were also fined $10,000, while a charge against runner Peter Jonas was dismissed.

The Crows had nine representatives in the June 2 State of Origin game between SA and WA. The Crows had a 6–3 win/loss record before the State game and a 2–11 record afterwards.

Tony Modra kicked three goals against Richmond in Round 12, taking his overall total to 302 goals.

Adelaide played what many fans believed was its worst game at home

1996

Andrew Jarman: dumped in 1996.

Fans still found something to cheer about.

Darren Jarman: back to South Australia.

He ain't heavy ...

The recruitment of Darren Jarman meant he was able to play alongside his brother Andrew for the first time since their successful days at North Adelaide until 1990.

Their old brotherly magic quickly came to the fore, never better than in the second series against Fitzroy when teamed in the forward lines and Darren kicked eight goals and Andrew six — two-thirds of Adelaide's total goal tally. It was one of the best goal-kicking performances by brothers in a match in the history of the VFL/AFL, and they loved every moment.

However, their tremendous combination didn't see out the season. While Darren played consistently well — he was the only Adelaide player to be named in the 1996 AFL All-Australian Team of the Year — Andrew seemed to become frustrated by the inconsistent opportunities he was given, and things came to a head late in the season when he chose to play for his SANFL club Norwood rather than be a last-minute replacement for an injured Crows' player.

Andrew copped a heavy fine — which he later successfully appealed against and was reduced — plus a two-match suspension from the Crows. Though Andrew played the last few games of the season, new coach Malcolm Blight later took a dim view of the controversy and chose not to retain him for the 1997 season.

It was a disappointing end to an otherwise impressive AFL career, and the brothers were split again. Darren went on to become a hero in Adelaide's 1997 Premiership win, while Andrew won his second Magarey Medal and played in Norwood's SANFL Premiership team.

Dr Matthew Liptak: club champion.

Beware the champion

Matthew Liptak won Adelaide's club champion award in 1996, a great achievement while doing his medical degree. The prolific ball-getting rover won the award by one vote from Nigel Smart and Darren Jarman, with Matthew Robran a further vote behind.

Liptak deserved the great honour, but might have taken notice of what happened to previous recipients after winning their awards. Chris McDermott and Tony McGuinness were de-listed by the club, Shaun Rehn was forced to endure two knee reconstructions and Matt Connell was plagued by persistent leg injuries the next season. And Liptak? He was restricted to just seven games in 1997 because of hamstring and Achilles tendon problems.

---

on June 30, losing to Melbourne by 51 points after leading by 19 points early in the third quarter. This was the first time the Crows had lost five games in succession.
Peter Vardy and Kane Johnson, who have gone on to become two key players for the Crows, made their AFL debut against Brisbane at Football Park on July 6.

It was hail the Crows and hail North Melbourne ... on them, that is. In the worst conditions at Football Park since the Crows' first game, 33,030 fans braved the abysmal elements on August 17, only to witness North Melbourne win by six points.
Within 24 hours of Adelaide's last loss of the season, Malcolm Blight announced that he would take on the role of coach in 1997. Blight had retired from coaching Geelong at the end of 1994 to take up a media position. In his six years with the Cats, they reached the finals five times.
Adelaide may have been down on the AFL ladder, but they led the way when it came to club memberships. Adelaide was easily on top with 42,283 members, followed by the West Coast with 26,663.
Darren Jarman polled the most votes of the Crows in the Brownlow Medal with 9 votes, three ahead of his brother Andrew.
In October, Chris McDermott became the first to receive Life Membership of the Adelaide Football Club. Tony McGuinness became the second and Andrew Jarman the third.

ADELAIDE

Malcolm Blight: an SA homecoming.

Nigel Smart: another fine year for one of the League's best backmen.

Pittman attack

Malcolm Blight, the Magarey and Brownlow Medallist, champion player and a fine coach at Geelong, did not return to Adelaide with a reputation for striking sparks and attacking his players.

So, the Crows must have wondered what struck them after his second-only home-and-away game at the club. After being well in contention midway through the last quarter against Richmond at the MCG, and losing by 28 points, Blight launched one of the most controversial attacks by a coach on one of his players – David Pittman.

Blight said: 'David Pittman was the most pathetic ruckman I have ever seen in my entire life in footy.'

Later, Blight apologised, explaining that he really meant to refer to Pittman's game that particular day. They sorted it out between themselves, and coincidence or not Pittman lifted his game as the season progressed. He said at the time: 'Malcolm and I discussed it; we know where we stand. You expect criticism in football. You don't just go weak at the knees.'

Port Adelaide's coach, John Cahill, said of the incident: 'I thought it was time a coach took a hard line. The Crows will only improve for what Malcolm did.'

New look, new approach

Once again the Crows' player list took on a vastly different look. Apart from the controversial departures of Chris McDermott, Tony McGuinness and Andrew Jarman, key players missing were David Brown and Scott Hodges, who moved to Port Adelaide, Jonathon Ross, who went to Collingwood, Greg Anderson (retired), Matthew Kluzek and Wayne Weidemann (de-listed).

Into the squad, through the draft, were Barry Standfield (Footscray), Brett James (Collingwood), Clay Sampson and Trent Ormond-Allen (Melbourne), Aaron Keating (Norwood), Tim Cook (Central District) and Nick Laidlaw (Sturt).

But the most significant changes proved to be the appointment of Malcolm Blight as coach, and Neil Craig as fitness coordinator.

When the Crows were going from bad to worse late in the 1996 season they were having some dreadful fade-outs.

Everyone had theories, and then coach Robert Shaw claimed that his players weren't fit enough. He was publicly ridiculed, but in time he was proven correct.

In racing terms, previously the Crows had been trained like sprinters ... they were renowned for starting a season well, but then faded badly. Under Craig they were trained like Melbourne Cup stayers and the ability to finish games – and ultimately the season – strongly became a new-found strength.

Blight, of course, was the major influence, and he used a shocking run of injuries (for the opening few games he was restricted to 24 players) to test almost everyone in the squad. This allowed him to discover his player stocks and in time, and with the return of key injured players, he was then able to work on the players he thought were best equipped to deliver his style of football.

Also, Blight encouraged his men to enjoy their football ... they trained and worked hard, and loved every moment. This rekindled the passion for football among the Crows, especially the senior players, and the enthusiasm was reflected on-field.

1997 HONOUR ROLL

Year	Pos	Leading Goalkicker	No.	Best & Fairest	Captain	Coach
1997	1st	Tony Modra	84	Andrew McLeod	Mark Bickley	Malcolm Blight

CLUB NEWS 1997

The Crows' former captain Tony McGuinness failed in his effort to be picked up in the February draft.

New coach Malcolm Blight looked ahead for 1997: 'I suppose deep down there was still something left - and the challenge of Adelaide. I would have loved to have been a Premiership coach, but it wasn't the burning thing that made me return. I think I came back because I had some energy to do it.'

Defender Nigel Smart started quite a trend by shaving his head. Those to follow early in the season included Rodney Jameson and Andrew McLeod.

Malcolm Blight's attack on ruckman David Pittman after the team's loss to Richmond in Round 2 was in turn attacked by his former 'Talking Footy' colleague, journalist Mike Sheahan. Sheahan wrote in the Melbourne *Herald Sun*: 'Pittman is the victim of the fiercest public attack by any coach on any player in my memory.'

The Crows' Round 4 loss to Port Adelaide caused the team to take a good hard look at themselves, according to Ben Hart. 'It definitely shocked a few blokes,' he said.

In Round 7 in the Crows defeat of Essendon at Football Park, Tony Modra kicked his 200th goal at Football Park. He kicked a total of five for the game and the club kicked a record 9.5 (59) in the last quarter to thrash the Bombers.

In May, captain Mark Bickley gave his impression of the differing coaching styles of Malcolm Blight and Robert

1997

Tony Modra hangs there, waiting, in the first of two showdowns against Port Power.

The power of two

As expected, the introduction of Port Adelaide into the AFL had a significant effect on the Adelaide Football Club. No longer were the Crows to dominate the sporting pages and prime-time electronic news services, and after six years of unrelenting exposure this was seen as a blessing.

Against widespread predictions, or fears, the club was buoyed by the fact it sold its home-match season tickets in record time, and its sponsorship base remained enormously strong.

The new home-town competition also had a positive effect on the Crows' players … they sensed they no longer had a mortgage on the local scene, and with some reputations suddenly being questioned they responded in terrific fashion.

Everything came to a head when they clashed in the fourth series, a contest dubbed as 'Showdown 1'. The Crows were weakened by the losses of Darren Jarman and big-men Shaun Rehn, David Pittman and Matthew Robran, yet were still expected to win against the vastly inexperienced Power.

Port performed magnificently and stunned the Crows by 11 points, 11.17 (83) to 11.6 (72), and many saw this as a huge embarrassment to them. However, Blight took it as another match that needed to be won and was lost, and left the amazing public reaction, an incredible week of stirring emotion, aside.

This loss proved to be a significant factor in capturing the ultimate prize, the Premiership. With their egos severely dented, the Crows knew they had to work much harder if they were to recapture their once-secure place on the mantel as the 'pride of South Australia'.

Come August, when they met again, Port looked like winning 'Showdown 2'. With heavy rain to come behind its back, and a lead of 23 points at three-quarter time, the Power looked 'home' again, but the Crows fought on tenaciously to hold it scoreless while they booted 4.6 to win by seven points, 9.11 (65) to 9.4 (58).

Bottoms up, as the Crows fight the Power.

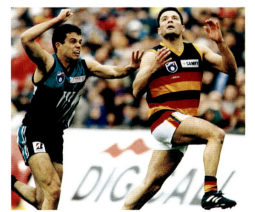
The Bond boys: Troy leads brother Shane.

The Bond boys, part 2: Troy marks.

Shaw: 'Malcolm Blight is very much an instructional coach on all the finer points of the game. Robert Shaw's was more of a fire-and-brimstone, us-against-them approach.'
In the *Footy Record* in June, Graham Cornes named his top 5 South Australian footballers never to play AFL: 1. Barrie Robran. 2. Neil Kerley. 3. Peter Carey. 4. Garry McIntosh. 5. Peter Marker.

Kane Johnson was nominated for the Norwich Rising Star award in June. Johnson, from Melbourne's Eastern Rangers, was selected at number 27 in the National draft in 1995 and played only two games for the Crows in 1996 due to a leg injury. In 1997 he secured his position as a defender, playing 19 games. Peter Vardy, another Adelaide Norwich Rising Star nomination, played all 22 games and kicked 26 goals.
Crows to represent South Australia in the State of Origin match against Victoria included: Mark Bickley, Ben Hart, Darren Jarman, Kym Koster, Matthew Liptak, Tony Modra, David Pittman, Shaun Rehn, Mark Ricciuto and Simon Tregenza.
In August, club chairman Bob Hammond spoke of the impact Malcolm Blight had had on the Crows in 1997: 'Malcolm has had a huge influence. He set an agenda and plan early in the piece. Everyone understood what was required and endeavoured to adhere to the plan.'
While Tony Modra was the first Crows player to win the John Coleman Medal, coach Malcolm Blight won it in 1982 playing for North Melbourne.

ADELAIDE

The Premiership

The Victorian dream was shattered … a Western Bulldogs versus St Kilda Grand Final was not to be. The Bulldogs captured the imagination of every sports lover who thrives on watching a battler succeed – and they had survived crippling financial ills and merger moves that threatened their existence.

Enter the Crows. Down 22 points at three-quarter time against the Bulldogs in the Preliminary Final, Darren Jarman was shifted to full-forward and booted two magical goals to snatch a two-point win, 12.21 (93) to 13.13 (91). It was a sensational comeback.

Now it was up to the Saints to fulfil the Victorian dream. They started Grand Final week with Robert Harvey winning the Brownlow Medal, and if the heart-felt emotion wasn't deep enough they shared Nicky Winmar's personal grief with the death of his inspirational father.

But in front of 99,645 fans, the biggest AFL Grand Final attendance since 1986, this tidal wave of emotion wasn't enough to lift the Saints as a disciplined, more focused Adelaide unit marched on to Premiership glory, winning 19.11 (125) to 13.16 (94).

It was an incredible triumph for Malcolm Blight, who after losing three Grand Finals during his six years at Geelong, captured his first Flag and joined an elite few who had coached a team to a Premiership in his first year at a club.

The Crows trained in front of their faithful fans at the Junction Oval in Melbourne.

Standing high above South Australia's new heroes was Andrew McLeod, who was rewarded with the Norm Smith Medal for one of the most outstanding individual performances seen in a Grand Final.

Adelaide's win was achieved without two of its best players throughout the year, playmaker Mark Ricciuto and John Coleman medallist Tony Modra, and without Matthew Liptak, who had won its club championship award the previous season.

Above: Mark Bickley (left) with Aaron Keating (near right). Left: Norm Smith Medallist Andrew McLeod.

Smart move

It must rate as one of the most daring, and successful, moves by a coach in an AFL Grand Final.

The Crows went into the Grand Final without their star full-forward Tony Modra, who injured a knee during the Preliminary Final against the Western Bulldogs, and later required surgery.

Regular ruckman Shaun Rehn was named there, but the popular belief was that Malcolm Blight would use Darren Jarman as the focal point, especially when considering he had been successful there in the past, including the last quarter of the Bulldogs match.

Instead, he opted for Shane Ellen, who had played most of his football on a half-back flank. In fact, before this game he had kicked only three goals in 37 AFL matches.

Ellen stunned everyone, kicking two of the Crows' first three goals, and kicked four up to three-quarter time before Blight made another significant move … switching Jarman to full-forward and Ellen to a forward flank.

Jarman kicked five of his six goals in a devastating last-term effort, and Ellen kicked another, taking their combined tally to 11 of Adelaide's 19 goals.

Darren Jarman: a game-winning streak.

1997

Adelaide celebrates the Crows' win.

Malcolm Blight and Mark Bickley hold the 1997 Premiership cup aloft in Adelaide.

Nigel Smart gets a taste for victory.

The succession Keating had to have

Aaron Keating will surely go down in history as one of the luckiest footballers.

In January, 1995, he was lucky not to suffer permanent brain damage after being struck repeatedly with an iron bar while being attacked by a group of thugs outside a Gold Coast nightclub.

Forced to play with a helmet, he was given an opportunity by Blight in the first game of the season and suffered a broken pelvis.

Keating was sidelined until two home-and-away rounds remaining, and played for Norwood's reserves in the SANFL. Remarkably, he was recalled for the Preliminary Final against the Western Bulldogs, replacing David Pittman who was suspended for one match.

Keating did well during his stints off the bench, and was able to keep his place in the side when Tony Modra was injured.

Suddenly, Keating is wearing a Premiership medallion after only his third AFL game, but it doesn't stop there. A week later he played his first League game for the season for Norwood and played in another Premiership side … that's two winning Grand Finals in only four senior games!

Party on

The reaction back home to Adelaide's Grand Final victory was nothing short of amazing; the most sensational since The Beatles hit town back in the sixties.

As soon as the final siren sounded thousands of armchair fans ran outside screaming for joy or drove through the city streets blasting their car horns and flashing their lights. Total strangers became instant friends as most of South Australia welled over with feelings of euphoria.

Parties raged throughout the night and during the week, with the grand finale being a ticker-tape parade – which was televised live throughout South Australia – for the team on the Friday.

More than 100,000 fans waving a sea of red, blue and gold coloured streamers and flags crammed the pavements down King William Street, massing at the Adelaide Town Hall. It was one of the most amazing scenes in Adelaide for a long time.

BRISBANE

MY CLUB
by Peter Blucher

For 10 years the Australian Football 'family' of Queensland wanted a VFL/AFL team. They got one in 1987. And for the next 10 years they watched as the club endured a roller-coaster ride through the highs and lows of football playing and club administration.

Twice the club teetered on the brink of collapse because of the perils of private ownership. It was like a soapie, and it was appropriate that the two founders were actor Paul Cronin, foundation chairman, and media magnate Christopher Skase, foundation deputy chairman. After a protracted licence battle, Cronin, from 'The Sullivans', commanded the Queensland VFL club.

Cronin 'recruited' Skase and they quickly settled on the name 'Bears'. They adopted the traditional Queensland colour of maroon and added a splash of gold, symbolising Queensland sunshine.

But the fledgling club, officially launched on 7 October 1986, for the 1987 season, was in conflict. It was named 'Brisbane', but was based on the Gold Coast, and adopted as a logo the koala, which wasn't really a bear. For those who yearned for a Queensland club in the VFL, the Brisbane Bears were hardly the real thing.

Skase insisted on the Gold Coast base and the VFL gave temporary approval to it, but as time passed it became evident that the club had no intention of relocating. By April 1988 the club had signed a 30-year lease at Carrara.

The dollar wasn't so mighty when, in 1989, the Skase empire collapsed. Behind him he left a reported Bears debt of $28 million.

The club would almost certainly have collapsed but for the intervention of the wealthy Gold Coast businessman Reuben Pelerman, who bought the Bears as a belated Valentine's Day present for his wife Anne.

Pelerman took over a club going nowhere. He was not the normal football club chief. Though honouring payments to players, more than once he threatened to close the operation. Four games into the coaching reign of Robert Walls in 1991, he suggested they shouldn't play any more that season, but should train extra hard to ensure the players were fit for 1992.

Pelerman reportedly lost $10 million before agreeing to transfer the licence to a traditional membership-based structure.

In the first five years the Bears finished 13th, 13th, 10th, 14th and 15th, and the club deficit approached $38 million.

The initial decision to base the Bears at Carrara did have its upside. They were in a favourable bargaining position when they finally did relocate to Brisbane, as the Gabba was planning a multi-purpose development program.

By switching to a traditional membership-based structure and relocating to Brisbane the woes of the early years were quickly forgotten. With the help of the AFL draft, the once 'Bad News Bears' had become an exciting force.

BRISBANE

Year Established	1986, merged with Fitzroy 1997
Joined VFL/AFL	1986
Home Grounds	Carrara, the Gabba
Premierships	see Fitzroy
Brownlow Medals	Michael Voss, 1996
Record home crowd	21,644 v Collingwood, 1996
Most games	Roger Merrett 313
Most goals	Roger Merrett 285
Notable supporters	Peter Hollingworth, Kieren Perkins, Cheryl Kernot, Greg Norman, Susie O'Neill, Patrick Rafter

The Gabba at night: a grand home for the Brisbane Lions.

Michael Voss: Brownlow winner, team leader.

Roger Merrett: the Bears' inspiration is with the Lions.

Alastair Lynch: a link with old and new.

BRISBANE

1987 Bears. Rear: Jamie Duursma, Mark Roberts, Stephen Reynoldson, Michael McCarthy, Neil Hein, Ben Harris, Adam Garton, Rick Norman, Ken Judge. Third row: Michael Gibson, Chris Waterson, Dale Dickson, Jim Edmund, Frank Dunell, Peter Smith, Alan Giffard, Robert Mace, Neal Gaghan. Second row: Rod McPherson, Stuart Glascott, Chris Stacey, Stephen Williams, Brenton Phillips, Tony Beckett, Craig Evans, Cameron O'Brien, David O'Keefe, Mark Buckley, Brad Hardie, Mark Withers. Front row: Gary Shaw, John Fidge, Geoff Raines, Mark Mickan (Capt.), Peter Knights (Coach), Mark Williams (Vice-capt.), Philip Walsh, Peter Banfield, Bernard Harris, Darren Carlson.

Peter Knights and Paul Cronin.

Brisbane Bears underway

If it was difficult to win the licence for a VFL club in Queensland, it was 10 times more difficult to start on hostile territory.

It was like the casting set for a new movie. So, how appropriate it was that former actor Paul Cronin, the inaugural chairman, was the 'director'. The leading man was former Hawthorn champion Peter Knights, the golden-haired boy with the perfect football pedigree. Former QAFL general manager Ken Murphy, once St Kilda boss, headed the administration team based at Gabba Towers, Brisbane.

A special draft, in which each existing club was to provide three players to the expansion club, was farcical. The mechanism intended to provide the core of the Bears' list originally unearthed more has-beens and rejects than the final list included.

A local Bear: Tony Beckett.

The Bears were established when transfer fees were outrageous, the club paying more than $1.3 million in year one. These fees included a reported $270,000 for Brad Hardie, $125,000 for John Fidge, $110,000 for Mark Williams and for Stephen Reynoldson, $85,000 for Bernie Harris, $80,000 for Geoff Raines and Mick McCarthy, $70,000 for Frank Dunell, $60,000 for Jim Edmond and Matthew Campbell, and $50,000 for Mark Mickan and Peter Smith. In year two, Warwick Capper cost a reported $420,000, Scott McIvor $80,000 and Roger Merrett $60,000.

The players moved to Brisbane on 3 January 1987, and made their 'home' for several months at the Brisbane Parkroyal Hotel. Training occurred at several grounds, including Kedron, Mayne and Mt Gravatt.

Mark Williams gets his jumper.

1987–1988 HONOUR ROLL

Year	Pos	Leading Goalkicker	No.	Best & Fairest	Captain	Coach
1987	13th	Jim Edmond	34	Phillip Walsh	Mark Mickan	Peter Knights
1988	13th	Warwick Capper	45	Mark Withers	Mark Mickan	Peter Knights

CLUB NEWS 1987–1988

Bears staffing includes former QAFL general manager Ken Murphy, Shane O'Sullivan, Mark Maclure (assistant coach) and Jim Sewell.

Collingwood captain and on-baller Mark Williams is caught in a contract dispute and is the first player to sign with the Brisbane Bears.

Mark Mickan, a ruckman from West Adelaide, is appointed the first captain of the Bears, with Mark Williams vice-captain and former Geelong key position player Steve Reynoldson as deputy vice-captain.

Jim Edmond kicks eight goals in the Bears' second game against Geelong at Kardinia Park. His effort in a magnificent 19-point victory would stand as the club's best for two and a half years until Brad Hardie's Round 10 effort against Carlton in 1989.

After back-to-back wins over North Melbourne and Geelong in the first two games and a Round 3 loss to St Kilda, the Bears lose their first home game at Carrara to Fitzroy 16.18 (114) to 20.9 (129) in Round 4. A week later against Melbourne, former Mayne (QAFL) wingman Tony Beckett becomes the first Queenslander to play for the Bears as they post their first home win 12.14 (86) to 12.9 (81).

Steve Williams, younger brother of vice-captain Mark Williams, makes his AFL debut in Round 3, as the popular pair from Adelaide become the only two brothers to play for the club in the 10-year Bears era.

1987 – 1988

The Carrara Stadium out in the Gold Coast countryside is a bit primitive, but has a fine playing surface.

The first game – and a great start for the Bears

On Friday night, 27 March 1987, a Bears team branded has-beens, rejects and misfits took on North Melbourne in their first game at the MCG. They were given no hope by the critics, yet triumphed 19.23 (137) to 15.14 (104) in superb fashion.

Half-forward Brenton Phillips kicked five goals to be best afield, while Bernie Harris, Phillip Walsh and Mark Williams were other stand-outs as the northerners led at every change.

It was an emotional coach Peter Knights who led his players and support staff in the first legitimate rendition of the club song, each clutching a piece of paper with the words to a tune they barely knew.

The first Bears team was:
B: Peter Banfield, Mark Roberts, Dale Dickson; **HB:** Matthew Campbell, Steve Reynoldson (dvc), Cameron O'Brien; **C:** Phillip Walsh, Geoff Raines, David O'Keeffe; **HF:** Brenton Phillips, Mick McCarthy, John Fidge; **F:** Mike Richardson, Jim Edmond, Neil Hein; **Foll:** Mark Mickan (c), Mark Williams (vc), Bernie Harris; **Int:** Brad Hardie, Chris Waterson.

The Bearettes burst out.

Jim Edmond is suspended for six weeks for striking Hawthorn's Russell Morris amid much controversy following the Round 12 clash at Carrara. It was the stiffest penalty imposed on a Bears player in the club's first five years.
The Bears beat Richmond by 56 points in Round 22 at the MCG to avoid the wooden spoon.
Philip Walsh wins the inaugural Bears Best and Fairest Award, polling 24 votes to nudge out Geoff Raines by two, with Mark Mickan and Mike Richardson tied for third on 17 votes.
In 1988 Essendon strongman Roger Merrett, high-flying Sydney full-forward Warwick Capper, prodigal son and Fitzroy Best and Fairest winner Scott McIvor and Hawthorn Premiership pair Rodney Eade and Rod Lester-Smith head the second wave of Bears recruits.
The scheduled Round 3, 1988 home clash with West Coast is transferred to Perth when Carrara is ruled unplayable due to torrential rain. Later, the club loses a fight to have the return match in Round 16 played at home on the Gold Coast.
Warwick Capper equals the club's single-game goalkicking record with eight goals against Richmond at Carrara in Round 11. It's the Bears' biggest return from the glamour recruit in his three years and 34 games with the club.
Mark Withers, who joined the Bears from Melbourne, wins 1988 Best and Fairest honours after Victorian squad selection mid-season.

BRISBANE

Peter Knights: the axe.

Norm Dare: stand-in.

Knights sacked, drama sets in

On 15 July 1989, the first night match was played at Carrara. Geelong hammered the Bears by 74 points, leaving them with a dismal 3–12 record. Four days later, Peter Knights was sacked as coach.

Paul Feltham, former North Melbourne Premiership player and the club's sports psychologist, took charge of the shocked club. Seemingly motivated by self-preservation, the players won five of their last seven games.

In October, Chief Executive Ken Murphy was replaced by John Dickson, the Marketing Manager. Shortly afterward Skase's empire collapsed, leaving the Bears with debts of $28 million. There was doubt whether the Bears could continue as Cronin stepped down and Skase fled the country.

The disarray continued. Feltham was not reappointed as coach and Norm Dare, the Bears Reserves coach, took charge.

In February 1990, businessman Reuben Pelerman rescued the club by becoming owner. A Board of Administration, headed by developer Noel Gordon, was appointed. In October, after the Bears finished with the 1990 wooden spoon, Andrew Ireland, ex-Collingwood player and QAFL official, was appointed CEO on the platform that the club be based in Brisbane.

Robert Walls was appointed coach and Dare assistant coach. Dare had asked Walls to take the senior position.

Glamour boy Warwick heads north

Brisbane Bears players had often been depicted in the sneering southern media as being more concerned with lemon rinses and solariums that the gym and the training track. Now they had a leader of the pack in the blond, bronzed Warwick Capper, he of the short shorts and white boots. He had been the darling of the chardonnay set in the Sydney stands as he took the big marks and, in season 1987, kicked 103 goals, only the second Swan, after Bob Pratt, to top the ton. Warwick came for big money, and it was assumed that he would both kick the goals and drag in the crowds. He did neither in a lacklustre 34 games, a highlight being his 8.3 in a destruction of Richmond in June 1988. A tally of 71 goals was not good enough, and he departed the Bears for another try with the Swans. There was speculation that some Bears resented Warwick hogging the limelight and the money, and didn't bother passing the ball to him.

Warwick and furry friend.

Man in charge Christopher Skase at a Bears function with Brad Hardie and Ted Whitten.

CLUB NEWS 1989–1994

SA defender Martin Leslie, the No. 1 pick in the first AFL Draft in 1987, joins the Bears in 1989 with WA pair David Bain and John Gastev.
Gold Coast product Marcus Ashcroft makes his AFL debut in Round 9, aged 17 years and 243 days.
In Round 10, 1989, Brad Hardie kicks a Bears-record nine goals and Warwick Capper six goals as they upset Carlton at Princes Park. Three days later Robert Walls is sacked as Blues coach.
In April, 1990 Roger Merrett replaces Mark Mickan to become the Bears' second captain, with Scott McIvor his deputy. A recently-retired Rodney Eade takes over as coach of the Reserves.
The Bears, in a rebuilding phase under coach Norm Dare, 'win' their first wooden-spoon after finishing 13th, 13th and 10th in the previous three years.
David Bain and Martin Leslie share the 1990 Best and Fairest award, while Bain is equal fourth in the Brownlow Medal with 15 votes.
Michael McLean joins the Bears in 1991, beginning a key association with the club in which he would establish himself as the 'Godfather' of the AFL's Aboriginal family. Other newcomers to the club include ex-Geelong pair Shane Hamilton and David Cameron, Hawthorn's Peter Curran and Woodville rookie Richard Champion.
Coached by Rodney Eade and captained by Rod Lester-Smith, the Bears win the AFL Reserves Premiership,

1989–1994

A tree full of old Bears

Bernie Harris: small and courageous.

Mark Mickan, the first captain.

Philip Walsh: the first club champion.

Rover David Bain.

Steve Reynoldson: vice-captain.

John Gastev: defender.

Reuben Pelerman: club saviour.

A matter of survival

In November 1991 the Bears made two decisions critical to the survival and well-being of the club – they swung from private ownership to a traditional membership-based structure and opted to move from Carrara to the Gabba. Without these two decisions the Bears would have almost certainly have folded.

A Heads of Agreement was signed with Reuben Pelerman, transferring the ownership of the club to the members. In December 1991 the club's first independent Board of Directors, headed by chairman Noel Gordon and deputy chairman Alan Piper, was established to operate the club on behalf of the 'owners'.

In season 1992, with the competition now operating under the Australian Football League banner, the Bears played at Carrara while final arrangements were made for the relocation to the Gabba. And on December 7 new football offices were opened on the Stanley Street side of the world-acclaimed cricket stadium.

At last the Bears had a home of which they could be proud. The Bears had begun an association with the Gabba, albeit briefly as they played four designated home games at the cricket ground on a trial basis.

1989–1994 HONOUR ROLL

Year	Pos	Leading Goalkicker	No.	Best & Fairest	Captain	Coach
1989	10th	Brad Hardie	54	John Gastev	Mark Mickan	P. Knights/Paul Feltham
1990	14th	Brad Hardie	37	D. Bain/Martin Leslie	Roger Merrett	Norm Dare
1991	15th	Laurence Schache	47	Michael McLean	Roger Merrett	Robert Walls
1992	14th	John Hutton	43	John Gastev	Roger Merrett	Robert Walls
1993	13th	Roger Merrett	60	Michael McLean	Roger Merrett	Robert Walls
1994	12th	Roger Merrett	41	Craig Lambert	Roger Merrett	Robert Walls

beating Melbourne 16.13 (109) to 11.9 (75) at Waverley.
A new jumper, featuring the traditional maroon of Queensland with a gold V and white trim, is unveiled in 1992.
In April 1992 teenage rookie Darryl White from Alice Springs kicks the AFL Goal of the Year against Fitzroy at Carrara in Round 3. His winning effort was the first goal of his career.

Michael Voss, aged 17 years and 11 days, becomes the youngest ever Bears player on debut against Fitzroy at Princes Park in Round 18.
Bears shed their Reserves side for financial reasons in 1993. They snare Nathan Chapman and Justin Leppitsch in the national draft.
Australia's 'most wanted' footballer, Nathan Buckley, agrees to join the club

for season 1993.
Matthew Campbell, the last of the original Bears, plays his last game for the club against Richmond at the MCG in Round 2 before a knee injury ends his AFL career.
For season 1994 Bears grab Richmond star Craig Lambert in the pre-season draft to complete a 'Super Six' recruiting package – Alastair

Lynch, Lambert, ex-Geelong skipper Andrew Bews, St Kilda's Gilbert McAdam and Collingwood pair Craig Starcevich and Troy Lehmann.
Bears launch a new club song in 1994, to the tune of 'Glory, Glory Hallelujah', to replace the dreadful old 'Dare to Beat the Bear'.
Chris Scott wins the 1994 Norwich Rising Star Award.

BRISBANE

The new Gabba

The Gabba as it has developed – lights, action and an intimate feeling.

Membership jump in Brisbane

The club's membership, a paltry 800 in 1992 at Carrara, jumped to 2600 in 1993 and 4700 in 1994. By 1995 it was 6500 and in 1996 it reached 10,400. In 1997 there were 13,800 Queensland-based members in an overall figure of almost 17,000.

Bears attendances jumped likewise, impeded only by a limited Gabba capacity in 1995 during redevelopment. In 1992 the reported average attendance at Carrara was 6499 – though debate raged on how many of these 'regulars' were mythical or freebies.

In 1993, when the capacity of the Gabba was 18,620, the average attendance was 11,097. In 1996, when the capacity swelled to 22,000, there were six sell-outs from 13 games and an average turnout of 18,672, including a ground-record 22,003 for the first Gabba final against Essendon in September.

In 1997, after the merger, there were seven sell-outs in 11 Gabba games and an average attendance of 19,500, taking the newly-named Lions past the rugby league Broncos as Brisbane's most-watched football team.

In 1981 Hawthorn and Essendon had done battle at the Gabba for VFL Premiership points. In 1982 Richmond and Carlton played an exhibition match there during the Commonwealth Games.

But there was a fundamental problem with the world-acclaimed cricket ground. It was too small. And it was shaped more like a pear, with no pocket at one end and too much room in the pockets at the other.

Before Australian football could make a permanent home at the Gabba in a co-tenancy that guaranteed ongoing Government funding, something had to be done. So, after much negotiation with Gabba Trust officials, the Bears signed a long-term lease, and a massive redevelopment program began.

On 5 February, 1993, the bulldozers began work on a $3.9 million development of the Gabba Oval. The greyhound track was removed to extend the playing arena, the Clem Jones Stand was upgraded, and a temporary stand was built on the Western Hill. Playing facilities were established beneath the new Bears Social Club, which was formerly the Gabba Greyhounds Club.

Two years later the Sir Leslie Wilson Stand and the Hutcheon Stand were demolished, to be replaced by a magnificent Northern Stand. Five giant towers provided lighting, and behind the traditional 'hill', in front of the old manual scoreboard, was built the world's biggest electronic scoreboard.

On 26 August 1995, amid the Bears' extraordinary late-season charge to their first finals appearance, the first night match was played at the Gabba. The home side won 17.14 (116) to 16.14 (110).

The next stage of the redevelopment, tipped to take total expenditure beyond $100 million, was scheduled to start in January 1998. The Northern Stand was to extend eastward to link up with the Lions Social Club, and westward to replace the temporary Western Hill Stand.

Importantly, throughout each stage of redevelopment the intimate atmosphere of the Gabba was retained. The public, corporate, player and media facilities grew to be the equal of any in the country, but in many ways it was still the same old Gabba!

The magnificent Northern Stand completes the transformed stadium.

CLUB NEWS 1995

Brisbane bows out of the Ansett Cup summer series of matches in the first round, losing to the eventual Cup-winners North Melbourne in a one-sided game, 17.18 (120) to 8.12 (60).

The day of the missing boots! When the Bears arrive at Optus Oval for the Round 6 clash with Essendon, property stewards are horrified to find the players' boots are missing. Only with the assistance of Essendon and host club Carlton were all players fitted out. Shaun Hart kicks five goals in borrowed boots in a stand-out performance, but the Bombers win by 28 points.

The Bears head to Perth in late May on the first 10-day interstate trip in AFL history. Drawn to play league newcomers Fremantle and West Coast at Subiaco on back-to-back weekends in Rounds 9 and 10, the club decides to stay over in the WA capital. They lose the first leg of the double-header by 66 points to the Dockers in dismal fashion, but are much better against the Eagles, despite a 45-point loss. The time spent in a virtual mid-season camp is to prove crucial to the success that was to follow.

Coach Robert Walls confirms in July he will not seek reappointment for 1996 and days later becomes the first person to coach 100 games for the Bears in the Round 14 visit to Geelong. A week later Walls coaches his 300th game overall and Roger Merrett, newly appointed assistant coach, skippers the Bears for the 100th time.

1995

Robert Walls: started the finals run with a thrilling victory.

Richard Champion: high on emotion.

Charge to the finals

Sunday 23 July 1995, an all too familiar day at the Gabba. The Bears trailed Hawthorn by 45 points at three-quarter time. The end of the season seemed a formality.

At three-quarter time coach Robert Walls spotted the Hawks huddling in the shade and pounced on it. 'They're tired', he told his troops. 'If we just keep persisting we can still win it!'

Kicking with the wind and to the east, the Bears added 9.7 to 1.3 in the final stanza to win it. It was an unforgettable day, and only the beginning. The Bears won six of their last seven, losing only to Carlton, and were in the finals for the first time.

On Sunday, September 10, the Bears met Carlton at the MCG. For nine years and 196 games they had waited. No fewer than 137 players had tried. At last they tasted finals football at headquarters.

The gallant Bears were beaten 12.5 (77) to 13.12 (90) by Carlton. But that didn't really matter. They made their mark.

A nervous weekend

Brisbane players and supporters had an agonising weekend as they waited to see if they had won a place in the eight. The team did the right thing by beating Melbourne in a Friday night match. But to make the eight, the lowly Sydney Swans had to knock out another contender, Collingwood.

It was all Collingwood at the start. But the Swans got going and ended up blitzing Collingwood. The Bears were in, and there were bear hugs all round.

Merrett – Lion-hearted

If, to the outside football world, the Brisbane Bears ever seemed to lack dignity or endeavour, there was one man in whom these qualities were always evident. Roger Merrett came to Brisbane after being discarded by Essendon in one of football's greatest pieces of misjudgement. He was a fearsome and effective centre half-forward with the Bombers, and he set about rebuilding his career by doing the same things he did down south – getting to the contests, getting his big body in the way of his opponents, taking the hard marks as well as the easy ones. He was a cheap buy for the Bears, but soon after he began in 1989 it became evident all around the club that here was a leader.

Merrett retired after the tumultuous 1996 season. He had played 313 games, and was to become an assistant coach to John Northey. It was certain his career would be tied up with the Brisbane Lions.

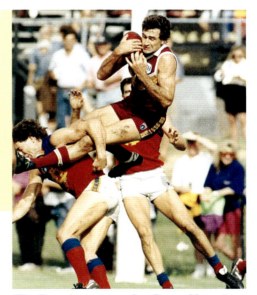

The Bears' great warrior, Roger Merrett.

1995 HONOUR ROLL

Year	Pos	Leading Goalkicker	No.	Best & Fairest	Captain	Coach
1995	8th	Roger Merrett	44	Michael Voss	Roger Merrett	Robert Walls

In its thrilling run to the finals the Bears won six of their last seven games, losing only to the eventual Premier, Carlton, in a tight game.
Alastair Lynch, despite having suffered with chronic fatigue syndrome for most of the season, posts the club's third goalkicking half-century.
Gilbert McAdam, who suffered a severe facial injury during the 1994 season, shows he is back to his uncanny best with some wonderful games in the all-important second half of the season.
Michael Voss becomes the youngest Bears Best and Fairest winner and only the third Queenslander to win a club B&F award, behind Jason Dunstall (Hawthorn) and Scott McIvor (Fitzroy).
Old warhorse Martin Leslie retires.
Morningside's Brett Voss, the younger brother of champion Michael, joins the club via a pre-draft concession for Queenslanders, along with North Brisbane's local hero Danny Dickfos, who for eight years had rejected countless AFL approaches.
In a remarkable double switch Brisbane Bears coach Robert Walls takes up the coaching position at Richmond, and Richmond coach John Northey takes the Brisbane position. Northey, experienced at Sydney, Melbourne and Richmond, is seen as an ideal replacement for the highly respected Walls.
The 1995 Qualifiying Final against Carlton is remarkable for the number of Brisbane supporters in the crowd at the Melbourne Cricket Ground.

BRISBANE

Savouring the moment: the Brisbane Bears on the ground before the start of the 1996 Preliminary Final.

A golden year in 1996

The Bears became a legitimate force in 1996, going within one game of the Grand Final in only the club's 10th season and the 100th of the VFL/AFL competition.

Under John Northey the Bears posted a seven-game winning streak on their way to third spot at the end of the home-and-away season and two Gabba finals. Only a loss to Collingwood at Victoria Park prevented them finishing top of the ladder.

On September 6, in a qualifying final sold out in 48 hours to a Brisbane public experiencing its first-ever finals fever, the Bears beat Essendon 15.11(101) to 15.10 (100) in front of a ground-record audience of 22,003.

A week later they did it again, the Bears obliterating defending Premiers Carlton 26.14 (170) to 10.13 (73) – the highest Semi-final score in history – under the Gabba lights.

But on September 21 the Bears' fairytale was cut short when they went down to North Melbourne 11.10 (76) to 17.12 (114) at the MCG. Michael Voss failed a fitness test in the warm-up as untimely injuries took their final toll. The margin reached 75 points shortly after half-time, before the northerners rallied.

The biggest live audience (66,719) in Bears history fittingly saw the last Bears game, before the birth of the Brisbane Lions via the Bears/Fitzroy merger.

It was a disappointing end, but they had rewritten the record books. The Bears had never finished higher than eighth, never won more than 10 games and never won a final. In 1996 they finished third with 17 wins and a draw, including two finals.

The Bears' Preliminary Final side was:
B: C. Scott, R. Champion, D. Dickfos;
HB: N. Chapman, M. Kennedy, A. Gowers;
C: C. McRae, A. Fletcher, N. Lappin;
HF: G. McAdam (*), D. Scott, D. White;
F: J. Leppitsch, A. Lynch (vc), S. Hart;
FOLL: M. Clarke, M. Ashcroft (vc), C. Lambert. **INT:** M. McLean (vc), R. Merrett (c), T. Lynch. * Replaced M. Voss.

A cruel blow: Voss injured.

1996 HONOUR ROLL

Year	Pos	Leading Goalkicker	No.	Best & Fairest	Captain	Coach
1996	3rd	Alastair Lynch	52	Michael Voss	Roger Merrett	John Northey

CLUB NEWS 1996

Brisbane hit the top of the Premiership ladder for the first time in 1996. Throughout the season they spend five weeks at No. 1.

In 1996, Brisbane club membership exceeds 10,000, nearly double that of 1995. Average Gabba attendances also jump by 8000 to 18,672, including six sell-out games.

In the Round 6 match full-back Richard Champion becomes the Bears' seventh 100-gamer. Andrew Bews plays his 250th AFL game, his 43rd for the Bears. Brisbane 17.8 (110) defeats Fremantle 12.13 (85) to become the first Brisbane team to win twice in the west in the same season. They had already beaten West Coast in Round 2.

Roger Merrett becomes the 32nd player to reach 300 VFL/AFL games in the Round 7 match against Hawthorn at the Gabba. The club celebrated the milestone by whipping Hawthorn 15.14 (104) to 5.11 (41).

In Round 11 Matthew Kennedy becomes the club's eighth centurion, and a week later Nigel Lappin becomes the first Bears player to win senior Victorian State of Origin selection. Overall, eight Brisbane players are chosen to play for their respective State of Origin teams.

A total of $27,000 in fines is handed out to the Bears club and players following the Round 15 clash against Essendon at the Gabba. The club is fined $10,000 over a melee, and Roger Merrett, Michael Voss, Craig Lambert,

1996

John Northey: experience at the helm as the Bears reach new heights.

Coach brings out best in a new Brisbane

The face is a little craggier, and he wears a cap as a concession to the Queensland sun, but the youth and spirit and determination of Brisbane coach John Northey is as strong as when he swooped on the ball on Richmond's half-forward flank, coached at Ballarat, took over the fledgling Sydney Swans, took moderate Melbourne teams to the heights in the finals, got Richmond up off the floor and took on the Brisbane Bears.

In a swap with Robert Walls, Northey headed North into the well-established football set-up at the Gabba. He had a team of experience, with Roger Merrett and old stagers like Craig Lambert, Andy Gowers, Andrew Bews, Scott McIvor and Alastair Lynch, as well as some amazing young talent in the likes of Michael Voss, Matthew Clarke, Justin Leppitsch, Darryl White and Co.

Northey, with his judgement, his stern but fatherly approach to his players, his great football thinking and his ability to put some steel into a team, had the Bears firing in 1996. He had almost an overabundance of talent at his disposal in 1997, but the players needed more than one season to shake down after the Brisbane-Fitzroy merger, and Northey is there to meld them into the formidable unit they must become.

Travel hoodoo

There was something that the Brisbane Bears just didn't like about hopping on a plane and flying interstate. After three away wins in 1987 and 1988 the club won just four games away from home in the next five years.

It started to turn around in 1994, when the Bears equalled early years, but slipped again in 1995, despite playing first-ever finals. Then, they managed just two away wins.

The hoodoo was put to rest in 1996, when the Bears won four games in a row interstate and went 6–1–5 in away games (including one finals loss).

Into the black

The Bears lost a reported $28 million in the Christopher Skase era of 1987–89 and Reuben Pelerman finished in the red ($10 million) for his 1990–91 venture.

In 1992, their first year as a membership-based club, still based at Carrara, they showed a profit of $75,853. In 1993, after relocation, they lost $52,788.

The Bears, more settled in 1994, finished $90,141 in the black before falling to a not-unexpected loss of $108,964 in 1995, hit by the reduced Gabba capacity.

In 1996 they finished $87,822 in profit pre-merger, and in 1997 the new Lions were set to show a record six-figure profit.

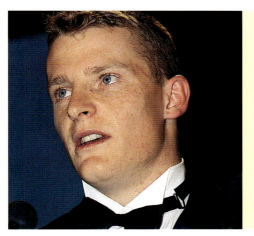

A Bears Brownlow for home-grown star

Michael Voss was the only Brownlow Medallist of the Bears era, sharing the award in 1996 with Essendon's James Hird. It was a huge triumph for the club, and for Queensland football, for Voss, born at Orbost in country Victoria, had moved to Queensland with his family at age 10 and did the bulk of his football learning via QAFL club Morningside.

Voss, then 21, was already the youngest winner of the Bears Club Champion Award in 1995, winning again in 1996. He won All-Australian selection in 1996, and when still only 21 was named a foundation co-captain with Alastair Lynch of the Brisbane Lions.

Other top-10 Bears finishes in the Brownlow Medal were McLean's 17 votes for equal fifth in 1991, David Bain's 15 votes for equal fourth in 1990, Roger Merrett's 14 votes for equal seventh in 1989 and Nathan Buckley's 14 votes for equal sixth in 1993.

Michael Voss on Brownlow night.

Andrew Gowers and Darryl White are each fined $3000. In a separate incident, Brent Green is fined $2000 for wrestling.
21-year-old Michael Voss becomes the Bears' first ever recipient of the Brownlow Medal, sharing the honour with Essendon's James Hird.
Shaun Hart posts his 100th game in the club's first Gabba final. Both Marcus Ashcroft and Alastair Lynch post their 150th AFL game. Brownlow Medallist Michael Voss and Craig Lambert are named in the All-Australian side.
The Bears post their first ever finals victory with a one-point win over Essendon. The game draws a record 22,003 spectators to the Gabba.
In a Semi-final clash against reigning Premiers Carlton, Brisbane produces what is arguably one of their greatest wins, beating the Blues 26.14 (170) to 10.13 (73). The Bears hadn't won against Carlton since 1991. In the same game Alastair Lynch becomes the third Bears player to post fifty goals in a season.
Roger Merrett receives a standing ovation at the MCG as he leaves the playing arena for the last time after the Preliminary Final. It was his 313th game.
Michael Voss completes back-to-back Best and Fairest wins. The Bears' first (and only) life memberships are awarded to Roger Merrett and property steward Graeme Smart.
The Bears finish the season in third place, losing the Preliminary Final to North Melbourne. They had never before finished higher than eighth on the ladder.

BRISBANE

Roger Merrett heads Bears top 10

Roger Merrett, seven-year captain, games record-holder (164) and leading goalkicker (285) of the Bears era, is unquestionably the club's all-time No. 1 player. Fittingly, he was the Bears' first life member after his retirement in 1996, and is a must at No. 1 in a Bears 'Top 10' list.

In rating the club's all-time top 10 players, history may say that Michael Voss was the best of them all. But in assessing only the Bears era, even with Voss' 1996 Brownlow Medal and 1995–96 Bears Best and Fairest wins, it is difficult to rate this ultra-classy youngster ahead of two old-stagers he holds in such high esteem, Merrett and Michael McLean.

The Bears' Top 10 players of the 1987–96 era, as selected by Peter Blucher, are:

1. Roger Merrett:
A windfall for the Bears in 1988 after he was prematurely axed after a long career at Essendon, which included a stint in the Reserves and the award of the Gardiner Medal for Reserves Best and Fairest in 1982. Was made captain in his first season. Brought some toughness and leadership to the mercurial Bears forward line, and became noted for his courage and ability to protect younger players. Retired with all honours after 313 League games in 1996, and took up the post of Assistant Coach of the Brisbane Lions.

2. Michael McLean.
The talented winger from Darwin revived his career after being discarded by the Footscray club in 1989 after 95 games. He had suffered injury problems at Footscray, but came to the Bears fully fit in 1991 and has given great service despite recurring injuries in recent times. Known as 'Magic' because of his ball-handling skills, he was Best and Fairest for the Bears in 1991 and 1993, and was still firing along as a veteran in 1997 after 15 seasons in the AFL. Noted for his leadership, on and off the field.

3. Michael Voss.  A superstar in the AFL at the age of 22, Voss has all the skills. He is a brilliant mark, a sure ball handler and a penetrating kick. In his midfield position he both launches attacks from the bounce and links the play. He was the youngest Bears player at 17 years and 11 days in 1992, and matured quickly to be Best and Fairest in 1995 and 1996. He shared the Brownlow Medal in 1996, and in 1997 was made co-captain of the Brisbane Lions with Alastair Lynch.

4. Scott McIvor.  A class player through the years with the Bears, he has been a regular at midfield in his early days. Born in Brisbane but began his career with Fitzroy, before returning north to the Brisbane Bears in 1988. He has been among the Brisbane best and fairest eight times in 12 seasons, and was Fitzroy Best and Fairest in 1987. With the merger he is the Brisbane Lions' games record holder by default. Struggled with injury in 1997.

5. Craig Lambert.
A tough rover and a great ball-winner, he had a six-year career with Richmond, and has won Best and Fairest honours at two clubs, the latest with the Bears in 1994. A vice-captain of the Brisbane Lions, he is moving into the veteran class but has a lot to offer with his on-field example and fighting spirit.

6. Matthew Clarke.
One of the younger brigade in the Brisbane Lions set-up. From South Australia, he was selected in the draft and made his debut in 1993. Now among the best ruckmen in the AFL, he is a fine athlete who can keep going all day, and is an excellent tap ruckman and a strong mark.

7. Marcus Ashcroft.
A loyal, outstanding home-grown product from the Gold Coast, he has had eight years with the team and is a veteran at age 25. Among the top performers every year, he is a great possession winner around the midfield and in a ruck roving role. A fine tagger but with all-round skills and a cool head. Vice-captain since 1994 and a strong part of Brisbane's rise to power.

8. Geoff Raines.  A football journeyman with his 254 games spread among four clubs, Raines reached a satisfactory conclusion to a brilliant career with his 59 games for Brisbane from 1987 to 1989. His polished play, which had earned him places in many Victorian teams, helped the football credibility of the fledgling Bears. Fast, balanced and a magnificent kick.

9. Brad Hardie.
Another highly qualified original with the Bears, and the first man to play 100 games with the club. Hardie was formerly a Western Australian star who joined Footscray. After a much-publicised break-up with coach Mick Malthouse he brought his Brownlow Medal-winning ability to the Bears. He combined immense strength with excellent ball-handling skills and judgement, and mostly utilised his abilities on the half-forward line.

10. Martin Leslie.
An All-Australian defender from Port Adelaide, Leslie played 89 games with the Bears (1989–93), and was joint Best and Fairest for Brisbane in 1990.

1996

Bears club records - 1987–1996

Most games: Roger Merrett (164)
Most goals: Roger Merrett (285)
Youngest player: Michael Voss – 17 years 11 days (1992)
Oldest player: Roger Merrett – 36 years 155 days (1996)
Highest score: 33-21-219 v Sydney (Gabba) Rd 8, 1993
Lowest score: 2-5-17 v Hawthorn (Princes Park) Rd 12, 1988
Greatest winning margin: 162 pts v Sydney (Gabba) Rd 8, 1993
Greatest losing margin: 164 pts v Geelong (Carrara) Rd 7, 1992
Longest winning sequence: 7 (1996)
Longest losing sequence: 12 (1990–1991)
Most seasons as coach: Robert Walls 5 (1991–95)
Most seasons as captain: Roger Merrett 7 (1990–96)
Most goals in a match: Brad Hardie 9 v Carlton (Princes Park) Rd 10, 1989
Brownlow Medallists: Michael Voss, 1996

BRISBANE

The merger

Throughout the 1980s and 1990s Melbourne struggled to accept that not all clubs could survive independently. But it was debatable whether a merger or a relocation was the more palatable option.

It seemed long-time battlers Fitzroy would do both. They would combine with the fledging Brisbane Bears to become the Brisbane Lions. The club had reached the end of the road in Melbourne. Relocation to Brisbane seemed the only option.

Late in the 1986 season Fitzroy president Leon Wiegard called a meeting of players at Wesley College. Scott McIvor, a Queenslander playing with Fitzroy, and later one of the Bears' all-time greats, was barely 20. But he remembers it well.

'Leon told us the club was in a position where they had no option but to go, and they were looking for support from the players. It was an overwhelming "yes" vote and we thought "That's it". As far as the players knew it was a done deal – Fitzroy was moving to Queensland,' McIvor said.

But a benefactor intervened and saved Fitzroy. An injection of cash, followed by more in ensuing years, couldn't solve the reality that the VFL foundation club didn't have the necessary financial backing.

Leading player: Club president Noel Gordon.

The Nauru Insurance Corporation saved Fitzroy Football Club with $1.25 million in 1994, but became the 'executioners' in 1996 by appointing an independent administrator to recoup the debt. It took all financial decisions away from club directors. An AFL offer of $6 million had been made 12 months earlier and was the 'carrot' for merging.

On 1 July 1996, the AFL Commission agreed in principle to a Fitzroy/North Melbourne union. Bears Chairman Noel Gordon offered Fitzroy administrator, Michael Brennan, what he considered a better financial deal. 'We felt if we could put a better offer in front of him he'd be compelled by law to say it was his preferred deal, remembering that he was in an awkward position because the only way he'd get his money was if the AFL provided the $6 million,' said Bears chief executive Andrew Ireland.

'We'd also been making a number of calls to other clubs, and it became quite evident that they would not support the extended player conditions stipulated by North. We believed we had the best offer and one that the clubs would accept', Ireland said.

Initially it was not well received on either front. In Brisbane there was resentment. The Bears had finally shed the laughing-stock tags. The maroon jumper with the gold V meant something. Why, asked supporters, give it away to join forces with a club battling on and off the field?

It would, Gordon said, guarantee the club's finances. 'We came out of private ownership [in 1991] with virtually nothing, and have had to operate on our year-to-year earnings. This secures our financial stability.'

The merger would also provide the club with a sizeable Melbourne support base, and an injection of eight quality Fitzroy players.

When the Brisbane Bears era of 1987–96 closed on 4 July 1996, the Brisbane Lions era began.

A long road to acceptance.

What some fans say

There was an indication of the acceptance of the merger by Fitzroy supporters in letters to the Brisbane Lions administration.

Wrote John Close of South Oakleigh: 'As a Fitzroy supporter in excess of 40 years I was apprehensive about the future. Remarkably, I have found myself as fanatical as ever with my new team. Any genuine supporter who has experienced the traumas of Fitzroy Football Club would have to appreciate our welcome to Brisbane, and the preservation of history.'

Daniel Martinez of West Sunshine wrote, 'Let me say how happy I've been by the way the whole merger issue has been handled by the Brisbane Lions administration. I truly believe that the Victorian membership will swell to at least 5–6000 in 1998 as many ex-Fitzroy people have taken the approach of "Let's see what happens in 1997."'

Dot Thompson, 76, a Fitzroy life member, admitted 'My first reaction was one of hatred. I looked at the jumper and listened to the song, and said to Deirdre [her daughter, another Fitzroy life member], "That's not half bad, is it?" and she replied "It's pretty damn good". And here I am, a fanatical Brisbane Lions supporter.'

CLUB NEWS 1996–1997

The Bears averaged five wins per regular season from 1987 to 1993. Since 1994 the average has been 12.

On 4 July 1996, following the appointment of Mr Michael Brennan to administer the affairs of the Fitzroy Football Club, it is announced that Fitzroy will merge with Brisbane. Three Fitzroy members will be on the club's new 11-member board.

Fitzroy play their last game against Fremantle before merging with Brisbane. Fitzroy supporters in Brisbane gather at the Brisbane hotel to farewell their team.

Brisbane enters the season with a new identity. After merging with the 113-year-old Fitzroy Football Club, the Bears are now the Lions.

The Brisbane Lions' new jumper is closely modelled on the old Fitzroy jumper, with the Lion emblem on the chest. The Brisbane Lions announce that the Best and Fairest award will be called the Merrett/Murray Award to recognise champions of both constituent clubs.

The club theme song remains to the tune of 'La Marseillaise'. The words start; We are the pride of Brisbane Town. We wear Maroon, Blue and Gold/ We will always fight for victory/ like Fitzroy and Bears of old.

1997. In Round 13 Brisbane beats Collingwood for the only the third time in club history. The scores are Brisbane 11.22 (88) to Collingwood 11.7 (73). An away win against the Pies remains as elusive as ever.

1996 – 1997

In the midst of merger turmoil, Brisbane defeats Fitzroy in Round 20, 1996. Matthew Clarke wins this ruck contest.

The birth of a new – and old – club, the Brisbane Lions

The 'marriage' of the Brisbane Bears and the Fitzroy Lions and the subsequent 'birth' of the Brisbane Lions was a landmark chapter in football history and there were inevitable rough spots. But the Lions, less than 12 months old, were worth it in the long term.

Chairman Noel Gordon, chief executive Andrew Ireland and Coach John Northey admitted it took much longer to overcome 'merger-itis' than they anticipated. But the merger consolidated expansion in Queensland, and upheld the tradition of one of football's foundation clubs.

Still, to quantify the success of the Brisbane Lions in their 1997 rookie season under foundation co-captains Alastair Lynch and Michael Voss is a three-fold process. It is about the present, on and off the field, and it is about the future.

In a cold, analytical sense year one of the merger club was perhaps a disappointment. A team ranked among the Premiership favourites in pre-season betting finished eighth, fortunate to scrape into the finals and eliminated by eventual Grand Finalists St Kilda on the first weekend in September.

If the 'marriage' was just about wins and losses there may be grounds for some counselling. But it was not.

It was about consolidating a base for continued football expansion in the fledgling Queensland market, and upholding the wonderful tradition of one of the game's foundation clubs.

In that sense, it was an inevitable winner.

And if veteran Essendon coach Kevin Sheedy is any sort of judge, the merger club will become a legitimate AFL superpower. In March 1997, after the Lions had eliminated the Bombers from the Ansett Cup pre-season competition, Sheedy suggested it was just a question of who would meet Brisbane in the Grand Final.

It was an extraordinary statement, and would prove to be a long way wrong. But when reminded of his error at the end of the year, Sheedy said: 'I wasn't wrong – I was just 12 months early.'

The Queensland-based membership of the club jumped from 10,400 to 13,800. Average Gabba attendances climbed from 18,672 in 1996, with six sell-outs among 13 games (including two finals), to 19,500 in 1997, with seven sell-outs among 11 games (no finals).

Clearly, for many former Fitzroy supporters, the appeal of AFL football in the wonderful intimate environment of the Gabba helped compensate for the change in name, song and jumper.

In Victoria, the membership of 3,200 helped the budget and when Brisbane tackled St Kilda at Waverley in the finals, there was a loud pro-Lions voice in the crowd that far, far out-pointed the Bears' minimal interstate support of previous years.

Ten players from the Brisbane Lions are called up to play for their respective State of Origin teams in mid-June.
The Brisbane Lions sign a sponsorship deal with Puma in June that will operate from seasons 1997 to 2000.
Brisbane had been hoping for a late season revival to lift its Premiership hopes, but the team seemed to run out of steam in Round 19. After having thrashed Hawthorn in the previous week at the Gabba, it succumbed to North Melbourne at the MCG, 17.14 (116) to 9.5 (59).
In Round 20 Daniel Bradshaw soccers a goal in the dying seconds that allows Brisbane to sneak in for a draw against Port Adelaide, with the scores locked on 13.15 (93) apiece. Brisbane had been kept in the game, and the finals race, by an eight-goal third quarter.
John Northey coaches his 300th game in Round 21, but the team does not help his coaching woes as it goes down to Essendon by four points in another Gabba thriller, 16.10 (106) to 15.12 (102).
Brisbane sneaks into the final eight, but the scoreline in its last home-and-away match does not offer much hope for progress through the finals series. In a capitulation in Perth Brisbane is beaten by the West Coast Eagles 18.12 (120) to 11.15 (81).
The end of the season marks the retirement of one of Brisbane's great players, Michael 'Magic' McLean, after 183 games. At 32 McLean succumbs to a long run of injuries that has restricted him to only six games in two years.

BRISBANE

The Lions emerge: the strength and the style of the new team is evident in this Round 10 picture.

Promises not fulfilled in 1997

A football team must be accountable in the win/loss column. Accordingly, coach Northey and his troops were disappointed with an overall 1997 result of 10 wins, one draw and 12 losses.

Northey suggested too many of his players suffered a hangover from the Bears' success of 1996, when they went within one game of the Grand Final. They expected just to flick a switch in 1997 and turn it on without the same appetite for hard work, sacrifice and mateship.

There is a suspicion, too, that the arrival of eight ex-Fitzroy players created an environment of selfishness. No fewer than 34 listed Lions of 1997 had played 14 or more senior games in 1996. Clearly, 34 into 21 didn't go. Perhaps some were playing more for themselves than the team. Certainly, they were nothing like as tight as they had been.

Whatever, there were two words which categorized the Lions' 1997 season – injuries and under-performance. Together, they combined to ambush a campaign that promised so much.

Coach Northey would not accept an extraordinary tally of injuries as the sole reason for the team's disappointing result. But drawing a parallel between the absentee list and the success ratio leads to a legitimate case of 'If only …'

A football club is no different to any other sort of business. When understaffed, the business doesn't function at full capacity. And nor did the Lions as they travelled through three distinct periods of the season.

They won just two of their first eight games as they battled a heavy early-season injury toll, and then took the points in six of their next seven to move to an ominous third on the ladder as the side started to take on some degree of consistency.

Significantly, in Round 15 in Melbourne they obliterated the Western Bulldogs, then leading the ladder, by 64 points. And in Round 16, just prior to the start of their second wave of injuries, they out-gunned eventual Premiers Adelaide by 31 points at the Gabba. The thought was emerging: 'The Lions will win it from here,' as they moved to an ominous third on the ladder.

Effectively, though, the Lions' season ended at Round 17, when they lost six key players. Michael Voss, Craig Lambert, Shaun Hart and Andrew Bews each suffered long-term injuries as the Lions were beaten by St Kilda at Waverley, and in the QSFL Brad Boyd and Chris Scott suffered a further recurrence of long-term hamstring injuries that would end their season.

Thereafter, the Lions could manage just one win and one draw from their last seven games. It seemed certain their season was over when they lost a virtual 'final' against West Coast in Perth in Round 22, but, with a miserable 0–1–3 record in August, they sneaked into the finals after a freakish sequence of upsets in the last round of the home-and-away season.

But it was a hollow inclusion. After a gallant effort from a grossly under-manned side, in which they led top side St Kilda by five points at half-time in the Qualifying Final, they were eliminated by 46 points.

1997 HONOUR ROLL

Year	Pos	Leading Goalkicker	No.	Best & Fairest	Captain	Coach
1997	8th	Justin Leppitsch	50	Michael Voss	Alastair Lynch	John Northey

1997

The Lions celebrate a great win over the Bulldogs in the run-up to the finals.

Overall, the Lions would beat each of the finalists except West Coast in a 6–5 record against the top eight bettered only by the Bulldogs (7–3) and Geelong (6–3).

But they were twice beaten by ninth-placed Essendon, managed just a draw from two games against 14th-placed Port Adelaide, had a 1–1 split with 15th-placed Hawthorn, and played non-finalists Melbourne, Fremantle, Richmond, Collingwood and Carlton just once for a combined 3–2 record.

Of the 'recruits', Brad Boyd, the ex-Fitzroy captain, missed all but 20 minutes of the year, Simon Hawking played no Senior games and Jarrod Molloy, the best-performed of the 'old' Lions, managed just 10 games in between a broken scaphoid and a knee reconstruction. Only Chris Johnson (19 games), and Scott Bamford (11) played more.

Of the 'locals', Brownlow Medallist Michael Voss missed the last six games, vice-captain Craig Lambert missed seven games, Andy Gowers missed 15, Andrew Bews missed 10 and Ben Robbins missed eight.

Michael McLean, a dual Bears B&F winner, finished his season and his career before quarter-time in round one, and Trent Bartlett, regarded as a key figure of the future, didn't manage even that much. Chris Scott played just five games (and only one full game) and Steven Lawrence missed the first 14 rounds before coming back from two knee reconstructions.

Matthew Clarke stayed fit enough long enough to become the inaugural winner of the Merrett/Murray Medal as the Lions' club champion.

Victorian State of Origin representative Nigel Lappin was runner-up from 'Mr Consistency' Marcus Ashcroft, who also was judged 'Most Professional Player'.

The emerging Justin Leppitsch was fourth in the B&F and topped the goal-kicking list with 50, while Danny Dickfos was fifth in the B&F and judged 'One-percenter of the Year'. Craig Lambert was sixth in the B&F, cut down by late-season injury for the second year in a row when in a winning position.

Daniel Bradshaw, who had played three Bears games as a 17-year-old in 1996, kicked 35 goals in 16 games in 1997 to rank second on the Lions' goalkicking list and fifth in voting for the Norwich Rising Star Award. History may show he is even better.

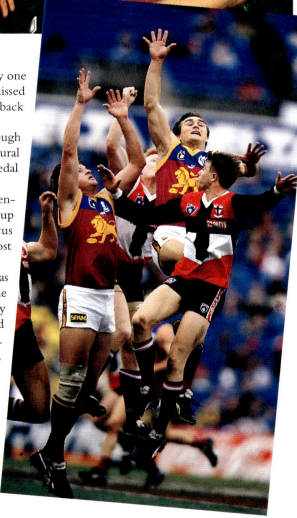

1997 aspirations end at the hands of St Kilda.

CARLTON

MY CLUB
by Garrie Hutchinson

The first thing anyone asks you, or used to, in Melbourne was 'Whodoya barrack for?' When I answer, 'Carlton, of course,' some people, with long suburban memories, say 'Dincha useta barrack for Esse'don?' And the answer is yes, I did. I am one of those who made the switch, and like many religious conversions, it took place on a road.

Saul who became St Paul was on the road to Damascus. I was on the road to Carlton.

It was the middle of a winter night in 1967, and the road was Mount Alexander Road, which leads through the heart of Essendon past Royal Park and the corner where I had once dismounted the 59 tram to go to University High School, the place where I was infected with a taste for bohemianism. John Coleman had once attended Uni High, and when I was there football legends such as 'Gags' Gallagher and the Keddie brothers walked the Oval like giants, already playing League Football. Brent 'Tiger' Crosswell was there too.

On this night I walked, it was after the trams were locked in their sheds. I had left, or was forced to leave home – some differences over politics, hair length, ambitions. I was a student at Melbourne University, but not for much longer.

I was headed for a friend's house in Carlton, and passed a number of old Carlton football grounds. Royal Park, where the club began and where early President and comedian George Coppin had sold Burke and Wills their camels, the University where the Blues had played a couple of seasons at the Madeleine Street ground, site of Newman College, and Princes Park itself.

This was football country, and had been as long as Carlton and football had existed.

While walking Mount Alexander Road, I had plenty of time for reflection, and one of the things I thought about was Essendon – the suburb, the football club, the politics, the social life, the childhood. It seemed to me that I was leaving all that behind, and that I was about to make a new life in Carlton. If that was the case I felt that I should make a wholehearted change.

I embraced the suburb and its football

The greatest – Alex Jesaulenko.

team, and have stuck to it through success and political embarrassment ever since. That's 30 years, boy and man, to the stage where having had the outer demolished almost under my feet, I now buy seats in the Legends stand.

I didn't know much about the history of Carlton Football Club at that time, but I did

CARLTON

Year established	1864
Joined VFL/AFL	1897
Home grounds	Princes Pk, Optus Oval
Premierships	1906, 1907, 1908, 1914, 1915, 1938, 1945, 1947, 1968, 1970, 1972, 1979, 1981, 1982, 1987, 1995
Brownlow Medals	Bert Deacon 1947, John James 1961, Gordon Collis 1964, Greg Williams 1994
Record home crowd	47,415 v Geelong, 1963
Most games	Bruce Doull, 356
Most goals	Stephen Kernahan, 738
Notable supporters	Past: Sir Robert Menzies, Professor Manning Clark. Present: B. A. Santamaria, Malcolm Fraser, David Boon, Jo Bailey, Mark Woodforde, Richard Pratt, Dean Jones

know that supporting the club involved a certain number of political paradoxes for me. At the time of the Vietnam War and conscription, Carlton's No. 1 ticket holder was the recently retired Prime Minister Sir Robert Menzies. Presidents and No. 1 ticket holders, then as now, represented the blue-blood side of Australian life.

But I knew having been in the outer a few times already that the fraternity represented there was of a different sort. Beyond the members at Carlton was a wild bunch of people, barrackers, bards, bohemians and bluestockings.

And this was football, modern football. This was the club that had changed the face of the game, and concepts of club loyalty, by recruiting Ron Barassi in 1965. Barassi to Carlton was in football terms the first act in the renovation of Carlton – and was accompanied by the first tentative moves by renovators of the suburb.

In the sixties it was still widely regarded as a slum, and certainly the places I lived in, with rotten floorboards, outside dunnies and

The heroes. Above: Stephen Kernahan and barrackers with the 1995 cup. Below: Brent 'Tiger' Crosswell.

an Early Kooka in the kitchen corner, were often beyond renovation.

Carlton the team and the suburb soon came to represent for me the whole bohemian thing – learning to eat out as cafes sprang up, arguments over football and politics in the dingy, grubby pubs, exercising literary and poetic skills in the outer and in little theatres such as La Mama. And Princes Park with its extraordinary passing parade of pseudo-, mock- and genuine footy intellectuals inhabiting the old press box wing *was* football.

Success seemed to come to the team (like most stand up and barrack supporters I had nothing to do with the machinations of the Club) and the suburb and the gang of supporters at the same time as the sixties wound into the seventies, and beyond.

The glory days of football on a Saturday afternoon in the outer with a bunch of mates coincided with my prime footy-going years, my 20s and 30s, and with everything that was happening in Carlton for writers, actors, filmmakers, drunks and painters.

Football represented something about an increasingly tolerant Australia in the 1960s and 1970s. The club might have been managed by a succession of 'entrepreneurs' but the broad church in the outer tolerated them, and occasionally even met them. Football in Melbourne crosses all social, cultural and political divides – and none wider than those at Carlton.

At Princes Park, on the wing near the Press Box was where I worshipped (except in Grand Finals) the heroes that set the standard of greatness (and style) in football for me – Jezza and Big Nick, Tiger and Syd, Wallsy and Gags, Serge and Swan – they were my yardsticks, and probably still are. Add a handful of later heroes, Mr Doull and the Dominator, Fitz'n'Sticks, SOS and the first football 'God', Ken Hunter, Braddles and Diesel and you have most of my dream team.

A dream team set in the history of football, Melbourne and me.

Our oldest home ground, near the Burke and Wills Memorial, Royal Park.

CARLTON

Left: Ted Prevot (l) and George Coulthard. Centre: 1880 team. Right: George Coulthard in 1880.

George Coulthard – the first Carlton legend

The remarkable sportsman George Coulthard was born at Boroondara on 1 August 1856, and packed a good deal of fun into the 27 years allowed him, before he died of tuberculosis in Carlton on 22 October 1883. He was a first-class cricketer who played six games for Victoria and one Test for Australia, and was three times Champion of the Colony in 1876, 1877 (a Carlton Premiership year) and 1879. The *Australasian* said of him in 1879: 'He is the grandest player of the day. It is doubtful if, for general excellence, his equal has ever been seen.'

As a cricketer he made 31 and took 3/29 on debut in a game against South Australia in November 1880 – the first first-class game between the two colonies. He had previously umpired in several matches involving the touring England team under Lord Harris – including the infamous game against NSW in February 1879 where a decision to give Australian captain Billy Murdoch out run out caused a near riot, and the cancellation of the Second Test. Only great diplomacy by Murdoch in England that year got Test cricket back on the rails. Perhaps gratitude, but surely not form on the cricket field caused Coulthard to be selected in a the first Test played at Sydney in February 1882. He made 6 batting at eleven and did not bowl.

As footballer he was a 'follower', a ruck-man fast, tough and skilful – and rarely took a backwards step. In 1882 he had a dispute with the import from Hotham, Joey Tankard, causing both players to be suspended for most of the season. Tankard went back to play for Hotham, and in the first game back from suspension for both players on 12 August 1882, they came to blows again and were suspended by the VFA for the rest of the season. It was Coulthard's last game for Carlton.

The wild men of Royal Park

The Triangle Ground, Princes Park.

Carlton's first home ground was in Royal Park, not far from the spot where Burke and Wills set off on their epic journey in 1859, and where the monument now stands. Carlton players known as 'wild men' played on the rough and sloping ground in 1864. Between the foundation of the club and the first game played at modern Princes Park on 22 June 1897 (against Collingwood – Carlton lost) the club played at a number of different places in Carlton. They included the Madeleine Street oval, where Newman College now stands at the University of Melbourne in Swanston Street (north); the southern end of Princes Park; and what was then known as 'the triangle' – the area of land where University Women's College was later built.

CLUB NEWS 1864–1896

At a meeting on 17 May 1865 at the University Hotel in Lygon Street Carlton, Ben James was elected Carlton's first secretary and James Linacre was invited to be President.

Theatrical entrepreneur, comedian, politician and property developer George Coppin was elected President of the Carlton Football Club on 13 March 1866 and presented a football as a trophy in intra-club practice games. T.S. Marshall played for the 'Vice-President's 20'.

Carlton had its first win over Melbourne on 22 June 1867, two goals to nil. The other two games against that team were drawn.

Carlton won its first trophy, the South Yarra Challenge Cup in 1871, captained by Jack Donovan and wearing a dark blue cap – the origin of the Blues, the old dark navy Blues. The team, however, was equally well known as the 'Butchers' because it wore tight-fitting blue dungaree jackets reminiscent of that trade.

Carlton went through the 1874 season undefeated, becoming the premier team in the colony. Eminent cricketers Tom Kendall and Harry Boyle played for Carlton

Carlton changed from grey socks and the blue jackets and blue caps to blue and white hooped socks, blue guernseys, blue caps and blue knickerbockers – truly the Blues in 1875.

Carlton won the inaugural Premiership of the Victorian Football

1864 – 1896

Carlton: the 1871 premier team.

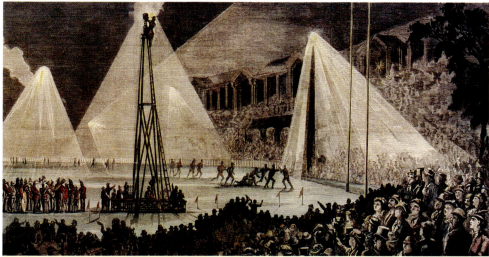

Lights, but not much action in 1879

1879 was a big year for electricity. Large areas could be lit economically. In 1879 the first electric light company was formed in Melbourne, the Australian Electric Light Co.

Not surprisingly, just about the first electrical action in Melbourne was to light a sporting event, not a city street. In 1879 three football matches took place at night, at the MCG.

The MCG was illuminated by carbon arc searchlights apparently mounted on high towers around the arena. Details of the height and number of towers are sketchy, and whether the whole of the MCG was lit, or a smaller area inside the ground, is also not known. Carlton played in the second of the three games.

On 13 August Carlton defeated Melbourne three goals to one, George Coulthard kicking all three in front of 7000 fans.

The electricity was supplied by a Professor Pepper, and in the Carlton game the teams used a white-painted football until it burst, when a brown one was used. Perhaps that is why it was so difficult to see. A contemporary account said: 'This ball was scarcely discernible in the fitful and unsteady light the machines gave. A goal by Coulthard relieved the monotony, and when the white ball once more enlivened matters a second goal was gained by Coulthard.

'The game will not count in the season's competition, and it cannot be pronounced a success from a football point of view. People could scarcely see the players, or the players the ball. Some considerable improvement will have to be made in the lighting before the game can be played to advantage under electric light.'

But the season continued. Carlton lost to Geelong at the Corio Oval and had the third VFA game against Melbourne abandoned when Carlton objected to Melbourne using a player without a clearance or residential qualification.

In 1879 Carlton were runners-up to Geelong, having played 22 games, winning 16, losing four with two drawn.

They kicked a record 82 goals and only had 17 kicked against them. No finals were played in this season.

Carlton's first Premiership Cup

The first organised competition began with a meeting on 16 May 1870 when the senior football club secretaries met and agreed on rules for a Challenge Cup, among them the first use of a central umpire. South Yarra won the 1870 competition, after some disputation, and the Cup became known as the South Yarra Challenge Cup. At the beginning of 1871 it was agreed that the two teams with the most wins in that season would play one 'grand match' for the Cup. Carlton met Melbourne in the 'grand match' of 1871, played on the neutral Albert Park ground. Jack Donovan of Carlton won the toss, and kicked with a gale. Play began at 3 o'clock and went on till 6. Carlton 'supported one another extremely well, and they went in extensively for small kicks from one to the other, giving marks this way'. Carlton scored two goals to nil to win the game. In the last hour 'spectators closed in on the ground in a disgraceful manner and at length it looked as if the game was being played on a crowded street rather than a regulation football ground.'

Association in 1877 and George Coulthard was named Champion of the Colony for the second year in succession (he won again in 1879). Carlton players Jack Donovan, William Lacey and George Robertson were champions for the three seasons before Coulthard – five Champions in a row.

Carlton in 1877 was the first Victorian club to play in NSW. In two games against Waratah they won under Victorian rules and lost playing rugby.

The University kicked Carlton off Madeleine Street oval in 1878 and the club was granted permissive occupancy of 11 acres at the southern end of Princes Park by the Melbourne City Council, after support by a petition from 3500 ratepayers and supporters. No permanent fences were allowed and no trees could be destroyed.

The Princes Oval, with a portable picket fence, was opened by the Lord Mayor on 3 May 1879.

Carlton won its second VFA flag in Queen Victoria's Jubilee year, 1887, by defeating Fitzroy before 20,000 people, 8.13 to 1.6, in the last game of the season. Future Carlton coach Jack Worrall was Fitzroy's best – while starring for the Old Dark Navy Blues were Jack Baker, 'Dolly' Batters, Sam Bloomfield, Mick Whelan, Tommy Leydin and Billy Strickland.

A mid-season trip to Tasmania after eight wins in succession in early 1888 precipitated a slump. The *Australasian* noted 'Tasmania and a fortnight's break in training played sad havoc with their efficiency.' Carlton finished fourth.

CARLTON

The Blues show their force in the triple Premiership years.

Raising the 1906 Flag.

The champions among the champions

Although Carlton played like a 'well-oiled clock, playing team ball, shining in clusters rather than bright particular stars' in the triple-Premiership years of 1906, 1907 and 1908, 'each hero deserves to have his name inscribed on the Scroll', according to Centre in the *Argus*. He wrote of the 1906 heroes:

Mallee Johnson – 'the white-haired boy who strides across the sward in three and a half steps, added more shine and polish to his already brilliant career. His passing was poetic. He brought down aces and bowers from nowhere ... He rang the bell every time. He cakewalked down the aisle. Whether soaring into the clouds, striding gaily round the lawn, on the blob or guarding the citadel, one of the loveliest features of the scenery was Mallee's genial smile.'

Mick Grace – 'Many a time and oft has the Gladiator Micko dragged a smouldering game out of the fire of Fate with his ice-cold thinking apparatus. He could be put in charge of a first-class volcano or earthquake and it wouldn't disturb his summer dreams. His rocket-like flights toward the azure and his happy knack of always being where he should be kept the good news going round.'

In the centre Wee Rod McGregor 'acquired the habit of grabbing the globe and spinning it where it should go, doing the right thing like clockwork. By the last quarter he was in about 17 pieces, but he managed to bring the various sections of himself down to the starting machine, and the majority of him finished like a Sheffield Handicap.'

Eli 'Pompey' Elliott kept 'prancing with the spheroid til the bell ... The Brewers' rucks never missed the trams. Jinks and captain Flynn, who handled the team like Napoleon, Wellington, Julius Caesar, Great Scot, Kitchener and Jim Flynn rolled into one big ball of bulging brain, grafted like bullocks and handed out the gay globule to Elliott til the rover's arms must have been tired taking it.'

'Mick' Grace.

Jack Worrall: first coach

Jack Worrall richly deserved all the bouquets and medals and tokens of esteem the Carlton multitude sprinkled on his shrine. He was 'the man that did'. 'Jack Worrall entered, and the scene was changed. The ghost-like Brewers rose from the Egyptian sepulchre. They were not dead but sleeping. For the past four years they have often been near the giddy top, but somebody, usually Fitzroy, shoved them down. At last Jack took his waistcoat off to the business. He talked. He grafted. He advised. He said things. He did things. And behold, they were dealing out Free Beer in Carlton last Saturday.'

Above: Carlton 1906 honour board.
Left: A uniform variant.

CLUB NEWS 1897–1908

Carlton lost 5.6. (36) to Collingwood 6.4 (40) in the first game on the new home ground at Princes Oval on 22 June 1897.

Carlton won two games in its first VFL season – defeating St Kilda twice. St Kilda failed to win a game at all.

Carlton lost to Essendon the next week, apparently following a pencilled note in the dressing room at East Melbourne: 'Don't waste time trying to pick up the ball. Take your kick and we are sure to win.' The Blues lost 1.3 (9) to 10.17 (77).

The VFL reduced the number of players permitted in a team from 20 to 18 in 1899, and Carlton brought in ten new players – but only won four games for the season.

14-year veteran Peter Williams starred in Carlton's first win in 1899 2.6 (18) to South Melbourne 0.5 (5). This Williams played 34 VFL games – after some 200 in the VFA, following his debut in 1888.

The Blues played in the finals in 1899, as all eight teams did, defeating Melbourne in one of the three games but losing to eventual Premiers Fitzroy by one point.

In 1902 former Fitzroy champion (and Test cricketer) Jack Worrall was appointed Carlton secretary, and in taking over team selection, recruitment and training methods became Australian football's first coach. He believed in long kicking, discipline and handballing only to get out of trouble.

1897–1908

Everyone is on the blue tram in 1906

When Carlton won its first VFL Premiership in 1906, a writer under the nom de boot of Centre, obviously a Carlton fanatic, wrote what is regarded in many circles as the finest (and funniest) match report ever written for the magazine Melbourne Punch. Trams of the day were colour coded – the blue tram travelled from the city up Royal Parade to Carlton.

'Carlton … ain't they blitherers?' 'Never mind the behinds. Fifteen to six … Wot the …' 'And then Bruce got the ball …' 'Would 'ave won it if it 'ad snowed …' 'Used to play for Carlton meself. They was a good team then. Coulthard …' 'I 'ad a few. We ain't won for nineteen years.

'On Saturday's dewy eve such scraps of dialogue were heard all over this great great city. No matter where you turned even in the pubs, your eardrums were tickled with: 'Grace', 'Great game,' 'Jack Worrall', 'Bongo' and other classic sounds that pattered like a rain of Grand Italian Opera. Everybody was decorated with blue and white ribbons. Their talk was blue. Everybody wanted to get into the blue tram and have a ride. At the finish they were drinking blue beer: it tasted blue, anyhow. Most people in Melbourne seemed to barrack for Carlton.

'The last, fatal quarter … was accompanied by wild warcries and chants of triumph, and waving of flags, scarves, brollies, other people's tall hats, bits of the fence, husks of grandstand, and anything else lying handy. After 19 dormant years, the Old Blues were sailing gaily up the happy Harbour for home and beauty, and a large scent of mixed ale was wafted to and fro on the summer zephyrs. That globule had been sent through the sticks so often that it seemed to know the way. That last quarter crystallises into one beautiful picture of white pants dancing on the lawn, and blue guernseys shoving about a battered piece of leather as though they were jugglers …

'Carlton certainly put up one of the finest

1906 Premiership team. Backs: Clark, Norman, Gillespie, Beck. Half-backs: Payne, Johnson, Hammond. Centres: Bruce, McGregor, Kennedy. Half-forwards: Caine, Marchbank, Grace. Forwards: Lang, Topping, Little. Followers: Flynn (C), Jinks. Rover: Elliott. Carlton 15.4 (94) defeated Fitzroy 6.9 (45).

exhibitions this wondering world has ever seen. They forgot nothing from the wine cellar to the gilded dome. It was a greater and finer exhibition than the Pyramids or the Crystal Palace of the Taj Mahal or the Melbourne Waxworks. The Blues kept juggling the globule till curfew tinkled in the twilight. Nobody had ever seen such a finish to a final game. They were actually handballing, handing the orb round as though it were a cheese sandwich, passing like passengers through turnstiles all in turn, judging the spot, and shoving it right through the gaudy uprights without frightening the children. They couldn't go wrong. It was a cinematograph performance. People opined they were posing for the photographer.

'They were too good …'

1897–1908 HONOUR ROLL

Year	Pos	Leading Goalkicker	No.	Best & Fairest	Captain	Coach
1897	7th	Wally O'Cock	13		Jimmy Aitken	
1898	7th	Tommy O'Dea	8		Ernie Walton	
1899	7th	Henry Thompson	8		Ernie Walton	
1900	7th	Joe Sullivan	18		William Stuckey	
1901	7th	Joe Sullivan	14		William Stuckey	
1902	6th	Fred Webber	11		Joe McShane	John Worrall
1903	3rd	Joe Sullivan	27		Joe McShane	John Worrall
1904	2nd	Mick Grace	26		Joe McShane	John Worrall
1905	3rd	Frank Caine	25		Jim Flynn	John Worrall
1906	1st	Mick Grace	50		Jim Flynn	John Worrall
1907	1st	Frank Caine	32		Jim Flynn	John Worrall
1908	1st	Vin Gardiner	34		Fred Elliott	John Worrall

Under Worrall's direction Carlton finished in the top four for the first time in 1903, losing to eventual Premiers, Collingwood, by four points. Worrall recruited George Topping, Mick Grace, George Bruce and 'Shooter' Ford.
On 9 May 1903 Carlton's game against Geelong at Geelong was postponed because of a railway strike. The game was eventually played on 3 August even further away – at the SCG – with Geelong winning by 10 points.
Joe Sullivan had a chance to win the Second Semi-final against Collingwood at the Brunswick St Oval with the last kick of the game – but missed. It was his last game.
A rift in the club over accounting procedures used by Jack Worrall developed and he was sacked by the committee – but at the AGM before the 1904 season began, the committee was voted out, and a 'reform ticket' led by Henry Bourne Higgins, the Commonwealth Attorney-General, was voted in and Worrall continued as secretary–manager and coach. Carlton reached the Grand Final for the first time, losing to Fitzroy.
Soon to be great players 'Mallee' Johnson, 'Silver' Caine, Rod McGregor, Charlie Hammond and Norman Clark were recruited in 1905.
1908 Premiership team. Backs: Clark, Norman, Beck, Ford. Half-backs: Flynn, Payne, Jinks. Centres: Bruce, McGregor, Kennedy. Half-forwards: Lang, Marchbank, Gotz. Forwards: H Kelly, Gardiner, Topping. Followers: Johnson, Hammond. Rover: Elliott (C).

CARLTON

Above: Vin Gardiner (left) with Jim Marchbanks.

Viv Valentine.

A pleasant weekend

Despite missing the finals for the first time in 10 years, Carlton players enjoyed a pleasant end-of-season motoring weekend (pictured) to South Morang in 1913. The season had been plagued by yet more internal dissension. Some players, it appears, felt they were being ill-treated, but after hearing Billy Payne and George Topping speak to a special meeting of the club the dissenters agreed that their fears were unfounded. The end-of-season trip would have been part of the 'healing process' within the club. Injuries and the transfer of one or two key players also affected the team's performance.

The 1911 professionals

Rover Viv Valentine had a brilliant debut season for Carlton in 1911. Under new administration after the disturbances of 1909–10 that saw Jack Worrall retire as secretary and coach, Carlton maintained its high standard of play on the field – runners-up in 1909 and 1910, third in 1911 and 1912.

Valentine hailed from Tasmania, and played for that State in the 1908 carnival – and made the first of five appearances for Victoria in 1911. He starred in the 1911 Semi-final loss to Essendon.

Valentine was one of the players who benefited from the adoption of Rule 29 by the VFL, which stated that from May 1911, 'players shall play as open and undisguised professionals'.

So did League leading goalkicker for that season, Vin Gardiner, who kicked an extraordinary 10.11 of his 47 against a strife- and strike-torn St Kilda in 1911.

1909 – 1918 HONOUR ROLL

Year	Pos	Leading Goalkicker	No.	Best & Fairest	Captain	Coach
1909	2nd	George Topping	36		Fred Elliott	John Worrall
1910	2nd	Vin Gardiner	42		Fred Elliott	John Worrall
1911	3rd	Vin Gardiner	47		Fred Elliott	Fred Elliott
1912	3rd	Vin Gardiner	47		Jack Wells	Norman Clark
1913	6th	Vin Gardiner	27		Jack Wells	Jack Wells
1914	1st	William Cook	27		William Dick	Norman Clark
1915	1st	Herb Burleigh	46		William Dick	Norman Clark
1916	2nd	Vin Gardiner	44		William Dick	Norman Clark
1917	3rd	William Dick	22		William Dick	Norman Clark
1918	3rd	Ern Crowley	35		Rod McGregor	Norman Clark

CLUB NEWS 1908–1918

Before the siren sounded, thousands of fans left the MCG, bored with the ease of Carlton's win over Essendon in the First Semi-final of 1909. Carlton led by 41 points at three-quarter time, winning 14.8 (92) to 9.2 (56). No one left in the 1909 Grand Final, against South Melbourne, where the Blues lost by just 2 points – preventing a fourth Premiership in succession. South won 4.14 (38) to Carlton's 4.12 (36)

A large 'C' was ordered by the club committee to be placed on Carlton's dark navy blue jumpers in March 1909, but what appeared that season was the first version of the famous CFC monogram.

The Grandstand, named in later years for the stalwart captain of the 1870s and President of the 1910s, Jack Gardiner, was opened on 19 June 1909.

The winless Saints upset the top-of-the-ladder Blues in the last home-and-away match of 1910, 5.6 (36) to 2.12 (24), for their first victory in five seasons.

Runners-up again in 1910. Carlton 6.11 (47) lost a vicious Grand Final to Collingwood 9.7 (61), after being on top after the first round of matches.

Quick on the draws. Carlton drew its opening two games of the 1911 season. 6.9 (45) against Essendon 5.15 (45) in Round 1, and 10.6 (66) apiece against South Melbourne. With Collingwood, these were the three teams in the finals that season, Essendon winning. Viv

1909 – 1918

The 1913 Carlton team, shown at the Carlton versus Collingwood fixture at Victoria Park on 17 May 1913. In the presence of the Governor General, Carlton 6.8 (44) outscored Collingwood 5.8 (38). The team finished the season in sixth position.
Back row from left: Jamieson, Barningham, Gibbons, Mills, O'Brien, Gotz, Challis, Clancy. Middle row: Green, Dick, Wells (Capt.), Marchbanks, Gardiner, Moran. Front row: McDonald, Valentine, Triplett, Bruce.

Action from 1909.

Sgt Challis' last game

Captain Billy Dick led 16 of the 1914 Grand Final side into the 1915 season but was suspended halfway through the season. Vice captain, young Alf Baud, who first played in 1913, took over and led the team to a brilliant campaign.

Jack Worrall wrote that the Grand Final was a glorious contest, one of the grandest ever seen in the finals. Baud, Rod McGregor, Viv Valentine – and George Challis. Challis, a brave winger, was playing his 70th game for Carlton. Also a brave soldier, Sgt Challis was killed in France less than a year after the Grand Final.

Flying the Flag in 1914

Carlton underwent what newspapers called its 'annual upheaval' in 1914, with a new administration led by new President and former captain Jack Gardiner (right).

As ex-coach and victim of a previous upheaval, Jack Worrall noted in his role as football writer for the *Australasian* 'It is a great feather in the cap of the new committee, which rose to power on its indictment of the methods of its predecessors. In winning the Premiership it has justified itself in more ways than one.'

Success was also due to the recruitment of a new band of enthusiastic players (a process begun by the previous administration in 1913). Six new players played in the exciting draw against Collingwood in Round 1, a game which announced Carlton's return to the top. Paddy O'Brien was magnificent through the year, but especially in the Grand Final against South Melbourne.

Jack Worrall was somewhat critical of the skill of the team and the fact that success was mostly due to imported strength rather than the prowess of the athletes of the district.

He noted however that Carlton 'had a fine band of defenders, were up to the average across the centre, were burly and full of energy in the ruck, were competent in roving, but were heavy and slow forward.' They were well led by Carlton's captain Billy Dick (above).

Valentine made his debut in the South Melbourne match.

Vin Gardiner topped the VFL goalkicking in 1911 with 47, and kicked 10 of them in a farcical match against St Kilda when several Saints went on strike. Carlton won 18.21 (129) to 2.3 (15). Some of the St Kilda players were juniors scrounged from the district to fill the club's ranks.

With Carlton four points behind, Viv Valentine while attacking the goal took an extra yard to steady in the 1912 Preliminary Final against Essendon, was tackled and the bell rang. Essendon, under coach Jack Worrall, went on to win the Flag.

After 10 consecutive years in the finals, Carlton had to beat St Kilda in Round 15 of 1913 to stay in the final four, but lost on the last kick by a point.

Carlton's delegate to the VFL, former great wingman Ted Kennedy, moved the motion to set up the independent Tribunal in 1913.

Carlton completed a hat-trick of Jubilee Flags by winning the 1914 Premiership, in the club's Jubilee year. Carlton had also won the 1887 VFA Flag in Queen Victoria's Jubilee year, and the 1908 Flag in the Jubilee of Australian football.

Fitzroy won the 1916 flag after winning only five matches for the season. Carlton won 11 out of 15 home-and-away matches, but lost to Fitzroy in the Preliminary and Grand Finals. Only four teams played in 1916. Carlton finished third in 1917 and 1918, before the VFL was back in full operation.

CARLTON

Above: Paddy O'Brien. Below: Keith Shea. Centre: a rare picture of Horrie Clover in action. Right: 'Soapy' Vallence.

O'Brien 'an ornament'

Paddy O'Brien was a champion from the first game he played for Carlton in 1913, recruited from Yarraville from under Essendon's nose. He was a follower in his first seasons, running around at about six feet tall and 13 stone. He played in this position and in defence in the 1914 and 1915 Premierships, and became a permanent stalwart. O'Brien played 167 games, 1913–25, was captain in 1920 and 1924, and was a regular in the Big 'V'.

Legendary *Sporting Globe* writer 'Jumbo' Sharland enthused of him 'His big hands enable him to grasp the ball with great certainty and in his time he has taken many spectacular marks. He also makes great pace to the ball, and is unusually fast for a big man. He is fearless and will come through the pack with great determination. O'Brien is not a rough player and uses his weight with discrimination. Fellow players look up to him and opponents hold him in the greatest of respect. He is an outstanding footballer, a gentleman, and quite an ornament to the game.'

Carlton in Clover

'Clo-verrr!' was the cry from the outer at Princes Oval for 11 seasons as Horrie Clover flew for another spectacular mark, followed by a deadly accurate kick for goal. Clover was the best thing going on Carlton's forward line in the 1920s. He was leading goalkicker for six seasons, playing mostly from centre half-forward.

He was the League's top goalkicker in 1922, with 56 goals in an era when even full-forwards struggled to reach 50. Clover was tall, fast, a one-grab mark and a master of every variety of kick. Newton Chandler thought he was the true inventor of the drop punt.

He filled a great variety of roles at Carlton over the years – he was captain–coach in 1923 and 1927, secretary in 1925, secretary–player in 1926 and president in 1956 and 1957. He was often called upon when faction fighting threatened the club he loved.

Clover's last game was in the 1931 First Semi-final against Collingwood where he was injured (accidentally, he later said; Carlton fans disagreed at the time), which Carlton won by a massive 88 points.

Slippery 'Soapy' Vallence

Harry 'Soapy' Vallence played 204 games in the barren years between 1926 and 1938, when his last game was in the drought-breaking Premiership side. Soapy was that rare being in Carlton history, a consistent and long-lasting full-forward.

A big bloke, Soapy espoused the 'kick it long down the middle and I'll take the grab' school of forward play. He was Carlton's leading goalkicker eight times and topped the VFL list in 1931 with 86 goals. Between 1929 and 1938 Carlton players kicked seven goals on 31 occasions: 'Soapy' kicked 27 of those bags of goals.

He was runner-up in VFL goalkicking three times, and kicked 11 goals three times in his 722 for the Blues. Two of those efforts were in Finals, 11 in the Preliminary Final of 1932, following 11 in the First Semi-final of 1931, both games against Collingwood.

He favoured the right-foot torpedo punt, spiralling it through 722 times for Carlton. At a time when full-forwards had become the superstars of footy for the first time, Soapy was Carlton's stellar forward. His 722 goals were the most by a Carlton player until Stephen Kernahan passed the mark in 1997.

CLUB NEWS 1919–1938

Carlton 6.10 (46) lost the 1919 Second Semi to Collingwood 9.10 (64) after a courageous last-quarter fightback. Jack Worrall said the two teams met each other head on in that term 'like bulls'.

After the war, membership and admission prices went up. Members paid five shillings and sixpence. It cost sevenpence to get into the outer at Princes Park, and one shilling and threepence to get into the reserve.

Champion centreman Rod McGregor was forced to retire after receiving an injury in Round 1, 1920, the first game of his fifteenth season with Carlton.

A record crowd of 51,000 saw Carlton defeat Collingwood on 28 August 1920, 16.13 (109) to 7.15 (57).

Maurie Beasy made his debut for Carlton in the Second Semi-final in 1920 – Carlton defeated eventual Premiers Richmond 7.11 (53) to 4.6 (30) on a mud heap in front of 62,200 people. Jack Greenhill starred in the ruck. Collingwood won the Preliminary Final after a big first quarter – 12.11 (83) to 8.11 (59).

Lyle Downs, Carlton's brave and clever rover, collapsed and died after training on 7 July 1921, from a 'heart seizure'.

A white stripe. In the disastrous 1923 season, Carlton won only six of 16 matches, and finished third last. A white stripe was added to the collar of the navy blue – it survived until 1926.

Carlton made one of the great comebacks against Fitzroy in the opening round of 1924. Five minutes after half-

1919–1938

Great team goes under the weather

Alec Duncan.

Many observers rate the Carlton side of 1921 as the best team not to win a Flag for the Blues.

The captain was the rover and centreman Gordon Green, who played 92 games before and after the Great War, including playing in the 1914 Premiership side.

Alec Duncan was one of the Carlton 'talls'. He was marked a very good player in this, his first season, and played 141 games mostly at centre half-back.

On one wing was Newton Chandler, the grand old man of Carlton, who died at the age of 103 in 1997. He came from Porepunkah via Brunswick and played 69 games between 1919 and 1924.

In the Second Semi-final Carlton trailed 2.10 to 5.5 at half-time. In the interval, what was described as a curtain of hail travelled across Melbourne accompanied by torrential rain. The Blues went down by eight points, setting up a sensational grand finale to the season.

This game was one of the greatest ever played in the finals. Once again the weather intervened, and a terrific downpour in the third quarter turned the ground into a quagmire. With eight minutes to go Richmond was four points in front, and defending desperately. 'Their defence never slackened, though the bombardment increased in intensity. It was thrilling!' wrote Old Boy.

In the last seconds the ball shot towards Alec Duncan who seemed certain to take a mark within easy scoring distance. But Richmond's Hislop cut the pass off with a desperate lunge, and was racing away with the ball as the siren sounded. Carlton had lost the Grand Final.

1919–1938 HONOUR ROLL

Year	Pos	Leading Goalkicker	No.	Best & Fairest	Captain	Coach
1919	4th	Charlie Fisher	36		Charlie Fisher	Viv Valentine
1920	3rd	Horrie Clover	48		Paddy O'Brien	Norman Clark
1921	2nd	Horrie Clover	58		Gordon Green	Norman Clark
1922	4th	Horrie Clover	56		Horrie Clover	Norman Clark
1923	7th	Horrie Clover	28		Horrie Clover	Horrie Clover
1924	7th	Alex Duncan	27		Paddy O'Brien	Percy Parratt
1925	9th	Harvey Dunn	35		Ray Brew	Paddy O'Brien
1926	6th	Horrie Clover	38		Ray Brew	Ray Brew
1927	3rd	Harold Carter	33		Horrie Clover	Horrie Clover
1928	4th	Horrie Clover	41		Ray Brew	Ray Brew
1929	3rd	Harry Vallence	64		Ray Brew	Dan Minogue
1930	3rd	Les Allen	56		Ray Brew	Dan Minogue
1931	3rd	Harry Vallence	86		Ray Brew	Dan Minogue
1932	2nd	Harry Vallence	97		Colin Martyn	Dan Minogue
1933	4th	Harry Vallence	84		Frank Gill	Dan Minogue
1934	5th	Mick Crisp	44	Mick Crisp	Maurie Johnson	Dan Minogue
1935	4th	Harry Vallence	66	Jim Francis	Charley Davey	Frank Maher
1936	4th	Harry Vallence	86	E. Ansell Clarke	Jim Francis	Frank Maher
1937	5th	Harry Vallence	39	Don McIntyre	E. Ansell Clarke	Percy Rowe
1938	1st	Harry Vallence	81	Mick Crisp	Brighton Diggins	Brighton Diggins

Breaking the drought

Brighton Diggins, the South Melbourne star, was appointed captain–coach of Carlton in 1938 and welded a talented team into a free-scoring and powerful unit that lost just four games for the season. Soapy Vallence kicked 81 goals in a season observers thought was of the highest standard that had been seen for years. In the Carlton v Collingwood 'Grand Final preview' on May 21 Ron Todd kicked 11 for the Magpies and Soapy Vallence eight for Carlton – but Carlton won. In the Grand Final astute tactical moves by Diggins ensured Todd was curbed, and the injured Albert Collier was persevered with on the field, becoming something of a liability for Collingwood. Carlton played a long and direct game through Jack Wrout at centre half-forward. Soapy played wide on the flank, and full-forward Ken Baxter stuck to the goal square taking the run away from Collingwood full-back Jack Regan. In the event it was a hard-fought close encounter. Carlton snuck away in the second quarter, and were never quite headed. Collingwood got within four points late in the last quarter, but goals to best-on-ground rover Jack Hale, his second, and then to Ken Baxter (his third) amid high excitement gave Carlton its first flag in 23 years. The beer was blue in Carlton again.

---

time the Blues trailed 3.5 (23) to 14.6 (90) but kicked 12 of the next 14 goals to go down by just 2 points 15.13 (103) to 16.9 (105). In the return match versus the Maroons Carlton won handily, 15.14 (104) to 8.8 (56) led for the first time by the great Paddy O'Brien.

Up for the count. St Kilda Captain Wels Eicke claimed Carlton were playing 19 men in the second quarter of Round 12, 1924 – but when the umpire lined up and counted, he found just the statutory 18. Carlton were ahead seven goals to two at the time.

Before Jim Caldwell was appointed coach in 1925 two others were offered the job. First Paddy Scanlon couldn't get a clearance from South Melbourne, then Paddy O'Brien had the job withdrawn after the players failed to elect him either captain or vice-captain.

Alec Duncan had his finest match among many excellent games at centre half-back for Carlton in a great game against Collingwood in 1927, taking 33 marks – his aerial work was simply perfection. Some of his marks were 'hair raising', said one scribe.

Richmond captain–coach Dan Minogue was appointed Carlton coach in 1929. A physically fit Carlton side finished third. He coached Carlton to a losing First Semi-final in 1930 – the Blues were beaten certainties for the Flag. A record 23.17 was kicked against North Melbourne in this season.

Richmond defeated Carlton 13.14 (92) to 12.11 (83) in the 1932 Grand Final after the Blues snatched a five-point lead with six minutes to go.

CARLTON

Footy saves flier

By PERCY TAYLOR

Flying Officer Jim Knight (killed in action).

ERNIE PILKINGTON, regarded as the best wing man in Southern Tasmania when secured by Carlton, tells officials of his experiences at sea. He lost his Carlton jersey at sea, when his ship, Vendetta, was sunk, and said that by clinging to an inflated football for some time in the water was he able to save his life.

Carlton footballers have played their part in the present world crisis. Lieut Jim Park, one of Carlton's best players when he enlisted in 1940, was killed in action up north. He played 124 games from the time he joined the club in 1933. Later Flying Officer Jim Knight, who came to Carlton when Geelong did not form a team, was killed as the result of a flying accident, also up north. Both were held in high esteem by players and officials.

The Australasian, 3 June 1944.

Above: Ken Hands. Below: the umpires' whistles used in the Bloodbath Grand Final.

Big Bad Bob Chitty

Of all Carlton's tough guys, none was tougher than big, bad Bob Chitty. He famously chopped the top off his left-hand middle finger at the Maribyrnong munitions factory before the 1945 Preliminary Final, but played well in that hard game, as he did the next week in the Bloodbath. He received eight weeks and 27 stitches for his part in that fighting victory.

The next season, 1946, proved to be his last, when he was reported the first game back, and played only three games to total 139 in his career.

The next year his good looks and reputation saw him cast as Ned Kelly for £25 in a movie. While he looked the part with a ferocious beard, as Jack Dyer said of him, 'Chitty never needed armour.'

Chitty was recruited from Cudgewa in 1937, played as an attacking half-back and was best first-year player that year. Best and Fairest in 1941 and 1944, he was made captain in 1945, and led the charge to the finals. He died in 1985 aged 68.

The 'Bloodbath' Grand Final of 1945

In September 1945 the Second World War was over at last, and not surprisingly people's minds turned to the traditional September action. Although the 1945 Preliminary Final between Carlton and Collingwood was a boots'n'all affair, few of the extraordinary throng of 62,986 who turned up at Princes Park for the Grand Final thought it would be as rough and tough a game as it turned out to be.

Percy Beames said in the *Age* that Carlton made history – not for the number of reports by umpire Frank Spokes in the spiteful game, but for winning the Flag from fourth place on the ladder for the first time.

Veterans cannot recall who started the fights, but in the end Ted Whitfield from South was suspended for the entire 1946 season, and another two players were penalised eight weeks each. South's Herbie Matthews was severely reprimanded.

For Carlton, Ken Hands, who was KO'd early in the piece, was found not guilty, Bob Chitty and Ron Savage got eight each, and Fred Fitzgibbon (already serving three weeks) received another four for running on the field and joining in the melees.

The 1945 Premiers in a calmer atmosphere, at Princes Park.

As for the football: after an unimpressive first quarter Carlton nosed in front and stayed there for the rest of the game, despite fightbacks from South in more ways than one. Ken Hands was concussed and did not even remember his vital last-quarter goal.

CLUB NEWS 1939–1947

'Soapy' Vallence transferred to Williamstown for the 1939 season, kicking nine goals in his first outing.

Forward-pocket rover Mick Price kicked seven goals in Round 1, 1939 as the Blues kicked their then highest score against South Melbourne 20.22 (144) to 13.10 (88).

Carlton missed out on the 1939 finals after losing to Richmond in a tough, physical game in a bog at Punt Road.

Best news from 1940 was Jim Mooring's excellent debut in Round 1. Less exciting was the fact that Hawthorn recorded its first win over the Blues since joining the VFL.

Carlton finished 1941 on top of the ladder, defeating eventual Premiers, Melbourne, twice home-and-away, but crashing to them in the Second Semi, and then to Essendon in the Preliminary Final.

Paul Schmidt kicked 11 goals from the forward pocket against St Kilda on August 16.

The Round 2 Carlton v Richmond game was more like a casualty clearing station as 10 Carlton players and eight from Richmond were injured – including Carlton's Jack Hale whose broken leg ended his career.

Ollie Grieve and Bert Deacon made their debuts for Carlton in 1942.

Carlton could barely field a team against Essendon on 14 August 1943, eventually playing with 17 men but winning in a courageous performance, 10.10 (70) to 9.13 (67).

1939 – 1947

Ern Henfry chaired from the ground after the 1947 Grand Final.

Bert Deacon, gentleman

1939—1947 HONOUR ROLL

Year	Pos	Leading Goalkicker	No.	Best & Fairest	Captain	Coach
1939	5th	Ken Baxter	65	Frank Gill	Brighton Diggins	Brighton Diggins
1940	5th	Paul Schmidt	55	Jim Francis	Brighton Diggins	Brighton Diggins
1941	3rd	Paul Schmidt	77	Bob Chitty	Jim Francis	Perc Bentley
1942	5th	Paul Schmidt	47	Jim Mooring	Jim Francis	Perc Bentley
1943	4th	Jack Wrout	33	George Gneil	Jim Francis	Perc Bentley
1944	5th	Jim Mooring	42	Bob Chitty	Jim Francis	Perc Bentley
1945	1st	Lance Collins	49	Ron Savage	Bob Chitty	Perc Bentley
1946	6th	Ken Baxter	46	Jack Howell	Bob Chitty	Perc Bentley
1947	1st	Ken Baxter	42	Bert Deacon/Henfry	Ern Henfry	Perc Bentley

Bert Deacon had played just a handful of games after his debut in 1942 because of the war, and in 1945 had even been 'loaned' to Preston. But he was back to be part of Carlton's seven-game winning streak and the Grand Final. He was Carlton's first Brownlow winner, in 1947, another Premiership year, and would have won in 1946 as well had not 'Chooka' Howell taken votes from him. He played 105 games in 10 seasons as a quick, marking and attacking half-back. He was later a Secretary of the club before dying in 1974.

Last-kick Fred wins 1947 Flag

Fred Stafford kicks when it counts.

Carlton got its eighth last-minute victory of the 1947 season with a kick by half-forward flanker Fred Stafford with just 44 seconds of the Grand Final remaining. Essendon might well have had the game sewn up at half-time had it kicked straighter, and Carlton had been less accurate. At half-time Carlton was just 11 points behind, 8.0 (48) to 8.11 (59). An even third quarter followed, then with just 10 minutes left two goals down, Carlton through Jack Howell in the ruck, Ken Hands at centre half-forward and Ken Baxter (replacing the injured Bert Deacon and Ern Henfry in the centre), attacked incessantly. Davies kicked a goal, and missed from close in, and Baxter and Hands had shots that fell short. Then Baxter barged through in the ruck at a throw-in near Carton's goal and the ball came to Stafford.

Snap, goal, siren, Flag.

Collingwood lost to Carlton by 104 points in Round 12, 1943: 28.10 (178) to 11.8 (74) – the Blues' greatest winning margin.

Last kick of the day, out of the finals. Carlton were two Premiership points and percentage ahead of Footscray as they played in the last game of the 1944 season. Scores were level as 'Scray's Harry Hickey kicked at goal from 50 yards out. The siren sounded with the ball in flight. Carlton's Bob Chitty stopped the goal – but it rebounded from his shoulder and went through for a behind. Footscray in the finals – Carlton missed out.

After Round 11 in 1945 Carlton was ninth – but in an extraordinary turn-around won eight of the next nine games. It made the finals in fourth place, and went on to win the Premiership, taking the record to winning 13 of 14 games.

Early in the 1945 season Carlton suffered its worst-ever loss to Essendon, (by 100 points) and it was the Dons who inflicted the only loss in the latter half of the season – by three points.

Two losses in 1946, to North Melbourne in Round 16 and to Richmond in Round 18, stopped Carlton playing in the finals in a disappointing 1946 season.

Match of the 1947 season was the Collingwood v Carlton clash at Victoria Park on the King's Birthday weekend – despite the efforts of Ern Henfry, Ken Hands and Ken Baxter, Carlton lost 13.8 (86) to 16.16 (112). Carlton, however, finished on top of the ladder.

CARLTON

The Flag that flew away

Coach Ken Hands maintains that Carlton really should have won the 1962 Flag – a drawn Preliminary Final against Geelong meant that the Blues had yet another tough game before the Grand Final while their opponents had an extra week off to rest and recuperate from injury.

Carlton had had a tough First Semi-final against Melbourne, and perhaps were a trifle lucky to win. Umpire Schwab gave a 'ball-up' decision when Geoff Tunbridge was tackled after he spilled a mark, and Melbourne's Laurie Mithen was steaming in to kick a goal. That said, Carlton, with John Nicholls and Sergio Silvagni in the van, had staged a great last-quarter comeback to win by two points.

In the First Preliminary Final, Geelong jumped Carlton but were gradually pegged back. But in time-on in the last quarter – 27 and a half minutes to be exact – the Cats were two goals up. Maurie Sankey ran 30 yards without bouncing the ball for one goal, and then Turkey Tom Carroll snapped another in great excitement to draw the game. John James had a shot from 55 yards to win the game but didn't make the distance.

In the replay Geelong played an injured Doug Wade, but were without Polly Farmer. 28 minutes into the last quarter John James kicked the winning goal – but wait – Pomeroy to Wooller to Wade mark! 25 yards out!! No!!! The umpire's taken it off him and given it to full-back Peter Barry. Wade is supposed to have held Barry by the shorts – from the front position!

So, Carlton, exhausted, were in the Grand Final against Essendon who hadn't played for three weeks. The Essendon ruck division ran Carlton off their feet, and won the Grand Final by a handy 32 points.

Ollie Grieve.   Chooka Howell.   Bugsy Comben.

Keith Warburton: acrobatic forward.

1948–1965 HONOUR ROLL

Year	Pos	Leading Goalkicker	No.	Best & Fairest	Captain	Coach
1948	6th	Ken Baxter/Ray Garby	39	Jack Howell	Ern Henfry	Perc Bentley
1949	2nd	Ken Baxter	46	Ern Henfry	Ern Henfry	Perc Bentley
1950	8th	Ken Baxter	43	Arthur Hodgson	Ern Henfry	Perc Bentley
1951	7th	Keith Warburton	48	Jim Clark	Ern Henfry	Perc Bentley
1952	4th	Jack Howell	42	Ollie Grieve	Ern Henfry	Perc Bentley
1953	5th	Jack Spencer	32	Ken Hands	Ken Hands	Perc Bentley
1954	8th	Noel O'Brien	45	Bill Milroy	Ken Hands	Perc Bentley
1955	7th	Noel O'Brien	73	John James	Ken Hands	Perc Bentley
1956	5th	Kevin Hamilton	22	Doug Beasy	Ken Hands	Jim Francis
1957	4th	Gerald Burke	34	Bruce Comden	Ken Hands	Jim Francis
1958	7th	John Heathcote	19	Bruce Comden	Bruce Comden	Jim Francis
1959	3rd	Sergio Silvagni	40	John Nicholls	Bruce Comden	Ken Hands
1960	7th	Leo Brereton	44	John James	Bruce Comden	Ken Hands
1961	8th	Tom Carroll	54	John James	Graham Donaldson	Ken Hands
1962	2nd	Tom Carroll	62	Sergio Silvagni	Graham Donaldson	Ken Hands
1963	6th	Tom Carroll	27	John Nicholls	John Nicholls	Ken Hands
1964	10th	Ian Nankervis	18	Gordon Collis	Sergio Silvagni	Ken Hands
1965	6th	Bryan Quirk	29	John Nicholls	Ron Barassi	Ron Barassi

CLUB NEWS 1948–1965

Having won the 1947 Flag, Carlton experienced another slump in 1948, finishing in sixth place, two games behind Footscray in fourth. The Blues won only two of the first eight games, then won eight of the next 11. Not enough.

Carlton turned the tables on top-of-the-ladder North Melbourne in 1949, defeating them in the Second Semi by 12 points – 15.13 (103) to 14.7 (91). North had inflicted a hiding on Carlton in the last game of the season, winning 15.8 (108) to a miserable 7.10 (52). Coincidentally, 52 points is all the Blues managed in the Grand Final against Essendon, where they scored a tragic 6.16 (52) to Essendon's 18.17 (125).

Ken Baxter played his 153rd and last game for Carlton in the win over South Melbourne in the last game of the disappointing 1950 season. Baxter had played in the 1938, 1945 and 1947 Premiership sides.

Carlton defeated St Kilda 15.5 (105) to 9.11 (65) in the Blues' 1000th League match in 1951.

Ern Henfry was captain for the fifth season, but injury ended his season halfway through, and vice-captain Ken Hands took over.

On being passed a message that King George VI had died, midway through the 1952 annual general meeting, President Kenneth Luke immediately closed the meeting as a mark of respect.

Carlton defeated Hawthorn at Euroa 17.15 (117) to 11.14 (80) on 14

1948 – 1965

The Barassi Coup

Many scribes have remarked that modern football might be said to have begun with the 'snatching' of Ron Barassi for Carlton by George Harris' incoming regime. Harris (as President) and a new committee were elected on 7 December 1964, and soon afterwards new committee members had lunch with Barassi, where the possibility of the move was discussed. Later, after Barassi decided he might stay with Melbourne, president Harris had a three-hour phone conversation with him, and 'at the end of those three hours, Barassi was Carlton coach'. The news was announced on 23 December 1964. After the administrative turmoil at Carlton, it was another announcement that shook Carlton players and supporters as well as those at Melbourne – and every other team. Club loyalty had overnight become an outdated concept.

The twin colossi of football, Barassi and Whitten, meet and greet.

John James played tall

Champion defender John James won Carlton's second Brownlow in 1961, and a record third Carlton Best and Fairest. Although just 5' 9" he played 'tall' and was quick. He was often used in key positions, but was at his best on the half-back flank or in the back-pocket.

Gordon Collis' record

Gordon Collis was a great Carlton backman. He won the 1964 Brownlow by eight votes, polling in 11 of his 17 games, including seven 'three-voters'. After debuting in 1961 he had a poor year in 1963 – mainly due to poor eyesight. Contact lenses solved that problem in 1964. He retired injured in 1965 after 77 games, but made a comeback in 1967.

June 1952 in the 'National Day' round where all games were played outside Melbourne.

Inaccuracy cost Carlton dearly in 1952 – the Blues kicked 206 goals 305 behinds for the season compared to eventual Premiers Geelong's more efficient 250 goals 280 behinds. The most culpable example was in the First Semi against Fitzroy where Carlton 8.20 (68) lost by a point to a more accurate Fitzroy's 10.9 (69).

Freakish footballer Keith Warburton was badly injured in the 1952 First Semi-final, and was placed on the danger list in hospital. Bulletins were issued, calls made for blood donations as he fought for, and eventually won, his life. He returned to the Blues in 1953 but had to retire from League football in 1954 after a knock to the kidney.

Carlton finished three games outside the four in 1953 after a large exodus of senior players through transfer, retirement and injury. They included Ern Henfry, Ollie Grieve, Fred Davies, Fred Stafford, Ritchie Green and Arthur Hodgson.

Princes Park was chosen as the site for the 130,000 seat main stadium of the 1956 Olympics during the 1953 season, but lost the privilege to the MCG after political infighting. Carlton President Kenneth Luke told the 1953 AGM 'I always thought Carlton would be the people's ground. It is unfortunate that the Premier Mr Cain should say "the MCG or nothing" and not listen to our claims. But we can still make our ground bigger and better.'

CARLTON

It's all over, and Brent Crosswell and John Nicholls raise their arms in delight.

Big Nick: a looming presence.

Blues bounce back to win '68 Flag

After the disappointments of the 1967 finals series, where Carlton went out in 'straight sets', the Blues finished second behind Essendon. After a relatively easy win over the Cats in the Second Semi 13.17 (95) to 8.11 (59), the scene was set for a desperately hard-fought Grand Final against Essendon.

As it happened Carlton was 13 points up at half-time, and eleven at three-quarter time. The most heart-stopping 'bounce back' of the game was when a kick from 18-year-old star Brent 'Tiger' Crosswell landed in the goal square, with Carlton just seven points ahead halfway through the last quarter – and bounced backwards, to be cleared.

Attacking play from Alex Jesaulenko, John Nicholls, Gary Crane and Brian Kekovich saw more behinds kicked – and after two goals to the Bombers there was just a point the difference with time-on to play.

Dennis Munari kicked forward and the ball was rushed through for a behind. Essendon's young star forward Geoff Blethyn kicked out of bounds at the other end, Brian Kekovich did the same for Carlton. Percy Jones missed, and Crosswell kicked a point – and the siren sounded. Carlton won, but uniquely in a Grand Final, kicked fewer goals than their opponents. Carlton 7.14 (56) defeated Essendon 8.5 (53). Gary Crane was best on ground.

The Colossus of Carlton

From the day he arrived at Carlton in 1957, a year after his brother Don, to the day in 1974 when he walked (prematurely) from the Western Oval, having played his last game for Carlton, John Nicholls was Carlton. He wasn't that tall for a ruckman by modern standards – 6 feet 3 inches in the old measure – but he was big and broad with it. Legs like gum trees, and especially in his palmy years, a very good leap. But more than that he had a calculating football brain that invariably seemed to get him in the right position to left-palm the ball onto Adrian Gallagher's chest – while his right paw was doing something unspeakable to the opposing ruckman. His grip on the ball was vice-like. His big legs gave him plenty of torque, and he could gather the ball and punch out a handpass. He was excellent in the 1968 Premiership side, even better in 1970 and supreme as a player and coach in 1972 – the rock on which the club was built over 328 games and three Premierships.

1966 – 1970 HONOUR ROLL

Year	Pos	Leading Goalkicker	No.	Best & Fairest	Captain	Coach
1966	6th	B. Quirk/A Gallagher	24	John Nicholls	Ron Barassi	Ron Barassi
1967	3rd	Brian Kekovich	36	John Nicholls	Ron Barassi	Ron Barassi
1968	1st	Brian Kekovich	63	Sergio Silvagni	Ron Barassi	Ron Barassi
1969	2nd	Alex Jesaulenko	66	Garry Crane	John Nicholls	Ron Barassi
1970	1st	Alex Jesaulenko	115	Adrian Gallagher	John Nicholls	Ron Barassi

CLUB NEWS 1966 – 1970

A win on the MCG, at last. Carlton defeated Melbourne 11.13 (79) to 3.14 (32) on May 21 for the first victory on the 'G in 13 seasons.

John Nicholls had one of his best seasons in the Brownlow Medal count, finishing second behind Ian Stewart in 1966, 17 votes to 21.

The Barassi magic started to take effect in 1967 as Carlton did not lose a match until the Round 9 encounter with Richmond, where the Blues went down by two points – 14.7 (91) to 13.15 (93). This run included a draw against South Melbourne in Round 7, and a somewhat lucky win against St Kilda. John Gill kicked a goal on the stroke of half-time – after the siren failed to sound. A sign of the times : Alex Jesaulenko finished third in the Brownlow in his debut season.

Carlton's four games against ladder leaders Essendon in 1968 included the Second Semi-final and the Grand Final – both of which were won by the Blues. Importantly they were an improvement on the dismal early season encounter at Princes Park with a vicious cross breeze where the Bombers won 7.8 (50) to 1.11 (17), and the Round 14 encounter at Windy Hill where Carlton lost 7.13 (55) to 6.13 (49). The Blues went from 3.1 at quarter time to a very frustrating 3.12 at three-quarter time.

Carlton's membership sank to rock-bottom in 1968 – a Premiership year. Only 5724 people paid up.

1966 – 1970

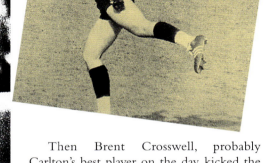

John Nicholls after the ball, backed up by Serge Silvagni. Right: Jezza hits the heights.

The grandest final of them all

Carlton fans were wildly enthusiastic about 1906, and deeply satisfied about 1945, and pretty relieved over 1968 – but nothing can describe the feeling of supporters, players, officials a) at half-time in 1970, and b) at the end of the game.

Half-time was a feeling of utter desolation, depression and despair. Carlton had lost the Second Semi to Collingwood after Collingwood surged away in the last quarter, 17.6 (108) to 17.16 (118). Alex Jesaulenko kicked a great bag of eight goals, but Peter McKenna kicked nine for Collingwood.

In the Grand Final in the first half it felt that both teams had carried on from where they left off – Carlton having disposed of St Kilda in the Preliminary Final, where Syd Jackson kicked six beauties and Brent Crosswell at the height of his athletic, larrikin powers, was best on ground.

At half-time the miserable score was Carlton 4.5 (29) Collingwood 10.13 (73) – many muttered about leaving and going to the pub, but there were too many people at the ground to get out – 121,696 to be precise, an all-time record, and one unlikely to be beaten.

Then came the message from the master coach. 'Handball on the backline. Get something moving.' And the last-minute change: the wispy blond 'Lightning' Ted Hopkins, on in place of Bert Thornley. 'Get ready, Teddy, you're on.'

Ted obliged with two goals in two minutes after hovering around the goal square. Then an uplifting goal came from Syd Jackson, one of the 'stolen generation' of Aboriginal children and among the first black players to find success through football.

Then Brent Crosswell, probably Carlton's best player on the day, kicked the fourth and the Blues were back in it.

Handball as an attacking weapon was supposedly invented in this game, but the breakthrough in reality was that five or six times in the second half Carlton players handballed on the backline, over the head of the man on the mark, and got a bit of run into their game.

Carlton was still 17 points down at three-quarter time, and 22 points down a few minutes later. If anything, the last-quarter fightback was more impressive than that in the third quarter. Jezza was at centre half-forward, Nicholls at full-forward, and this soon paid off with Jezza passing to Nicholls for a goal, then another to the big man, and Jackson passed to Hopkins for his fourth. Collingwood were by now just a point in front. Two minutes and time-on to go. A point to Collingwood. Then Crosswell put Carlton in front to a combination of pandemonium from Blues fans and a sickening silence from the Magpies. Jezza sealed the game by bouncing one through from a distance out – and the siren sounded. Carlton by ten points. It was the greatest, the grandest final ever.

Carlton kicked a club-record score of 30.30 (210) against the hapless Hawks 12.10 (82) in Round 2 1969 at Princes Park, after the 1968 Flag had been unfurled by VFL President Sir Kenneth Luke. Next home game was against Collingwood, where a sensational third quarter saw the Magpies kick 12.5 to Carlton's two behinds to come from behind.

The second game against Hawthorn proved in retrospect to be a disaster for Carlton because the Blues won too well again – 22.17 (149) to 11.14 (80). This had a catastrophic effect on Hawthorn's percentage allowing Richmond to jump into the finals in fourth place, on percentage.

Coach Ron Barassi made a comeback as a player after the 1969 Round 6 loss to Geelong – against his old team Melbourne. 'Barass' didn't see the game out but it inspired a win 14.24 (108) to 12.6 (72), and a winning sequence of nine games. Carlton finished second on the ladder to Collingwood – winning the Second Semi against the Magpies. Richmond however overcame Carlton in the last quarter of the Grand Final.

Alex Jesaulenko kicked 10 goals in Carlton's 23.9 (147) to 15.20 (110) win over Fitzroy in 1970 – the first Carlton player to kick 10 since Noel O'Brien in 1954 – also against Fitzroy. He brought up his hundredth goal with five against Melbourne on August 29. Jezza became the first (and only) Carlton player to kick one hundred goals in a season.

CARLTON

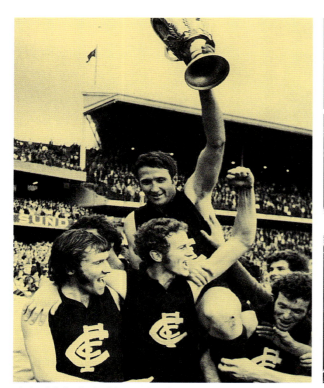

John Nicholls holds up the Cup that cheers.

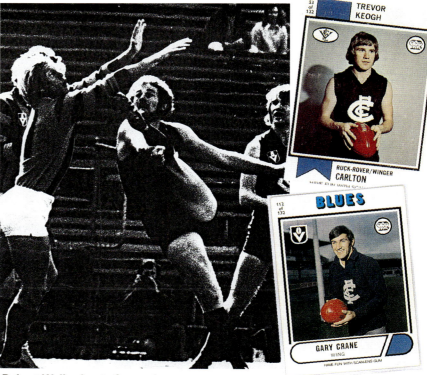

Robert Walls shoots for goal.

Nick beats Richmond with his football brain

Carlton played Richmond three times in the 1972 finals, for a draw, a hiding and a thrashing. Carlton had finished on top of the ladder, but only half a game clear of the Tigers. 1972 was the first year of the final five and the series was made even longer because of a drawn Second Semi – courtesy of a goal to Barry Armstrong in the last minute, 8.13 apiece. Richmond gave Carlton a hiding in the replay, easing up toward the end but still winning by 41 points.

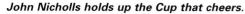

The thrashing occurred when Nicholls, now captain–coach, proved himself to be one of the more astute thinkers as well as one of the greatest players, in the game. It seems that before Carlton beat Richmond on the MCG, Big Nick had beaten them in his head. He told the team after the hiding in the Second Semi replay that Carlton could win the Grand Final, even before they had won the Preliminary Final.

The game plan was not to try and match Richmond defensively, but to go for outright attack, and simply outscore them. Nicholls put himself in the forward pocket, and young Percy Jones into the ruck (provided he shaved off his moustache) where he played the game of his life. Nick also kicked a modest six goals. So did Robert Walls in a range-roving performance at centre half-forward

It was hot football on a hot day, a game of skilful vengeance, where Big Nick, accused after the Second Semi replay of being too old and too slow, proved he was quick in imagination and too good to lose.

Stars shine in the 70s

Great full-back Geoff Southby was Carlton's Best and Fairest in 1972, his second award in a row after he won it in his debut year, 1971. He played 268 games in 13 seasons, and was plagued by a back injury in later years.

Robert Walls scored a goal with his first kick in League football as a skinny 16-year-old in 1967, and went on to play 218 games and kick 367 goals. He captained the side in 1974 and 1977, and coached the team between 1986 and 1989. He played in the 1968, 1972 and 1979 Premierships and coached the 1987 Flag.

High leaping David 'Swan' McKay first played for Carlton in 1969, and played 263 games, mostly on the forward line. He retired in 1981 after several seasons beset by ankle injuries. He was one of the most spectacular marks of his day, and played in four Premierships.

CLUB NEWS 1971-1975

Lost it in the fog. Carlton missed the finals in 1971 after a defeat by Fitzroy at the Junction Oval on 21 August 1971. A thick fog descended on the ground causing almost zero visibility. Fitzroy exploited the conditions better than the Blues, particularly the Carlton ruckman who let on to all and sundry that he had the ball. Fitzroy won 15.15 (105) to 11.16 (82).

Ron Barassi's contract as Carlton coach was not renewed after the 1971 season, and John Nicholls took over as playing coach in 1972.

Alex Jesaulenko literally won the game against Essendon in 11 minutes of the 22 July 1972 game. He kicked six goals, and gave three others away as Carlton kicked 12 straight in the second quarter, winning the match 20.13 (133) to 17.15 (117)

Greg Kennedy kicked 12.3 of Carlton's 24.12 (156) against Hawthorn's 11.22 (88) at Princes Park on 26 August 1972. This is the highest individual tally by a Carlton player after Horrie Clover's 13.3 in 1921.

Umpire Ian Coates was assaulted by a long-haired spectator after the drawn 1972 Second Semi-final between Carlton and Richmond at VFL Park. Barry Armstrong kicked the goal which levelled the scores in the last seconds of the game. 8.13 (61) each. Richmond thrashed the Blues in the replay, 15.20 (110) to 9.15 (69), inspiring Carlton's successful attacking strategy in the Grand Final.

1971–1975

Jezza: classic football hero.

Alex the Greatest

For many Carlton barrackers, the greatest player, bar none, in recent memory is Alex Jesaulenko. He represented all that was mercurial and brilliant in football; he was a player people came to watch because he did the unbelievable on a regular basis, and the unexpected 10 times a game.

Like Mozart, the greatest composer of all time, Alex Jesaulenko was born of Ukrainian parents in the Austrian city of Salzburg. He came to Australia as a young boy and grew up in Canberra.

There are a couple of persistent rumours about the young Jesaulenko, which lend an aura to his particular genius.

The first is that the baby Jezza spent some time with his family in a refugee camp in or near Carlton in the late 1940s – Camp Pell, or a camp in the Exhibition Gardens. The second is that he did not even pick up an Australian football until the ripe old age of 15. And the last one is that the prime Minister of the day Sir Robert Menzies personally intervened to have the Manuka-Eastlakes star and Commonwealth public servant transferred to Melbourne in time for the 1967 season.

The rest of his story is truthful, and needs no embellishment – the soaring marks, such as the mark of the century in the 1970 Grand Final, the hundred goals in a season, the ability to command the ball to do his will, the way his body worked its way untouched through marauding packs, as if he could disappear under ground and worm his way up in a clear space.

Not to mention the way he could bring the rest of the team into the play by direct involvement, or sheer example. When called upon to coach Carlton in 1978, it was his being shirt-fronted by Collingwood's Stan Magro that inspired a win that season, and eventually the Flag in 1979. He left in loyalty to controversial President George Harris but was still blue through and through. When called upon in another crisis after the sacking of Robert Walls in 1989, he came and the magic worked again. Carlton finished 8th in 1989 and 1990 before Jezza was replaced by David Parkin. Jesaulenko's legacy is loyalty over 256 extraordinary games and 424 goals – 115 of them in 1970, four Premierships – 1968, 1970, 1972 and 1979, some of the marks of the century. When it come to winning games by example or by individual brilliance, every Carlton player is measured against the standard of Jesaulenko – as in: 'Yeah, great mark, but not as good as that one of Jezza's.'

1971–1975 HONOUR ROLL

Year	Pos	Leading Goalkicker	No.	Best & Fairest	Captain	Coach
1971	5th	Alex Jesaulenko	56	Geoff Southby	John Nicholls	Ron Barassi
1972	1st	Greg Kennedy	79	Geoff Southby	John Nicholls	John Nicholls
1973	2nd	Brian Walsh	60	Peter Jones	John Nicholls	John Nicholls
1974	7th	Craig Davis	45	Bruce Doull	John Nicholls	John Nicholls
1975	4th	Robert Walls	59	Alex Jesaulenko	Alex Jesaulenko	John Nicholls

Richmond's tough-guy tactics saw Geoff Southby and John Nicholls flattened in the 1973 Grand Final. Southby was king hit, and captain–coach Nicholls was 'semi-comatose' and unable to change Carlton's tactics against the aggressive Tigers after being crashed to the ground by Laurie Fowler. Two important cogs in the Blues' machine, Trevor Keogh and Barry Armstrong, did not play because of injury, and Alex Jesaulenko and Neil Chandler were not 100 per cent fit.

The 'Grand Final Replay' in Round 3, 1974 was a vicious occasion with Robert Walls and two Richmond players Royce Hart (striking) and Francis Bourke (kicking) reported. Richmond won 18.11 (119) to 11.15 (81).

Carlton's 1974 finals campaign ended in a spray of inaccuracy in the Round 19 clash with Footscray. The Dogs were in the Five, a game ahead but with a lower percentage than Carlton. Carlton kicked 12 behinds in a row before kicking just their third goal in the last quarter. Footscray won 10.8 (68) to 4.20 (44).

Great, big John Nicholls retired as a player after an official 328 games on 3 August 1974. In a mark of the change of eras, Mike Fitzpatrick secured a clearance from Subiaco in WA on 4 April 1974 and played against Geelong.

Carlton kicked an all-time best quarter of 14.1 against Essendon in Round 14 at Windy Hill in 1975, winning the game 27.13 (175) to 15.5 (95). This is Carlton's highest score against Essendon.

CARLTON

Bruce Doull directs football traffic.

The Rhodes Scholar

Mike Fitzpatrick played 150 games for Carlton from 1975 to 1983, and was captain (1980–83) of the back-to-back Premiership sides, a feat no other modern Carlton captain has been able to achieve. Coach David Parkin once said, tongue in cheek, that Fitzpatrick, WA's 1974 Rhodes Scholar, was too intelligent to be a great footballer. The opposite was true – whether in the ruck or in the truly great performances at centre half-forward in the 1981 and 1982 finals, he was a terrific footballer because he had the sort of courage, skill and football brain of the big forwards who preceded and followed him – such as Stephen Kernahan and Robert Walls – and he also had leadership quality, enabling him to do the right thing in the big Final moments.

Bruce Doull lets the football do the talking

Few players have become legends as quietly as Bruce Doull. Over his record 359 games for the Blues he became something like Old Man River in the song. 'He don't say nuthin'; but must know somethin' … He just keeps rollin' along.' Maturing from a stringy and beardless youth in 1969 to the distinguished grey beard and head-banded head of his glorious maturity, Doull played football with the efficiency of an abacus and the strength and grace of a gymnast.

When football scribes write of players having the ball on a string, it is a concept which does not encompass or envisage Doull's special magic. He didn't need a string. He was seemingly able to hypnotise the ball and make it do his bidding.

He could attract it or repel it as he desired, punch it from a rival's hands with the accuracy of a wire-guided missile, and create space with more aplomb than Einstein.

Doull first arrived at Carlton from suburban Jacana in 1966, at the age of 16 when he had a try-out for the Under 19s. He had to work hard to establish himself as a senior player, which he did in 1971, playing 12 games – followed by a mammoth 26 in 1972. Doull broke Big Nick's Carlton game's record in Round 1, 1985 against Footscray – and still avoided the spotlight as assiduously as he did when he was a youngster wearing number four – which meant his locker was next to Big Nick's. He asked for a change and made 11 as famous as his mentor's number 2.

If there was to be a measure of football telepathy, efficiency, dependability, reliability, endurance, toughness and skill it would be a 'doull'. When assessing later backmen, we might say that he is '.75 doulls' – there will never be another 'one' like him. His record 356 games for Carlton is unlikely ever to be beaten.

CLUB NEWS 1976–1980

Hawthorn assistant coach David Parkin rejected an offer to coach Carlton in 1976, after the shock resignation of John Nicholls just before the opening round of the season. Ian Thorogood was then appointed, amid rumours of the call going out to Alex Jesaulenko.

In Round 10, 1976, Malcolm Blight created a football legend after North Melbourne was 13 points behind in time-on in the last quarter at Princes Park. He kicked a goal to put them a point behind, and then booted a mighty torpedo after the siren from 60 metres out. Aghast Blues fans saw the game slip away 11.15 (81) to 11.10 (76).

Carlton kicked its best fourth-quarter score, 12.6, against St. Kilda in Round 19, 1976, wining the game 22.19 (151) to 7.8 (50).

Former Collingwood full-forward Peter McKenna signed with Carlton after leaving the Magpies in a dispute over money in April 1977. He played eleven games and kicked 36 goals for the season, but never recaptured his great goalkicking form of his best years with the Magpies.

Carlton runner Craig Davis was fined $25 by the VFL for carrying too many messages (32) from coach Ian Thorogood in the first three quarters against Sth Melbourne in Round 5, 1977.

Alex Jesaulenko became Carlton's third coach in the first seven games of 1978, when he took over from Sergio Silvagni on May 11. Silvagni had stepped in when Ian Stewart resigned

1976–1980

Top: Geoff Southby with the Cup.
Above: Wayne Harmes, Ken Sheldon and Jim Buckley with the spoils of battle.

Alex Jesaulenko holds the 1979 Premiership Cup aloft.

1979: in Harmes' way for a mighty win

The 1979 Grand Final was won 15 minutes into the last quarter by a piece of play on which Grand Final legends are built. Carlton was just four points up, after seemingly having the game won at three-quarter time. Collingwood's never-say-die attitude saw them edge back from 21 points down, and the momentum was moving like a balance beam with extra grains of sand added to one end.

Enter the pocket battleship Wayne Harmes. He gathered the ball near the centre and kicked in the direction of the forward line. It was a wet and windy miskick, and slewed off towards the boundary line in the forward pocket. Seemingly appalled by his skill error, Harmes somehow defeated every law of football physics — the first one of which is that the ball is faster than the footballer — and made it to the boundary line just as the footy was about to cross. He dived and whacked the ball in the direction of the goal square, where Ken Sheldon accepted the miracle with delight and kicked his third goal, sealing the game. Was Harmes over the line? All that may be said is that the umpire did not blow his whistle. If he had, it would have spoiled one of the great moments in football.

Collingwood planned to grind Carlton into the mud, which they tried to do in a rough first quarter. The Blues couldn't raise a gallop in the heavy going, and were 28 points down after 20 minutes. Then Mike Fitzpatrick put the ball in Harmes' direction and he kicked the first goal, followed by Sheldon and Mark Maclure. Wayne Johnston zipped a pass to Jim Buckley and astonishingly Carlton was a point up at half-time. All the great names of the time were in action — and despite Collingwood's claw-back, the Blues were never in doubt. Johnston was best on ground. Harmes, Fitzpatrick, Buckley, Armstrong, Doull — stars.

1976–1980 HONOUR ROLL

Year	Pos	Leading Goalkicker	No.	Best & Fairest	Captain	Coach
1976	3rd	Robert Walls	55	Trevor Keogh	Alex Jesaulenko	Ian Thurogood
1977	6th	Mark Maclure	39	Bruce Doull	Robert Walls	Ian Thurogood
1978	4th	Rod Galt	48	Trevor Keogh	Alex Jesaulenko	Alex Jesaulenko
1979	1st	Ken Sheldon	53	Mike Fitzpatrick	Alex Jesaulenko	Alex Jesaulenko
1980	4th	Wayne Johnson	51	Bruce Doull	Mike Fitzpatrick	Percy Jones

because of ill health.

Under Jesaulenko in 1978 Carlton staged a revival following one win in six matches, defeating Collingwood at Victoria Park, and then defeating ladder leader North Melbourne.

Another win over Collingwood later in the season consolidated a place in the final five, and after winning the Elimination Final over Geelong, confidence was high that the dose could be repeated in the First Semi-final against Collingwood. It wasn't — the Blues went down and out of the finals, 15.18 (108) to 13.15 (93).

Carlton defeated Essendon in the first match played for Premiership points in March, when the Round 3 clash was brought forward to March 31, the Saturday before Round 1. Carlton won, 14.17 (101) to 11.14 (80).

Carlton rallied to defeat Collingwood in a vigorous game at Princes Park, inspired by the sight of Jezza flat out in the grass after being shirt-fronted by Stan Magro. Carlton won 18.15 (123) to 16.11 (107) in Round 10, 9 June 1979.

Reports in the *Age* on July 27 revealed that non-football business ventures associated with Carlton president George Harris and Carlton Marketing Services, such as the cheerleader troupe the Bluebirds, had lost money. The newspaper alleged that the Bluebirds, who cost $2000 a spot, lost $29,918.

Carlton lost only three games in the 1979 home-and-away rounds — and only one of these was by more than a goal. A Premiership was in sight.

CARLTON

'God' and the Dominator

Ken Hunter was the original football 'god', acquiring the honoured sobriquet in just about his first game for the Blues in 1981 which was against Richmond at Waverley. He was god because he had no fear of death or injury, and achieved immortality playing a decisive role in the back to back flags in 1981–82, and winning a Carlton Best and Fairest in his first season.

Hunter played 99 games for Claremont before the first of 147 for Carlton, mostly on the half-back flank, but later occasionally being thrown onto the forward line as the coach searched for a goal. He kicked seven against North Melbourne in 1983 and eight against Footscray in 1984.

An image of him is of a socks-down rag doll flinging itself skywards, oblivious of the pack roaring in from behind, landing sideways or on his head, but always getting up to take his awkward, loose-limbed but effective kick. He went directly at the ball wherever it was, often at a funny angle – there was something of the young Stephen Silvagni in the ageless Ken Hunter. He was a clamping tackler who appeared from nowhere. He had a loopingly direct handpass, and the sure sign of football divinity – he went where the ball was. With Bruce Doull kicking in from full-back after a behind, he had a nice routine. This involved running with his back to Doull and receiving the kick-in over his left shoulder at full pace, speeding through the centre. Nice trick.

Johnston on the rise. Ken Hunter in classic action.

Wayne 'Dominator' Johnston was the best big occasion player Carlton had in the 1980s because he was so explosive. He could win a match (and often did) with 10 minutes of football. In a game against Hawthorn, Carlton trailing badly at half-time he had 15 touches in 15 minutes of sustained ferocity, inspiring a 10-goal quarter. He kicked a few, gave a few away, tackled, smothered, skittled, passed and by-passed. He was everything and everywhere – and it wasn't even a Grand Final. Dom was a great exponent of the 'little things' the one-percenters at Carlton – chasing and spoiling, , smothering (a speciality), tackling and shepherding. He had a swinging left-foot kick, and loved to put them through the goals. Johnston was captain of Carlton 1984 and 1985, got 22 kicks in his first game, was a dominant influence in four winning Grand Finals and countless other big games, played 209 games, played the last three seasons after a back operation and suffered a series of injuries in 1989 and 1990 that eventually forced him to retire.

And the Buzz – Peter Bosustow.

1981–1985 HONOUR ROLL

Year	Pos	Leading Goalkicker		Best & Fairest	Captain	Coach
1981	1st	Peter Bosustow	59	Ken Hunter	Mike Fitzpatrick	David Parkin
1982	1st	Ross Ditchburn	61	Jim Buckley	Mike Fitzpatrick	David Parkin
1983	5th	Ken Hunter	43	Wayne Johnston	Mike Fitzpatrick	David Parkin
1984	4th	Warren Ralph	55	Bruce Doull	Wayne Johnston	David Parkin
1985	5th	Mark Maclure	48	Justin Madden	Wayne Johnston	David Parkin

CLUB NEWS 1981–1985

Unrest and upheavals at Carlton in the summer following the 1979 Premiership saw the departure of both coach Alex Jesaulenko and president George Harris. Mike Fitzpatrick was appointed captain, and Peter 'Percy' Jones coach. Jesaulenko went to coach St Kilda.

Despite the off-field activity Carlton began the season on scintillating form, winning the first five games. Carlton was in the battle with Geelong and Richmond for top spot in the last round – and missed out on percentage, after Fitzroy staged a spirited and high-scoring last-round game.

Finishing second was no help to Carlton in the 1980 finals series, losing the Qualifying Final 10.14 (74) to Richmond 18.8 (116), and then the First Semi-final to Collingwood 15.12 (102) to 22.20 (152).

With Carlton 13 points up in time-on in the game at Princes Park against Essendon, captain Mike Fitzpatrick was free-kicked by umpire Ian Robinson for time wasting, judging that he held on to the ball for too long while taking a kick after a mark. Neale Daniher for Essendon then managed to steal the game by kicking three goals in time-on. Essendon won 14.15 (99) to 15.8 (98).

Fitzroy gave Carlton a fright in Round 1 of 1982, drawing 16.17 (113) to 17.11 (113) Things looked more ominous after Carlton lost to Essendon in Round 2, 8.17 (65) to 13.13 (91).

1981–1985

Carlton hit the MCG with that winning look about the team.

Back-to-back

In 1981 Carlton finished on top of the ladder, nearly eight per cent ahead of Collingwood (who lost the last game to Fitzroy). The Blues defeated Geelong fairly easily, 16.17 (113) to 11.7 (73), Des English best on ground, with Bruce Doull, Ken Sheldon, Mike Fitzpatrick, Phil Maylin and first-year player and crowd favourite, David Glascott. Bosustow provided the extraordinary in this game, an improbable smother followed by an impossible goal.

The Grand Final dawned with Collingwood the favourites. The first quarter was described in the *Age* as being like a 'tug of war between two computers, each programmed to resist. Even the coaches were loath to change the system, fearing a short circuit. On and on it went. Ball smothered on boot. Promising run stopped in midstream. Likely mark thwarted by timely punch.' A point the difference.

The second quarter saw Collingwood nip away to a heartbreaking 21-point lead before Rod Ashman conjured a goal from nowhere, and Jim Buckley pinched one on the siren. At three-quarter time Collingwood was still nine points up. Fitzpatrick, in charge at centre half-forward, thought the game was lost, but coach Parkin had a glint in his eye, and conviction in his voice. Collingwood were tiring, he said, Carlton was fresher. Kick the first goal and we'll win. Sheldon did and we did! Bruce Doull the titan in defence won the Norm Smith, but Fitzpatrick was just about his equal up forward.

Back-to-back looked improbable, but they didn't count on Carlton's best big occasion player, Wayne Johnston, who had saved himself (he had served a two-week suspension) for as ferocious an opening to a Grand Final as has ever been played. He took a handball from Mark Maclure within seconds of the first bounce and squeezed a goal in while nearly wiping out the goal post. After the restart he tackled a Tiger so hard the ball squeezed out and Wayne Harmes kicked a goal. Then Mike Fitzpatrick, the scholarly centre half-forward, kicked an educated ball off the ground to Rod Ashman who kicked another. Then Ross Ditchburn and Ken Hunter were KO'd. Despite the fact that Richmond actually got to the front at half-time, Carlton fans felt we had the game won. We knew it after a superb third quarter where five goals were kicked to Richmond's nil, goals thanks to Bosustow, and the absence of them thanks to Doull.

The last quarter was the Dominator (should have been Norm Smith medallist), the Buzz, the captain and 'Chesty' – Peter McConville, who kicked the last goal.

How sweet it is – two in a row.

Michael Leunig's vision of the 1982 Grand Final.

Carlton kicked its second-highest score in Round 18, 1982 when it piled on 30.21 (201) to Footscray's 10.12 (72). This was also Carlton's greatest winning margin against the Dogs, 129 points.

A record 12.5 (77) first quarter against the Swans at Princes Park resulted in a scoreline of 27.23 (185), also a record in Round 9, 1982.

Carlton slipped to third spot later in the season, after losing to the revenge-minded Swans 9.18 (72) to 15 16 (106) in Sydney in Round 19, before a then-record crowd of 25,601. The Swans were pressing for a place in the five. Carlton bounced back by trouncing Richmond in the next round 13.14 (92) to 9.10 (64), thrashing North Melbourne 26.24 (180) to 17.8 (110) and Fitzroy 23.12 (150) to 17.9 (111) in the last round. Only Richmond, two games better on top of the ladder stood between Carlton and 'back-to-back' Flags.

Carlton won the pre-season Night Premiership in 1993, defeating Richmond 14.16 (100) to 10.6 (66). Suffering from triple-Flag hangover, Carlton crashed out of the day finals in the Elimination Final to Essendon, 12.9 (81) to 17.12 (114).

Bruce Doull passed John Nicholls' record number of games with his first game of 1984.

Carlton kicked a massive 31.13 (199) against North Melbourne's 9.8 (62) in Round 1, 1984 at Waverley – its highest score and greatest winning margin against the Kangaroos.

CARLTON

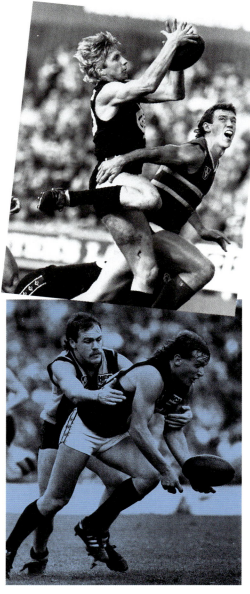

Six stars shine in 1987
Clockwise from top left: the hottest thing from the Latrobe Valley, terrific Tom Alvin; second generation Blues champ Stephen 'S.O.S.' Silvagni; elegant and tough David Rhys-Jones; the sublime runner Craig Bradley; the resilient and brilliant Ken Hunter and determined Jon Dorotich.

1986–1989 HONOUR ROLL

Year	Pos	Leading Goalkicker	No.	Best & Fairest	Captain	Coach
1986	2nd	Stephen Kernahan	62	C. Bradley/W. Johnston	Mark Maclure	Robert Walls
1987	1st	Stephen Kernahan	73	Stephen Kernahan	Stephen Kernahan	Robert Walls
1988	3rd	Stephen Kernahan	54	Craig Bradley	Stephen Kernahan	Robert Walls
1989	8th	Stephen Kernahan	59	Stephen Kernahan	Stephen Kernahan	Walls/Jesaulenko

CLUB NEWS 1986–1989

South Australian imports Craig Bradley, Stephen Kernahan, and Peter Motley played their first games for Carlton, joining other new recruits Adrian Gleeson, Peter Kenny and Jon Dorotich.

David Parkin and Robert Walls 'swapped' coaching jobs for 1986 – Parkin left for Fitzroy, and Walls returned to his original club, Carlton.

The Blues kicked a record third-quarter 12.2. (74) in Round 3 against St. Kilda in 1986, winning 24.13 (157) to 10.9 (69).

Some tremendous performances in the middle of 1986 by the old and new Blues saw Carlton into third place. Bruce Doull played his 350th game against North in Round 11, which was also David Glascott's hundredth.

Hawthorn defeated Carlton in awful wet and slippery conditions at Waverley for the 1986 night Premiership 9.12 (66) to 5.6 (36).

Carlton's highest score and greatest winning margin against Melbourne was kicked in Round 10, 1986, 25.15 (165) v Melbourne 6.13 (49) when Justin Madden rucked and laughed his way through a best-on-ground performance.

Disappointment is something of an understatement for the reaction to Carlton's capitulation in the 1986 Grand Final. Stephen Kernahan said, 'The Grand Final is the ultimate test and I know I felt shocking that we'd failed it'. Bruce Doull was badly beaten on the day, and retired with

1986–1989

Blues give Hawks a hot time in '87

Craig Bradley bubbles over on the siren.

Left: Kernahan greets the crowd. Above: joy in the dressing room.

Carlton finished third in 1986 with the new stars Stephen Kernahan and Craig Bradley shining brightly alongside such old Blue giants such as Bruce Doull and Ken Hunter.

A methodical demolition of Sydney in the Qualifying Final was followed by a surprising and as it turned out deceptive win over Hawthorn in the Second Semi – David Rhys-Jones had 31 possessions and seemingly no opponent, Doull thrashed Dunstall – who did not kick a goal – and it looked promising for the big one.

But looks were proved to be deceptive when in the Grand Final Dunstall kicked three in the first quarter, as Hawthorn jumped Carlton and never looked back. It was humiliating for the new players who failed on the day, but worse for Doull – it was his last game, as it was for stalwart Mark Maclure.

In 1987 the boot was not on the 1986 foot. Carlton finished on top of the ladder with a record 18 wins and 4 losses. Stephen Kernahan kicked 73 goals in his first season as captain, kicking the Blues into top spot with that goal against North Melbourne after the siren. While the drama of the final series unfolded for Melbourne, Carlton disposed of Hawthorn in a rousing fightback in the second half to win the Second Semi 11.14 (80) to 10.5 (65)

Grand Final day dawned hot and got hotter. Hawthorn had played the heart-stopping Preliminary Final against Melbourne while the Blues rested their team with seven new faces from 1986 in it. But it was the old campaigner Wayne Johnston who noticed at the opening bounce that there were too many Hawks in the centre square and got himself the first kick of the game. Hunter missed a shot after he marked the Dominator's kick – but Johnston made up with the next one, kicking it himself. He kicked two for the quarter. He also was reported for clobbering Hawthorn 'strong man' Robert DiPierdomenico, much to the delight of Carlton fans with long memories.

David Rhys-Jones was brilliant on Dermott Brereton, winning the Norm Smith Medal, and a nine goals to five second half saw Carlton comfortable winners 15.14 (104) to 9.17 (71). Captain Kernahan kicked three and played a focused game, while Bradley also kicked three goals, creating havoc with his running. Tom Alvin also swooped off the half-back line. The game was over early in the last quarter when Dermott Brereton patted Rhys-Jones on the head after out-pointing him in a contest for the ball. Blues too hot.

356 magnificent games. Rod Ashman (236 games) also retired. Even the solid win over Hawthorn in the Second Semi-final (as well as the defeat of Sydney in the qualifying final) were in retrospect none too convincing.
Mark Maclure was deposed as captain at the end of 1986 and retired with 243 games. Stephen Kernahan was appointed in just his second season with the Blues.
Tragedy for Carlton and Peter Motley when he was terribly injured in a car accident on May 7. He was widely regarded as having more potential even than Craig Bradley – who gave Motley his 1987 Premiership Medal. Earlier (February), dual Premiership player and gallant defender Des English was diagnosed with a type of cancer. His courageous and successful battle against it in 1987 was an inspiration to his team-mates.
The new captain more than justified his position by securing top spot for Carlton in 1987 with a kick after the siren in the game against North Melbourne in Round 22. Stephen Kernahan marked a lob from Justin Madden, the siren sounded and he steered through a difficult shot to win the game 20.9 (129) 19.11 (125).
After a shocking start to the 1989 season, culminating in a loss to the Brisbane Bears at Princes Park, coach Robert Walls was replaced. Alex Jesaulenko made a comeback as coach. Carlton won 18 and drew one of the next 34 games for Jezza, finishing eighth in 1989 and 1990.

CARLTON

From left: the captain Stephen Kernahan, Scott Camporeale, Andrew McKay and Stephan Silvagni.

The greatest season

By virtually any measure Carlton was far and away the best team of 1995, and statistically one of the best of all time. No other team had won 20 home-and-away games, or 16 games in a row including the Grand Final. 23 from 25 – and the two losses were real doozies.

Rounds 1 to 7 resulted in seven wins, and some spectacular highlights. The campaign opened with captain Kernahan's 200th game, and Matt Clape and Scott Camporeale's first. Against Footscray in the third game, Kernahan kicked a lazy 10, and the team had a massive 154 possessions more than their opponents in a 98-point win.

But in Round 8 Sydney walloped Carlton 21.6 (132) to 8.12 (60) and the next week was even less explicable. The free-scoring Blues managed a preposterous 3.6 (24) to St Kilda's 11.14 (80) at Waverley in the next game – a nervous hiccup?

It seemed so when in Round 9 the Blues thrashed Hawthorn in a highly satisfying manner by 102 points, Kernahan, Pearce and Hanna each kicking five goals.

Then came the surge to the Flag, as irresistible as a king tide.

First Melbourne, then a heart-stopper against Geelong – a win by three points in the game of the season, and the Grand Final preview. 'Harry' Madden played his 300th in front of 85,000 in a cracker of a game against Richmond at the MCG, where Anthony Koutoufides had 34 touches and 10 marks.

Adelaide managed to give Carlton a 29-point start in the third quarter, which had become a 22-point deficit for them by three-quarter time. In Round 17, 1995, Best and Fairest Brett Ratten managed 44 possessions (but no Brownlow votes!), Bradley 37 and Kouta 33 with 14 marks, in a 97-point win over Fitzroy. Footscray, Brisbane and North were all accounted for – followed by the terrific contest at Subiaco where Carlton won by a point in an extremely tense and exciting game. This was what finally convinced supporters that '95 was going to be a Blue year. After beating Essendon in Round 22, Carlton overcame a nervous disposition to beat Brisbane in the Qualifying Final; 13.12 (90) to 12.5 (77) and then account pretty easily in the end for North Melbourne 18.10 (116) to 8.8 (56), winning on a wet MCG night.

So Carlton was in the Grand Final, after a grand season.

CLUB NEWS 1990–1996

Alex Jesaulenko's coaching career ended after the 1990 season, David Parkin was reappointed, and while a clean-out of players was undertaken, Carlton won only eight games, finishing in the lowest position, eleventh, in the history of the club in the VFL/AFL.

Mark Arceri kicked Carlton's only face-saving goal (in the last quarter) in perhaps the most dismal performance of the 1990s – 1.10 (16) to Footscray's 8.9 (57), Round 11, 1991.

On 12 February 1992 Greg Williams was deregistered until April 30 after admitting he gave League incorrect information about his 1990 payments with Sydney. Williams scored his first win in a Carlton jumper in the furnace of the Collingwood centenary match in Round 8 – 83,000 people watched Carlton win 16.9 (105) to 9.18 (72). Kernahan bagged seven goals, Williams 33 possessions.

Stephen Silvagni kicked eight goals and beat four opponents in Round 2, 1992 as Carlton 17.13 (115) defeated Hawthorn 12.17 (89).

The 1992 All-Australian team included Mil Hanna and Stephen Kernahan. Kernahan signed new three-year deal for Carlton on 22 September 1992, following speculation that he would move back to Adelaide.

Carlton had second spot, and the double chance, but after beating Essendon in the Qualifying Final and Adelaide in the Second Semi, they

1990-1996

Sweet 16

The inspirations. Dean Rice's smother and Bradley's calm first goal. Silvagni on Ablett's hammer. The captain robbed of a goal, gets it back straight away, thanks to Greg Williams. Kernahan returns the favour and gives one to Diesel. Brad Pearce zips out on a lead and bags his first. All the forwards are getting near the footy, and the backline is as well knit as one of my mother's jumpers. Not a hole to be seen.

And the 'starting four' in the middle, led by Justin Madden, engineer of the engine room, were just magnificent. Brett Ratten, Greg Williams, Craig Bradley and Fraser Brown take turns to smuggle the ball out of the centre.

If Dean is the backline general, and Kerna is on the forward line, then Craig Bradley is directing traffic and organising moves all over the ground – but especially in the middle.

Spalding's sensational smother and goal kicked off the second quarter. Then Madden goals, and writing is starting to appear on the wall. Rice and a couple from the Captain sew up the first half.

Forty points in front, can't read the Record, surely they can't do an '89 on us, Geelong aren't Carlton '70 after all ... first goal of the third is important.

The captain gets it, and then Diesel turns on a show in the forward pocket, artfully grabbing the short kick in and a few minutes later juggling a mark in the goal square to dazzle another one.

The quarter is capped off by Campo rightly getting a Grand Final goal in his first season, Williams getting one from the visionary kick of Bradley, and giving one to Pearce. It's all over now.

But I want the first goal of the last quarter. It's Bradley who gets the treatment, the 50-metre penalty and the first goal – and finally, it's Carlton's sweet sixteenth Flag.

1990–1996 HONOUR ROLL

Year	Pos	Leading Goalkicker	No.	Best & Fairest	Captain	Coach
1990	8th	Stephen Kernahan	69	Stephen Silvagni	Stephen Kernahan	Alex Jesaulenko
1991	11th	Stephen Kernahan	46	Justin Madden	Stephen Kernahan	David Parkin
1992	7th	Stephen Kernahan	83	Stephen Kernahan	Stephen Kernahan	David Parkin
1993	2nd	Stephen Kernahan	68	Craig Bradley	Stephen Kernahan	David Parkin
1994	5th	Stephen Kernahan	82	Greg Williams	Stephen Kernahan	David Parkin
1995	1st	Stephen Kernahan	63	Brett Ratten	Stephen Kernahan	David Parkin
1996	6th	Stephen Kernahan	56	Stephen Silvagni	Stephen Kernahan	David Parkin

That winning feeling: Greg Williams and the captain; Peter Dean; the Blues brothers.

were lethargic in the 1993 Grand Final. Essendon humiliated them 20.13 (133) to 13.11 (89).

An MCG crowd of 85,381 saw the Blues make it eight in a row when they defeated Collingwood 14. 13 (97) to 7.12 (54) in Round 17, 1994.

Greg Williams scooped the pool in 1994, winning not only his second Brownlow Medal (with 30 votes), but also every major Melbourne media award.

After 8 consecutive wins in mid-season, top place beckoned in the last round of 1994 – but Carlton lost to Essendon in the last round of the year – which happened to be in September. The Blues then were very disappointing in losing the two finals, to Melbourne in the Third Qualifying Final 14.12 (96) to 18.15 (123) and then to an injury-riddled Geelong in the Second Semi-final – 10.12 (72) to 15.15 (105).

In 1995, Stephen Kernahan and Greg Williams were contracted to the Blues until retirement.

Carlton's 1995 pre-season injury list grew to awesome proportions after Stephen Kernahan, Andrew McKay and Fraser Brown were injured in the Carlton v Collingwood round robin challenge at Waverley. In all, 12 senior players were out.

The 1996 finals were a re-run of disappointing 1994, except that the defeats were even heavier – West Coast defeated Carlton in the Qualifying Final 18.17 (125) to 10.10 (70) and Brisbane won at a canter, 26.14 (170) to 10.13 (73).

CARLTON

Craig Bradley with Ansett Cup.

Premiership Blues

By the end of the ordinary season many Blues fans found it difficult to recall that Carlton had actually won a Premiership cup that season. But Carlton had indeed defeated Geelong in the Ansett Australia Cup 14.13 (97) to 5.10 (40) on the night of March 21. Along the way Carlton had good wins over Melbourne, Fremantle and St Kilda. Craig Bradley won the Michael Tuck Medal as best player on the ground in the Grand Final win.

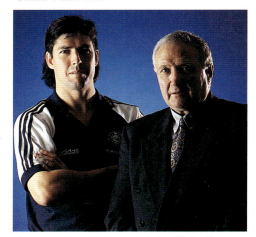
Stephen Kernahan and John Nicholls.

Blues Legends

In April, Carlton supporters voted for the top 25 Blues from the 1010 who have played over the past hundred years or so. Of the 1997 players Stephen Kernahan, Stephen Silvagni, Justin Madden, Greg Williams and Craig Bradley were named. Named in the Carlton Hall of Fame and honoured in the Legends Stand are Jesaulenko, Nicholls, 'SOS', Bradley, Kernahan, Johnston, Vallence, Deacon and Doull.

The light-blue M&M strip.

Diesel's last lap blues with the tribunal

Dual Brownlow Medallist and 1995 Norm Smith Medallist Greg Williams had a horror start to what proved to be his final season for Carlton. He was reported after the game by the AFL – not the umpire – in the Easter Monday game against Essendon for 'unduly interfering'

The Diesel: vintage finish.

Kouta's boots cause blue.

Sponsorship blues

On top of the shock of seeing Old Dark Navy Blues in a light blue in the game against Adelaide (luckily it was a win), another sponsorship wrangle arrived in the shape of Kouta's boots. Carlton were paid $300,000 to wear jumpers in the shade of light blue M&Ms, though no one was sure how much Anthony Koutoufides made from his three-striped Adidas boots while the rest of the team were in club sponsor Nike boots.

Kouta's manager threatened Kouta would strike in the Round 7 clash with Richmond if he couldn't wear the stripes, while Carlton thought it threatened their sponsorship. The primacy of club and individual contracts, and the role of player managers was at the centre of this (and the alleged dispute with Stephen Silvagni later in the season). Eventually common sense prevailed and both Kouta and the club played out the season.

with umpire Andrew Coates. The tribunal suspended him for nine weeks, but Carlton obtained a temporary injunction from Mr Justice Nathan which allowed Diesel to play on until the case was heard by the full Supreme Court. Carlton lost the game against Essendon and also the game the next week against North Melbourne where Williams was reported and suspended for three weeks for kneeing Dean Laidley. Hedigan J. reserved his decision in May, and then overturned the tribunal decision saying that no tribunal could have found Williams guilty on the evidence before it. The AFL, its rules under threat, appealed and the full bench of the Supreme Court overturned Williams' appeal with a 2–1 majority in July. Williams had to serve the remaining weeks of his suspension. Williams' retirement (after a couple of vintage games at the end of the season) brought the matter to a close.

1997

The 1997 Blues

1997 was a disappointing year for Carlton on and off the field. The club desperately needed a turnover of its ageing superstars. At the same time it was reluctant to force them out, preferring to repay the players' loyalty with support for each player to make his own decision in his own time.

Genial giant Justin Madden was the first to go on July 7, after 332 games, and two Carlton Premierships, as well as the Presidency of the AFL Players' Association.

Stephen Kernahan after another injury-interrupted season became Carlton's greatest goalkicker, eclipsing Soapy Vallence's 722 goals against Richmond in Round 6. Even more significant was that in his 250th game (against Adelaide in Adelaide), 'Sticks' became the longest-serving captain in League history – his 225th game as the Blues skipper, since taking over in 1976. He retired in his own time, in Grand Final week.

Greg Williams brought up his 250th game against Essendon, with 109 for Carlton on July 12. Williams was given a hint that he might not be required in 1998. He said 'I'm 34, I've got a sore knee and I'm having a bit of trouble with incentive.' Mil Hanna and Earl Spalding also retired; Luke O'Sullivan and Rohan Welsh were de-listed.

Stephen Silvagni's heroic effort at full-forward against the Eagles at Subiaco, when Carlton won 12.14 (86) to 11.13 (79) revived memories of 1995 and 1993, when big wins in the west heralded greater things. However, the Blues only won three of the next nine games. Losses included terrible results against Melbourne, and even worse a fade-out against Richmond at home (of all places) in Round 22, which prevented another finals campaign. Silvagni was great at both ends of the ground all year. Michael Sexton was the best centre half-back in the competition – but missed the last four games with injury. Ang Christou had a bad back injury for most of the season. Brett Ratten won the club's Best and Fairest award for the second time, beating the other star of the season, the ageless Craig Bradley.

Above: Stephen Silvagni flies. **Inset:** Brett Ratten passes.
Below: Greg Williams leaves. **Right:** some big victories.

1997 HONOUR ROLL

Year	Pos	Leading Goalkicker		Best & Fairest	Captain	Coach
1997	11th	Anthony Koutoufides	28	Brett Ratten	Stephen Kernahan	David Parkin

COLLINGWOOD

MY CLUB
by Michael Roberts

Loved and reviled, admired and despised – often all at the same time – the Magpies have long prided themselves on being the most famous sporting club in the country. It is a claim supported by a huge army of fanatical supporters, and by the even larger pool of other fans who like nothing better than seeing Collingwood go down.

Of course, that meant nothing to a five-year-old back in the mid-1960s. Then, like every child growing up in suburban Melbourne, I was faced with one of the most difficult, and ultimately significant, choices of my life – that of which VFL team to support.

Many Collingwood supporters, I would learn later, were born into the black and white, either by virtue of family links or the suburb in which they were born. Mine was a simple case of sibling rivalry. My older brother barracked for Essendon, and in one of the first matches in which I took an interest, the Bombers were opposed to Collingwood. Like all 'narky' kid brothers, I simply started barracking against my brother's side. Had the Bombers been playing Fitzroy that day, I would now be without a team. Instead I have spent more than 30 years following one of the most fascinating sporting clubs in the world.

Of course fascinating doesn't necessarily equate with successful – at least not in the modern era. For example, West Coast Eagles have been incredibly successful, but they are hardly fascinating.

Collingwood, on the other hand, is always a story – even when they are losing. Nothing is ever done in half measures at Victoria Park. In all ways, Collingwood is football writ large.

And that, ultimately, is one of the great joys of being a Collingwood fan – there is simply never a dull moment. The lows seem somehow lower, and the highs higher. The scandals are more outrageous, the infighting – think of 1976, '82, '86 – more bitter and savage. The players are never simply average, despite mounting evidence to the contrary; they are either 'champions' or 'duds'. And, as every good media mogul knows, a big Collingwood story is good for sales, or ratings. That means we're never out of the spotlight for very long.

Collingwood has always had strong support. In its very first season as a football club, 1892, the *Australasian* noted that 'Even the best game between other clubs could not tempt Collingwood supporters into deserting their team for a week.'

Collingwood wanted its own team primarily because Fitzroy, its neighbour and rival, had one. It was a matter of civic pride. People might have been quick to deride the suburb, but the footballers were not to be dismissed so lightly.

So when the club began winning, the supporters were quick to crow – as underdogs suddenly on top are prone to do. And as the team kept winning, so did the arrogance grow. Winning became a way of life.

What footy was given was a large pool of fanatical, loyal Magpie fans, and a larger pool who couldn't stand their success, their arrogance, their supporters or their sometimes physical tactics on the field. It was often said that many footy fans, after checking their own team's results, would next check on the Collingwood game in the hope they had lost.

But when the Big Drought hit, the going became harder. Even the famed Flag of 1990 didn't return things to their natural order, for the team has continued to struggle. Since 1958, the Maggies have won only one Flag, while Carlton have won eight, Essendon five, Richmond five, Hawthorn nine. Yet through it all the black and white army has remained remarkably loyal, passionate and committed. And for that you have to admire us, whatever you think of our club.

Today, of course, the Magpies' footballing pre-eminence is under threat, if not already gone. Other Victorian clubs have more members. So do some interstate clubs – and they have more money, too. Some, even, like Adelaide, are probably more hated.

The game has changed, but somehow, I know the loyalty and passion of Collingwood supporters will continue to be a part of football for as long as the game is played.

COLLINGWOOD

Year Established	1889
Joined VFL/AFL	1897
Home Ground	Victoria Park
Premierships	1902, 1903, 1910, 1917, 1919, 1927, 1928, 1929, 1930, 1935, 1936, 1953, 1958, 1990
Brownlow Medals	Syd Coventry 1927, Albert Collier 1929, Harry Collier 1930, Marcus Whelan 1939, Desmond Fothergill 1940, Len Thompson 1972, Peter Moore 1979
Record home crowd	47,651 v Sth Melbourne, 1948
Most games	Tony Shaw, 313
Most goals	Gordon Coventry, 1299
Notable supporters	Past: ,John Wren, Archbishop Daniel Mannix Present: David Williamson, Elle McFeast, Daryl Braithwaite, Brian Naylor, Frank Galbally

Above: The forward troops of the Magpie army prepare for battle.
Inset: The men who built a legend: Jack McHale and the team of 1929.

Gavin Brown: inspirational leader.   *Peter Daicos: magic to follow.*   *Tony Shaw at the Grand Final parade.*

COLLINGWOOD

The 1891 Britannia team, soon to be part of the new Collingwood.

Bill Strickland: from Carlton.

A new club is founded

Collingwood's formation was based in part on the old Britannia Football Club, a junior club that played at Victoria Park but which also had links with Fitzroy.

With Fitzroy having had its own senior football team from 1883, there came from the municipality of Collingwood a growing push for the establishment of a senior football team that would carry the name of its district. A group of citizens met in mid-1889 and resolved to push for Collingwood's entry to the VFA, with the assistance of Britannia.

This first push was rejected by the VFA, but the Collingwood locals persisted. Two years later, in 1891, the VFA changed its rules to allow for the admission of a thirteenth club.

Those behind the Collingwood push asked if Britannia would be admitted as a Collingwood team if Victoria Park was improved and upgraded to meet VFA standards, and they were given the go-ahead.

Not all at Britannia were happy with the move, but Collingwood's civic leaders were determined. In early 1892, as a public meeting overwhelmingly endorsed the formation of Collingwood, Britannia disbanded. That decision caused further dissension. Some members went to Fitzroy (taking the match bell with them!) and others to the fledgling club Collingwood.

Strickland inspires

Collingwood went through five captains in little more than its first 12 months.

Former Britannia legend Bill Dean was chosen as the team's captain, but only led them in a practice match. Former Fitzroy player Joe Delahunty was next chosen, but he was too ill to lead the team in its first matches and Tasmanian George Watt filled in. Ken McPherson was appointed for 1893, but lasted only a few games before handing over to Bill Strickland, a former Carlton champion who was to prove one of the most important figures in the Club's early years.

First game – v Carlton

A carnival atmosphere pervaded Victoria Park on 7 May 1892, when more than 16,000 people came to the first official match of the Collingwood Football Club. Fittingly, it was played against Carlton. The Magpies lost that first game by two goals to three, with Alf Toll kicking the first goal and Bill Proudfoot the second. Critics were universal in their praise of the new club and the brave manner in which they fought.

Magpie fans had only to wait a few weeks for their team's first win, when they beat Williamstown in Round 5 by four goals to three. The pickings were slim until Round 14 when the Pies beat St Kilda. They finished the season on a high by beating Carlton, but still finished in last place.

The heartland: a view over Collingwood in the 1890s.

CLUB NEWS 1892–1896

A meeting of prominent Collingwood citizens in June 1889 decides to push for establishment of a senior football team to carry the Collingwood name.

The public meeting at Collingwood Town Hall on 12 February 1892 endorses formation of Collingwood Football Club. A local MP rouses the already enthusiastic crowd with the declaration that 'The very name of Collingwood would strike terror into the hearts of opposing players.'

The first committee meeting of the Collingwood Football Club, is held at the Grace Darling Hotel on 11 March 1892.

Collingwood's first practice game is played against the Clifton Hill Juniors in the Darling Gardens on 16 April 1892. The Magpies win nine goals to three, after meeting in the Yarra Hotel before the game to elect a captain.

Collingwood's first game in senior competition is played against Carlton in the Victorian Football Association on 7 May 1892.

Collingwood's first win in the VFA (over Williamstown) on 28 May 1892 inspires hopes of a successful first season, hopes that go largely unfulfilled as the team wins only one of its first 14 matches.

Collingwood finishes off its debut season in fine style with its first win over Carlton, but the team still finishes bottom of the ladder, having earlier beaten Williamstown and St Kilda.

Carlton's Bill Strickland arrives in April 1893 to assume the Collingwood

1892 – 1896

Bill Proudfoot: the protector.

Bill Proudfoot's day

It isn't often that players have to come to the aid of an umpire – let alone save his life.

But that's just what Bill Proudfoot did at Arden Street in 1896, when a mob of enraged North Melbourne fans invaded the field after their team's loss. Proudfoot, a giant of a man and a policeman by profession, tried to protect the umpire with one arm while fending off a flurry of blows from fists and sticks with the other. Umpire Roberts suffered only minor injuries, but Proudfoot was so severely beaten that he collapsed upon reaching the dressing room. One observer noted that the ump 'would probably have been killed' but for Proudfoot's help.

Later in life, Proudfoot was awarded a bravery medal from the Royal Humane Society after saving several people on a tram by stopping a pair of bolting horses in Swanston Street.

The 1896 Premiership team defeated South Melbourne before both teams joined the VFL.

1896 Premiership

Collingwood's first Premiership flag was also its last, at least in the VFA.

It was secured on an abnormally hot October day in 1896 before 12,000 fans at the East Melbourne Cricket Ground, when Bill Strickland led his charges to a victory over South Melbourne, six goals to five.

The two teams had finished on equal points at the end of the home-and-away season, necessitating a 'Grand Final' play-off. The score was locked at five goals all for much of the final quarter, before the Magpies' Danny Flaherty goaled from a free kick just minutes before the end.

Strickland, named Champion of the Colony for the season, was again a major contributor on Grand Final day. He was given much of the credit for the Premiership for telling his men to 'go easy' in the third quarter, thereby saving their energy for the last. It was a strategy that worked perfectly, South tiring noticeably late in the game.

Strickland was ably supported by the high marking defence work of Jack Monohan, who changed the game when swung into attack in the final term, and the clever play of Charlie Pannam and Dick Condon.

Victoria Park in 1900, with a new 'ladies' grandstand in the foreground.

captaincy, becoming the first great Magpie leader. Under his leadership, the team wins seven games in 1893.
Ern 'Bud' Copeland becomes Collingwood secretary in 1895, a post he will hold for 29 years during which time he will play a major role in the transformation of the club to one of the powers of the competition.
In August 1895, Captain Bill Strickland reports one of his own players, wingman Charles 'Buffer' Sime, for using bad language during a game. Sime is called upon to apologise to both Strickland and to the Committee.
Rover Jack McInerny, a former Britannia player who crossed to Collingwood in 1892, is expelled in September 1895 for having taken a bribe in a game against North Melbourne earlier in the season. McInerny is subsequently 'blacklisted' by other senior clubs until he finds a home at Prahran in 1899.
Collingwood becomes one of the founding members of the new Victorian Football League in a meeting at Buxton's Art Gallery in Swanston Street on 2 October 1896. Collingwood has become a key player in the formation of the new League, confirming its rise to a position of power.
The Collingwood side defeats South Melbourne to take the VFA Flag on 3 October 1896. The local community rejoices, with more than 2000 attending the victory celebrations at the Town Hall. A succession of parties, banquets and dinners follows, as the players are feted as local heroes.

COLLINGWOOD

Dick Condon (rear) seems to be aggrieved in a match against Fitzroy.

Fred Leach: enigmatic genius.

Condon – a brilliant troublemaker

The most brilliant – and controversial – Collingwood player of the era was undoubtedly Dick Condon. He is still regarded as one of the most talented players the club has ever produced. But he was also one of the game's great troublemakers – coming to blows with his own team-mates, trying to lead his team from the field during a game and falling foul of umpires and committeemen alike.

A rover/centreman with pace, extraordinary agility and silky ball skills on both sides of his body, Condon was one of the most dangerous players in the VFL. Many contemporaries regarded him as the best they had seen.

But his disciplinary problems were never far from the surface. In 1895 he was hauled before the committee for failing to obey the captain (Strickland) during a match. In 1900, while captain, he was suspended for three weeks for abusing an umpire. Soon after his return he got involved in a three-quarter time fight with one of his own players.

Later that same season, he tried to pull his players off the field in protest at the umpiring. The following week he abused umpire 'Ivo' Crapp ('Your girl's a bloody whore!') – and the VFL suspended him for life!

The suspension was lifted in May of 1902, and Condon returned to play a key role in the Premierships of 1902 and 1903. He coached the Club in 1905–06, but in the latter year was again suspended for causing dissension.

He left the club at the end of 1906 and spent a year in Tasmania – umpiring! He returned to Victoria in 1908 and joined Richmond without a clearance – an appropriately controversial note on which to end a controversial career.

Dick Condon.

A brief career

Fred Leach was the first of Collingwood's tragic heroes. He was the most brilliant of three brothers to play for the Magpies, a phenomenally talented but enigmatic genius who became the most feared centreman of his day. But he missed many games through illness and injury, and others through sheer whimsy – like taking a mid-season holiday in 1901, the year in which he was named the VFL's champion player. He retired in the middle of 1903 at the age of just 25, after only 83 games. Five years later he contracted typhoid fever and died. His life, like his career, was tragically brief.

A Sydney game

The VFL's push into the Sydney market began way before the advent of the Swans. In May of 1903 Collingwood and Fitzroy played a match for Premiership points at the SCG. Fitzroy won 7.20 to 6.9, but the game was perhaps more memorable as the first occasion on which numbers were worn by the players.

CLUB NEWS 1897–1903

Collingwood becomes the first VFL team to start a season as 'reigning Premier', and plays its first game on 8 May 1897 in the newly-formed Victorian Football League against St Kilda at Victoria Park. The Saints are no match for the Magpies, who finish with a comfortable 25-point victory.

Collingwood Council's Victoria Park committee offers the Magpies a £20 incentive in Round 9, 1898 if they beat arch rivals Fitzroy in their second meeting of the year – such was the rivalry between the geographical neighbours. Although the ploy worked – Collingwood won – the incentive was widely criticised in an era of amateurism and never repeated.

In 1898, Archie Smith becomes the first Magpie to top the VFL's goalkicking table, with 31 goals. In the same year, Dick Condon is chosen by sportswriters as 'Champion of the Colony'.

Collingwood plays in its first VFL Grand Final on 7 September 1901, going down to the crack Essendon outfit by 27 points.

In a controversial finish to the game against Fitzroy on 20 July 1901, the bell rang after just 20 minutes of the final term, with Collingwood five points up and the ball in Fitzroy's attack. Despite Fitzroy's complaints, the result stood.

In 1902 Charlie Pannam becomes the first player to play 100 VFL games. Ted Rowell, a champion athlete as well as a wonderful footballer, is named the

1897–1903

Back-to-back Flags

Having waited six seasons for its first taste of VFL Premiership success in 1902, the Magpies backed up with another triumph the very next season – giving it back-to-back Flags.

The 1902 Grand Final, against Essendon, attracted a then-record crowd of 35,000 to the Melbourne Cricket Ground. But they saw a one-sided game in which the Magpies won by 33 points. Star centreman Fred Leach performed a great stopping job on the legendary Albert Thurgood.

The Magpies' second Flag was a much closer affair, against their greatest rivals of the time, Fitzroy. It was a tight match all day, and when the siren blew the Magpies were three points up, with the Maroons' Gerald Brosnan kicking for goal. Brosnan's kick missed narrowly – legend has it that the lace of the ball brushed against the post – and the Woods were home by two points.

Ted Rowell Accused

1902 was a big season for Ted Rowell, the half-forward who later became a champion full-back. He not only won the VFL goalkicking and was named by the press as Champion of the Colony, he also competed in the Stawell gift for the first time. But the biggest drama came early in the season when, after a rare poor performance against Fitzroy, Rowell was accused of 'playing dead'. Incensed at the accusations – he swore his poor form was due to blows on the head – Rowell resigned. The Collingwood committee hastily met and accepted Rowell's explanation, and he returned to the team.

High-flying action as Collingwood has control in the 1902 Grand Final.

Collingwood went to Tasmania in 1902 and returned with a new invention, the stab pass, (a short, spearing kick to a team-mate). They perfected it against weak opposition and, still seasick from the voyage home, used it to devastating effect against Geelong. The team is pictured in the snow at Mt Wellington.

1897–1903 HONOUR ROLL

Year	Pos	Leading Goalkicker	No.	Best & Fairest	Captain	Coach
1897	3rd	Archie Smith	15		Bill Strickland	
1898	3rd	Archie Smith	31		Bill Proudfoot	
1899	4th	Archie Smith	17		Dick Condon	
1900	4th	Archie Smith	21		Dick Condon	
1901	2nd	Edward Rowell	31		Bill Proudfoot	
1902	1st	Edward Rowell	33		Lardie Tulloch	
1903	1st	Edward Lockwood	31		Lardie Tulloch	

champion of the colony for the 1902 season and also shares the title of VFL's leading goalkicker with his former opponent from the Kalgoorlie goldfields, Essendon's Albert Thurgood. Both kicked 33 goals.

Collingwood wins its first VFL Flag in 1902.

A young kid from the Coburg Juniors, Jock McHale, makes his debut for the Magpies against Carlton in Round 1, 1903. Carlton wins, but a great career is launched.

Premiership points are at stake when Collingwood plays Fitzroy in Sydney on 23 May 1903.

In September 1903, Bill Proudfoot plays in the finals under an alias, 'Wilson', after the police force decides that its members (Proudfoot was then a constable) are not allowed to play football. The force's ruling kept Proudfoot out of action for much of the home-and-away season, but 'Wilson' is an excellent contributor in the finals. The ruse, obvious to everyone, is repeated early the following season until the police force changed its ruling.

Collingwood wins its second VFL flag on 12 September 1903.

Edward Lockwood, a goalsneak who crossed to Victoria Park from Geelong in 1902, heads the 1903 VFL's goalkicking ladder with 35 goals. In all, Lockwood kicks 83 goals in his 53 games with the Magpies and was a valuable recruit. His brother, George, crossed with him at the same time and played in the Premiership teams of 1902–03.

COLLINGWOOD

A new grandstand! Collingwood members had a treat in store in 1909, with the construction and opening of a 1500-seat grandstand. Remarkably, the entire construction process took only six weeks. The cornerstone was laid on March 13 (in a ceremony which included a man being shot out of a cannon), and the new stand was opened and ready for use in time for the Round 1 game against Fitzroy.

Turmoil at the Top

The 1906 season was not one when the famed Collingwood spirit was seen at its best advantage.

The problems started with the sacking of controversial coach Dick Condon midway through the season. This followed an earlier three-week suspension when the committee considered him to have been the cause of dissension in the team. 'Rosie' Dummett was chosen as a replacement captain, but he, too, resigned before the season was out after a bout of poor form.

Centre half-back and vice-captain Jack Monohan then stood in for a few games – despite also having been suspended during the season for causing dissension – before ruckman Arthur Leach stepped into the position and the infighting seemed to stop.

The cause of all the problems has never been made clear, but it certainly created enormous inner turmoil. Given all the unrest, the Pies' efforts in finishing third for the season seem quite remarkable.

Monohan: dissension.

Bare knees

The Magpies started a new trend in 1907 when they took to the field with their bare knees exposed. Until this time, footballers' legs had been encased in a combination of knickers and stockings. But Collingwood's decision to start 1907 with loose shorts that finished above the knee and long socks stunned the footy world.

George Angus.

CLUB NEWS 1904–1910

Former captain Bill Strickland is appointed Collingwood's first 'coach' in 1904, taking charge of the team briefly late in the season. Dick Condon was appointed playing coach for 1905.

Round 7, 1906 sees the debut of Dick Lee, a promising young forward from the Rose of Northcote Football Club. Lee plays the last 12 games of the year and at the age of just 17, wins the club's goalkicking title with 35 goals.

Legendary full-back Bill Proudfoot plays his last game in 1906, qualifies for 15 years service, then retires. For the past two seasons he had played rarely, holding himself officially 'in readiness' to play if required, in order to make his 15 years. The controversial Dick Condon leaves at the end of the season for Tasmania.

In 1906 three-game player Thomas Nelson puts new words to the Boer War song 'Goodbye Dolly Grey' and produces the now famous – or should that be infamous – 'Good Old Collingwood Forever'.

Two club stalwarts departed in 1907. Charlie Pannam and Jack Monohan both crossed to the VFA – Pannam to Richmond (via Ballarat) after Round 1 and Monohan to Brunswick a week later. Pannam captained the Tigers when they joined the competition in 1908 and Monohan became a goal umpire.

With Condon's departure, the popular and highly regarded Ted Rowell takes on the job as playing coach in 1907.

1904 – 1910

Cheeky Charlie

In an era when Collingwood had fast, skilled players like Dick Condon, Fred Leach, 'Buffer' Sime and Ted Rowell, Charlie Pannam still stood out.

Pannam's career started in the club's VFA days on the wing, where he was renowned for his lightning dashes down the ground. But as his pace slowed in his later years, he moved to the half-forward flank where he was canny enough to top the League's goal-kicking table in 1905 with 38 goals.

Pannam was famous – or maybe infamous – for the sly tactics he often employed to upset opponents. Unlike his troubled teammate Condon, Pannam was rarely caught.

Pannam's characteristics surfaced in later members of the dynasty. His two sons, Charlie Jnr and Alby, played nearly 280 games between them, and his grandsons, Ron and Lou Richards, totalled nearly 400 games, with Lou in particular turning 'sneaky' into an art form. Charlie's brother, Alby, also played for the club around the turn of the century. Charlie left Collingwood after two games of the 1907 season and made the short trip down Punt Road to Richmond.

Charlie Pannam.

The contest is torrid as Carlton and Collingwood ruckmen vie for the ball.

1910 Grand Final – a violent affair

Every footy fan knows of the infamous 1945 'bloodbath' Grand Final. But the 1910 Grand Final was every bit as violent. Collingwood's 'Flapper' Hughes was flattened before the game even started, and team-mate Richard Daykin then knocked out his assailant.

The second half was riddled with sly bumps and punches. By the last term the game had degenerated into what one newspaper described as 'the most disgraceful scene ever witnessed in a Melbourne football final'.

The problems started when the Pies' Tom Baxter and Carlton's Jack Baquie became entangled after Baquie had taken a mark. The Carlton man elbowed Baxter as the pair grappled. Blows were traded freely as other players joined the melee.

Magpie defender John Shorten ran the length of the ground and belted Baquie with a hefty blow to the face. Carlton's Percy Sheehan then whacked Shorten in the ribs, while Baquie staggered to his feet, knocked 'Flapper' Hughes out cold and then collapsed alongside him. Only when umpire Elder bounced the ball did players remember there was a game to be won.

Fortunately, Collingwood was the team to do it, by 14 points.

1904 – 1910 HONOUR ROLL

Year	Pos	Leading Goalkicker	No.	Best & Fairest	Captain	Coach
1904	3rd	Charlie Pannam	24		Lardie Tulloch	Bill Strickland
1905	2nd	Charlie Pannam	38		Charlie Pannam	Dick Condon
1906	3rd	Dick Lee	35		Arthur Leach	Dick Condon
1907	4th	Dick Lee	47		Arthur Leach	Edward Rowell
1908	4th	Dick Lee	54		Edward Drohan	Edward Rowell
1909	3rd	Dick Lee	58		Bob Nash	George Angus
1910	1st	Dick Lee	58		George Angus	George Angus

Former Collingwood captain Lardie Tulloch, now an umpire, takes charge of the 1907 Carlton v South Melbourne Grand Final just three years after his retirement from league football.
Popular follower George Angus takes over the playing coach duties from Ted Rowell in 1909. He holds the post until Jock McHale's appointment in 1912.
Collingwood again plays a game in Sydney (this time exhibition), downing Geelong at Erskineville Oval on 14 August 1909.
Collingwood trainers provide an oxygen tank in the rooms at half-time of the Semi-final against South Melbourne in September 1909, hoping players will 'top up' during the long break. Most ignore the opportunity, and the Pies go down by 21 points.
Dick Lee tops the VFL goalkicking table for the fourth time in a row with 58 goals in 1910, also winning the award of Champion of the Colony.
Treasurer and former player Bob Rush develops the Collingwood motto, *Floreat Pica* – 'May the Magpies Prosper'.
The League's hearing into the reports from the 1910 Grand Final was almost as dramatic as the game itself. Shorten and Sheehan were each suspended for a season and a half, and Baxter and Baquie for a season. But Baxter's suspension was later revoked when Daykin wrote to the VFL claiming it was he – not Baxter – who had been involved in the stoush. The League quashed Baxter's suspension and let Daykin off for his courage in coming forward!

COLLINGWOOD

Jock McHale, seen here swooping on the ball, has achieved deserved fame as the longest-serving coach in VFL/AFL history – a staggering 38 years. He was also an outstanding player, either in the centre or at half-back. As with his coaching, endurance was a strong point. In his 15 years of full availability as a player he managed 259 of a possible 275 games, including a phenomenal 191 in a row between 1906 and 1917 – a record that was later surpassed by 'Skinny' Titus and, of course, Jimmy Stynes.

The great Dick Lee

There was no finer footballer in the era spanning World War One than Collingwood's mercurial Dick Lee.

Lee matched spectacular, high-flying acrobatics with superb ground-level skills and unerring accuracy in front of goal, whether by punt or place kick.

He made his debut in 1906 soon after he turned 17, and topped the VFL's goalkicking for the first time the very next season, and for the next three seasons. By the time his career finished after the 1922 Grand Final, he had topped the table six more times, captained the team and represented his state every year from 1908 to 1922. His career tally of goals stood at 707, the last of those registered with his final kick in League football.

Lee's records would probably have been even more phenomenal had it not been for a succession of serious injuries – most notably an infected shin and a 'big knee' – that forced him out for almost two full seasons.

But it didn't stop him. And neither could the best defenders. He would take marks from the most improbable of positions, and thread through goals from similarly unlikely angles.

Following division

Two of Collingwood's most loyal servants during this era were the ruck/rover combination of Les Hughes and Percy Wilson. Hughes, an ungainly but effective tap ruckman, joined in 1908 and played 225 games before retiring in 1922. Wilson, a fearless rover, followed his former Collingwood Trades team-mate to Victoria Park in 1909 and rose to lead the club to the 1917 Premiership. He played 183 games before becoming Melbourne's 1921 playing coach.

Flapper Hughes: hard-working ruckman.

Dick Lee. Was he the best of all time?

CLUB NEWS 1911–1924

Dick Lee injures his knee while representing Victoria in the 1911 interstate carnival, and damages it more severely in the first few minutes of the Grand Final. He misses all but one match of the 1912 season and retires, frustrated at his injury problems. But a doctor decided Lee's career can be saved, and puts him under the knife for football's first known cartilage operation. Lee gets back onto the field late in 1913.

George Angus has crossed to coach Williamstown in the VFA in 1912, and his position as playing coach is taken by Jock McHale. It is to be another 38 years before Collingwood has to bother appointing another senior coach (and even then they botch it).

Dick Lee, in his first full season back in the VFL in 1914, resumes his love affair with the big sticks and kicks 57 goals to be the VFL's leading goalkicker. He also takes one of the most famous marks in VFL history, against Carlton at Victoria Park.

Collingwood goes down to arch rival Carlton in the 1915 Grand Final, after best friends Paddy Rowan and Doc Seddon had to be fetched from the army camp at Seymour, having endured a 10-mile route march on the morning of the match.

Dick Lee confirms his re-emergence among the game's elite in 1915, again being voted Champion of the Colony and once more heading the VFL's goalkicking table (jointly) with 66 goals.

1911–1924

Deserting the club

When Collingwood skipper Dan Minogue left for the First World War after a game against Carlton midway through 1916, he was chaired from the field and farewelled as a hero. When he returned to footy four years later, he was every inch the villain – at least as far as Magpie fans were concerned.

Minogue stunned everyone at Victoria Park, and his legion of adoring fans, by seeking a clearance to Richmond upon his return in 1919. The club opposed his application, forcing him to stand out of football for an entire season, but by 1920 he was at Punt Road.

Although he never publicly aired his reasons for leaving, Minogue may have been upset with the club's treatment of teammate and close friend Jim Sadler, who struggled to get a game in Minogue's absence.

Minogue turns villain.

Apart from Dan Minogue, the Magpies also lost captains Con McCarthy and Tom Drummond to more lucrative offers.

But the two departures that hurt most were those of Bill Twomey Snr and Charlie Pannam Jnr. They spent much of their careers on opposite wings, and played their final matches in the losing 1922 Grand Final to Fitzroy. The brilliant Twomey left at age 22 to pursue a career in athletics while the equally gifted Pannam accepted a well-paid position as South Melbourne's playing coach. But Collingwood fought Pannam's move, and he was prevented from playing for South for fully three seasons. Bill Twomey left a legacy to Collingwood of four talented sons, three of whom played senior footy for the club.

Bill Twomey.

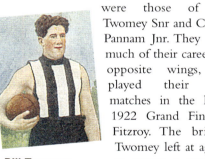

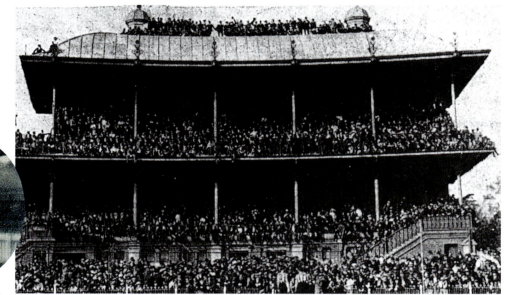

Perching-room only at the MCG for the 1919 Grand Final.

Flags of 1917 and 1919

Of all Collingwood's Premierships, it is those of 1917 and 1919 that have received least recognition, perhaps because the 1917 Flag was won in restricted wartime conditions. But these wonderful Collingwood teams included outstanding players such as Dick Lee, Charlie Pannam, Harry Saunders, Percy Wilson and Harry Curtis. They were teams good enough to play in four successive Grand Finals, losing Flags to South Melbourne and Richmond.

In 1917 they beat Fitzroy by 35 points, and Richmond by 25 in 1919. They finished on top of the ladder in each of the seasons.

1911–1924 HONOUR ROLL

Year	Pos	Leading Goalkicker	No.	Best & Fairest	Captain	Coach
1911	2nd	Tom Baxter	31		George Angus	George Angus
1912	7th	Les Hughes	13		Jock McHale	Jock McHale
1913	4th	Les Hughes	22		Jock McHale	Jock McHale
1914	5th	Dick Lee	57		Dan Minogue	Jock McHale
1915	2nd	Dick Lee	66		Dan Minogue	Jock McHale
1916	3rd	Dick Lee	48		Dan Minogue	Jock McHale
1917	1st	Dick Lee	54		Percy Wilson	Jock McHale
1918	2nd	Tom Wraith	26		Percy Wilson	Jock McHale
1919	1st	Dick Lee	56		Con McCarthy	Jock McHale
1920	2nd	Ted Utting	23		Dick Lee	Jock McHale
1921	3rd	Dick Lee	64		Con McCarthy	Jock McHale
1922	2nd	Gordon Coventry	42		Con McCarthy	Jock McHale
1923	5th	Gordon Coventry	36		Percy Rowe	Jock McHale
1924	6th	Gordon Coventry	28		Charlie Tyson	Jock McHale

Half-forward 'Paddy Rowan' is killed in action in France in 1916. Paddy's real name was Percy Rowe, but he adopted the alias so his mother would not know he had come to the city from Bendigo to box, and also to avoid clearance problems with the South Bendigo Football Club.

In 1916, Dick Lee is once again the VFL's leading goalkicker, this time with 48 goals, and he repeats the performance with 54 in 1917 and 56 in 1919.

In Round 3, 1917 Jock McHale misses his first game as a player since Round 13, 1906.

Collingwood wins its fifth VFL Flag in 1919, beating Richmond by 25 points, 11.12 (79) to 7.11 (53)..

A thick-set full-forward from Diamond Creek named Gordon Coventry plays his first game for Collingwood in 1920. Coventry later described the match as one of the most inglorious debuts any player could possible have made.

Dick Lee becomes the VFL's joint leading goalkicker (with Rankin of Geelong) with 64 in 1921.

In Round 1, 1922 Gordon Coventry's older brother, Syd, joins him at Victoria Park after the club overcomes clearance difficulties with St Kilda.

Collingwood misses the finals for the second year in succession in 1924, the first time ever in the club's VFL history.

'The Prince of Secretaries', Ern Copeland, retires in 1924 after 29 years in the position, having won a reputation for fairness, business acumen and administrative skill.

COLLINGWOOD

George Clayden.   Frank Murphy

The class of 1925–26

Collingwood's amazing run of success in the late 1920s was born out of its rare double failure when it missed the finals in both 1923 and 1924. That failure rocked the club, and the president and secretary were immediately replaced.

More importantly, a string of new players were introduced. Tough man George Clayden and full back Charlie Dibbs made their debuts in 1924, and

Charlie Dibbs.

were followed the next year by the great Albert Collier, centre half–forward Frank Murphy and first rover Bill Libbis. Harry Collier joined in 1926, as did centreman Jack Beveridge. Back-pocket Harry Rumney came on board for the start of 1927.

With Gordon and Syd Coventry already at the club, these players formed the core of the team that became known as 'The Machine'.

Bill Libbis.

Gordon Coventry looks hard to handle as he shoots for goal at Victoria Park.

The Coventrys were Collingwood

There were no more important figures in the club's years of domination than the legendary Coventry brothers, Gordon and Syd.

They came from Diamond Creek, Gordon late in the 1920 season and Syd a couple of years later via Tasmania and a clearance dispute with St Kilda. Before long they had established themselves as the key players in the Magpie line-up.

Gordon's record is simply phenomenal. He played for 18 seasons, and his 306 games stood as the club record until Tony Shaw broke it nearly 60 years later. He kicked 1299 career goals – still the League record – won the VFL goalkicking six times and the Collingwood goalkicking 16 times. He was the first man to top the ton, a feat he achieved four times in all. He kicked 50 or more goals in a record 13 consecutive seasons, and kicked 100 goals against every VFL team bar one. With a big backside and huge hands that gave him a vice-like grip, he has been likened to a more cumbersome version of Jason Dunstall.

Syd, too, was an outstanding footballer, a follower who was good enough to win the Brownlow Medal in 1927. But in the Collingwood pantheon he stands tallest as a leader who helped shape a team still regarded as one of the best of all time. The power of Syd's leadership is reflected in the fact that the team won Flags under him in each of his first four seasons as captain. Victoria, too, did not lose an interstate match while under his control. He was also revered as a warm, kind man held in universally high regard. And when his on-field career finished, he spent a further 24 years in administration, including 13 as president.

Syd Coventry: most successful leader.

CLUB NEWS 1925–1928

Syd Coventry says he will take a lucrative job in 1925, coaching in the country with Horsham. Collingwood convinced him to stay by saying it wouldn't clear him, and by offering him substantial 'expenses' to travel back to Melbourne.

A raw, strong key-position player from Ivanhoe named Albert Collier plays his first game for Collingwood in Round 1, 1925. He lines up at full-forward against Essendon, but his day proves embarrassing when, having taken a fine mark, he 'toe-ends' his attempted place kick straight to the man on the mark.

Harry Collier, smaller and faster but just as tough as Albert, joins his brother in the senior side at Victoria Park in 1926. Harry's progress had been stalled in 1925 by a pre-season knee injury.

Gordon Coventry finally starts to come of age as a League footballer, and his 83 goals for the 1926 season is enough to give him the title of the VFL's leading goalkicker for the season. It is also the highest season's tally on record to that time.

The club takes 25 of its senior players on a mid-season trip to Western Australia in August 1927. The trip, timed to coincide with the interstate carnival, was designed to help bond the players after the upheavals at the end of 1926. The long train trip over, and the boat trip back, had the desired effect – the players returned a closer, more committed unit. Many believe it was the start of the four-in-a-row record.

1925–1928

A bribery scandal

Collingwood became embroiled in a bribery scandal after the 1926 Grand Final loss to Geelong when captain Charlie Tyson was accused of having 'played dead'. Proponents of the theory pointed to Tyson's poor game, some questionable moves he made during it, Collingwood's decision to dump him from the list before the next season and the new car he was driving around the following year.

The story became part of football folklore. But Richard Stremski, in *Kill for Collingwood*, conducted the first thorough examination of the claims and came down on Tyson's side. As in the case of similar accusations levelled against rover Tom Baxter after the 1911 Grand Final, it seems Tyson may have been unfairly tainted.

A line-up of the great Collingwood men of 1928, with mascot.

Charlie Tyson: jury still out.

Back-to-back Flags of 1927–28

Having finished runners-up in both 1925 and 1926, the Magpies were determined to make amends in 1927. That they did – waltzing away with both that Premiership and another the following year.

The 1927 Flag was won in the most appalling conditions, with the game played in freezing temperatures and torrential rain that had fallen for much of the week, turning the MCG into a quagmire. All thoughts of science went out the window as players from both sides just moved the ball forward any way they could, while trying to keep their feet. In the end it seemed a miracle that three goals had been scored, with the Magpies winning 2.13 to Richmond's 1.7.

The ladder the following season was the same as it had been in 1927 – Collingwood on top with 15 wins, one game clear of Richmond. And again it was these two teams that met in the Grand Final.

But this time there was no rain or mud to quash Grand Final day expectations, and the Magpies proved themselves clearly superior with what was at that stage the highest ever finals score of 13.18 (96). The bulk of the goals, as always, came from Gordon Coventry, who bagged a finals-record of nine. Richmond fought hard, but were simply no match for the pace, strength and teamwork of Jock McHale's machine.

The Copeland Trophy

The man known as 'The Prince of Secretaries', Ern Copeland, was given a wonderful testimonial evening when he finished his 29-year stint as secretary at the end of 1924. But he was honoured more permanently for his contribution to Collingwood in 1927 when the club's Best and Fairest award was named after him. Syd Coventry was the first recipient.

Ern Copeland.

1925–1928 HONOUR ROLL

Year	Pos	Leading Goalkicker	No.	Best & Fairest	Captain	Coach
1925	2nd	Gordon Coventry	68		Charlie Tyson	Jock McHale
1926	2nd	Gordon Coventry	83		Charlie Tyson	Jock McHale
1927	1st	Gordon Coventry	97	Syd Coventry	Syd Coventry	Jock McHale
1928	1st	Gordon Coventry	89	Harry Collier	Syd Coventry	Jock McHale

Syd Coventry's brilliant 1927 season is capped off when he wins the Brownlow Medal – the first Collingwood player to achieve the honour.
Gordon Coventry proves that the 100-goal barrier is close to being broken with a 97-goal season in 1927, and once again is the VFL's leading goalkicker.
In July 1928, players threaten to strike over a proposed pay cut. A players meeting after training discusses the possibility of strike action, but such action is averted when Syd Coventry refuses to accept any strike motion as valid.
Two Collingwood players allegedly take bribes to 'play dead' in the final match of the 1928 season, against Carlton. Collingwood could not lose top spot, and the result (a Carlton win) gave them a spot in the four.
Collingwood and Melbourne play the first tie in finals history in their 1928 Semi-final. The Magpies win a tight replay by just four points.
Collingwood wins the 1928 VFL Premiership, with Gordon Coventry bagging a record nine goals for the game. But the real hero is tough follower Percy Rowe, who asks to be stationed alongside Coventry and spends the afternoon shielding him from Richmond defenders, winding up black and blue – but with a Premiership medal.
Gordon Coventry once more heads the VFL's goalkicking table in 1928, but again the magical ton proves just out of reach. He finishes with 89 goals.

COLLINGWOOD

Syd Coventry is chaired from the field.

All-conquering team, 1929

There is a good case to be made for Collingwood's 1929 team to be regarded as the best ever in VFL/AFL history.

For a start, they remain the only team in more than 100 years of competition to go through the home-and-away season undefeated. They might well have gone through the whole year undefeated, too, but for some complacency creeping into the team for its semi-final against Richmond. They finished three games clear of their nearest rivals (Carlton), with a whopping percentage of over 170. And they were rarely stretched in any of their games during the year.

The exception, of course, was the shock semi-final defeat to a physical Tiger outfit. In the wake of that 62-point flogging, the Magpies brought in three new players, including two renowned for their vigour.

Then Jock McHale showed a flash of tactical brilliance by playing the great Gordon Coventry, the man who had just become the first player to kick 100 goals in a season, as a decoy full-forward! The result was that half-forward 'Tubby' Edmonds slotted five goals and the Pies careered away to win by 29 points, thus fulfilling their pre-season commitment to equal Carlton's record Premiership treble of 1906–08.

Albert and Harry look like they mean business as they take the field for a 1930 final.

The Colliers – born to Collingwood

Syd Coventry might have provided the leadership and Gordon Coventry the goals, but it was another pair of brothers who provided much of the spirit of the famous Collingwood sides of this era.

Harry and Albert Collier were born in Collingwood and went to school opposite the Victoria Park ground. They spent every spare minute at the ground, watching training, having a kick or selling *Footy Records*. They wanted nothing more than to wear the famous black-and-white jumper.

Both wound up doing so with great distinction. Harry was a feisty, courageous rover who played 255 games, kicked 299 goals and led the club for five years. He was so honoured to play for the club he was shocked to learn he would be paid. Albert was the most feared big man of his day, a tough 'enforcer' who won the 1929 Brownlow as a centre half-back. Harry tied for the medal in 1930, lost on countback and was later awarded it retrospectively.

Albert stunned the club when he left to play in Tasmania in 1931–32, lured by money during the depths of the depression. But he returned in 1933. He and Harry formed a revered leadership team.

They were straight shooters who looked after their mates and who believed that the jumper came first, last and everywhere in between.

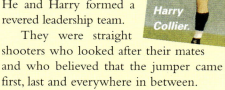

Harry Collier.

1929–1930 HONOUR ROLL

Year	Pos	Leading Goalkicker	No.	Best & Fairest	Captain	Coach
1929	1st	Gordon Coventry	124	'Leeter' Collier	Syd Coventry	Jock McHale
1930	1st	Gordon Coventry	118	Harry Collier	Syd Coventry	Jock McHale

CLUB NEWS 1929–1930

More creature comforts for Magpie fans with the opening of another new grandstand in 1929.

Gordon Coventry kicks 16 goals against Hawthorn on 27 July 1929 to break the VFL match record for goal.

Collingwood wins the 1929 VFL Premiership, equalling Carlton's three-in-a-row record and edging in front of Fitzroy for most Flags.

Charlie Ahern, one of three players brought in to the team after the 1929 shock defeat in the Second Semi, breaks his wrist while playing an otherwise outstanding game in the Grand Final. It was only his third game – and it proved to be his last. The arm became infected and Ahern died the next year.

In 1929, Albert Collier becomes the second Collingwood player to win the Brownlow Medal, following Syd Coventry's victory two years earlier. Gordon Coventry finally achieves in 1929 what many had long thought impossible – the scoring of 100 goals in a season. Coventry's total of 124 was nearly double that of his nearest rival, Carlton's 'Soapy' Vallence, who steered through 64.

Bob Ross wins the 1929 award as Best and Fairest in the Seconds competition.

Syd Coventry applies for, and is accepted into, the position as playing coach of Footscray in 1930. But the League blocked the move after Collingwood protested; in those days it was not thought to be in the best

1929–1930

1930 – and it's four in a row

One of the most telling things about the achievement of one of football's most remarkable feats is that no one was surprised it happened.

By the time the 1930 season rolled around, the Pies had assumed such a hold over the rest of the competition that few doubted their capacity to set the four-in-a-row record. What couldn't be guessed, perhaps, was how long that record would stand.

Admittedly, the 1930 victory wasn't quite as emphatic as that of 1929. The team only grabbed top spot on the ladder on percentage from Carlton, but wound up facing fourth-placed Geelong in the Grand Final. And while the eventual five-goal margin might have been unexceptional, there was something unusual about the victory – it was achieved without coach Jock McHale.

McHale was at home for the historic game, restricted to his bed by a severe bout of the flu. In his absence, Treasurer Bob Rush stepped in and delivered a stirring half-time speech of which McHale himself would have been proud. He needed to, because the Pies at that stage were 21 points behind and staring defeat in the face.

But with Rush's words ringing in their ears, the Colliers and Coventrys inspired an eight-goal third quarter that secured the game, and the 1930 Premiership. The record of four Flags in a row was Collingwood's. And it has stayed that way.

Collingwood salutes its heroes.

Harry Chesswass. **Len Murphy.**

The unsung heroes

It's easy to overlook the contribution of Collingwood's unsung heroes to their four-in-a-row victories.

But players like Bruce Andrew, Percy Bowyer, Harry Chesswass, Bob Makeham and Len Murphy should not be forgotten. They were all fantastic servants for the club who played important roles in at least two of the Premiership wins. Some, like Murphy and Bowyer, were still around for the club's next burst of success in the mid-1930s.

Andrew was a speedy wingman later famous as an administrator and 'World of Sport' commentator, Bowyer a reliable ruck-rover, Chesswass a centreman/half-forward who was vice-captain for a couple of seasons and Murphy and Makeham tall, strong follower/forwards. All can be proud of their contributions.

Bruce Andrew. **Percy Bowyer.**

---

interests of the game to allow a player to switch clubs without the blessing of his original club.
In 1930, club secretary George Connor resigns pre-season after being found to have embezzled funds. He is replaced by Frank Wraith, one of the most influential of all Collingwood officials.
The man who would become known as the Prince of Full-backs, Jack Regan, makes an inauspicious debut in 1930 – failing to get off the bench.
Gordon Coventry breaks his own League record with a massive 17 goals against Fitzroy on 19 July 1930. In all VFL history, only one man has ever kicked more goals.
Collingwood wins its fourth VFL Premiership in a row in 1930, setting a record that has never been broken.
Harry Collier ties for first place in the 1930 Brownlow Medal with Stan Judkins and Allan Hopkins. Judkins is awarded the medal on a countback, but Collier receives his retrospectively many years later – and steals the evening with a prolonged speech.
Gordon Coventry again tops the ton in 1930, this time with 118, and again is the VFL's leading goalkicker.
On 9 December 1930, former full-back Harry Saunders dies just four years after retirement, at age 32, after contracting pancreatitis. He had battled the illness for some time, but returned from work at CUB one Friday feeling sick. Three days later, he was dead. On the day of his funeral, CUB accorded him the rare tribute of closing down the brewery operations as a mark of respect.

COLLINGWOOD

Back-to-back Flags

Up to World War Two, Collingwood was not a team easily satisfied by success. With only one exception (1910), every time the club won a Flag it followed with another almost immediately. And from 1927–30, of course, they added two more for good measure.

It happened again in the mid-1930s. Having not played in a Grand Final since the 1930 triumph, the Magpies found themselves up against South Melbourne in 1935. This time, for once, they were not favourites, having finished the season a game behind the Bloods. But the famous pre-game injury to Bob Pratt, when he was struck by a brick truck after getting off a tram, changed the equation.

The Pratt-less South could only manage seven goals – their lowest haul all year – while Jack Regan quietened South's other gun forward, Laurie Nash. Phonse Kyne, Marcus Whelan and the Colliers were brilliant, however, and the Pies won by 20 points.

The next year, true to form, they did it again. Once more they had finished below South on the ladder, but outplayed them in both the Second Semi and Grand Finals, winning the latter by 11 points. The star was Alby Pannam, whose pace and cleverness brought him five goals.

The win gave Collingwood six Flags in 10 years. The Magpies also played in 11 Grand Finals in 15 years from 1925.

A classic mark by Ron Todd.

Todd takes over up front

Ron Todd's emergence as the game's best full-forward in the late 1930s continued a Magpie domination of the goalkicking tables that had been evident from the earliest days of the VFL.

When Todd topped the table in 1939 with his second consecutive 120-goal haul, it gave the Magpies 22 goalkicking honors in the 43 years the VFL had been operating.

It started with a few one-off victories to names like Archie Smith, Ted Lockwood, Ted Rowell and Charlie Pannam. But when Dick Lee came along, Victoria Park became the unofficial home of the game's best forwards.

Lee won (or shared) the title 10 times in his 17-year career. Two years before Lee retired, Gordon Coventry made his first, uncertain steps into League football. By the time Lee retired, Coventry was just about ready to take over, his own time at the top giving the Pies a further six goalkicking titles.

Then, just as the baton had passed smoothly from Lee to Coventry, so did it pass from Coventry to Todd. He, too, started his career two seasons before the incumbent finished, and was so well primed to take over that he kicked 120 goals in each of his first two seasons as the club's full-time full-forward.

The chain was broken, of course, when Todd deserted to Williamstown, and it was to be another 30 years before the club could again claim to have a star spearhead.

1931–1939 HONOUR ROLL

Year	Pos	Leading Goalkicker	No.	Best & Fairest	Captain	Coach
1931	4th	Gordon Coventry	67	Harold Rumney	Syd Coventry	Jock McHale
1932	3rd	Gordon Coventry	82	Syd Coventry	Syd Coventry	Jock McHale
1933	6th	Gordon Coventry	108	Gordon Coventry	Syd Coventry	Jock McHale
1934	4th	Gordon Coventry	105	'Leeter' Collier	Syd Coventry	Jock McHale
1935	1st	Gordon Coventry	88	'Leeter' Collier	Harry Collier	Jock McHale
1936	1st	Gordon Coventry	60	Jack Regan	Harry Collier	Jock McHale
1937	2nd	Gordon Coventry	72	Des Fothergill	Harry Collier	Jock McHale
1938	2nd	Ron Todd	120	Des Fothergill	Harry Collier	Jock McHale
1939	2nd	Ron Todd	121	Marcus Whelan	Harry Collier	Jock McHale

CLUB NEWS 1931–1939

Albert Collier stuns the football world in 1931 by leaving to play in Tasmania for two seasons, work proving impossible to find in Melbourne during the depression.

With the depression hitting hard, the club faced financial difficulties in 1932 and had to impose a mid-season pay cut on the players. Many were unhappy, and were late onto the field for one match while debating possible strike action. In the end no strike eventuated, and the lost wages were made up after the team appeared in the finals.

Albert Collier returns from his sojourn in Tasmania in 1933, but nearly heads to St Kilda, until the club finds him work.

Jack Regan wins State selection in 1933 as a forward, where he had been playing after disappointing early showings at full-back. During the game, Richmond and Victorian captain Percy Bentley swung Regan to full-back, and he played so well there that he returned to the last line of defence when resuming his duties with Collingwood.

Collingwood introduces a schoolboy competition as curtain-raiser to its senior matches in 1934, replacing baseball. The schoolboy curtain-raisers prove highly successful, and help produce stars like Des Fothergill, Len Fitzgerald and Bill Twomey. The matches last until the mid-1950s, when the League introduces the Under 19 level competition.

1931 – 1939

After 16 years without a charge, Gordon Coventry boils over in 1936 and is supended for eight weeks by the VFL tribunal.

Suspensions a blow to Flag hopes

The club's run of success in the mid-to-late 30s might have been even greater but for a succession of cruel and controversial blows delivered by the League's tribunal.

The first came in 1936 when Gordon Coventry, the proverbial 'gentle giant', was reported for striking Richmond full-back Joe Murdoch. Coventry claimed Murdoch had been hitting him on a painful outbreak of boils on the back of his neck, and that he had been concussed by another blow to the back of the head. But the tribunal gave no account to any provocation and suspended Coventry for eight weeks – despite a previously unblemished 16-year record.

The following season, Albert Collier was accused of spitting on a female fan as he left the field at half-time at Arden Street. North Melbourne laid a charge of 'unseemly conduct' against Collier, but Collier informed the hearing he had received legal advice they could not hear the case, and left. The tribunal suspended him for eight weeks anyway – not on the original charge, but for walking out.

The next year it was Albert's brother, Harry, who copped a ridiculously long suspension. This time it was the Carlton club that laid a charge the umpires had missed, when Harry whacked a Carlton player in frustration after the Pies had lost a game they appeared to have had sewn up. Harry pleaded guilty, but despite a 13-year clean record was rubbed out for the rest of the year – 14 matches in all.

Polished centreman Marcus Whelan won the 1939 Brownlow Medal. Although he played his best football in the centre, the classy Whelan was strong enough in the air to play at full-back on occasions.

Prince of full-backs

Although the selectors who chose the AFL's 'Team of the Century' in 1996 might not agree, there is little doubt that Jack Regan was the prince of full-backs. In a career that spanned 17 seasons, Regan reigned supreme, despite having to pit his talents against great full-forwards like Pratt, Mohr, Vallence, Moloney, Titus and Margitch. He was a magnificent high-flying mark and a superb drop kick. He was quick, graceful and skilled, and preferred to back his judgement and outmark the forwards, even when flying from behind. With this attitude, his duels with South's mercurial Bob Pratt quickly became the stuff of legend, and crowds packed the grounds to watch them in action.

Jack Regan: all the skills.

Phonse Kyne, a ruckman, makes his debut in 1934.

Round 10, 1934 produced one of the most infamous matches in Collingwood v Carlton history, highlighted by an all-in brawl that one newspaper described as 'the most disgraceful scene in the history of the game'. It left Syd Coventry unconscious, nine other players injured and three reported.

The great Syd Coventry had retired in 1935 and crossed to Footscray to take on a coaching position, after agreement between the two clubs that he would not return to the field as a player. Harry Collier assumed the captaincy for the 1935 season.

Collingwood players take a two-week trip through Brisbane, Sydney and Newcastle in 1935, forging close bonds similar to those formed by the 1927 trip to WA.

Collingwood wins the 1935 VFL Premiership, and the celebrations pass into Magpie folklore. A piano is wheeled out into the middle of Victoria Park, and as Harry Collier is driving home after more celebrations on the Sunday, he rams his car into Archbishop Mannix's fence! Collier later has to retrieve the bumper bar of his car from the local police station.

On 3 October 1936 Collingwood wins its sixth VFL Premiership in 10 years, a record only equalled by Melbourne in the decade from 1955.

Gordon Coventry retires in 1937 with a career tally of 1299 goals. In his last season, he once more tops the competition goalkicking with 72 goals.

COLLINGWOOD

Fothergill and Todd costly defectors

The 1940s could not have started worse for Collingwood. Within 12 months they had lost their two most brilliant footballers in controversial circumstances.

First Ron Todd, who had farewelled the 1930s with a brace of 100-goal seasons, stunned the football world by crossing to VFA club Williamstown without a clearance before the start of the 1940 season. One year later, his good friend Des Fothergill – the reigning Brownlow Medallist – joined him.

They were by far the two most exciting footballers Collingwood had at that time, and they remain two of the most talented ever to have pulled on the guernsey. Both were attracted by the huge sums of money on offer at Williamstown, but both in the process diminished their place in history.

Todd was one of the best high marks the game has ever seen, taking freakish grabs week after week. Although he was at Collingwood for four years, in only two of those did he get to play as permanent full-forward. In that time he averaged more than six goals a game.

Fothergill, a sublimely talented half-forward who also played Shield cricket, won the Copeland trophy in his first season and two more in his next three seasons. He also added a Brownlow for good measure. Like Todd, Fothergill was a darling of the Victoria Park crowds.

He was far too good for the VFA, and

*Above: Fothergill: sublimely talented.
Left: Ron Todd in his new Williamstown strip.*

won that competition's best player award in his first year. He then served in the war, and injured his knee playing in a services game. The injury hampered him for the rest of his career, which he resumed at Collingwood when the war finished.

Todd was not so lucky. A comeback attempt in 1945 was spurned, and he was virtually barred from the club until the 1960s.

The coaching fiasco

In March of 1950, pre-season at Collingwood was proceeding pretty much according to plan. Then the unthinkable happened – Jock McHale retired, and all hell broke loose.

Jock had been in the job for 38 years – and the Club was seemingly unprepared for the succession. Almost everyone expected Phonse Kyne to get the job – he'd played for 15 years, been captain for four, won three Copelands and was universally admired.

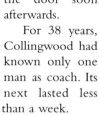

Phonse Kyne.

But some of the Committee had all but promised the job a few years earlier to Bervin Woods, a loyal and likeable bloke who had played more than 100 games and coached the seconds since 1943. When his appointment was announced, the club tore itself apart.

Within hours, a special meeting had been organised by outraged members. The Committee was hopelessly and bitterly divided. At a practice match the next day Woods was booed, and Kyne carried from the field shoulder-high.

Woods had no choice but to resign, which he did the very next day. His supporters on the Committee – including the president and treasurer – followed him out the door soon afterwards.

For 38 years, Collingwood had known only one man as coach. Its next lasted less than a week.

Bervin Woods.

CLUB NEWS 1940–1943

Albert Collier is forced to quit by the Collingwood committee after the final practice match in 1940. Bitterly disappointed, he plays 11 games with Fitzroy in 1941, then coaches successfully at Camberwell in the VFA, Kyneton and Sea Lake.

Des Fothergill wins the 1940 Brownlow Medal, in the first ever tie for the award (i.e. he and South's Herbie Matthews could not be separated on 32 votes, even by countback). Fothergill also finished fifth in the competition goalkicking.

In Round 6, 1940 Harry Collier retires after 255 games and 299 goals. He coached Essendon Reserves the following season, but remained a club icon until his death two years ago.

In Round 6, 1941 Lou Richards made his debut for Collingwood, against Carlton, having played in the Magpies' Reserves Premiership the previous season.

On 24 May 1941 Collingwood defeats Melbourne by a point in a Lightning Premiership played to raise patriotic funds.

In 1942 legendary trainer Wal Lee, father of Dick Lee, finally hangs up the towel and retires as the Magpies trainer after 50 years in the job.

In 1944 Collingwood misses the finals for the fifth year running – the first (and so far only) time this has happened in the club's history. After playing in five successive Grand Finals from 1935–39, the team finishes

1940 – 1953

Richards – Mr Personality

Collingwood has produced no better-known figure in its history than Lou Richards. Indeed, it is debatable if the game itself has ever produced a bigger personality.

Lou Richards.

But while most readers would be familiar with Louie's outrageous antics on TV, radio and – a little further back – in the pages of the *Sun*, he remains most loved at Collingwood for his period there as a player.

Lou and his brother Ron were the third generation of the famous Pannam/Richards dynasty, following in the footsteps of Charles Snr, Albert, Charles Jnr and Alby, who all played for the Magpies. He was Collingwood born and bred.

Richards' career stats are impressive; 15 years, 250 games, captain for four, 425 goals. And while the Richards' mythologising might have inflated – a little – his skills as a footballer, there is no denying the passion and leadership he showed as a player.

His contemporaries agree he was a magnificent, inspirational leader. And yes, that probably included the legendary cheekiness, the 'sledging', the occasional rough stuff. They were all part of Louie the footballer.

And Louie the Personality? That, as they say, is another story again.

Death of McHale, Wren

There was an eerie aftermath to the Pies' 1953 Premiership, with the death within days of two of the club's most famous figures.

Jock McHale died of a heart attack just days after the triumph. Soon after, John Wren – he of *Power Without Glory* fame – also passed away. It seemed that both had held out just long enough to see their beloved Magpies once more at the top.

Above: The crowd takes to the field in the exciting aftermath of the win over Geelong. Inset: Mick Twomey marks strongly.

'53 Flag after 'drought'

Every Premiership is significant, but Collingwood's 1953 triumph was particularly important because it signalled the Magpies' re-emergence as a power in football, after 17 years without a Flag – a period which at the time seemed like 'forever', but which in later years paled into insignificance beside The Great Drought.

They had surprised the highly fancied Geelong in the Second Semi-final and repeated the feat two weeks later with a 12-point win. Des Healey, Bob Rose, Thorold Merrett and skipper Lou Richards were all instrumental in the victory.

1940 – 1953 HONOUR ROLL

Year	Pos	Leading Goalkicker	No.	Best & Fairest	Captain	Coach
1940	8th	Des Fothergill	56	Des Fothergill	Jack Regan	Jock McHale
1941	5th	Alby Pannam	42	Frank Murphy	Jack Regan	Jock McHale
1942	10th	Alby Pannam	37	Alby Pannam	Phonse Kyne	Jock McHale
1943	10th	Alby Pannam	41	No Award	Jack Regan	Jock McHale
1944	10th	Lou Richards	28	No Award	Pat Fricker	Jock McHale
1945	3rd	Des Fothergill	62	No Award	Alby Pannam	Jock McHale
1946	3rd	Des Fothergill	63	Phonse Kyne	Phonse Kyne	Jock McHale
1947	5th	Neil Mann	48	Phonse Kyne	Phonse Kyne	Jock McHale
1948	3rd	Lou Richards	44	Phonse Kyne	Phonse Kyne	Jock McHale
1949	4th	Jack Pimm	34	Bob Rose	Phonse Kyne	Jock McHale
1950	7th	Lou Richards	35	Charlie Utting	Gordon Hocking	Phonse Kyne
1951	3rd	Maurie Dunstan	40	Bob Rose	Gordon Hocking	Phonse Kyne
1952	2nd	Maurie Dunstan	43	Bob Rose	Lou Richards	Phonse Kyne
1953	1st	Bob Rose	33	Bob Rose	Lou Richards	Phonse Kyne

eighth, fifth, eleventh, eleventh and tenth in the next five.

In Round 15, 1946 Jack Regan plays his last senior match. He had played 177 games in 12 years until the war intervened in 1941. He returned to lead the side in 1943 and finished his stint with six more games in 1946. He later became a much loved and respected football secretary at Collingwood.

In Round 17, 1946 Bob Rose made his Senior debut for Collingwood, against Footscray, having come to the city to pursue his promising boxing career.

On 3 April 1950 Jock McHale retires. Long-serving committeemen Bob Rush (treasurer for more than 40 years), Frank Wraith (secretary) and Harry Curtis (president and former player), were forced out in the turmoil following Bervin Woods' short-lived appointment as his replacement.

In 1950, schoolboy star Len Fitzgerald stunned the club by announcing he was accepting employment in South Australia. Fitzgerald who first played as a 16-year-old in 1945, took up with Sturt, where he won three Magarey Medals.

In 1951, Captain Gordon Hocking injured his knee while leading Victoria against WA, all but ending the career of one of the toughest and most revered Magpies of his era. A ruckman who toiled long and hard against players much bigger and stronger, Hocking was all heart, all Collingwood and greatly loved.

Ruckman Neil Mann, one of the best players in the Grand Final win of 1953, was third in Brownlow Medal voting.

COLLINGWOOD

Rival coaches Smith and Kyne.

Rivalry with Melbourne

Collingwood has always had its share of fierce rivals, most famously, of course, Carlton. But in the club's early days it was Fitzroy, and in the late 1920s it was Richmond. And in the late 1950s to early-1960s it was Melbourne.

The Collingwood–Melbourne rivalry became, for a decade, the most publicised in football. The teams met in no fewer than five Grand Finals in the 10 years from 1955-64, with the Demons winning all but one, and played in numerous other classic matches.

More sets of brothers

The Magpies have an unsurpassed record when it comes to famous sets of brothers – from the Leaches, Pannams, Lockwoods, Coventrys, Colliers, Murphys and Richards to latter-days siblings like the Richardsons, Shaws and, now, the Roccas.

But in the 1950s, Victoria Park was awash with brothers from two families who, for a time, seemed as if they could just about provide enough players for an entire team. There was the Twomey clan – Bill, Pat and Mick – all sons of a former champion in Bill Snr. Bill Jnr was probably one of the most talented players ever to play for the club, and he managed 189 often brilliant games from 1945–58. Mick, a taller, high-leaping player, played 158 times, while Pat, a centreman/flanker, managed more than 50. All played in the '53 flag together.

Then there were the Roses from Nyah West. Bob, of course, is a club legend, but Kevin totalled 159 games from 1958–67 (and is current club president), Bill played more than 30 games between 1950–55 and Ralph managed 23 games in 1962–63. Another brother, Colin, played in the Reserves.

But of all these, no one would dispute that Bob Rose was the most famous. A fast, tough, feisty rover, Rose became the most feared small man in the game.

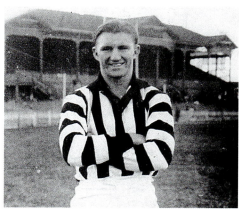

Bob Rose: Magpies champion.

Mick Twomey flies high.

1954–1964 HONOUR ROLL

Year	Pos	Leading Goalkicker	No.	Best & Fairest	Captain	Coach
1954	7th	Keith Bromage	22	Neil Mann	Lou Richards	Phonse Kyne
1955	2nd	Ken Smale	47	Des Healey	Lou Richards	Phonse Kyne
1956	2nd	Ken Smale	33	Bill Twomey	Neil Mann	Phonse Kyne
1957	5th	Ian Brewer	26	Murray Weideman	Bill Twomey	Phonse Kyne
1958	1st	Ian Brewer	73	Thorold Merrett	Frank Tuck	Phonse Kyne
1959	4th	Murray Weideman	36	Thorold Merrett	Frank Tuck	Phonse Kyne
1960	2nd	Murray Weideman	30	Ray Gabelich	Murray Weideman	Phonse Kyne
1961	9th	Kevin Pay	31	Murray Weideman	Murray Weideman	Phonse Kyne
1962	7th	Murray Weideman	48	Murray Weideman	Murray Weideman	Phonse Kyne
1963	8th	Terry Waters	50	Des Tuddenham	Murray Weideman	Phonse Kyne
1964	2nd	Terry Waters	43	Des Tuddenham	Ray Gabelich	Bob Rose

CLUB NEWS 1954–1964

Collingwood loses the Grand Final to Melbourne in 1955. The match is famous for the horrific clash between Des Healey and Frank Adams that saw both players stretchered from the ground. It ended Healey's career.

In 1955, two of Collingwood's greatest ever small-men, Bob Rose and Lou Richards, retire from League football with more than 400 games and 630 goals between them.

In Round 10, 1958 a record home-and-away crowd of 99,346 cram into the MCG for the Queen's Birthday clash between Collingwood and Melbourne. The Demons won with two late goals after Collingwood had grabbed the lead in time-on.

In 1958, for the first time, the captain is chosen by the committee, rather than the players. The result is that Bill Twomey is replaced in the role by Frank Tuck.

On Grand Final morning in 1958, the *Sun* newspaper publishes a list of players and their guernsey numbers, in contravention of a League ruling. The VFL responds by forcing most players to change their numbers for the Grand Final, including Ron Barassi swapping his famous No. 31 for a No. 2. The move causes mass confusion among fans at the game.

The unheralded Ian Brewer heads the VFL goalkicking list with the comparatively modest tally of 73 goals. The talented full-forward had headed the club's goalkicking table with the

1954–1964

Heroes of the decade at home at Victoria Park. Collingwood's 1958 Premiership was one for those who believe in fate – and maybe miracles. Melbourne had won Flags in 1955, '56 and '57 – a win in 1958 would equal the Pies cherished four-in-a-row record of 1927–30. And nobody gave the Pies much chance of stopping the Demons taking that record. It looked grim at quarter time, when Melbourne led 5.1 to 2.2. But Murray Weideman, Bill Serong and Barry 'Hooker' Harrison unsettled the Demons with some strongarm tactics. By half-time the Woods had piled on five goals and edged to a two-point lead. In the third quarter they added another five goals to just two points and the game was as good as safe. The exhausted Pies managed only one point in the final term, but it was enough.

Thorold Merrett goes

Champion wingman Thorold Merrett retired after breaking his leg against Carlton in Round 8, 1960. He had played 180 games and received two Copeland Trophies.

Harrison the hero

Grand Finals can make heroes out of ordinary men. And that's happened to Barry 'Hooker' Harrison on Grand Final day in 1958.

Harrison was a tough, aggressive ruck-rover of limited ability but with enormous heart. On The Big Day in '58 he tagged the great Ron Barassi, and drove him to distraction to such a degree that the champion had relatively little impact on the game. Along with team-mates like Murray Weideman and Bill Serong, Harrison started any number of fights that day, but sagely left the Melbourne players trying to finish them. He was reported for hitting Barassi but somehow escaped with a reprimand.

This was the culmination of Harrison's first season in League football, and he never again reached the same heights. In the years that followed he battled injuries, and an increasingly vigilant umpiring fraternity, and finished with just 55 games. But Magpie fans will always remember him as one of the true heroes of '58.

'Hooker' Harrison hangs on.

princely total of 26 in 1957.
Premiership hangover for the Pies, who start the 1959 season with five successive losses before finally notching a win against Footscray in Round 6.
Collingwood registers the lowest Grand Final score since 1927, managing only 2.2 (14) for the day against Melbourne in 1960.
Skipper Murray Weideman turns his off-field attentions to pro wrestling in 1962, making a short-lived, but profitable, career out of meetings with such names as the Zebra Kid.
Ballarat youngster Des Tuddenham debuts for the Pies, on the bench against Geelong in 1962.
The club is torn apart by factional dealings in 1963, as it searches for a new president to replace the retiring Syd Coventry. Tom Sherrin eventually won the battle from Jack Galbally, who was then Labor Party leader in the Legislative Council, but players, coaches and long-serving members all became embroiled.
'The Bear', Ray Gabelich, stuns the football world and his team-mates during the 1964 Grand Final, with a run and goal from the half-forward flank that has passed into football folklore. The lumbering giant nearly lost the ball on each of his three bounces, but remained composed long enough to goal, exhausted, from the square and put the Pies in front with just minutes remaining. It was not enough to win the game, however, with Melbourne back pocket Neil Crompton kicking the match-winning goal.

COLLINGWOOD

A never to be forgotten scene: Bob Rose in despair after the 1970 Grand Final loss.

Peter McKenna: pop star status.

Birth of the Colliwobbles

Ill fortune plagued Collingwood during the 1960s and 1970s. Magpie fans in that period had to endure a succession of heartbreaking finals losses and internal squabbles.

The Pies lost the 1964 Grand Final by four points after leading with just a few minutes left. Two years later they let St Kilda in by a solitary point for the Saints' first Flag. And then, of course, there was 1970, when a 44-point half-time lead evaporated in the face of a Carlton onslaught.

But it wasn't just those games that gave rise to the famous Colliwobbles. In four other seasons as well the Pies capitulated in finals after dominating the home-and-away season.

The first came in 1969 when Collingwood finished on top but went out of the finals in 'straight sets' to Carlton and Richmond. In 1971, the team lost only three of its first 17 matches and were Flag favourites; they promptly lost four of the last five matches and staggered into the finals in fourth place, for another early exit.

In 1972 the Magpies finished third, but again lost both finals matches. And in 1973, after again finishing on top of the ladder, the Pies once more went down in successive finals, blowing a six-goal half-time lead in the Preliminary Final against Richmond.

The evidence had mounted too heavily; the Colliwobbles were born.

McKenna – the superstar

Peter McKenna was more than just a goal-kicking full-forward in the 1970s. McKenna had a remarkable public profile. He released a couple of records that sold well. He co-hosted (briefly) the Saturday morning children's cartoon program that would become 'Hey Hey It's Saturday', before being replaced by a stuffed pink ostrich. He won successive 'popular footballer' competitions.

Girls would run onto the ground before matches just to kiss him. It was like Beatlemania revisited. And through it all he kept kicking goals – 97 in 1969, then 143, 134, 130 and 86. A pop star to be sure, but an outstanding footballer as well.

The Greening incident

The football world was shocked on 8 July 1972, when young champion John Greening was knocked unconscious behind the play in an incident with St Kilda's Jim O'Dea.

Greening suffered cerebral concussion, did not regain consciousness for 24 hours, and was expected to be permanently disabled. Remarkably, he recovered to play again – in a memorable and emotionally-charged return match against Richmond in 1974. But his career never regained ground, and he managed only eight more games. Greening had been in top form in 1972, and may well have won the Brownlow but for the incident (he finished seventh despite playing only 13 games), which all but ended what had shaped as one of the great Collingwood careers.

Len Thompson, five-times winner of the Copeland Medal, received the highest accolade with a Brownlow Medal in 1972. Thompson is noted not only for his size and rucking ability, but for his safe marking and agility on the ground.

CLUB NEWS 1965–1976

A youngster by the name of Peter McKenna is given his first game for Collingwood in Round 1, 1965. Placed at centre half–forward, he does not kick a goal.

Collingwood springs a surprise in its 1965 Preliminary Final line-up by including 18-year-old ruckman Len Thompson for his debut.

Collingwood tours Japan and plays exhibition matches in 1965.

Collingwood breaks with tradition in 1969 by paying big money for an interstate recruit, Subiaco's Peter Eakins. The move sparks a rash of pay demands, and Eakins is never a success in the VFL.

Two of the club's biggest names, Des Tuddenham and Len Thompson, go on strike in 1970 looking for improved contracts. They did not attend training during for three weeks, but returned to the fold in March, with all players having received a better pay deal.

Tuddenham is replaced as skipper by Terry Waters, and Thompson as vice captain by Wayne Richardson.

In 1970, Peter McKenna becomes the first Collingwood player since Ron Todd to kick 100 goals in a season. He goes on to total 143, second to Peter Hudson's 146.

Terry Waters quits as captain after being dragged during a game in 1971. He is replaced as skipper by Wayne Richardson, and does not play again that season. He finishes his career with six games early in 1972.

1965 – 1976

Fabulous Phil Carman

Collingwood thought it had found a new Messiah when 'Fabulous' Phil Carman arrived at Victoria Park from Norwood in 1975. Carman was magical that first season, winning the Copeland Trophy and finishing just three votes behind the Brownlow winner, despite having missed seven games with a broken foot suffered in a State game.

Carman was brilliant, athletic, superbly gifted and capable of playing anywhere from centre to full-forward or on the ball. It soon became clear why the Pies had fought so hard to get him over from SA, even making him stand out of football for a year in a clearance wrangle.

But Carman also proved undisciplined and hard to manage. He never regained the form of 1975, and was eventually off-loaded to Melbourne after the 1978 season.

Max Richardson: refused to play. Right: Wiedeman and Clarke

1976 – the Magpie annus horribilis

Season 1976 was one of the most tumultuous in the club's history. The team was tearing itself apart. So, too, was the club. Many of the players were resentful of the salary being paid to Phil Carman, especially because Carman was a loner. Rumours circulated that players would not kick to him on the field; there were even punch-ups at training.

Meanwhile the Richardsons, Wayne and Max, were dropped for the first time in their careers. Wayne responded with a public outburst that cost him a four-match suspension. Max refused to play in the Seconds.

Through all this, coach Murray Weideman and president Ern Clarke were at war, with Weideman declaring publicly that he would not continue to serve as coach under Clarke. The two papered over the cracks publicly, but by May Clarke had gone. The team won its first wooden spoon.

Fabulous Phil flies high.

1965 – 1976 HONOUR ROLL

Year	Pos	Leading Goalkicker	No.	Best & Fairest	Captain	Coach
1965	3rd	Dave Norman	32	Trevor Steer	Ray Gabelich	Bob Rose
1966	2nd	Ian Graham	58	Terry Waters	Gabelich/J. Henderson	Bob Rose
1967	4th	Peter McKenna	47	Len Thompson	Des Tuddenham	Bob Rose
1968	7th	Peter McKenna	64	Len Thompson	Des Tuddenham	Bob Rose
1969	3rd	Peter McKenna	97	Barry Price	Des Tuddenham	Bob Rose
1970	2nd	Peter McKenna	143	Peter McKenna	Terry Waters	Bob Rose
1971	4th	Peter McKenna	134	Wayne Richardson	Waters/W. Richardson	Bob Rose
1972	4th	Peter McKenna	130	Len Thompson	Wayne Richardson	Neil Mann
1973	3rd	Peter McKenna	84	Len Thompson	Wayne Richardson	Neil Mann
1974	4th	Peter McKenna	69	Wayne Richardson	Wayne Richardson	Neil Mann
1975	5th	Phil Carman	41	Phil Carman	Wayne Richardson	Murray Weideman
1976	12th	Phil Carman	35	Robert Hyde	Des Tuddenham	Murray Weideman

Bob Rose quits as senior coach in 1971 after another strife-torn and heartbreaking season. Rose coached the Magpies to three Grand Finals, and lost them by a combined total of 15 points. He is replaced as senior coach by Neil Mann.

In 1971 Peter McKenna kicks his second ton – 134 goals – but again it is eclipsed by Hudson, who finishes with 150.

In 1972 Des Tuddenham crosses to Essendon as captain–coach, as part of a deal struck before the 1971 season in the wake of Waters' appointment as captain. Tuddenham returned to Collingwood in 1976.

In 1972 Peter McKenna at last wins the VFL goalkicking with 130 goals.

Ruckman Len Thompson, his confidence boosted by new coach Neil Mann, wins the 1972 Brownlow Medal – the club's first since Des Fothergill back in 1940.

Peter McKenna is controversially left out of the team to play Richmond in the 1973 Preliminary Final and replaced by 16-year-old Rene Kink. McKenna had been affected by flu, but claims he was available to play.

Peter McKenna wins the 1973 VFL goalkicking with 86 goals.

Tom Sherrin stands aside as president in 1974, to be replaced by the 'damn the tradition' forces of Ern Clarke.

Murray Weideman arrives as senior coach in 1975 to take over from Neil Mann.

Collingwood finishes last on the VFL ladder for the first time in 1976.

COLLINGWOOD

Champion centre half-back Billy Picken takes one of his characterisically strong marks.

Peter Moore

Peter Moore was a fans' favourite in the late 1970s and early 1980s, his agility, athleticism and spectacular high marking stamping him as a precursor to the Corey McKernans of the 1990s. Moore won the Brownlow in 1979, but began to fall from favour when he became embroiled in the dispute with Tom Hafey in 1982. At the end of that year he stunned Magpie fans by crossing to Melbourne for big money, and won another Brownlow there in 1984.

Peter Moore hits the heights.

Hafey's Heroes '77–81

Collingwood's performances between 1977 and 1981 were phenomenal. It started with a dramatic turnaround in 1977.

The team that finished last in 1976 took the competition by storm a year later to finish on top of the ladder at the end of the home-and-away series. There had been few changes – only a new coach in Tom Hafey, and some 'steel' from the West in the form of defenders Stan Magro and Kevin Worthington.

Hafey teams of '77–81 were far from the most talented, but were often the most desperate, the most disciplined and spirited. Sadly, spirit wasn't enough in the five Grand Finals the team played during that period.

The class of '86

There wasn't much for Magpie fans to cheer about in 1986, with the club teetering on the verge of bankruptcy and the team missing the finals on percentage.

But early on Grand Final day the Collingwood Under 19s took off the Thirds' Premiership. Hardly a cause for mass celebration, but the real significance of that win would be realised four years later.

The Class of '86, as they came to be known, produced a number of players who were central to the Magpies' drought-breaking Senior Premiership in 1990. Gavin Brown, Mick McGuane, Gavin Crosisca and Damien Monkhorst were all part of that Under 19s Flag-winning combination.

1977–1989 HONOUR ROLL

Year	Pos	Leading Goalkicker	No.	Best & Fairest	Captain	Coach
1977	2nd	Peter Moore	76	Len Thompson	Max Richardson	Tom Hafey
1978	3rd	Peter Moore	54	Ray Shaw	Len Thompson	Tom Hafey
1979	2nd	Craig Davis	87	Peter Moore	Ray Shaw	Tom Hafey
1980	2nd	Craig Davis	52	Peter Moore	Ray Shaw	Tom Hafey
1981	2nd	Peter Daicos	76	Mark Williams	Peter Moore	Tom Hafey
1982	10th	Peter Daicos	58	Peter Daicos	Peter Moore	Hafey/Mick Erwin
1983	6th	Michael Richardson	49	Bill Picken	Mark Williams	John Cahill
1984	3rd	Mark Williams	53	Tony Shaw	Mark Williams	John Cahill
1985	7th	Brian Taylor	80	Mark Williams	Mark Williams	Bob Rose
1986	6th	Brian Taylor	100	Wes Fellowes	Mark Williams	Rose/Leigh Matthews
1987	12th	Brian Taylor	60	Darren Millane	Tony Shaw	Leigh Matthews
1988	4th	Brian Taylor	73	Peter Daicos	Tony Shaw	Leigh Matthews
1989	5th	Brian Taylor	49	Gavin Brown	Tony Shaw	Leigh Matthews

CLUB NEWS 1977–1989

Peter McKenna, a hero to legions of Magpie fans, leaves the club in a 1977 pay dispute. To make matters worse, he heads for arch enemy Carlton, where he manages 11 games and 36 goals.

On 10 September 1977 the Magpies beat the Hawks in the Second Semi-final, but star forward Phil Carman is reported for striking Michael Tuck. He is subsequently rubbed out for two weeks, missing both Grand Finals.

Collingwood and North Melbourne draw the 1977 Grand Final after 'Twiggy' Dunne levels the scores with just seconds left. The Pies lose the replay by 27 points, in a match remembered for Phil Manassa's famous long run and goal from the half-back line.

'Too short, too fat and too slow', Tony Shaw, younger brother of Ray, makes his senior debut against Footscray in Round 19, 1978. It marks the start of a remarkable career that will see Shaw finish with the club's games record, the captaincy and eventually the job of coaching the side. His leadership in the 1990 Premiership year stamped him as one of the club's greatest.

The club loses patience with the unpredictable and temperamental Phil Carman in 1978, clearing him to Melbourne in exchange for Ross Brewer and cash.

Collingwood kicks a new club-record score of 31.21 (207), defeating St Kilda by a mammoth 178 points at Victoria Park in Round 4, 1979. On debut was a young but freakishly skilled centre-

1977–1989

The packed annual general meeting.

There's only one Collingwood player in this picture, but he happens to have the ball.

New Magpies

The Collingwood Football Club was not a good place to be in season 1982. The team fell into a huge hole, winning only one of its first 10 games, and player discontent was rife. Captain Peter Moore was at loggerheads with coach Tom Hafey, and other senior players were unhappy. The spirit had broken down, and Hafey was sacked mid-season.

But he wasn't the only casualty. The administration of president John Hickey was also doomed, overwhelmed by the New Magpies juggernaut that swept aside an entire committee.

The New Magpies were headed by Ranald Macdonald and included businessmen Bill Weston, Alan McAlister and Ian McPherson, and former players Terry Waters, Len Thompson and Brian McKenzie. Spurred by the sacking of Hafey, they rode to power on promises of modernisation and aggressive recruitment. The fans loved it. Their petition of no-confidence in the existing 12-man board led to the September meeting at which they were overwhelmingly voted into power.

Four years later, however, and the New Magpies dream had ended, with the club within touching distance of bankruptcy, Macdonald forced to quit and other members of the 'magnificent seven' having already departed.

The Macedonian Marvel

No Collingwood player more excited the fans during the 1980s than the Macedonian Marvel, Peter Daicos.

Daicos was a footballing freak. Old timers rank him alongside Des Fothergill, Bill Twomey Jnr and Phil Carman in terms of sheer talent. His ball-handling, field-kicking and evasive skills were of rare quality, and his goalkicking something else again. He had the ability to do the seemingly impossible on a regular basis, whether racking up heavy possessions in midfield or snagging goals on the forward line.

By 1990, Daics had become a permanent forward, and his 97 goals that season were a major part of the club's Flag assault. And very few of those goals were forgettable. He kicked them from everywhere that season – torps from outside 50, dribbled miracles from the boundary, lightning quick snaps out of packs.

The fans loved him like they had no other since Peter McKenna, and especially at Victoria Park, where he always seemed to produce something extraordinary.

Daics finished his career with 250 games and 549 goals. Through the 80s he struggled with a succession of debilitating injuries, including two serious knee problems and shin splints, that threatened his career.

BT gets ton

Brian Taylor proved Richmond wrong when he topped Collingwood's goalkicking list every year from 1985 top 1989. In 1986 he scored exactly 100 goals to top the VFL list and win the John Coleman Medal.

Death of Tom Sherrin

Tom Sherrin, 'elder statesman' and president of Collingwood from 1963 to 1974, was killed in a car crash in 1978, while returning from a Collingwood v Geelong game at Kardinia Park. Mr Sherrin, 60, was a principal of the Sherrin football manufacturing firm.

man/forward from Preston RSL, Peter Daicos, who had 25 possessions.

In 1979 Peter Moore becomes the seventh Collingwood player to win the Brownlow Medal.

In May, 1982 Tom Hafey is sacked as coach after the club wins just one of its first 10 matches. Mick Erwin fills in until the end of the season, then South Australian John Cahill takes on the job.

In July 1982 the 'New Magpies' officially announce their formation, and their intention to take over the running of the club.

On 15 September 1982 the New Magpies are swept to power by club members, with all members of the existing committee voted out.

Reserves player John Bourke earns his place in history when, in May 1985 during a televised Seconds match, he kicks and pushes the field umpire. The VFL Tribunal suspends him for 10 years.

In 1985 Bob Rose is appointed Senior coach for the second time.

Former Hawthorn champion Leigh Matthews joins the club in 1986 as assistant coach to Bob Rose.

Bob Rose resigns after a bad loss to North, and is replaced by Matthews.

On 14 April 1986 Ranald Macdonald resigns as president, and general manager Peter Bahen is sacked as the club nearly folds under financial pressures, the players being forced to take a 20 per cent pay cut (those who wouldn't then left for other clubs). By this stage the club debts had blown out to $2.9 million, and only the largesse of the club's bankers saved it from extinction.

COLLINGWOOD

Worth waiting for. Tony Shaw holds the Premiership trophy on high.

Shaw and team-mates celebrate.

The Flag brings joy and relief

The emotion when the final siren went on Grand Final Day, 1990, was joy, elation and excitement. But mostly, it was relief.

The Collingwood team of 1990 was neither the best, nor most talented, team in VFL/AFL history. But it is hard to imagine there has ever been one more desperate.

The inspiration came from Tony Shaw, Craig Kelly, Denis Banks and Darren Millane – the 'hard' men of the club (Millane was so 'hard', in fact, that he played the finals series with a broken thumb). They drove, cajoled and pressed their team-mates to play with the kind of fierce desperation that characterised their own games – the sort that wins finals. There were no 'easy' balls to be had against Collingwood, and no soft options.

The drive came from a trio of interstaters – Graham Wright, Tony Francis and Scott Russell. Wright on a wing and Francis and Russell on-ball were superb all season, getting mountains of effective possessions.

And the magic? That, of course, came from the one and only Peter Daicos. He kicked 97 goals for the year as a permanent full-forward or forward-pocket, often left alone with a defender near the goal mouth.

The reward? A place in the history books, and eternal gratitude from the most famous army of supporters in football.

Shaw jumps all obstacles

For much of his career, Tony Shaw struggled to achieve football credibility. The 'too short, too fat, too slow, can't kick' tag had stuck so well that his achievements (such as the 1984 Copeland) were downplayed or disregarded. But by his second Copeland, in 1990, no one was making the same mistake.

His resurgence started in the late 1980s, when he became one of the most prolific possession-getters in the League. In 1990 he was the inspiration behind the Premiership win, with a Norm Smith Medal to show for it.

In 1994, he broke Gordon Coventry's club games record of 306, and later that season bowed out after the finals loss to West Coast in Perth. Tears were shed as he left the field that day – on both sides of the fence.

Club centenary

Collingwood celebrated its centenary in style in 1992, but not always to great effect. The May 7 game against Carlton – exactly 100 years to the day since the teams first met, in what was Collingwood's first-ever game – was the highlight, with enormous hype and a huge crowd at the MCG. But it didn't help the Collingwood team on the field, which fell to their arch rivals by 33 points.

1990–1996 HONOUR ROLL

Year	Pos	Leading Goalkicker	No.	Best & Fairest	Captain	Coach
1990	1st	Peter Daicos	97	Tony Shaw	Tony Shaw	Leigh Matthews
1991	7th	Peter Daicos	75	Tony Francis	Tony Shaw	Leigh Matthews
1992	5th	Peter Daicos	52	Mick Mcguane	Tony Shaw	Leigh Matthews
1993	8th	Saverio Rocca	73	Mick Mcguane	Tony Shaw	Leigh Matthews
1994	8th	Saverio Rocca	49	G. Brown/N. Buckley	Gavin Brown	Leigh Matthews
1995	10th	Saverio Rocca	93	Saverio Rocca	Gavin Brown	Leigh Matthews
1996	11th	Saverio Rocca	66	Nathan Buckley	Gavin Brown	Tony Shaw

CLUB NEWS 1990–1996

On 30 May 1990 former great full-back and later VFL Commissioner, Jack Hamilton, dies in a car accident near Whittlesea. Hamilton was a fine player, with more than 150 games to his credit. But he achieved wider fame in his VFL roles, renowned for his quick wit and performances reading the votes on Brownlow Medal nights.

The 8 September 1990 drawn Qualifying Final with West Coast throws finals schedules into chaos and precipitates introduction of 'extra time' in subsequent finals series.

Peter Daicos kicks 13 goals against Brisbane at the Gabba in 1991, including one goal so preposterous that he apologises to opponent John Gastev!

On 7 May 1992 Collingwood plays its Centenary match at the MCG against Carlton.

In May–June 1993 Collingwood is plunged into a racism row after taunts from the crowd to Nicky Winmar, who responds by baring his torso to the crowd, proclaiming his pride at being black. The situation is exacerbated by remarks made by Allan McAlister in TV interview, and a 'curse' is placed on the club. It struggles to win matches while the curse remains in place.

In October 1993, the Magpies pull off the recruiting coup of the season by enticing Nathan Buckley to don the black and white jumper for the 1994 season. Buckley responds by sharing the Copeland Trophy with Gavin Brown in his first season at Victoria Park.

1990 – 1996

Good old Collingwood forever, they know how to play the game …

Alan McAlister's greatest day.

Right: Sav Rocca bagged nine in the epic Anzac Day clash with Essendon in 1995.

Death of Darren Millane

6 October 1990. Darren Millane throws the ball into the air as the siren goes to signal the end of Australian football's most famous Premiership drought.

Fast forward one year and one day later and Darren Millane is dead, killed in the early hours of the morning on his way home from a night club when his car hit the back of a semi trailer.

The football world was thrown into mourning. The *Herald Sun* was flooded with death notices, and more than 5000 crammed into the Dandenong Town Hall for the funeral. The 1990 Premiership Flag, which he had done so much to bring back to Victoria Park, was lowered to half-mast in his honour.

Daics says goodbye

It was an emotional moment before the mega-clash with Carlton on the Easter weekend of 1994, when the Macedonian Marvel, Peter Daicos, bade farewell to his legion of fans. Daicos had been sacked just weeks earlier, and had considered nominating for the draft. But the thought of playing against Collingwood proved too much, and Pies fans gave him the send-off he deserved during a lap of honour before the Carlton game. Mick McGuane followed up soon after with his own 'tribute' – a seven-bounce goal that quickly passed into footy folklore.

Daics with daughter Madison.

In December 1993, Collingwood members vote to move most of their home games from Victoria Park to the MCG, after a bitter and at times questionable campaign. The move left traditionalists angry, but the turnstiles at the 'G' kept clicking.

In February 1994, Collingwood plays an Aboriginal all-star team in Darwin as part of its reconciliation after the racism incidents of 1993. The event is a huge success, with 15,000 attending. Peter Daicos is axed from senior list (along with Micky Gayfer) in 1994, sparking an outcry from Magpie fans.

Tony Shaw played his last game on 11 September 1994, retiring with a club record of 312 games beside his name.

In October 1995, Leigh Matthews was sacked as Collingwood coach, despite McAlister's 'coach for life' commitment after the '90 Flag. Matthews develops a handy career in the media. Tony Shaw is appointed to replace him.

The most-quoted president in the AFL, Allan McAlister, steps down from his position in 1995 and is replaced by Kevin Rose. Journalists suddenly find quotable quotes a little harder to get.

The quietly spoken but inspirational Gavin Brown succeeds Tony Shaw as captain in 1996, but has a poor first year, dogged by injury.

Nathan Buckley brightens up the tail-end of another disappointing year in 1996 by announcing he has rejected overtures from Port Adelaide and will re-sign with Collingwood for a further three years.

COLLINGWOOD

Fans turn out for 'last game' at Victoria Park

Fremantle's visit to Victoria Park in Round 15 became one of the biggest days of the year for the Magpie faithful. First, the team finally broke its six-game losing streak with a 100-point thumping of the hapless Dockers. Secondly, hero Nathan Buckley played his 100th game, picking up a handy 44 possessions along the way. And thirdly, there was once again speculation that this might be the Club's last match at Victoria Park. That speculation ensured a big crowd and an almost carnival atmosphere. But although it seems certain that Vic Park is living on borrowed time, it is unlikely to have seen its last AFL match just yet. That day, which will be a sad one for many Magpie fans, probably won't come until the proposed Docklands Stadium is up and running.

Team of the Century

One of the big marketing exercises of the year for Collingwood was the selection of its 'Team of the Century'.

Miffed at the fact that no Collingwood player won selection in the AFL's all-time team in 1996, the Magpies decided to choose their own 'best ever' line-up. And what an exercise it turned out to be!

Names like Bob Rose, Peter Daicos, Albert Collier and Dick Lee were always going to make it, but some of the other spots proved more problematic. The most contentious decisions surrounded the selection of Nathan Buckley and Darren Millane, and the omission of Gavin Brown. The final line-up chosen was:
B: Rumney, Regan, S Coventry
HB: Buckley, A Collier, Picken
C: Merrett, Rose, Millane
HF: Fothergill, Weideman, Lee
F: Daicos, G Coventry, Kyne
R: Thompson, Tuddenham, H Collier
Int: T Shaw, Whelan, W Richardson
Coach: Jock McHale

Darren Millane. Albert Collier. Jock McHale. Nathan Buckley. Tony Shaw.

Harold Rumney.

Peter Daicos.

Anthony (left) and Saverio Rocca.

The Rocca Bros show

Collingwood has had many famous sets of brothers over the years. When Anthony Rocca joined big brother Sav at Victoria Park in 1997, fans hoped for another set that would soon become famous.

They quickly assumed a huge following, especially after some early promising performances from Anthony – most memorably his 70-metre torpedo against Essendon on Anzac Day.

By year's end the jury was still out; Sav's kicking had let him down too often, and Anthony's fitness was a major problem. But they remain the Club's best hopes yet in the key forward positions.

1997

1997 Promised much, delivered little

Collingwood's 1997 season was played out to much the same script as the entire period since the 1990 Premiership – it promised much, delivered little and disappointed greatly.

There was no outrageous sense of pre-season optimism. Anthony Rocca was the only recruit expected to make any major impact, and the general feeling was that a finish in the lower reaches of the eight was about as good as the Club could expect.

But those modest expectations were blown out of the water in the first eight rounds, after which the Pies stood atop the ladder with six wins and two losses.

Tony Francis and Scott Russell were back to their exhilarating best, the Rocca boys were causing touble up forward, Paul Williams was producing those electrifying runs and Gavin Crosisca was leading a committed defence.

It was the last two of those wins that really set the bandwagon rolling. Victories on successive Friday nights over North Melbourne and the Western Bulldogs had been so impressive that even the sceptics had to concede that the Pies looked a real threat for the Flag. They were aggressive, fast, skilful and kicked bags and bags of goals.

But no sooner had that concession been made than the side's season fell apart. They lost their next six in a row – including one at Victoria Park – to slide out of the eight. Big wins over Fremantle and Melbourne raised false hopes of a late charge, but losses to St Kilda and Carlton just about ended the season.

Still, the competition was so tight that the Pies still had a slim finals chance going into the last match of the year, against the Crows in Adelaide. They should have won, too, holding the lead until late in the match when a stupid 50-metre penalty gifted the Crows a rare goal. As it turned out, Collingwood would have made the finals had they won. But in the end the cards just didn't fall their way – or they just weren't good enough. It was that kind of season.

Unfortunately, the magic didn't eventuate for the Magpies in 1997.

Paul Williams.

Nathan Buckley.

Saverio Rocca.

1997 HONOUR ROLL

Year	Pos	Leading Goalkicker	No.	Best & Fairest	Captain	Coach
1997	10th	Saverio Rocca	76	Nathan Buckley	Gavin Brown	Tony Shaw

ESSENDON

MY CLUB
by Rohan Connolly

Success is all relative. Tell people these days that you barrack for Essendon, and you'll get the sort of blank, faintly bored look that must greet English fans of soccer giant Manchester United, or kids in the US who follow basketball's mega-powerful Chicago Bulls.

The Essendon of the 1990s is a leading corporation, big, popular and usually well-performed; a safe bet for a supporter. But it wasn't like that for all of us.

Like so many football fans, I had little choice over my allegiance. My parents had arrived from Western Australia in the 1950s to settle in Marco Polo St, Essendon. Not only were the Bombers the local church of worship, they happened to wear the same jumpers as Dad's WAFL side, Perth. Blood ties ran thick. So did red and black ones.

But that was little comfort to the youngest of four kids whose awakening to the joys of football at the age of five happened to coincide with the 1970s, the second-worst decade in Essendon's entire history. It was Richmond, Carlton, Hawthorn and North Melbourne that then ruled the roost.

My older brother Steve had carried proudly the No. 23 of Bomber champion and captain Ken Fraser. By the time I inherited it, and began wearing it proudly behind the Napier Street goals at Windy Hill on a weekly basis, it was occupied by the rather more modest talents of Peter Hickmott.

My compensation would come towards the end of the decade as I watched a band of young kids, in some cases only a couple of years older than me, mature together into one of the greatest combinations football has seen.

The 'Baby Bombers' - high-flying Paul Van Der Haar, feisty wingman Merv Neagle, crafty Glenn Hawker, 'Nobby' Clarke, Shane Heard and a 15-year-old schoolboy genius called Tim Watson – joined established up-and-comers like Simon Madden and Terry Daniher in a precocious, unpredictable team that had that touch of youthful rebellion about it.

They were forever scratching at the doors of the establishment, copping the odd hiding but beginning to pull off more than their share of audacious victories, 15 of them in a row and a Night Flag and one of the greatest comebacks in history against Carlton during Kevin Sheedy's memorable first season as coach in 1981.

At three-quarter time of the 1984 Grand Final, they were no closer to breaking through, trailing Hawthorn by 23 points having kicked only five for the match. But an amazing burst of 9.6 and one of the game's unforgettable moments from brilliant centreman Leon Baker duly delivered the

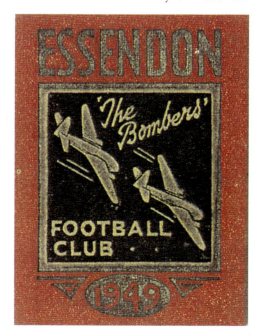

ESSENDON

Year Established	1873
Joined VFL/AFL	1897
Home Grounds	Windy Hill, MCG
Premierships	1897, 1901, 1911, 1912, 1923, 1924, 1942, 1946, 1949, 1950, 1962, 1965, 1984, 1985, 1993
Brownlow Medals	Dick Reynolds 1934, 1937, 1938; Bill Hutchison 1952, 1953; Graham Moss 1976; Gavin Wanganeen 1993; James Hird 1996
Record home crowd	87,638 v Collingwood, 1993
Most games	Simon Madden, 378
Most goals	Simon Madden, 575
Notable supporters	Joan Kirner, Louise Asher, Peter Costello, Michael Wright, Andrew Peacock, John Barnaby

dream and carried both the team and this nervous 19-year-old across the threshold of adolescent angst to adult achievement. Now we were the big boys.

So it followed in the record-breaking 11-goal exclamation mark to the last quarter of the 1985 Grand Final, a 78-point thumping of the Hawks for back-to-back Premierships, and in a string of regular finals appearances since.

But however successful or not it has been through the course of 125 years, Essendon has always seemed to stand for either skill, flair or aggression, and sometimes, like in those glorious days of 1984–85, all at once. But always at least some remarkable characteristic; never merely mundane efficiency.

Even back as far as 1891–94, when Essendon was the king of Association football with four successive Premierships, it drew crowds with an exciting, open brand of football and the brilliant goalkicking of Albert Thurgood.

Its brilliant 'Mosquito Fleet' ran rings around its bigger, slower opposition in

Dick 'King Richard' Reynolds.

breathtaking fashion when the club won back-to-back Premierships in 1923–24 and when Essendon again dominated football between 1946–51, winning three Premierships, it had arguably the most eye-catching footballer of all time, the brilliant spearhead John Coleman.

As recently as 1993, Essendon again stunned the football world, climbing from eighth to a Flag on the back of the wizardry of Michael Long and yet another crop of talented and precocious kids – James Hird, Mark Mercuri, Joe Misiti, Ricky Olarenshaw, Dustin Fletcher and David Calthorpe. How many other sides so inexperienced would have overhauled the 42-point deficit the Baby Bombers II faced at half-time of that year's Preliminary Final?

Now a new crop of youngsters with names like Lloyd, Lucas and Caracella are threatening to turn the AFL on its ear as another potential Premiership combination takes shape.

Essendon, the club I came to know as downtrodden, has the biggest membership of any Victorian club, consistently packs the MCG and when it defeated arch-enemy West Coast in the 1996 First Semi-final, turned one of the world's largest sporting stadiums into a giant swirling cauldron of black and red passion.

That colourful explosion said everything about what the Dons have been even for those of us who have endured the odd barren spell. Life as an Essendon supporter is one of adventure; exciting, dramatic, sometimes controversial, tragic, but never, never dull.

James Hird Essendon's modern champion.

Che Cockatoo-Collins.

Early star Jim Anderson.

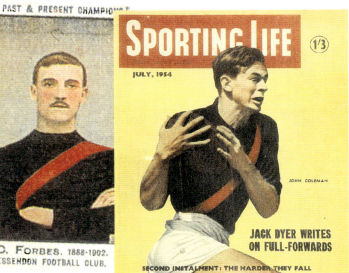

Albert Thurgood. **Tracker Forbes.** **John Coleman: top full-forward.**

ESSENDON

Birth of a club

Essendon the football club grew from a meeting held at the home of well-known brewery family, the McCrackens, whose Ascot Vale property hosted a team of local junior players. The McCracken family loomed large in the formation of and running of the club.

Robert McCracken: founder.

Robert McCracken, owner of several city hotels, became Essendon's first president, and his 17-year-old son, Alex, its secretary. He would follow his father into the same post, and later become president of the newly-formed VFL. Alex's cousin, Collier, who had already played with Melbourne, was the team's first captain.

Its first official game was in 1873. Essendon played 13 matches in its first season, winning seven, drawing four and losing only two. In 1875, the club changed the design of its guernsey to the black with red sash that has remained the official uniform since.

In 1877, Essendon joined the newly formed Victorian Football Association, playing 19 games for eight wins and a finish in fourth place.

It began to attract large crowds, and in 1882, accepted an invitation from the East Melbourne Cricket Club to use its more suitable facilities. There Essendon would stay until its return to its heartland at the Essendon Recreation Reserve some 40 years later.

The team gets together in 1873, the first year of the Essendon Football Club.

Kings of the Association

Essendon ruled football's roost in the 1890s, winning four VFA Premierships from 1891–94, losing only three of 77 matches over the period and playing a string of 57 matches without tasting defeat between July 1892 and September 1894.

The Same Old, as Essendon was known, was a crowd favourite, attracting big audiences with its exciting, fast style of football. Its string of success began in 1891 when it lost only one match and tied two more (behinds were not counted then) and in which it was the only team to handle one of the wettest seasons in history, conclusively topping the ladder and winning the Premiership (there were no finals).

In 1892, the new top-dog took on an even more formidable appearance when young forward Albert Thurgood joined the club, which beat off a swag of rivals for the schoolboy champion's services.

He kicked 56 at centre half-forward in his first year, and together with stars like full-back 'Ned' Officer, big-man Charles Forbes, cool-headed captain and defender Alick Dick, brilliant centreman Bill Crebbin and wings Stewart Angwin and George Stuckey, helped take Essendon to a second successive title, again losing only one game.

The following season, Essendon managed to improve even on that, going through the year undefeated for a Premiership hat-trick. Thurgood improved on his tally still, and Essendon's dominance raised concerns that the competition may have become too one-sided.

They were not alleviated by the events of 1894 and Essendon's fourth consecutive Premiership. When Geelong defeated Essendon at Corio in the final game of the season (Premiers were still the top team on the ladder), it was the first time the Same Old had lost a match since July 1892.

The East Melbourne Ground became home to Essendon in 1882.

CLUB NEWS 1873–1896

Essendon became the first Association club to kick 10 goals in a match in 1879, when it thrashed Hawthorn 10 goals to one. But only a few weeks later, it was handed a taste of its own medicine, when it was thrashed by Carlton, 10 goals to three.

Essendon lost the last game of 1882 against Geelong at Corio after having played matches in Tasmania, arriving back by boat only just before the game after 12 hours at sea in a rough crossing of Bass Strait. Several Essendon stars were too ill to play, and more played under duress.

By 1884, Essendon had established itself as one of football's most popular clubs. When it drew with Geelong at East Melbourne before more than 16,000, one of the biggest to have then attended a football match.

Essendon played a controversial draw with undefeated South Melbourne in 1885, when it protested after the match that one of its goals had been incorrectly ruled a behind. The field umpire supported its claim, and the game was awarded to Essendon. But a week later, the Association changed its decision, ruling that the goal umpire's decision was final.

There was humiliation for Essendon in 1886, when it was thrashed in the final game of the season by Geelong's massive 15 goals to nothing.

In 1891, Essendon was leading Fitzroy four goals to two when Fitzroy players noticed its opponent appeared to have

1873 – 1896

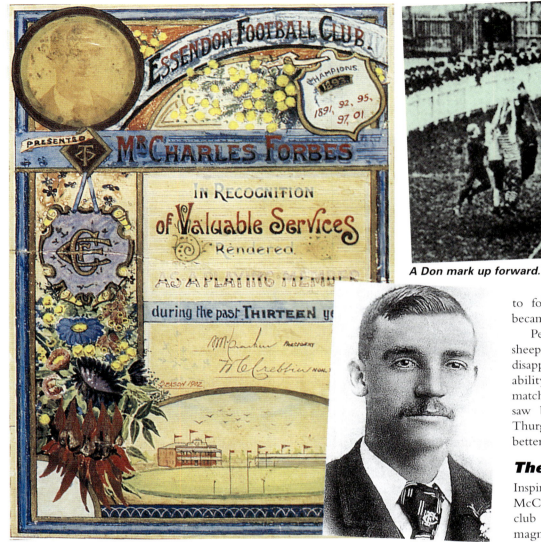

The club thanks 'Tracker' for services rendered. Inset: Tracker Forbes.

A Don mark up forward.

Overhead Commotion

Charles Pearson's impact on the game stretched far further than his winning of the 1886 award for the 'Best in the Colony'. Nicknamed 'Commotion', Pearson is credited with having introduced the high mark to the game.

His spectacular jumps to catch the ball overhead introduced a whole new exciting dimension to the game, one that still enthrals the football public more than a century later. Team-mates soon began to follow suit as Pearson's dashing style became the talk of football.

Pearson, who worked on a Queensland sheep station, played only sporadically, and disappeared for four years at the peak of his ability before returning to play some matches early in 1891. One team-mate who saw both Pearson and the great Albert Thurgood play nominated Pearson as the better player.

The Same Old

Inspired by Essendon's founding family, the McCrackens, the curious nickname for the club stuck well and truly after the club's magnificent run of four consecutive Association Premierships in the early 1890s.

While some critics bemoaned Essendon's success, and its likely detrimental impact on crowds, the club's games continued to draw well as its winning run continued, moving its growing support base to verse. A supporter penned a song known as 'Same Old Essendon' which supporters would sing at East Melbourne games. Essendon would be known as the Same Old until some time after it had moved back to its true home in 1922.

'Tracker' Forbes a ruck champion

Known as 'Tracker', Charles Forbes was Essendon's first champion ruckmen, and a crucial factor in the club's four successive Association Premierships between 1891–94. At 6ft 3in (190.5 cm) he dominated the ruck, and his strong marking and courage were an inspiration.

Forbes' work with his ruck partner Fred Ball and rover Colin Campbell was superb and he won the Champion of the Colony award in 1891, and represented the colony in 1893–94.

Forbes was with Essendon when it took the step into the VFL, playing in the first and 53 subsequent League games, and was a star in the club's historic first-season Premiership.

too many players on the ground. But the umpire decided to wait until half-time for a player count, and one Essendon player disguised himself in an overcoat and escaped out a side window.

Schoolboy champion Albert Thurgood joined Essendon in 1892 with immediate impact, his brilliant high-marking and incredible long-kicking feats dominating the competition. He kicked 56 goals from centre half-forward, the first player to kick more than 50 goals in a season.

Thurgood rose to even greater heights in 1893, smashing his previous record with 63 goals, and kicking an astonishing 12 of the 14 goals Essendon scored against Richmond in the final game of the season.

On 1 September 1894, Essendon lost a controversial match against Geelong. It ended an astonishing run of 52 matches without defeat, which had begun back on 9 July 1892. In its magnificent four-season run of Flags, Essendon lost only three of 95 games.

Essendon trailed Richmond 2.4 to 3.3 at half-time of an early-season 1896 match, but on lining up at interval it was discovered Richmond had an extra player on the field, and it was stripped of its score.

On the eve of the 1896 Premiership play-off, Essendon joined other strong clubs Melbourne, Geelong, Collingwood, South Melbourne and Fitzroy at a meeting leading to a break-away group of clubs, which would invite Carlton and St Kilda to join them in forming the VFL.

ESSENDON

An Essendon high mark in the match against Melbourne.

The first and the best

Essendon played its first VFL match against Geelong at Corio Oval, and emerged victorious, 7.5 (47) to 3.6 (24). Forward Norman Waugh scored the Dons' first League goal.

But Essendon finished the home-and-away rounds in second position behind Geelong, winning 11 of its 14 matches. That left those two teams, plus Melbourne and Collingwood, to fight out a round-robin finals series, the Premiership to be decided not in a Grand Final, but by the team finishing a game clear of the rest.

Essendon had to play Geelong in its first finals match, and was in deep trouble at three-quarter time when it trailed by 10 points, having kicked just one goal for the match. But in a sensational burst inspired by ruckman Charles Forbes, the Dons kicked four goals in the last term to win by six points.

In the second round of finals, Essendon played Collingwood, and this time led at the final change, both teams having kicked four goals. But the Dons charged home, booting 5.5 to the Woods' three points to win by 40 points.

That meant a win in the third-round final against Melbourne would give Essendon the Premiership. And incredibly, the Dons triumphed again.

Melbourne hit the post three times. Essendon had a goal disallowed because the bell had signalled the end of a quarter. And the one deciding goal for the match came in extraordinary fashion when Essendon's Forbes marked close to the goal square. It was an easy kick, and players began to move back to the centre.

But Forbes' kick miscued, and Edgar Croft, standing alone near the behind post, marked it to seal the club and the League's first Premiership, the scoreline an amazing 1.8 (14) to 0.8 (8), still the lowest tally for a finals match.

A second Pennant

Essendon was unlucky not to achieve back-to-back Pennants in the first two years of VFL competition. It finished on top of the ladder after the home-and-away matches, again winning 11 of its 14 games.

Another, more complex method of finals had been introduced weighted heavily in favour of the minor-rounds Premier, giving the Dons every chance of winning their second Premiership. But Fitzroy's form during the play-off rounds was impressive, and it headed its sectional ladder, Essendon second.

Essendon then had the right to challenge Fitzroy for the Premiership, but the Dons were jumped by a team in top touch and, held goalless after half-time, lost the Grand Final by 15 points, signalling a period of struggle for Essendon.

By the turn of the 20th century Essendon was again a contender and in 1901, inspired by the brilliance of champion centre half-forward and leading goalkicker Albert Thurgood, the Dons were into the Grand Final against Collingwood at South Melbourne.

The quicker Essendon, suited by the conditions, got an important break with three goals to none in the first quarter. Then Thurgood kicked two quick goals and at half-time the Dons led by a healthy 29 points with Collingwood goalless.

The Woods had one last effort, holding Essendon to just two points while reducing the margin to 19 points at the final change. But an early goal to Thurgood put the result beyond dispute, Essendon winning its second Premiership by 27 points. Again in 1902, the Dons' bid for back-to-back Pennants was foiled at the final hurdle, Collingwood gaining Grand Final revenge by 33 points.

But having won two Premierships, along with Fitzroy, and having appeared in five of six finals series, Essendon had established beyond dispute its place as a VFL power.

CLUB NEWS 1897–1910

On 4 September 1897, before only 3800 people at South Melbourne, Essendon defeated Melbourne 1.8 (14) to 0.8 (8) in its final play-off game to win the first Premiership in the newly-formed Victorian Football League.

Essendon threatened to forfeit the 1898 Premiership rather than play Fitzroy at the St Kilda ground that had already been top-dressed for cricket and was unfit for football. Doubt remained until the morning of the match, but Essendon took to the dust-bowl-like field and lost by 15 points.

In 1899 against Fitzroy, Essendon recorded its lowest score for a game of League football, managing only nine behinds.

Albert Thurgood returned to Victorian football for one game in 1899, and with a vengeance the following season. In June 1899, at the East Melbourne ground, Thurgood launched a place-kick recorded at 107 yards two feet one inch (98.5 metres). After a run of injuries in 1900, Essendon took to the field one man short against Collingwood. During the first quarter, club secretary and former star Bill Crebbin, who hadn't played since 1895, volunteered to fill the gap.

Essendon finished third in 1900 when it lost a thrilling divisional play-off to Melbourne, 5.13 (43) to 7.3 (45), playing most of the match one man short after an injury to 'Newhaven' Jackson.

In 1900, Essendonians disenchanted by the team's playing at East Melbourne

1897–1910

Thurgood (standing left) looks every inch a champion with the team at three-quarter time.

Albert 'The Great' Thurgood

By the time he came to play VFL football, Thurgood had already long been considered the best player of his time, having won the Champion of the Colony award in 1893–94. He played a key role in Essendon's outstanding run of four successive Premierships in the VFA between 1891–94.

A spectacular high mark and possessing superb balance and ball skills, Thurgood was proficient on the left and right sides, and a superb long kick, who for three years headed the Association goalkicking honours.

Thurgood had been playing in Western Australia for three seasons when the VFL began, and when he returned to Melbourne in 1898, League residential rules prevented him playing for Essendon. He stood out of football for a year.

His greatness brought Essendon its second VFL Premiership in 1901. Both he and the Dons were in sparkling early-season form until Thurgood was injured in a match against Collingwood. Without his talent, the Dons slumped dramatically, but recaptured their lustre on his return, scraping into fourth place and a crack at another Premiership.

Though Essendon went into its semi-final against Fitzroy an underdog, it emerged a dramatic one-point victor, with Thurgood's performance hailed as one of the greatest individual efforts of all time. The champion forward scored five of Essendon's six goals and had a hand in the other, played at centre half-back when the Dons kicked against the wind and also had a run in the ruck.

In the Grand Final against Collingwood, Thurgood kicked two quick goals to all but put the Grand Final out of the reach of the Woods, then added a third nail in the coffin in the last quarter. He kicked half his side's six goals. One of his place kicks, against the wind, was measured at 93 yards (85 metres).

Thurgood put the seal on an outstanding effort when he won the Champion of the Colony award for the third time.

In 1902, he was involved in controversy when he became the first Essendon player suspended. He retired at the end of the season, but made a shock comeback in 1906, at 36, when the Dons were depleted by injury, adding eight more games to his outstanding record.

Thurgood died in a car accident in 1927 at the age of 57.

Albert Thurgood.

1897–1910 HONOUR ROLL

Year	Pos	Leading Goalkicker	No.	Best & Fairest	Captain	Coach
1897	1st	Norman Waugh	23		George Stuckey	
1898	2nd	C. Moore	20		George Stuckey	
1899	5th	Arthur Cleghorn	15		George Stuckey	
1900	3rd	Albert Thurgood	25		George Stuckey	
1901	1st	Fred Hiskins	34	Albert Thurgood	Tod Collins	
1902	2nd	Albert Thurgood	32		Tod Collins	
1903	6th	Michael Madden	15	Hugh Gavin	Jim Anderson	
1904	4th	Michael Madden	25		Jim Anderson	
1905	4th	George Barker	29		William Robinson	
1906	4th	Norman Yeo	31	Jack Dookie McKenzie	Jack McKenzie	
1907	8th	Jim Martin	16		William Griffith	
1908	2nd	Dave Smith	26	Bill Busbridge	William Griffith	
1909	4th	Pat Shea	40	Bill Busbridge	William Griffith	
1910	4th	Albert Armstrong	30		Alan Belcher	

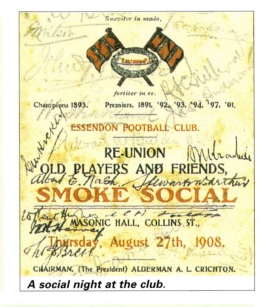

A social night at the club.

formed a new team to play in the VFA, known first as Essendon Town and later as Essendon A.

Essendon won its second VFL Premiership before 30,031 spectators at South Melbourne on 7 September 1901 when it defeated Collingwood by 27 points, 6.7 (43) to 2.4 (16).

Albert Thurgood was suspended for three matches for striking in 1902. In two of the three matches Essendon fielded a player mysteriously called 'Goodthur'. The replacement was not, however, Thurgood.

Essendon played a 1904 Premiership match against Melbourne at Moore Park in Sydney. It lost the game, played before the Governor-General and Governor of NSW. The players then had to return to Melbourne by sea, arriving only on Thursday and losing the next game, against Fitzroy.

After finishing a dismal last in 1907, Essendon staged a recovery in 1908 to reach the Grand Final, falling to the more finals-hardened Carlton at the MCG before nearly 50,000 people by only nine points, 3.8 (26) to 5.5 (35).

There was internal conflict in 1909, when player Len Bowe objected to a reprimand he had received from his captain, Bill Griffith. At a players' meeting, Griffith asked to resign the captaincy, but his team-mates would not allow him, and order was restored.

Essendon lost the 1910 First Semi-final to Collingwood by 58 points, 5.7 (37) to 14.11 (95), the fifth time in the past seven years Essendon had been eliminated in the first week of the finals.

ESSENDON

A desperate struggle against Collingwood on Essendon's backline.

Worrall at Fitzroy.

Worrall factor lifts Dons

Essendon hadn't won a Flag for 10 years when the club beat off a host of eager rivals to sign up three-time Carlton Premiership coach Jack Worrall in 1911.

After a draw against Worrall's old club in the first game, Essendon lost only two games for the rest of the season, demanding attention as early as Round 4, when it thrashed Collingwood by 85 points.

The Dons won 10 games in a row and finished the home-and-away rounds on top of the ladder. It met Worrall's old side, Carlton, in the Second Semi-final. After trailing all day and by eight points at three-quarter time, Essendon's final-term burst of 5.6 gave it victory and a Grand Final berth by 21 points.

On Grand Final day, Essendon took on Collingwood in wet and slippery conditions, which didn't suit the Dons' fast, skilful style. The Dons were also without key big-man Alan Belcher. But Essendon jumped Collingwood nevertheless, holding its opponent goalless for a 16-point half-time lead, with ruckman Fred Baring and champion little-man Ernie Cameron starring.

The Dons relaxed and held only a slender three-point lead at the final change, with Collingwood looking the fresher side. But the Woods missed three easy chances, goals to Bill Walker and Pat Shea gave Essendon breathing space, and the Dons withstood a late surge by Collingwood to win their first Pennant for a decade.

Essendon struggled through the following season and limped into fourth position, but surprisingly defeated top team South Melbourne by 12 points. Again, master coach Worrall was confronted by his old club, Carlton, in the Preliminary Final, and again he emerged triumphant against the odds.

The Dons lost wingman Fred O'Shea in the first minutes and 1912 Champion of the Colony Ernie Cameron with a broken leg in the final minutes, Essendon hanging on by four points playing two short. O'Shea, who could barely hobble, took a mark and goaled, staggering and falling again in the act.

Champion defender Bill Busbridge was also out of the Grand Final injured, which made Essendon's 14-point victory over South Melbourne all the more meritorious.

The Dons took over in the second term, little-man Percy Ogden dominating, and while squandering scoring opportunities, still led by 20 points at the final change. Victory was sealed in the last quarter by a magnificent solo run and goal by Fred Baring. Essendon had won its fourth VFL Pennant.

Fred O'Shea, Michael Madden, Ernie 'Ginger' Cameron.

CLUB NEWS 1911–1920

Essendon defeated Collingwood to win the 1911 Premiership, then travelled to South Australia to play local Premier West Adelaide in a match billed as the 'Championship of Australia'. With a depleted side, Essendon lost by three points.

Essendon lost a controversial match against St Kilda in 1912 when a clear Essendon goal was disallowed and a free kick given to a St Kilda player who hadn't tackled the Essendon goalscorer.

Essendon won its second successive and fourth overall VFL Premiership in 1912, beating South Melbourne 5.17 (47) to 4.9 (33) before 54,463 people at the MCG, at that time the largest crowd to have attended an Australian sporting event.

The attempt at a Premiership hat-trick was derailed when Essendon could finish only eighth, hampered by internal dissent. Premiership defender Les White had a dispute with the club mid-season, seeking a clearance to St Kilda, which he was eventually granted.

In a 1914 match against South Melbourne, Essendon captain Alan Belcher was struck by a spectator who had run on to the ground during the match. Belcher turned and chased the offender and, for retaliating, was reported for unseemly conduct. He was cleared.

Essendon big-man Fred Baring was selected in the Australian Test cricket team to tour South Africa in 1914, the

1911-1920

The distractions of football can't compete with the call of war.

Halt! – World War One

When World War One began on 1 August 1914, attendances at VFL matches fell by 60 per cent within a couple of weeks. By the following season, the conflict had already cost millions of lives, and lost Essendon the services of many players, who went to fight in Europe.

University disbanded in 1915, attendances had halved, clubs fell into debt, and in July of the same year, at a meeting of VFL delegates, a majority (but not the required three-quarters) voted to suspend the competition altogether.

Early in 1916, Essendon players resolved that they would not play unless all played strictly as amateurs, and that the League would hand over gate receipts and membership subscriptions to the Patriotic Funds. The VFL would not accept the resolution, and so Essendon dropped out of the competition, which by now was left with only four teams.

The Dons were absent again in 1917, but re-entered the League for the 1918 season. Having missed two seasons of League football, and without many top players who were away fighting, Essendon won only three matches and took out the dreaded wooden spoon. Within a few years, they would again win the Premiership.

A fine sportsman

Considered one of the finest players to represent Essendon, Bill Busbridge was a centre half-back and follower who played his first Senior match for the club at just 16. He was quick, an excellent mark and kick and was also renowned for fair play and sportsmanship.

Busbridge twice won the Champion of the Colony award for the best player in Victoria, and represented the state in three seasons, including his last. He seriously injured a knee in 1910 and missed two months, then missed the first 14 matches of 1911 before being talked into a comeback and playing a key role in Essendon's first Premiership for a decade. Sadly, Busbridge's knee gave way again in 1912, finishing his career and putting him out of the Dons' back-to-back Premiership-winning team.

Busbridge: career cut.

A real all-rounder

Although Cyril Gove played just 28 senior games for Essendon from 1913–15, he remains one of the most celebrated Dons of the era and a great all-round sportsman.

On one very busy Saturday in May 1915, Gove proved it. First, Gove rode a horse in a hurdle at Moonee Valley in a race starting at 2 p.m. Gove finished third, and was whisked away to play for Essendon against South Melbourne. Although the Dons lost, Gove was one of the best players afield. But he still hadn't finished. That evening, at Melbourne Stadium, Gove missed out by only a few points on becoming the state's amateur boxing champion.

It is believed he slept well that night.

1911–1920 HONOUR ROLL

Year	Pos	Leading Goalkicker	No.	Best & Fairest	Captain	Coach
1911	1st	Albert Armstrong	34		Dave Smith	John Worrall
1912	1st	Jack Kirby	45	Ern Cameron	Alan Belcher	John Worrall
1913	8th	Jack Kirby	29	Fred Baring	Alan Belcher	John Worrall
1914	6th	Ernie Lumsden	28	Alan Belcher		John Worrall
1915	8th	William Walker	14	Alan Belcher		John Worrall
1916–1917		Club in recess during World War One				
1918	8th	Norm Hall	15		Fred Baring	John Worrall
1919	6th	Dave Walsh	15		Percy Ogden	John Worrall
1920	6th	Frank McDonald	33	Jack Garden	Percy Ogden	Percy Ogden

Dons insuring him against injury. But Baring never made the tour, which was cancelled because of the impending Great War.

Member of Essendon's founding family and VFL president Alex McCracken died at his mansion in North Essendon after a short illness in 1915.

In its first season back in the VFL in 1918 Essendon, with many top players still in service, could win only three matches for the season. Of the 41 players used during the season, 12 would play only in 1918.

Future Essendon great Tom Fitzmaurice made his debut in 1918 after having been overlooked by Carlton three years earlier. His mobility for a big-man and strength in the air had an immediate impact.

Essendon captain and champion rover Percy Ogden was a runaway winner of the rover's category in the *Sporting Globe*'s 'best footballer' poll in 1919.

Arthur Crichton, who had been Essendon's president for the previous 12 years, died in 1919. He was replaced at the helm of the club by Bill Raper, who had played for Essendon during its Association days.

In a Premiership spree up to 1912, John Worrall coached five Pennants in seven seasons – a hat-trick to Carlton and back-to-back Premierships for the Dons. After that, in the war-interrupted years, he could take the club to no higher than sixth, but held the post until he retired in 1919.

ESSENDON

This tranquil Essendon landscape was destined to become home for the Dons.

Essendon moves to Windy Hill

Essendon had played its home matches at East Melbourne from 1882 until 1921, but in 1922 the Dons moved back to their heartland. The local council put up 12,000 pounds worth of improvements to the existing Essendon ground on the corner of Brewster and Napier Streets, including a grandstand, fencing for the playing field and the ground as a whole, and, naturally, turnstiles to charge admission.

The team's return was greeted with instant enthusiasm from both current and would-be supporters of Essendon, whose overwhelming support helped catapult the team into the finals for the first time since 1912 in its first season at its true home.

Essendon's first game at Windy Hill was against 1921's runner-up Carlton. The Dons emerged with an 18-point win in front of an excellent crowd of 21,000. It was just a taste of the tremendous home-ground advantage Essendon would enjoy right up until it left the ground 70 years later for the roomier spaces of the MCG.

Tom Fitzmaurice: bitter departure.

A top backman

A high-flying ruckman initially, Tom Fitzmaurice became a top centre half-back in his second stint with Essendon, which came after he had been transferred to Sydney in his employment in 1921.

It was a leg injury which forced Fitzmaurice into defence, but the Dons reaped the benefits. His defensive marking, strength and agility when the ball hit the ground were outstanding.

Fitzmaurice starred in the Bombers' back-to-back 1923–24 Premierships and both seasons won the Champion of the Colony award as the best player in Victoria. But he left Windy Hill at his peak for Geelong at the end of the 1924 season after the acrimony that surrounded the club's 1924 Premiership win. He had played 85 games for the Bombers and represented Victoria in five different seasons.

A speedy rover

Rover/forward Keith Forbes was one of the outstanding VFL players of the 1930s. Forbes was runner-up in both the 1930 and 1935 Brownlow Medals, won two Essendon Best and Fairests and was runner-up in two more.

After having been told by South Melbourne that he was too small, the 171-centimetre Forbes started with the Bombers in 1928. A smart and speedy rover, he soon made his mark with the Dons where his lightning-quick dashes made him a joy to watch.

Forbes, who captained the club in 1934–35, was also very good around goal. In 152 games, he notched up 415 goals and four times was Essendon's leading goalkicker.

After leaving Essendon, Forbes was captain–coach of North Melbourne in 1938–39, and he also played with Fitzroy.

CLUB NEWS 1921–1937

There was a sensation in Essendon's match against Richmond in 1921 when the Tigers scored a behind and Bomber full-back Albert Day, noticing that the ball had been punctured on its return from the crowd, kicked it gently to the umpire to inspect it. But a Richmond player intercepted the 'pass', and ran in and scored a goal, which, incredibly, was allowed.

Essendon 'won' its third wooden spoon in 1921 after losing to fellow struggler St Kilda. The Bombers won only three matches for the season.

Essendon decided to move back to Essendon from East Melbourne towards the end of 1921 after considering a plan to move to North Melbourne and effectively merge with the aspiring VFL club.

Bomber full-forward Greg Stockdale won the VFL goalkicking in 1923 with 68 goals, at the time a League record.

In a new finals system, Essendon played its last finals match in 1923 against Richmond knowing it could lose by 45 points and still win the Flag.

Essendon fell short of a Premiership hat-trick when it lost the 1925 semi-final to Collingwood by just 10 points.

A host of star players left Essendon for the 1926 season, but the Bombers made the finals regardless, beating Geelong in the First Semi-final, then losing a thrilling Preliminary Final to Melbourne by three points. The Demons would go on to beat Collingwood for the Premiership.

1921 – 1937

Essendon's small-men rule the 1923 Final against Fitzroy.

The mosquito fleet wins back-to-back Flags

In 1923 a supreme combination of speedy little-men became known affectionately as 'the mosquito fleet'. The mosquito fleet – Charlie Hardy, George Shorten, Jack Garden, Jim Sullivan, Vince Irwin and Frank Maher – ranged from just 160 to 167 centimetres, but their pace and elusiveness as a group made them close to unstoppable.

In 1923 the Dons kept the Lions goalless in the third term to lead by 10 points and, in a thrilling last term, goaled twice to seal the club's fifth VFL Pennant. The tally would become six in 1924, when the Dons defeated Richmond on finals percentage.

1921 – 1937 HONOUR ROLL

Year	Pos	Leading Goalkicker	No.	Best & Fairest	Captain	Coach
1921	9th	Frank McDonald	17		Percy Ogden	Percy Ogden
1922	3rd	Jack Moriarty	36		Syd Barker	Syd Barker
1923	1st	Greg Stockdale	68	Tom Fitzmaurice	Syd Barker	Syd Barker
1924	1st	Tom Jenkins	50	Tom Fitzmaurice	Syd Barker	Syd Barker
1925	4th	Tom Jenkins	37	Greg Stockdale	Frank Maher	Frank Maher
1926	3rd	Greg Stockdale	36	Joe Harrison	Frank Maher	Frank Maher
1927	8th	Jack Vosti	35	Frank Maher	Frank Maher	Frank Maher
1928	5th	Greg Stockdale	39	Norm Beckton	Frank Maher	Charlie Hardy
1929	6th	K. Forbes/Len Johnson	40	Howard Okey	Norm Beckton	Charlie Hardy
1930	6th	Keith Forbes	54	Keith Forbes	Norm Beckton	Charlie Hardy
1931	6th	Ted Freyer	50	Tom Clarke	Garnet Campbell	Garnet Campbell
1932	6th	Ted Freyer	52	Syd Carman	Garnet Campbell	Garnet Campbell
1933	12th	Ted Freyer	51	Paddy Walsh	Garnet Campbell	Garnet Campbell
1934	10th	Ted Freyer	61	Dick Reynolds	Keith Forbes	Charlie May
1935	8th	Keith Forbes	52	Keith Forbes	Keith Forbes	Charlie May
1936	8th	Ted Freyer	50	Dick Reynolds	Jack Baggott	Jack Baggott
1937	10th	Keith Forbes	44	Dick Reynolds	J. Baggott/K. Forbes	Jack Baggott

Norm Beckton: 1929 captain.

The bribery scandal

You'd think a club which had won its second consecutive Premiership wouldn't have too much to be worried about, but Essendon's 1924 Flag 'celebrations' ended almost before they began. After the Finals loss to Richmond, players argued and, in some cases, exchanged blows.

The following week, Essendon played VFA Premier Footscray for charity, and the latter, on the brink of admission to the VFL, was keen to make its point.

Essendon kicked only four goals and was soundly beaten by 28 points, with sections of the crowd jeering Essendon players. Fists flew again in the dressing rooms, with accusations that a number of Essendon players had received money to play poorly.

Though the club officially denied the allegations, several leading players who had not taken part in 'the sting' confirmed them. Champion centre half-back Tom Fitzmaurice was so incensed by events that he left the club.

So divisive was the scandal Essendon would not win another Premiership for 18 years.

After having played in the previous five finals series, Essendon could finish no higher than eighth in 1927.
Top forward and sometime defender Greg Stockdale left Essendon for VFA club Northcote in 1929. Stockdale kicked 189 goals in 106 games for the Dons.
Essendon blew its chance of making the 1931 finals when it lost to Melbourne in 1931 by one point, after claiming a point kicked by Ted Freyer had not been registered. The Bombers' protest was dismissed by the VFL.
After finishing sixth for four seasons in a row, Essendon reached a nadir in 1933 when it finished 12th, its lowest position to that time, to take the wooden spoon. The Dons won only two matches for the season, although they did unveil a future star, teenage sensation Dick Reynolds.
At 19 and in only his second season of League football, Reynolds won his first Brownlow Medal in 1934.
Full-forward Ted Freyer kicked 12 goals in Essendon's 1935 opening-round demolition of Melbourne.
Jack Baggott, a versatile player and fine mark, was appointed Essendon captain-coach for 1936. He retired as a player during the 1937 season, and resigned as coach early in 1939.
Essendon wingman Ted Bryce was suspended for 18 matches in 1936 after being found guilty of kicking a Carlton player.
Dick Reynolds won his second Brownlow Medal in 1937, a clear four-vote winner over South Melbourne's Herbie Matthews.

ESSENDON

The 1942 team, with Dick Reynolds as captain–coach, photographed at Windy Hill.

Percy Bushby on the ball in '46.

Two more Flags liven up grey days

Though World War Two cast a pall over the nation, Essendon managed to maintain its position as a football heavyweight. It won the 1942 Premiership, played off in the 1941 and 1943 Grand Finals and won the first post-War Premiership in 1946.

With triple Brownlow Medallist Dick Reynolds still the game's foremost little-man and now captain–coach, Essendon emerged as a power again when it lost to Melbourne in the 1941 play-off. Already fielding stars like defender Wally Buttsworth and forwards Gordon Lane and Ted Leehane, when the Bombers added 18-year-old little-man Billy Hutchison to the blend in 1942 it had the right ingredients.

Though the Bombers surprisingly lost the Second Semi-final to Richmond after having finished clear ladder leader, they narrowly defeated South Melbourne in the Preliminary Final to earn another shot at the Tigers, this time making amends.

After a tight first term, the Dons turned up the heat with a six-goal second quarter to go to the break with a 34-point lead, Lane booting three goals and Reynolds starring. When they added another six in the third term to Richmond's one, it was all over, the final margin a convincing 53 points.

That result would be reversed the following year when Essendon suffered a heartbreaking loss in the 1943 Grand Final to Richmond by just five points.

Essendon scored a run of eight wins early in the 1946 season, and headed the ladder at the end with its fast-flowing brand of football revolving around small-men Reynolds, Hutchison and Jack Cassin.

There was a hard slog to get to the Grand Final after Essendon drew a magnificent Second Semi-final against Collingwood, the Dons having trailed most of the day. In a wet, slogging replay, the Bombers emerged 19-point winners.

It was Melbourne the Dons would take on in the Grand Final. After a sensational first quarter in which a combined total of 15 goals were kicked, and a dour struggle in the second, Essendon exploded after half-time, booting an astonishing 11.8 (a Grand Final record) in the third quarter alone. Lane went on a rampage, booting seven goals to equal the individual record for a Grand Final as his side went on to win by 63 points, having kicked a record 22.18 (150).

1938–1946 HONOUR ROLL

Year	Pos	Leading Goalkicker	No.	Best & Fairest	Captain	Coach
1938	7th	Tom Reynolds	68	Dick Reynolds	Len Webster	Jack Baggott
1939	6th	Tom Reynolds	71	Dick Reynolds	Dick Reynolds	Jack Baggott
1940	3rd	Edward Bryce	48	Hugh Torney	Dick Reynolds	Dick Reynolds
1941	2nd	Tom Reynolds	65	Wally Buttsworth	Dick Reynolds	Dick Reynolds
1942	1st	Tom Reynolds	61	Dick Reynolds	Dick Reynolds	Dick Reynolds
1943	2nd	Tom Reynolds	31	Dick Reynolds	Dick Reynolds	Dick Reynolds
1944	3rd	Roy Powell	42	Perc Bushby	Dick Reynolds	Dick Reynolds
1945	8th	Bill Brittingham	48	Wally Buttsworth	Dick Reynolds	Dick Reynolds
1946	1st	Bill Brittingham	66	Wally Buttsworth	Dick Reynolds	Dick Reynolds

CLUB NEWS 1938–1946

Six-time leading club goalkicker Ted Freyer left Essendon in acrimonious circumstances to play for VFA club Port Melbourne in 1938.

Dick Reynolds won his third Brownlow Medal in 1938, only the second man to do so after Fitzroy champion Haydn Bunton.

Essendon coach Jack Baggott resigned mid-season in 1939 after a disagreement with selectors over training methods. At 25, Reynolds took over the job as captain–coach of the Bombers.

Essendon reached the finals for the first time in 14 years in 1940. The Bombers beat Geelong by 18 points after making an early break, but lost the Preliminary Final to eventual Premier Melbourne by just five points.

The Bombers reached their first Grand Final since 1924 in 1941, but Melbourne stole a march in the first half and won, easing up, by 29 points.

The 1942 finals were played at Princes Park. After a shock loss to Richmond in the Second Semi-final, Essendon broke through to beat South Melbourne in the Preliminary Final by 28 points, the Bombers' first win at the ground since 1925.

The Dons were required to play one more match after their 1942 Premiership triumph over Richmond; a match to raise funds for the War effort against a services team which included many League stars. Essendon won that as well, by 27 points.

1938–1946

Reynolds the record breaker.

Dick Reynolds: zest for football.

The great career of 'King Richard' Reynolds

In the long and successful history of the Essendon Football Club, no name looms larger than that of Dick Reynolds or 'King Richard' as he came to be known – such was his sustained brilliance over such a long period.

Reynolds' career statistics do most of the talking. He played 320 VFL games from 1933–51, which remained a League record for nearly 20 years after he retired. He won three Brownlow Medals in 1934, 1937 and 1938.

He won a record seven Essendon Best and Fairests. He led Victoria and played for the state in nine different seasons. He took over as captain–coach in 1938 and led his team to four Premierships. He retired as a player after the 1950 Grand Final but returned to the field at 36 for the 1951 play-off against Geelong, nearly leading his team to another Premiership. As non-playing coach, he would take it to two more Grand Finals.

One of the finest rovers, and later half-forward and ruck-rovers, of all time, Reynolds' strength and fierce competitiveness allowed him to take on and beat bigger opponents, and his speed and exciting dashes forward made him a universal football favourite. Few players have matched his skill or record before or since.

At the time of his retirement, no player had played more games, taken his team into as many successive Grand Finals or won his club's Best and Fairest as many times. Only the great Haydn Bunton had won as many Brownlows. But you wouldn't hear Reynolds blowing his trumpet about it. For most Essendon supporters, his modest and gentlemanly ways off the field took the points as well. VFL football has seen few bigger or better stars.

New stars arrive

Essendon emerged from the horrors of world war with a golden era looming not only as the likes of Jack Cassin, Rawle and Lambert returned from battle, but through the introduction of talented youngsters such as Bob McClure, Jack Jones and George Hassell. The new talent complemented perfectly the established stars, all living in the giant shadow of the greatness of Reynolds and Hutchison.

Gordon Lane was a top centre half-forward who saved his best for the biggest occasion, booting a combined 13 goals in the Bombers' Grand Final wins of 1942 and 1946.

Bill Brittingham was a very good full-forward, whose kicking caused him problems but who became a top full-back. He played at full-forward in the 1946 Flag and 1948 defeat and was full-back in two more Premiership wins.

Wally Buttsworth was a leading centre half-back, tough and hard-hitting but a top mark and beautiful drop kick, who won the Best and Fairest in 1945 and 1947 and played State football.

Bill Brittingham: top forward.

Fighting and reports marred the Dons' first-round win over South Melbourne in 1943. South's Jack 'Basher' Williams received an eight-game suspension for striking four Essendon players in retribution for an incident in the previous year's Preliminary Final.

Australian Test cricket wicketkeeper Gil Langley played four games for the Dons in 1943, including a spot as 19th man in the beaten Grand Final team.

Essendon played two draws in 1944, against St Kilda and Fitzroy. Against Fitzroy the Dons were one point down with the siren about to sound when Noel Smith marked close to goal and converted. But the umpire ruled that he had run around the mark and made him kick again. This time he scored only a point.

A big last quarter took Essendon to a 49-point win over Footscray in the 1944 First Semi-final, but were blown away in the Preliminary when Richmond slammed on eight goals to nothing in the first quarter, to lose by 21 points.

Essendon missed the finals for the only time in the 40s in 1945, when it suffered a mid-season slump and could finish no higher than eighth.

Essendon players who went to war included Ray Watts, who was taken prisoner after being shot down over Germany, and Keith Forsyth who was a prisoner of war in Singapore and spent two years on the Burma Railway. Other Bombers involved in the war effort included Bill Pearson, Harold Lambert, Keith Forbes, Ted Leehane, Keith Rawle and Chris Lambert.

ESSENDON

Heartbreak Grand Finals

Though enjoying the most successful period in its history, Essendon would still lament the loss of Premierships that should have been won, including two Flags which it effectively lost by one point.

In 1947 the Bombers had several stars unavailable through injury, having to recall Reserves captain–coach Jack Cassin. They were underdogs, but started brilliantly, only inaccuracy denying a bigger lead.

At half-time, it was 8.11 to Carlton's 8.0, and at three-quarter time, the Bombers were still only 11 points clear. With nine minutes to play, Carlton goaled, and the Dons were under siege. Attack after attack was repelled, until with just 44 seconds left on the clock, Carlton half-forward Fred Stafford snapped with his left foot from 25 metres to give the Blues victory by just one point.

Essendon lost only two games for 1948, thrashed Melbourne by 36 points in the Second Semi-final, and was red-hot favourite for the Flag. But again inaccuracy was to prove tragically costly, scoring 2.15 to half-time. Late in the last quarter, Melbourne managed to draw level, 7.27 (69) to 10.9 (69), for the VFL's first drawn Grand Final.

Essendon was supremely confident it would win the replay. Too confident. On a wet, difficult day, it was Melbourne that ran away to a 39-point win.

Reynolds and Coleman lead the rebound

Such profound Grand Final disappointments might have broken a lesser club, but Essendon knew it had the capacity to stamp on this era the dominance its record suggested. And the gut-wrenching losses of 1947–48 were swept away with two of the most conclusive Premiership wins of the day as the Bombers went back-to-back in 1949–50.

The arrival of sensational full-forward John Coleman had solved the one obvious problem the Dons had – kicking goals – and, flaw corrected, his team-mates who had suffered the pain of the previous two years cashed in when it counted most.

Essendon thrashed Collingwood by 82 points in the First Semi-final, but almost blew the Preliminary Final against North Melbourne when its five-goal lead by was slashed to a matter of points before the Bombers regained their composure to win by 17.

But on Grand Final day there would be no respite. Essendon was up against Carlton, the angst of the '47 loss still burning on the Bombers' minds, and their performance was emphatic. After an even first term, Coleman and masterful little-man Bill Hutchison took charge in the second, the Bombers leading by 27 points at half-time.

Ruckman Bob McClure was in control as Essendon continued to score at will. The Dons led by 57 points at the final change and were able to turn their attention to giving Coleman the four goals required for

Coleman's 100th goal, in 1949 Grand Final.

his century. That milestone was reached with just moments remaining. The final margin was a stunning 73-point victory, a Grand Final record.

In 1950, Essendon not only took out the Senior Premiership, but the Reserves and Under 19 Flags as well. The Seniors lost only one of 20 home-and-away games, and this time Coleman finished the year with 120.

Again there was a scare in September, when only a goal in the final minute of the Second Semi-final against North Melbourne put Essendon into the Grand Final, but when it played the Roos a fortnight later, there would be no such flutters. The Bombers rammed on seven goals in the first quarter of a spiteful match, emerging bruised, but with a 38-point victory.

It was Essendon's seventh successive Grand Final (including a replay) between 1946–51, and its third Premiership win in the era.

1947–1951 HONOUR ROLL

Year	Pos	Leading Goalkicker	No.	Best & Fairest	Captain	Coach
1947	2nd	Ted Leehane	50	Bill Hutchison	Dick Reynolds	Dick Reynolds
1948	2nd	Bill Hutchison	52	Bill Hutchison	Dick Reynolds	Dick Reynolds
1949	1st	John Coleman	100	John Coleman	Dick Reynolds	Dick Reynolds
1950	1st	John Coleman	120	Bill Hutchison	Dick Reynolds	Dick Reynolds
1951	2nd	John Coleman	75	Norm McDonald	Bill Hutchison	Dick Reynolds

CLUB NEWS 1947–1951

Essendon suffered an injury hoodoo in 1947 which kept players such as George Hassell, Gordon Abbott and Harry Equid out for long periods, and forced the Bombers on Grand Final day to select Reserves captain–coach Jack Cassin, who had retired from senior football.

The Bombers led North Melbourne by 44 points at three-quarter time of the Round 6, 1947 match, but in an incredible turnaround, were held scoreless while the Roos slammed on 8.4 to win by eight points.

Two goals in time-on of the last quarter of Essendon's final-round 1947 match against Collingwood gave the Bombers double satisfaction in confirming second place and the double chance, and dumping the Magpies out of the finals by half a game.

Veteran big-man Percy Bushby and talented forward Harry Equid left Essendon after the 1948 season. Equid was the Bombers' last true exponent of a disappearing football art – the place kick.

Essendon was criticised for taking a trip to Brisbane mid-season in 1949, but after being thrashed by 95 points against Geelong, won its next 11 games straight, including two finals, to take the Premiership.

In 1949, the Bombers became only the second side, following Carlton in 1945, to take the Premiership having finished the home-and-away games in fourth position.

Champion centre half-back Wally

1947–1951

The Coleman phenomenon

If Essendon hadn't already realised it needed a quality full-forward, the heartbreak of 1947–48 made it blatantly obvious. But even insiders who knew the talent of the 20-year-old from Hastings couldn't have dreamed of just what John Coleman would bring not only to Essendon, but to football as a whole.

Incredibly, Bomber officials hadn't been overly impressed with his talents during practice matches in the previous two years. However, VFL football had an overnight sensation when in his first game of Senior football in Round 1 of 1949 he kicked 12 goals against Hawthorn.

Coleman's spectacular high-marking and prodigious goalkicking, combined with a fierce competitive nature and boyish good looks brought football to a whole new, young legion of fans, who followed him from goal square to goal square.

His fairytale start to League football continued when he brought up his 100th goal in the dying seconds of Essendon's record Grand Final win over Carlton the same season. He won the club Best and Fairest and represented Victoria. It was a debut from heaven.

Far more was to follow. In 1950, Coleman booted 120 as the Dons went back-to-back. He kicked 75 for 1951, 103 in 1952 (kicking 30 alone in the final three home-and-away games), and in his final full year, 1953, he kicked 97.

Neither did controversy leave him untouched. His suspension from the 1951 finals series for four weeks was widely believed to have cost Essendon what would have been the second leg of a Premiership hat-trick. The Bombers could kick only 10 goals in an 11-point loss to Geelong on Grand Final day.

And just as he burst into League football, so was Coleman's career snuffed out with tragic swiftness. In Round 8 of 1954 he seriously damaged a knee in a match against North Melbourne. The masterful full-forward had kicked 14 goals just the week before.

Testament to the Coleman legacy is his career record of 537 goals from only 98 games: nearly five-and-a-half per game, an average second only to Hawthorn's Peter Hudson. He kicked a bag of 14 goals once, 13 twice, and kicked 10 or more 10 times.

But Coleman would again emerge as a pivotal Essendon figure, this time as coach, where his nous and hard edge brought two more Premierships. Popular with the public, successful in business, Coleman remained one of football's heroes until his tragically early death from a heart attack in 1973 at the age of just 44.

Left: Coleman marking against Footscray, and as a magazine hero. **Below:** Coleman suspended on the eve of the 1951 final series.

Coleman marks against Collingwood in the 1950 Grand Final.

Business as usual.

Buttsworth and top forward Gordon Lane were two familiar faces missing when the 1950 season began. Lane kicked a match-winning seven goals in the 1946 Grand Final and 256 in total from 131 games. Buttsworth was one of the League's top defenders in the 1940s, tough but a sound mark and good kick. He played 188 games and won two Best and Fairests.

In July 1950, captain–coach Dick Reynolds broke Richmond legend Jack Dyer's VFL games record of 310 senior appearances.

John Coleman broke his finger in Essendon's final home-and-away game of 1950 against St Kilda, and it remained in plaster during September, save for the Bombers' two finals matches against North Melbourne.

North turned nasty in the final term of the 1950 Grand Final with the game lost; Coleman, Reynolds, Bert Harper, Ron McEwin and Ted Leehane all receiving heavy knocks.

Bomber forward Ted Leehane finished his career with the Dons after the 1950 Grand Final. The fast-moving, high-marking centre half-forward or spearhead kicked 139 goals from 83 games, and played in the 1942, 1949 and 1950 Premiership sides.

After having retired as a player, coach Reynolds caused a sensation by being named as 19th man for the injury and suspension-hit Bombers in the 1951 Grand Final. At 36 years of age, Reynolds came on late in the game and contributed to the Dons' comeback, but Geelong won by 11 points.

ESSENDON

The downturn

After the most successful era in Essendon's history, the fall from grace was swift. Not only did the Bombers fail to compete in the 1952 Grand Final, the first time they hadn't made the play-off since 1945, but they missed the finals altogether, finishing a dismal eighth.

John Gill.

In 1953, Essendon returned to September action, but only for one week, bundled out in the First Semi-final by Footscray. In 1954, devastated by the career-ending knee injury to John Coleman, the Dons again missed out, finishing sixth. They scraped into the finals in 1955, but lost to Geelong by eight points, and finished sixth again in 1956.

Fred Gallagher.

After playing in seven successive Grand Finals (including a draw) from 1946–51, Essendon would have to wait six years before it again made it to the biggest game of the season, this time against Melbourne.

Meanwhile, the club was building up its playing stocks. It had two of the great ruckmen of the time in the talented John Gill, a fine high mark and the awkward Geoff Leek, who matured into one of the finest tap ruckmen of all time. Up forward there were the likes of Fred Gallagher, who kicked 12 goals in a game against Geelong in 1957, and the brilliant flanker Hughie Mitchell, while the centreline was stacked with talent in Peter O'Sullivan, Jack Clarke and Reg Burgess.

Geoff Leek.

North players line up like schoolboys while the umpire counts the heads.

The captain calls a player count

Essendon was playing North Melbourne at Windy Hill for a spot in the 1958 finals when the result momentarily became overshadowed by one of the most sensational incidents seen on a VFL football ground.

North Melbourne's Brian Martyn was felled and was being attended to, 19th man John Waddington ran on to the field as a replacement. After receiving advice from his runner, Essendon captain Jack Clarke asked field umpire Barbour for a count of the North players.

Barbour, under the rules, obliged, but found that there were indeed only 18 North Melbourne players on the field.

What the Bombers had failed to notice was that immediately before Martyn had been injured, North's Albert Mantello had left the field, some distance from the Reserves bench. Waddington was his replacement.

It was only the second time in League history a count of players had been called, but North shrugged off the distraction to record a season-ending 18-point defeat of Essendon. To add to the home team's embarrassment, Bomber coach Dick Reynolds said after the match that he had not issued instructions for the count.

1952–1960 HONOUR ROLL

Year	Pos	Leading Goalkicker	No.	Best & Fairest	Captain	Coach
1952	8th	John Coleman	103	Bill Hutchison	Bill Hutchison	Dick Reynolds
1953	4th	John Coleman	97	Bill Hutchison	Bill Hutchison	Dick Reynolds
1954	6th	John Coleman	42	John Gill	Bill Hutchison	Dick Reynolds
1955	4th	Hugh Mitchell	51	Bill Hutchison	Bill Hutchison	Dick Reynolds
1956	6th	Graham Willey	33	Bill Hutchison	Bill Hutchison	Dick Reynolds
1957	2nd	Fred Gallagher	34	Reg Burgess	Bill Hutchison	Dick Reynolds
1958	5th	John Birt	31	Jack Clarke	Jack Clarke	Dick Reynolds
1959	2nd	Ron Evans	78	Hugh Mitchell	Jack Clarke	Dick Reynolds
1960	4th	Ron Evans	67	Reg Burgess	Jack Clarke	Dick Reynolds

CLUB NEWS 1952–1960

Brilliant full-forward John Coleman topped the century for the third time in 1952, booting 103 goals on some of the wettest, heaviest grounds football had seen for many years.

Essendon thrashed eventual Premier Geelong by 67 points in a 1952 Premiership points match, played in Brisbane in an attempt to popularise the game in non-football territory. Coleman kicked 13. In October the same year, Essendon and Richmond played an exhibition match under lights at the Showgrounds, only the second night game to be held in Melbourne.

In Round 15 of 1953 against Geelong, a dangerously-packed crowd of 41,000 people crammed into Windy Hill, many angry at being unable to see. The Health Commission subsequently cracked down on overcrowding.

Essendon made the 1953 finals, but lost by eight points to Footscray in a low-scoring First Semi-final, 5.11 (41) to 6.13 (49).

Coleman, who missed out on a fourth century of goals by only three, won the VFL goalkicking for the fourth time in his five-year VFL career.

Aboriginal star Norm McDonald left the club for country football in 1954. He played 128 games, mainly on a half-back flank, his lightning pace making him one of the game's most spectacular defenders. He won the 1951 Best and Fairest, played for Victoria in 1952, and starred in the 1949 and 1950 Premiership wins.

1952 – 1960

Jack Clarke

A sporting natural (and brother of Olympic athlete Ron) Jack Clarke joined Essendon at the tender age of 14 and immediately made his presence felt at junior level, winning two Under 19 Best and Fairests.

Lightly-built but courageous and possessed of a brilliant football mind, Clarke made the centre his own and was a spectator favourite. He was also a consummate big-game performer, starring in two Bomber Grand Final wins.

Six times in his superb 263-game career, Clarke finished runner-up in the Essendon Best and Fairest, winning the award in 1958 and 1962.

Clarke captained the Bombers from 1958–64 and played for Victoria every year between 1953–62, captaining the State in three different seasons.

Not quite good enough in 1957 and 1959

A decade that had turned sour began to offer some hope when, after contesting the 1956 finals, Essendon finished the 1957 home-and-away rounds second to Melbourne.

The Demons were hot, but the Bombers stunned them on Second Semi-final day with a nine-goal second-quarter blitz. The lead was enough for Essendon to withstand a bold comeback and win by 16 points.

But Essendon was taught a lesson by the Melbourne side when it mattered most, on Grand Final day – overrun by 61 points.

In 1959, the Bombers came home with a rush, losing only one of their last seven home-and-away games. New stars in spearhead Ron Evans and tough centre half-back Ian 'Bluey' Shelton captured the limelight.

The Dons barely snuck into the finals, but then beat Collingwood and Carlton to make the Grand Final.

But motivation or not, the Melbourne team Essendon confronted on Grand Final day was in line for its fourth Flag in five years, and playing its sixth consecutive Grand Final. It appeared not to matter early on when the Dons, inspired once again by champion little-men Clarke and Birt, led by 13 points at quarter-time.

Bob Suter fails to hold Barassi down.

But the super Melbourne side began to flex its muscle, Ron Barassi kicking three quick goals. The Dons stayed in front until late in the third term, when they conceded three more quick and very costly goals to go to the final change six points down. Disappointingly, that was the end of the contest. Melbourne slammed on six goals to one for the last quarter to run away to a 37-point win. Another opportunity had been lost.

Bill Hutchison

Arriving at Essendon as an 18-year-old wingman, Hutchison would become one of the most brilliant rovers of all time.

Lightly-framed, but lightning quick and with superb skills, 'Hutchy' became the linchpin of some of the club's greatest sides.

He played 290 games for Essendon, not retiring until age 34 at the end of the 1957 season. By then he had won the 1953 Brownlow Medal, finished runner-up in two more, won six club Best and Fairests, captained the Dons since 1951, and played 30 times for Victoria.

Hutchison played in a Premiership in his first season of VFL football. His last game, 16 seasons later, would also be a Grand Final: his 10th. In 1989, the VFL ruled that all players beaten for the Brownlow on countbacks, as Hutchison had in 1952, were to be awarded retrospective medals. Hutchison became a dual medallist. Sadly, he had passed away seven years earlier. His medal was accepted by his widow, Nell.

Coleman was tragically lost to football after seriously injuring his knee in Round 8 1954 against North Melbourne. He had already kicked five goals for the match. Coleman would not play again, leaving amazing career figures of 537 goals in only 98 matches, an average of 5.48.

Essendon scraped into the 1955 finals series by just 0.06 per cent, but lost the First Semi-final to an injury-weakened Geelong by eight points, the same margin by which it had fallen short in the corresponding game two years earlier.

Essendon lost a thrilling but controversial match by one point to Melbourne in Round 14, 1957. The Bombers were penalised for deliberate out of bounds in the dying seconds and the resultant free kick from boundary line sailed through. Angry Essendon supporters pelted umpire Schwab with rubbish and bottles.

Ruckman Geoff Leek, never the most reliable kick, claimed he was hampered by the thick fog at Geelong when he attempted to kick for goal from point-blank range. Somehow he missed!

Star defender Bob Shearman asked to be released to play in South Australia at the start of 1960. When his clearance was refused he stood out of football until Round 11, when he returned to Windy Hill to play out the season.

Essendon defeated red-hot Flag favourite Melbourne in the final round of 1960, but had to play Collingwood the following week in the First Semi-final, and lost another close finish, this time by nine points.

ESSENDON

Bombers go ballistic at the 1962 Grand Final. Inset: John Coleman salutes win.

Fraser and Davis

Barry Davis.

Ken Fraser and Barry Davis were the glittering stars of the 60s. Fraser was an outstanding centre half-forward hailing from the local area who marched straight into the Seniors in 1958 and stayed there. Fraser played in the 1962 Premiership team then won successive Best and Fairests with his marking and ground skills. In his first season as captain, Essendon won the 1965 Premiership, and his absence with a leg injury from the 1968 Grand Final was almost as costly as John Coleman's absence from the 1951 play-off.

Fraser was twice runner-up in the Brownlow Medal, spent four seasons as Bomber captain, and represented Victoria in six seasons. He retired after 198 games before the 1969 season.

Davis, also a local, was a cool half-back, whose dashes out of defence and long-kicking were a key part of a superb half-back line comprising Alec Epis and Ian 'Bluey' Shelton.

In only his second season, 1962, Davis was a star in a Premiership side, repeating the performance in 1965. In 1973, under the controversial 10-year rule, Davis left for North.

Twice Davis was the runner-up in the Brownlow, and he won three Essendon Best and Fairest awards.

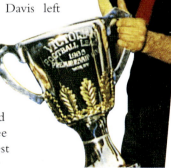

Ken Fraser holds the prize.

1960s: more Flag success

Essendon won two Flags in the first half of the 1960s under new coach John Coleman.

Coleman's first season at the helm in 1961 saw the Bombers slump to seventh, but next year a Premiership came out of nowhere.

The Dons began in spectacular fashion with seven straight wins and later peeled off another run of eight victories on end.

Essendon was a warm Flag favourite against Geelong in the Second Semi-final. The Bombers bolted in the second half, slamming on 7.15 to 1.4 to run away by 46 points. The Cats and Carlton drew in the Preliminary Final, forcing Essendon to wait three weeks between games. But when the Dons took on Carlton on Grand Final day, they were primed.

Ruckman Geoff Leek was a huge source of drive as Jack Clarke, John Birt and Hugh Mitchell tore the Blues apart. Essendon led by 34 points at quarter-time, was still 20 points to the good at the last change, and went on to a 32-point victory.

Just as stunning as Essendon's 1962 re-emergence was its failure to contest the following season's finals, nor to do any better than fourth in 1964. More disappointment looked to be in store in 1965 when the Bombers limped into the last finals spot. Instead, they became only the third team to win the Premiership from fourth position.

The Dons went into the First Semi-final underdogs but thrashed Geelong by 52 points. Then, a fortnight later, they disposed of Collingwood in a spiteful Preliminary Final by 55 points. And on Grand Final day, despite Cinderella team St Kilda's superior season, it was the hardened Essendon which again emerged triumphant, this time by 35 points.

Crucially, the Bombers started better, and although wasting chances, maintained a narrow lead of eight points at half-time. The Dons sank St Kilda with a supreme third quarter which yielded 5.8 to just 1.3 for a match-winning 37-point lead.

That was reduced by only two points in the final term, as a jubilant Essendon bench congratulated Coleman on his second Flag as coach.

CLUB NEWS 1961–1968

New coach John Coleman had his plans for the 1961 season disrupted by a bout of hepatitis, which forced a reorganisation of the coaching panel. After a delayed start to his duties, Coleman assumed the reins.

A long layoff for Essendon ensued from the 1962 Carlton and Geelong Preliminary Final draw. The Bombers tried to keep the players motivated with a varied training program that included sea bathing, various sports and a practice match.

Half-forward Terry Rogers was unlucky to miss the 1962 Premiership after kicking two goals and playing well in the Second Semi-final. He hurt his leg in a practice match against Melbourne during the Bombers' week off.

Veteran big-man Geoff Leek retired before the 1963 season having played a major role in the 1962 Flag. The ruckman played 191 games over 12 seasons and, despite his awkward style, was a superb palmer of the ball.

Vigorous big-man Don McKenzie was reported for striking a boundary umpire during the Round 7 1963 match against Collingwood. The tribunal took only four minutes to dismiss the charge.

Valuable defender Ian 'Bluey' Shelton missed the 1964 season after Shelton, working a tractor on his Avenel property, was hit in the eye by a steel fragment.

Coach John Coleman, no friend of the umpires, was reported twice during the 1964 season. The first time

1961 – 1968

John Somerville down, after a mysterious fainting fit.

The Somerville incident

John Somerville was a tall, deceptively fast and long-kicking half-forward who was a key to Essendon's 1965 Premiership plans. But he missed out on a deserved Flag, and the Dons were forced to rewrite their forward strategies, after Somerville was sensationally flattened behind play just 10 minutes into the 1965 Preliminary Final against Collingwood.

With the ball 40 yards upfield, the forward flanker was sprawled unconscious on the ground, Collingwood opponent Duncan Wright standing impassively nearby. Essendon supporters could scarcely believe their eyes when their attention was finally drawn to Somerville's slumped figure, and Wright, who was questioned by police after the game, was vigorously jeered every time he went near the ball thereafter.

Somerville was taken straight to hospital with severe concussion. The incident, far from unsettling Essendon, seemed only to motivate the Bombers further, and they went on to a resounding 55-point win. But a week wasn't long enough for Somerville to recover from the force of the blow, and he was an unlucky absentee from Essendon's 12th Premiership side.

Near miss in 1968 final

Essendon had a new coach for 1968, former champion centreman Jack Clarke. The Clarke-coached Bombers got off to a great start with five straight wins, then won another string of nine games on the trot, led by the great form of Davis and youngsters like Ken Fletcher and Robin Close.

The Dons had beaten Carlton twice during the season, stumbled badly against them on Second Semi-final day, but got another chance in the big one after comfortably disposing of Geelong. This time they were underdogs; being without injured skipper Fraser, and having to include bespectacled schoolboy full-forward Geoff Blethyn for only his second game.

But on a windswept MCG not conducive to any sort of cohesive football, the 17-year-old excelled, booting four goals on cagey Carlton full-back Wes Lofts. Essendon trailed by 11 points at three-quarter time, got closer still after reserve Bruce Lake marked and goaled, then drew within one point after Blethyn goaled.

There followed only points, and a couple more close shaves, before the siren left the Bombers an agonising three points short. To rub salt into the wound, it was the first time in a Grand Final the losing side had kicked more goals than the victor.

1961 – 1968 HONOUR ROLL

Year	Pos	Leading Goalkicker	No.	Best & Fairest	Captain	Coach
1961	7th	Hugh Mitchell	33	John Birt	Jack Clarke	John Coleman
1962	1st	Charles Payne	39	Jack Clarke	Jack Clarke	John Coleman
1963	5th	Charles Payne	36	Ken Fraser	Jack Clarke	John Coleman
1964	4th	Hugh Mitchell	32	Ken Fraser	Jack Clarke	John Coleman
1965	1st	Ted Fordham	54	John Birt	Ken Fraser	John Coleman
1966	3rd	Ted Fordham	76	Don McKenzie	Ken Fraser	John Coleman
1967	6th	Alan Noonan	40	John Birt	Ken Fraser	John Coleman
1968	2nd	Alan Noonan	51	Barry Davis	Ken Fraser	Jack Clarke

Barry Davis: schoolboy star, long kicker.

was for misconduct in crossing the boundary line during play, the second following an altercation between Coleman and Geelong players in the losing First Semi-final. This time he received a severe reprimand.

Essendon finished the home-and-away season fourth in 1966, but there would be no repeat of the previous season's achievement. The Bombers beat Geelong in the First Semi-final by 10 points, but in wet conditions were thrashed by 42 points by St Kilda in the Preliminary Final.

Veterans Jack Clarke and Hugh Mitchell were sensationally omitted from Essendon's team after just two games in 1967, both retiring immediately. Clarke had played 263 games, skippered the Dons for seven seasons and won two Best and Fairests. Mitchell played 224 games and won the 1959 Best and Fairest.

Essendon unveiled several new stars in 1967 but missed the finals for the first time since 1963, finishing sixth after having at one stage slipped as low as 11th.

In Round 3 of the 1968 season, Essendon humiliated Carlton at a windswept Princes Park, restricting the Blues to a pitiful 1.11 (17) for the game for a resounding 33-point win.

The Dons scored a controversial two-point win over Richmond in Round 7 of 1968 at Windy Hill when half-forward Geoff Gosper snapped for goal, only to watch it scrape the goalpost. But amazingly, the goal umpire signalled a goal, and the Dons hung on to win.

ESSENDON

Ugly brawls at Windy Hill

Essendon was involved in two of the most controversial on-field incidents of the 1970s in successive seasons, both at Windy Hill.

On 18 May 1974, federal election day, the Bombers and Richmond brawled as they left the ground at half-time, after an altercation between Tiger strongman Mal Brown and Essendon's Graeme Jenkin. An unsightly skirmish involving not only players, but officials and spectators, resulted in League and police investigations. Seven people from either club were brought before the tribunal and five suspended.

Essendon runner Laurie Ashley was outed for six matches; fitness adviser Jim Bradley likewise; rugged defender Ron Andrews also got six while John Cassin was cleared.

The following year, a similar ugly scene exploded during the second quarter of a game against Carlton, this time after Essendon's Dean Hartigan and Carlton's Craig Davis had been knocked out. Nine players from either side were reported. Incredibly, the Blues also had time in the second term to slam on an incredible 14 goals, finishing the match with 27, while Essendon's reputation took another nosedive.

The strikers stand by. From left, Gosper, Gerlach, McKenzie, Pryor and Davis.

The players' strike

The Bombers fell to sixth in 1969, and their 1970 campaign was thrown into turmoil before the season even began when five senior players – captain Don McKenzie, Geoff Pryor, Daryl Gerlach, Barry Davis and Geoff Gosper – sought pay increases.

The five had asked the club for three dollars for each training session instead of the standard one dollar, and basic match payments of $40, increases that VFL regulations would not yet allow. The players subsequently submitted their retirements. The whole club threatened to split apart when, on the Thursday night before the first game of the season, the five turned up for training but were not invited to the players' dinner.

McKenzie, Pryor, Gerlach, Davis and Gosper were not selected, and watched from the outer as the Dons lost by 49 points. When several days later, the VFL agreed to increase minimum payments to $35, and the Essendon committee established a testimonial fund, the row was settled.

The pattern of disruption and disappointment, however, had also been set, and a disastrous year finished with the Bombers a dismal 11th. Sadly, coach and club legend Jack Clarke lost the job. His replacement in 1971, John Birt, did little to turn fortunes.

Not again! St Kilda's Carl Ditterich and Simon Madden come to blows.

1969 – 1980 HONOUR ROLL

Year	Pos	Leading Goalkicker	No.	Best & Fairest	Captain	Coach
1969	6th	Alan Noonan	43	Barry Davis	Don Mckenzie	Jack Clarke
1970	11th	Geoff Blethyn	33	Daryl Gerlach	Barry Davis	Jack Clarke
1971	11th	Alan Noonan	31	Barry Davis	Barry Davis	John Birt
1972	5th	Geoff Blethyn	107	Neville Fields	Des Tuddenham	Des Tuddenham
1973	5th	Alan Noonan	63	Andrew Wilson	Des Tuddenham	Des Tuddenham
1974	8th	Alan Noonan	77	Graham Moss	Des Tuddenham	Des Tuddenham
1975	8th	Alan Noonan	48	Graham Moss	Des Tuddenham	Des Tuddenham
1976	10th	Geoff Blethyn	39	Graham Moss	Graham Moss	Bill Stephen
1977	9th	Max Crow	38	Simon Madden	Ken Fletcher	Bill Stephen
1978	10th	Wayne Primmer	47	Ken Fletcher	Ken Fletcher	Barry Davis
1979	5th	Terry Daniher	57	Simon Madden	Ken Fletcher	Barry Davis
1980	7th	Simon Madden	45	Tim Watson	Simon Madden	Barry Davis

CLUB NEWS 1969–1980

The Essendon community was plunged into mourning in 1970 when promising young player Doug Tassell, who had played 20 games, was killed in a car accident.

Geoff Pryor, one of five Essendon players who went on strike at the start of season 1970, resigned as a player after being dropped from the Senior side.

Essendon scored a Round 3 draw with Collingwood in 1971. But the Dons were humiliated in the return game at Victoria Park, the Magpies booting 30.20 (200) to win by a massive 147 points.

In 1972, Essendon celebrated the centenary of its formation with a series of balls and functions to mark the occasion. Long-serving club secretary Bill Cookson retired.

Geoff Blethyn became only Essendon player besides John Coleman to kick 100 goals in a season, finishing with 107, second only to Collingwood's Peter McKenna in 1972.

Essendon mourned another great when John Coleman, only 44, died prematurely from a heart attack at his Dromana hotel days before the start of the 1973 season. Players observed a minute's silence before the first game.

Cans and fists flew during a heavyweight contest at Western Oval between Don McKenzie and Footscray ruckman Barry Round.

Essendon and Carlton set a VFL Park attendance record on Anzac Day 1975 when 77,770 people crammed into the

1969 – 1980

The Tuddy years

Essendon's on-field credibility was sinking fast when it landed the biggest recruiting coup since Ron Barassi's switch from Melbourne to Carlton in the mid-60s. The Dons lured Collingwood legend Des Tuddenham across as captain–coach for the 1972 season, the first 'outsider' to lead the club in over 30 years.

Des Tuddenham.

Almost immediately, a transformation came over Windy Hill. With virtually the same players as the previous season, Tuddy took his new team on a winning streak. Essendon, buoyed by the form of exciting young players like spearhead Geoff Blethyn, centreman Neville Fields and Ken Roberts, led the ladder at the end of Round 10.

That grand early form fell away, and it was only a thrilling last-round victory over Tuddenham's old side at Windy Hill that guaranteed the Dons a spot in the First Elimination Final under the new final five system. Essendon was subsequently thrashed by St Kilda but its rise from 11th to fifth won the club new respect in the football world.

The next year, despite losing star defender Barry Davis and full-forward Blethyn, Essendon finished the home-and-away games even higher, but again lost to St Kilda in the Elimination Final, this time by 67 points.

That seemed to take the sting out of both coach and his team. The Bombers were a disappointing eighth in 1974, and finished similarly in 1975, during which the feisty Tuddenham made his players crawl around on hands and knees at training after one bad loss. Although he had been contracted until 1977, Tuddenham was sacked.

The Baby Bombers

While the 1970s didn't get a lot better for Essendon, under the coaching of Bill Stephen the club managed to unearth a group of highly-talented youngsters, who might at least give some semblance of hope for the future.

In a massive turnover, 15 senior players from 1976 didn't play a Senior game in 1977, as the selectors decided to punt on youth.

While big-man Simon Madden had already been playing at Senior level for four years, 1977 saw his youthful exuberance complemented by the addition of fellow youngsters such as high-flying blond-haired Paul Van Der Haar, Merv Neagle and Shane Heard. Incredibly, in Round 7, the Dons trialled a 15-year-old boy from Dimboola, Tim Watson, who immediately looked right at home playing against men in some cases twice his age.

The youngsters still copped their share of big defeats, but the Dons began to pull off some unexpected upsets against highly rated opposition, becoming stronger still in 1978 for the addition of Terry Daniher, recruited from South Melbourne, and Glenn Hawker.

By the time the club, now under the coaching of Barry Davis, made the finals for the first time in six years in 1979, Essendon could at least look ahead to the next decade with genuine optimism.

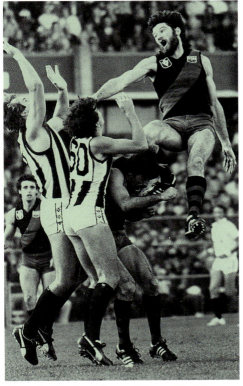

Jumping-jack ruckman Simon Madden.

Graham Moss wins Brownlow

About the one bright spot for Essendon during this dark period in its history was the performance of prized Western Australian recruit Graham Moss. The Claremont ruckman was immediately sensational on debut in 1973, and became one of the VFL's best ruckmen with his smart positioning and brilliant palming of the ball. He was pipped only on the final vote of the evening for the Brownlow Medal by North Melbourne's Keith Greig.

The consistent big-man virtually propped Essendon up for four years. He was equal third in the 1975 Brownlow as his team crumbled around him. In 1976, as his side performed even worse, Moss won the medal outright, the first Western Australian to do so.

Sensationally, within weeks of becoming only the club's third medallist, Moss announced that he was returning to his native state. Essendon was shattered.

---

stadium to watch the Bombers score their fourth win on end to start the year.
The introduction of colour television prompted Essendon to change its uniform for the 1975 season, switching to red shorts for home games. The Dons reverted to black again in 1982.
Little-man Wayne Primmer became a short-lived goalkicking sensation early in 1978 when he three times booted bags of seven goals as a ground-level goal-sneak.
Essendon and St Kilda played a spiteful match at Moorabbin in Round 7 which saw young Bombers Merv Neagle and Terry Cahill knocked out, and after which Essendon president Colin Stubbs accused the Saints of 'playing like animals'.
Essendon was at rock bottom after being thrashed by nearly 100 points by Fitzroy early in 1979, but a players' meeting called by captain Ken Fletcher had a dramatic impact. The Bombers rattled off nine wins on the trot to move to second on the ladder.
After another good start by Essendon to a season in 1980, brilliant but erratic star recruit Phil Carman was suspended for a massive 20 matches for headbutting a boundary umpire at Moorabbin. The Dons imploded once more. They finished seventh with 10 wins – but were 12 Premiership points behind sixth-placed South Melbourne.
Coach Barry Davis resigned at the end of the 1980 season after the Dons failed to make the finals. He was replaced by former Richmond Premiership player and captain Kevin Sheedy.

ESSENDON

Formidable foes. The implacable young Bombers close in on Warwick Capper of the Sydney Swans.

The big turnaround

Early in new coach Kevin Sheedy's tenure at Windy Hill, it appeared little had changed. After six rounds of 1981 the Bombers were a dismal 1–5, with Sheedy suggesting he might even return to the playing field.

That didn't happen, but an amazing Essendon turnaround did. By Round 20, the Bombers had racked up 13 straight wins.

The Dons, thanks to Neale Daniher, then beat Carlton by a point and thrashed South Melbourne by 111 points to register a 15th successive victory, a club record.

Just as stunningly, that was where the party ended. A knee injury Daniher sustained in that crushing win would prevent him playing again for four years. A loss in its final round match against Geelong lost the all-important double chance.

An amazing season ended abruptly with a loss to Fitzroy in the Elimination Final.

The amazing Timmy Watson.

A victory lap of the MCG in 1984 after a stunning last quarter.

CLUB NEWS 1981–1986

Essendon won its first Night Premiership and first Flag of any description since 1965 when it shrugged off a slow start to defeat Carlton by 24 points on a winter's evening at Waverley in June 1981.

Essendon journeyed to the Gabba in Brisbane to play for Premiership points in Round 14, defeating the Hawks by 18 points. They also played the first regular Sunday game at the MCG against Collingwood in Round 18 in front of 64,000 people, winning by 19 points.

Brilliant utility Neale Daniher jogged off Windy Hill in the Bombers' Round 21 1981 thrashing of South Melbourne with what was described at first as a 'jarred knee'. Instead, he required a total reconstruction and didn't play another Senior game for three years.

Essendon won 16 home-and-away games but still missed out on the double chance in 1982. Again it lost an Elimination Final as a result, this time to North Melbourne by 13 points.

Controversy exploded on the eve of the 1983 finals, when the *Sun* claimed that a hitman was operating in the VFL. The finger of accusation subsequently pointed at Roger Merrett. Not only did the big forward reject the charges, he began to play his best football for the club at the same time.

Essendon reached its first Grand Final since the 1968 play-off against Carlton, coming from fifth in 1983, but was humiliated by a record 83-point margin against a hungry and fresher Hawthorn.

1981–1986

No holds barred in the Bombers and Hawks melee.

Simon Madden takes a big one.

Back-to-back in 1985

In 1983, the Bombers finally broke through, defeating Carlton in the Elimination Final, nemesis Fitzroy in a bruising First Semi, then disposing of North Melbourne on Preliminary Final day by a massive 86 points.

The Bombers' first Grand Final appearance for 15 years resulted in one of its biggest humiliations – an 83-point thrashing at the hands of Hawthorn.

Few teams in League history have been as universally acclaimed as the Essendon back-to-back Premiership sides of 1984–85.

The core of the side was by now supplemented with the necessary missing parts – a classy centreman in Leon Baker, a boom full-forward called Paul Salmon and a couple of precocious kids, Mark Harvey and Mark Thompson.

Essendon swept through 1984, finishing on top, and was troubled by only one side – Hawthorn – which defeated the Dons twice in the home-and-away games, and again by eight points in a classic Second Semi-final.

On Grand Final day the deja vu was overwhelming. At three-quarter time, the margin was still 23 points in Hawthorn's favour.

The Bombers were about to unleash one of the most memorable last quarters in Grand Final history. Leon Baker put the Dons closer with a clever snap and Peter Bradbury added another. Minutes later Thompson kicked a goal and, after only eight minutes, Essendon had hit the front when Baker executed a superb blind turn to thread through his fourth goal of the match. At the end it had added 9.6 in a stunning burst that delivered a Premiership and wiped away 19 years of Bomber misery.

Few teams have been as dominant as the Dons in 1985, who lost only three matches out of 24 and finished three games clear on top of the ladder.

The finals proved more of a celebration than a contest as Essendon made short work of Hawthorn in the Second Semi-final by 30 points. Two weeks later, the Bombers went into their third successive play-off against Hawthorn as the hottest of favourites.

Apart from a wild brawl at the start, everything went according to plan. With Simon Madden magnificent in the ruck, Paul Salmon dominant at full-forward and Baker and Watson on fire, Essendon took control. The Bombers exploded with a final-term avalanche of 11 goals, marching to a crushing 78-point win over Hawthorn.

Essendon had won back-to-back Flags for the first time in 35 years, and if that fact alone wasn't enough to enshrine the Bombers' standing in football history, the final 30 minutes of the 1985 season made the point.

1981–1986 HONOUR ROLL

Year	Pos	Leading Goalkicker	No.	Best & Fairest	Captain	Coach
1981	5th	Tony Buhagiar	42	Neale Daniher	Simon Madden	Kevin Sheedy
1982	5th	Simon Madden	49	Terry Daniher	N. Daniher/Ron Andrews	Kevin Sheedy
1983	2nd	Terry Daniher	63	Simon Madden	Terry Daniher	Kevin Sheedy
1984	1st	Paul Salmon	63	Simon Madden	Terry Daniher	Kevin Sheedy
1985	1st	Mark Harvey	48	Tim Watson	Terry Daniher	Kevin Sheedy
1986	5th	Alan Ezard	47	Glen Hawker	Terry Daniher	Kevin Sheedy

Veteran defender 'Rugged Ronnie' Andrews left Windy Hill for arch-rival Collingwood after failing to get a game in the 1983 Grand Final. He played 151 games for the Bombers, earning a reputation as one of the toughest players the game had seen.

Paul Salmon went from relative obscurity to superstardom almost overnight in a spectacular start to the 1984 season. He had 63 goals on the board from 13 games before a serious knee injury that required a reconstruction put him out of action for 12 months.

Essendon won its second Night Flag in four seasons under Kevin Sheedy in 1984, beating the Sydney Swans in the Grand Final by 51 points, 13.11 (89) to 5.8 (38).

Neale Daniher returned to Senior football in Round 9 of 1985 against Melbourne. It was his first game since Round 21 1981. Tragically, just weeks later in a June night game against SA club Norwood, Daniher damaged his knee again, seriously enough to require a third reconstruction.

After achieving back-to-back Premierships, Norm Smith Medallist Simon Madden and coach Kevin Sheedy both turned their back on enormous offers from the Edelsten-backed Sydney Swans to stay at Essendon.

Serious injuries to Paul Van Der Haar, Tim Watson and Darren Williams early in 1986 put the Bombers behind the eight-ball in their bid for a Premiership hat-trick. Essendon scraped into fifth, where it lost a rain-soaked Elimination Final to Fitzroy by one point.

ESSENDON

Three champion imports: David Grenfold, Michael Long and Darren Bewick.

Changes must be made

While the Baby Bombers of 1977 had carried all before them for the best part of a decade, 1987 marked a symbolic change in Essendon's selection policy. Partly through age, but mostly through injury, Essendon's engine room had begun to look ragged.

Tim Watson, Darren 'Daisy' Williams, Simon Madden, Roger Merrett, Mark Harvey and Leon Baker were all cut down with serious injury, and from being labelled one of the greatest teams in history, Essendon in the space of a year had begun to find itself on the wrong end of results: such as a 114-point thrashing and a record 163-point humiliation at the hands of the rampant Sydney Swans in 1987.

Not for the first time, the club turned to youth. The year saw the introduction of the fourth and youngest Daniher brother, Chris, a determined kid from Ringwood called Gary O'Donnell and a tough cookie from the country, Dean Wallis.

Over the following two seasons the club complemented the youth push with some shrewd interstate recruiting. In 1988, Port Adelaide wingman and Magarey Medallist Greg Anderson joined the Bombers, along with relatively unknown but highly-rated Western Australian little-man Darren Bewick.

The next season, South Australian pair David Grenvold and Kieran Sporn arrived at Windy Hill, along with eagerly-anticipated Northern Territory speedster Michael Long. By the time the spectacular Derek Kickett joined the Dons from North Melbourne for the 1990 season, and lanky Sandgroper Peter Cransberg made an immediate impact, the Dons had in short time turned over the core of their team. The result was a rise again from mediocrity to Flag contention.

Gary O'Donnell's promise.

The big letdown

In 1990, with the renamed AFL's first Premiership on the line, Essendon was determined to repeat its capture of the first VFL Flag back in 1897.

The Dons withstood their sternest test yet in Round 19 in a gripping but gruelling slog with Collingwood on a sodden Waverley. The finals beckoned, and in the last game, some senior players were rested.

No one had counted on West Coast and Collingwood tying the Qualifying Final, giving top-placed Essendon an agonising three weeks off. The extraordinary layoff took its toll as the Bombers lost to Collingwood in the Second Semi-final and had an unconvincing Preliminary Final win over West Coast.

It didn't seem to matter 10 minutes into the 1990 Grand Final, by which time Bomber full-forward Paul Salmon had had four shots for goal, kicking two. An ugly quarter-time brawl unsettled the Bombers far more than their opponents, and a series of stupid free kicks and 50-metre penalties quickly gave Collingwood a five-goal lead.

Essendon finished with only five goals in the 48-point drubbing, allowing a hated rival one of its most famous victories.

Greg Anderson chases.

CLUB NEWS 1987–1992

Sydney delivered one of Essendon's most embarrassing defeats when it went on the rampage at the SCG in Round 17, 1987 for 36.20, just two points short of the record score, and thrashing the Bombers by 163 points.

Favourite son Roger Merrett left Essendon for Brisbane at the end of 1987. Merrett's aggression and strength at centre half-forward made him a key to the Premiership sides of 1984–85, and at his best he was considered the most valuable player in the League.

Another Bomber favourite, Leon Baker, retired at the end of 1988. Though a late starter in the VFL at 27, the cool and classy centreman was a crucial part of the 1984–85 Premierships. His fourth, inspirational goal in the '84 Grand Final was one of football's most memorable.

Glen Hawker, also a big contributor to the 1984 Premiership, left Essendon for Carlton at the end of 1988. He won the 1986 Best and Fairest.

A wet winter and a muddy Windy Hill led to some extraordinary scorelines during 1989, including Essendon's five-point win over Footscray despite kicking only three goals – 3.10 (28) to 3.5 (23) – and a thrashing of West Coast in which the interstate visitors were held to a miserable 1.12 (18).

The Bombers made the 1989 finals, the first time in three years, and thrashed Geelong in the Qualifying Final, only to beaten and bruised in the Second Semi against Hawthorn the

1987–1992

The move to the MCG

As a one-time suburban Victorian competition stretched its wings to all points of the country, so had Essendon outgrown the atmosphere-charged but pokey confines of its beloved Windy Hill. Its shift to the MCG for the 1992 season coincided with the opening of the new Great Southern Stand, and would soon prove one of the shrewdest commercial decisions in the club's history as the Bombers' ever-growing membership base flocked to watch their team in comfort.

Essendon's Windy Hill, where the club returned in 1922 after its time at East Melbourne, had been the scene of some of the club's most unforgettable moments, but the move to the game's home not only enabled the Dons to offer far superior corporate and membership facilities and boost its revenue significantly, but also to tailor a fast-running, skilled side more suited to a big finals-type ground.

It was that familiarity which played no small part in Essendon's success early on in its tenure at its new home.

The great duo Simon Madden and Terry Daniher before their last game for the Dons.

All good things must end

Simon Madden carved a niche as one of the all-time great ruckmen in 378 games for Essendon. Terry Daniher completed 313 games, likewise as one of the club's fiercest competitors and greatest leaders. Tim Watson, with 307 games, was one of the greatest ruck-rovers the game, let alone the club, had seen.

When the former pair bowed out of AFL football in the final game of 1992 against Geelong at Waverley, and Watson, a shock retiree 12 months earlier, joined them on a lap of honour, the emotion of Bomber fans was overwhelming.

Between the three of them, they played a tick under 1000 games. Six Premierships. Nine Best and Fairests. All captains of the club. All regular state players. And, of course, the sources of so many fond memories.

No three players symbolised more Essendon's climb from a chopping block of the 70s to a power of the 80s. And few players in the League remained as universally liked by their peers and public. No wonder the Geelong fans were cheering as well.

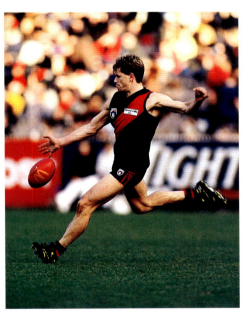
Mark Harvey: courageous.

1987–1992 HONOUR ROLL

Year	Pos	Leading Goalkicker	No.	Best & Fairest	Captain	Coach
1987	9th	Paul Salmon	43	Mark Thompson	Terry Daniher	Kevin Sheedy
1988	6th	Paul Salmon	37	Tim Watson	Terry Daniher	Kevin Sheedy
1989	3rd	Paul Salmon	39	Tim Watson	Tim Watson	Kevin Sheedy
1990	2nd	Paul Salmon	43	Mark Thompson	Tim Watson	Kevin Sheedy
1991	6th	Simon Madden	42	Alan Ezard	Tim Watson	Kevin Sheedy
1992	8th	Paul Salmon	59	Mark Harvey	Mark Thompson	Kevin Sheedy

following week, and cleaned up by the hungry Cats in the Preliminary Final.
Paul Van Der Haar, suspended for three weeks for striking in the 1989 Second Semi-final, won an extraordinary 11th-hour reprieve when the club successfully argued that he had been concussed at the time of the report, and unaware of his actions. But Van Der Haar was still too sick to play and the Dons lost their last chance.
Essendon kicked off the new decade in successful fashion, winning the first trophy of the 1990s and under the AFL banner, defeating North Melbourne 17.10 (112) to 10.16 (76) in the Grand Final of the pre-season night series.
Collingwood and Essendon played to a sold-out Waverley on a Sunday afternoon in Round 19, the match telecast live even in Melbourne. The Dons won the epic struggle by six points.
'The Flying Dutchman' Paul Van Der Haar retired after the 1990 Grand Final, bringing to an end a spectacular 201-game career which netted him 278 goals and legendary status as a 'reveller'.
Essendon and West Coast played one of the games of the 1991 season at Windy Hill, where the Bombers were left with barely a dozen fit players, but the major talking point was the Dons' pre-game tactic of tying down the windsock to keep the Eagles' guessing.
After trailing by 47 points 5 minutes into the last quarter, Essendon defeated Melbourne by one point on Anzac Day 1992. The Dons booted seven goals in 12 minutes, with Wanganeen sealing the match.

ESSENDON

The new baby Bombers of 1993 celebrate the sweetest of victories.

Michael Long: created spark.

The fairytale Flag in 1993

Even the optimists around Windy Hill had trouble seeing the Bombers finishing any better than fifth or sixth pre-season 1993. While the end of a disappointing 1992 had unearthed some promising youngsters, this was a side clearly in transition.

The new breed – star-in-the-making James Hird, silky-skilled Mark Mercuri, schoolboy full-back Dustin Fletcher, speedy wingman Rick Olarenshaw, prolific midfielder Joe Misiti and nuggetty little-man David Calthorpe – had between them played only 11 senior games at the commencement of 1993. Within six months, they would all play key roles in one of the club's proudest moments, along with the un-retired Tim Watson, back for a final fling.

While the potential of the raw, exciting Bomber line-up was quickly realised in a night Premiership win, the Dons struggled early in the season, sinking as low as 11th after seven rounds. The turning point came in an amazing game against Geelong at the MCG, where the freakish Gary Ablett booted 14 goals for the Cats, yet somehow Essendon, inspired by 10 from its own spearhead, Paul Salmon, still managed to win.

There followed a run of 11 victories in the next 13 games. The irresistible enthusiasm of the youngsters and the out-and-out class of players such as Michael Long complemented perfectly the coolness of old heads Mark 'Bomber' Thompson, Mark Harvey and Gary O'Donnell in defence.

Even when half-a-dozen injuries threatened to bring the revival to an end, with a depleted line-up just going down to Carlton in the first-ever night final at the MCG, replacements such as David Flood and Chris Daniher rose to the occasion.

A sterner test still awaited Essendon at half-time of the Preliminary Final when it trailed the upstart Adelaide by a whopping 42 points before a stunned home crowd. Gradually, both it and the Dons found some life thanks to some blistering work in the centre from Long and some sharpshooting from Darren Bewick. Fittingly, it was the returned prodigal son Watson, roving his own miskick, who clinched a famous victory, Essendon having added 11.3 to the Crows' 2.4 after the long break.

The anxieties of Carlton, which had enjoyed a week off, were realised within 10 minutes of the start of the Grand Final, by when Paul Salmon had goaled, and Long followed up with a dazzling run, weave and goal from the wing which had the crowd roaring. The Dons were hot, and by quarter-time already led by five goals.

When a run of three unanswered Carlton goals reduced the gap to five goals late in the third quarter, an instant thumping reply from Calthorpe and another from Misiti were the symbolic nails in the coffin.

The last quarter was a 30-minute celebration, the last act a double from Norm Smith Medallist Long to Brownlow Medallist Gavin Wanganeen for one final goal to make the margin 44 points. Essendon's 15th Premiership had been won.

CLUB NEWS 1993–1996

Essendon won another Night Flag in 1993 when it defeated Richmond by 23 points in the Grand Final at Waverley before a crowd of 75,533.

The Bombers played an amazing draw with Carlton in Round 2, 1993 at the MCG, when Blues' skipper Stephen Kernahan kicked out of bounds on the full from only 30 metres out after the siren.

A dramatic last-minute victory over West Coast at the MCG in 1993, thanks to a Paul Salmon goal, sent coach Kevin Sheedy into a jacket-waving frenzy of delight, a gesture now mimicked *en masse* by the crowd every time the Bombers play the Eagles.

Sheedy coached his 300th game of football with Essendon in 1993, and was officially honoured by the club.

Derek Kickett, whose spectacular brand of football had made him a Bomber favourite, was controversially omitted from the 1993 Grand Final side after having played each of the preceding 23 games. He resigned from the club in protest, and joined Sydney in 1994.

Essendon took out another pre-season Premiership in 1994, this time beating Adelaide in the Night Grand Final by 34 points. It was the third successive League Premiership (night or day) won by the club.

Tim Watson played his 300th game in Round 2 of 1994 against Fitzroy, becoming only the fourth Essendon player alongside Simon Madden, Dick Reynolds and Garry Foulds to achieve

1993–1996

1993–1996 HONOUR ROLL

Year	Pos	Leading Goalkicker	No.	Best & Fairest	Captain	Coach
1993	1st	Paul Salmon	65	Gary O'Donnell	Mark Thompson	Kevin Sheedy
1994	10th	Scott Cummings	32	James Hird	Mark Thompson	Kevin Sheedy
1995	5th	James Hird	47	James Hird	Mark Thompson	Kevin Sheedy
1996	4th	James Hird	39	James Hird	Gary O'Donnell	Kevin Sheedy

Michael Long and Gavin Wanganeen.

The Medallists

Essendon couldn't help winning awards during the mid-90s. A sensational 1993 was capped by inspirational Aboriginal back-pocket Gavin Wanganeen claiming the Brownlow Medal.

Five days later, his close mate Michael Long, in the Year of Indigenous People, took out the Norm Smith Medal with a stunning Grand Final performance. In a year the Bombers took out everything, Tim Watson even won Father of the Year.

In 1994, David Calthorpe capped a magnificent debut for Victoria by winning the E. J. Whitten Medal. The following season Long finished equal second in the Brownlow in his comeback year, and in 1996 James Hird added a Brownlow Medal to three consecutive Best and Fairests when he tied with Brisbane's Michael Voss.

The night the lights blew

There seemed nothing terribly exciting about Essendon's Saturday night game against St Kilda on 8 June 1996, at least until the 22-minute mark of the third quarter. With the Bombers leading a lacklustre contest by 20 points, the Waverley lights went out and a whole stadium was plunged into chaotic darkness.

As players rushed from the field and rowdy fans souvenired point posts and lit bonfires, officials of both clubs, the AFL and the electricity people scratched their heads wondering what to do next.

Eventually, venturing into the previously unheard of, the League settled on a Tuesday night 'conclusion' of two 12-minute halves with time-on, with fans admitted free, and both clubs allowed to select players who hadn't lined up on the Saturday, a decision which enabled the Dons to play superstar James Hird.

Finally, about 72 hours after it started, the longest game in League history ended, Essendon running out a 22-point victor.

The injury toll

Serious injuries, often to key players, seemed to be a curse at Essendon for most of the 90s. None epitomised the jinx more than Long who, just four months after the pinnacle of his career, damaged his knee in a meaningless February 1994 practice match, forcing a knee reconstruction.

The medical room overflowed regularly that year, with Paul Salmon, Mark Thompson, Mark Harvey, Mark Mercuri, Dustin Fletcher, Tim Watson and Rick Olarenshaw all sidelined for lengthy periods.

Little changed the following season when Darren Bewick fell victim to the 'big' knee, and Harvey, Salmon and Thompson all missing for long spells. When the Bombers took on Richmond in a sudden-death final, Bewick, Long and Damian Hardwick were already missing, and Gary O'Donnell, Barry Young and Ryan O'Connor out of action well before the end. Without an interchange, a five-goal lead was turned on its ear as the Dons were worn down by the Tigers.

In 1996, Bewick returned with an astonishing nine goals in the Centenary re-enactment game against Geelong. Tragically, the same Wednesday evening, Long suffered a serious and season-ending knee injury again.

Essendon made it to the '96 Preliminary Final against Sydney without Long, the classy Mercuri or Paul Barnard. During the game, Bewick, Matthew Lloyd, Dean Wallis, Denham, Wanganeen and Hardwick all suffered injuries that would have kept them out of a Grand Final, had the Dons not gone down by a point.

---

the landmark with the Bombers alone.
Essendon and Collingwood played one of the AFL's most breathtaking games, a spectacular draw, on Anzac Day 1995 at the MCG before 94,825, the second-biggest home-and-away crowd in League history.
A major controversy about racism in football exploded in May 1995 when Michael Long accused Collingwood ruckman Damien Monkhorst of racially abusing him, sparking an investigation and the eventual implementation of potentially serious penalties for players who use racial abuse on the football field.
Giant forward/ruckman Paul Salmon left Windy Hill for Hawthorn at the end of 1995, after 13 years, two Flags, 209 games and 509 goals for the Bombers.
Essendon won the first (and what may turn out to be the only) AFL Lightning Premiership, played over an unfortunately wet February weekend as a forerunner to the 1996 night series. The Bombers beat Geelong, Sydney, Fremantle then Brisbane to take the title.
The Bombers were the unluckiest side of 1996. Having to travel to Brisbane for their first final, they hauled back a five-goal deficit but lost by one point after a Gavin Wanganeen shot in the final seconds hit the post. Incredibly, two weeks later it happened again after the Dons had led Sydney by two goals with just four minutes of the Preliminary Final left. Tony Lockett kicked a point after the siren to deny the Bombers a Grand Final appearance.

ESSENDON

The Bombers look ahead

Damian Hardwick in defence.

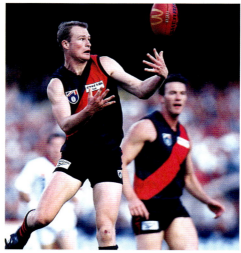
Sean Wellman up forward.

Blake Caracella: midfield talent.

Ryan O'Connor: more to come.

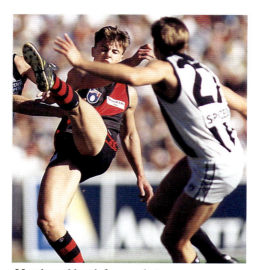
Matthew Lloyd: forward star.

Dustin Fletcher: champion full-back.

Disaster then daylight

Essendon was a clear Premiership favourite after three rounds of the 1997 season. It had outlasted a better-prepared Carlton in a magnificent opening to the year at the MCG, beaten Port Adelaide in the SA club's first home match, then blown away reigning Premier North Melbourne by 42 points in a highly impressive performance.

But no sooner had the pundits begun pencilling Essendon in for at the very least a Grand Final spot, that its season began to crumble under the weight of injuries. The very next week, against Geelong, the Bombers lost Brownlow Medallist James Hird and Norm Smith Medallist Michael Long with serious injuries.

It was the beginning of an incredible run of misfortune which saw more key players like Mark Mercuri, Darren Bewick and Stephen Alessio all miss large chunks of the season. Essendon's performance with such weakened line-ups deteriorated accordingly.

The Dons would win only three of their next 15 games, the dramatic downturn including a humiliating 97-point loss to Fremantle in Perth and a 50-point drubbing at the hands of Port Adelaide – on the MCG, of all places.

There were rumblings off the field as well, as football manager Danny Corcoran departed in acrimonious circumstances, and both assistant coach David Wheadon and recruiting manager Noel Judkins left for Collingwood.

Towards the end of the season it was a different Essendon again. It was a youthful and exuberant combination that racked up wins in three of their last four matches, including an amazing come-from-behind effort to beat Brisbane at the Gabba, and a win over eventual Premier Adelaide in their last game of the year.

While Best and Fairest winner Sean Denham and consistent midfielder Joe Misiti were the engine room for the Dons all year, much excitement surrounded the performance of boom full-forward Matthew Lloyd, who finished the season with 63 goals.

Versatile big-man Scott Lucas and cool-headed forward Blake Caracella both finished in the top 10 in the Best and Fairest, while at the end, the feisty Gary Moorcroft and newcomers like Andrew Ukovic, Chris Heffernan and Daniel McAlister all began to make their mark.

1997

Mark Harvey retires

Although Essendon had already been knocked out of 1997 finals contention, its final-round match at Optus Oval against Adelaide was a huge game nevertheless: the 400th coaching engagement for Kevin Sheedy and the final game for Bomber warrior Mark Harvey.

Harvey debuted for Essendon in 1984 at 19, and helped turn the course of that season's Grand Final after coming off the interchange bench. He finished with 206 games over 14 seasons, a figure which would have been far greater but for shocking injuries, including three broken legs, a serious knee problem and illness.

Harvey had fought the eating disorder bulimia for several years during the late 80s and early 90s, but got his life and career back on track when he was moved to defence from half-forward. He was a key leadership figure in Essendon's 1993 Premiership.

Daniher dynasty ends

When Chris Daniher retired at the end of the season, it meant that in 1998, for the first time for more than 20 years, the name Daniher would not grace the Essendon Senior list.

Chris, the youngest and least feted of the Daniher clan in his early career, became one of the Bombers' hardest-working on-ballers during the 1990s, playing 124 games and a key role in Essendon's amazing 1993 Premiership win.

Chris Daniher.

Terry was the first Daniher to represent the Dons, after crossing from South Melbourne for the 1978 season. He would be joined at Windy Hill by exceptionally-talented younger brother Neale the following year. Anthony and Chris would not join them until 1987, Anthony leaving Sydney after already playing 115 senior games, and Chris arriving from the Daniher farm at Ungarie.

Neale, whose career was ruined by three knee reconstructions, played 82 senior games, Terry finished his League career at the end of 1992 with 313 games to his name, and Anthony retired at the end of 1993 with 224 games. Between them, the four Danihers played 743 League games.

Mark Harvey's farewell and Kevin Sheedy's 400-game milestone.

Kevin Sheedy nears club record

Football coaching is apparently one of life's most tenuous occupations. Try telling that to veteran Essendon coach Kevin Sheedy. The best-known coach of the modern era in 1997 completed his 17th season at the helm of the Bombers, with at least one, and possibly more, years to go.

Sheedy had already established a reputation when he was snapped up by Essendon at the end of 1980. His methods began to kick in as the young Bombers launched a stunning run of victories (15 in a row) and delivered the club's first Night Premiership.

The seal on Sheedy's reputation as a master tactician was set on Grand Final day 1984, when, faced with a second successive Grand Final pasting from Hawthorn, the Essendon coach threw most of his defenders forward, with Bill Duckworth (who would win the Norm Smith Medal), Paul Weston and Peter Bradbury all playing crucial roles in the memorable comeback win.

The master of cunning has carried and exploited a reputation for versatility ever since, and has become something of an ideas man for football in general.

Sheedy has managed to reinvent himself as coach, as well as his teams, several times over during his reign. In 1997, Sheedy again pushed through a talented crop of youngsters upon whom the club's immediate future hangs.

An outgoing and at times eccentric ambassador for Essendon and for the game, Sheedy finished the 1997 season only 20 games behind Dick Reynolds' club record of 420 games as coach. He has coached three day and five night Premierships.

The final game of the season, against Adelaide, was not only the last for Essendon hero Mark Harvey, but the 400th for the Bomber coach. After another memorable victory, Sheedy's 251st from the coach's box, both were carried from the field.

Year	Pos	Leading Goalkicker	No.	Best & Fairest	Captain	Coach
1997	14th	Matthew Lloyd	63	Sean Denham	Gary O'Donnell	Kevin Sheedy

FITZROY

'Fitzroy is not a Club big in numbers, but what we lack in numbers we make up for in goodness, you [the players] are the core of that goodness.'
Len Smith

MY CLUB
by Rick Lang

To a child in the 1970s, Flinders St train station was the heart of football come winter Saturdays. Fanatical supporters of the 12 clubs draped in their team's colours converged here for connections to the suburban grounds of Melbourne. Generations of rivalries fuelled the hopes and anticipation of supporters, creating an atmosphere that can only be generated by a football crowd.

Fitzroy supporters were always the most colourful, the bright colours contrasting against the darkness of the Collingwood and Carlton fans. Our home ground was the Junction Oval on the St Kilda line. I remember counting the supporters, hoping to board a carriage with more of 'us' – though usually there were more of 'them'.

Returning to Flinders St after a victory at the 'Junction' was loud! Scarves and flags flew from windows, the 'red-rattler' shook with elated renditions of our song. If we lost we were quiet but my father made sure we still wore the colours proudly, we still supported.

In defeat we always try.

As long as I can remember we were always outnumbered, but as supporters we made up for it with colour and passion. Almost in defiance I wanted people to know that I barracked for Fitzroy. Only a Fitzroy supporter knows the feeling of being one out, not just in your grade but the entire school. Fitzroy people share a special bond.

Most people consider that Fitzroy supporters have been starved of success, and while this might be true in terms of ultimate success, we are blessed with richer memories than most. Lack of success has given a greater appreciation of victory. Great wins and glorious moments are savoured and remembered in absolute detail. My most treasured and tragic memories are of single goals in games, the 'special goals'.

Allan Ruthven achieved everything at Fitzroy. He won a Premiership and a Brownlow, and in 1952 he won a final off his own boot. He also kicked one of the greatest goals of our history, a desperate last-minute goal in the mud against Footscray in 1953. It was our only score of the day saving us from humiliation. We didn't win but there was a hero to cheer.

Fitzroy kicked a VFL-record score against Melbourne in 1979 and of the 36 goals we kicked that day Harvey Merrigan's record breaker will always be the one I cherish. It was my first 'special goal'. I enjoyed school the following Monday.

Ross Brewer's fluke goal in the First Semi of 1981 cruelly stole what should have been 'my' first final win at the MCG. This was the first time I ever cried at the football. Old timers' hatred of Collingwood is due to geography, mine can be attributed to that moment.

When Gary Pert goaled giving Collingwood the lead against us in 1992 I was devastated. How could 'our' Perty beat us? When Paul Roos replied within a minute a tragic defeat became glorious victory. That's joy!

Haydn Bunton.

FITZROY

Year Established	1883
Joined VFL/AFL	1897
Home Ground	Brunswick St Oval, Princes Park, Junction Oval, Victoria Park, Western Oval
Year merged	1996
Premierships	1898, 1899, 1904, 1905, 1913, 1916, 1922, 1944
Brownlow Medals	Haydn Bunton 1931, 1932, 1935; 'Chicken' Smallhorn 1933; Dinny Ryan 1936; Allan Ruthven 1950; Kevin Murray 1969; Bernie Quinlan 1981
Record home crowd	34,765 v Essendon, 1923
Most games	Kevin Murray, 333
Most goals	Jack Moriarty, 626
Notable supporters	Past: Henry Bolte, John McEwan, Ross Faulkner, Ossie Porter Recent: Bert Newton, John Waters, Barry Dickins

My most celebrated 'special goal' will always be Micky Conlan's winner in the 1986 Elimination Final. Ask any Fitzroy supporter about this goal and it will be replayed with passion and a clarity of detail that will take you to the rain-soaked terraces of Waverley on that jubilant day.

Allan 'the Baron' Ruthven.

Fitzroy fans turn out for the first-ever AFL game in Canberra, 1995.

But the greatest victories were survival itself. The wonderful euphoria of hearing the news that your club has been saved. Precious moments. I defy anyone to tell me a Grand Final win is the ultimate feeling.

Only Fitzroy supporters know the gut-wrenching anguish worrying about the survival of your club. The hours spent hoping for miracle rescue plans. I dreamed of winning Tattslotto so I could rebuild the Brunswick St Oval and bring Fitzroy 'home' where we belong.

Brunswick St, the ground of champions where Trotter, Freake, Bunton, 'Butch' and Murray made us proud. We might not be able to argue with other supporters about great sides but we match anyone champion for champion.

I always dreamed of watching us play at Brunswick St. My favourite memory of the ground is of a training session in late 1993. Hundreds of supporters cheering the sight of a knight in shining armour on a silver horse, symbolising the saviour of Fitzroy. Bernie Ahern, a Collingwood supporter, but still a hero. He gave us the gift of watching our team again. I will never forget the atmosphere that night. I now know the feeling of victory at home. One year later the people of Nauru gave us the same gift. But it was not enough.

'Chicken' Smallhorn.

It is impossible to describe the numbness I felt at Subiaco Oval for Fitzroy's last game. An angelic voice sang Auld Lang Syne and I realised that this was the end. Later that night supporters filled the Brisbane Hotel. The stirring anthem of Fitzroy was sung with more emotion than I remember it ever being sung on the red-rattlers. The song, written over 40 years ago, was never more accurate than this day.

Win or lose, we do or die. This was our saddest loss.

Kevin Murray spoke about the pride he felt to have been associated with Fitzroy, the pride of playing for the supporters, how he was happy that the merger gave Fitzroy the chance to continue playing. He reminisced about all the good things of Fitzroy. Pride and goodness. Len Smith was Kevin's first coach at Fitzroy (Under 19s). Kevin Murray is the epitome of the Fitzroy Football Club.

We sang the song again. Kevin smiled as a tear rolled down his cheek. The proudest of all Fitzroy people supports the Brisbane Lions. Fitzroy will never die.

Fitzroy Fitzroy, the club we hold so dear.

Bernie Quinlan.

Kevin Murray: 1969 Brownlow, 333 games.

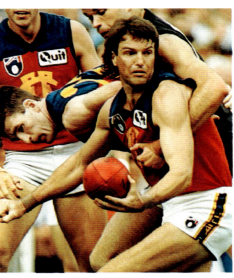
Paul Roos.

FITZROY

It was two in a row in 1899 when Fitzroy defeated South Melbourne by one point.

A club is formed

Fitzroy Football Club was founded on Wednesday, 26 September 1883, when a meeting convened by George Toms unanimously agreed to form a senior football club to represent Melbourne's oldest suburb.

A Provisional Committee worked tirelessly establishing the club. The rules of the Melbourne FC (1879) with some alterations were adopted and club colours of maroon and blue were chosen, forcing the players' jerseys and stockings to be ordered from England.

Players from other senior clubs were enticed, with the majority of the initial team coming from local junior club Normanby. Fitzroy Cricket Club agreed to share the facilities of the Brunswick St Oval and the club established the ground as its home.

The Victorian Football Association amended its rules in February 1884 and accepted Fitzroy into its competition as a senior member. Fitzroy was now ready to compete against its neighbouring districts in the popular winter game.

Years at the top

Nicknamed the Maroons due to their distinctive canvas jerseys, Fitzroy matched their older rivals from its very first season. Led by Paddy McShane and good recruiting, seven victories in 1884 convinced locals the club was a serious competitor.

A new grandstand and cable tram along Brunswick St saw support grow as the team's performances consolidated. Under new skipper John Worrall the team climbed to fourth place with 11 wins in 1887.

Worrall was a nuggetty rover and the club's first star, and was twice named as Champion of the Colony in 1887 and 1890. His absence in 1888 (to play Test cricket) coincided with the club occupying tenth place, its worst ever VFA result.

The committee responded by employing a professional trainer to condition the players, resulting in a climb up the ladder. A memorable season in 1895 saw the club finish on top of the ladder after losing only one game, securing the club's first Premiership. The captain, Tom Banks, known for his fearless play and dashing runs from defence, was widely regarded as the driving force behind the win.

The Maroons take on Geelong in 1902 at the Corio Oval.

Tom Banks: captain 1892–95.

CLUB NEWS 1883–1910

The hot barrackers of Fitzroy rejoiced on 31 May 1884 after the club secured its first victory over a senior club. They defeated Melbourne four goals to one, signalling the young club had come of age.

A Fitzroy v Carlton contest in 1885 prompted one reporter to object to the tactics of both clubs. Fitzroy instructed 'Dummy' Muir to watch Baker of Carlton and the Blues had a player watch Paddy McShane with the four 'taking a lively interest in each other's movements' – tagging had begun!

A tour to the northern districts of NSW in early 1888 saw Fitzroy amass a record score when they potted 22 goals to nil against Newcastle, at Newcastle. Fitzroy also defeated a touring English rugby team in an exhibition match in Sydney.

Blows were struck in August 1889 when Fitzroy secretary C.S. Cock alleged the Fitzroy timekeeper was blocked from ringing the bell at the proper time. Carlton won 6.7 to 5.11 amid claims the last quarter lasted two minutes longer than it should have.

Star forward Jim Grace won his second consecutive VFA goalkicking championship with 49 goals in 1891, including a record tally of 11 against Richmond. Grace was the club's most successful forward in the VFA, bagging 248 goals and leading the club goalkicking seven times.

Jim's brother Mick was declared Champion of the Colony in 1899. The

1883–1910

The glory years

The club in its formative years boasted many leading players and strong local support was reflected with a large membership.

When a mooted breakaway competition was formed at the end of 1896, Fitzroy was one of the first clubs invited to participate and became a foundation member of the Victorian Football League.

Fitzroy began its league career with a win over Carlton, 6.13. (49) to 2.4. (16), but after a mediocre season finished in sixth position on the ladder.

Disappointed, the club adopted a more professional approach to the following season, increasing the players' fitness. The hard work was rewarded with 10 victories in the home-and-away season. The club won its way into the inaugural VFL Grand Final played at the St Kilda Cricket Ground. It led opponent Essendon at every change, winning by a comfortable 15 points. The Grace Brothers, Jim (with two goals) and Mick were the heroes.

Fitzroy defended its title the following season aggressively and entered the Grand Final as favourite. With rugged half-back Pat Hickey defending stoutly, it defeated South Melbourne by one point.

Carlton's Snell leads Fitzroy's McSpeerin (left) to the ball in the 1904 Grand Final.

Fitzroy qualified for the major rounds in the next four seasons, contesting Grand Finals in 1900 and 1903. In 1903 the club played and defeated Collingwood at Moore Park, Sydney, in a game that saw players wear numbers for the first time.

Star of the era was the magnificently skilled and prolific goalscorer rover Percy Trotter. With Trotter and skipper Gerry Brosnan firing, Fitzroy again won back-to-back pennants. Season 1904 began with a 94-point victory over Carlton and ended when the Maroons again defeated Carlton in the Grand Final, this time by four goals.

The following season Fitzroy qualified in second place, and victories over Essendon (43pts), Carlton (27pts) and Collingwood (13pts) in consecutive finals secured them top honours in a memorable season, capped by Percy Trotter being named as the 'Champion Player'.

At the conclusion of the tenth VFL season Fitzroy had contested seven of the nine Grand Finals played and had established itself as one of the most progressive and successful clubs in Victoria.

1897–1910 HONOUR ROLL

Year	Pos	Leading Goalkicker	No.	Best & Fairest	Captain	Coach
1897	6th	Chris Kiernan	11		William Cleary	
1898	1st	Chris Kiernan	18	Mick Grace	Alex Sloan	
1899	1st	William McSpeerin	18	Pat Hickey	Alex Sloan	
1900	2nd	Chris Kiernan	21	Mick Grace	Alex Sloan	
1901	4th	Gerald Brosnan	33		William McSpeerin	
1902	3rd	Percy Trotter	22		William McSpeerin	
1903	2nd	Percy Trotter	27	Percy Trotter	Gerald Brosnan	
1904	1st	Percy Trotter	36	Jim Sharp	Gerald Brosnan	
1905	1st	Alf Wilkinson	30	Les Millis	Gerald Brosnan	
1906	2nd	Percy Trotter	28	Les Millis	Ernest Jenkins	
1907	5th	Jim Sharp	24	Barclay Bailes	Ernest Jenkins	
1908	7th	Wally Johnson	27	Herbert Milne	James Sharp	
1909	6th	Robert Briggs	26	Bill Walker	James Sharp	
1910	8th	Robert Briggs	31	Herbert Milne	James Sharp	

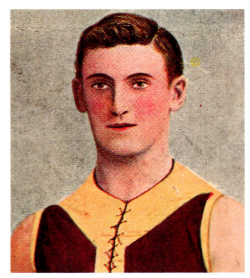

Percy Trotter: superlative form in finals.

popularity of the two was captured in lyric by admiring supporters: 'Other clubs may have their stars; But Fitzroy have their aces; Other clubs may put on airs; But Fitzroy have the Graces.'

The only scoreless quarter in the history of the VFL was played between Fitzroy and Collingwood in 1901. A fierce rivalry existed between the two neighbours, and residents either side of Smith St took a keen interest in their clashes.

Fitzroy and Collingwood played the first VFL game for Premiership points in Sydney when they clashed on 23 May 1903. The Maroons proved too strong, winning 7.20 (62) to 6.9 (45).

In Round 7, 1903 against Geelong, Bill McSpeerin became the first player to represent Fitzroy in 100 league games. Another 109 players achieved this milestone with the club.

Joe Johnson, believed to be the first Aborigine to play VFL football, made his debut on 7 May 1904. He played a total of 55 matches with the Maroons as a flanker, including the 1904 and 1905 Premierships.

Fitzroy annihilated Melbourne on 25 August 1906, recording their first victory by a margin greater than 100 points. Percy Trotter bagged five gaols in Fitzroy's huge score of 17.18 (120). Melbourne managed just 2.1 (13).

'Boxer' Milne and Barclay Bailes became the first Fitzroy players to play for Victoria, in the 1908 Jubilee anniversary carnival. The States and New Zealand contested for a prize named in honour of Fitzroy Secretary Con Hickey.

FITZROY

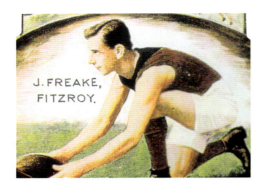

The Unbeatables

Nicknamed the Unbeatables, the Fitzroy team of 1913 produced the most remarkable season in the club's history. Possessing the perfect balance of speed and strength and a deadly attack of Freake, Toohey and playing coach Percy Parratt, it won a club-record 18 matches and the Premiership.

Parratt and Freake had perfected their productive partnership during the 1912 pre-season when Parratt was impressed by Freake's goalkicking accuracy. Parratt's passes were delivered with such precision that if Freake failed to mark the ball his opponent almost certainly conceded a free kick, and Freake usually converted.

The 1913 Grand Final was played before a record crowd of 59,479, who saw Fitzroy start powerfully, leading at half-time 4.8 (32) to St. Kilda's 5 behinds. The Saints rallied to within one point during the last quarter before the Lions steadied with goals to 'Bull' Martin and 'Yorky' Shaw, sealing a 13-point victory 7.14 (56) to 5.13 (43).

Another Premiership in 1916 wasn't quite as convincing. Due to war, only four teams participated in the season: Fitzroy, Collingwood, Carlton and Richmond. The Maroons started well winning their first two games followed by a draw; however, their form fell away and they lost the last nine games of the season.

Luckily, all teams made the finals, and Fitzroy's form improved dramatically, winning its way into the Grand Final. Played against Carlton, the sixth game between the two for the season, the momentum gained carried the Roys to a 29-point victory and the unique distinction of being Premiers and wooden spooners in the same season!

1911–1941 HONOUR ROLL

Year	Pos	Leading Goalkicker	No.	Best & Fairest	Captain	Coach
1911	5th	Bruce Campbell	25	Jack Cooper	Harold Mclennan	Geoff Moriarty
1912	5th	Jim Freake	53	Harold McLennan	Jack Cooper	Geoff Moriarty
1913	1st	Jim Freake	56	Harold McLennan	William Walker	Percy Parratt
1914	3rd	Jim Freake	47	Jack Cooper	Percy Parratt	Percy Parratt
1915	3rd	Jim Freake	66	George Holden	Percy Parratt	Percy Parratt
1916	1st	Tom Heaney	27		Wally Johnson	Percy Parratt
1917	2nd	Jim Freake	37		George Holden	George Holden
1918	5th	Jim Freake	29	Jim Freake	George Holden	George Holden
1919	5th	Bob Merrick	42	Gordon Rattray	Wally Johnson	T. Melling/Holden
1920	4th	Bob Merrick	53	Len Wigraft	Percy Parratt	Percy Parratt
1921	5th	Bob Merrick	32	Gordon Rattray	Parratt/Chris Lethbridge	Percy Parratt
1922	1st	Bob Merrick	47	Jim Atkinson	Chris Lethbridge	Vic Belcher
1923	2nd	Jim Freake	45	Goldie Collins	Gordon Rattray	Vic Belcher
1924	3rd	Jack Moriarty	82	Len Wigraft	Jim Atkinson	Vic Belcher
1925	5th	Jack Moriarty	63	Len Wigraft	Jim Atkinson	Chris Lethbridge
1926	8th	Jack Moriarty	48	Horrie Jenkin	Bill 'Bull' Adams	Vic Belcher
1927	9th	Jack Moriarty	83	Jack Moriarty	Len Wigraft	Vic Belcher
1928	8th	Jack Moriarty	68	Charles Chapman	Gordon Rattray	Gordon Rattray
1929	11th	Jack Moriarty	58	Arthur Batchelor	Charles Chapman	Freake/Ringrose
1930	9th	Charles Chapman	46		Colin Niven	Colin Niven
1931	10th	Jack Moriarty	53		Colin Niven	Colin Niven
1932	10th	Jack Moriarty	81		Haydn Bunton/Sexton	Frank Maher
1933	6th	Jack Moriarty	70		Jack Sexton	Frank Maher
1934	8th	Len 'Apple' Pye	39	Haydn Bunton	Cashman/Fred Davies	Cashman/Wigraft
1935	7th	Dinny Ryan	46	Haydn Bunton	Charles Cameron	Percy Rowe
1936	12th	Haydn Bunton	33		Haydn Bunton	Haydn Bunton
1937	7th	Haydn Bunton	37		Haydn Bunton	Gordon Rattray
1938	10th	Fred Hughson	62		Frank Curcio	Gordon Rattray
1939	8th	Clendon Denning	37		Frank Curcio	Gordon Rattray
1940	7th	Claude Curtin	56		Frank Curcio	Dan Minogue
1941	7th	Claude Curtin	65		Frank Curcio	Dan Minogue

Percy Parratt: in partnership with Freake.

CLUB NEWS 1911–1941

Radical changes occurred when a new committee came to power in 1911. The club's first coach (ex-player Geoff Moriarty) was employed, and the players' uniforms were modernised. The players wore woollen maroon jumpers with a navy yoke and white shorts in all games.

A fire in the cricket pavilion in August 1913 destroyed the football club's five hard-won Premiership pennants, including the 1895 pennant, the first flag awarded to any team for a Premiership win.

Fitzroy was able to redecorate the new room with a great end to the 1913 season. The team took the Premiership and Jimmy Freake topped the VFL goal-kicking list with 56 majors. One trophy not allowed inside was the prize awarded to 'Yorky' Shaw for his sterling play in the Grand Final – a bicycle!

Bob 'Bloater' Merrick bagged 12 goals as Fitzroy thrashed Melbourne by 125 points in Round 14, 1919. Merrick's dozen was the most scored by a player at Brunswick St and helped the Maroons to its first 20-goal score.

A contingent of 53 players and officials went on a mid-season holiday to Perth in 1922. Travelling by train, a four-day journey, Fitzroy played matches in Perth and Kalgoorlie for a 2–2 result, before returning home in time to defeat the Magpies 11.13 (79) to 9.14 (68) in the Grand Final.

A record crowd of 34,765 somehow managed to squeeze into the

1911 – 1941

Another good year: Fitzroy beat Collingwood to win its seventh VFL Flag.

1922 – a seventh VFL Premiership

Fitzroy gained a fearsome reputation with its barnstorming performances in 1922. Big and strong, it simply outmuscled its opposition, earning the tag 'The Man's Team'. Players like Len Wigraft and Chris Lethbridge took Fitzroy into the Grand Final against bitter rival Collingwood with a direct no-nonsense style. Lethbridge in particular preferred to run through his opponent rather than go around him! Trailing at half-time, it was the old firm of Parratt and Freake who swung the game Fitzroy's way. The duo produced a devastating third quarter and combined to score seven goals, helping the Roys to an 11-point victory and their seventh VFL Flag.

Medals, medals, medals

Even when looking at a still photograph the elegance and grace of Haydn Bunton is obvious. He won a remarkable three Brownlow Medals, one in each of his first two seasons (1931 and 1932) and another in 1935, averaging over a vote per game for his entire career. A move to Western Australia in 1938 saw him win three Sandover Medals, making him the most decorated player in the history of the code.

Bunton was definitely the brightest, but not the only Fitzroy star or medallist in the 1930s. 'Chicken' Smallhorn claimed the Brownlow in 1933 with his dashing wing play. A grand clubman, he played 150 games for the club he dearly loved. Wingman Doug Nicholls crossed to Fitzroy from Northcote after winning the VFA's equivalent award in 1929 and 1930, and Jack Sexton came to the club as winner of the 1931 Magarey Medal.

'Dinny' Ryan impressed the umpires with his fine overhead marking and won the 1936 Brownlow Medal, the fifth to a Fitzroy player in six seasons!

Haydn Bunton with Fitzroy legends Percy Trotter (left) and Con Hickey.

Bunton's 1931 Brownlow certificate.

Brunswick St Oval in June 1923. The ones who could see any of the play saw Fitzroy defeat Essendon by 23 points.
According to Roy Cazaly, Gordon Rattray invented the torpedo punt while a student at Wesley College. Rattray played 87 games for Fitzroy, captaining the side in 1923, and again in 1928 as a playing coach.
In the first-round Fitzroy v Carlton match in 1924 both sides piled on over 100 points each, the first occurrence of this in VFL. Jack Moriarty bagged seven goals and ended his first season in the maroon and blue with a record 82 goals.
Googly-eyed Moriarty equalled the club record of 12 goals in 1928 against North Melbourne at Arden St. His career tally of 626 goals remains a club record, as does his nine club goalkicking awards.
Aboriginal wingman Doug Nicholls joined Fitzroy in 1932, fresh from tent boxing with Jimmy Sharman. Sharman agreed to release him on the condition that the club found him a job. He became assistant curator at the Brunswick St Oval.
Searching for an aggressive mascot to replace the Maroons tag, the club agreed to a suggestion from Dr Cec Raphael, so from 1939 the inspiring cry of 'Carn the Gorillas' was yelled by the Fitzroy faithful.
The close of the 1941 season saw the addition of a navy FFC monogram to the jumper with the yoke going straight across the chest instead of being pointed.

FITZROY

The Gorillas' 1944 Premiership team.

Fred Hughson: an inspirational leader.

Premiers in 1944

Piece by piece Secretary Perce Mitchell rebuilt the Fitzroy team at the beginning of the 1940s. He assembled a team of exciting youngsters and surrounded them with experienced players that he recruited from other clubs. The jigsaw was complete at the end of 1942 when Fred Hughson accepted the offer to be captain-coach of the team – an offer that shocked Hughson but one he accepted.

Hughson was greatly admired at Fitzroy as a man and as a footballer. Fearless, he always protected his smaller team-mates and had a booming kick. His leadership was inspirational and his teams played with great spirit and loyalty.

Mitchell's hard work was rewarded with the 1944 pennant. The Grand Final, against Richmond, remains the fondest memory for those supporters lucky enough to have witnessed it. The stories tall and true from that day are legend.

Despite a tram strike and oppressive heat, 43,000 people crammed into the Junction Oval for the game. Richmond, coached by Jack Dyer, had been installed by the press as favourites for the Flag.

Hughson gambled and chose to kick against the wind in the first quarter, a move that paid off as a pumped-up Fitzroy only trailed by one goal at quarter time. It was a close game and fiercely physical all day but once in front, Fitzroy refused to give in.

Giant ruckmen Bert Clay was unstoppable, providing plenty of ball for the rovers. Bruce Calverley dominated the midfield with Ken Sier and Keith Stackpole dangerous up forward. Hughson at full-back kept Jack Dyer to one goal and Fitzroy recorded a joyous 15-point victory.

The people of Fitzroy celebrated the victory, with premiership dinners and dances stretching out over the weeks that followed. Hughson's gamble had paid off and Fitzroy had triumphed again.

The Baron

Allan Ruthven, nicknamed after nobility, played like an aristocrat for 15 grand seasons. A local schoolboy star, the Baron came to Fitzroy in 1940 and was later granted the prized No. 7 guernsey (in 1945) worn by childhood hero Haydn Bunton. Like Bunton, he was a brilliant and courageous rover.

In his 222 games he achieved every honour available to a footballer. He was a member of the 1944 Premiership team, winning his first of five Best and Fairest awards that season as well leading the goalkicking. He captained and coached Fitzroy and represented Victoria on 17 occasions. His artistry and fairness were rewarded with a Brownlow Medal in 1950.

CLUB NEWS 1942–1966

Club stalwart Frank Curcio led the RAAF team to the 1942 Inter-Services League Premiership at the Brunswick St Oval in what could be deemed Fitzroy's unofficial 10th flag. The team contained no fewer than nine 'Royboys, including Norm Hillard and Len Smith.

Captain–coach Fred Hughson had no time for a breather at half-time of the 1943 match against South Melbourne. The crowd at Brunswick St were treated to a challenge between four footballers and two American servicemen to see who could propel their code's ball the furthest. Hughson set an official world record with his drop kick measuring 89 yards 11 inches!

1944 was a stellar year for Fitzroy. It kicked its highest score in Round 11, 25.29 (179), helping it to a 123-point victory over Geelong and a record season percentage of 131.2. The Premiership 'double' was achieved for the only time the Seniors defeated Richmond 9.12 (66) to 7.9 (51) a week after the Reserves defeated Collingwood 11.12 (78) to 9.9 (63).

Frank Curcio became the first player to play 200 games for the club, in Round 2, 1946. Unfortunately the team lost to Collingwood at Victoria Park.

With Vic Chanter at full-back Fitzroy were the only team to hold the great John Coleman goalless in his VFL career in the Round 10 match in 1952 at Brunswick St, helping the 'Roys to a 52-point victory.

1942–1966

Fitzroy's characters

Master coach Len Smith's football principles and philosophies continue to influence coaches to this day. His coaching career began at Fitzroy with the Under 19s and he became senior coach from 1958 until 1962.

His astute coaching is regarded as the main reason behind Fitzroy's success during this period. He spent hours preparing for games, developing elaborate strategies to confuse opponents. His teams were fast and used the flip pass with great effect, often beating teams with greater ability.

The players at Fitzroy respected him deeply, but were not averse to a bit of a lark. The introduction of television coincided with an era of great showmen and larger-than-life characters in the last great production at Brunswick St.

Big Norm Johnstone and 'Butch' Gale greeted visiting teams in their own special way, while Vic Chanter was employed to guard the opposition stars!

The 'Baron' played a starring role, while club darling Billy Stephen performed as the straight man with his reliability in the back-pocket.

Tony Ongarello's high flying marks dazzled the crowds, but his kicking provided the comic relief. Kevin Wright's routine included brushing his teeth at half-time.

Even the audience provided cameos, celebrating each of Owen Abrahams' goals in song: 'Abby, Abby my boy.'

The club jumper got into the act, improving its image with a change to a white monogram in 1956, the same year Kevin Murray won his first Best and Fairest and developed his liking for the microphone.

The team entered the big stage of finals in 1958 and 1960, but the night Premiership in 1959 was their greatest prize of the era.

As with all great shows the end must come. Sadly 1966 was the finale for Brunswick St and the curtain closed on a magnificent theatre.

Len Smith instructs Graham McKenzie, Kevin Murray, Butch Gale and Kevin Wright.

1942–1966 HONOUR ROLL

Year	Pos	Leading Goalkicker	No.	Best & Fairest	Captain	Coach
1942	5th	Claude Curtin	61		Maurie Hearn	Dan Minogue
1943	3rd	Jack Grant	42	Fred Hughson	Fred Hughson	Fred Hughson
1944	1st	Allan Ruthven	46	Allan Ruthven	Fred Hughson	Fred Hughson
1945	6th	Allan Ruthven	42	Allan Ruthven	Fred Hughson	Fred Hughson
1946	8th	Claude Curtin	56	Allan Ruthven	Fred Hughson	Fred Hughson
1947	3rd	Eddie Hart	64	Norm Johnstone	Fred Hughson	Fred Hughson
1948	7th	Eddie Hart	61	Allan Ruthven	Allan Ruthven	Charles Cameron
1949	7th	Eddie Hart	53	Allan Ruthven	Norm Smith	Norm Smith
1950	5th	Eddie Hart	50	Bill Stephen	Allan Ruthven	Norm Smith
1951	5th	Eddie Hart	65	Vic Chanter	Allan Ruthven	Norm Smith
1952	3rd	Tony Ongarello	50	Neville Broderick	Allan Ruthven	Allan Ruthven
1953	6th	Joe Hickey	40	Don Furness	Allan Ruthven	Allan Ruthven
1954	11th	Allan Ruthven	31	Bill Stephen	Allan Ruthven	Allan Ruthven
1955	9th	Norm Johnstone	32	Don Furness	Bill Stephen	Bill Stephen
1956	8th	Tony Ongarello	33	Kevin Murray	Bill Stephen	Bill Stephen
1957	11th	Owen Abrahams	31	Graham Campbell	Bill Stephen	Bill Stephen
1958	4th	Tony Ongarello	53	Kevin Murray	Alan Gale	Len Smith
1959	5th	Kevin Wright	43	Ron Harvey	Alan Gale	Len Smith
1960	3rd	Kevin Wright	36	Kevin Murray	Alan Gale	Len Smith
1961	5th	Owen Abrahams	32	Kevin Murray	Alan Gale	Len Smith
1962	10th	Wally Clark	21	Kevin Murray	Owen Abrahams	Len Smith
1963	12th	Gary Lazarus	35	Kevin Murray	Kevin Murray	Kevin Murray
1964	12th	Kevin Murray	27	Kevin Murray	Kevin Murray	Kevin Murray
1965	11th	Gary Lazarus	32	Norm Brown	Ralph Rogerson	Bill Stephen
1966	12th	Gary Lazarus	43	Norm Brown	Rogerson/John Hayes	Bill Stephen

After 11 behinds in a row it was worth a try! Placing the ball on the ground Tony Ongarello stepped back, drew a breath, ran in and booted a goal. He liked it and so did the crowds. They counted his paces 10,9,8 – with every place kick until the last one, in Round 4, 1955.

The Lion became the official emblem of the club at the 1957 annual meeting.

The king of all beasts was chosen to reflect the club's 'never-say-die spirit' and give it a more aggressive image.

Len Smith had a dream start to his league coaching career with a 120-point victory over North Melbourne in 1958, 23.21 (159) to 5.9 (39), before taking the Lions into the finals that season.

A Night Premiership was won by Fitzroy in 1959 when they defeated Hawthorn 10.10 (70) to 4.16 (40) at the Lakeside Oval. Kevin Wright with four goals was the hero.

The 1960 Second Semi-final between Fitzroy and Melbourne saw the first and only occurrence of brothers, Len and Norm Smith, coaching opposing sides in a final. Unfortunately younger brother Norm won the family battle for the Demons.

A better result in 1960 was achieved by ex-player Laurie Morgan (33 games 1937–39) when he won two gold medals in the Equestrian event at the Rome Olympics.

The last-ever League match at the Brunswick St Oval saw St Kilda 17.22 (124) defeat Fitzroy 5.10 (40) on 20 August 1966, bringing to an end Fitzroy's 83-year association with the ground.

FITZROY

Kevin Murray, lionheart

As Kevin Murray stepped on to the ground for the 300th time his adoring fans raised a banner that read: 'Fitzroy is my life' – a fitting tribute to a man who devoted his heart and soul to the Fitzroy Football Club.

The most celebrated career in the history of the club had its origin in 1955, when as a 16-year-old, his determination was rewarded with his first senior game. His trademark tattoos and ferocious style of play thrilled supporters. Playing as a half-back flanker his long arms and excellent judgement allowed him to out mark taller opponents.

For 18 seasons he drove himself relentlessly, his braveness and courage never doubted once in 374 games for club and State. Even a debilitating back injury which forced him to play in a back brace couldn't diminish his performances.

Only playing in two finals, he cherished the opportunity to play for Victoria. The highlight of his career came in 1969 when he proved to be one of the all-time most popular winners of the Brownlow Medal. The old warrior was genuinely respected by all football supporters.

His durability allowed him to retire at the end of 1974 as the VFL games record holder. That record has since been passed, but his grand contribution to Fitzroy is reflected in the club record books:

Kevin Murray: popular Brownlow Medallist.

Most matches (day)	333
Most Best and Fairests	9
Most matches as captain	159
Most Brownlow votes	178
Most consecutive matches	168
Most interstate matches	24

Superboot

Bernie Quinlan was the ultimate football all-rounder, who crossed to Fitzroy in 1978. His impact on a struggling team was stunning and immediate. He is the only man to kick 100 goals in a season, play 300 games and win a Brownlow, achieving all of these milestones after his 30th birthday.

Tall and versatile he could play in every position. His Brownlow year in 1981 saw him playing as a ruck-rover, but it was as a forward that he was most dangerous. With a classical kicking style he propelled his towering torpedo punts as high as the clouds, enabling him to score goals from anywhere.

Quinlan's superboot defies a young Silvagni.

The Lion kings

Fitzroy and Richmond clashed in the first ever Sunday match, played before royalty at the MCG on 5 April 1970. The Sunday game was something of a novelty and attracted a large crowd.

Appearing after half-time groomed and showered, the players were introduced to the Queen and the Royal party by a nervous President Ern Joseph, who was forced to improvise many of their names! Princess Anne said to Richmond's Bill Barrot, 'I understand there were a couple of punch-ups before we got here. Do you think there will be any more?'

The Lions were Kings of the day, winning 16.20 (116) to the Tigers' 14.12 (96).

Club president Ern Jospeh introduces the players to the Queen.

CLUB NEWS 1967–1985

Fitzroy began a new life playing home games at Princes Park, Carlton in 1967 and added a lion to the left breast of the players' jumpers. Another move in 1970 saw the club play their home games and set up their administrative base at the Junction Oval in St Kilda.

Carlton travelled to the Junction Oval in the last round of 1971 requiring a victory to make the finals. Heavy fog engulfed the ground after half-time making vision almost impossible. Fitzroy adjusted better, winning 15.15 (105) to 11.16 (82), thanks to some innovative and selective lighting arrangements when kicking for goal.

Kevin Murray played his 300th match for Fitzroy in Round 11, 1973 versus Geelong at Kardinia Park. The Cats won 16.8 (104) to 11.15 (81), but as usual Kevin was among the best players.

More uniform changes in 1974 with red and gold replacing maroon and white in readiness for colour television; gold shorts were even worn in away games with matching hooped socks.

With Harvey Merrigan at full-back, Fitzroy ended Peter McKenna's VFL-record streak of scoring a goal in 120 consecutive games in Round 4, 1974.

The appointment of Graham Campbell as caretaker coach during the 1974 season led to the only ever occurrence of two players coaching each other in VFL/AFL history. Kevin Murray coached Campbell in 1963 and was still playing when Campbell took over in 1974.

1967 – 1985

The glamour team

Fitzroy bounced back into the spotlight in 1979 with big-name recruits Quinlan, Walls and Richardson. The courageous rover Garry Wilson, in his ninth season with the club, came within one vote of winning the Brownlow Medal. In 1979 the team won 15 games (many by large margins), including a club-record nine in a row. Crowds of more than 50,000 flocked to VFL Park to see Fitzroy take on top teams Carlton and Collingwood. The highlight of the year was the 81-point thrashing of Essendon in the Elimination Final, the club's first final victory since 1952.

Fitzroy entered the 1980s as the glamour side of the competition. Quality players Wilson, Micky Conlan and Laurie Serafini had the Lions playing attractive football and new coach Robert Walls took them into the finals in 1981, '83 and '84.

The club celebrated its centenary in 1983. Bernie Quinlan became the first Fitzroy player to kick 100 goals in a season and his heroic last-quarter in the Qualifying Final against eventual Premiers Hawthorn almost took Fitzroy all the way.

Courageous rover Garry Wilson.

Finals Fights

The 1978 Night Grand Final provided a fairytale result. Opponents North Melbourne, the reigning day Premiers, were regarded as the giant of the competition but were slain by underdog Fitzroy. Led by its band of unknown youngsters and the unwanted Robert Walls, the Lions scored the last 13 goals, creating a record winning margin of 76 – 13.18 (96) to 2.8 (20).

In 1979 Fitzroy reached the day finals for the first time since 1960, missing out on the double chance through a last round loss to Geelong at Kardinia Park, in a game in which they were leading by 27 points with only 10 minutes to play. They came back and crushed Essendon in the Elimination Final but then fell to Collingwood in the First Semi.

After a shocker of a year in 1980, Fitzroy finished in fifth position in 1981 and history repeated itself when they defeated Essendon in the Elimination Final, and again lost to Collingwood in the First Semi-final, this time by one frustrating point.

Collingwood was Fitzroy's nemesis again in 1984, beating Fitzroy in the Elimination Final. It was the ninth Fitzroy finals loss at the MCG, the fifth inflicted by the Magpies.

```
A VFL RECORD
              G    B    P
FITZROY      36   22   238
MELBOURNE     6   12    48
```

What a win!

The Fitzroy v Melbourne clash in Round 17, 1979 at VFL Park provided the club with two VFL records. Bobby Beecroft kicked 10 goals in Fitzroy's 36.22 (238) to 6.12 (48) victory. Harvey Merrigan kicked the goal that secured the VFL record for the highest score in a game on the way to a record winning margin of 190 points.

1967 – 1985 HONOUR ROLL

Year	Pos	Leading Goalkicker	No.	Best & Fairest	Captain	Coach
1967	11th	Gary Lazarus	36	Norm Brown	Kevin Murray	Bill Stephen
1968	11th	Doug Searl	36	K. Murray/John Murphy	Kevin Murray	Bill Stephen
1969	10th	Doug Searl	77	Kevin Murray	Kevin Murray	Bill Stephen
1970	9th	Alex Ruscuklic	49	John Murphy	Kevin Murray	Bill Stephen
1971	6th	John Murphy	47	John Murphy	Kevin Murray	Graham Donaldson
1972	8th	Garry Wilson	37	Garry Wilson	Kevin Murray	Graham Donaldson
1973	8th	Garry Wilson	43	John Murphy	John Murphy	Graham Donaldson
1974	11th	David Wall	35	Harvey Merrigan	John Murphy	Donaldson/Campbell
1975	9th	Renato Serafini	34	Warwick Irwin	John Murphy	Kevin Rose
1976	11th	John Murphy	35	Garry Wilson	John Murphy	Kevin Rose
1977	10th	Bob Beecroft	59	John Murphy	John Murphy	Kevin Rose
1978	9th	Bob Beecroft	65	Garry Wilson	Harvey Merrigan	Graham Campbell
1979	4th	Bob Beecroft	87	Garry Wilson	Ron Alexander	Bill Stephen
1980	12th	Bob Beecroft	63	Garry Wilson	Ron Alexander	Bill Stephen
1981	4th	Bernie Quinlan	73	Ron Alexander	Garry Wilson	Robert Walls
1982	6th	Bernie Quinlan	53	Matthew Rendell	Garry Wilson	Robert Walls
1983	4th	Bernie Quinlan	116	Matthew Rendell	Garry Wilson	Robert Walls
1984	5th	Bernie Quinlan	105	Ross Thornton	Garry Wilson	Robert Walls
1985	9th	Bernie Quinlan	84	Paul Roos	Matthew Rendell	Robert Walls

Graham Campbell coached Fitzroy to the 1978 night Flag, giving him a hand in every Fitzroy Premiership in any grade between 1945 and 1981. He played in the 1955 Under 19s and 1959 Night Premierships, and coached the Reserves to the 1974 Premiership.

Season 1979 was a record-breaking year for the Lions. They amassed 2699 points in the home-and-away rounds, with their high scoring continuing into the finals. Their first-quarter total of 9.4 (58) in the Elimination Final was a VFL record, and their 81-point winning margin over Essendon was the greatest winning margin achieved by the club in any finals game.

Fitzroy inflicted the greatest-ever defeat over a team on top of the ladder when they thrashed North Melbourne by 150 points in Round 13, 1983 at the Junction Oval. The win boosted Fitzroy's percentage enough to take over as league leader.

The Fitzroy club celebrated its Centenary year in 1983 with teams from all three grades playing off in the finals for the only time ever. Bernie Quinlan also became the first Fitzroy player to kick a ton in a season, when he slotted 116 goals.

Bernie continued kicking goals in 1984. His 11 at the MCG against North Melbourne in Round 21 helped him reach his second ton a week later in the last-ever game at the Junction Oval. Fitzroy defeated St Kilda in a day when three results went the club's way, lifting it into the finals after being in last position at the halfway mark of the season.

FITZROY

Roos Roos Roos

In 269 games for Fitzroy, Paul Roos' attacking style of play redefined the role of centre half-back in league football. An excellent high mark with an uncanny ability to 'read the play', he repelled opposition attacks at will. His amazing stamina allowed him to roam all over the ground gathering bucketloads of possessions which he delivered with precision. His play was so damaging to other sides that they were forced to tag him in a bid to curb his influence on games. Always backing him up was full-back Gary Pert. The two developed a great partnership and together led Fitzroy to many stirring victories with attacking defence.

Paul Roos arrived at the Junction Oval in 1980, a Doncaster youngster zoned to play with the Lions. He began in the Under 19s and made his debut in the Seniors in 1982 on the wing before he went on to play centre half-back. In 1986 he came within one vote of winning the Brownlow Medal. The umpires overlooked him in the final game of the season against Sydney, in which many commentators rated him best on ground.

Bernie Quinlan and Bernie Harris celebrate the Lions' win in the 1986 First Semi-final.

The last finals fling

Emotion is such a powerful force it can sometimes produce superhuman efforts. In 1986 it drove Fitzroy, close to extinction, to one last shot at glory. Clawing their way into the finals it met reigning champs Essendon in a torrid Elimination Final, stealing victory in the dying seconds with a Micky Conlan goal. Another nailbiter followed, and once again the Lions pushed themselves to victory. Limping into the Preliminary, battered and bruised, it threw everything at the Hawks before going down courageously. Fitzroy's Michael Reeves was knocked out by Robert DiPierdomenico almost before the game began and injuries took their toll during the game with both full-back Gary Pert and captain Matt Rendell reduced to hobbling pace. The injury-depleted Roys were gallant, but went down by 56 points.

The dream was over but the supporters' hearts were swollen with pride by a team that refused to let their club die without a fight.

Paul Roos: 14 years with Fitzroy.

1986–1996 HONOUR ROLL

Year	Pos	Leading Goalkicker	No.	Best & Fairest	Captain	Coach
1986	3rd	Richard Osborne	62	Paul Roos	Matthew Rendell	David Parkin
1987	11th	Richard Osborne	62	Scott McIvor	Matthew Rendell	David Parkin
1988	12th	Richard Osborne	60	Darren Kappler	Paul Roos	David Parkin
1989	6th	Richard Osborne	68	Gary Pert	Paul Roos	Rod Austin
1990	12th	Paul Roos	49	Scott Clayton	Paul Roos	Rod Austin
1991	14th	Darren Wheildon	29	Paul Roos	Richard Osborne	Robert Shaw
1992	10th	Richard Osborne	58	Paul Roos	Paul Roos	Robert Shaw
1993	11th	Alastair Lynch	68	Alastair Lynch	Paul Roos	Robert Shaw
1994	14th	Darren Wheildon	26	Paul Roos	Paul Roos	Robert Shaw
1995	16th	Chris Johnson	25	Brad Boyd	Brad Boyd	B. Quinlan/A. McConnell
1996	16th	Anthony Mellington	22	Martin Pike	Brad Boyd	M. Nunan/A. McConnell

CLUB NEWS 1986–1996

Fitzroy and Essendon battled out the closest Elimination Final in history with the Lions winning by one point in 1986, 8.10 (58) to 8-9 (57). A five-point victory over the Sydney Swans the following week at the MCG was to be Fitzroy's 34th and last final victory.

The first night game at Waverley played for Premiership points in Round 3, 1987 resulted in a 74-point victory for the Lions over North Melbourne. The club also played in the first-ever match at Waverley v Geelong in 1970 and the first-ever match played under lights v North Melbourne in the AMCO Cup night series in 1977.

Fitzroy christened another venue in Round 4, 1987, this time in Queensland when they played the Brisbane Bears at Carrara Oval, winning 20.9 (129) to 16.18 (114) before a crowd of 22,684.

A last Premiership came to the club when Fitzroy, coached by Robert Shaw, won the Reserve Grade Grand Final in 1989, defeating Geelong 17.12 (114) to 16.16 (112). It allowed club legends Micky Conlan, Leon Harris and Ross Thornton to retire with a victory lap of the MCG with a Premiership Cup.

A one-point victory over North Melbourne in Round 14, 1993 was the club's 31st victory by this margin, the most by any side. Eight weeks later the club recorded its ninth 100+ point victory when it defeated the Brisbane Bears 22.15 (147) to 5.13 (43) at Princes Park.

Fitzroy and West Coast played the

1986–1996

The prophetic banner for the Centenary Match.

The end of old Fitzroy

The 113th and final season for Fitzroy provided many moving moments. The club's last-ever victory against Fremantle was followed by scenes of unbridled delight; hundreds of supporters remained on the ground long after the siren to savour the winning feeling one last time.

Equally emotional was Fitzroy's last game in Melbourne, without a doubt the saddest day in 100 years of AFL football. It was a day when supporters came to pay their respects to something that had become more than a football club. To reflect on the glorious moments that brought so much joy, and to say farewell. Not only personally, but on behalf of their ancestors who bequeathed them the pleasure of being a Fitzroy supporter. Most came to say 'Thank you for the memories'.

The symbolism of Fitzroy's last-ever game was ironic. Formed over a century ago with a desire to defeat its neighbouring suburbs, it played its final match 2000km away against a club two years old.

Fremantle FC hosted Fitzroy on Sunday, 1 September 1996, and marked the occasion with a moving tribute before and after the game, a gesture appreciated by the 1000 Lion supporters present.

The players, with the club's emblem tattooed on their arms, entered the ground through a banner displaying the names of every player who played 90 or more games for Fitzroy. As always the team performed with pride, and although unsuccessful they did manage to 'win' the final quarter, with their last-ever goal kicked by Simon Atkins.

The appointment of an administrator forced a July 4 deadline to decide Fitzroy's future. Extensive negotiations with North Melbourne collapsed and a late merger offer from Brisbane was endorsed by the AFL and its member clubs. The Brisbane Lions were created with a commitment to preserve 113 years of tradition and the spirit of the Fitzroy Football Club.

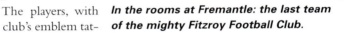

In the rooms at Fremantle: the last team of the mighty Fitzroy Football Club.

Emotional scenes at the last game played in Melbourne.

first and only AFL match in Canberra at the Bruce Stadium, the 19th VFL/AFL venue that Doug Hawkins played in his career – the most by any player.
The AFL celebrated its centenary season in 1996. Fitzroy is one of only three clubs to participate in all 100 VFL/AFL seasons.
18 May 1996. Fitzroy celebrate its 869th and final victory when it defeats Fremantle 16.11 (107) to 10.16 (76) at the Western Oval. Anthony Mellington kicked six goals and Nick Carter was named as Best Player on the Ground. Fremantle had recorded its first-ever victory against Fitzroy the previous season.
2 September 1996. Fitzroy legends Kevin Murray, half-back flank, and Haydn Bunton, half-forward flank, were selected in the AFL's team of the century.
4 July 1996. The AFL member clubs endorse a merger between Fitzroy and the Brisbane Bears.
25 August 1996. Fitzroy plays its last match in Melbourne at the MCG against Richmond, losing 28.19 (187) to 5.6 (36) before a crowd of 48,884.
1 September 1996. The 1928th and final match is played by Fitzroy (10.11 (71)) at Subiaco Oval in Perth against Fremantle (24.13 (157)).
18 September 1996. Martin Pike is the last winner of the Fitzroy Best and Fairest award, with Matthew Primus and Scott Bamford filling the places.
1 November 1996. The Brisbane Bears and the Fitzroy Football Club trading as the Brisbane Lions Australian Football Club formally becomes the first official merger between two AFL clubs.

FOOTSCRAY

Bulldog supporter for life

MY CLUB by Ray Stevens

My first recollections of barracking for the red, white and blue date back to the early 1960s. My older brother Doug came home to Shepparton with some souvenir flags from the 1961 Grand Final.

I was hooked from that point on. I remember attending a football clinic at Deakin Reserve with my mates. We were about 12 years old at the time. John Jillard and Kevin Delmenico took the clinic and I had my photo taken for the local newspaper. I showed that newspaper article to all and sundry. I still do today.

I loved listening to the broadcast of the games on the radio (when you could pick it up). If we were going badly or lost I would knock the radio over or, in later years, throw it to the ground. Such was my passion.

I couldn't wait to see my beloved Bulldogs on the Saturday night replay (a rarity in the 60s) and then watch 'World of Sport' footy panel on the Sunday.

I marvelled at the brilliance of Ted Whitten and the teamwork and marking power of John Schultz. I remember attending my first game in 1969.

The same year Kevin Murray pipped Georgie Bisset for the Brownlow. It was round 19, Ted Whitten's 313th game. Whitten played at full-back on a young up-and-coming Essendon forward by the name of Alan Noonan. He gave him a football lesson. I was absolutely stoked.

Unfortunately for me it was to be the only time I saw Ted play. I still have fond memories of that day and of the personal autograph he signed for me.

Two finals appearances and a swag of lean years followed. Personally, I think the '85 side is the best I have seen. They really played attacking football and had some true champions in Hawkins, Royal, Hardie, Beasley and powerhouse full-back Rick Kennedy. Losing the 1985 Preliminary Final was heartbreaking. We really could have tested Essendon in the Grand Final.

My other biggest memory is the mournful and gut-wrenching feeling I had on hearing the news that Footscray was to merge with Fitzroy. I walked around for some time in disbelief. 'This couldn't possibly happen to my team,' I thought. Football was part of me, part of my character.

It felt like I had something cut from my own being. I was so relieved to hear that a group of supporters had organised a rally for the following Sunday. I swore then and there that I would do everything in my power to help the cause.

It's historic that we survived. I became an active member of the Bulldog Taskforce '89 and have since been involved in restoring and maintaining the Footscray Football Club's proud history.

FOOTSCRAY

Year established	1875–76
Joined VFL/AFL	1925
Home Ground	Western Oval, Yarraville, Optus Oval
Premierships	1954
Brownlow Medals	Alan Hopkins 1930; Norm Ware 1941; Peter Box 1956; John Schultz 1960; Gary Dempsey 1975; Kelvin Templeton 1980; Brad Hardie 1985; Tony Liberatore 1990; Scott Wynd 1992
Record home crowd	42,354 v Collingwood, 1955
Most games	Doug Hawkins, 329
Most goals	Simon Beasley, 575
Notable supporters	Past: H.V. McKay, William Angliss Present: Ernie Sigley, Merv Hughes, Collette Mann, Craig Parry, Alison Durban

Spirit of the team

I have barracked for the Bulldogs for as long as I can remember. Our family has a history of four generations of supporting Footscray, beginning with my great-grandma, who is 86 years old, through to me.

My dad and I often listen to the games on the radio. It's a really nerve-racking feeling. Because we live at Bunbartha which is about 200 km north-east of Melbourne we only see the Bulldogs play five or six times a year. My brother Jared and I are junior members; Dad, Nan and Great-Grandma are all adult members. They love the football. Nan's favourite player is Brad Johnson. She never stops talking about him. My favourite player is Chris Grant.

Our new coach Terry Wallace has put confidence and spirit into the players, which has them playing a terrific style of football.

Brad Matthews – 15 years of age

Bulldogs all, at the last game at Whitten Oval. Jared and Brad Matthews (bottom and far right), with grandma Valda Alford, father Peter, great grandma Mona Stevens and cousin Jaye (bottom left).

Charlie Sutton, Premiership captain–coach, leads the Bulldogs out in '54.

Sons of the West

Sons of the West, Red, White and Blue,
We'll come out snarling,
Bulldogs through and through.
Bulldogs bite and Bulldogs roar, we give our very best,
'Cos you can't beat the boys of Bulldog breed,
We're the team of the mighty West.

Standing commitment

I came to barrack for the Bulldogs because I lived in nearby Eleanor St, West Footscray. I read about the team in the local paper and decided to go and watch them. This was in 1942. My mother thought I was at the Saturday Matinee. At 16 I went to work at Southern Can and met people to go to the football with. In 1943 we wore our blue skirts, white blouses and red cardigans. That same year I bought my first membership ticket. I still have it.

Harry Hickey was a star player in those days and I absolutely adored him. I had him autograph my Footscray doll once. It took a fair amount of daring from my friends before I went through with it. Since those days I have always been a follower of the No. 7 jumper. However my favourites were Harry Hickey, Roger Duffy, Doug Hawkins and now Scott West. I used to write to Doug Hawkins often. I have become good friends with his wife Raelene and the family. I always tell people I am his second mother. He was such a skilled player, he should have won a Brownlow. He was a real lovable larrikin. I am very proud of him. His final series in 1985 was brilliant.

Following Footscray and going to the footy has always been my passion and main priority. We never make arrangements or organise anything during footy season.

Beryl Cox – Springvale

The Bulldogs and us:

Being lifelong supporters of the Footscray Football Club, we have cherished coming to play for the Western Bulldogs.

Initially as children we were both very fanatical supporters, going to every game possible, be it rain, hail or shine. We watched our heroes play, and after the final siren we relived the day's happenings by having a kick with our fathers until dark on the sacred turf of the Western/E.J. Whitten Oval.

Having been given the opportunity to play for our club means a whole lot more to us. Now children (like we had done years earlier) look at us as their heroes and when the final siren sounds they too may relive the day's happenings as we did when we were children playing out our dreams. We hope that they may well be tomorrow's heroes and play for the mighty Bulldogs just like us.

The Western Bulldogs has become an extension of our family, a family that we are very proud of.

Brad Johnson and Rohan Smith – 1990s players

FOOTSCRAY

President James Cuming received this tribute upon Footscray's first VFA Premiership in 1898.

The first Footscray Premiership team. Captain Dave De Coite is fourth from left, centre row.

The genial James Cuming was President of the Footscray Football Club for a record 17 years, from 1895 until his death in 1911. He often entertained the players, or 'my boys', as he called them, along with club officials at 'smoke' nights.

First VFA game

Led by stand-in captain 'Ducky' Cameron, Footscray made a memorable start as a senior club in the Victorian Football Association. Playing St Kilda at the Western Reserve, the local boys wasted no time racking up three goals in succession. The Saints responded with three quick goals, before Footscray kicked the winning goal just before time. The boys from the 'borough' of Footscray had made an auspicious debut, winning 4.11 to 3.10. In this era behinds were recorded but didn't count toward the score.

The Premiership hat-trick: 1898–1900

Not long after the breakaway of clubs to form the VFL, Footscray began assembling a formidable combination – one that would take them to three consecutive Premierships.

In the deciding match for the 1898 Premiership, Footscray more than doubled North Melbourne's score 6.12 (48) to 3.5 (23). No Grand Finals were played during this time, the Premiership going to the club that finished on top of the ladder at the end of the season. The 'Tricolours' as Footscray were known, had played 17 games for 13 wins to claim the flag.

In 1899, the Footscray side was further boosted with the recruitment of champion backman Joe Marmo and crack full-forward Lou Daily. Daily, who wore a woollen cap with a tassel in the centre when he played, topped the Association goalkicking in his two years (1899–1900).

These recruits further complemented Dave De Coite's captaincy, the brilliance of Billy Robinson, the spirit of 'Skeeter' Armstrong and the redoubtable combination of 'Paddy' Hinch and 'Ching' Harris in the last line of defence.

It is not hard to understand why Footscray became such a VFA power. Unsung heroes in 'Nance' Williams, Davey Drew, Charlie Brockwell, Billy McCarthy and Pat Shanahan added further to the Tricolours' awesome depth.

In winning their second Premiership, the Tricolours lost only three games. They performed even better the following season, losing only one game to complete the Premiership hat-trick.

Footscray's domination was such that the team won 46 of the 54 matches played between 1898–1900 – the reward for which

CLUB NEWS 1886–1911

1886. Footscray joined the VFA in 1886 with four other clubs – South Williamstown, Prahran, Port Melbourne and St Kilda (which was re-entering the competition).

1891. Only 12 players turned up to play an away game against St Kilda. St Kilda's ground was found to be in a deplorable state – pools of water everywhere. With rain teeming down, the Footscray skipper objected to his side playing. The umpire, however, rejected his complaint so the dozen Footscray players took on the 20 from St Kilda and were, not surprisingly, held scoreless – St Kilda winning 10 goals (5 behinds) to nil.

1894. Footscray, undefeated in the first four games of 1894, faced South Melbourne in Round Five for the team's first 'match of the day' in the VFA. The Footscray players acquitted themselves well, drawing the match 5 goals apiece. The season proved to be Footscray's best yet, the Tricolours finishing with a new-found respect and fifth spot on the ladder.

Club nicknames. In the early VFA years, Footscray had several nicknames. The most common were 'Scray' and 'Tricolours'. At other times the team members were referred to as the 'Saltwater lads', 'Bone-millow fellows', 'Representatives of Stoneapolis' and the 'Men from the land of boulders'.

1900. Footscray's Billy Robinson was regarded as the champion player in the

1886 – 1911

Stalwarts Joe Marmo and 'Ching' Harris.

1908 – the 'century makers' put on a show

The VFA provided the masterstroke of 1908 when it transferred the scheduled Grand Final between Footscray and Brunswick from Saturday to the public holiday on Monday, at the MCG.

Melbourne was in the grip of American Fleet week. On the morning of the match, the crowds flocked to see American marines march through the city. That afternoon 41,000 people crammed into the MCG to watch the Tricolours take on the 'Brickfielders'.

Footscray's side was a champion team being coined 'the century makers' for their ability to kick high scores during the season. In one match they kicked a club and Association record 28.20 (188) to North Melbourne's 4.4 (28). Champion full-forward Jack Hutchinson kicked 16 goals that day – another record. He kicked 68 for the season but, strangely, none in the Grand Final.

Footscray defeated Brunswick for the Premiership 9.10 (64) to 6.4 (40). The Tricolours had an array of Grand Final stars including ruckman Art Gregory and rover Roy Cotton. Tom Sevior, 'Ching' Harris, 'Soldier' McCarthy and the lion-hearted Joe Marmo held the backline together.

'Intercolonials' – fierce western rivals

Such was the intense interest and rivalry aroused by clashes between Footscray and its VFA neighbour Williamstown, their matches were facetiously known as the 'Intercolonial'.

The games between the two teams were characterised by their spite – the battle for the ball often being secondary to pugilistic displays of violence. Footscray's first win over Williamstown in 1889 was cause for great celebration, with players being feted at the Royal Hall that night.

The two clubs did bury the hatchet, albeit temporarily, when a spirit of sympathy prevailed after both clubs were excluded from the clubs that formed the VFL. A benefit match was played to aid Williamstown, with players from both sides revelling in each other's company at a 'smoke' night after the game.

The bribery scandal

It was rumoured prior to the clash with top side Richmond in 1902 that an attempt would be made to induce some Footscray players to play 'stiff'. The rumour was proven correct, with several Footscray players refusing to accept the bribery money when approached.

Star backman 'Paddy' Hinch, though, took the half sovereign on offer and indignantly told astonished 'Richmondites' he intended to play his heart out. At half-time Hinch handed the money to VFA secretary Tom Evans and an impromptu inquiry was held – without a satisfactory outcome.

The second half of the game developed into a deplorable fight scene. Richmond, however, went on to win the match and the Premiership that year. Footscray charged 'Fishy' Taylor of the Richmond club with bribery and he was brought to justice by the VFA's investigation committee. The Association, proving the charge, disqualified Taylor for life.

A local Footscray paper remarked, 'It was a "fishy" bit of business altogether and the punishment was well deserved.'

VFA for season 1900. For business reasons though, Robinson left the Tricolours for Essendon (VFL) the following year and played in the 1901 Essendon Premiership side. He went on to captain the Dons in 1905.

Changes of guernsey. Footscray has always worn the colours red, white and blue. However, in the early years in the VFA the guernsey varied quite a bit. An early design had perpendicular stripes. An alteration in 1894 saw a royal blue guernsey with red and white sash. In Premiership years 1898–1900 the club sported a red guernsey with a red, white and blue sash. In 1901, it is believed Susan Gerrard, owner of a local knitting business, redesigned the guernseys to be blue incorporating a red and white hoop, a style that remains in vogue to this day.

1903. Ted Stephenson gave one of the great individual performances in 1903. He kicked 10 goals and hit the post twice in Footscray's 12.12 (84) to 1.1 (7) win over Essendon Town.

1906 runners-up. Led by Arthur 'Nance' Williams, Footscray lost the 1906 Grand Final to West Melbourne 5.9 (39) to 7.8 (50) after suffering injuries to players at vital stages in the last quarter.

1908: first coach. Jim Cassidy became Footscray's first coach in 1908–09. Cassidy also coached the Tricolours in 1912–15, 1918, and 1926, Footscray's second year in the VFL. Bob Nash, father of Laurie, captain–coached the Tricolours in 1910–11.

FOOTSCRAY

Vernon Banbury – the darling of the gods

Footscray's most brilliant player during its VFA years was half-forward of five Grand Finals and three Premierships, Vernon Banbury. Banbury's career spanned two periods, 1910–14 and 1919–22.

Described as the 'prettiest footballer in the Association', Banbury's endless array of tricks left many an opposition defence floundering and supporters of both sides spellbound. A local paper observed that, 'Banbury is the follower's joy. He has a thorough grasp of the spectacular in football, he believes in preference to evolutions, and twists before kicks.'

Dubbed the 'Darling of the Gods' for his genius on the football field, Banbury's career ended in shame, being banned for life by the VFA for attempting to bribe Port Melbourne players prior to the 1922 Grand Final.

1913 – a fifth Premiership

With less than five minutes remaining, Footscray trailed North Melbourne by 12 points in the Grand Final of 1913. The Tricolours had only made the Grand Final after defeating Essendon Association by two points in a thrilling Semi-final.

The Tricolours held on in a thriller, winning 10.14 (74) to 11.7 (73). In both finals, Footscray had scored fewer goals than the opposition but still won on total points.

The 1919 team. Imports and returned men strengthened the ranks.

1919 – the Peace Premiership

The war over, Footscray entered the battle for the 'Peace Premiership' of 1919 with renewed vigour. With players returning from the battlefields of Europe and an aggressive recruiting policy, Footscray strengthened its player ranks.

Much to the dismay of VFL clubs, the Tricolours lured ruckman 'Chook' Howell and gun full-forward Harry Morgan from South Melbourne. Howell proved to be one of the club's great ruckmen, while Morgan's 72 goals for the season was a remarkable total for the era.

Playing North Melbourne in the Grand Final, the Tricolours were never in danger of losing. They had stars on every line. In defence Jack Meuleman, 'Piggy' Grierson and champion Norman Ford stood firm. 'Tattles' Patterson's high marking and wing play earned him the title of best man on the ground. Vernon Banbury's cleverness proved decisive as did Vic Samson and rover Johnny Martin's work in the packs.

Captain Johnny Craddock kicked four goals in the Tricolours' 8.17 (65) to 6.7 (43) victory.

Inspiring the Tricolours to the Premierships of 1913, 1919 and 1920 was dynamic captain Johnny Craddock. Powerfully built and as tough as nails, Craddock was regarded as a 'human cyclone when roused'.

A Braybrook boy, Craddock was the protector of the team. His deeds inspired the term 'bulldog tenacity', a famous Tricolour catchcry of the era.

Craddock demanded 'fitness and guts' from his players. Any team captained by Craddock was characterised by its fighting spirit and whirlwind finishes.

CLUB NEWS 1912–1924

1912. Footscray unveiled its new brick grandstand and scoreboard in the opening game against Melbourne City in 1912. The scoreboard worked overtime on the day, with Footscray winning 19.20 (134) to 3.3 (21).

1912 Runners-up. Footscray met Essendon Association in the Grand Final of 1912. In a desperate effort to curb Essendon's champion Dave McNamara, the Tricolours lured ex-Carlton captain Fred Elliott out of retirement to mind him. The move backfired. McNamara kicked three goals (for 107 for the season) and the Tricolours lost 9-8 (62) to 5-11 (41).

1914 Runners-up. North Melbourne defeated Footscray in the 1914 Grand Final 12.14 (86) to 7.9 (51). A good deal of betting took place on the outcome of the match, much of it by Footscray players.

Hail Footscray. In the Final of 1921, Footscray were staging a 'typical bulldog finish' when an almighty hailstorm swept the ground causing the game's abandonment. The game against Williamstown was replayed the following week with the 'villagers' winning by three points. As minor premiers, Footscray had the right of challenge to a Grand Final. Again Williamstown won.

Call to Duty. Many players at Footscray served their country with distinction during the First World War. One such player was 'Tattles' Patterson who was awarded the

1912 – 1924

1920 Premiership team – a long and controversial battle for the Flag.

Battle for 1920 Flag

For the scheduled Second Semi-final of 1920 between Footscray and North Melbourne it took three weeks to decide a winner. Rain caused postponement of the game the first week with the ground an inch under water.

The following week the game ended in controversial circumstances. With Footscray five points up, Considine of North Melbourne had just marked within range on the final bell, when the crowd rushed the ground. Arguments raged as to whether the mark was taken before or after the bell, and it was clear that Considine would not be able to attempt a shot on goal.

The task of clearing the arena became impossible and umpire Hurley abandoned the game with Considine unable to take his kick and the result in dispute. The VFA later ruled the match would be replayed. The Footscray committee met and it was only on the casting vote of chairman Alf Greenwood that Footscray agreed to play.

Footscray finally won the replay – a goal in the last minute from Roy Park giving the Tricolours a four-point win. Formerly of University and Melbourne, Park joined Footscray, where he had a medical practice.

Park again proved the hero in the subsequent Grand Final against Brunswick. With his team trailing by 20 points early in the last quarter, Park kicked the last four goals of the game to give Footscray a remarkable Premiership victory.

Footscray humbles VFL winner Essendon

Saturday, 4 October 1924 is remembered as the greatest day in Footscray's distinguished history as a VFA club.

Arising from a suggestion made by Australia's Queen of Opera, Dame Nellie Melba, a match was arranged for charity – pitting the 1924 VFA Premiers, (Footscray), against VFL premiers, (Essendon). The match was billed as the 'Championship of Victoria' and was the first time the Premiers of each competition had met.

Played in front of 46,100 people at the MCG, the game was evenly balanced at half-time. In the second half the Tricolours mesmerised not only Essendon, but the crowd with dazzling chains of handball, piling on six goals to one. Footscray stars included Vic Samson, rover Alex Eason, captain–coach Con McCarthy and defender Norman Ford.

Essendon had been run to a standstill as delirious Footscray and VFA supporters celebrated the 9.10 (64) to 4.12 (36) victory. For those stalwarts of the red, white and blue, the unimaginable had happened – they had dethroned the might of the League. The *Australasian* declared that 'Footscray made hacks of the mighty Essendon.'

However, much controversy surrounded the victory. Ten years later, Essendon champion half-back Tom Fitzmaurice declared that the game had been fixed, prompting strong rebuttals from other players involved in the match.

Vic Samson first played for Footscray in 1912. He developed into one of the game's great followers, with his characteristic strength and amazing reserves of stamina. His last-quarter performances were legendary. Samson appeared in nine Grand Finals and five Premierships for the Tricolours (1913, 1919, 1920, 1923 and 1924). He retired in 1926 after playing a further 27 games when Footscray entered the VFL. A teetotaller and non-smoker, he was also a champion gymnast, swimmer and diver.

Belgian 'Croix de Guerre' in 1918, for bravery in the face of enemy fire.
Winning Streak. Footscray won their last 48 home games in the VFA. The winning streak began in August 1919.
1922 Runners-up. Footscray lost the 1922 Grand Final to Port Melbourne, 9.6 (60) to 8.10 (58), but the real drama took place after the game. President George Sayer and player Vernon Banbury were charged with attempting to bribe several Port players to play 'dead'. The VFA suspended Banbury for life but exonerated Sayer.
1923 Premiers. Footscray won a spiteful Grand Final over Port Melbourne 7.10 (52) to 5.8 (38). In the second quarter, the two ruckmen, Howell and Bissett stood 'toe to toe … and pummelled each other until first aid men, supporters and finally a police constable had to force them apart.' Seven players in all were reported in one of the most violent Grand Finals.
Minor Premiers. Footscray topped the VFA ladder after the home-and-away season in five consecutive years (1920–24).
Footscray's VFA record. Footscray played 680 games in the VFA (1886–1924). Of these they won 394, 24 were drawn, two abandoned and 260 lost. At the Western Reserve the Tricolours won an impressive 218 of 302 games played.
1924 Premiers. Footscray trounced Williamstown in the 1924 Grand Final. The Tricolours won 11.11 (77) to 3.4 (22) after keeping the seasiders goalless in the first three quarters.

FOOTSCRAY

VFL admittance at last

Footscray's first VFL side – strong, determined, but losers on the day.

In January 1925, the city of Footscray received its wish. The Footscray Football Club, along with the North Melbourne and Hawthorn clubs, was admitted to the VFL competition.

However, the elevation to League ranks came at a cost. Champions Norm Ford, Alex Eason and Jack O'Brien were banned from playing in the VFL competition for contravening transfer rules when they crossed to Footscray from League clubs, without a clearance, years earlier. The flick pass, Footscray's secret weapon, was banned and the VFA even refused to present the 1924 VFA Premiership medallions to the club, regarding Footscray's desertion as treason.

Brilliant ruckman Con McCarthy won the VFA's Best and Fairest (Recorder Cup) in 1923, and achieved great success in his four years as captain–coach (1922–25).

McCarthy was also Footscray's captain–coach in its first season in the VFL. Though bowing to 'father time' one year later, he can lay claim to having played a prominent role in Footscray's transition to being a VFL club.

Round 1, 1925, first VFL game

Footscray's opening game in League company, against Fitzroy, was given 'match of the day' status. The biggest crowd of the day (28,000) crammed the Brunswick Street Oval, to witness history in the making.

Footscray's first team in the VFL contained only four new players. There were established stars in Jack Meuleman, Vic Samson and captain–coach, Con McCarthy. Forward, George Bayliss, had the honour of securing the Tricolours' first goal in the VFL. Among the other forwards was emerging champion, Allan Hopkins, who finished the game as Footscray's best. Fitzroy led all day to win by nine points, 8.15 (63) to 8.6 (54).

All in Footscray hailed the game a big success. 'No district in Australia takes its football so seriously as Footscray,' said the *Sporting Globe*. The Footscray supporters felt relieved after that first match, as the team had shown it could compete against such an illustrious old club as Fitzroy.

1925–1938 HONOUR ROLL

Year	Pos	Leading Goalkicker	No.	Best & Fairest	Captain	Coach
1925	11th	Allan Hopkins	40		Con McCarthy	Con McCarthy
1926	10th	A. Hopkins, Les Chapple	42		McCarthy/Allan Hopkins	J. Cassidy/S. Saunders
1927	10th	Les Chapple	32	Ivan McAlpine	Paddy Scanlon	Paddy Scanlon
1928	7th	Alby Morrison	50	Albert Outen	Paddy Scanlon	Paddy Scanlon
1929	9th	Alby Morrison	50	William Russ	Allan Hopkins	Alec Eason
1930	11th	Alby Morrison	48	Ivan McAlpine	Allan Hopkins	Allan Hopkins
1931	5th	Alby Morrison	36	Allan Hopkins	Bill Cubbins	Bill Cubbins
1932	7th	Les Dayman	37	Ivan McAlpine	Bill Cubbins	Bill Cubbins
1933	7th	Alan Rait	59	Alby Morrison	Ivan McAlpine	Bill Cubbins
1934	9th	Alby Morrison	46	Norm Ware	B. Cubbins/A. Morrison	Alby Morrison
1935	11th	Joe Ryan	25	George Bennett	Alby Morrison	Alby Morrison
1936	10th	Arthur Olliver	37	Alby Morrison	Stan Penberthy	Syd Coventry
1937	11th	Arthur Olliver	39	Norm Ware	Syd Dockendorff	Coventry/J. Kelly
1938	4th	Charlie Luke	44	Norm Ware	Roy Evans	Joe Kelly

CLUB NEWS 1925–1938

Round 2, 1925. In winning their first game, Footscray 10.10 (70) defeated South Melbourne 8.12 (60) at the Western Oval.

Round 16, 1925. Footscray won its fourth game in its inaugural VFL season beating Hawthorn 15.10 (100) to 10.10 (70). 'The outstanding individual effort in the game was by Allan Hopkins, who gave a masterly display on the forward line and scored nine goals from eleven shots.'

1926. In the news story of 1926, the VFL threatened Footscray with expulsion if it did not remove elected President George Sayer from office. A hidden clause, apparently given upon Footscray's entry to the League, was that Sayer would never hold any official role at the club. In the immediate interests of the club, Sayer stood down, and in a barbed response to the VFL's actions, the *Footscray Advertiser* noted, 'He has been dethroned by an autocracy as unprincipled as it is apparently powerful.'

September 1927. 'Ivan McAlpine has gained President Dr McCarthy's Cup for the most consistent player.' Thus, McAlpine became the first official winner of the club 'Best and Fairest'.

1928: the catchcry. 'Three cheers for the Red, White and Blue,
Success to our colours so true.
Wherever we go, we'll let them all know
We belong to the Red, White and Blue.'

1925 – 1938

Footscray full-forward Alan Rait.

Battle of full-forwards

The Round 8 clash of 1933, between Footscray and Carlton at Princes Oval, provided one of the great exhibitions of Australian football. Carlton won a high scoring affair, 21.13 (139) to 17.14 (116), but it was the battle of the full-forwards that captured the imagination of the crowd.

Footscray's first-year spearhead, Alan Rait, had been recruited from North Hobart after kicking nine goals for Tasmania against Victoria in 1932. With a quick lead and an ability to take 'corkscrew leaps', Rait dazzled the crowd with a goalkicking display, the equal of which is rarely seen.

With the brilliance of Allan Hopkins and Norm Ware pumping the ball forward, Rait potted 10 goals from all angles. At the other end, Carlton's legendary full-forward Harry 'Soapy' Vallence steered through nine goals to lead the Blues to victory.

Allan Hopkins

The classy centreman Allan Hopkins was Footscray's first genuine superstar in the VFL competition. His career, which began in the VFA, spanned the years 1923–34, and included 151 games and 205 goals in the VFL.

Hopkins began as a half-forward, but developed into one of the games great centremen when switched to that position in an interstate game. Nicknamed 'Banana legs' because of his bandy legs, Hopkins grew up living in the caretaker's house at the Western Oval, where his father was the groundsman.

He won a Best and Fairest in 1931, topped the goalkicking (1925–26), captained the club (1926, 1929 and 1930) and was even persuaded to coach the club in 1930.

At the 1930 interstate carnival, 'Hoppy' was awarded the title of 'Champion of Australia'. He was regarded as being a most unlucky player, finishing runner-up in the Brownlow Medal in three consecutive years (1929–31). The VFL, in an unprecedented move, awarded Hopkins a commemorative certificate.

In 1989, the VFL awarded retrospective Brownlow Medals for players that lost the medal on countback. Hopkins received one for his 1930 season as captain–coach.

1935 – change of guernsey

A new guernsey was adopted for season 1935, featuring vertical stripes of red, white and blue. It was hoped the guernsey would give the players a more 'conspicuous' appearance on the field. After only one season of wear, the club reverted to the old design of horizontal hoops. The 1935 guernsey had mysteriously been shrunk in the wash prior to the 1936 season.

1938 First Semi-Final

Footscray made its first appearance in a VFL finals series when it met Collingwood in the 1938 First Semi-final. A record Semi-final crowd of 67,566 packed the MCG.

A major setback for Footscray was the loss of regular full-back Alf Sampson to injury. A remarkable scoreline had developed by half-time. Collingwood, with amazing accuracy led 9.1 (55) to Footscray's contrastingly inaccurate 6.11 (47). Footscray hit the lead with two goals early in the third term, but it was Collingwood's seven unanswered goals for the remainder of the quarter that swung the game.

In the end, the Magpies won comfortably, 18.9 (117) to 10.16 (76). The centreline of Bob Spargo, captain Roy Evans and Jim Miller did best for the Bulldogs. Jim Greenham provided solid support from a back flank. Cliff MacRae, with five goals, was Footscray's only clear winner up forward and Norman Ware battled stoutly in the ruck. Coach Joe Kelly was justifiably proud of his boys – they had risen from 11th in 1937 to contest the finals one year later.

Alby Morrison

Local boy Alby Morrison became one of the most versatile big-men of Footscray In a career spanning 224 games and 369 goals, Morrison won two Best and Fairest awards (1933, 1936), was leading goalkicker five times (1928–31, 1934), captain (1934–35, 1937), and playing coach (1934–35). Morrison first played in 1928 and retired as a 37-year-old in 1946.

1928. Footscray's 1928 season was remarkable for its close finishes. The Tricolours figured in nine games in which the final margin was four points or less. Footscray won three games by one point, one game by two points and another by four points. On the other hand, they lost two games by a solitary point, one by three points and one by four points.

5 July 1930. The Boys' Band from Hyde St State School made a brave showing during the half-time interval, playing several selections.

1932. Footscray has a record-high club membership (6031), the largest in the VFL.

May 1935. Syd Coventry, the famous Collingwood player, is appointed non-playing coach. 'The coup was the "talk of the town" … a feature of the move was the sportsmanship of Alby Morrison, the retiring coach.' Morrison, who stepped into the breach when Bill Cubbins resigned as coach during the 1934 season, willingly stood aside for the Collingwood legend.

Out of debt. Footscray town clerk John Gent arranged a Debt Abolition Appeal to help wipe out the club's debt of £1000. In March 1937, Gent handed to the club a cheque for £400, raised during the Appeal.

April 1937. The Footscray club motto, *Cede Nullis*, which translated from the Latin means 'Yield to None', is adopted. The idea of a club motto came from secretary Sam Ramsay, who chose the winning entry from numerous applications.

FOOTSCRAY

Ambrose Palmer's injuries

Fifteen minutes into the 1939 season, Ambrose Palmer, a triple Australian boxing champion and the idol of the Footscray home crowd, was accidentally sandwiched between two Essendon opponents in a horrifying collision, the force of which literally burst the back of his skull.

Palmer received stitches to wounds, a black eye and multiple fractures of the jaw and skull in one of the worst football injuries ever seen. He returned to the field the following year and eventually retired during the 1943 season after 82 games.

Boys of the Bulldog breed

Footscray was originally known as the 'Tricolours' because of its red, white and blue guernsey. It wasn't until 1938 that the club officially adopted the 'Bulldogs' as a nickname and mascot.

The bulldog connection, though, stretched back to the club's formative years. A song, 'The Boys of the Bulldog Breed', was the rage in the 1880s and it was said the club adopted the song as their battle cry. The bulldog theme was revived in the latter years of the VFA, when under Johnny Craddock's captaincy, the team's play displayed a fighting spirit, suitably coined 'Bulldog tenacity'. A flag emblazoned with this term and showing a bulldog's head, was presented to President David Mitchell after the 1920 Premiership victory. Mitchell had a bulldog head printed on the 1921 membership ticket, and the local paper declared that Footscray would now be called the 'bull dogs'.

Norm Ware's Brownlow

In 1941, champion ruckman Norman Ware was appointed Footscray's playing coach. In the same year he also became the first Footscray player awarded the Brownlow Medal, polling 23 votes to beat South Melbourne's Herbie Matthews by one vote.

The win was fitting reward for Ware's consistency. In his first 10 seasons, Ware finished in the top 10 in the Brownlow voting seven times, and won Footscray's Best and Fairest award five times.

Tall for his era, at 6 foot 4 and a half inches (191 cm), Ware was known as a superb mark and penetrating kick. Recruited from Sale in 1932, Ware led his side to the 1942 finals and retired as a player after the 1946 First Semi-final, his 200th game.

1939–1953 HONOUR ROLL

Year	Pos	Leading Goalkicker	No.	Best & Fairest	Captain	Coach
1939	11th	Charles Page	31	Harry Hickey	Roy Evans	Joe Kelly
1940	6th	Charles Page	52	Norm Ware	Norm Ware	Joe Kelly
1941	6th	Alan Collins	35	N. Ware/Arthur Olliver	Norm Ware	Norm Ware
1942	4th	Norm Ware	51	Edward Ellis	Norm Ware	Norm Ware
1943	6th	Alan Collins	41	Alan Collins	Arthur Olliver	Arthur Olliver
1944	4th	Bill Wood	51	Arthur Olliver	Arthur Olliver	Arthur Olliver
1945	5th	Joe Ryan	37	Harry Hickey	Arthur Olliver	Arthur Olliver
1946	4th	Bill Wood	52	Joe Ryan	Arthur Olliver	Arthur Olliver
1947	9th	Bill Wood	75	Joe Ryan	Harry Hickey	Jim Crowe
1948	4th	Bill Wood	41	Harry Hickey	Arthur Olliver	Arthur Olliver
1949	9th	Arthur Olliver	28	Wally Donald	Arthur Olliver	Arthur Olliver
1950	10th	Bill Wood	45	Charlie Sutton	Arthur Olliver	Arthur Olliver
1951	4th	C. Sutton/Alby Linton	23	Jack Collins	Charlie Sutton	Charlie Sutton
1952	10th	Roger Duffy	20	Jack Collins	Charlie Sutton	Charlie Sutton
1953	3rd	Jack Collins	50	Harvey Stevens	Charlie Sutton	Charlie Sutton

CLUB NEWS 1939–1953

Lucky for some? Footscray's policy of not issuing the No. 13 guernsey to its players due to it being considered unlucky changed when Robert 'Bluestone' Flanigan (1936–40) insisted 13 was his lucky number. A fractured skull, a broken jaw, broken wrist and removal of a knee cartilage later, Flanigan was discarded by Footscray after the club tired of 'paying for everything but his burial'.

Harry Hickey's kick. Fourth-placed Carlton met fifth-placed Footscray in the last round of 1944 to decide which team would play in the finals. With the scores level, Footscray's Harry Hickey marked about 50 metres out, as the final bell was ringing. Hickey's kick floated across the behind line and was marked by Carlton's Bob Chitty. After consultation between the goal and field umpires, a point was signalled, and the Bulldogs clinched fourth spot – and a finals appearance.

1944. First Semi-final. Footscray's third appearance in a Semi-final was a forgettable one. Playing Essendon at St Kilda, the Bulldogs managed only one goal to half-time. Essendon piled on 6.11 in the last quarter to win 14.17 (101) to 8.4 (52).

1946. Footscray began the season in a blaze of glory winning their opening nine games – a club record.

1946. Round 18. Footscray kicked their highest score, 23.27 (165), in a 112-point win over Hawthorn. The bulk of the goals were shared by three players

1939–1953

Arthur Olliver's miskick

When Arthur Olliver marked at the top of the goal square into time-on in the last quarter of the 1946 First Semi-final against Melbourne, Footscray's first victory in a VFL finals match seemed assured.

Unfortunately for the Bulldogs, the unthinkable happened. Olliver slipped as he took the kick – the ball skewing out of bounds on the full.

Melbourne rebounded with a four goals and one behind in the remaining four minutes, to steal an impossible 17.18 (120) to 15.12 (102) victory.

The loss left Footscray stunned and, for Olliver, it was a cruel injustice. He had toiled manfully to be the side's best player, yet the popular captain–coach truly felt the devastation of that miskick. Many felt the 1946 side was to that time Footscray's best-ever chance at Premiership success.

Melbourne player and 1946 Brownlow medallist Don Cordner recalled in sympathy that, 'We were gone if Arthur had goaled. But he was that tired he could hardly move. Arthur stood there with tears streaming down his face. He realised what that kick meant to Footscray.'

Charlie Sutton (right) takes charge of the team on the training track at the Western Oval.

Charlie Sutton is coach

The appointment of the dynamic Charlie Sutton as captain–coach of Footscray in 1951 ushered in a new era for the club.

Faced with the challenge of rebuilding the side after the retirements of club stalwarts Olliver, McDonnell, McCankie and Rees at the end of the 1950 season, Sutton brought together a bunch of kids, mainly from the local district, and moulded them into a power.

The new wave of young guns, including Whitten, Collins, Henderson, Box, Gallagher and Edwards, injected the side with fresh enthusiasm. Blended with regulars in Sutton, Donald, Martin, Bryden, McLaren and Bill Scanlan, the new-look Bulldogs surged into the finals in Sutton's first year as coach. The young Bulldog side was only overrun in the last quarter of the First Semi-final against Essendon, going down by eight points, 8.13 (61) to 8.5 (53).

When Sutton addressed the new players the following season, he told them, 'You have made the list in the finest club in Australia, and you have got something to uphold. Think of nothing when you are playing but of the red, white and blue jumper you are wearing.' Under Sutton, the club was in good hands.

Defence of the century

In the middle of the 1950s Footscray could claim to have had 'The Defence of the Century'. The 1954 combination of backs Donald, Henderson, Bryden and half-backs Martin, Whitten and Gallagher is without doubt Footscray's greatest-ever backline.

Round 5, 1953, v Fitzroy

In round 5, when Footscray played host to Fitzroy, so much rain fell that the drains at Footscray could not cope with the deluge. The entire outer wing became submerged in water, in some places a foot deep.

Alan Ruthven's face-saving goal was Fitzroy's only score for the day – and the lowest score by any club this century. Footscray won 10.6 (66) to 1.0 (6).

– Alan Collins bagged 9.3, Jim Thoms 6.7 and Norm Ware 6.4.
1947. Bill Wood created a club record – 75 goals in a season – when he kicked four goals against Fitzroy full-back Fred Hughson in the last round. The previous record of 72 goals was kicked by Harry Morgan in 1919, when Footscray was an Association team.
Semi stumbles. The hoodoo of the First Semi-final continued to haunt the Bulldogs when they met Collingwood in 1948. Footscray suffered its fifth consecutive Semi-final loss, 17.17 (119) to 12.12 (84).1950.
New Australians. 'Footscray Football Club is all out to make migrants in this district real "Bulldog" supporters. The posters printed in German and Polish, in the colours of FFC, which are to be posted amongst migrants accommodated locally, will exhort them "as new Australians, to play and follow Australia's national football game."'
1950. The Bulldogs disappointed by winning only five games for the season, but were unlucky in losing six games by four points or less.
1951. When Ted Whitten was refused leave to play in the Semi-final against Essendon because of army National Service, the Prime Minister, Bob Menzies, stepped in and granted Whitten permission.
Round 11, 1951. Essendon defeats Footscray 9.10 (64) to 7.14 (56). Unofficial records indicate Bill Scanlan at centre half-back had between 20 and 28 marks during the game, including 10 in the last quarter alone.

FOOTSCRAY

Jack Collins
Games: 154 Goals: 383
Best and Fairest: 1951, 1952.
VFL Leading Goalkicker 1954 & 1957

Collins had been a top-line player well before his goalkicking exploits from full-forward. In his early years Sutton used Collins at centre half-back and centre half-forward with enormous success.

It wasn't until Collins received a slight knee injury prior to the interstate carnival in Adelaide in 1953 that Collins was used at full-forward. Collins takes up the story from here. 'I read in the paper that I had been dropped from the state team. I was pretty savage, I can tell you. I was determined to play [on the carnival weekend] with Footscray against Carlton.

'Footscray selectors were a little bit reluctant to play me at centre half-forward because they thought twisting and turning at centre half-forward might aggravate the knee. It wasn't 100 per cent right. Of course I played against Carlton at full-forward. It was my first game at full-forward and I kicked seven goals.

'It caused a hell of a stir. Carlton believed I deliberately dropped out of the state side so I could play against them, which wasn't the case They did bring a rule that any player that wasn't fit to play could not play with his team. In my case I didn't drop out of the side - they dropped me, without even examining me.

'That's how I came to be at full-forward. I played most of my football at full-forward other than a time in '56 when I got a depressed fracture of the cheekbone and Max Cross came in and played full-forward. I finished up back at centre half-forward again.'

Jack Collins was an outstanding player for Footscray between 1950–58. He later served 8 years as secretary of the club and as president for 7 years between 1967–73. Although he won the VFL leading goalkicker award twice, the crowning glory was surely his 7 goals in the 1954 Premiership victory.

Another great grab by Collins.

A grand season

Harvey Stevens.

Sutton had developed a team he felt could go all the way in 1954. Few observers doubted his prediction. However, by Round 2 of the season and two sound defeats, the prediction was taking on an all too familiar look.

In the third game, the Bulldogs were pitted against South Melbourne. The return of Jack Collins seemed to do the trick. His eight goals for the game was the tonic the Dogs needed, and they came out 87-point winners. 'We have come back,' announced Charlie Sutton 'and we will carry on from where we left off last season.'

The Bulldogs went on to secure second spot on the ladder after winning 11 games and drawing the Round 16 fixture against North Melbourne.

The first task was to defeat Geelong and move into Footscray's first VFL Grand Final.

Second Semi-final win

Footscray were all class as they went about their business in the Second Semi-final. The game was tight all day, until the Bulldogs pulled away from Geelong in what many described as a masterly display of systematic football. The backs were again supreme, winning the ball well and delivering into the forward line with long accurate kicks. Stevens was dominant in the ruck while Collins and Box put in their usual faultless displays.

Only for inaccurate kicking in the final quarter, the Dogs would have won by even more than 23 points. Footscray was only two weeks away from its ultimate dream.

1954 HONOUR ROLL

Year	Pos	Leading Goalkicker	No.	Best & Fairest	Captain	Coach
1954	1st	Jack Collins	84	Ted Whitten	Charlie Sutton	Charlie Sutton

CLUB NEWS 1954

Round 1, 1954. 'Footscray Football Club experienced its greatest shock for many years when the Bulldogs were soundly beaten by St Kilda in a game regarded as "a sitter" for the locals.'

Round 3. Jack Collins returned after suspension and took nine marks and kicked eight goals in Footscray's thumping 87-point win over South Melbourne. The win was Footscray's first for the season and boosted their percentage from 81.2 to 131.5.

Round 4. By half-time, full-forward Jack Collins had nine goals on the board against Carlton. 'Collins, who is essentially a team man,' was swung into the ruck in the third term and helped quash the rampaging Blues. Collins returned to the forward line in the last quarter but failed to add to his total as the Bulldogs went on to record an 11-point victory.

Big 10 for the big V. Footscray's Jack Collins kicked 10 goals in just over three quarters as Victoria thrashed South Australia.

Sept. 3. 'Football fever has hit Footscray … not only have the Bulldogs made the final four for the first time in successive years — for the first time since joining the VFL they have gained the much-prized "double chance".'

Sept. 3. 'Footscray undoubtedly has the best goal-to-goal line of all finalists … It is extremely fortunate that every member of the team is now playing at his top and it is doubly fortunate

1954

The 1954 Premiership team at their final training, the day the bikes rolled into the Western Oval.

The big day – a Footscray Flag at last

As Charlie Sutton led his red, white and blue charges onto the MCG, the crowd rose as one with wild cheering. It seemed that the greater proportion of the crowd supported the Bulldogs.

Footscray was very hard at the football. Charlie Sutton had encouraged his players to get in early and hit the Demons with everything. 'Shop early and avoid the rush,' Charlie had told his players.

Two marks followed by goals from Jack Collins saw the Bulldogs push ahead. Goals to Kerr and Stevens from boundary throw-ins were followed by another by Collins and smart play from McCarthy set up Duffy for a goal.

Melbourne had succumbed to the fast-running, well-organised Bulldogs, who finished the quarter full of running to lead by 29 points.

Footscray had learnt well from the previous game. They were exploiting the more attacking side of the MCG on the members wing, their use of hard running and sharp disposal bringing the forwards into play.

Melbourne attacked continually, but stout defence by Whitten, Henderson, Donald, Martin and Gallagher continued to turn them out. Some outstanding marking from Bryden and continued dominance of Stevens in the ruck proved a stumbling block for the Demons.

Although Melbourne had shown a far more determined approach and outscored the Bulldogs for the quarter, they still trailed by 23 points at half-time. During the break Charlie Sutton urged his players on to greater deeds. This was their best Premiership chance.

The Bulldogs came out full of running. Box was dominating in the centre while Reynolds, McCarthy, Kerr and Ross were creating numerous opportunities for their forwards. Half-forward Stockman chipped in to kick the Dogs' ninth. A goal to Sutton soon after had given the Bulldogs a six-goal buffer midway through the third term.

Henderson and Whitten continued to hold sway across the backline. Gilmore and Cordner were in turn making their presence felt with some fine marking. Goals to McLean and Johnson of Melbourne were answered through Collins and Sutton.

In the final term Kerr, who had roved tirelessly all day, was in the thick of things again. Martin's clearing run landed with Edwards and on to Collins for the crack forward to bring up his sixth and seal Melbourne's fate.

As Collins marked again and passed the ball to Gilmore the siren sounded to give the Bulldogs victory. In the excitement, Gilmore threw the ball high into the air, missing out on what would certainly have been a goal.

Little did it matter. Charlie's boys had finally done it. The sight of seeing Charlie Sutton being chaired from the ground bought tears to the eyes of the many supporters who had waited for this historic moment.

Left: John Kerr – best on ground.

Charlie Sutton leads the team out.

that there is only one casualty in the camp – Charlie Sutton.'
Final session. Footscray's final hit-out prior to the Grand Final was a training session at the Western Oval. Bill Long, the organiser for the Sydney to Melbourne bike race, decided to end the race at the Western Oval. A crowd of 18,000 turned out.
Team selection for Grand Final. The Bulldogs made one change to the winning Semi-final team. 'With Sutton to come in, Lionel Ryan looks the unlucky player to be omitted.' First-year player Lionel Ryan was indeed the unfortunate player who made room for Charlie Sutton – the Bulldog captain–coach had missed the previous two games with a leg injury.
The Celebrations. Footscray's great victory on Grand Final day was almost overshadowed by the farcical celebrations that followed. A pre-arranged Premiership dinner at the Mayfair Hotel in the city went askew. A hastily arranged civic reception at the Footscray town hall petered out when the sound system failed and the gathering of supporters at the Western Oval, looking to kick on, fizzled out when police ushered the people home. Despite promises of a party, the club had nothing organised.
Oct. 8. 'Apart from the maintained brilliance of the 1953 stars, Footscray's rise to fame this year was due in no small measure to the vastly improved play of ruckmen Brian Gilmore and Arthur Edwards, rover John Kerr and wingman Doug Reynolds.'

FOOTSCRAY

Unfurling the Flag

A crowd of 30,000 plus assembled at Footscray's first home game of season 1955 to witness the ceremony of unfurling the 1954 Premiership Flag. As the players and officials formed a square, the club President's wife, Mrs Grobbecker, stepped forward to unfurl the flag. Her simple speech said it all: 'Today I'm sure, is a proud and happy day for the people of Footscray, and I feel highly honoured for the privilege of unfurling our premiership pennant.'

After a sensational first quarter and a half that saw the reigning Premiers kick nine goals before the Tigers kicked their first, the Bulldogs went on to record a sound win 16.16 (112) to 12.9 (81). Star full-forward Jack Collins kicked eight goals for the day.

Cartoonist Sam Wells' depiction of Charlie Sutton, pocket tank.

Charlie Sutton – spirit of Footscray

If anyone characterised the 'battler of the Bulldog breed' it is Charlie Sutton, the captain–coach who took the Bulldogs to their only Premiership in 1954. Sutton came from Spotswood in 1942, and his career was interrupted by war service. On his return he found that he was battling for a game as a centreman, but his hard-as-nails, stocky body became a terrifying weapon in the back pocket. His strength was acknowledged by an almost permanent place in Victorian State teams, and his appointment as captain–coach of Footscray in 1951. His coaching style and his speech was straightforward, like the man. He backed his players and asked them to have confidence in themselves. 'Forget names and reputations. You can do it.'

He put himself on the half-forward flank in the Grand Final of 1954 and told his charges to concentrate on the ball. 'I'll look after the rough stuff,' he said, and bowled over a few Demon stars early in the game. His inspiration and his three goals took Footscray to its most ecstatic moment in football.

Sutton, a club man before everything, lost his coaching place in 1957 and was refused admittance to the rooms on the grounds that he might upset the new coach Ted Whitten. He went in anyway and told Whitten: 'Good luck son! In future take your time when you talk to the players.' He said of his sacking: 'I felt the boys were going rather well and I was happy they were keeping their feet on the ground. You don't push too soon.' He put all these troubles behind him as he came to coach the club again in 1967–68 and served the club as a committeeman and President.

The Sutton record

Year	W	L	D	Position
1951	12	6	–	4th Lost First Semi
1952	5	14	–	10th
1953	13	5	–	4th Lost First Semi
1954	11	6	1	1st Won Second Semi Won Grand Final
1955	12	6	–	5th Missed 4th by 0.6%
1956	11	7	–	3rd Won First Semi Lost Preliminary Final
1957	7	4	1	3rd place end Round 12

1955–1957 HONOUR ROLL

Year	Pos	Leading Goalkicker	No.	Best & Fairest	Captain	Coach
1955	5th	Jack Collins	60	Peter Box	Charlie Sutton	Charlie Sutton
1956	3rd	Max Cross	52	Don Ross	C. Sutton/Wally Donald	Charlie Sutton
1957	6th	Jack Collins	74	Ted Whitten	Harvey Stevens/T. Whitten	Sutton/Whitten

CLUB NEWS 1955–1957

Post 1954 win. Footscray Mayor Fred Peart hands the keys of the city to Footscray Premiership coach Charlie Sutton after the Bulldogs' demolition of Melbourne in the 1954 Grand Final.
A young Ted Whitten wins the first of his five club Best and Fairest awards, back-pocket Wally Donald is runner-up and Best Clubman is taken out by Angus Abbey. Abbey's son Ross would later play 123 games for the Bulldogs between 1971–81.
Jack Collins wins the goalkicking award for the VFL, kicking 84 goals for the season. He would again win the award in 1957 with a tally of 74 goals. Collins finished his career with 383 goals.

1955 pre-season. Half-back flanker Alan Martin takes up a lucrative country coaching post. He is the only Premiership player to make himself unavailable for the 1955 season.
Long-time club identity and Premiership secretary Roy Russell collapsed and died after a committee meeting at the Footscray Town Hall. Russell had acted in the role of treasurer, Secretary and VFL delegate during his time as a hard-working dedicated Footscray committeeman.
Peter Box wins the 1955 Best and Fairest award. Champion full-back Herbie Henderson is runner-up.
Dogs miss the final four by a record narrow margin of 0.6%.
1956. Footscray coach Charlie Sutton played his last game against South

1955–1957

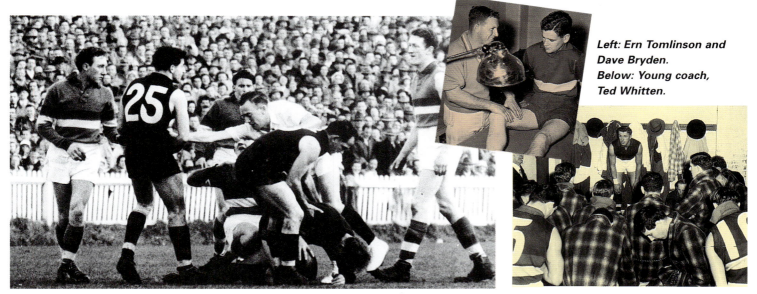

A dust-up with Carlton – plenty of spirit in the Dogs, but no Grand Final.

Left: Ern Tomlinson and Dave Bryden.
Below: Young coach, Ted Whitten.

A slow fade-out after the Premiership

Footscray was expected to carry on their fine form into the 1955 season. It was felt that their long kicking and high marking style would hold them in good stead.

Membership rose to 12,315 – a VFL record. But, as early as the first game (a 56-point thrashing of Collingwood at Victoria Park), Charlie Sutton was concerned: 'That's the bloody worst thing that happened to us today,' he said, standing with club secretary Roy Russell. 'The big thing we have to watch now is the bloody complacency.' The following week Footscray did it again, tearing their Richmond opponents apart.

Sutton's fears became reality during the next three weeks, when the Bulldogs lost all three games. A six-game winning streak mid-season put the Bulldogs back in the race for the four. In the final round Footscray needed a percentage boosting victory over North Melbourne. The players duly delivered a 60-point win, but Essendon beat Hawthorn to cling to fourth spot.

In 1956, Footscray scored a hair-raising two-point win over Geelong to get into the Premiminary Final against Collingwood. The strong Melbourne side was already through to the Grand Final, waiting for the winner.

Playing a quick-moving, running style of game, Collingwood jumped the Bulldogs in the early stages. At the quarter's end Collingwood led by 19 points.

A revitalised Footscray came out firing in the second quarter. Ted Whitten led from the front, ably supported by his half-backs in Gallagher and Stockman, who were both holding their individual opponents.

Footscray capitalised on this solid play and attacked continually throughout, though they kicked poorly. For all their dominance in the second quarter, Footscray managed only 2.8, giving them only a one-point lead at half-time.

All hope of playing in another Grand Final slipped away under a third-term Collingwood onslaught. Rawson had stood firm on his wing all day while Whitten, Donald Gilmour, Stockman and Gallagher worked tirelessly. Collingwood ran out easy winners 15.6 (96) to Footscray's 7.15 (57).

Peter Box: a fine kick.

Box's Brownlow

Centreman Peter Box showed that courage and persistence pay off, earning a Brownlow Medal for his brilliant 1956 year. The skilful, long-kicking centreman was in a car crash in 1952, and had a long fight to regain his fitness. But his hard work gave him a lean, well-muscled frame and he starred in the 1954 Grand Final. He played 107 games before retiring in 1957. Box always seemed well balanced, and could break away onto either foot and deliver a long drop punt accurately.

Melbourne at the Albert Ground in Round 5 of the 1956 season. In a match that the Bulldogs controlled for most of the day, the Swans stormed home. However, Charlie's determined teammates held on to give their mentor a fitting finale to his career, recording a 10-point victory.

In the Round 7 clash at Western Oval Charlie was afforded a guard of honour as he ran onto the ground and circled the ground in front of 30,000 adoring fans prior to the Dogs' clash with Carlton. In a thriller Carlton got up to win the match with a last-throw-of-the-dice effort that saw John James record a point from a kick off the ground.

The Round 18 clash with Carlton promised to be another classic final-round encounter. The Bulldogs were sitting fifth with 10 wins, while Carlton through the agency of a win over the Magpies in Round 16 occupied fourth spot. Victory would give either side the opportunity to take their place in the finals. A crowd of 45,000 packed into the Carlton ground to witness the Bulldogs play a characteristic defensive style game limiting the Blues to a meagre six goals for the game. Whitten played his typical stout game, repelling many Carlton attacks. The Dogs ran out winners by 17 points.

1956 First Semi-final heart-stopper. Footscray fought back to draw level with Geelong at the last change, and they remained close from there on. When Geelong's Rayson missed a snap on the siren, Footscray won by two points.

FOOTSCRAY

The great 'E. J.' – Ted Whitten

E. J. flies high over John 'Jerker' Jenkins.

Games: 321 Goals: 361
Player 1951–70, Capt: 1967 & 68
Capt/Coach: 1957–66, 69–70
State Rep: 29 times
Best and Fairest: 1954, 57, 58, 59 & 61

A sensational player: a great leader who gave his all in every contest. Often described by team-mates and opponents as the greatest player to have played. The stand-out player in the 1950s and 60s. A mobile versatile player who was equally at home at centre half-back or centre half-forward. Ted's love for big-time football was borne out in his unabashed pride for the big white V. Whether as a player, coach or selector, Ted gave of his best always for Victoria and Victorian football.

As a player Whitten had few peers. His uncanny balance and ability to read the play was second to none. Able to take strong marks or do the spectacular, he was able to play anywhere and do almost anything when the situation demanded something special. Whitten played for the Bulldogs for 20 seasons, accumulating accolade after accolade. Unfortunately, his leadership of the team, verbal battles with umpires and often tough on-field tactics precluded him from winning the game's highest individual honour, the Brownlow Medal. He played hard, tough, uncompromising football that often saw him gesturing with umpires as his opponent lay prostrate on the ground beside him. Footscray's 1941 Medallist Norman Ware held Whitten in the highest regard, clearly considering Whitten an 'honorary' member of the Brownlow Medal Club.

Whitten was a truly colourful character of the game, so aptly named 'Mr Football'.

Nights to remember

It could have been expected that having made the 1961 Grand Final with such a young and 'talented' side that the 'Scray' would be a side to contend with for some years to come. However, it was not to be.

Throughout the 1960s the club struggled to match it with the likes of Richmond, Carlton, Geelong and Collingwood.

Bulldog fans did, however, receive some consolation in the form of four Night Premierships, in 1963, 1964, 1967 and 1970.

Ruckman John Schultz was a popular winner of the Brownlow Medal in 1960.

1970 The last hurrah

Whitten's last game could not have been more sentimental nor sensational. Retirement was forced upon him by a committee that felt coaching was fast becoming a non-playing domain.

Footscray defeated a determined Hawthorn led by David Parkin by 3 points in a slog-fest in the Western Oval mud. Whitten's three-quarter time address etched itself in his players minds:

'It's got to be a do or die effort. It's got to be a determined effort. You've got to show all the guts and determination you've got in your body. You've got to inspire me with this last-quarter finish. You've been in front all day and you've got to stay there.'

The final quarter saw only 5 points kicked. Footscray managed 3 of those, winning a tight one by three points.

Whitten was carried shoulder high by Gary Dempsey to a specially erected dais in front of the John Gent stand. Whitten expressed his sorrow at playing his last game but took time to thank the supporters who had stuck by him. 'You are fantastic … magnificent is the word … I

love you all,' he said, before stepping from the dais to jog the last few yards and run up the players' race for the last time.

CLUB NEWS 1958-1970

Premiership President Otto Grobbecker passed away after a protracted illness. Grobbecker had served the Footscray Football Club well over many years. Two stints as President in 1947–49 and 1953–55 culminated in a Premiership in 1954. Otto also acted as club secretary between 1956–58 before his illness saw him retire.

1959. Former champion full-forward Jack Collins takes over as club Secretary, acting in that role until the end of the 1966 season before being appointed President, a role he carried out for seven years. Jack's input to the club both as a player and administrator spanned 23 years.

Wooden spoon goes to Footscray for the first time, after only three wins for the season. They had victories in Rounds 5 and 16 over South Melbourne and a nine-point win against top-of-the-ladder Melbourne.

1962. Footscray turned on a great display against Hawthorn in the Grand Final replay, Round 1 1962. The Bulldogs won the game using its superior pace, matching it against the aggressive vigour of Hawthorn. Final scores Footscray 12.8 (80) to Hawthorn 6.11 (47).

The 1962 season had its highs and lows. After defeating the reigning Premiers twice and eventual Premiers Essendon by 37 points in Round 17, defeats at the hands of down the ladder teams St Kilda and Collingwood in rounds 16 and 18 respectively ended

1958–1970

Hawthorn ends Flag dreams

Supporters, players and administrators alike were unable to contain their joy at the Bulldogs reaching only their second Grand Final.

After their resounding win in the 1954 Grand Final, it had been expected that the Bulldogs would feature in many more during the coming years. Alas, it was not to be. Loss of form by top-line players, players taking on lucrative country coaching positions, unrest with the appointment of a very young and inexperienced Ted Whitten as coach coupled with lazy attitudes soon saw the might of Western Oval fade into past memories.

Whitten was now required to regroup and formulate a new combination. By 1961, with a young and relatively inexperienced team, Whitten began moulding a running group of players. With the reintroduction of the flick pass and some sound performances from Brownlow Medallist John Schultz, the Dogs were able to make it to their second Grand Final.

Hawthorn had made the Grand Final via a convincing win against Melbourne in the Second Semi-final, while the Bulldogs had to stave off a determined St Kilda in the

Merv Hobbs' great mark.

First Semi before easily accounting for a leg-weary Demon side in the Preliminary Final.

Grand Final day was hot and fine as Ted Whitten, followed by his blond vice-captain John Schultz, ran onto the MCG to a hero's welcome. Red, white and blue colours filled the stadium as the 100,000-strong crowd waited in anticipation of the contest about to begin.

The Bulldogs were playing a good running style of football that was paying dividends, with Footscray leading at quarter time by 10 points.

The second quarter was all Hawthorn early. Edwards was now getting on top of Spargo and drove the Hawks into attack on a regular basis. However, the Hawk forwards couldn't convert their play into goals, kicking five points in a row. Hobbs had been busy throughout the quarter, as had Graeme Ion.

The Dogs' only goal for the quarter came from a Hoiles mark mid-term that found Whitten. His kick into the goal square saw McKellar free-kicked from the spillage, and the subsequent goal gave the Bulldogs an eight-point break at half-time.

The Bulldogs match committeeman Clarrie Shields remembered the rooms as looking like a battlefield. The long finals campaign was starting to take its toll.

The second half began with Edwards repeatedly winning the ball and bringing his team-mates into the game. Unable to contain him, Whitten and Jillard both made attempts at taking Edwards out, but all to no avail. The supremely fit Hawk champion bounced back to lead the Hawks to a resounding victory over the gallant young Bulldog team that gave its all throughout the finals series. The Bulldogs had tired noticeably after the main interval, the previous two weeks taking its toll.

A reception at the Footscray Town Hall after the game was well attended by officials and supporters. Captain–coach Whitten announced 'I'm sorry for you people that we did not win.'

Whitten, along with Gardiner, Ware and Schultz performed well, while Evans and Hoiles battled hard. A lack of a key goal-kicking forward and physical strength was the Dogs' final downfall in a season that ended at the hands of a tough opponent.

1958–1970 HONOUR ROLL

Year	Pos	Leading Goalkicker	No.	Best & Fairest	Captain	Coach
1958	11th	Jack Collins	49	Ted Whitten	Ted Whitten	Ted Whitten
1959	12th	Ray Baxter	35	Ted Whitten	Ted Whitten	Ted Whitten
1960	10th	Ray Baxter	37	John Schultz	Ted Whitten	Ted Whitten
1961	2nd	Ted Whitten	42	Ted Whitten	Ted Whitten	Ted Whitten
1962	5th	Ted Whitten	38	John Schultz	Ted Whitten	Ted Whitten
1963	9th	Merv Hobbs/G. Bisset	16	Ray Walker	Ted Whitten	Ted Whitten
1964	7th	George Bissett/Whitten	24	John Schultz	Ted Whitten	Ted Whitten
1965	10th	Merv Hobbs	24	John Schultz	Ted Whitten	Ted Whitten
1966	10th	Kevin Jackman	28	John Schultz	Ted Whitten	Ted Whitten
1967	12th	George Bisset	27	John Jillard	Ted Whitten	Charlie Sutton
1968	10th	Ted Whitten	36	David Thorpe	Ted Whitten	Charlie Sutton
1969	11th	George Bisset	45	George Bisset	Ted Whitten	Ted Whitten
1970	7th	George Bisset	45	Gary Dempsey	Whitten/Stuart Magee	Ted Whitten

the season on a disappointing note.
Roy Evans (captain of Footscray's 1938 first finals team) coached the reserves to their first Premiership since 1945.
1963. Former top player Jim Miller becomes President in 1963. Miller acts in this role for the next four years.
1966. John Schultz wins the Best and Fairest award for the fifth time, equalling Ted Whitten's record.

The old cowshed, a landmark in the outer at the Barkly Street end of the Western Oval, was pulled down and replaced by rows of concrete steps.
Ted Whitten played his 272nd game against Carlton at Princes Park, breaking Arthur Olliver's long-standing club games record.
1969 pre-season. Up-and-coming ruckman Gary Dempsey was severely burned in bushfires that threatened the family's Lara-based property. A courageous Dempsey fought back and regained his position by Round 1 1970.
Ted Whitten plays his 300th VFL game, joining an elite group of players to have achieved that mark.
Rover George Bisset is narrowly defeated in the Brownlow by Fitzroy stalwart Kevin Murray. Bisset was looked upon as being a little unlucky after being reported in the Dogs' Round 14 clash. Bisset was found not guilty, however he would have been ineligible to gain votes on the day.
1970. Gary Dempsey gains state selection and his first club Best and Fairest award, and is runner up to South Melbourne's Peter Bedford for the Brownlow Medal.

FOOTSCRAY

The 1976 team: battled into the five, but lost to Cats.

Finals but no joy

In 1974, all three Footscray sides made the finals for the first time. Ex-Collingwood champion Bob Rose was in charge and had developed a good running style of play.

The Bulldogs' late string of victories put them in the finals for the first time in 13 years. But whatever chance Footscray had of winning the 1974 Elimination Final against Collingwood was blown away with atrocious kicking in the second term. After trailing the Pies by 17 points at quarter time, the Dogs proceeded to kick 1.10, while Collingwood's 5 straight goals put them on the way to a 69-point victory.

In 1976 the team wilted under Geelong's pressure to lose the Elimination Final by seven points.

Administrative troubles

Instead of the club blossoming from its finals experiences, it quickly went back to old habits. In-fighting over debts began with the social club. The club had locked the social club doors in 1976, ultimately locking its members out.

Players had grown tired of poor treatment and administrative blundering, many seeking and gaining clearances. Threats of player strikes, the quitting of captain Laurie Sandilands, Warwick Roach's resignation in 1978 as general manager six months into the job and finally the walking out of coach Goggin six days into the season had destabilised the club once more. Although club legend and vice-president Ted Whitten had resigned, president Dick Collinson held steadfastly to his position.

Players were becoming rebellious, the stability of the club and its future having been sorely tested throughout the past few years. It wasn't until reserves coach Don McKenzie stepped in to take over the side that tempers and feeling came under some control once more.

The highlights of the season were the team's record-breaking VFL score of 33.15 (213) against St Kilda in round 13, and Templeton's 15-goal performance.

1971–1984 HONOUR ROLL

Year	Pos	Leading Goalkicker	No.	Best & Fairest	Captain	Coach
1971	8th	Bernie Quinlan	48	David Thorpe	Gary Dempsey	Ted Whitten
1972	7th	Laurie Sandilands	39	Peter Welsh	Gary Dempsey	Bob Rose
1973	9th	Laurie Sandilands	34	Gary Dempsey	David Thorpe	Bob Rose
1974	5th	Laurie Sandilands	50	Gary Dempsey	Laurie Sandilands	Bob Rose
1975	7th	Laurie Sandilands	47	Gary Dempsey	Laurie Sandilands	Bob Rose
1976	5th	Kelvin Templeton	82	Gary Dempsey	Laurie Sandilands	Bill Goggin
1977	7th	Kelvin Templeton	40	Gary Dempsey	Gary Dempsey	Bill Goggin
1978	11th	Kelvin Templeton	118	Kelvin Templeton	Gary Dempsey	Goggin/Don McKenzie
1979	9th	Kelvin Templeton	91	Ian Dunstan	Geoff Jennings	Don McKenzie
1980	10th	Kelvin Templeton	75	Kelvin Templeton	Geoff Jennings	Royce Hart
1981	11th	Jim Edmond/S. Loveless	25	Ian Dunstan	Geoff Jennings	Royce Hart
1982	12th	Simon Beasley	82	Ian Dunstan	Kelvin Templeton	Hart/Ian Hampshire
1983	7th	Simon Beasley	69	Brian Royal	Jim Edmond	Ian Hampshire
1984	7th	Simon Beasley	61	Andrew Purser	Jim Edmond	Michael Malthouse

Gary Dempsey won the 1975 Brownlow Medal with the highest vote yet recorded. The great ruckman was noted for his stamina and his marking ability, particularly in defence in last-quarter efforts.

CLUB NEWS 1971–1984

1972. Ted Whitten is replaced as coach by ex-Collingwood champion Bob Rose. The committee hoped to gain a fresh approach to the game. The move proved successful with a fifth-position finish by the Dogs in 1974. Their first finals appearance since their 1961 finals campaign resulted.

1973. Champion rover George Bisset is cleared to Collingwood after 166 games and 288-goal career with the Bulldogs. Bisset craved the opportunity to play in finals football. He achieved his dream with Collingwood in his first year with that club.

1973 captain and prolific kick-winner David Thorpe is cleared to Richmond. Thorpe's apparent clashes with the administration and desire to play finals football were the catalyst behind the decision to move on. Thorpe went on to play in Richmond's 1975 Premiership team.

Star South Australian recruit Neil Sachse was tragically injured during only his second game. Sachse crashed awkwardly into a pack, suffering spinal injuries that ended his career.

1976. Barry Round is cleared to South Melbourne. His ongoing battle to play a major role as a ruckman with the Bulldogs was thwarted by the outstanding form of Gary Dempsey.

Scraped in. The Bulldogs scraped into the final five due to an Alan Stoneham goal after the siren in Round 21, and a draw against Carlton in the final round.

1971-1984

Clearance sale

Between 1973 and 1986 Footscray effectively cleared or simply let go more than 15 quality players – players that would take out football honours with other clubs.

Players lost were of the calibre of George Bisset – to Collingwood, Gary Dempsey – North Melbourne, Bernie Quinlan – Fitzroy, Barry Round – South Melbourne, Alan Stoneham – Essendon, Robert McGhie – Richmond, David Thorpe – Richmond, Ian Low – Collingwood, Wayne Foreman – Essendon, Denis Collins – Carlton, Peter Featherby – Geelong, Laurie Sandilands – Collingwood, Kelvin Templeton – Melbourne, Brian Wilson – North Melbourne, Ian Dunstan – North Melbourne, Ray Huppatz – North Melbourne, Jim Edmond – Sydney, and of course, Brad Hardie – to Brisbane.

After topping the VFL goal-kicking in the previous two years, Kelvin Templeton played even better in 1980 when moved to centre half-forward. His just reward was the Brownlow medal.

Royce, Bluey and Mickey

It was hoped that the 1980 appointment of Richmond champion Royce Hart might put new life the Bulldogs. However, his disciplinarian approach did not work on the young players remaining at his disposal after 24 players were cut. The one thing the Dogs didn't have was time (something Hart required) – they expected results.

The Dogs lost their first 11 straight before putting together some good wins. The move of Templeton to centre half-forward was the only positive in another dismal year.

Worse was yet to strike the Kennel in 1981 – they were only able to win two games. By Round 10 of 1982 the Bulldogs had hit rock bottom with one win. The committee demoted Royce Hart to reserves coach. He never took up this option and was effectively sacked.

Workhorse ruckman and veteran of 224 games with Geelong and Footscray Ian 'Bluey' Hampshire was approached to take over.

Hampshire's coaching career ended as abruptly as it had commenced. After a reasonably successful 1983 season that saw Footscray gain some respectability with 10 wins, Hampshire's position looked safe. Bluey himself unloaded a shock wave before the start of the 1984 season. His resignation left Bulldog board members scurrying to find a replacement. Hampshire cited work commitments and a lack of support from certain quarters of the club for his shock announcement.

Approaches were made to Don Scott, Kevin Bartlett, Phil Cleary and finally Mick Malthouse. A disciplinarian and believer in hard work, Malthouse (supported by some sound recruiting from Shane O'Sullivan) placed the Bulldogs in its best position for many years – eventually culminating in the Preliminary Final against the Hawks in 1985.

George Bisset.

Left: Bluey Hampshire.
Right: Peter Featherby.

1977. Supporters are puzzled by the clearance of leading kick-winner Peter Featherby to Geelong after only 42 games.
Gary Dempsey wins his sixth Best and Fairest award in 1977, passing the record five wins held jointly by Ted Whitten and John Schultz.
1978. Denis Collins is cleared to Carlton five days into the season. Rover Huppatz is leased to North Melbourne. Bernie Quinlan (Fitzroy), and Laurie Sandilands (Collingwood) all departed the Western Oval through dispute with the club or as an avenue for the club to raise funds. Quinlan continued to play outstanding football culminating in the sharing of 1982 Brownlow Medal honours with friend and former team-mate Barry Round.
Round 13 v St Kilda. Footscray kicks a VFL record 33.15 (213), full-forward Kelvin Templeton bagging 15 goals.
1983. Captain Jim Edmond would have been ecstatic at his first-quarter 5-goal haul and the team's 10-goal blitz of Richmond in the opening quarter of their Round 5 contest. Edmond went on to kick a further two and take best on ground honours, with the Bulldogs scrambling home to a 2-point victory after a spirited Tiger fightback.
$21,000 Bonus. Sponsors Eastcoast offered the Footscray players a $21,000 incentive for their players' trip fund if they were able to take out the final three matches in 1983. They achieved the task, although not without some good fortune and great come-from-behind football.

FOOTSCRAY

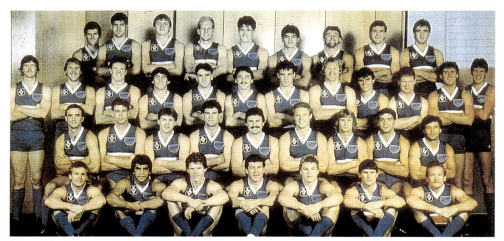

The 1985 team revived the Bulldogs' fortunes under coach Mick Malthouse.

Bulldogs gallant to the end in 1985

After being totally dominated by a rampant Hawthorn combination in the Qualifying Final, the Bulldogs hit back savagely against North Melbourne in a classic finals encounter. Hawkins, Maylin, Wallis and Royal racked up numerous possessions and sent the ball forward regularly. Footscray ran out easy victors by 30 points.

Footscray supporters flocked to Waverley for the rematch with high expectations of seeing the red, white and blue take victory and go on to only their third appearance in a Grand Final in their 60-year history.

Essendon had accounted for Hawthorn fairly easily the week before, buoying hopes of the Bulldogs reversing the drubbing from the Hawks in the earlier Final.

The first half was hard, tough football. Hardie proved unpassable, causing Matthews to be benched, while Hawkins handed out a football lesson to DiPierdomenico on his wing. The Bulldogs had worked themselves to an eight-point lead by the first change.

As expected, the Hawks fought back and by half-time had gained the ascendancy again, albeit by only four points.

The third quarter was sheer pressure. Hanging on grimly, the Hawthorn took a one-point lead into the final stanza. A goal by Beasley kept the Dogs within touch, but the Hawks replied through McCarthy and again when Matthews went to the forward pocket.

An attempted spoil by Sewell and Hardie fell to free-running Matthews who goaled to put the Hawks in a commanding position at the 10-minute mark. Purser replied to drag the margin back; however, goals to Dunstall and Judge sealed the Bulldogs' fate for 1985.

Hardie affair splits club

When Brad Hardie suffered burns to 65 per cent of his body at the age of 15, it could have ended a promising football career. The former South Fremantle junior began in sensational style, winning the 1985 Brownlow Medal – only the second player to achieve this in his first year of VFL football. Hardie had a nonchalant, free-running style of play, often backing his judgement and ability to read the game against that of his opponent.

Hardie's fall from grace was just as sensational. In Round 20 against Carlton at Waverley in 1986 a fired-up Malthouse dragged Hardie after what he saw as loose and undisciplined play. Hardie's act of defiance (taking off his jumper and waving it at the coach's box) was not to be tolerated by Malthouse. Hardie's departure from the Western Oval, transferred to Brisbane for a reported $270,000, split administrators and supporters alike.

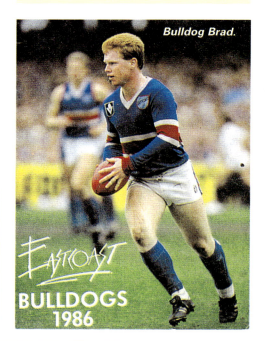

Bulldog Brad.

1985–1989 HONOUR ROLL

Year	Pos	Leading Goalkicker	No.	Best & Fairest	Captain	Coach
1985	3rd	Simon Beasley	105	Doug Hawkins	Jim Edmond	Michael Malthouse
1986	8th	Simon Beasley	88	Brad Hardie	Rick Kennedy	Michael Malthouse
1987	7th	Simon Beasley	73	Tony McGuinness	Rick Kennedy	Michael Malthouse
1988	8th	Simon Beasley	82	Terry Wallace	Rick Kennedy	Michael Malthouse
1989	13th	Adrian Campbell	21	Terry Wallace	Steve Wallis	Michael Malthouse

CLUB NEWS 1985–1989

1985. Hardie wins Brownlow. The fiery redhead from South Fremantle became only the second player to win the coveted Brownlow Medal in his first VFL season.
Simon Beasley wins Coleman Medal for leading goalkicker in the VFL with 105 goals. Beasley steered through his 100th goal in the First Semi-final against North Melbourne, setting the Bulldogs up for a 5-goal winning burst in the third term. He also kicked 12 goals in a match twice during 1985, against Richmond in Round 7 and Melbourne in Round 15.
1986. Doug Hawkins goes down with a serious knee injury in Round 21 versus Collingwood at the MCG.
Hardie dispute escalates. With little hope of a solution being found, the committee finally cleared Hardie to Brisbane for a reported $270,000.
1987. Hawkins makes his long-awaited return in Round 11 against West Coast. When coach Malthouse released Hawkins onto the ground and into his customary position on the wing, the pro-Footscray crowd erupted, the wave of euphoria sweeping the team along. West Coast were unable to match the Dogs, Hawkins gaining many possessions.
1989 Round 20. Despite suggestions that the Footscray club would fold, and that it would be playing its last game, a crowd of only 8673 bothered to turn out to watch Footscray's crushing defeat of Richmond 15.17 (120) to 3.11

1985 – 1989

A smiling Leon Wiegard and an apprehensive-looking Nick Columb announce the proposal.

The power of the people

When Nick Columb joined Leon Weigard and VFL boss Ross Oakley for the announcement of the impending merger of the Fitzroy and Footscray football clubs, many felt it was 'a done deal'. Whatever the case, the VFL was close to achieving its desire of having two Melbourne-based teams merge, making way for another interstate team.

However, they hadn't bargained on the people, of their emotion and strength, their love for the game, their team, their colours. As the news of Footscray's demise and the impending merger started to sink in, people from all walks of life rallied. On October 8 they met at the Western Oval, 10,000 strong.

Frank Mullholland started proceedings with his protest song 'Footscray Town'. First Dennis Galimberti, then Peter Gordon addressed the crowd. Gordon gave the impression of a fighter, a man ready to put himself on the line. It was a sight to behold for all red-blooded Doggie supporters. Being part of that crowd made people realise it wasn't over.

Gordon insisted that the target of $1.5 million could be reached. He spoke of believing in the ability of the ordinary supporter in the outer and how business could help. With emotions running high, he introduced the Footscray team for 1990 and his nine-member board. 'This may be the last time you see a Footscray team assembled on the Western Oval,' he said. 'It's up to you.'

His announcement of Terry Wheeler as coach for 1990 brought thunderous applause. Wheeler had earned a healthy respect from many Bulldog fans for his wise management of the 1989 Reserves and for taking Williamstown to a VFA Premiership.

After the rally all thoughts were channelled to finding out how people could help. The drill hall on the corner of Barkly and Gordon (appropriately named) Streets became the workplace for accepting donations, handing out tins for collection of money and for people to meet for support and discuss the campaign. The offices of Slater and Gordon became the headquarters for operations.

As people filed away from the Western Oval that day, new hope had sprung into their thoughts . 'Maybe there was a chance we could save the club?' they thought. People volunteered their services to stand on corners, and outside the TAB, or doorknock to ask for donations. Others worked around the clock organising functions, setting up dances, hastily putting together raffles, cooking cakes – anything to support the cause.

The Battle of Barkly St

The *Western Times*, the *Mail* and the *Western Independent* ran stories urging Footscray supporters to 'Dig Deep'.

'Footscray is not just a football club. It is a symbol of the western suburbs,' argued Brendan Donohue, political reporter for the *Sunday Age*. The union movement threatened to ban work on the Great Southern Stand. Joan Kirner, Labor MLA for Williamstown, offered her support for the campaign and secured sponsors from local industries.

The campaign was gaining momentum. There was no stopping the people's express from here. $1.15 million was quickly raised, a business plan put in place and a list of sponsors named. The VFL had no choice but to concede that Footscray was still alive.

When news broke that Footscray Football Club had been saved people were beside themselves with joy. We've done it, – The spirit of the Dogs lives on, – I don't care if we never have another victory, as long as we keep playing – Three cheers for Footscray – all were common cries from the thousands of Bulldog supporters who joined the throngs to celebrate Footscray's second greatest victory. A victory for the people by the people.

Terry Wheeler aptly summed it up. 'I've seen many games won on emotion … and we've just seen a football club saved on emotion.'

Peter Gordon.   **Irene Chatfield.**

---

(29). Garry Linell writes in the *Age* '…saddest of all is that the suburb of Footscray has turned its back on the Western Oval and its football team.'
1989 – coach goes. Mick Malthouse, dispirited by Footscray's lack of money, supporters and winning players, resigns after six seasons, having had 67 wins, 66 losses and two draws.
October 2 – the news is out. The press carries definitive news that the Footscray Football Club will merge with Fitzroy. The team will be the Fitzroy Bulldogs and be based at Princes Park.
October 3. A Bulldog Connection Committee meets to discuss how to block the merger.
October 5. Supporter Irene Chatfield acts as Plaintiff for the 'Save the Dogs' movement in an action lodged with the Victorain Supreme Court, claiming that the VFL was acting 'irregularly' in winding up the club.
October. A 'board in exile' comprising Peter Gordon, Tony Hannabery, Peter Welsh, Ron Coleman, Don Gibson, Lynne Kosky and Dennis Galimberti is appointed.
October 8. The rally of supporters at the Western Oval collects $450,000. The club was estimated to need to raise at least $1.3 million in 17 days to discharge its debts.
Celebration. The legends match held days after the victory became a celebration day for many, and raised a further $75,000. On Saturday, October 28 a victory parade marched down Barkly Street to Footscray Mall.

FOOTSCRAY

Stalwarts of the fighting Bulldogs

Dancing Dougie Hawkins

The larrikin from Braybrook represented the soul of Footscray in modern times, as much as Charlie Sutton and Ted Whitten had done in the past. On an emotional day in 1994 he passed the club record of 321 games held by Ted Whitten and went on to play 329 games over 17 seasons before he was virtually discarded by the club, and went over to Fitzroy to finish his career. Who else in a Fitzroy jumper would be cheered by Footscray supporters as he danced again, in alien colours, on the Doug Hawkins wing at Western Oval. He had endured a total knee reconstruction and resisted lucrative lures to stay with Footscray, and inspire his team-mates with his pace, ball handling, marking, baulking and weaving skills. He captained the club from 1990 to 1993.

Terry Wheeler

After coming from Warburton, Terry Wheeler's first kick in the big league came from a typical Dempsey palm. 'Stand there, son' said Dempsey to Wheeler when he first got a run at VFL Park in Round 7, 1974.

Wheeler went on to become a formidable 157-game back-pocket player during the 70s. He would later return as Reserves coach to Mick Malthouse and finally take on the enormous task of rebuilding a demoralised Bulldog combination after a very poor 1989 season and amidst the turmoil, frustration and finally ecstatic joy of the '89 fightback campaign.

Terry Wheeler gave his players, the team and supporters time to 'savour the moment'. He loved a sense of occasion and he believed in it. He took them to the 1992 Preliminary Final, but was a victim of the team's decline in later years.

Steven MacPherson

Steve MacPherson had the important ability to inspire players around him with his uncompromising football. He came from Tasmania in 1982 and always had the ability to succeed, although he did not always take to club discipline. His career seemed to be going nowhere by 1991, when coach Terry Wheeler told him that the only position he was being considered for was the back pocket. He took the news to heart, and emerged as a strong team leader and an influence in Footscray's revival. His reformation included playing an influential part in the Footscray club's Care For Kids program.

Scott Wynd

Scott Wynd has been the most influential player in the Bulldogs' rise in the 1990s. The blond, athletic ruckman was zoned to North Melbourne, but was overlooked and at the age of 18 he was free to join the club of his choice. He went to Footscray in 1988, where his outstanding ruck work, strong marking and round-the-ground play were recognised with numerous club awards and the 1992 Brownlow Medal. He was made captain in 1994, but was restricted for several seasons by persistent knee injuries. His presence and consistent form in 1997 took Footscray close to the top.

'The human clamp' – Tony Liberatore

A pocket dynamo. The human clamp. The most difficult opponent I've ever had – opponents' expressions on Tony Liberatore. Any of these descriptions fit Libba to a T. Discarded by North Melbourne, Liberatore has become one of the fiercest competitors the game has seen.

His reading of the ball enabled him to be at the fall of the ball and administer one of his trademark bone-crunching tackles, turning many a defensive situation into attack. Tony's quest to prove that he could play the game at the highest level paid off with two Gardiner Medals (Reserves Best and Fairest) and a Brownlow in 1990.

CLUB NEWS 1990–1996

1990. The Bulldogs take a big step towards their on-field resurrection with 12 wins and a creditable seventh spot finish for the season. 17-year-old Chris Grant makes his debut. Grant went on to become the youngest player to kick 50 goals in a season, and, was voted AFL Rookie of the Year. **Steven Kolynuik** kicks the match-winning goal to snatch victory from eventual Premiers Collingwood in the dying minutes of their Round 17 match at the MCG. Kolynuik had marked way out on an acute angle. Knowing the clock was running down, Kolynuik baulked Wright on the mark, took two bounces, steadied and drilled the ball through the two big sticks

1992. A resounding 27-point win over the Adelaide Crows in Round 1 at Football Park gave supporters a taste of what was to come for the 1992 season. Doug Hawkins was in outstanding touch along with young guns Grant and Cameron.

In Round 21 the Bulldogs again showed their persistence with a hard-fought victory in the wind and rain of the Western Oval against a determined Eagles combination. The victory cemented a top three placing for the Dogs. In what was a low-scoring game the Dogs ran out winners by 30 points.

1993 First operating loss since 1988 devastates President Peter Gordon **Fitzroy** is invited to share the Western Oval.

Doug Hawkins is chaired from the

1990 – 1996

The team thanks their supporters after bowing out of the 1992 finals campaign.

Ted Whitten says goodbye.

Battles of the 90s continue

Terry Wheeler's Bulldogs developed a confidence that had been missing from the club for some seven seasons.

In 1992, the Bulldogs were faced with the prospect of entering the finals against Geelong without their Captain Scott Wynd. Young ruckman Justin Charles would be asked to fill the void. Whatever dominance the Bulldogs had in the first half was eroded quickly by the more skilled and superbly fit Geelong during the third and final quarters. They ran away with the Qualifying Final with 15 goals to three in the second half.

The Bulldogs hurdled St Kilda in the First Semi-final with surprising ease, and faced Geelong again in the Preliminary Final. Wheeler's dream of taking the Dogs all the way to the big day in September hinged on the team's ability to close down dangermen Ablett and Brownless up forward.

To do this Wynd would need to shut out Barnes and the on-ballers Hocking and Bairstow. A determined effort early saw the Dogs hanging in. But a six-goal onslaught in the second term saw the Bulldogs drop off the pace.

Wheeler's last onfield act was to take his players across to supporters at the Ponsford Stand end, giving the supporters a chance to say thank you. The red white and blue army duly payed respect, cheering their boys as they trudged dejectedly from the MCG for the last time in 1992. A season that saw sixteen wins and six losses coupled with three finals appearances had been more than was initially expected.

Memories of a champion

As the hearse carrying E.J. Whitten to his final resting place moved ever so slowly across the top of the Geelong Rd bridge people waved their last farewells. The crowd that gathered in the John Gent stand reminisced about the feats of the great E.J. Whitten.

They remembered the 75-yard goals he kicked with that howling and bitterly cold Western Oval wind. They remembered a scrawny 17-year-old kid being knocked unconscious in his first game, of a 23-year-old coaching men much older. And the way he manipulated the rules when introducing the flick pass.

They talked about E.J.'s ability to take control of a game, as if he were the appointed umpire. They cringed when discussing the bone-crunching clashes he had with the likes of Mopsy Fraser and Eric Guy. Most in attendance remembered Ted's love for the game, his love of the red, white and blue, of the very people of Footscray itself.

Many a humorous moment filled the afternoon. Memories of Ted's stint on 'World Championship Wrestling' and his running verbal battles with Mal Brown and Neil 'Knuckles' Kerley on State of Origin footy. It was these memories that helped people come to terms with the loss of one of their own. A champion, everyone's childhood idol, a legend, their hero.

1990 – 1996 HONOUR ROLL

Year	Pos	Leading Goalkicker	No.	Best & Fairest	Captain	Coach
1990	7th	Chris Grant	51	Peter Foster	Doug Hawkins	Terry Wheeler
1991	10th	Doug Hawkins	38	Tony Liberatore	Doug Hawkins	Terry Wheeler
1992	3rd	Danny Del-Re	70	Scott Wynd	Doug Hawkins	Terry Wheeler
1993	9th	Danny Del-Re	36	Leon Cameron	Doug Hawkins	Terry Wheeler
1994	6th	Chris Grant	71	Chris Grant	Scott Wynd	Wheeler/Alan Joyce
1995	7th	Richard Osborne	53	Scott West	Scott Wynd	Alan Joyce
1996	15th	Jason Watts	44	C. Grant/Jose Romero	Scott Wynd	Joyce/Terry Wallace

Western Oval after playing his 300th game. Hawkins went on to break Ted Whitten's long-standing club record of games (321) finally playing 329 games with the Bulldogs before ending his career with Fitzroy in season 1995.

1994. Subiaco Fiasco: After winning four games in a row leading up to the final home-and-away fixture against the Eagles at Subiaco, Bulldog fans were well pleased with the team's efforts. However, the half-time brawl against the Eagles that saw Grant, Southern and MacPherson fronting an AFL investigation and subsequent 61-point loss left the Bulldogs in disarray, just six days before the Qualifying Final against Geelong.

1995. Six straight losses faded into memory as the Bulldogs kicked 37 points clear of Collingwood at Waverley. **Communications breakdown,** and Hawkins walks from the Kennel a dejected and disappointed man. Hawkins finally nominated for the draft and was picked up by Fitzroy.

Club stalwart Beryl Cox purchased a Lions membership along with her Footscray one, supporting Doug for the season he spent with Fitzroy.

1996. The dismal performances of a team seemingly heading nowhere were quickly shaken off when new Bulldog coach Terry Wallace took over. **Chris Grant falls** one vote short of sharing Brownlow honours with Michael Voss and James Hird. Hird secured the 3 votes while Grant received 2 in the Essendon v Footscray game in Round 22.

FOOTSCRAY

Terry Wallace: tough approach.

1997 in review

More than a few eyebrows were raised when pre-season training for 1997 commenced on 6 October 1996. Coach Terry Wallace embarked on a program aimed specifically at improving the players' general fitness and skills levels. Wallace planned to revamp the structure of the side and implement a game plan that would provide more run and flexibility across all lines.

Camaraderie engendered by the arduous pre-season threatened to falter at the first hurdle. A ticketing fiasco at the club's new Optus Oval home ground left many a fan with a bitter taste in the mouth – although this wasn't as hard to swallow as Winston Abraham's last-minute goal for Fremantle that deprived the Bulldogs of victory.

The players hit back with three thrilling victories, over Sydney, Richmond and Melbourne. There is no doubt that the side had been transformed over summer into an attacking unit.

When the Bulldogs defeated Geelong in Round 11, they went to the top of the ladder – a position they held for another three rounds. They were sitting pretty.

After a soft win against Carlton in Round 14, the Bulldogs' form suddenly dropped away. They suffered four straight losses, and crashed out of the eight when Richmond defeated them at Optus Oval.

After beating Melbourne, the Western Bulldogs emphasised their return as a finals candidate with a thumping victory over Adelaide at Football Park. Despite the predicted aggressive tactics of Hawthorn in the last round, the Bulldogs managed to win and clinch third spot on the ladder with 14 wins, eight losses.

Taskforce to the rescue

By mid-1996 the club's situation was becoming desperate. Rumours of mounting debt, talk of mergers and of discontent from players who would be uncontracted at season's end dominated supporter discussions. Yet under all of this Terry Wallace was able to stabilise the on-field performances and achieve a high level of competiveness from his team.

By September Denis Galimberti had stepped down from his position with the club and Peter Gordon stated his intentions to resign from the Presidency before the forthcoming AGM. These people were among those who had ultimately saved the club in 1989. A miracle of no less impact was again required if the Bulldogs were to grace the fields of AFL football in 1997.

The miracle came in the form of a Taskforce group headed up by former players Rick Kennedy and Ray Baxter and backed by long-time supporters and past committeemen David Smorgon and Alan Johnstone. The group comprised over more than 30 influential business people and long-time supporters of the Red, White and Blue.

They set about changing the image of the club and its home base. David Smorgon spoke of the need for unity and positive attitudes. The name Footscray was removed from the team's playing name and changed to Western Bulldogs. However, the club was to continue trading under the traditional name Footscray Football Club.

Home games were switched to Optus Oval to attract sponsorships and make available better amenities for all supporters. A more upbeat playing strip was created from a mix of the past, present and future. The coach and players were encouraged to be open in their approach to the media and play an aggressive, attacking style of football.

They were now representing the western region of Melbourne, not just the immediate surrounds of Footscray and Maribynong River.

David Smorgon and the new symbol.

The Docklands stadium may be the new home in the inner-west for the Bulldogs

1997

A wet Saturday on August 22 and the victorious Bulldogs and 28,000 supporters say farewell at the last AFL game on the Western Oval.

Overwhelming Sydney

A near faultless display of football in the first term saw the Bulldogs totally dominate proceedings in their Second Qualifying Final encounter against the Sydney Swans. It was a devastating performance that highlighted the abundant talent that the Bulldogs had. This was not a snarling, biting team of triers, but a genuinely talented combination.

Matthew Dent and Leon Cameron oozed class on the wing and across half-back, delivering the ball with pinpoint accuracy. With Wynd falling back across Lockett, and also dominating the centre bounces, the Bulldogs either won first use of the ball or would quickly turn a Swans attack into a forward thrust of their own. Grant was particularly damaging up forward and Smith created havoc with his sustained pace and his ability to finish off his work.

By the 15-minute mark of the first term the Bulldogs had the Swans looking like a disorganised rabble. A nine goal to nil first term left little more for the crowd than to stand and applaud a record-breaking performance. The Western Bulldogs' win was only the team's second in seven finals in the 90s.

The Western Bulldogs' physical and hardline approach to their game in 1997 attracted the attention of more than just the umpires. After the Round 7 game against Hawthorn, the AFL charged Chris Grant with striking, despite the umpires not having made a report. The ramifications of the one-week suspension were felt on Brownlow Medal night, when Grant polled the most votes (27), but was ineligible.

So near at season's end

Not since Billy Brownless' after-the-siren goal in 1994 had Bulldog supporters felt like this. Only this time the stakes were higher. There would be no Grand Final. No September glory.

They had just seen their team sqaunder a wonderful opportunity of playing for the ultimate prize. Chris Grant, Rohan Smith, Tony Liberatore and Scottie West were devastated, the pain obvious in their outward displays of emotion.

It was soul-destroying stuff. In the crowd, a young girl stood crying as an ashen-faced father and his mate looked on in despair. So close yet so far away. The game that had been won for the better part of the day was now lost. A feeling of total dismay and emptiness crept across the sea of red, white and blue supporters.

It had been a lacklustre affair in the first term, with neither side showing any dominance. It was the Crows who kicked three of the first four goals before the Bulldog machine moved into overdrive. After injuring his shoulder again Jose Romero was replaced by Mark West, and his hard-running approach to the ball gave new bite to the Bulldogs around the packs. The Dogs were now controlling every situation and put on on eight goals to the Crows four in the second quarter. The 31-point half-time lead would surely be too much for the Crows to peg back.

The game had now become a dour struggle, but the Bulldogs still led by 22 points

The opening minutes of the final term saw the Bulldogs push forward on countless

Rohan Smith: Bulldogs' dynamic runner.

occasions. First Cook marked 30 metres out, only to miss. Then Romero hit the post. Young gun Nathan Brown ran onto a loose ball but couldn't find the handle and Tony Liberatore kicked one that looked like a goal, the sealer, but was adjudged to have sailed over the post.

Minutes later Jarman goaled for the Crows and a sniff of victory filtered through their camp. The Bulldog players had visibly slowed. Adelaide were making one last effort to stay in the finals race.

A goal to Smart and another to Goodwin put the crows within a kick before the 20-minute mark of the last quarter. Another attempt from Mark West running into goal 35 metres out went astray. The next six minutes felt like an eternity for Bulldog fans as their players struggled to stay in the game. The Crows' Kane Johnson, roaming free across centre, ran through half-forward before delivering to Jarman, who kicked truly. The final blow had been dealt to the Western Bulldogs.

1997 HONOUR ROLL

Year	Pos	Leading Goalkicker	No.	Best & Fairest	Captain	Coach
1997	3rd	Simon Minton-Connell	43	Scott West	Scott Wynd	Terry Wallace

FREMANTLE

MY CLUB
by Les Everett

There's some explaining to do if you support one of the AFL's new teams. If you're over 25 you can't say you've grown up barracking for Adelaide, Brisbane, Fremantle, West Coast or maybe even Sydney – following one of these clubs is the result of a decision made as an adult.

I grew up supporting East Perth in the WAFL and it's important to point out that my support for the Royals was as passionate, illogical and all-consuming as that exhibited by any Carlton, Collingwood or Essendon fan. I'm still emotionally scarred by the period 1966 to 1969 when East Perth lost four consecutive Grand Finals.

The expansion of the VFL hit home for Western Australian football followers with the formation of the Eagles and their entry into the national competition in 1987. The effect on the local competition was devastating. Suddenly the team you had grown up supporting was playing in a second-rate competition in front of dismal crowds and the atmosphere had all but disappeared.

For many WA fans the adult decision to barrack for the Eagles was simple – they were Western Australians barracking for the WA club against the bitter enemy – Victorians. Some were happy to ditch the VFL club they had followed for life in favour of the locals.

Of course not all WA footy followers jumped into bed with the Eagles. Some kept up their support for another VFL team. Some hated what the expanded VFL did to local football and never embraced the VFL/AFL. Others may have had a reaction something like mine.

I never really followed a VFL team – I was an admirer of Essendon when fellow Boulder boy Alec Epis played there; had a passing fling with Geelong because of Polly Farmer; an early seventies tumble with Carlton due to Syd Jackson and a much later one-season-stand with Essendon in 1993 which ended when the Bombers ran onto the ground in the Grand Final minus Derek Kickett. So I was a prime candidate for taking on a new local team in the national competition.

So why not the Eagles? Maybe it started with the launch – a showy affair that could just as easily have been launching a new fizzy drink.

It seemed to me that those in charge of the new VFL club believed they were the product of some sort of immaculate conception – as if football hadn't existed in WA before the Eagles came along.

Something else annoyed me too – you were expected to barrack for the Eagles and asked to explain yourself if you didn't. In the past I might have hated East Fremantle and despised West Perth but I never questioned people's right to follow such stupid teams!

I watched the progress of West Coast in 1987 with a kind of benign indifference but by 1988 I'd become passionate – barracking with gusto for whoever was playing against the Eagles.

Obviously I was in need of a team to barrack for in the AFL but I was not going to unconditionally take on the newcomer when it arrived. As fate would have it I was close at hand for some of the key moments in the birth of WA's second AFL club.

On 14 December 1993 a phone call alerted me to a big announcement to be made at Subiaco Oval. I was able to get away in my lunch break and hear Ross Oakley announce the new team would be based in Fremantle. Look closely at the TV footage of this historic event and you'll clearly see my leg.

As the club began to take shape it began to appeal to me. Gerard Neesham was made coach and I thought he was the right person for the job in cultural and football terms. Besides, I'd briefly played in the same football team as him back in 1974.

On 12 July 1994 I was at the 'strictly embargoed media launch' of the club name, logo and colours. It was to be the Fremantle Football Club, nickname the Dockers, and the jumpers, home-and-away with plenty of purple, looked all right. It had all been thought up by a marketing firm and

'Grinder', the Freo mascot.

FREMANTLE

Year Established	1995
Joined VFL/AFL	1995
Home Grounds	Subiaco Oval, WACA
Premierships	Nil
Brownlow Medals	Nil
Record home crowd	39,844 v West Coast, 1995
Most games	Dale Kickett, 63
Most goals	Peter Mann, 79
Notable supporters	Ric Charlesworth, Jerry Ellis, Luc Longley, Johnny (JJ) Miller, Tim Winton

Ben Allan leads the Dockers out for the first training session.

Traditional rivals already!

although no wharfie was able to recall the term Docker in use on the Fremantle waterfront, we accepted it. At least Dockers was better than Cobras (a touted possibility).

On Monday, 31 October 1994 the Dockers began to look like a footy team. And a Fremantle team. The first training run was at Fremantle Oval and a large group of hopefuls tried their luck. They were led out onto the track by the captain Ben Allan; Dale Kickett was there, staying in the background on his last chance in the AFL; it was a surprise to see Matthew Burton – he stooped but couldn't remain inconspicuous. A big crowd of supporters looked on, some already decked out in the colours.

As the Fremantle's Football Club grew it became apparent that the club was willing to acknowledge its links with the WAFL and to celebrate its connection to Fremantle's football heritage.

On the field, where it really matters, the Dockers have provided plenty of thrills and heartbreaks and they've done it all with a certain charm. Every week there's the chance to see Dale Kickett emerge from a situation that would've trapped anyone else; Craig Callaghan and Luke Toia climb smiling from the bottom of a pack; the unknown Shane Parker make a superstar look silly; Stephen O'Reilly beat a top full forward and then run from defence or carefully crafted moments of skill from Gary Dhurrkay.

Yes, it's been a long journey, but I reckon I'm there now. I still barrack for East Perth, I still hate the Eagles, but there's a new positive force in my football life these days – I follow Fremantle.

A Docker puts his hair where his loyalty lies.

No finals, but some good performances to celebrate for the cheer squad in 1997.

EAST FREMANTLE

East Fremantle legend Jack Clarke takes a kick for WA.

Brian Peake: a great Shark.

The legends and larrikins of the old West

Football fans across the country are starting to appreciate what a derby means with the ferocity of matches between Fremantle and West Coast.

The intensity of matches between the home town AFL rivals steps up markedly when they are opposed to each other. So you can just imagine the tension between two clubs from the same city.

The AFL rivalry has been spawned from a near century-old battle between the two Fremantle clubs in the WAFL, East and South Fremantle. As much as anything, performances in those games built or destroyed reputations in the port city and victory provided more than mere bragging rights until the next confrontation.

If football is the game of the working class, then its heart must surely beat in Fremantle. It is a town with a rich history in the game. A town that has produced more than its share of legends and larrikins, heroes and villains.

Right from the time that East Fremantle (now the most successful club in senior Australian Football ranks behind the SANFL's Port Adelaide) won its first Premiership in 1900, the Sharks have forged a proud history.

Its early record was built around the efforts of magnificent achievers like the Doig family, a relationship which began when Hooky Doig played in the club's second season, 1899, and continued with his three sons Norman, Billy and Edgar adding to the legend.

Hooky's brother Scotty began as a half-back flanker in the club's first season and played until 1911. Then, there was Charlie, another brother, who was an early champion on a wing or as a forward.

Scotty's son Ron was bound residentially to South Fremantle so he played with that club and was brilliant and versatile half-forward, who tragically died after being injured in the 1932 Second Semi-final.

Charlie Doig later served as president from 1924–36, and his sons Charlie Jnr and George had a wonderful and lasting impact at East Fremantle. Charlie was versatile, strong and skilful and won the Fairest and Best award in his second season, was captain of the unbeaten 1946 Premiership team and coached the club to the 1954 Flag.

George could lay claim to being the first genuine superstar of the game in WA, kicking 106 goals in his first season in 1933 and by the time he retired in 1941 he had a total of 1111 against his name.

Of course there have been many other great players since with the likes of Jack Sheedy, Jack Clarke, Ray Sorrell, Norm Rogers and George Prince being outstanding contributors through the 50s and 60s.

Clarke holds the distinction of winning the most All-Australian blazers through the carnival system, earning that honour four times. A truly great player, his rivalry with East Perth's Graham 'Polly' Farmer is legendary.

More recently the Sharks have produced outstanding players like Brian Peake, Doug Green, Tony Buhagiar, Michael Brennan, Chris Mainwaring, Peter Wilson, Paul Harding and Andrew Purser.

East Fremantle had won 10 Premierships before their port neighbours celebrated with successive Flags in 1916–17, but Souths' greatest era was from 1947–54 when the Bulldogs played in seven of the eight Grand Finals for six Premierships.

That success was forged in the main by two men: Sir Ross Hutchinson (who also coached West Perth and East Fremantle to Premiership glory), and Clive Lewington, perhaps the club's favourite son.

Nipper Truscott: Easts coach 1916–1922.

SOUTH FREMANTLE

Brownlow winner Brad Hardie.

John Todd: a Sandover at 17.

Nicky Winmar: first games for Souths.

Lewington, who had the distinction of kicking five goals with his first five kicks in League football, played only four games as a full-forward before carving out a niche for himself across the centreline.

It was as a centreman that Lewington won the 1947 Sandover Medal under Hutchinson's tutelage and two years later he took over as captain–coach, winning a Premiership in his first year. That was the first of four Flags under his direction.

During that era some of the greatest players who ever represented the club were at the height of their powers, with champion rover Steve Marsh, legendary full-forward Bernie Naylor, Des Kelly and Lewington all supreme.

Undoubtedly the story of this period was Marsh. A magnificent player in Kalgoorlie, he was convinced to try his luck with East Fremantle. He was to meet a friend outside the Fremantle town hall who would introduce him to the club's coach, Jerry Dolan.

Marsh's mate never turned up so he ventured to Fremantle Oval alone. Souths and Easts shared the ground then, and because the South Fremantle rooms were opened first he wandered in and began training.

Marsh played 226 games and in six Premierships with the Bulldogs, winning the 1952 Sandover Medal. In 1956 he switched to East Fremantle as coach and broke an 11-year Premiership drought in his first season.

In 1955 South discovered perhaps the greatest of them all, a brilliant young centreman by the name of John Todd. Balanced, brilliant and brash, Todd won the Sandover Medal as a 17-year-old in his first season. A knee injury early in his career dampened his impact, but he is still regarded with the likes of Farmer and Barry Cable.

Four years after his debut he was captain–coach of Souths, but had to wait until 1997 to lead the Bulldogs to a Premiership. He coached East Fremantle to the Flag in 1974 and then won four Premierships with Swan Districts, 1982–84 and again in 1990.

More recently Souths stars have been the likes of dual Sandover Medallist Stephen Michael, champion centreman Maurice Rioli, Brownlow Medallist Brad Hardie and star midfielder Nicky Winmar.

Yes, Fremantle has made a wonderful contribution to the game and the club now is poised to make its mark in the AFL as a combined entity.

Bernie Naylor: kicked 23 goals for South Fremantle against Subiaco in 1953.

FREMANTLE

John Todd: six South Fremantle Flags.

Above: Phil and Jim Krakouer.
Right: Graham Melrose – the East Fremantle rover played 111 games for North Melbourne.

Gone Over East – a prelude to the new WA teams

With the 1980s came a realisation within WA football that things had to change.

The game no longer had a divine right to survival and there loomed a real risk of self-destruction. Press the wrong button and the very fabric of a competition approaching its 100th season would disintegrate.

Clubs that had traded on their capacity to produce players for the VFL market, reaping the benefits of staggering transfer fees, were gagging on the thick chequebooks of the Melbourne clubs.

Many of them lived beyond their means and as happened to so many of the State's high-flying corporate figures of that time, sooner or later the high life would catch up with them.

While the boardrooms of the eight WAFL clubs were no doubt reverberating to the discussions detailing the delicate position of Australian Football in a State which had been infatuated with the game for close to a century, most people outside the inner sanctum were oblivious to the looming strife.

That instability was also reflected on the field, with five clubs sharing the seven Premierships determined before the arrival of West Coast into an expanded VFL competition in 1987.

There was more than merely a superficial transformation with some of the game's least successful clubs – Claremont, Subiaco and Swan Districts – emerging to enjoy a reign of power and sharing Premierships with the moderately successful South Fremantle and the competition benchmark, East Fremantle.

It was a time when the Perth clubs – Perth, East Perth and West Perth – which had won seven Premierships between them in the 70s, struggled to compete. The wheel had turned and they had been unable to cling on for the ride.

The decade began with Mal Brown, who coached East Perth to the 1972 Premiership, leading South Fremantle to its first Flag in a decade.

It was a year in which South Fremantle and Swan Districts, coached by John Todd, clearly emerged as the outstanding teams. Not since Haydn Bunton Jr led Swans to its first three Premierships from 1961–63 had the boys from Bassendean been so formidable. Indeed, for much of that time they were the competition whipping boys. But 1980 was different.

Swans won their first 12 games, earning a $20,000 bonus from one of the League's sponsors and was a club reborn. Souths won its final 12 games, the last of them against Swans, which nonetheless won the minor Premiership.

But Brown had timed Souths' run to a treat. The Bulldogs eclipsed Swans by 10 points in the Second Semi-final and, with

Warren Ralph as a Blue.

Ken Hunter: a great went over east.

WAFL IN THE 1980s

Polly Farmer and Ron Alexander. Centre: Mal Brown at the mike as East Perth claims the 1972 WAFL Premiership. Right: Maurice Rioli.

the benefit of a week's break, crushed their Grand Final opponents by 58 points. The game was virtually secured with an inspired 8.7 yield in the second quarter when Maurice Rioli gave one of his spellbinding big-game performances.

In 1981, another club that had struggled for close to a decade emerged from the shadows. Claremont won 19 of its 21 games, including their last 14 which translated to the last 12 qualifying rounds, the Second Semi-final and Grand Final.

That Tigers outfit, coached by 1976 Brownlow Medallist Graham Moss, was star-studded. Phil and Jim Krakouer, Michael Aitken, Wayne Blackwell, Gary Shaw, Warren Ralph, Steve Malaxos and Allen Daniels all went on to play in the VFL with varying degrees of success.

Of course Moss and full-back Gerald Betts (Collingwood) had already achieved that distinction, taking to 10 the number of players to rise to that level.

The Grand Final was memorable for a couple of reasons. The first was an all-in brawl in the opening minutes and the second was South Fremantle's wasteful second-term effort when it kicked 6.12 with the wind at its back.

Again Rioli was simply magical and he shared the Simpson Medal with Shaw. A year later he would win the Norm Smith Medal in a losing Richmond effort against Carlton.

After threatening to crack their fourth Premiership for a couple of years, Swans finally achieved it in 1982. And having tasted the sweetness of success it gorged itself by launching a polished defence of its crown in 1983 and then backing up to win a hat-trick.

It was a time when it built a strong rivalry with Claremont, beating the Tigers in '82 and '83.

With Todd and captain Graham Melrose leading the charge, the drought was ended emphatically when Swans led 14.15 to 4.10 at three-quarter and went on to win by 49 points. Wingman Phil Narkle completed an outstanding season for the club by winning the Sandover Medal.

In 1983 Swans came from the First Semi-final to triumph – beating East Fremantle, South Fremantle and Claremont (by 21 points) to earn consecutive titles.

Key players in the rebirth of Swans included Narkle, Leon Baker, Tony Solin (now Fremantle's runner), Murray Rance, Alan Sidebottom, Don Holmes, Gerard Neesham and Michael Richardson.

The hat-trick was completed when Swans destroyed East Fremantle in the opening quarter of the 1984 Grand Final, kicking 10.7 to 0.3 in an amazing initial onslaught.

The theory that a club must first lose a Grand Final before it can win one was emphasised in 1985 when Ron Alexander led the Sharks to their 26th Premiership in the WAFL's centenary season.

East Fremantle survived a late charge from Subiaco to win by five points.

In 1986, the year Mark Bairstow won the Sandover Medal, the roles were reversed when Bunton ended a barren 13-year period for Subiaco. It was fitting that Bunton should lead the club to a Flag because many people believe his role was significant in 1973 when Ross Smith was at the helm when Subiaco ended a 49-year torment.

Bunton coached the Maroons in 1972 before heading back to South Australia.

Subiaco was always in charge of the Grand Final against East Fremantle, winning the last Premiership before the arrival of the Eagles, 19.16 (130) to 8.13 (61).

Alexander's Sharks were conquered, but the coach received some consolation when he was appointed the Eagles' inaugural mentor.

Peter Bosustow.

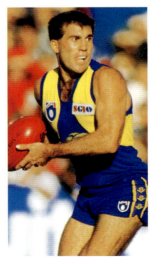

Steve Malaxos.

FREMANTLE

The first line up for the pre-season match against Essendon.

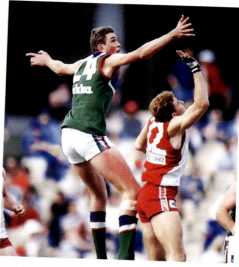
'Spider' Burton gets another hit-out.

The Dockers sail into the AFL

After the gala launch, the parties and the announcements about the size of squad, the uniform and the office bearers, the people of Fremantle finally had something tangible by which to identify the AFL's newest franchise.

On October 31 about 2500 fans drifted in to Fremantle Oval for the Dockers first training session. Finally the people who could not find a place in their hearts for West Coast had a team they could embrace.

The state was polarised.

Like the Eagles, this Fremantle team would play Richmond in its first game. Unlike the Eagles of 1987, Fremantle would play its first match at the MCG – the AFL depriving it of the right to launch its beginning on home soil.

Perhaps with that in mind a couple of pre-season matches became the launching pad for a new club. The first opportunity came on February 11 when the Dockers tackled Essendon at East Fremantle Oval.

It was fitting that Essendon should be the first challenge, given that Kevin Sheedy had long supported the arrival of a second team out of Perth. The Dockers won the game handsomely against an experimental Bombers line-up, but the result was not the only important factor on Docker Day.

At half-time, with the Dockers leading by 53 points, the club's rope and anchor crew were seen for the first time and the theme song was launched by Dave Warner. As spectators filed out of the ground after a 50-point win, many fans were heard singing, humming and chanting the song – testimony to its immediate acceptance.

The Dockers devotees were delighted with the form of the previously unheralded Craig Burrows, who won the Channel 7 Medal as best afield at centre half-forward, while Peter Bell, Travis Edmonds, Quentin Leach, former Bomber Tony Delaney, Scott Edwards, Ben Allan and Winston Abraham were strong contributors.

Two weeks later, the Dockers played the match that truly launched them into the AFL – an Ansett Cup showdown with St Kilda at Fremantle Oval.

After leading by two points at half-time, the Dockers slipped to a 35-point defeat as Stewart Loewe dominated with a nine-goal performance. It was also a game when the Dockers found themselves a cult hero in the shape of angular

The rope and anchor crew.

Ben Allan: returns.

CLUB NEWS 1995

Colours purple: When the Fremantle Football Club settled on the colours for its strip it incorporated the port and starboard colours of red and green with a dark purple version of the workman's blue singlet. Also included was the red and white ghost of the original Fremantle Football Club, born 100 years earlier.

Food for thought: It wasn't just the new style or bright colours of Fremantle that caught the eye in their first match – against Richmond on April 1. It was the three-quarter time energy food – which included mango, pineapple, honeydew melon and plums. The Tigers won by just five points 12.18 (90) to 12.13 (85) at the MCG, as 26,219 fans watched.

Victory at last: Fitzroy became Fremantle's first victims in their third match, losing 11.12 (78) to 18.13 (121) at the Western Oval. Winston Abraham kicked three goals.

Local derby: 41,601 fans, including Prime Minister Paul Keating, turned up to watch the first West Coast/Fremantle local derby at Subiaco. The Dockers seemed overawed by the occasion and lost 9.12 (66) to 23.13 (151). Winston Abraham was suspended for three matches for striking Peter Matera.

Top Dockers: The inaugural Fremantle club champion award, which attracted more than 1000 people to the Fremantle Passenger Terminal, also saw the formation of a new club – The Top Dockers. Positions in this team within the team were won by players finishing

1995

The Dockers' first AFL bounce.   *Winston Abraham on the run.*   *The Dockers first AFL night game, against St Kilda.*

ruckman Matthew 'Spider' Burton.

Previously on the West Coast list and cut without an opportunity, big 'Spider' produced an exceptional performance and was quickly embraced by the Fremantle faithful.

With the preliminaries out of the way, it was time to start planning for the first game against Richmond at the MCG on 1 April 1995. The Dockers almost made fools out of pundits across the nation with a spirited performance before losing by a tantalising five points.

Richmond held sway for most of the match, but the Fremantle grit was evident as it refused to yield.

Ten Dockers played their first AFL game on that day – Abraham, Bell, Burrows, Burton, Scott Chisholm, Gary Dhurrkay, Edwards, Leach, Jamie Merillo and David Muir.

Round 2 provided the Dockers with their first home game when they hosted Essendon at the WACA Ground and the first phase of what looks like evolving into a strong rivalry was forged with the clubs competing for the Albert Thurgood Challenge.

A legend at both Essendon and Fremantle at the turn of the century, Thurgood was a common thread between two worthy clubs.

Skipper Ben Allan played his 100th game, but the Dockers were wasteful early and paid a price for their inaccurate first term return of 3.8, eventually losing an entertaining contest by nine points.

Again Burton was a star and with Scott Chisholm also weaving some magic in defence the Dockers were finding some early heroes.

The form of Fremantle in the first two rounds suggested it was close to a breakthrough – and it came against Fitzroy at the inhospitable Western Oval in Round 3. A sizzling first-quarter burst with the breeze set up victory as Allan, Dale Kickett and Winston Abraham provided the impetus for victory.

Backed up by a brilliant 19-point win over Geelong in Round 4, the Dockers were on their way and Perth began to brace itself for its first Western Derby. After the Geelong success came a two-point loss to Footscray, again at the Western Oval, and this time Allan tried to snatch victory with a 65-metre torpedo after the siren, but the task was always going to be beyond him.

So the Dockers had won two and lost three – by a total of just 16 points – and had quickly arrived as a credible outfit.

A thumping victory over Sydney gave them the perfect prelude to the first derby against the Eagles. West Coast, a seasoned and tough campaigner, rose to the occasion and won by 85 points in a game which was merely part of Fremantle's learning curve.

Subsequent victories over Brisbane and St Kilda gave Fremantle a 5-5 win–loss ratio after 10 rounds, a better start than most people were predicting before the season. But there was also going to be a lean spell and it came with the Dockers losing seven on the trot.

In the end the Dockers finished with an 8-14 record to be 13th on the ladder.

1995 HONOUR ROLL

Year	Pos	Leading Goalkicker	No.	Best & Fairest	Captain	Coach
1995	13th	Peter Mann	33	Peter Mann	Ben Allan	Gerard Neesham

in the top five in the club's Fairest and Best count. The first five, in finishing order, in the debut season were Peter Mann, Dale Kickett, Ben Allan, Scott Chisholm and Stephen O'Reilly. Chisholm also won the Dockers Beacon as the outstanding first year player.

History made: While the record books will probably show the Dockers played their first game against Essendon, perhaps St Kilda in the Ansett Cup or even Richmond in the season proper, the club's first outing was against the Northern Territory in Darwin. The NT team won that game, in sloppy conditions, by a point. Playing in Darwin was probably a reflection of Gerard Neesham's liking for the Top End. The destination for his end of season trip is generally a remote part of the country.

A night to remember: The Dockers might have been just two games old when they played Essendon at the WACA Ground on 21 April 1995, but skipper Ben Allan celebrated his 100th game. The former Hawthorn star had returned home to Perth to play under Neesham, a close friend of the Allan family through water polo connections and a man who influenced Allan's early career at Claremont.

Wolf man: Clinton Wolf's career was all too brief, a back injury causing him to call an early end to his AFL aspirations. After just four games, in fact. But he still had time to create a lasting impression at Victoria Park. In the Round 7 game, Wolf took spectacular marks and also won the crowd over with his willingness for a physical confrontation.

FREMANTLE

Faces in the crowd at the WA derby.

Prolific Dale Kickett gets another kick.

Second-year blues for the green, purple and white

The AFL's laws generally prevent large overhauls of a playing list, but Fremantle took advantage of its position as it geared towards 1996.

The club's football department had taken on board lessons learned in its baptismal season and massively turned over 20 players. Some were forced through injury and the reduction of the club's list from 50 to 46, but others were simply culled.

Gerard Neesham and his match committee had seen enough of some players under training conditions and performances in the WAFL to determine that speculative selections in the initial 50-man squad would not come off.

So the Dockers were busy in the football marketplace, searching for players who could carry them through to the upper echelon of the AFL table.

In the main the replacements were again young, emerging players like Greg Harding, Steven Koops, Daniel Parker, James Clement, Trent Carroll, Michael Clark, Gavin Mitchell and Clive Waterhouse.

Having played one season, the Dockers hierarchy had a better understanding of what was required. What it did mean though was that a large percentage of the squad remained in the developmental phase.

After being forced to wait until Round 7 in their debut season to tackle local rivals, West Coast, because of the redevelopment of Subiaco Oval, the Dockers had an early opportunity in 1996.

Fremantle fans went into the opening game against West Coast with high expectations, and the players responded positively. The Eagles needed to summon every gram of their defensive nous to keep the Dockers at bay, eventually recording a 22-point victory.

The trend established in the first season continued in the second, that margin again cutting in half the difference between the two sides in their previous meeting.

It was, however, to prove a testing season for the Dockers and they were unable to match the eight wins achieved in 1995. They won seven games and again finished 13th on the table, though on many occasions they looked and played much better than that figure would indicate.

The cold, hard win–loss statistics do not truly reflect the season. Again the Dockers were treated cruelly by fate in the close matches – one-point losses to Essendon at the MCG and to Brisbane in Round 21, when Shaun Hart soccered a goal off the ground in

David Hynes stretches for a mark.

CLUB NEWS 1996

Pre-season quadrella: Fremantle won all four official pre-season games, against Port Adelaide, Essendon, Hawthorn and Fitzroy.

Joint connection: John Todd might have been the second coach of West Coast, but he was linked to Fremantle in 1996 when he was inducted into the club's hall of champions. Todd was a legend of the port city, being the youngest player to win the Sandover Medal, a feat achieved as a 17-year-old in 1955. Also inducted into the hall of champions was former Geelong captain Brian Peake, Nipper Truscott and legendary full-forward Bernie Naylor. The inaugural inductees were Clive Lewington, Steve Marsh, Jack Clarke, Jack Sheedy and Stephen Michael.

Docker debuts: For the Round 1 derby game against West Coast, five players made their Docker debut – Gavin Mitchell, Greg Harding, Brad Rowe, David Hynes and Tony Godden – and so did the mascot 'Grinder' who preceded the rope and anchor crew onto the ground in the pre-game build-up. The Dockers lost 6.9 (45) to 9.13 (67).

Sydney sojourn: At a time when Sydney has created one of the great home-ground records in modern football, Fremantle has defied that level of performance, never losing to the Swans. In 1996, the Dockers built on its imposing feats against one of the competition's emerging powers by recording a Round 2 victory in the harbour city.

Away record: Winning away from

1996

Kingsley Hunter: great determination.

Tony Delaney in possession.

Stephen O'Reilly: on the mark.

the dying seconds. Just one of those seasons.

After the defeat by the Eagles, it was off to Sydney for the daunting task of tackling one of the toughest assignments in the game, even though the Swans were coming off an opening-round hiding from Adelaide.

The Dockers eventually stormed to a 21-point victory with their small running players and their defence ruling the roost.

They backed it up with a 53-point win over Carlton, a victory largely attributable to the dominance of rising ruck star Daniel Bandy over Justin Madden. As well, Peter Mann proved a reliable target in attack, kicking four goals.

So the start to the season was bright enough. After losing to Collingwood in Round 4 the Dockers went to 3–2 when they romped to a 37-point win over Melbourne at the WACA Ground. Just three points up at three-quarter time, the Dockers exploded in the final term as Winston Abraham inspired his team-mates with some magical moments.

Losses to Brisbane, Adelaide and Fitzroy had the Dockers on the ropes, however, with the loss to Fitzroy particularly hurtful on a day Scott Watters played his 100th AFL game.

Fremantle responded to that embarrassing defeat – which would prove to be Fitzroy's last triumph – by dishing out a 54-point hiding to Richmond on a day it was without its stars in Ben Allan, Mann, Abraham and Shaun McManus.

Gary Dhurrkay stepped forward to pilot the way and the Dockers rode to victory on the back of a seven-goal third-quarter surge.

Then came the trough. Seven losses on the trot, the last of them to West Coast when the Dockers again had problems kicking goals. The Eagles stymied Fremantle's free-flowing method and reduced it to a war of attrition, winning 12.10 (82) to Fremantle's 7.6 (48).

The chance of a final eight position was all but gone, though the Dockers could retain some respectability with an encouraging finish to the season. That came with another victory against Sydney in Round 17 on a day when Jeff White was the star in attack, kicking four goals.

Losses to Carlton, Melbourne and Brisbane were interspersed between victories over Collingwood and Fitzroy to close out the season. Down by two points at three-quarter time against the Pies in Round 19, the Dockers kicked four goals to one in the last stanza to stride to victory.

That success was largely generated by the long – Matthew Burton – and the short of it – Luke Toia.

On the way to a 53-point win.

1996 HONOUR ROLL

Year Pos	Leading Goalkicker	No.	Best & Fairest	Captain	Coach
1996 13th	Kingsley Hunter	33	Stephen O'Reilly	Ben Allan	Gerard Neesham

home was proving a problem for the Dockers. That success against Sydney was its only victory outside of WA in 1996 as they lost to the likes of Fitzroy, Footscray and Melbourne on Victorian soil. That saw the Dockers finish in the exactly the same position they occupied in their first season – 13th.

Genuine Legends: Two players from the original Fremantle Football Club, Albert Thurgood and David 'Dolly' Christie, were named in the first AFL Hall of Fame.

Friendly foes: If a friendly rivalry can exist in the cauldron of the AFL it is developing between Fremantle and Essendon. The two clubs have fought some exciting finishes – none more so than the 1996 Round 11 showdown at the MCG – the Dockers lost by a point.

Club champion: The role of the full-back is often under-played in football, but the Dockers paid due notice to the efforts of champion defender Stephen O'Reilly when he won the second Fairest and Best award at Fremantle. O'Reilly, whose dashing runs out of defence were a feature – particularly against Sydney star Tony Lockett – won the 1996 award ahead of Dale Kickett, who for the second year in succession was runner-up.

Docker Beacon: The award for best first year AFL player went to Gavin Mitchell – who played 21 games and represented WA in the State of Origin. Mitchell was originally from Broome and made it when convinced by Gerard Neesham to give WAFL football another try.

FREMANTLE

The team bursts through the banner in Round 22, but fails to break Melbourne.

Matthew Burton: the spider.

Fremantle 1997: nearly there

When Fremantle had time to sit down and reflect on the 1997 season, the bitterness of missing out on a place in the finals was tempered by an awareness that its quest was ruined by two factors. One was beyond its control and the match committee was working fastidiously to rectify the other.

Much was written about the injury problems of West Coast, Essendon and Brisbane, but the Dockers were hit almost as hard as any of them. At times they were down to 22 or 23 fit players and it's extremely difficult to gather any momentum when there is a constant turnover of players.

It was not so much the length of the casualty list, but the calibre of players afflicted. Skipper Peter Mann's usually reliable hands copped an accidental kick from Ben Allan shortly after surgery, making it even tougher for Mann to have an impact.

Allan himself had problems with a debilitating knee injury. That was something the Dockers had budgeted for and he did remarkably well to play 17 games. In crunch matches in the early stages of the season it was Allan who lifted the Dockers, providing the spark which so often was the difference between victory and defeat. But he tired at the end of the season, his battle-weary body symptomatic of the team's end-of-season nose-dive.

The other problem was one which was not peculiar to just 1997, but has been a sore point with the club since its inception. There was no stand-out forward who could consistently kick goals. Only three times in the season did the Dockers surpass 100 points – against St Kilda under lights at Subiaco Oval on Anzac Day, against the struggling Melbourne in Round 7 and then against a depleted Essendon in Round 12 at Subiaco Oval.

Daniel Parker was given the initial responsibility of lining up at full-forward. Tall, strong and athletic, he is an outstanding prospect, but was not yet ready to shoulder the burden of team spearhead.

Later, after recovering from ankle surgery, Kingsley Hunter assumed the role and showed enough to suggest he could be the answer. The Dockers certainly looked more potent when he was standing in the square.

Again the season started with great enterprise, and a first-up victory over the Western Bulldogs at Optus Oval was just the start they needed. The value of that win would be emphasised later in the season as the Doggies carried all before them.

They backed up with a solid performance against Hawthorn and were almost favourites going in to the first Western Derby. The Eagles were coming off a trouncing by Geelong and the Dockers were full of confidence.

There were encouraging early signs, but eventually the Eagles overpowered them to win by 40 points. The most distressing aspect of the defeat was that it spelled the end of the season for brilliant young winger Shaun McManus. He went down in almost exactly the same spot as West Coast's Glen Jakovich a year earlier and suffered the same agonising result – a knee reconstruction.

The Dockers could not string more than two wins together, but offered their supporters great hope with some memorable performances. Fremantle showed that it could win tight matches, particularly when considering the four-point win against the Bulldogs to open the season.

Clive Waterhouse gave the best performance of his short career as the Dockers overcome St Kilda by a goal and then, three weeks later, beat Brisbane with a major after the siren. Quentin Leach took a strong mark in the dying seconds and as he was wandering back to take his kick the siren sounded.

Wills a wizard

The surprise performer for Fremantle, particularly early in the season, was Andrew Wills. So good was his early form that he was selected in the Victorian state-of-origin squad. He also led the Brownlow Medal count in the middle stages, and had it not been for a niggling groin injury, he might have capped off his year with football's most cherished individual honour.

1997

A wild celebration after Quentin Leach kicked the winning goal against Brisbane.

Quentin Leach: matchwinner.

About 35 metres from goal, on a 45 degree angle the pressure was intense.

Leach, as steady as you like, wandered in kicked accurately and triggered scenes of great elation. Coach Gerard Neesham said later that he could not have wished for any better man to have the ball in his hands under such circumstances. Essentially a half-back, who had kicked only 20 career goals to that stage, Neesham still regarded him as the best kick for goal in his team.

Then there was the victory over Sydney which kept intact the Dockers' unbeaten record against the Swans, further triumphs against Hawthorn and the Western Bulldogs and another one against Richmond.

Three games out there was a real chance for the Dockers to secure a place in the finals series for the first time.

Even after losses to St Kilda and Geelong there was some hope. If the Dockers could beat Melbourne in the last qualifying game, they would almost certainly make it.

Unfortunately, the Demons were just as keen to prevent that happening and eventually overran the tired Dockers, whose brave quest had come to a disappointing end.

Nevertheless it was still a remarkable season, one which will be remembered for the impact of youngsters like Heath Black and Jess Sinclair, the emergence of Greg Harding as one of the game's outstanding half-backs, the continued development of Luke Toia, Clive Waterhouse, Mark Gale and Craig Callaghan as tenacious midfielders, the rise of Andrew Wills as a team leader and the impressive durability of Shane Parker.

Most of all, though, it was the year when Dale Kickett shone. He won the club champion award and was an integral part of a Dockers' defence. After being runner-up in the first two seasons – to Peter Mann and Stephen O'Reilly – he finally savoured the moment.

Dale Kickett: top Docker at last.

Finally the bride

Twice the bridesmaid, finally the bride. That was the situation for brilliant Dockers defender Dale Kickett. Runner-up twice in the club's Fairest and Best award, he won the mantle after a magnificent 1997 season. Kickett polled 96 votes to win from Shane Parker (76), Craig Callaghan (74), Andrew Wills (72) and Greg Harding (63). Kickett is the only player who has finished in the club's top five vote-winners in each of the Dockers' three seasons.

1997 HONOUR ROLL

Year	Pos	Leading Goalkicker	No.	Best & Fairest	Captain	Coach
1997	12th	Kingsley Hunter	32	Dale Kickett	Peter Mann	Gerard Neesham

Geelong

For almost 14 decades, there has been a remarkably consistent image of the football club based in Victoria's largest provincial city, both for Geelong supporters and for football followers generally. The club's decision-makers have promoted an attractive, exciting, free-spirited style of play which has resulted in numerous successful eras, punctuated by some periods of under-achievement and frustration.

Geelong has always been able to attract, or develop, a sprinkling of players renowned for their amazing talent, flair, and (unfortunately) inconsistency. Many icons of Australia's greatest sporting institution hail from Geelong: Wills, Brownlow, the McShanes, Young, Burns, the Rankins, the Easons, Todd, Greeves, Hickey, Jennings, Flanagan, Smith, Davis, the Hoveys, the Goggins, Wade, Farmer, Newman, the Nankervises, Ablett, Couch, the Hockings … the list is seemingly endless.

People who attend Geelong matches have never been deprived of entertainment. Even when the team has not been winning there have been controversies, brilliant passages of play, characters strutting their stuff or records being established.

The consistent recruitment of left-footed goal-sneaks has been a feature of the club's ethos. 'Southpaws' such as Teddy Lockwood, Cliff Rankin, Arthur Rayson and his son Noel, John Sharrock, David Clarke and Ronnie Burns have provided opposing defenders with a century of headaches. Geelong's ultimately successful teams have combined the acknowledged champions with highly reliable workhorses who have been content to perform out of the glare of the spotlights.

Geelong is a team with strong ties, a team that commands the greatest respect and loyalty from the people of its home town. For well over a century, the people of Geelong have had their spirits elevated by the success of their football team. A stroll down Moorabool Street on a Monday morning following a significant Cats' victory is a revealing experience. The place buzzes. People enthusiastically discuss the details of the match played hours earlier, and smiles are exchanged between strangers. Economically, it has been shown that more money is circulated in the district when the club is performing well, as the supporters are more relaxed and optimistic. Conversely, poor performances by the team tend to encourage general pessimism within the community. Smiles turn into frowns and conversation does not flow as easily.

Following Geelong's spectacular rise up the ladder in Malcolm Blight's first season as coach in 1989, which saw it narrowly lose a thrilling Grand Final against Hawthorn, Geelong was on the up. Just months later, the city plunged into one of its darkest eras.

MY CLUB
by Col Hutchinson

GEELONG

Year Established	1859
Joined VFL/AFL	1897
Home Grounds	Corio Oval, Kardinia Park
Premierships	1925, 1931, 1937, 1951, 1952, 1963
Brownlow Medals	Edward Greeves 1924; Bernie Smith 1951; Alistair Lord 1952; Paul Couch 1989
Record home crowd	49,109 v Carlton, 1952
Most games	Ian Nankervis, 325
Most goals	Gary Ablett, 1021
Notable supporters	Geoffrey Blainey, John Button, Ian Cover, Tony Street, Jill Birrell

Not only did the club slip dramatically down the ladder, but an economic calamity enveloped the district with the collapse of the Pyramid financial group. Thousands of local investors lost large sums of money.

Although the city has not yet fully recovered economically, there is little doubt that the Cats' consistently positive performances, resulting in seven finals campaigns over the past nine seasons (including four

Old Malop St, Geelong – the heart of the heartland.

Aaaaaablett takes a screamer.

A sea of support as Gary Ablett tops 1000 League goals.

Grand Final appearances), have assisted in the recovery process.

The one frustration has been the lack of a Premiership during that period. More than a third of a century has passed since the victorious 1963 team stood on the steps of City Hall, overwhelmed by the roar from more than 10,000 supporters who were there to welcome their heroes home. The community craves the incredible atmosphere that followed each of Geelong's six winning League Grand Finals.

Every true Geelong supporter waits impatiently for the seventh magic moment.

Unique achievements:
Seven VFA Premierships in a nine-year span.
Restricting an opposing team to the lowest ever League score (St Kilda 0.1 (1) in 1899).
The longest sequence of wins in League history (23 in 1952–53).
The highest-ever League score (37.17 (239) against Brisbane in 1992).
The longest sequence of goals uninterrupted by a behind (15 against St Kilda in 1979).
The two highest-ever scoring aggregates for a League season (3558 points in 1992 and 3452 points in 1989).
The only two cases of a goal tally of 500 or more for a League season (527 in 1992 and 503 in 1989).

Geelong team leaders from left Couch, Bews, Bairstow, Hinkley, Ablett and Stoneham.

Bernie Smith: all class.   **Bunny Eason: early champion.**   **The big Cat: Polly Farmer.**

GEELONG

Geelong players in the early 70s at the Argyle Ground, Aberdeen St.

The first kick

'Football: Admirers of the new game are requested to attend a meeting to be held at the Victoria Hotel at 7:30 on Monday evening. 18th July. A. M. Mason, Secretary.

The above notice was the first step towards the establishment of the Geelong Football Club in 1859.

The first 'kick' took place on the Corio Cricket Ground on the following Saturday, 'with, however, more ardour than skill'.

Enthusiasm waned and it was not until May of the following year that more decisive steps were taken. The club's first documented match occurred in 1860 in a paddock on the corner of Aberdeen and Pakington Streets, adjacent to the Argyle Hotel. Geelong and Melbourne played a scoreless draw.

One spectator later observed, 'There is one very objectionable feature in their play – I allude to that of charging with their arms straight out, and their fists closed as if they are going to participate in a free fight! They also want practice at Geelong, then they would abandon the habit of playing so much with their hands.'

A train ride away

The opening of the railway link between Geelong and Melbourne in 1857 was pivotal to the development of Victoria's most important provincial centre. With the journey taking little more than an hour to complete, the train really opened up opportunities for sporting participation.

Train travel and Australian football had their origins in the Corio Bay district within the space of a year or two. Regular matches between Geelong and metropolitan clubs could be organised quite easily. When the line to Ballarat was completed in 1862, the range of possible football rivals was increased even further.

Geelong in the VFA

On 7 May 1877 the secretaries of the eight senior football clubs, including Geelong, met for the purpose of forming the Victorian Football Association. Its aims were to promote and extend football throughout the colony, to have complete control of intercolonial matches, to supervise the revision of the laws of the game and to protect its interests. Previously, none of those areas had been coordinated effectively.

Wills the player

Tom Wills.

Tom Wills captained Geelong in several matches during 1860 before moving to Queensland to take up a pastoral run. In 1864 he returned to Victoria to play mainly with Geelong. He captained that club for six years and played an estimated 172 matches. He was a brilliant ruck player.

Peter the Great

Peter Burns.

Peter Burns' performances at full-back and as a follower were brilliant. He possessed a strong physique and great skill and dash. He staved off opposition attacks most effectively and was a fine high mark, a great kick and a smart ball handler. He loved to make attacking runs out of the backline. Known universally as 'Peter the Great', his retirement was forced by a serious leg injury.

Triple Champion

Jim Wilson.

Jim Wilson's kicking ability was outstanding. He was well known for gaining long distance into the teeth of strong winds. He played with great distinction from 1877 until 1882. In his last three years he won a trio of Champion of the Colony awards and captained the team to two Premierships and a second placing.

CLUB NEWS 1859–1896

1859: Geelong Football Club was formed, with Tom Wills playing a key role in the establishment and development of the code in the district. Initially, the club uniform consisted of a blue shirt and cap, but later in the season bright crimson became the team colour.
1860: Geelong and Melbourne met in a keen contest at Argyle Square. The match ended in a scoreless draw.
1862: Henry Harrison captained the club in his only season with Geelong. Red caps and blue trousers were worn.
1863: A white shirt with a blue stripe formed the uniform. The club won the Challenge Cup for best performed team.
1864: The Challenge Cup was successfully defended.
1865: Scarlet shirts and red caps with blue and white stripes were worn.
1871: The club, now wearing blue, played its first matches at Corio Oval when Argyle Square was unavailable.
1872: Geelong became known as the 'All Whites'. Tom Wills won the Champion of the Colony award.
1876: Navy blue and white hooped guernseys were worn for the first time. Tom Wills played his last game.
1877: The Victorian Football Association was formed, with Geelong as a foundation member.
1878: All home matches were now played at Corio Oval. The club won its first VFA Premiership, with A. Christie equal leading goalscorer for the competition. Percy Douglass won the Champion of the Colony award.

1859–1896

The 1884 Premiership team – one of the many successful Geelong teams in the VFA.

The top VFA team

Geelong 1884 Premiership team was among those that won seven Flags in nine years. Geelong was far and away the best team in the VFA competition from its inception in 1877. Its superiority may have been because the Geelong men lived a more regular life in the provincial centre and were able to get together to train and improve their team play. The great support for the team in the city of Geelong was also a factor, and the home-ground advantage after visiting teams had arrived by train from Melbourne. Geelong won Premierships in 1878 and 1880, three in a row in 1882, 1883 and 1884 and another in 1886.

Forty years a leader

Charles Brownlow was to have more than 40 years association with the club as player, coach and administrator.

As a coach Brownlow revealed his tactical genius. In the early years teams lined up in their defensive half at the start of play, rugby style, and wandered all over the field. Brownlow instructed players to take up specific field placings and to play the ball to position to avoid packs. The tactic enabled the club to remain undefeated in 1886.

The fair Geelong (1886) – a poetic tribute

What now, they cry, and wherefore is the din? The game is lost, the Pivot's scored a win! Uplift McShane, and loud his praises roll, A demon bribed must have kicked that goal. Geelong, Geelong – no Sleepy Hollow there, Victoria's glory in her games you wear. Throughout the world the sportsman's latest son tells loud the prowess of the fair Geelong.

Seaside colours – blue and white

It is believed that the basic Geelong uniform of blue and white hooped guernseys and socks, first worn in 1876, represents seagulls flying over the waters of Corio Bay.

Initially, the colour bands of the guernseys were relatively narrow, and a matching striped cap was standard headgear. Later, canvas lace-up sleeveless guernseys were introduced, and players often wore blue short-sleeved vests underneath. Several changes to the guernseys were to be made over the next few decades.

In 1912 guernseys were numbered for the first time. Shirt-weight guernseys incorporating wider stripes and more prominent numbers were brought into use in 1968.

Dark knickerbockers (below knee length) were part of the original uniform. In 1907 the shorts crept up to knee-length, and from that time on have become progressively briefer.

Dave Hickinbotham in the colours of Geelong.

The young Charles Brownlow.

1880: After winning a second VFA Premiership in 1879, Geelong made it three in a row in 1880. Percy Douglass was leading goalscorer for the competition and James Wilson won the Champion of the Colony award.
1881: James Wilson was the Champion of the Colony for the second time.
1882: The club won the VFA Premiership, with Hugh McLean leading goalscorer for the competition. James Wilson was awarded his third consecutive Champion of the Colony award.
1883: The club won the VFA Premiership. Phil McShane was leading goalscorer for the competition.
1884: The club won its third successive VFA Premiership. Phil McShane was leading goalscorer for the competition. Jack Kerley won the Champion of the Colony award.
1886: A new grandstand was opened at Corio Oval. The club won its seventh VFA Premiership in nine years. Phil McShane became the first player in history to register 50 goals in a season.
1887: Tom McShane was leading goalscorer for the competition. His five brothers, Henry, Jack, Phil, Joe, Tom and Jim also played for the club.
1888: A crowd estimated to be 32,000 watched South Melbourne defeat Geelong at the Lake Oval. The boundary fence collapsed.
1889: The club administration first discussed the idea of forming a new competition and inviting other strong clubs to join.
1895: Dave de Coite was the leading goalscorer for the competition.

GEELONG

Geelong leads VFL push

The Geelong Football Club was instrumental in the formation of the Victorian Football League toward the end of 1896.

Geelong had been a foundation member of the Victorian Football Association in 1877. By the early 1890s the stronger clubs in the competition were burdened with an obligation to 'prop up' the remaining clubs financially. Geelong, which had won seven Premierships in nine years, was losing patience with the situation.

A meeting of delegates of the six strongest VFA clubs was arranged for Friday, 2 October 1896. The *Argus* reported the proceedings:

'The project of forming a new football association, which has been quietly discussed for some time past, took definite shape last night.

'An alteration having been determined on, two courses were open – either to retain the association in its present form and divide the clubs into A and B sections, or to reduce the number of clubs playing, and leave the rejected to take their own course.

'The latter was the step determined on. Geelong, as a club credited with having done more for Victorian football than any other, should not, it was thought, suffer through having failed so badly this season, and will be just as well suited by the proposed alterations in rules as any club in the competition.'

A tense battle on the forward line as Geelong plays University at Corio.

The first matches

Geelong did not begin its first VFL season well, as the *Australasian* reported: 'Prior to the match [against Essendon at Corio on 8 May 1897], the Geelong team had not once got together, and some of the players had no practice whatever.'

The *Geelong Advertiser* also reported hiccups with the new rules in the first games: 'When the play began both teams displayed a desire to revert to the old style of 'little marking'. However, Mr Crapp, the field umpire, had mastered the new rules, and he gave a very good interpretation of them.'

The *Advertiser* told of teething problems with transport in these early days: 'The game [against Fitzroy at Corio on 19 June, 1897] was not commenced until 3.44 p.m. owing to the special train bringing the Fitzroy team being detained, and the players struggled in the dark against each other in the last quarter.'

A win over Carlton at Corio Oval in Round 4 began a remarkable turnaround. The Pivotonians did not lose again in the home-and-away series, winning 11 matches in succession and finishing on top of the ladder.

1897–1910 HONOUR ROLL

Year	Pos	Leading Goalkicker	No.	Best & Fairest	Captain	Coach
1897	2nd	Eddy James	27	Joe McShane	Jack Conway	
1898	4th	Eddy James	26		Jack Conway	
1899	3rd	Eddy James	31		Jack Conway	
1900	5th	Ted Lockwood	24		Peter Burns	
1901	3rd	Charles Coles	24		Henry Young	
1902	7th	Ike Woods	16		Henry Young	
1903	4th	Ike Woods	34	Teddy Rankin	Henry Young	
1904	7th	Ike Woods	20		Henry Young	
1905	6th	Ike Woods	19	Henry Young	Henry Young	
1906	7th	Les Roebuck	21	Henry Young	Henry Young	
1907	6th	Tom Sherry	18		Henry Young	
1908	10th	Tom Hardiman	25		Henry Young	
1909	9th	Percy Martini	17		Henry Young	
1910	5th	Percy Martini	51	Dick Grigg	Bill Eason	Dave Hickinbotham

CLUB NEWS 1897–1910

Making a point: Only 300 people bothered to attend Corio Oval on 9 September 1899 to watch Geelong play St Kilda in the last home-and-away round. Early in the opening quarter the Saints rushed the ball into their forward line to register the first behind of the match. That was to be their only moment of glory, as the locals piled on a record 23 goals 24 behinds in the most one-sided contest in League history. St Kilda's final score of one point remains an all-time low. Geelong muscle-man forward, Jim McShane, with 11 goals, became the only player to reach 'double figures' in a match during the first 18 seasons of League competition.

Flat as a tack: Champion centreman, Firth McCallum, experienced a rare quiet game against Fitzroy on 9 May 1901. McCallum's many admirers were puzzled by his surprising lack of form, but unusual circumstances accounted for his lethargy. He had been working at Lorne as a carpenter, and, due to a misunderstanding, had missed a ride home. His only alternative was to walk many kilometres through the Otway Ranges to meet the train. No wonder he lacked energy on the field!

Kicked out: In one 1903 encounter between Geelong and Collingwood, two players failed to obtain a single kick for the entire match. They were direct opponents, Arthur Pincott (Geelong) and Ted Lockwood (Collingwood).

1897 – 1910

The proud Geelong team under the leadership of Teddy Rankin and 'Tracker' Young.

Teddy Rankin: great ball handler.

Always the bridesmaid

The League prepared for the first finals series in football history. A round robin series would determine the 1897 Premiership winner. Local officials, players and supporters could hardly disguise their elation when it was announced that Geelong's first finals encounter, against Essendon, would be played at Corio Oval.

Tragically for them the team failed to capitalise on the home ground advantage and the Dons were victorious, scoring 5.5 (35) to Geelong's 3.11 (29). Although Geelong went on to win its two other finals, Essendon remained undefeated, and claimed the first League pennant.

Giant full-forward Eddy James became the competition's inaugural leading goalscorer by booting 27 of his club's 111 goals for the season. He repeated the achievement two years later with a tally of 31.

In 1901 the club again participated in the finals but was eliminated by Collingwood 6.9 (45) to 3.6 (24) to be placed fourth.

Geelong next appearance in a final was on the first Saturday in September, 1903. It was a memorable occasion for champion Teddy Rankin. When he lined up at the beginning of play at the MCG he became the first Geelong player to reach the 100 League match milestone. Unfortunately for him, and for the club, Geelong went down to Fitzroy by 52 points.

The club from Corio Bay was not to make another appearance in the finals for nine years.

Brilliant Teddy Rankin

Teddy Rankin was a brilliant utility player, best suited to roving. He ran with a crouched style and was a marvellous ball-handler. His wonderful judgement, good spring, excellent kicking and seemingly unlimited stamina made him a champion for two decades. In a wet, muddy VFA match against Fitzroy at the Brunswick Street Oval in the 1890s he originated the technique of touching the ball on the ground instead of bouncing it as he ran.

Wooden spooners

In 1906 a club-record number of 43 players were tried, 23 of them first-year recruits.

The unwanted 'wooden spoon' was collected in 1908, when the team managed just two wins from 18 games. The only real highlights were Teddy Rankin's 150th League match and 'Tracker' Young's captaincy of Victoria in the first-ever football carnival series at the MCG.

In 1910 Percy Martini became the first player in blue and white hoops to boot 50 goals in a League season.

Henry 'Tracker' Young

The skilful tap ruckman gave his club 20 seasons of magnificent service before retiring at the end of 1910. He played vigorously but within the rules, and his fanaticism for physical fitness allowed him to play four quarters on the ball. Smaller team-mates appreciated his willingness to clear a path for them with strong shepherding. He was a magnificent mark, and his leadership qualities saw him elected captain for nine consecutive seasons.

Single-handed: During a match against Fitzroy on 11 May 1907 Peter Stephens, on the backline, sustained a painful hand injury and Geelong was left with 17 men on the field. After having his hand bandaged Stephens was instructed to go to the forward line to provide moral support for his team-mates. He was able to do more than that. With one hand he created havoc by scoring a match-winning five goals.

Protest upheld: In Round 6 of 1909 the final scoreboard showed St Kilda one point ahead of the home team. Prior to the match Geelong officials had warned the Saints not to play 'Ginger' Stewart, who had been suspended by a Bendigo Tribunal following an incident in a local match. The advice was disregarded. Geelong's protest to the League was upheld and the match points were awarded to the Pivotonians.

One-eyed: Ernest 'Bung' Newling possessed an unusual nickname. The courageous Geelong half-back gave excellent service in 150 matches during an 11-season career, beginning in 1900. He displayed great concentration, speed and cleverness despite the fact that he possessed sight in only one eye!

Back-seat coach: Geelong's first non-playing coach, Dave Hickinbotham was appointed in 1910. He stated publicly that his role was to supervise training, coordinate team selection and to provide pre-match advice to the players. It was his firm belief that all positional moves during a match should be made by the captain.

GEELONG

Joe Slater: fallen star.

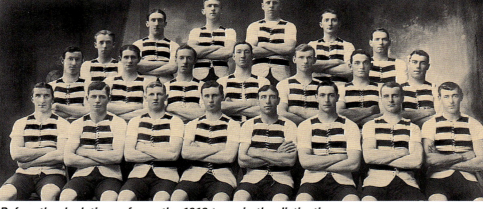

Before the depletions of war, the 1912 team in the distinctive guernsey.

Time off for war

Australia's involvement in World War One coincided with the commencement of the 1914 football season. Concern for the tragic battles at Gallipoli cast gloom on recreational activities and for the next four years declining emphasis was placed on the importance of sport.

Many League players enlisted for military service and most clubs were confronted with a shortage of on-field personnel. Geelong decided not to field a team in 1916 due to such difficulties. Although the situation had hardly improved, it returned to the competition a year later. A club-record low of 25 players were selected during the 15-round 1917 season.

William Landy: killed in action in France.

Hickinbotham lifts side

Dave Hickinbotham worked hard in his role as the club's first non-playing coach to improve the team's performances, and in 1910 ten wins were achieved. Although only eight victories eventuated the following season there were positive signs emerging. Future champions Les Armstrong, Alec Eason, Harry Marsham and George Heinz were beginning to realise their potential.

Players wore numbers on the backs of their classy lace-up style guernseys for the first time in 1912. Previously, spectators and umpires often experienced difficulty in identifying team members during play.

At the beginning of 1912 Hickinbotham decided to step down and Bill Eason took over the reins as captain–coach. Eason proved to be truly inspirational. The team won 11 times to gain a finals berth, but wasted numerous opportunities in the First Semi-final against Carlton, booting only four goals from 23 scoring shots to go down 4.19 (43) to 10.11 (71).

Eason was a highly skilled centreman and slashing half-forward; a brilliant, attacking player, able to baffle opponents with his quick turns and speed. At times he was switched to the half-back flank. In Round 15 of 1914 he became the first Geelong player to play 200 League matches.

1911–1920 HONOUR ROLL

Year	Pos	Leading Goalkicker	No.	Best & Fairest	Captain	Coach
1911	6th	Percy Martini	40	Dick Grigg	Bill Eason	Dave Hickinbotham
1912	4th	Percy Martini	41		Bill Eason	Bill Eason
1913	5th	Percy Martini	46		Bill Eason	Bill Eason
1914	4th	Percy Martini	45	Dick Grigg	Billy Orchard	Bill Orchard
1915	10th	Tom Brownless	25	Alec Eason	Bill Orchard	
1916		Club In Recess During World War One				
1917	5th	Percy Martini	24	Bert Rankin	Henry Marsham	
1918	7th	Percy Martini	24		Jim Kearney	
1919	8th	Percy Martini	19		Jim Kearney	
1920	7th	Cliff Rankin	48	John Jones	Alec Eason	

CLUB NEWS 1911–1920

57 varieties: George Heinz was an excellent rover/forward for Geelong from 1910 until 1914, playing 87 matches and booting 71 goals. He joined the military forces early in World War One and had his surname altered to Haines by deed poll, because of anti-German feeling at the time.

After the bell: Geelong's first home match of 1911 was against Melbourne in Round 2. A large crowd of about 10,000 was entertained by a 'nail-biter'. The Redlegs were a point in front and Geelong had the ball deep in attack when the final bell tolled, much to the disappointment of the locals. However, Field Umpire Lardie Tulloch, a former Collingwood player, saw fit to award a free kick to Geelong's Bert Whittington. He managed to steer the ball through for a behind to level the scores, 7.12 (54) apiece.

Ball-burster: Joe Slater was a highly effective, versatile centreman and flanker who possessed superb skills. Playing for the Pivotonians against Richmond at the Punt Road Oval he let fly from the middle of the ground with one of those kicks that went on, and on, and on … It sailed through for a goal from 78 metres out!

Own goal: Cheeky champion rover, Alec Eason, was on the wrong end of an umpiring decision in a match against Richmond at the Punt Road Oval in 1914. He made a desperate attempt to thwart a Tiger scoring attempt by booting the ball backwards

1911–1920

The rucks go up in a match at Corio Oval, this time between Geelong and St Kilda.

A riot at Corio

A match between Geelong and Carlton at Corio Oval on 18 August 1917 erupted into a riot. Remarkably, no player was reported.

'Saturday's match was the roughest seen on the Oval for years,' reported the *Geelong Advertiser*. 'Presumably Ellingsen (Geelong) did something that roused the resentment of some of his opponents. This led to much ill-feeling. In the first quarter Martini (Geelong) and Martin (Carlton) exchanged blows, and when the latter subsided McDonald (Carlton) took his place. Later on Ellingsen and Kiely (Carlton) had a set-to. From hence onward the game became very rough. Several of the players, instead of going for the ball, deliberately went for their opponents.

'There were faults on both sides. In the last quarter O'Brien (Carlton), who is a very powerfully built man, charged Collins (Geelong), injuring his face and causing blood to flow. Collins retaliated by pushing at his aggressor, and both rolled on the ground. Several other players joined in, and the crowd swarmed onto the ground. Play was suspended for some time, and it was with difficulty that the few police present, assisted by the Geelong secretary (Mr Charles Brownlow) and some of the Geelong players, cleared the field.

'When the Carlton players were entering the reserve at the finish of the game, W. Dick their captain, savagely struck at one of the barrackers, who was annoying him. Although there was no difficulty in detecting the chief offenders, neither the steward nor the umpires reported any of the players for rough play. Stewards were appointed by the League specially to put down such blackguardism. After Saturday's experience their services might well be dispensed with.'

Alec 'Bunny' Eason, champion rover

As one of Geelong's really great rovers, Alec 'Bunny' Eason lacked nothing in dash, skill and courage. His fitness allowed him to play on the ball for four quarters, and his pace worried all opponents. He stab-kicked particularly well, was cool and resourceful and had excellent judgment.

Amazingly, he had only three digits on his right hand, the others having been lost in an accident. He was always vocal on the field and some of his team-mates claimed that he was the only player in history with the ability to run half the length of the field and talk non-stop at the same time!

Grigg, a smart utility

Dick Grigg was regarded as one of the League's most accomplished and fairest players. Being well suited to the ruck or centre half-back, he also contributed well as a half-forward and half-back flanker. The durable player missed only four matches in the 11 seasons from 1904 until 1914. In that time he played 130 consecutive matches – a Geelong record. After seven years out of League circles he made a brief comeback to play the final two games of 1921, at the age of 35.

through for what should have been a rushed behind. Instead, both Field Umpire Jack Elder and the officiating goal umpire thought that Richmond's Hughie James had kicked the ball and awarded a goal. Richmond won the match 10.17 (77) to 6.17 (53).

Major problem: There have been two occasions in League history Geelong has failed to score a goal in a match. On 24 May 1899 at Corio Oval, Fitzroy 4.8 (32) defeated the home team 0.8 (8). Firth McCallum was unlucky not to score full points late in the match, his shot just grazing a goal post. On 31 May 1919 a large crowd watched St Kilda register a winning score of 6.10 (46). The visitors coped with the strong cross wind much better than the Pivotonians, who could manage only 18 behinds.

Famous families: Four sons of former players turned out for Geelong in 1917. They were Bert (son of Jack) Davie, Jim (son of Dan) Kearney, Bert (son of Teddy) Rankin and Jack Baker Jnr (son of Jack Baker).

Early Start: Geelong players had to set their alarm clocks ahead of normal schedule on the last Saturday in May 1920. The League had determined that the game would start early, at 10:45 a.m. The Prince of Wales was visiting Melbourne and was due to be paraded through the city during the afternoon, and this arrangement would allow people to watch the football prior to the royal procession. Several Geelong players appeared to be slow to 'wake up' and the Roys won the game 13.18 (96) to 8.8 (56).

GEELONG

Knocked out by Tigers

Under new 1921 captain and top full-back Harold Craven, Geelong qualified for finals participation for the sixth time in its 24 seasons at League level.

Sadly, Richmond defeated it easily in the First Semi-final, 16.19 (115) to 6.18 (54). Champion forward Lloyd Hagger had a day that he would prefer to forget, scoring two goals 10 behinds.

Only five victories from 16 attempts were achieved in 1922, however future stars Arthur Coghlan, Eric Fleming, 'Joker' Hall, 'Wingy' Stevenson and 'Jocka' Todd all made their League debut.

Arthur Coghlan.

The origin of 'The Cats'

From its very earliest years the Geelong team was usually referred to as the Pivotonians.

The term 'Cats' originated from an incident on 30 June 1923, when a black cat followed the Collingwood Juniors team onto the ground, and they started playing well.

Melbourne *Herald* cartoonist, Sam Wells, took up the idea and in his Friday evening cartoon suggested that a black cat would bring Geelong good luck. Geelong had won only two of its seven matches, but it managed to defeat the Blues 13.15 (93) to 13.10 (88). Captain Bert Rankin quipped that the black cat had helped the team to win.

The adoption had immediate results, with Geelong winning four successive matches. The idea developed momentum, and by the 1950s the Geelong Football Club and The Cats were synonymous.

Cats and Fords.

Last-kick victory

An incident in the game against Fitzroy on 12 July 1924 resulted in a change to the rules. Geelong's Eric Fleming had taken a mark just before the bell.

'For several seconds,' reported the *Geelong Advertiser*, 'play was held up while Fitzroy players (11 of them) crowded in front of Fleming. The centre half-forward made as if to kick, but protested against Fitzroy players encroaching over the mark. He then put his boot to the leather, but the ball bounced harmlessly off the crush of players in front of goal. The bell rang and the umpire awarded Fleming another kick. This time he made no mistake.'

Geelong won the match 9.14 (68) to 9.11 (65). The following week the League made a ruling that only one player was allowed to stand on the mark.

Eric Fleming.

A rough game against North

North Melbourne, in its first season in the VFL, was in for a rough game when it came up against Geelong on 1 August 1925 at Arden Street. The *Geelong Advertiser* reported that 'Johnston (North Melbourne) came into contact with Coghlan (Geelong), and there was an outburst of hooting when the North Melbourne man went down … There was another outburst from spectators when Russ (North Melbourne) in front of the press-box, rolled along the ground holding his head.'

Coghlan and Thomas of Geelong were both suspended for the remainder of 1925 and all of 1926. The suspensions were considered by many to be excessive, and a public meeting was called to protest. 'A resolution urged the Geelong football Club to endeavour to have an appeal board constituted by the League,' the *Advertiser* said. 'Those present at the match agree that the men primarily responsible for the trouble at North Melbourne were not reported at all.'

First Brownlow to 'Carji' Greeves

A highlight of the 1924 season was the awarding of the inaugural Brownlow Medal to Edward 'Carji' Greeves. An outstanding centreman with great courage, anticipation and acceleration, Greeves had the ability to read the play expertly. His kicking style was classic. As well as winning the inaugural Brownlow Medal in 1924, he finished second in that award on three occasions (1925, 1926 and 1928).

In 1928 he was invited to the United States to instruct in the art of kicking. In 1930 he suffered a serious knee injury which was to end his career prematurely.

Stan Thomas.

CLUB NEWS 1921-1925

New record: Cliff Rankin created a Geelong record when he kicked 63 goals for the 1921 season.

Badly shaken: In Round 9, 1924, South Melbourne hosted Geelong at the Lake Oval. During the second quarter it was alleged that South defender Arthur Hando deliberately shook a goalpost as a shot from Cat Arthur Pink was about to cross the goal line at the eastern end of the ground. The ball hit the upright and Geelong lost the match by three points. The club immediately protested to the League. The case could not be proved but Hando was warned never to attempt such action in the future.

Nothing in reserve: Geelong was awarded the 1924 Seconds (Reserve Grade) Premiership in controversial circumstances. The team was scheduled to meet Essendon at Kardinia Park in the last round of a 'Round Robin' series. The Dons refused to play in the Cats' home territory and forfeited the match to give their opponents the Flag.

What a ripper! In the opening round of 1925, newly admitted League club North Melbourne was handed a tough first-up assignment – Geelong at Geelong. The Cats were red-hot favourites. However, the Shinboners caused the upset of the decade, winning the game 9.13 (67) to 8.11 (59). Hundreds of Geelong members stormed out of Corio Oval in disgust, before the end of play. Some actually tore up their membership tickets,

1921–1925

Lloyd Hagger and Cliff Rankin are confident at three-quarter time.

The Cats grab Flag in 1925

The 1925 Geelong team had given its loyal supporters a great run for their money. It was the first of the top-class, speedy sides for which Geelong is renowned. The team won 15 games, including a great run of 12 games straight, and lost only two. Lloyd Hagger, 'the Mighty Splinter', kicked 78 goals, more than any other Geelong player before. Last but not least, the team broke a 28-year drought to win the Premiership Pennant.

The Geelong players bounced away to a good lead and preserved it with slick passing, completely bamboozling the Collingwood players. Typical of Geelong's play was a freakish mark taken by Ferguson: somehow, he managed to take the mark while lying on the ground on his back. With Collingwood concentrating on keeping top-scorer Hagger out of the game, Cliff Rankin kicked the goals.

Geelong outscored the inaccurate Pies to hold off a typical Collingwood finishing burst, and won 10.19 (79) to 9.15 (69).

Geelong went mad, and thousands gathered at the railway station to cheer their heroes. The celebrations went on for weeks.

A cheer from the supporters.

Bert Rankin left out

Bert Rankin.

In a controversial move, Geelong's selectors decided at the eleventh hour before the 1923 First Semi-final against Fitzroy to drop captain Bert Rankin from the team. Bert's brother Cliff chose not to play as a result.

'Cliff intimated during the morning that he would not be available, as he considered he would not do himself nor his team justice in view of the fact that he would be troubled by the thought that his brother Bert had not been chosen,' reported the *Advertiser*.

Geelong went on to lose the match 14.13 (97) to 8.14 (62). Bert Rankin had played his last match for the club, after outstanding service as a centreman in 132 matches.

Cliff Rankin

The resourceful full-forward/half-forward flanker was a most efficient goal-sneak, kicking 400 goals for the club. He preferred to make position cleverly and wait for crumbs rather than to fly for big marks. His left-foot kicking was superb.

Many of his 63 goals for the 1921 season (a new record for a Geelong player) were scored from place-kicks. He became captain-coach in 1925 with immediate and spectacular success, the club winning its first League Premiership that year under his guidance.

Cliff Rankin.

1921–1925 HONOUR ROLL

Year	Pos	Leading Goalkicker	No.	Best & Fairest	Captain	Coach
1921	4th	Cliff Rankin	63	Billy McCarter	Harry Craven	
1922	8th	Cliff Rankin	42	Keith Johns	Harry Craven	
1923	4th	Cliff Rankin	43	Billy McCarter	Bert Rankin	Bert Taylor
1924	5th	Lloyd Hagger	42		Lloyd Hagger	Lloyd Hagger
1925	1st	Lloyd Hagger	78		Cliff Rankin	Cliff Rankin

vowing never to support the club again. They must have felt foolish on Grand Final day just over five months later.
Fast out of the blocks: The crisp sea breeze from Corio Bay on the second Saturday in July 1925 did wonders for the Cats. In the opening quarter of their match against the ruffled Swans they piled on 11 goals from 15 scoring shots before the visitors could bother the flag-wavers. Geelong went on to win by 93 points, the final tally 18.13 (121) to 3.10 (28).
Tuned in: The first radio description of a League match involving Geelong occurred on Grand Final day 1925, when two metropolitan stations covered proceedings. Mr A. N. Bishop described play for 3AR and 'Jumbo' Sharland, who had retired as a Cats player earlier in the season, called the action on 3LO.
Burning the midnight oil: Geelong citizens certainly took their football seriously during Grand Final week, 1925. At that time most people were obliged to work on Saturday mornings and rush off to the football at 'knock-off' time. During the week leading up to the Grand Final industries operated up to 6 p.m. each night, an hour later than usual, so that the employees and employers could have the day off on Saturday. The time was needed to travel to the MCG early to secure a good position, as there were no seat bookings for the finals at that time. The people's enthusiasm was understandable, as Geelong was participating in its first ever League Grand Final in 28 years of competition.

GEELONG

Geelong's great forward George Moloney flies high at Corio Oval.

'Jocka' Todd: never ruffled.

A build-up to the Flag

At the beginning of 1926 the club was confident of winning its second consecutive Premiership flag. Geelong suffered only three defeats in the home-and-away matches, and just missed finishing on top of the ladder. The finals system allowed a second chance to the top team only, and a defeat by Essendon in the First Semi-final, 7.15 (117) to 10.10 (70), resulted in elimination.

Sadly, 1927 told an almost identical story, bundled out by Collingwood in the Second Semi-final, 16.18 (114) to 7.6 (48).

Everyone in the Western District would prefer to forget the 1928 season. The club could manage only six victories to finish a lowly ninth. At least the fans were kept excited with seven encounters decided by seven points or fewer, but, to their frustration, six of them were losses.

The pattern of a roaring start to the season, followed by a string of losses, was repeated in 1929, but greater team maturity and confidence achieved a Grand Final berth against Collingwood in 1930. The Cats outclassed their opponents in the first half but missed numerous ridiculously easy scoring shots. Such wastage proved costly. After halftime Collingwood took over completely, winning the game 14.16 (100) to 9.16 (70).

The greatest full-back

Veteran Cats' followers generally rate the lean defender as the club's greatest full-back. He used fine judgement, brilliant high marking and concentration to restrict the classiest opposition key forwards to meagre goal tallies. His long drop-kicking was a delight to watch, and his spoiling defensive punches propelled the ball almost as far as disposals by foot. Never ruffled, he was rarely guilty of giving away a costly free kick.

Railway bonanza

During the 1920s trains carried crowds to League matches. A total of 5396 people travelled by train from Geelong to the 1926 Semi-final at the MCG, while 5100 took advantage of the same method of travel to the 1925 Grand Final when Geelong beat Collingwood. At least 20 per cent of the 24,000 spectators at the Geelong v Carlton match at Corio Oval on 3 September 1921 were transported from Melbourne and the Western District by train.

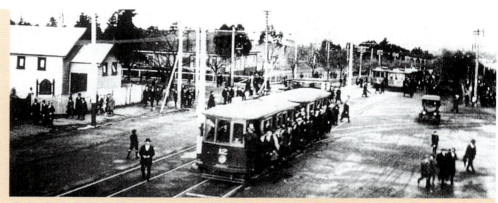
A crowded tram in Geelong as everybody heads to the football.

CLUB NEWS 1926-1931

Breaking the cycle: Cliff Rankin inspired Geelong to victory against Fitzroy at the Brunswick Street Oval in June 1926 by booting six goals. A nasty accident earlier in the week obviously had not affected his performance: he suffered abrasions when the fork of his bicycle broke as he was riding to work.

No charge: The Geelong committee invited champion centre half-back Tom Fitzmaurice to take up coaching duties at the beginning of 1928. He accepted on one condition – that the money set aside for his coaching services be shared equally among the players. Agreement was reached and the weekly fee of 12 pounds was split between the 18 selected men.

Off target: Fitzroy literally kicked away its chances of defeating Geelong at Corio Oval on 26 May 1928. Although they had two more scoring shots than the home team, the Roys were defeated by a massive 83 points! It was a dull, windy day and the ball was slippery. Play was delayed at one stage when a goal umpire straightened a behind post; bent, no doubt, by a wayward Fitzroy kick. Geelong obviously coped with the conditions much better, scoring 19.8 (122) to 2.27 (39). The visitors did not register their second goal until time-on in the last quarter.

Cold fingers: The following week Geelong travelled to the Punt Road Oval on a freezing, wet day. This time

1926 – 1931

The 1931 team. Pace, skill and teamwork were the keys to success.

1931 Grand Final

Geelong was the form side for 1931, winning 15 home-and-away games, and losing only three.

However, Geelong's confidence was badly dented by Richmond in the Second Semi-final, when the Tigers romped away 15.9 (99) to 10.6 (66). Richmond immediately became hot favourites for the Premiership.

They looked even greater certainties the following week, when Geelong qualified for the Grand Final with a win by only six points over the underdogs, Carlton, in a tough and tense Preliminary Final. Carlton staggered Geelong by scoring 7.5 (47) to nil in the first quarter, but Geelong showed its spirit and determination to turn on a devastating second quarter, scoring eight goals to Carlton's one and snatching the lead. The Cats defied Carlton to take it back, but the Blues couldn't prevail against the stronger Cats, who won the match 11.17 (83) to 11.11 (77). Geelong went (slightly apprehensively) into the Grand Final.

Players, officials and supporters need not have worried. The Cats had learned the dangers of a slow start, and took the initiative from the first bounce. As the match advanced, so did Geelong's lead. It had superior pace, marked better, and dazzled Richmond with a devastating second-quarter burst. A goal by Metherell and another 'impossible' goal by Maloney just before the half-time siren had the Cats ahead by seven points. From there on they never relinquished the lead.

Wingman Jack Carney provided the drive for Geelong with his electrifying dashes. Richmond also had problems matching Jack Collins, a great natural footballer who alternated between centre half-forward and centre half-back. Captain Ted Baker was a clever rover, and 'Carji' Greeves was another menace on the centre-line. The defence was very strong, and every player did his job in achieving the final score of Geelong 9.14 (68) to Richmond 7.6 (48).

George Moloney.

The team was: **Backs:** M. Lamb, G. Todd, H. Hardiman
Half-backs: J. Williams, R. Hickey, R. McDonald
Centres: J. Carney, E. Greeves, J. Walker
Half-forwards: L. Hardiman, J. Collins, R. Troughton
Forwards: J. Evans, G. Moloney, T. Quinn
Rucks: A. Coghlan, L. Metherell
Rover: J. Baker
19th Man: F. Mockridge

1926 – 1931 HONOUR ROLL

Year	Pos	Leading Goalkicker	No.	Best & Fairest	Captain	Coach
1926	4th	Lloyd Hagger	56		Cliff Rankin	Cliff Rankin
1927	3rd	Lloyd Hagger	55	George Todd	Cliff Rankin	Cliff Rankin
1928	9th	Jack Chambers	29	Reg Hickey	Tom Fitzmaurice	Tom Fitzmaurice
1929	7th	Jack Plunkett	29		Arthur Coghlan	Arthur Coghlan
1930	2nd	Bill Kuhlken	57	George Todd	Arthur Coghlan	Arthur Coghlan
1931	1st	George Moloney	74	George Todd	Ted Baker	Charlie Clymo

Richmond coped better in the slushy conditions, winning by 16 points. No doubt the fact that several Tigers wore woollen gloves contributed to their victory. Had Geelong kittens worn mittens the result may well have gone the other way.

No longer a Saint: In the third round of 1929 the Cats won a thriller at Junction Oval. When the final bell tolled they were three points in front, defeating St Kilda 8.12 (60) to 8.9 (57). Many St Kilda supporters blamed field umpire Les Reynolds for their team's defeat, accusing him of bias. They reacted in a hostile manner, gathering outside the umpires' dressing room to shout abuse. Poor Les was unable to leave the venue until 6:40 p.m., after the supporters had dispersed. Truth is often stranger than fiction: he was a former St Kilda player!

Travelling in style: Charlie Clymo, a Bendigo goldminer, played 43 matches and scored 21 goals for St Kilda from 1907 until 1909, after being recruited from Eaglehawk. The Saints regarded him highly enough to provide one of the state's few motor cars of the time to transport him home in time to begin a midnight shift underground, after a match against Geelong at Corio Oval. Later, he developed a fine reputation as a coach in country Victoria, and Geelong saw fit to appoint him as non-playing coach in 1931. Remarkably, he guided the Cats to the Premiership in only one season, and did not seek reappointment, preferring instead to return to 'the bush'.

GEELONG

George Moloney leads into space to take a strong chest mark.

So-so seasons frustrate the Cats

The seasons from 1932 to 1935 were all in the same pattern: a promising start followed by a disastrous finish. Wins in each of the first five matches of 1932 raised hopes of another Premiership, but a run of four losses in five contests meant the team missed the final four by a cat's whisker. Geelong's percentage of 139.7 at the end of the 1932 rounds was superior to all other clubs; still a record for a club failing to qualify for the finals. They had top forwards in George Moloney and Jack Evans, but couldn't capitalise on their work.

Percy Parratt, 1935 coach.

After late-season fade-outs in 1933 and 1934, former Fitzroy champion Percy Parratt took over as coach in 1935 – but no wins in the last eight rounds left the Cats in ninth place. Such frustrating seasons did not dampen the enthusiasm of their supporters for their close-fought games, according to the *Geelong Advertiser*.

'Spectators [at the 18 June 1932 away match v South Melbourne] who had thrilled at the tremendous pace of the earlier stages wondered that players had anything left for the supreme finishing effort that followed, and throughout the final term there was a succession of breathtaking incidents that had the huge crowd in a state of wild excitement.'

Dibbs loses way

Former Collingwood star full-back Charlie Dibbs was brought to the club as captain–coach in 1936, but after a sound start with three consecutive victories something went wrong. Five losses in as many games saw the matter come to a head on 17 June 1936.

The *Geelong Advertiser* noted that 'Charlie Dibbs, who has been coach of the Geelong Football Team this season, has resigned that position and his appointment as Captain. Making this announcement yesterday, club officials said that Dibbs had reached the decision because he was not in the best of health, and consequently, was unable to give the required concentration to the duties of coaching and leading the team.

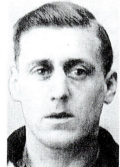

Charlie Dibbs.

'Dibbs apparently has felt the strain of coaching and leading the team when he has not been enjoying perfect health, and it was reported that in the last few days he had felt the need to relax, and had kept to his room.'

Reg Hickey was appointed to replace Dibbs as captain–coach. Dibbs did not play for Geelong again. Back under Hickey, the team responded positively. In 1937 the Cats won 15 of their 18 home-and-away games to finish on top of the ladder. They had won their last 12 home-and-away games in succession, and then easily disposed of Melbourne in the Second Semi-final.

Reg Hickey.

1932–1937 HONOUR ROLL

Year	Pos	Leading Goalkicker	No.	Best & Fairest	Captain	Coach
1932	5th	George Moloney	109	George Moloney	Reg Hickey	Reg Hickey
1933	3rd	George Moloney	68	Les Hardiman	Reg Hickey	Arthur Coghlan
1934	3rd	Jack Metherell	45	Reg Hickey	Reg Hickey	Arthur Coghlan
1935	9th	Jack Evans	32	Fred Hawking	Reg Hickey	Percy Parratt
1936	5th	Jack Metherell	58	Tommy Quinn	Charlie Dibbs/Hickey	Dibbs/Reg Hickey
1937	1st	Jack Metherell	71	Tommy Quinn	Reg Hickey	Reg Hickey

CLUB NEWS 1932–1937

Leather poisoning: George Moloney, a freakish full-forward brought from Western Australia, possessed the ability to snap amazing goals over his shoulder from seemingly impossible positions. In a remarkable span of eight days in August 1932 at Corio Oval, he scored 10 goals 10 behinds against Melbourne, and 11 goals from 20 scoring shots against Fitzroy.

Daily goals: A tall, rangy recruit from Collingwood, Lou Daily was selected in the forward pocket by the Cats in the opening round of 1934 against St Kilda at Corio Oval. Without a doubt he was best man on the ground. Although he only had 14 kicks, 12 of them were scoring shots (10 goals, 2 behinds). That was to be his only notable match for the club. After just 18 more goals in as many matches he disappeared from the League scene at the end of the season.

No training: The first Saturday in August 1935 was bitterly cold. In fact, the icy wind restricted the MCG attendance for the Victoria v South Australia match to a meagre 7864. The home state's captain, Geelong's centre half-back Reg Hickey, almost missed the match. He was to travel to Melbourne by train, but arrived at the station in time to see the last carriage disappearing into the distance. In desperation he contacted a friend, who rushed him to the ground by car, and he was able to lead his state to a 29-point victory.

1932 – 1937

The 1937 team. Standing: Everitt, L. Hardiman, Muller, Hore, Hickey (capt.), Sellwood, Dougherty, Metherell, Mahon, Hawking, Arklay, Evans. Front row: H. Hardiman, Wills, Quinn, Slack, Coles, Grant, Abbott.

The greatest game of all

'The greatest game of all' – that's how they described the thrilling 1937 Grand Final when Geelong overcame its great rival, Collingwood, for its third Premiership. The game had everything. The teams were evenly matched, both playing brilliant, clean football.

At three-quarter time, the teams were level on 80 points. Only Geelong's great accuracy had kept it with Collingwood, who had already won the previous two Premierships and was going hard for the hat-trick.

Geelong captain–coach Reg Hickey decided on a desperate plunge, and turned his side inside-out. Hickey switched full-forward Les Hardiman to centre half-back, Joe Sellwood from centre half-back to centre half-forward; Gordon Abbott from centre half-forward to the ruck, and Jack Evans from the ruck to full-forward.

The result of the moves was almost incredible. Average players suddenly became match-winners. The entire side revved up its play. Geelong, which had been struggling to open up a gap of more than a few points, streaked away with a sustained burst of non-stop teamwork.

Collingwood died hard, as always. Only its determination kept it in the game, as it frantically tried to find a solution to Geelong's sudden breakaway. The Magpies tried their own moves, but they didn't help. Unlike their fast Geelong opponents, most of the Black and White players already were very tired. They had tried their hardest, and couldn't raise any further effort.

As Geelong's confidence rose, Collingwood's dwindled. The rejuvenated Geelong side stormed home clear winners, slamming on six goals to one in the last term for a final score of 18.14 (122) to 12.18 (90).

When the final bell went, Geelong had won its 14th game straight for the season. It was a fitting end to a great season, in which they topped 100 points in more than 12 games, and had kicked more than 90 points in six other games.

The team:
Backs: B. Hore, R. Hickey, A. Everett
Half-backs: J. Grant, J. Sellwood, T. Arklay
Centres: L. Slack, F. Hawking, A. Muller
Half-forwards: J. Wills, G. Abbott, C. Coles
Forwards: J. Metherell, L. Hardiman, J. Evans
Rucks: H. Hardiman, G. Dougherty
Rover: T. Quinn
19th Man: G. Mahon

Reg Hickey

Reg Hickey was an excellent team player whose clearing dashes were inspirational. He could kick well with either foot and it was almost impossible to tackle him. He played a key role in Geelong's 1931 and 1937 Flag teams, was captain in 1932, captain–coach in 1936 and was non-playing coach of the club when it won the 1951 and 1952 Flags. Best and Fairest for the Cats in 1928 and 1934, he played a then club-record 245 games and represented Victoria 18 times.

Not-so-crowded house: Geelong's last home match of a very disappointing 1935 season was against Hawthorn, which had won only three of its 16 matches. When field umpire Bill Blackburn, flanked by his boundary and goal colleagues, walked out onto Corio Oval, he must have thought that he was at the wrong venue. A mere 2500 fans had bothered to travel to witness the contest. To rub salt into the already raw Geelong wounds the humble Hawthorn contingent was 28 points ahead when the final bell echoed across Eastern Park. It was to be the visitors' first and only win at Corio Oval, taking the match 13.9 (87) to 7.17 (59).

Get off the ground! During the third quarter of the Cats' match at Windy Hill in 1935, there was a diversion when hundreds of small boys jumped the fence at various points around the arena. They made their way across the playing field to the outer wing, where a collection of papers and small parachutes had fallen from a miniature balloon employed as an advertising gimmick. The crowd roared with laughter as the police chased the small boys, who quickly made off with the prizes.

A sign of the times: During the final quarter of Geelong's match against St Kilda at Corio Oval in 1936, a hailstorm swept across the ground. It was almost impossible for spectators to see any action. Some of the players rushed to the scoreboard wing and jumped the fence to shelter behind a galvanised iron sign.

GEELONG

The grandstand at Corio Oval, Geelong's home over the early decades.

Last game at Corio Oval

The loss of Les Hardiman and Jack Metherell prior to the commencement of the 1938 season had reduced the team's goalscoring potential, while the acquisition of Jack Butcher strengthened the defence. Geelong made it to the finals, but the Blues broke a sequence of seven victories in the Second Semi-final. A week later Collingwood shattered Geelong's hopes for another Flag, defeating it in the Preliminary Final 21.9 (135) to 14.14 (98).

The club had to face 1939 with the loss of Abbott, Coles, Collins, Evans and Peter Hardiman. Only George Gniel and Jim Knight could be regarded as star recruits. Not surprisingly, the club slid down the ladder, finishing in seventh place with the same number of wins.

Champions Reg Hickey and Tommy Quinn announced their retirement after the Round 4 loss to Richmond in 1940, apparently under pressure from the Committee who considered them to be beyond their best. Geelong still performed well despite these losses, making it to the finals only to lose to Essendon in the First Semi-final, 10.14 (74) to 13.14 (92).

The game against Footscray in Round 17, 1940 turned out to have greater significance than anyone knew. Geelong scraped through in a thrilling finish, defeating the Bulldogs 12.17 (89) to 11.18 (84). No one was aware at the time that Geelong would never again play a League game at the historic ground.

Humble war years

Clyde Helmer.

As Australia's involvement in World War Two became deeper, the importance of League Football changed. More and more players were enlisting, and match attendances were in decline. Several match venues, including the MCG and Corio Oval, were taken over as defence forces training bases. Some fine men from the Geelong club gave their lives – Clyde Helmer, Jack Lynch, Ralph Lancaster and Jim Knight.

In 1941 with new coach Len Metherell and a relocated home ground, Kardinia Park, the team struggled to win just three times for 10th place.

Ralph Lancaster.

Due to wartime transport restrictions and a severe shortage of players Kardinia Park went into a two-year hibernation in 1942 and 1943. The League Premiership was contested by just 11 clubs.

After Christmas 1943 Geelong applied for inclusion in the fixtures for the forthcoming season. One or two clubs were keen to exclude the Cats from the competition and the club officials had to use all its persuasive powers to gain readmission.

Jim Knight.

Geelong Headquarters

Originally, the Geelong Football Club was based at Argyle Square, in Aberdeen Street, Newtown. In 1878 an administrative oversight saw it lose tenancy of the Argyle ground – non-payment of dues prompted the owner to plough up a portion of the field to prevent the playing of matches. Soon afterwards, Geelong adopted Corio Oval for training and all home fixtures.

The club enjoyed great success at its new headquarters near the shores of Corio Bay, one of Australia's most picturesque grounds. Spectators were able to position their horses and buggies on low embankments in the outer and watch the match in comfort while seated in their vehicles.

The Cats were forced to find new headquarters at the end of 1940 when Corio Oval was required by the military authorities as a training establishment. The decision to use Kardinia Park 'temporarily' as an alternative home ground was made in 1941, although the facilities were basic.

CLUB NEWS 1938-1950

Running into form: Speedy Geelong utility Jack Grant won the 1938 Stawell Gift. At the opening match of the season against Melbourne at Corio Oval he gave a demonstration run and completed a lap of honour wearing his treasured sash. He decided to take two weeks' break before making himself available for football.

No blues with Blues: The 1938 Second Semi-final was played in a splendid spirit, and there were no spiteful incidents of any kind. In fact, when Laurie Slack of Geelong fell heavily near the centre, Carlton's captain Brighton Diggins ran over to help, and when Carlton's Jack Hale went down with a cramp in the leg, Cat Allan Everett gave him assistance until the trainers reached him.

Making a bunny of himself: When Geelong played Melbourne at Kardinia Park in 1941 players could have been forgiven for thinking they were playing in the country. A rabbit bobbed up during the game, was neatly taken by a boundary umpire and handed to some eager boys on the other side of the fence. A sheepdog also made itself at home on the ground at the start of the game. Efforts to coax it off were unsuccessful and it was not removed until half-time.

Secret service: Coach Tom Arklay had not played since 1941, but due to the poor performance of the team he was a last-minute inclusion to play against Collingwood at Victoria Park in

1938 – 1950

Top recruits

Jim Fitzgerald.

The football recruiting officers began to smile in 1946 when they attracted future top-liners Fred Flanagan and Russell Renfrey to the club. There were signs of improvement in Geelong's fortunes when four wins were achieved for the season, including a resounding 39-point victory in Round 10 over eventual Premiership winner, Essendon.

Marty Lynch, Sid Tate and classy left-footer Leo Turner made their debuts with the club in 1947. In the fifth round the supporters who travelled to the Lake Oval had good reason to celebrate on the train home that night. Geelong's victory over South Melbourne was its first 'away' success since its Round 12, 1940 defeat of Carlton at Princes Park.

Lindsay White.

A memorable moment came in the last match of 1947 against Carlton at Kardinia Park. Late in the last quarter, with his team four points down, Lindsay White marked 60 metres out. He used a beautiful drop kick to bring up his tenth goal for the day and victory for the Cats, 17.7 (109) to 16.11 (107). Eleven wins and seventh place were encouraging achievements for the Cats.

The 1948 season was disappointing, with only seven wins and ninth place achieved. One highlight: Lindsay White was awarded League goalscoring honours with 86 goals in 16 appearances, including five 'bags' of seven or more.

Some future stalwarts of the Geelong club line up as young players with the 1948 team.

Reg Hickey the coach as club builds list

Geelong appointed Reg Hickey as non-playing coach in 1949. Terry Fulton, Russell Middlemiss and Neil Trezise were added to the list of senior players, and Geelong's prospects looked good for the coming season. After Round 15 Hickey's methods had produced nine wins, and a finals berth appeared almost certain. However, the loss of top centre half-back John Hyde through injury seemed to upset the team's balance and four consecutive losses dashed the team's hopes.

In 1950 George Goninon was recruited from Essendon to add goalscoring power. The team finished the home-and-away series in fourth place, and performed excellently to defeat Melbourne by 44 points in the First Semi-final. Unfortunately, the Cats were defeated by North Melbourne in the Preliminary Final, 12.11 (83) to 14.16 (100).

After a drought of 14 years, loyal supporters were about to enjoy two years of 'football heaven'.

1938 – 1950 HONOUR ROLL

Year	Pos	Leading Goalkicker	No.	Best & Fairest	Captain	Coach
1938	3rd	Clyde Helmer	74	Tom Arklay	Reg Hickey	Reg Hickey
1939	7th	Norm Glenister	36	Jack Grant	Reg Hickey	Reg Hickey
1940	4th	Jack Grant	47	Tom Arklay	Reg Hickey	Reg Hickey
1941	12th	Lindsay White	67	Jim Knight	Tom Arklay	Len Metherell
1942-1943		Club in recess due to World War Two				
1944	12th	Lindsay White	60	Jim Munday	Jack Butcher/Arklay	Tom Arklay
1945	11th	Vic Nankervis	43	Jim Fitzgerald	Jack Butcher	Jack Williams
1946	10th	Russ Renfrey	28	Geoff Mahon	Jack Grant	Tommy Quinn
1947	7th	Lindsay White	76	Lindsay White	George Gneil	Tommy Quinn
1948	9th	Lindsay White	86	Bruce Morrison	Lindsay White	Tommy Quinn
1949	8th	Lindsay White	53	Fred Flanagan	Jim Fitzgerald/Tom Morrow	Hickey
1950	3rd	George Goninon	45	John Hyde	Lindsay White	Reg Hickey

July 1944. Listeners to the broadcast of the match by 3GL did not hear his name mentioned throughout the whole of the match. For private reasons, Arklay had asked that his name not be broadcast.

Four of the best: Geelong certainly had a vintage year for quality recruits in 1948. Bruce Morrison, Bernie Smith and Bob Davis (all first-year players) finished first, second and third respectively in the Geelong Best and Fairest award. John Hyde was also in his first season. All four eventually won Best and Fairest awards, participated in excess of 100 League matches and were key members of the 1951 and 1952 Premiership teams. Morrison, Smith and Davis represented Victoria, Davis was Victorian and All-Australian captain in his last season and Smith won the 1951 Brownlow Medal.

Caught behind: Footscray's Whitten Oval has always had a reputation of being a very windy football ground. In many matches there, teams have found great difficulty in kicking against strong northerly winds. During the Round 16 match in 1948 Geelong full-back Bruce Morrison must have become frustrated in his attempts to kick into the teeth of the gale howling down the ground that day. It was almost impossible to put the ball to boot with any certainty. On one occasion his kick-off from the goal-square sailed back over his head to score another Footscray behind. Not surprisingly, three footballs were lost over the fence that day.

GEELONG

No trouble for Fred

Fred Flanagan.

Fred 'Troubles' Flanagan, so called because he always seemed to be terribly worried about something before he took the field, was remarkably consistent throughout his 10-season career. He ranks with Jack Collins as Geelong's greatest-ever centre half-forward. He was highly skilled in all areas and developed the habit of flying for a mark and landing to face the direction of his disposal. He has the remarkable distinction of representing Victoria in each of his nine full seasons. He captained the highly skilled Premiership teams of 1951 and 1952, but business commitments forced his retirement while still in top form during the 1955 season.

Smith's Brownlow

After playing his early football as a centreman, Bernie Smith was switched to the back-pocket where he became an instant star, and in 1951 became the first player to win the Brownlow Medal in that position. His most remarkable attributes were uncanny anticipation and quick-thinking. He seemed to have

total control of the ball before it even touched his hands. At times he appeared to take unwise risks, but inevitably turned last-ditch defence into exciting attack. His cooperation with full-back Bruce Morrison was a delight to watch.

A wonderful moment at Geelong – raising the 1951 Premiership Flag.

Speed the key to Geelong team

Speed and sensational ball handling were Geelong's secret weapons in 1951.

This Geelong team was no fluke. Reg Hickey had planned it, step by step. Geelong sides were traditionally fast. This was the answer, but it was not blind speed. Hickey carefully chose his speedsters, and then drilled them. Every kick and every move was part of the pattern. Mobile rucks and a long-striding half-back line got the ball forward, and the forwards fanned out to provide a host of opportunities.

Geelong gained its first Grand Final berth in well over a decade, playing Essendon on 29 September 1951. In the first quarter the Cats sprayed their shots, but still galloped away to a good lead. Essendon took advantage of Geelong's inaccuracy to come back strongly in the second quarter and hit the front. Geelong steadied, rammed on 5.3 to two points in the third quarter, and then won 11.15 (81) to 10.10 (70).

CLUB NEWS 1951-1952

All-time low: One of the few lowlights of the time occurred on the first Saturday of August, 1951 at Kardinia Park. More than 26,000 people watched Collingwood win a thriller by just two points in very heavy conditions. The home team's score of 3.11 (29) remains its lowest ever home score for the 506 contests between 1941 and 1997.

Welcome home: Many of the 12,000 people who welcomed the Geelong Premiership team on its arrival back to Geelong after the 1951 Grand Final stood for up to three hours outside the City Hall. The huge crowd packed Gheringhap St and stretched from Malop St to Ryrie St. They cheered wildly when the team, led by the captain, Fred Flanagan, arrived on the steps of the hall one hour behind schedule. The outburst of cheers reached a peak as St Augustine's Band struck up 'See The Conquering Hero Comes'.

Father Bob: More than 1000 people were at Kardinia Park the following morning when the Premiership celebrations were continued. Highlight of the celebrations was the burial of a 'Bomber' – a model aeroplane made especially for the occasion. From the dressing room it was carried to the arena, preceded by players and officials, and during the procession the bell in the time keeper's box was tolled. As 'Father' Bob Davis covered the bomber with earth in the centre of the arena there was a loud blast from the siren.

1951–1952

Even faster in 1952

The Geelong speed machine hit its top in 1952, the Cats winning 16 home-and-away games and easily taking the Premiership.

The team had changed very little from the 1951 combination. Veteran ruckman Tom Morrow had retired and the very promising youngster, Norm Sharp, took his place. Russ 'Hooker' Renfrey was a ruck-rover, and dashing Geoff Williams had clinched a place on the half-back line.

Once again, Collingwood was Geelong's victim, both in the Second Semi-Final and the Grand Final. Each time Geelong showed its obvious superiority by more than doubling its opponent's score. The Magpies pitted their courage and determination against Geelong's superior speed, skill and system, but it wasn't enough. Geelong established an early lead, and the result was a foregone conclusion.

Flanagan is chaired aloft.

The Pies must have wondered if Geelong held something against them: the Cats had already taken the 1925 and 1937 Premierships from them!

Jack Jennings: over 25 years as president.

Jack Jennings' Reign

Jack Jennings has followed the fortunes of the Geelong Football Club since 1925.

He has seen most of Geelong's matches since the 1925 Grand Final – a remarkable record. He became officially associated with the club in 1930 as a Second Eighteen committeeman. In 1944 he was elected to the Senior committee.

He became club president in 1945 and remained in that capacity until the end of the 1970 season – a record term of 26 seasons. He was also a vice-president of the VFL for six years, the last two as senior vice-president.

In 1970, due to the illness of the president of the VFL (Sir Kenneth Luke) it was Mr Jennings' honour to be introduced to the Queen and Prince Phillip during their visit to the MCG to witness the Richmond v Fitzroy match.

He is a holder of the ANFC Merit Award for service to football and a life member of both the AFL and the Geelong Football Club.

Bobby Davis on the run.

The Geelong flier

Bob 'Woofa' Davis established himself as a fine half-forward flanker as soon as he joined the club in 1948. His strength, pace, flair and penetrating disposal made him a key forward-line player. He was appropriately dubbed the 'Geelong Flier'.

Late in his career, when the club was struggling to win matches, he became an outstanding utility player, filling the roles of full-back, centre half-back and ruck-rover with distinction. His leadership was first class, and he was a cheerful character around the club. In 1958 he was appointed All Australian captain during his final season as a player. His 1960–65 coaching stint yielded Geelong's 1963 Premiership.

1951–1952 HONOUR ROLL

Year	Pos	Leading Goalkicker	No.	Best & Fairest	Captain	Coach
1951	1st	George Goninon	86	Bernie Smith	Fred Flanagan	Reg Hickey
1952	1st	George Goninon	59	Geoff Williams	Fred Flanagan	Reg Hickey

Satisfying treble: With the Premiership, the Brownlow Medallist (Bernie Smith), and the League's leading goalkicker (George Goninon with 86 goals) all residing at Kardinia Park in 1951, the Cats had produced a rare treble.

Packed out: On 30 August 1952 Geelong was scheduled to meet Carlton at Kardinia Park in an important match for both clubs in preparation for the finals. An amazing total of 49,107 spectators passed through the turnstiles. The record crowd represented 70 per cent of Geelong's entire population. Thousands of the latecomers had no hope of viewing play and left the ground in frustration to listen to the match on radio. The Cats cruised to a 45-point victory.

Ghost city: Bounce-off time in Melbourne was switch-on time in Geelong on Grand Final afternoon, 1952. Radios went into action as the crowds roared at the MCG. Scraps of commentary floated through the still air through open windows. Ryrie St at 3.30 p.m. was a remarkable sight. Tramlines seemed to stretch like bush railway lines into empty horizons. One reporter counted one car, one parked motorcycle, three Chinese seamen and a dog between the Post Office and the Geelong Theatre. When the final siren blew more than 72 km away, and the radios brought the result, the silent tension seemed to lift from the city.

New Men: Four new players in the 1952 Premiership team were N. Sharp, G. Williams, D. Palmer and S. Smith.

GEELONG

Polly Farmer's ruck magic

New coach Bob Davis started a vigorous recruiting campaign in 1960 and netted the likes of John Brown, Terry Callan, John Devine, Stewart Lord and Peter Walker, then a year later Doug Wade, Tony Polinelli and Roy West.

The cream was introduced to the cake with the arrival of Graham 'Polly' Farmer from Western Australia in 1962. Many people believe that Farmer was Geelong's greatest player, despite his relatively short six-season career. He is regarded as the greatest exponent of handball in the history of football and was one of the first players to use it as a method of attack. He would frequently handpass 30 to 40 metres to team-mates in better positions. His ruck work was also revolutionary. He developed the technique of leaping for the ball slightly earlier than his opponents and gaining a 'ride' higher into the air. Often he would, in preference to a conventional tap-out, roll the ball down one arm and handpass to a team-mate running past. Geelong was never out of the finals during his League career.

Polly Farmer and his great rival, John Nicholls.

Was it a mark?

Geelong followers will ever say that they were robbed of a Grand Final appearance by Umpire Irving's decision in the last stages of the 1962 Preliminary Final replay.

The *Geelong Advertiser* reported, however, that the 'first reaction of Geelong supporters on Saturday after the initial disappointment of defeat by Carlton in the Preliminary Final replay was praise for the gallant play of the Geelong team. The terrific finish during which only points separated the teams and the lead changed several times, had all the elements to make it live long in the memories of those present.

'It included a controversial decision by Umpire Irving. With Geelong five points in arrears after John James (Carlton) had snapped the goal that gave his team the lead in the time-on period, Wooller broke clear and sent the ball towards Doug Wade and Carlton full-back Peter Barry.

'There appeared to be no more than the usual amount of jostling for position by either Wade or Barry, and Wade marked cleanly. To his amazement, Irving awarded a free kick to Barry, indicating that Wade had infringed the five-yard shepherding rule.'

Geelong lost the match 10.13 (73) to 10.18 (78).

1953–1963 HONOUR ROLL

Year	Pos	Leading Goalkicker	No.	Best & Fairest	Captain	Coach
1953	2nd	George Goninon	65	Peter Pianto	Fred Flanagan	Reg Hickey
1954	3rd	Fred Flanagan	55	Norm Sharp	Bernie Smith	Reg Hickey
1955	3rd	Noel Rayson	80	Geoff Williams	Bob Davis	Reg Hickey
1956	4th	Noel Rayson	41	Bernie Smith	Bob Davis	Reg Hickey
1957	12th	Fred Wooller	56	Bob Davis	Bob Davis	Reg Hickey
1958	12th	Neil Trezise	27	John O'Neill	Bob Davis	Reg Hickey
1959	10th	Fred Wooller	27	Colin Rice	Neil Trezise	Reg Hickey
1960	9th	Fred Wooller	29	Fred Wooller	Ron Hovey	Bob Davis
1961	6th	Doug Wade	51	John Yeates	Bob Davis	Bob Davis
1962	3rd	Doug Wade	68	Alistair Lord	John Yeates	Bob Davis
1963	1st	Doug Wade	48	Graham Farmer	Fred Wooller	Bob Davis

Doug Wade gives the umpire his view.

CLUB NEWS 1953–1963

Undefeated: Geelong holds a long-standing League record. From 12 July 1952 when it defeated Collingwood at Kardinia Park until 25 July 1953 when it outplayed Footscray at the same venue, 23 consecutive wins were achieved. The Magpies broke the sequence seven days later, beating the Cats 10.15 (75) to 7.13 (55). If a tied match against Essendon in Round 11 of 1952 is taken into account, the Cats remained undefeated in 26 successive encounters. Russell Renfrey was the only player to participate in all 26.

Geelong Flyer derailed: As Geelong's Bob Davis and Norm Sharp raced to stem a Footscray attacking move during the 1956 First Semi-final they collided head-on. Both lay motionless on the ground. In the confusion following the incident, Bulldog Max Cross picked up the ball and scored a vital goal. It was a costly accident for Geelong, as for a few minutes they only had sixteen men participating. Davis recovered rather shakily and again went into the fray, but it was some time before Sharp was lifted in a very groggy condition to his feet. He tried to make good but was obviously injured. Just before the end of the quarter trainers again went to him and signalled for a replacement. Footscray won the match by a whisker, scoring 5.13 (43) to 6.5 (41).

The not-so-cunning Fox: The huge crowd watching the 1962 Second Semi-final at the MCG was amused by

1953 – 1963

The victorious 1963 Geelong team with coach Bob Davis.

Fred Woolmer.

Bill Goggin in the clear.

The Cats 1963 Flag triumph

As with the 1951 and 1952 Premierships, there was a lot of thought and care put into the 1963 combination. Davis gathered together a fast side, not as fast as 1951–52, but with more physical strength. Polly Farmer made the team tick.

A strange feature of the 1963 Premiership was that Geelong had to beat Hawthorn three times in succession to take the title. The Cats met the Hawks in the last home-and-away game and won 13.12 (90) to 6.16 (52). A fortnight later they won 14.17 (101) to 11.16 (82) in the Second Semi-final.

In the Grand Final it was the Hawks' strength against Geelong's skill. In the first quarter Hawthorn hit Geelong hard and often. Gradually, the Cats took the sting out of Hawthorn and by half-time they led by 16 points. The Hawks threw everything at them, but slowly and surely it was Hawthorn that was fading.

Geelong was fitter and fresher for the last quarter, and unleashed a dazzling burst to kick 6.6 to three points, to finish 15.19 (109) to the Hawks' 8.12 (60).

The team was **Backs:** I. Scott, R. West, J. Watts; **Half-backs:** S. Lord, P. Walker, J. Devine; **Centres:** H. Routley, A. Lord, J. Brown; **Half-forwards:** J. Sharrock, F. Wooller, G. Hynes; **Forwards:** C. Rice, D. Wade, J. Yeates; **Rucks:** G. Farmer, P. Vinar **Rover:** W. Goggin; **19th & 20th men:** K. Goodland, T. Polinelli.

Alistair Lord's Brownlow

Alistair Lord became the Cats' third Brownlow Medallist in 1962, winning the award by an extraordinary 6 votes. After beginning as a dangerous half-forward flanker, the consistent ball-winner had been switched to the centre with immediate success. He was a strong mark, could run all day, and had the ability to continually pump the ball deep into attack with long drop-kicks. During 1962 he averaged 30 kicks per match. Lord's twin brother Stewart was almost as good a player, an attacking half-back flanker with brilliant marking and ball skills.

Goggin – a top rover

As possibly the finest rover in Geelong's history, Bill Goggin possessed crisp ball control and great speed. His deadly stab passes usually hit team-mates on the chest – it would be interesting to know how many times he directed the ball perfectly to Doug Wade. Few players possessed as much courage as the slightly built on-baller. There is little doubt that Graham Farmer and Bill Goggin formed the greatest ruck and rover team ever.

an unusual incident. Cat wingman John Fox commenced an amazing run around the members' stand wing. Clearing from goals, he 'touched down' twice, then with the ball tucked under his arm, he belted along the wing for at least 30 metres, until Umpire Nunn called the inevitable halt and paid a free kick against him. Fox had played rugby in NSW during his adolescence.

Sorry, wrong number: Early in the 1962 season Geelong played Richmond at the Punt Road Oval. During a scrimmage, a boundary umpire saw a punch thrown and reported star Cat centre-man, Alistair Lord for striking his opponent, Basil Moloney. At the tribunal hearing Alistair's identical twin brother, Stewart claimed that he was the one involved in the incident. There was no video evidence available and the case was dismissed. At the end of the season Alistair was awarded the Brownlow Medal. He may well have become the first ineligible player to gain the most votes had his brother not supported him four months earlier.

Season's most important kick: If Hawthorn's Youren had kicked accurately late in the Round 7 match of 1963, Geelong would not have participated in the finals at all. He ran into an open goal late in the match but scored a behind, and the siren sounded with scores level at 9.12 (66) apiece. The draw left Geelong half a win ahead of Essendon and with an inferior percentage at the end of the home-and-away rounds. But for the their lucky escape, the Cats would have missed the big one.

GEELONG

The blue in the race

Tempers flared in a close contest between North Melbourne and Geelong on 27 June 1964, with the conflict spilling over into the players' race, when North Melbourne coach Alan Killigrew was allegedly punched by a Geelong player.

Geoff Rosenow.

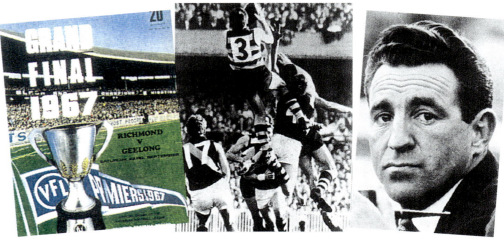
A 1967 souvenir. *Ken Newland marks.* *Peter Pianto.*

'Geelong relaxed dangerously,' reported the *Geelong Advertiser* 'in a torrid final term at Kardinia Park on Saturday, and was lucky to defeat a tenacious North Melbourne.

'It was a match filled with fire and incident, highlighted with the police taking the name of a North Melbourne player and followed by a scuffle in the players' race afterwards. Both incidents were unfortunate and leave sour memories of what otherwise was thrilling football.

'The first occurred at half-time when police questioned a North Melbourne player, and a senior policeman said later that the player could be charged with assault, following an incident which took place during the second quarter.

'The second incident occurred in the players' race where it is understood a Geelong player (Geoff Rosenow) and the North Melbourne coach (Alan Killigrew) were involved in a brief scrimmage. Killigrew emerged with a bleeding nose.

'As a result, North Melbourne players and officials did not go into the Geelong rooms as is customary after the match, and the players left the ground without communicating with the home team.'

Brave fight for 1967 Flag

The team played excellent football in 1967, with Wade back to his best and Wade and Sharrock providing lethal scoring power. Despite three losses in four contests mid-season, the Cats' form going into the finals was very good Magnificent wins over Collingwood and Carlton earned them a place in the Grand Final against Richmond.

The Premiership decider was a ripper. It had everything: vigour, skill, excitement and controversy. Several doubtful umpiring decisions swung the pendulum the Tigers' way in the vital last few moments. A running shot at goal by Bill Goggin appeared to go through for full points, but a mark to Richmond full-back, Fred Swift near the goal line was allowed.

When the final siren blared the Tigers were nine points in front, but it was an honourable loss.

Wade ended the season with 96 goals to be the top goalscorer in the competition.

1964–1975 HONOUR ROLL

Year	Pos	Leading Goalkicker	No.	Best & Fairest	Captain	Coach
1964	3rd	Doug Wade	41	Graham Farmer	Fred Wooller	Bob Davis
1965	4th	Gareth Andrews	35	Peter Walker	Graham Farmer	Bob Davis
1966	4th	Doug Wade	52	Denis Marshall	Graham Farmer	Peter Pianto
1967	2nd	Doug Wade	96	Bill Goggin	Graham Farmer	Peter Pianto
1968	3rd	Doug Wade	64	John Newman	Bill Goggin	Peter Pianto
1969	4th	Doug Wade	127	Doug Wade	Bill Goggin	Peter Pianto
1970	5th	Doug Wade	74	Bill Goggin	Bill Goggin	Peter Pianto
1971	10th	Doug Wade	94	David Clarke	Bill Goggin	Bill McMaster
1972	10th	Doug Wade	90	Ian Nankervis	Doug Wade	Bill McMaster
1973	11th	David Clarke	45	Bruce Nankervis	Geoff Ainsworth	Graham Farmer
1974	6th	Paul Sarah	32	Bruce Nankervis	John Newman	Graham Farmer
1975	11th	L Donohue/I Nankervis	29	John Newman	John Newman	Graham Farmer

CLUB NEWS 1964–1975

Ryan incident: Geelong trailed Collingwood by five points in April 1967 when Bill Ryan marked on the siren. His first kick was touched by Magpie defender Terry Waters, but the umpire ruled that Waters had run over the mark. Ryan reloaded and kicked again. His goal secured victory by a single point, 13.13 (91) to 13.12 (90).

High marks: Burly centre half-forward Bill Ryan was one of Geelong's greatest exponents of high marking. One of his most outstanding performances was as a back-pocket against Hawthorn in Round 17 of 1968, when he took the amazing total of 22 marks to help foil star Hawk full-forward, Peter Hudson. He also gathered 31 kicks – a rare tally for a big man in the last line of defence. Ryan's consistency was demonstrated in 1971 when he marked the ball 211 times in 21 matches.

Another first: Geelong met Fitzroy in the inaugural match played at Waverley Park on 18 April 1970 in uncharacteristically hot, sunny conditions for a venue in the middle of the Mulgrave rain-belt. Doug Wade booted the first goal after two minutes of play, and the Cats won easily by 61 points, the final score 17.12 (114) to Fitzroy's 7.1 (53).

Inside out: On Tuesday, 15 September 1970 Fitzroy and Geelong fought out a thriller in a night match at the Lake Oval. Geelong champion Doug Wade inadvertently provided a humorous moment during the first quarter.

1964–1975

Finals fade-outs in 1968–69

Season 1968 commenced without the services of Farmer, who had returned to the West. Speaking of West, he had also hung up his boots. Recruits included 'Bluey' Hampshire and Phil Stevens. The team ended the season with a 24-point loss to Essendon in the Preliminary Final.

Hosking, Marshall and Sharrock all announced their retirement in 1969, and unfortunately, no new players of note came to the club. Doug Wade had an outstanding year, booting 127 to win League goalscoring honours once again.

Every Geelong supporter would prefer to forget the 1969 First Semi-final against the Tigers. In the club's most dismal finals performance it submitted meekly by 118 points, going down 7.7 (49) to Richmond's 25.17 (167). At least Wade tried hard, scoring five of his team's seven goals.

A classic Doug Wade mark.

A great full-forward

Burly full-forward Doug Wade performed with remarkable consistency for a decade. He will always be remembered for lightning leads, super-strong marking and booming, deadly-accurate torpedo punt kicks. Never prepared to meekly accept niggling tactics from unscrupulous opponents, he used his great strength and fiery temperament to his team's advantage. Often, he played the forward role like an aggressive defender.

John (Sam) Newman

Using Polly Farmer as a role model, the Geelong Grammar athlete developed into a fine ruckman with excellent palming, marking and kicking ability. He knew how to position himself correctly in contests and read the play to perfection. During the 1967 First Semi-final he suffered a serious kidney injury which threatened his football career, but he fought back courageously to win the club Best and Fairest award the following season. He endured severe ankle problems later in his career, which restricted his mobility and kicking distance, but not his effectiveness. In his last few seasons he played creditably at centre half-forward. Newman played 300 games for Geelong.

New coach, but no joy

New coach Bill McMaster was faced with a handful of aging champions and very few promising young players in 1971. As many as 42 different men were tried during the season, but of the new ones only Rod Blake, David Clarke and Michael Woolnough would become consistent performers. Only two wins were achieved in the first 17 matches of 1971, and a 10-match losing sequence at the beginning of 1972 was not a good membership ticket sales promotion.

Rod Blake.

'Polly' returned to the club as coach in 1973. Team improvement was evident, with eleven wins leaving Geelong not far out of the final five.

A frustrating drop in performance in 1975 made drastic changes imminent. Although the recruiting campaign continued, with Bryan Cousins and Graeme Landy joining the club, 15 losses and a dismal percentage of 78.2 were a poor return.

The apple core incident

An unusually good shot at Kardinia Park may have decided a close-fought game between Geelong and South Melbourne in Round 20 of 1970. The *Geelong Advertiser* asked: 'Did an apple core cost Geelong victory on Saturday and a place in this years finals? We'll never know. "The Apple Core Incident" occurred as Doug Wade was taking a kick at goal 30 yards out and 15 yards from the boundary. As he dropped the ball to his boot, an apple core, thrown by a spectator, struck the ball fair and square. It slid off the side of his boot and was lost to the South defence. Said Wade in the dressing rooms after the match: "He did a William Tell on me."'

Playing in an unfamiliar role as centre half-back, the burly Cat started off playing in a sleeved guernsey. He soon signalled to a trainer that he wanted to switch to a sleeveless version. He hurriedly donned the replacement garment as the ball unexpectedly came towards him. The crowd howled with laughter as it became obvious that he had put the guernsey on inside-out!

Two-man forward line: Centre half-forward Bill Ryan and full-forward Doug Wade turned on an unforgettable combined performance in two matches against North Melbourne during 1971. In Round 9 at the Arden Street Oval each scored seven of their team's 16 goals for the match. In the return encounter at Kardinia Park, Wade took 12 marks, had 20 kicks and scored 13 goals, Ryan took 18 marks, had 25 kicks and scored 7 goals. The pair scored 20 of Geelong's 24 goals. Only six of the team's 40 goals for the season against the Kangaroos were registered by players other than the amazing duo.

Dream debut: David 'Rocky' Armour made his League debut at Collingwood in Round 8, 1974. He came on as a reserve at quarter time to replace Peter Doyle, who had sprained an ankle. Positioned on the half-forward flank he capitalised on every opportunity that came his way, scoring goals with his first two kicks in League football. He managed to score four goals one behind with his first six kicks – a truly memorable performance. But despite the good start, he played only 19 games.

GEELONG

Rod Olsson: new approach.

Olsson and Goggin

Two coaches between 1976 and 1988 brought different concepts to the club, but without Premiership success.

The appointment of former Hawthorn ruck-rover Rod Olsson as coach for the 1976 season brought a totally new approach to the Geelong team. He instilled confidence in individuals to use more imagination and initiative. The team played fast, attractive football for the majority of the season, finishing fourth after the home-and-away schedule. North Melbourne ended their season with an easy victory in the First Semi-final.

The improvements were not to continue. The team put in ordinary performances for the next few years, with the only finals achievement a berth in the Elimination Final in 1978, where the Cats went down to Carlton 9.18 (72) to 15.15 (105).

Prior to the 1980 season the Committee decided to replace coach Olsson with legendary rover, Bill Goggin. He was able to capitalise on his predecessor's sound basis to produce positive on-field results, but the Cats were unable to lift themselves to become Premiership contenders.

Hafey and recruits

Geelong had a dismal season in 1982 under the captaincy of Brian Peake. At no stage did the team perform with any consistency. Seven wins and ninth place gave supporters little reason to be optimistic.

New direction came in the form of highly experienced coach, Tom Hafey, who had a reputation as a 'players' man' and was appointed coach for the 1983 season. The team began in a blaze of glory, winning its first four matches using a Hafey-inspired direct style. Lack of consistency from that point, not helped by injuries to important players, saw the club finish ninth.

The opening match of 1984, against Fitzroy, unveiled the attributes of three highly publicised recruits: Mark Jackson, Greg Williams and Gary Ablett. Each performed brilliantly. Between unusual gestures 'Jacko' scored nine goals, while the other pair, with veteran, Michael Turner, formed one of the most talented centrelines ever seen in League football.

Unfortunately, Williams injured a knee in Round 12, and was unable to play for the rest of the year. Ablett was unavailable due to suspension in five games, and consistent performers Turner and Toohey missed the latter part of the season because of injury. Under the circumstances the Cats did fairly well to miss a place in the finals by percentage only.

Jacko gives Gary a lift.

1976–1988 HONOUR ROLL

Year	Pos	Leading Goalkicker	No.	Best & Fairest	Captain	Coach
1976	4th	Larry Donohue	105	Ian Nankervis	Bruce Nankervis	Rod Olsson
1977	8th	Larry Donohue	63	Ian Nankervis	Bruce Nankervis	Rod Olsson
1978	5th	Larry Donohue	95	David Clarke	Ian Nankervis	Rod Olsson
1979	6th	David Clarke	40	David Clarke	Ian Nankervis	Rod Olsson
1980	3rd	Terry Bright	59	Rod Blake	Ian Nankervis	Bill Goggin
1981	3rd	Terry Bright	48	Peter Featherby	Ian Nankervis	Bill Goggin
1982	9th	Michael Turner	40	John Mossop	Brian Peake	Bill Goggin
1983	9th	Terry Bright	26	Ray Card	Ian Nankervis	Tom Hafey
1984	6th	Mark Jackson	74	Gary Ablett	Michael Turner	Tom Hafey
1985	6th	Gary Ablett	82	Greg Williams	Neville Bruns	Tom Hafey
1986	9th	Gary Ablett	65	Paul Couch	Michael Turner	John Devine
1987	6th	Bruce Lindner	62	Mark Bos	Damian Bourke	John Devine
1988	9th	Gary Ablett	82	Mark Bos	Damian Bourke	John Devine

CLUB NEWS 1976–1988

On target: Geelong holds the League record for scoring the most consecutive goals without a behind to interrupt the sequence. In Round 5, 1979 the Cats visited Moorabbin, where they had enjoyed little previous success. They played superbly to win by 30 points. No doubt, excellent accuracy contributed significantly to their success. From the eight-minute mark of the second quarter until 22 minutes into the final term they added 15 goals straight! Geelong 22.10 (142) defeated St Kilda 17.10 (112).

Tied up: Geelong was involved in a drawn match each season from 1960 until 1964. No other club has experienced such thrillers in five consecutive years. Strangely, the Cats also hold the record for the greatest 'drought' of drawn results. Between draws with Essendon at Windy Hill in Round 2, 1969 and Round 6, 1987, Geelong played 406 consecutive matches without producing a tied result.

Strike me! Zane Taylor made his League debut for Geelong in Round 1, 1980 against South Melbourne at Kardinia Park. Unfortunately, he provided one of the rare instances of a player facing the tribunal after an incident in his first match. Taylor was found guilty of striking Swan Michael Wright and suspended for four matches.

The Sidebottom affair: For the 1981 Preliminary Final showdown against the Magpies, Geelong initially named their best performer from the week before,

1976-1988

Geelong and Hawthorn sort themselves out at the end of the melee.

Bloodbath match leads to police action

The game against Hawthorn at Princes Park on 15 June 1985 was marred by an extraordinary degree of violence, with two players suffering broken bones and five players reported for a total of eight incidents on 17 report sheets.

The match was compared by the media to the 'Bloodbath' 1945 Grand Final, which was played at the same ground between South Melbourne and Carlton. Geelong's Mark Jackson was the main offender with eight charges from four incidents. He was found guilty of striking Gary Ayres, Chris Mew, and Chris Langford twice, and was suspended for eight matches.

Hawthorn's Leigh Matthews escaped a report when the umpires missed a nasty incident which left Geelong's Neville Bruns with a broken jaw and concussion. Matthews was later deregistered for four weeks by the VFL Commission for conduct unbecoming. He was also charged with assault after a police investigation into the incident.

Matthews pleaded guilty to the charge and was fined $1000. Matthews himself had suffered a broken nose in a clash with Geelong's Steve Hocking.

John Devine

The club decided in 1986 that it was time to try another coach: tough, loyal former defender, John Devine.

At the beginning of the season he told the players that he would demand full commitment to the football at all times. Some criticised him for lacking a tactical approach, but he had to contend with the unexpected loss of Williams, Toohey and Bolton to Sydney. The team did not win until Round 6, and it struggled to finish ninth with seven wins.

In 1987, 11 wins and a tie left the club just half a win away from finals action. With only a minute remaining in the last match, at home against Hawthorn, the Cats held a three-point advantage and looked set for September action. Jason Dunstall spoilt the party by slotting a quick pair of match-winning goals to put the Hawks in front 19.12 (126) to 17.21 (123).

Six wins in the first 10 games of 1988 were followed by a season-ruining run of losses. Devine's contract was not renewed.

Ian Nankervis

The lightly built boy from Barwon began as an elusive half-forward flanker who occasionally shared roving duties with Bill Goggin. After eight years of moderate success, his career appeared to be coming to a conclusion. In an inspired move, Nankervis was tried as a back-pocket, with instant success. His concentration, superb fitness, anticipation and running ability were utilised to make him a revolutionary player in what previously had been considered a defensive field position. A further eight seasons of determination and creative play ensured his place among the club's all-time greats.

Michael Turner

Lightning pace, spectacular marking and great evasion skills made the classy wingman one of the club's most effective midfielders. He did well in the centre or as a goal-sneak, and captained the Cats in 1984 and 1986. He played for Victoria in 11 games, and was All-Australian player in 1979.

Turner lays a tackle.

David Clarke, then unaccountably omitted him at the last minute. His intended replacement, Garry Sidebottom, was not told that he was to play, and stayed at home. Goggin had to summon forward Peter Johnston to fill the position.

Eight of the best: The incomparable Gary Ablett had played only 15 League matches when he gained selection in the Victorian State of Origin team for the first time in 1984. On July 17 of that year the Vics met the Sandgropers at Subiaco in front of 42,500 football lovers. In a high-standard, closely contested match Ablett revealed the class that he was to display consistently for the next 12 seasons. His State of Origin debut, which produced eight spectacular goals, was one of the most outstanding in more than two decades of State of Origin matches.

Give me some advice, Dad! Bert Rankin, Cliff Rankin and Michael Turner are the only Geelong captains whose fathers played at League level for the club. The Dads were Teddy Rankin and Leo Turner. Three Geelong captains had sons who later played for the Cats: Teddy Rankin (Bert, Cliff and Doug), Harry Marsham (Alan), Jim Kearney (Dan) and John Yeates (Mark).

Good start: The following Geelong players won the club Best and Fairest award in their first season: Jim Munday (1944), Bruce Morrison (1948), Geoff Williams (1952), Roy West (1961), David Clarke (1971) and Gary Ablett (1984). The youngest winner was Clarke, at the age of 19. The oldest was Billy Carter, who won in 1923 at the age of 35.

GEELONG

1989 – a year of high-voltage football

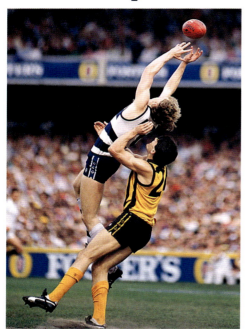
Billy Brownless stretches out.

The appointment of 1989 coach Malcolm Blight heralded the most entertaining decade in the club's history. Never before had supporters enjoyed such a sustained period of prolific scoring, witnessing regular displays of the finest skills in the world's greatest game.

The club entered the finals from third position with justifiable optimism. The Cats then played a nightmare Qualifying Final against Essendon. Completely outclassed, they lost 11.15 (81) to 24.13 (157).

Melbourne was eager to meet the seemingly dispirited Geelong in the First Semi-final. Little did the Demons realise what the cunning Blight had stored up his sleeve. They knew that Couch and Bairstow were key team members, and had assigned specialist taggers to negate them. In a master move Blight sat both on the interchange bench at the start of play, leaving many of the Melbourne players bewildered. Geelong quickly gained a scoreboard advantage and romped home by 63 points.

In the Preliminary Final the Cats achieved one of the greatest reversals in football history. Inspired by a rampant Gary Ablett, who bagged eight spectacular goals, the Cats totally humiliated the Bombers, who scored 10.10 (70) to the Cats' 24.20 (164).

The scene was set for a classic Grand Final between Hawthorn and Geelong. From the opening bounce, when Mark Yeates collided with Dermott Brereton, to the thrilling final seconds, when David Cameron's goal reduced the margin to six points, everyone who attended or watched on television was enthralled. Geelong lost honourably, the final score 21.12 (138) to 21.18 (144) Ablett's effort in booting nine goals earned him the Norm Smith Medal.

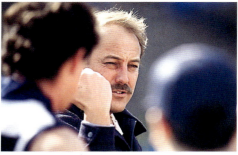
Blight with the troops.

So near and yet so far

Most Geelong supporters, although disappointed by the 1989 Grand Final loss, could not wait for the 1990 season to arrive. What a let-down it was! A combination of complacency and a series of injuries resulted in a forgettable winter. Eight wins and 10th place were the rewards.

Third place and an exciting Elimination Final victory over St Kilda in 1991 set the town ticking once again. A courageous effort in the Second Semi-final resulted in narrow two-point defeat, and the team was finally eliminated by West Coast in the Preliminary Final, 11.13 (79) to 8.16 (64).

The home-and-away games of 1992 were almost a replica of three seasons earlier. A League-record season aggregate of 3558 points was capped by a brilliant finals series, unhappily ending in a heavy Grand Final loss.

Malcolm Blight decided to place a much greater emphasis on defence in 1993. Few of his men were able to adapt, and their confidence was disintegrating. A disastrous loss to St Kilda in Round 16 precipitated a meeting between players and coach to thrash out their differences. At the meeting Blight declared that he would return to his earlier philosophy of all-out attacking football.

The players responded positively, winning the last five games, four of which were against teams in the top five. Although the Cats were clearly the form team, time had run out, and they missed the finals by a percentage of less than five.

Couch – Mr Consistent

Paul Couch, the ever-smiling centreman, was a consistent performer who was able to adapt to on-ball and forward roles in the latter stages of his career. His strength, superb ability to read the play, quick hands and immaculate disposal by foot were his trademarks. He could affect a deceptive lack of pace. Few other champions have been as capable of booting the ball 50 metres or more with pin-point accuracy from a two-step approach when under pressure in a pack. He was at his best in 'heavy traffic' and when the ground conditions were damp.

CLUB NEWS 1989–1996

Perfect match: In Round 6 of 1989, Princes Park hosted one of the best-quality League matches ever seen. The Geelong team drove to the ground knowing that it had not defeated Hawthorn there for six years. In an enthralling display of power football the Cats piled on 17 first-half goals to hold what appeared to be a match-winning 49-point lead. They also booted the opening bull's-eye of the third term, but their opponents were not giving up. The switch of Gary Ayres into the centre during the second half swung the game dramatically. In an exciting conclusion the Hawks were eight points ahead at the end. Geelong's losing score of 25.13 (163), to the Hawks 26.15 (171), was the highest ever recorded.

Best of the best: G. Ablett, Esq. will be remembered forever for his miraculous forward play, but his performance as a centreman at Subiaco in 1992 was possibly his most effective in a 248-match career. Against West Coast he distributed 27 penetrating kicks, took eight telling marks and fed out nine constructive handpasses to help his team record a memorable away victory of 20.11 (131) to 15.17 (107). Oh, by the way, he slotted five goals as well.

Putting the score on the board: On 3 May 1992 Geelong travelled to Carrara to play Brisbane. The Cats began well, scoring 7.4 (46) to 2.2 (14) in the opening quarter. It was the

1989 – 1996

A mighty leap from Gazza.

One lap too many as the Cats go down again in 1994.

Gary Ablett – the greatest

Ablett is regarded by many as the player with the widest range of skills ever to play Australian football. His pace, strength, courage, guile, elusiveness, long kicking with either foot and spectacular (often one-handed) marking thrilled one and all.

A life of service

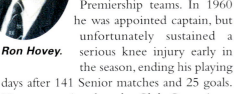

Ron Hovey.

In 1948 the 15-year-old Ron Hovey joined Geelong Thirds (Under 19s). Three years later he made his senior debut. During his 10-season career he gave the Cats consistent service as a half-forward flanker/centreman/back-pocket. He was a member of the 1951 and 1952 Premiership teams. In 1960 he was appointed captain, but unfortunately sustained a serious knee injury early in the season, ending his playing days after 141 Senior matches and 25 goals. He was appointed to the Club Committee, and was elected Club President in 1988. He retains both roles to this day.

Back-to-back Grand Finals

Geelong finished fourth after 13 home-and-away victories in 1994. In a thrilling Final series, two out of the three finals were won by a single goal scored after the siren. After that, the Grand Final against West Coast was an anti-climax for all Geelong supporters. The Eagles were far too accomplished, beating the Cats 20.23 (143) to 8.15 (63).

Malcolm Blight resigned at the end of 1994 and Gary Ayres was a worthy replacement as coach. He was able to develop greater consistency in his players' performances, with the team not losing two successive matches during the 1995 season.

Second place on the ladder was an accurate indication of Geelong's form leading into the 1995 finals. The Cats easily accounted for the Bulldogs in the Qualifying Final, and a huge 89-point victory over Richmond in the Preliminary Final gave Geelong a place in its fourth Grand Final in seven years. Another disaster!

The team submitted meekly to Carlton by 10 goals without any worthwhile excuses, finishing with just 11.14 (80) to the Blues 21.15 (141).

1989–1996 HONOUR ROLL

Year	Pos	Leading Goalkicker	No.	Best & Fairest	Captain	Coach
1989	2nd	Gary Ablett	87	Paul Couch	Damian Bourke	Malcolm Blight
1990	10th	Gary Ablett	75	Barry Stoneham	Andrew Bews	Malcolm Blight
1991	3rd	Billy Brownless	81	Garry Hocking	Andrew Bews	Malcolm Blight
1992	2nd	Billy Brownless	79	Ken Hinkley	Mark Bairstow	Malcolm Blight
1993	7th	Gary Ablett	124	Garry Hocking	Mark Bairstow	Malcolm Blight
1994	2nd	Gary Ablett	129	Garry Hocking	Mark Bairstow	Malcolm Blight
1995	2nd	Gary Ablett	122	Paul Couch	G. Hocking/Ablett/K. Hinkley	Gary Ayres
1996	7th	Gary Ablett	69	Garry Hocking	G. Ablett/B. Stoneham	Gary Ayres

beginning of an unprecedented scoring spree. The visitors added nine goals in the second term and seven more in the third to establish a 102-point advantage by the last break. By registering a remarkable 14.2 in the next half-hour they drew level with the all-time League record score of 238 points, which was established by Fitzroy almost 13 years earlier. With seconds of the match remaining Billy Brownless managed another behind to break the barrier, Geelong finishing 37.17 (239) to the Bears' 11.9 (75). Ablett contributed nine goals for the day.

Level pegging: On 8 June 1996 fans at Kardinia Park witnessed a thrilling tie between Geelong and Brisbane, the Cats finishing with 14.4 (98) to the Bears' 15.8 (98). It was only the third time in 490 encounters at the venue that the scores were level at the end of a match. In the opening round of 1957 Footscray 10.17 (77) and Geelong 11.11 (77) had different scores but identical tallies. The Hawks and the Cats shared the match points in Round 7, 1963 with 9.12 (66) apiece. Prior to the 1996 season, Geelong's most recent drawn match had been against Essendon at Windy Hill in the sixth round of 1987, when the Cats scored 13.18 (96) to the Bombers' 14.12 (96).

Not quite there: The team managed 13 wins in 1996 to finish seventh. Their final game for the season was a disappointing and one-sided Qualifying Final in which the eventual Centenary Premiers, North Melbourne, won by 10 goals.

GEELONG

The changing of the guard

In his two previous seasons as Senior coach, Gary Ayres worked determinedly to modify Geelong's style of play.

He asked his players to become more accountable for their direct opponents even if it meant sacrificing some aspects of attacking football. At the same time he encouraged them to play positively whenever an opportunity arose. Young players in particular adapted well to the change in approach. An excellent fitness level allowed the team to score vital goals late in quarters. Rarely were the Cats defeated in a tight finish. Generally, team scores were significantly lower than in the previous ten years, but gone were the widely fluctuating winning and losing margins and lapses in concentration during matches.

The 1997 season saw a changing of the

Liam Pickering: up there.

Gary Hocking: thinking ahead.

guard at Kardinia Park. Gary Ablett did not make a senior appearance during 1997, a faulty knee forced Paul Couch into retirement after just five matches, and nagging injuries restricted performances by Billy Brownless.

Perhaps the greatest positives for the year were the emergence of Ronnie Burns, who notched a half-century as a goal-sneak, Leigh Colbert, who demonstrated versatility and courage, Steven King, who developed rapidly as an excellent ruckman, Ben Graham, who continued to mature as a top full-back, and the consistency of midfielders Glenn Kilpatrick, Liam Pickering and Garry Hocking. The team's defensive unit led by Ben Graham, Brad Sholl, Brenton Sanderson, Tim McGrath and Michael Mansfield became the tightest in the club's recent history.

Barry Stoneham is back.

Garry 'Buddha' Hocking

The chunky ruck-rover is the perfect example of a 'hard at the ball' type. His polished skills elevate him to the elite class. Despite lacking leg-speed, and occasional careless tackling, he is breathtakingly effective at feeding the ball out to team-mates from congested situations and to link play in lightning fashion with beautiful kicking with either foot. The umpiring fraternity obviously recognises his unquestioned value to his team, having allocated in excess of 100 Brownlow Medal votes, resulting in no fewer than five 'top five' placings in a space of six seasons.

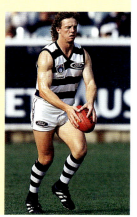

1997 HONOUR ROLL

Year	Pos	Leading Goalkicker	No.	Best & Fairest	Captain	Coach
1997	5th	Ronnie Burns	50	Liam Pickering	Barry Stoneham	Gary Ayres

1997

A day out at Kardinia Park

There's still a good country feel down at Kardinia Park, where rabbits were occasionally traversing the field in the 40s, and the pine trees in the park rear over the grandstands. The trees held their share of spectators in the old days, but the Social Club and the Ford Stand have since barred any chance of a free look at the footy.

The view from the stand is across a low landscape of rooftops, with the occasional tower and spire to split the grey sky that arches down to the flatlands around Corio Bay. On the other side of the ground the long mound that was a viewing platform for the outer has been replaced by terraced rows of blue plastic seating.

Geelong at home has attracted a sell-out crowd again. In truth these seats are pretty well taken up each year by the faithful. Someone in the press box remarks that the entitlement to a Geelong seat is passed down in the last will and testament. Judging by the grey heads predominating in the members stands, there will be some beneficiaries quite soon.

The Seniors come out and the crowd gives a big welcome to the midfield powerhouse, Garry Hocking, who hits the pitch for his 200th game. He has been an inspiration for 10 years, with his fearless work in the packs, his sure touch and his team instincts. His value at centre bounces has been enormous, but he has also lifted the side with brilliant goals and terrific link work. Liam Pickering, ever reliable ruck-rover, comes out for his 100th game, many of them in the best player class.

The crowd seems in a relaxed mood. The Cats are at home and on top of the ladder. It is with some surprise, but little alarm, that the Tigers go to the front and have 7.1 on the board to the Cats 3.2 by quarter time. The Cats seemed a bit sluggish in midfield and, although Derek Hall is marking everything up forward, their moves are meeting with strong Tiger resistance. Hall is not flamboyant, but he puts himself where the ball is, and is probably the most reliable mark in the Geelong side – invariably a one-grab man. But his fellow forwards, Burns, Barnes and Corrigan are not firing, and Barry Stoneham wastes some big marks with poor kicking. Down the back Tim McGrath and Michael Mansfield are having to work hard to stop the Tigers.

The black and yellow banners are beginning to wave in the outer as the visiting Tiger supporters, jammed into the pockets of standing room, are finding their voice.

A few moderate changes by coach Gary Ayres seem to balance things up in the second quarter. Colbert on the backline and Carl Steinfort on the rampaging Wayne Campbell seem to stem the flow, and the whole team is playing more tightly, tackling hard.

Suddenly Richmond unravels as a series of wayward handballs, two from their captain Matthew Knights, brings a turnaround and a goal to the new forward star Paul Lynch. The Cats are in front, and the Hickey Stand is booming with noise.

Tim McGrath: hard worker.

Lynch, a boy from the Western District of Victoria, seems typical of the Geelong types who have appeared down the years, and have given the club its peculiar stamp of the country. His father, a dairy farmer, had a stint with Essendon, but Paul has come through the Cats' Under 19s and Reserves into the Seniors. He has a clean-cut, country boy look and is broad shouldered, muscular and pacy. He is another of the young Cats who have, surprisingly, taken Geelong from a fading combination last year, to the top of the ladder and finals favourites with six rounds to go.

The others on the field today who have lifted the Cats' fortunes are Martin McKinnon, Paul Corrigan, Carl Steinfort, Steven King and Glenn 'Oysters' Kilpatrick, a high-velocity centreman who is now ploughing through the packs and picking up possessions, .

Steinfort's effort in shutting down Wayne Campbell has been part of the game's turnaround. He is pumped up at three-quarter time, listening to the coach and ready to go out and finish the job.

King is probably Geelong's biggest find of all, a second-year ruckman who, at 18, displays a lot of maturity. He is a very tall and well muscled, with an old-fashioned manliness of appearance that would have fitted into a Geelong team of the 20s or 30s. He does everything: marks and kicks well, is a fine palmer and a sure ball handler.

Then there's Ronnie Burns, over from the West and a mite older, but with only two years at Geelong. He's the magician of the forward line, not getting many touches today, but always looking likely to cut loose, run rings around an opponent and score.

That's seven newer players to back up the more experienced, but still quite youthful, men of the team. Gary Ablett is gone, but the forward line at the moment looks more versatile with Hall, Burns, Hocking, Leigh Colbert and John Barnes. Paul Couch is gone, his knee too painful to see the season out, but there are others who are coming up to emulate the silky skills that won him a Brownlow. The speculation is that gallant and much-loved forward, Bill Brownless, might find it hard to fit back into the team and play the two games he needs to make 200.

In the last quarter the full flow of Geelong sweeps Richmond aside. Chains of handpasses are moving the ball through to the centre and into attack; marks are being taken everywhere; ball handling, tackling and shepherding are the best of team play.

There is quiet calm in the Geelong coach's box, despair at Richmond. In a triumphant end to it all, Garry Hocking finds the ball in a crowded pack, is suddenly in space and kicks a last goal deep into the Hickey Stand.

He is chaired off by his team-mates, having souvenired the ball, and gives a shy wave to the cheering crowd. In the dressing room it's all a bit exuberant, but business as usual. This team has become used to winning.

Outside there is similar satisfaction and the folk with the rugs and baskets head for the car park and home to a nice, country style Saturday night. – **John Ross**

HAWTHORN

MY CLUB
by Damien Cash

When the Hawthorn Football Club joined the League in 1925 it was nicknamed the 'Mayblooms' (after the Hawthorn bush) before becoming the 'Hawks' in 1943. Until recent times, Hawthorn neither bloomed in May, nor swooped in September. It was not a winning team. But the club song, which originated in the 1950s, proclaimed 'We're a happy team at Hawthorn' and in those years the club president, Dr A. S. Ferguson, would tell new players: 'If you embrace Hawthorn, Hawthorn will embrace you.' Hawthorn was the 'family club'. And like a family, Hawthorn provided a culture of acceptance which encouraged loyalty, tolerance, discipline, a sense of responsibility, pride and an appreciation of the importance of pulling together with common purpose and identity.

The spirit of 'family' was nurtured in the 1950s by players sharing meals and after-dinner singalongs with coach Jack Hale and his wife. In more recent times, a ritual of barbecued sausages at Hawthorn's training sessions continued the sharing tradition and widened its application to supporters and other members of the brown and gold community. When the wealthy Carlton club booked the plush Southern Cross Hotel in misguided anticipation of winning the 1986 Premiership, the Blues' brewer president scoffed at the thought of Hawthorn enjoying their victory at a 'BYO'. But the Hawks really were having a great time. They brought their own Flag.

A 'family first' philosophy meant putting the club before most individual or external values. As with any football club, Hawthorn has had its share of problems over the years, but there has been genuine success in keeping most of these 'in-house' or settled early. Both off-field and on, Hawthorn likes to run smooth and quiet. The club prefers not to 'squeal' when the ball doesn't bounce its way. You take defeat on the chin. And you don't get too carried away with victory, praise or criticism. 'Savour the moment, but remember there are losers in the next room,' Allan Jeans reminded his players after Hawthorn thrashed Essendon in the 1983 Grand Final. There was no 'witch hunt' or impassioned purge two years later when Essendon returned the compliment. Hawthorn simply assessed the situation with calmness and reason.

Keeping your feet on the ground is vital to success in any pursuit, and Hawthorn has benefited from a generally stable line of presidents and coaches, some of unusually high calibre. Football knowledge has been only a part of what has distinguished Hawthorn's greatest leaders. John Kennedy and Allan Jeans imbued their charges with rarer qualities of personal 'character'. They fostered a generation of modern League coaches, including David Parkin, Gary Ayres, Peter Knights, Terry Wallace, Ken Judge, Leigh Matthews, Gary Buckenara and Rodney Eade. Each of these Hawthorn 'graduates' has in turn influenced other League clubs.

Even in the greedy 1980s there was evidence that playing for the guernsey still meant something at Hawthorn. Jason Dunstall rejected a $2 million contract to join the Brisbane Bears. And he was a Queenslander! Leigh Matthews and Peter Knights could have named their price. Hawthorn paid its champions well, but somewhat less than they might have earned elsewhere. Money wasn't everything. Hawthorn didn't believe in buying Premierships. The club prided itself on sound financial management and there was uproar when some questionable building contracts led to heavy losses in 1993. The big purchases of Peter Hudson, Gary Buckenara and John Platten were exceptions to the more usual Hawthorn style of developing the League's designated recruiting zones and rearing talent in the Under 19s and Reserves. By the time a player broke into senior ranks, he was determined to keep his place, and usually did.

The modern play-on game, with its emphasis on supreme fitness and attack-at-all-costs, owes much to coaching strategies developed at Hawthorn, which climaxed in the 1980s when the Hawks won four of their seven consecutive Grand Finals. It was hard to imagine that this was the club that originally created all kinds of records for losing, and still holds the AFL record for the longest time out of the finals, 32 consecutive seasons from 1925 to 1956. But with nine Flags since 1961 and a record 13 successive finals series appearances from 1982 to 1994, Hawthorn made up for all those long years in the football wilderness. The happy team became a winning team.

HAWTHORN	
Year Established	1873
Joined VFL/AFL	1925
Home Grounds	Glenferrie, Princes Park, Waverley
Premierships	1961, 1971, 1976, 1978, 1983, 1986, 1988, 1989, 1991
Brownlow Medals	Col Austen 1949, Robert DiPierdomenico 1986, John Platten 1987
Record home crowd	53,962 v Collingwood, 1990
Most games	Michael Tuck, 426
Most goals	Jason Dunstall, 1200
Notable supporters	Past: Sir Henry Winneke Present: Gareth Evans, Jeff Kennett, Bryce Courtenay, Ian Baker-Finch, Andrew Gaze, Lloyd Williams, Pat Cash

The Hawks hit the ground for the 1988 Grand Final.

Waving in a victory over the Brisbane Lions.

Hawks up and away. Stewart Stewart, Ted Poole and Jim Francis

Noel Voigt. Ian Law. Peter Hudson. Graham Arthur.

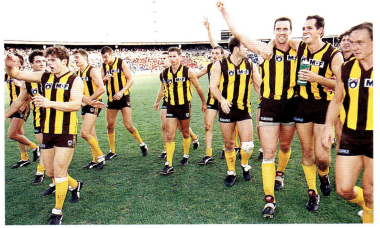
A win for the 'new Hawks' in 1997.

HAWTHORN

Grace Park, Hawthorn, in 1887.

Hawthorn's paddock pioneers

The origins of the Hawthorn Football Club can be directly traced to 1902, when the present club was formed to enter the Metropolitan Junior Football Association, now the Victorian Amateur Football Association (VAFA). But Hawthorn acknowledges earlier, more tenuous origins among the various small clubs that competed in the local district during the late nineteenth century. These 'forerunners' included the Glenferrie and Riversdale clubs, Hawthorn Rovers, Glenburn, Hawthorn Trades Club, and a Hawthorn Football Club in the 1870s and another in the 1890s.

What seems to be the oldest Hawthorn club emerged when twenty men signed up as members at the Hawthorn Hotel on 28 February 1873.

The *South Bourke Standard* reported that members purchased a football the next day and headed for 'Mr King's paddock to practise, whereupon a few noses were broken and two or three teeth dislocated, but all agreed that the ball was a great success …' A 'ferocious and exciting scratch match' was played at the Hawthorn Cricket Ground on April 5 and another a few weeks later in the paddock below Hawthorn Grammar School in Power Street.

Only one player could mark the ball, but everyone had a go, even the local dogs. About six goals were kicked in the Power Street match, all of them disputed. The paddock was a little rough. A cart track to the brick kilns ran through the middle, and there was a tense moment when the ball bounced off the nose of a woodcarter sitting on top of his load. 'Why the —— don't you play on public property?' he yelled.

The first serious match was played in King's paddock against Studley Park on April 30. Neither side scored for the entire match. Unfortunately, Mr King's six-foot fence was smashed by a couple of horseriders skylarking and King was furious. That was the end of using his paddock for a while.

Hawthorn lost one-nil to Carlton Imperial in their next game, then drew with Essendon, one goal apiece. Hellicar kicked Hawthorn's historic first goal.

Hawthorn ended its first season with ten losses, five draws and no wins. Five games were won in 1874 and three in 1875. After the original club languished, the Riversdale Football Club changed its name to Hawthorn in 1889. As the 'yellow and blacks', the club won its first game against the 'Dingoes' at Grace Park in May 1889 (3.9 to 0.1). Whatever bite Hawthorn had that day was soon lost. The club had to be 'revived' at a public meeting at the Hawthorn Town Hall in 1893, but to little avail.

All that changed on 9 April 1902, when about 150 people gathered in the Hawthorn Town Hall to support the creation of a united Hawthorn Football Club from the assortment of small clubs in the area. After much difficulty, a team was entered in the Metropolitan Junior Association, another in the Eastern Suburbs Association, and a third, a trades team, would play off on Wednesday afternoons.

The catalyst for the club's formation appears to be the Hawthorn Council's purchase of land at Grace Park, which meant the club could eventually have its own ground. High-powered patrons included the Hon William Knox MHR, Sir Frederick Sargood, Edward Payne MLA and Cr Barbour MLA, and three Hawthorn councillors were among 16 'Vice-Presidents'. If the new club ever ran short of players, there was a football team or more within the administration.

The Firsts played at the Hawthorn Cricket Ground, which later became Glenferrie Oval from 1905. The Seconds, called the Hawthorn Rovers, played in Grace Park Reserve.

In *For the Love of the Game* (1992) VAFA historian Joseph Johnson notes Hawthorn was a popular club, admired for its friendliness, sportsmanship and fairness. But it was just an average team on the field, even after a merger with the Boroondara Club in 1905. Hawthorn's best Metropolitan Association seasons were 1907 (third) and 1913 (fifth). Still, there was plenty of local enthusiasm. In April 1912 the club boasted 600 members, and coach Eddie Drohan, the former Fitzroy and Collingwood champion, had over 100 players on his list.

CLUB NEWS 1873–1913

Hawthorn's first distinguishing 'uniform' was a white cap with a blue Maltese cross in 1873. The 1875 version was blue knickerbockers, light blue and white striped guernsey and hose, and cap. Club colours were yellow and black in 1889, red and blue in 1893 (the club was briefly known as the redlegs), blue and white in 1902, black guernsey with a red sash (on their amalgamation with Boroondara in 1905 and blue and gold in 1913.

Michael O'Grady MLA was Hawthorn president in 1876. Reginald Thompson was captain. The club's main 'playground' was Grace Park, and 80 members had subscribed 3s.

For some strange reason, the whole Hawthorn side failed to appear for a game against an Essendon district side in 1877.

On 16 June 1877 a Hawthorn 25 played 20 from Melbourne at the MCG. According to the *Australasian*, the Hawthorn 'boys' were no match for the Melbourne 'men', who 'put the leather behind time after time'.

In 1893 Hawthorn president James Westley prophesied that the club would one day compete against teams like Essendon and Geelong, and perhaps even play internationally.

Cam's Paddock in Urquhart Street was rented by Hawthorn as a playing field for one pound a week for 1893.

There was chaos in 1895 when the Hawthorn and Austral teams turned up to play in the same uniforms. The

1873 – 1913

Lost heroes

Football in Hawthorn was simply too unimportant to warrant much coverage in the newspapers. The deeds of Hawthorn heroes went mostly unrecorded and are as lost in football history as knickerbockers and lace-up guernseys.

Hawthorn's best mark in 1873, a player named Anderson, was said to be able to jump six feet in the air. The Cleverdon brothers, E. H. Prevot, Willis, Roberts, C. F. Taylor and 'Master Harry' starred in Hawthorn's drawn game against an Essendon side in 1873.

The *Footballer* in 1876 described Hawthorn captain R. Thompson as 'a good strong player'; vice-captain L. Suward was 'an excellent place kick'; Demaine, the goal sneak, 'very plucky'; J. C. Brooke, 'always gets his kick'; G. O'Connor, 'a good rough player'; and J. Snowball, 'very reliable, a long low kick'.

The pick of Hawthorn's early crops went to VFA, or later, VFL clubs, especially Melbourne. The 1893 Hawthorn captain Jack Geddes was reputedly the outstanding player among the junior clubs, but he left Hawthorn after internal strife in the mid 1890s.

In 1913 Hawthorn temporarily clinched the Geelong champion Joe Slater, who agreed to play as an amateur after a little persuasion from Hawthorn secretary R. W. Lord. When Slater broke his collarbone playing against Collingwood District, he ignored medical advice and returned to the field after the bone was set.

'We have a good lead,' he said, 'and we have to keep it. With one man off the field they would have a loose man, but if I am in there they will have to put someone to mind me, and I can keep him quiet.'

Hawthorn won, of course, but lost Slater to Geelong when he had fully recovered. It took World War One to kill him.

The Hawthorn Reserves team of 1913, in Eastern Suburbs competition.

The Hawthorn Rovers

Hawthorn's Reserves team, the 'Hawthorn Rovers', played in the Eastern Suburbs Association from 1902–13 against clubs like Auburn, Camberwell and Richmond Juniors, and were Premiers in 1904 and 1905.

An old Scotch College player, Charlie McBean, was captain. Among his players was J. W. 'Bill' Kennon, who was President of Hawthorn when it entered the VFL in the 1920s. Generally, the Rovers tended to distinguish themselves in fields other than football. Russell Martin became a Supreme Court Judge. Vernon Ransford became a Test cricketer and secretary of the Melbourne Cricket Club, and several others became fine cricketers, including Archie Dean, 'Hughie' Carroll and Lindsay Main.

Years later Kennon told journalist 'Old Boy' (R. W. E. Wilmot) about playing Richmond Juniors, who arrived sporting headbands reading 'Today, every man must do his duty'. 'And, by Jove,' said Kennon, 'they did it. I know I was unconscious after the game and it took some time to bring me round. In fact, it was reported I was dead, but it was not as serious as that.'

Looking back

A. S. Cleverdon was one of three footballing brothers who played for early Hawthorn sides in the 1870s. At the age of 82 in 1940 Cleverdon recalled those days in a letter to the *Australasian* newspaper:

'About 66 years ago my people came from South Melbourne to Hawthorn. Jack, my elder brother, played for South Yarra First Twenty before he started with Will with the Glenferrie Football Club, as it was then called. The game at that time was played in a paddock which is now Manningtree Road, and in one corner was a fair-sized waterhole, and at times players got a good ducking. My brother Jack is living in America … Will kept on playing, and later on, when I left school, I played with the team as well in Grace Park. I was on the wing. Will in the ruck. Jack Clark was captain and it was called the Glenferrie Football Club First Twenty. My word, what great times we had.'

---

match was drawn.

In 1898 the *Boroondara Standard* reported that Hawthorn players were so hopeless that 'twenty Chows would shamefully beat them'.

Temperance was the issue in 1902, when Hawthorn committeeman J. C. Watts resigned in protest at club meetings being held at the Langham Hotel in Burwood Road.

In 1903 Hawthorn mayor, George Swinburne MLA, became club president. The Swinburne University of Technology in Hawthorn is named after him.

In 1904 Hawthorn was fined three times for failing to provide a venue for games. Port Rovers enjoyed a walkover when Hawthorn could provide no suitable ground.

When Hawthorn's new ground opened at Grace Park on 5 May 1906, the club captain was rover Tom Ferguson, whose son 'Sandy' would become Hawthorn president in the 1950s.

Between 1905 and 1907 Hawthorn City was used as the club title. The name persisted unofficially for many years afterwards.

In a 1908 Hawthorn game, the captains decided to abolish half-time interval. It was not against the rules, but didn't become a regular feature.

Hawthorn was defined as a 'junior' club in terms of status, but the Metropolitan Association allowed three 'senior' players to compete in member teams. In 1913 the limit was raised to five.

HAWTHORN

This portrait of the 1922 team hangs in the Past Players' Rooms at Glenferrie Oval.

1925–1949 HONOUR ROLL

Year	Pos	Leading Goalkicker	No.	Best & Fairest	Captain	Coach
1925	12th	L. Woodford	20		Jim Jackson	Alec 'Joker' Hall
1926	11th	Bert Hyde	27		Dan Minogue/C. Nott	Minogue/P. Burke
1927	12th	Bert Hyde	41		Pat Burke	Dan Minogue
1928	12th	Bert Hyde	62		Bert Sutton/M. Sellars	Bert Sutton
1929	10th	Bert Hyde	52		Bert Chadwick	Bert Chadwick
1930	10th	Bert Hyde	52		John 'Jiggy' Harris	John 'Jiggy' Harris
1931	11th	Jack Ryan	39		John 'Jiggy' Harris	John 'Jiggy' Harris
1932	12th	Jack Ryan	37	Stan Spinks	Bert Mills	Jim Jackson
1933	11th	Ted Pool	27	Bert Mills	Bill Twomey	Bill Twomey
1934	11th	Jack Green	80	Ernie Loveless	Bert Mills	Bill Twomey
1935	10th	Jack Green	63	Bert Mills	Ivan McAlpine	Ivan McAlpine
1936	9th	Norm Hillard	26	Leo Murphy	Ivan McAlpine	Ivan McAlpine
1937	8th	Norm Hillard	31	Leo Murphy	Ivan McAlpine	Ivan McAlpine
1938	11th	Alby Naismith	30	Stan Spinks	Bert Mills	Ivan McAlpine
1939	10th	Alec Albiston	37	Bert Mills	Len Thomas	Len Thomas
1940	9th	Alby Naismith	25	Andrew Angwin	Bert Mills	Bert Mills
1941	12th	Alec Albiston	57	Alec Albiston	Bert Mills	Bert Mills
1942	11th	Alec Albiston	32	Jack Barker	Jack Carmody	Roy Cazaly
1943	5th	Wally Culpitt	43	Jim Bohan	Robert Williams	Roy Cazaly
1944	11th	Wally Culpitt	57	Jack Blackman	Jim Bohan	Tommy Lahiff
1945	10th	Alec Albiston	66	Jim Bohan	Keith Shea	Keith Shea
1946	12th	Albert 'Butch' Prior	52	Alec Albiston	Jim Bohan	Keith Shea
1947	11th	Albert 'Butch' Prior	67	Wally Culpitt	Alec Albiston	Alec Albiston
1948	11th	Albert 'Butch' Prior	47	Kevin Curran	Alec Albiston	Alec Albiston
1949	12th	Albert 'Butch' Prior	48	Col Austen	Alec Albiston	Alec Albiston

A brown and gold Association

The Hawthorn Council enthusiastically backed Hawthorn joining the Victorian Football Association (VFA) in February 1914. A dozen or more colour combinations were debated before the gathering accepted Mr J. Brain's suggestion of brown guernseys with a gold V and white knickers.

Port Melbourne 16.8 (104) defeated Hawthorn 9.9 (63) in the club's VFA debut match on Easter Monday 1914. There were 3000 people at the first home game at Glenferrie Oval next week, and Association eyebrows were raised when the newcomers beat Port in a return bout on 20 June.

But the 'Mayblooms', as Hawthorn were known, finished second-last in their first season and last in the next. Then World War One severely interrupted the club's development. Fifteen players and two committeemen joined the AIF and there was no competition in 1916–17.

Over 140 games between 1914 and 1924 in the VFA, Hawthorn won 57, lost 81 and drew twice. The club finished sixth in 1921 and 1922, and again in 1924, its last year before joining the VFL.

The VFL was a more prestigious competition than the Association. Local Hawthorn councillors, representing many middle-class and professional people, knew the value of status. And they knew about money. League teams brought bigger crowds and therefore greater revenue. So when Hawthorn made a move for VFL membership in 1919–20, its proposal included plans for a council-owned ground with 45,000 seating capacity.

The effort was stepped up after 1923, when Hawthorn enjoyed its most successful VFA year, finishing fourth. Finally, on 9 January 1925 the VFL agreed to expand the competition and admit Hawthorn, Footscray and North Melbourne.

CLUB NEWS 1914–1949

As a team of gentlemen, Hawthorn was sometimes shocked by the undue roughness displayed by certain VFA teams. The club protested to the Association in May 1921.

On 5 August 1922, Hawthorn's 30.31 (211) demolition of Prahran set a VFA record for high scoring. Prahran kicked only 6.9.(45)

Former South Melbourne defender Arthur Rademacher briefly became Hawthorn coach late in 1921 and played two games while Jim Jackson remained Hawthorn captain.

In June 1923 someone rang the bell eight minutes early as Brighton stormed home against Hawthorn at Glenferrie. Hawthorn won the replay three weeks later.

Hawthorn met Footscray 15 times in the VFA for 15 losses. When they met in the VFL in 1925, Hawthorn 10.13 (73) defeated Footscray 8.10 (58) – Hawthorn's first League win.

In Hawthorn's VFA years, the club's best players graduated to the VFL. Cyril Gambetta was a brilliant mark who became a champion centre half-back for St Kilda in the 1920s.

Big-man George Rudolph served his football apprenticeship with Hawthorn in the VFA. As a Richmond player in the late 1920s he became a 'hero' of the young Jack Dyer.

Glenferrie Oval was top-dressed for the cricket season before Hawthorn met North Melbourne on 7 August 1926. All play had to be confined to

1914–1924, 1925–1949

Brown and gold men all: Bert Hyde, H. Mills, J. Ryan, S. Stewart and S. Spinks.

Nice guys – who finished last

Hawthorn ended its 25th year in the VFL the way it began: with a 'wooden spoon'. Between 1925 and 1949 Hawthorn finished last or second-last 17 times, and collected the spoon on eight forgettable occasions.

The club won only three games in its first season. The former Collingwood and Richmond champion Dan Minogue took over as captain–coach in 1926, but had the misfortune to preside over a run of 16 losses.

Under Bert Sutton in 1928 Hawthorn couldn't manage a single win. But Bert Hyde kicked 62 goals in for the season and booted six for Victoria in their win over WA.

The drought was broken under coach Bert Chadwick in June 1929, when Hawthorn defeated South Melbourne in Round 7. Hawthorn were now 'cert's for the four' joked the newspapers.

Things really began to look up when wingman Stan Spinks emerged in 1932 as one of the few players in the League who could beat the great Haydn Bunton. Spinks was twice runner-up in the Brownlow Medal in the 1930s. The club had plenty of men who could kick and mark, but only a handful with any football sense. Most ran with the ball instead of kicking to advantage, and according to press reports, everyone 'went up for marks like schoolboys'.

When Hawthorn almost beat Carlton in May 1936 the *Hawthorn Standard* headline screamed: 'Hawthorn Astounds Football World'. Fifteen Hawthorn players, more than any other club, polled in the 1937 Brownlow medal, and in 1938 the club triumphed for the first time over Melbourne at the MCG. It also lost ten in a row that year.

Hawthorn finally bloomed in May 1939 when the brown and gold defeated Carlton (by three points) in front of Prime Minister Menzies. Hawthorn president Jacob Jona called it the most significant day in the club's history. Hawthorn was in 'the four' at last.

Col Austen: finally a Brownlow in 1989.

To open season 1940, Hawthorn recorded its then-highest League score, against North Melbourne, 25.11 (161) to 13.11 (89). For the first time, Hawthorn was on top of the ladder. It finished the season ninth, but notched up seven wins and found a goalkicker and future captain in Jimmy Bohan.

The 40s were largely bleak. Typical of the club's poor fortune was half-back flanker Col Austen, who lost the 1949 Brownlow Medal on countback to Ron Clegg.

The 'Moderne'-style grandstand at Glenferrie Oval was opened on 25 June 1938.

the wings and flanks to avoid the 'glue-pot' centre. A social game at 'Woop Woop' was how one newspaper described the scene.
During the 1931 season, fiery defender Edward 'Tich' Utting became the first Hawthorn player to reach 50 games.
In 1933 Hawthorn reversed its colours to a brown V on a yellow background, earning the nickname 'mustard pots'. The earlier style (yellow V on brown) returned in 1934.
Hawthorn's run of wins against Essendon, Geelong and Fitzroy in 1935 was described as 'a fine advertisement for non-payment of players'. The 'hat-trick' came after the players were told there was no money to pay them.
It was not until 1937 that Hawthorn was able to pay its players the £3 per match payment established by the League in 1930.
With Roy Cazaly as coach, the 1942 season was the first in which Hawthorn won more games than it lost (nine wins, six losses) and the club finished fifth. In May 1943 Cazaly announced the end of the nickname 'Mayblooms', and Hawthorn became the Hawks.
When Wally Culpitt shifted from the backline to full-forward in 1943 he kicked nine goals in his first game and 43 for the season.
Hawthorn's clash with Richmond on 24 June 1943 was the first time the club had ever been billed in the VFL's main game, or 'match of the day'. The Hawks lost by 19 points.

HAWTHORN

Upheaval in 1950

Hawthorn's world was shattered on the eve of the 1950 season, when news broke that the 1949 captain Alec Albiston and star of the season Col Austen had both been 'sacked'.

At issue was the appointment of Kevin Curran as captain for 1950. Albiston had believed he had been promised the captaincy by new Hawthorn president Dave Prentice. Both Albiston and Austen were so disgusted at Curran's appointment that they refused to play under him. The Hawthorn committee then gave both players open clearances. And both men walked, Albiston to North Melbourne and Austen to Richmond.

The real story of this upheaval may never be known. Some say sectarian and personal issues were involved. Key members of Hawthorn's administration denied that any promise was made, but Albiston was adamant.

Hawthorn's abysmal performance in the 1950 opening round against Geelong illustrated the problems at the club. Hawthorn scored only one goal in the first quarter (against Geelong's six) and did not goal for the next two. At three-quarter time the Hawks were 1.11 to Geelong's 17.19. Despite losing by 80 points, new Hawthorn coach Bob McCaskill was apparently not despondent, but as the *Sporting Globe* declared, 'Even a McCaskill can't turn water into wine.'

Underlying tensions surfaced in the fourth round when Curran 'collided' on field with Austen, who was playing for his new club. Austen's flattening merited a four week suspension for Curran.

Hawthorn lost every match for the season in 1950. Newspapers had a field day. The *Globe* joked that 'not even Superman' could make a team of Hawthorn the way they were playing. The *Argus* called on other clubs to help 'save' Hawthorn.

Big backman and war hero Kevin Curran.

Alec Albiston, nicknamed 'Hungry'.

Morale couldn't have sunk much lower. As Bob McCaskill told the *Globe*'s Hec de Lacy: 'I am face to face with a club that expects to be beaten and likes to be.' The players accepted defeat. They didn't know anything else. The committee expected them to lose. Even the barrackers expected them to lose, however much they lived, and died, in hope.

Jack Hale, who became coach after McCaskill's death in June 1952, later reflected: 'They were prepared to settle on the best terms with the opposition. As long as they had a nice, friendly game, and everybody behaved themselves, they were happy.'

Both Hale and McCaskill had to 'kick a few shins', as Hale put it, to transform the 'Happy Team' into a winning team.

New boys make mark

Two gleams of hope for Hawthorn in 1950 were rugged newcomers, ruckman John Kennedy and Roy Simmonds, a 'pocket-Hercules' rover from Cohuna who became a champion half-back flanker. 'Simmo' was Hawthorn's Best and Fairest in 1956.

Kennedy took the award in his first three seasons, and again in 1954. He played 165 games before hanging up his boots in 1959, and went straight on to become Hawthorn's coach in 1960. He attempted to overcome Hawthorn's skills limitations by making the players fitter than other VFL teams, and therefore more suited to the play-on, attacking style of football that is now a hallmark of the modern game. But the strategy almost came undone at the outset when Hawthorn lost their first five matches under Kennedy's coaching. The club and players persevered with him and the new style of play and were rewarded one year later with that elusive first Premiership.

CLUB NEWS 1950–1960

On the recommendation of coach Bob McCaskill in 1950, Hawthorn changed its uniform, replacing the dark brown and gold V guernsey with gold and brown vertical stripes. Players were sometimes reminded that the colour was gold, not yellow.

Pat Cash starred in Hawthorn's first win since 1949, when the Hawks defeated St Kilda, 12.15 (87) to 9.10 (64) on 5 May 1951. Cash, Hawthorn's new forward, played his part in the four-goal surge in the second quarter that put the Hawks in front.

Goals were like gold in 1952, when Hawthorn's leading goalkicker was Kevin Coghlan, in his first season after being recruited from Collingwood. His tally was 19 goals for the season.

During June 1953 Jack Hale responded to complaints from clubs concerning Glenferrie Oval's small size by pointing out that Hawthorn had to play there every second week.

Dr A.S. 'Sandy' Ferguson, who took over from Dave Prentice as Hawthorn president in late 1953, told players: 'Embrace Hawthorn and it will embrace you.'

Composer Jack O'Hagan, of 'Road to Gundagai' and 'Our Don Bradman' fame, wrote the Hawthorn club song, 'We're a Happy Team at Hawthorn', to the tune of 'Yankee Doodle Dandy' in 1956.

Hawthorn forward Pat Cash was a lawyer who became first president of the Australian Football Players'

1950 – 1960

'Candles' lights Hawks

There's an old saying that it takes just one candle to overcome a world of darkness. It took only one to light up Hawthorn's long night: Clayton 'Candles' Thompson, a 6ft 5in ruckman and full-forward from the South Australian club Sturt.

'Candles' was Hawthorn's first recruiting 'coup'. He was described by Kevin Hogan in the *Sun* as 'the biggest football prize landed by any League club for many years'. To snare him, the club had to raise £750, organise a job for him as a wool classer at Dalgety's and beat a determined syndicate from the Melbourne Football Club. Ironically, 'Candles' was snuffed by Melbourne's Denis Cordner when making his debut for Hawthorn as a ruckman in May 1954. He earned only three kicks in the first half and was obviously nervous, but he starred against Geelong a fortnight later, where he booted the winning goal and was best man on the ground.

'Candles' played 51 games between 1954 and 1957, and kicked 54 goals. He never quite lived up to Hawthorn's high hopes, but generated an enthusiastic feeling among players and barrackers that the club was finally 'on the way.'

The supremely fit Brendan Edwards puts some getting-fitter Hawks through their paces.

Hail 'P.T.' – the fitness revolution

In May 1959 coach Jack Hale revealed the 'secret' of Hawthorn's recent success. 'Scientifically-based Physical Training'. Circuit training was first introduced at Hawthorn, by Brendan Edwards, a physical education teacher. Once the sceptical Hale was convinced, he invited Melbourne University's Albert Willee to devise a set of exercises. It all sounds very ordinary today, but in 1959 it was nothing short of revolutionary.

'Candles' Thompson and proud officials.

1950 – 1960 HONOUR ROLL

Year	Pos	Leading Goalkicker	No.	Best & Fairest	Captain	Coach
1950	12th	Gordon Anderson	21	John Kennedy	P O'Donohue/K Curran	Bob McCaskill
1951	11th	Pat Cash	26	John Kennedy	P O'Donohue/K Curran	Bob McCaskill
1952	11th	John McDonald	25	John Kennedy	Peter O'Donohue	McCaskill/Hale
1953	12th	Kevin Coghlan	19	Ted Fletcher	Ted Fletcher	Jack Hale
1954	9th	Kevin Coghlan	27	John Kennedy	Ted Fletcher	Jack Hale
1955	8th	Kevin Coghlan	28	Graham Arthur	John Kennedy	Jack Hale
1956	7th	John Peck	31	Roy Simmonds	John Kennedy	Jack Hale
1957	3rd	Terry Ingersoll	33	Alf Hughes	John Kennedy	Jack Hale
1958	6th	John Peck	27	Graham Arthur	John Kennedy	Jack Hale
1959	7th	Garry Young	35	Allan Woodley	John Kennedy	Jack Hale
1960	5th	Garry Young	36	Brendan Edwards	Graham Arthur	John Kennedy

Association in 1956, but the VFL opposed the union's registration.

Signs of a brighter future in 1956: Hawthorn's Reserves reached the Semi-final; Garry Young was leading Reserve Grade goalkicker; and Under-19 player Gary Rasmussen won the Morrish Medal. Among the new boys in the Seniors was Brendan Edwards, who went on to play 109 games.

In response to League requests to foster the game among the young, during 1956 Hawthorn began training 50 schoolboys each Thursday.

The Hawks' 1957 hopes initially fell with news that star recruit, 18-year-old ruckman John Winneke, would play with University due to his law lectures falling on training nights.

John Kennedy captained Victoria against Tasmania in July 1957, leading a last-quarter fightback that saw the Vics reverse a 15-point deficit to a 36-point win.

In driving rain and bitter cold, Hawthorn lost by 30 points to Fitzroy in the 1959 Night Grand Final. Fitzroy's opening term of 6.1 to Hawthorn's 0.1 set the dismal scene.

John Winneke joined Hawthorn in April 1960, after legal studies had kept him from the team. He played 50 games and was the champion ruckman in the 1961 Premiership side.

Victory at Victoria Park. The Hawks managed to defeat the Magpies in their own nest for the first time on 23 July 1960, winning 7.16 (58) to 7.15 (57). Clearly, both sides' kicking let them down.

HAWTHORN

Above: Getting behind the Flag; players and club officials alike.
Left: Souvenir football from Hawthorn's first Premiership.

Triumph as Graham Arthur holds the 1961 Premiership Cup aloft.

Kennedy's Commandos charge into history

After finishing the season on top of the VFL ladder, Hawthorn came of age in the 1961 finals series, defeating Melbourne by just seven points in the Second Semi-final, then capping off a glorious year with a convincing 43-point win over Footscray in the Grand Final, 13.16 (94) to 7.9 (51).

But it almost didn't come off. The Hawks jumped out to an early lead when Ian Law goaled in the opening minutes, then Footscray took control around the packs and were two goals ahead at the first change. In the second term Hawthorn kicked five behinds in a row. Full-forward John Peck missed one from 10 yards out, but the brown and gold men refused to let their grab at history slip away.

Despite numerous forward-line errors, Hawthorn maintained the pressure. Footscray's plucky rover Merv Hobbs was slowed after a heavy clash and at half-time the Hawks were only eight points down.

Coach John Kennedy made several key changes, including switching Peck into the ruck to help John Winneke overcome the brilliant John Schultz. With Hawthorn more able to dominate the bounces, centreman Brendan Edwards led a second-half charge. He goaled twice immediately, and the Hawks stormed on to seal the Flag with a six-goal third quarter to Footscray's one.

The last term proved the benefits of Kennedy's commando-style fitness regime. Footscray, apart from Ted Whitten, looked tired on the hard MCG surface in the late-September heat. The Hawks remained full of running, with Edwards best-on-ground and almost everyone in the Hawthorn team contributing to the victory. Hawthorn's major goalkickers were Morton Browne (3 goals) and the two Ians, Mort and Law, who bagged two each.

For Hawthorn, 1961 was the moment of triumph. It was the waking from a dream. For so long this club had been the laughing stock of the League. They were the whipping boys, the perpetual wooden spooners, football's ugly ducklings. No more.

1961 HONOUR ROLL

Year	Pos	Leading Goalkicker	No.	Best & Fairest	Captain	Coach
1961	1st	John Peck	49	Ian Law	Graham Arthur	John Kennedy

CLUB NEWS 1961

Sports writer Hugh Buggy once declared that VFL cheer squads really began with 'that Hawthorn teenage choir who chanted the name Hawthorn after every goal the Hawks kicked in 1961'.

Sir Henry Winneke, whose son John played in the 1961 Grand Final, became first chairman of Hawthorn's support group, the 'Confreres' in 1961.

During 1961 Hawthorn purchased a house in Linda Crescent, opposite Glenferrie Oval, for construction of the future Hawthorn Football Club Social Club premises.

Two future coaches who broke into senior ranks in 1961 – David Parkin, a local boy who captained the team, played 211 games, and coached the 1978 Premiers, and Alan Joyce, who played 49 games and coached the Hawks to a Premiership in 1988. Neither played in Hawthorn's 1961 Premiership, but Joyce was named as an emergency.

Hawthorn's 1961 Premiership ended Melbourne's reign of glory, the longest in League history, which was marked by five Demon flags in seven years. The *Herald*'s Alf Brown had nominated the Hawks as the biggest threat to the Demons back in April – and they defeated Melbourne in Round 2 at the MCG by 32 points, and at home in Round 13 by 18 points.

On 29 July 1961 Hawthorn rose to the top of the VFL ladder with a seven-point win over Fitzroy.

1961

Club president Dr Ferguson is crowned.

The 1961 Premiership team: winners, every one.

Looking back on the team that learned to win

The historian Professor James Griffin attended De La Salle College, Malvern (Jack Dyer's old school) during the 1940s with John Kennedy and Pat Cash. 'The brothers who taught us believed that sport bred character,' says Griffin. 'So did John, unshakeably.' Griffin remembers that none of the three barracked for Hawthorn in those days because 'we liked winners', but Hawthorn was the nearest ground to all their homes, and they developed a kind of affection for the underdogs. Griffin transferred his allegiance to the Hawks when Kennedy and Cash began to play in 1950–51.

Of that glorious first Premiership year, Griffin recalls: 'We lost four of the first eight games in 1961. We were not as good as we thought. Those backs, commandos to a man, who thumped when they tackled, all lacked brilliance. But Round 9 began a sequence of 12 wins leading to the Grand Final and Premiership. It was a long, exhilarating crescendo of rugged contests. The crucial game was the second-last round against St Kilda at Glenferrie. It was a bloodbath – for St Kilda, that is. From memory, more than half their players had first aid after the match – all quite fair, of course. Except, perhaps, Ian Mort's pursuit of Eric Guy as though he were a forward, not a half-back.'

In the Grand Final, Hawthorn, with a week's rest, seemed a lay-down misere for the Flag. However, before half-time, nerves saw the Hawks fumbling – with a glorious exception of Edwards in the centre of the ground clearing 20 kicks and scoring two goals before half-time. They were eight points down but the fittest side ever was not going to lose, we knew that.

'It was fashionable to say Hawthorn lacked skills. The backs relied on limitless courage and aggression as well as safe hands, but the centreline of Youren-Edwards-Fisher was capable of 80 possessions a match against anyone, while the half-forward line of Mort-Young-Browne (average weight, 14 stone), highly skilled, also put heavy pressure on any would-be intimidatory backs. Then there was the high-flying Winneke, palming ambidextrously to the almost zany acrobatics of Ian Law, with Peck and Arthur alternating as followers and full-forward! No skills? Nonsense! They just did not play to look good.'

The Premiership contenders' line-ups

	Hawthorn		Footscray
B	R. Poole, L. Kaine, G. Cooper	B	C. Evans, B. Lee, N. Ware
HB	S. Hay, J. McArthur, C. McPherson	HB	J. Jillard, J. Hoiles, B. Ion
		C	I. Bryant, R. Spargo, J. Gardiner
C	C. Youren, B. Edwards, J. Fisher	HF	B. McKellar, G. Ion, J. Quarrell
HF	I. Mort, G. Young, M. Browne	F	E. Whitten (c), J. Slatter, K. Beamish
F	J. Cunningham, J. Peck, M. Hill		
Ruck	J. Winneke, G. Arthur (c), I. Law	Ruck	J. Schultz, C. McDonald, M. Hobbs
Reserves	P. Hay, R. Nalder	Reserves	K. Duff, C. Stewart
Coach	J. Kennedy	Coach	E. Whitten

Club history was made on 5 August 1961, when Hawthorn notched up its seventh straight win, defeating North Melbourne by 53 points.
A record home crowd of 34,500 saw Hawthorn kick five goals in eight minutes during a sensational 8.1 last-quarter burst in Hawthorn's win over St Kilda at Glenferrie Oval on August 19.

Hawthorn wrapped up the 1961 season by winning its last ten home-and-away-games. The Grand Final victory completed the club's longest-ever winning sequence of 12 games in a row.
During the Grand Final Footscray failed several times to stop Hawthorn's Brendan Edwards. The most serious occasion was when Bulldog captain–coach Ted Whitten charged the Hawk centreman from about 30 yards away. Edwards was severely knocked, but remained on the ground.
After Hawthorn's Premiership win, over 5000 fans enjoyed barbecues and other celebrations at Glenferrie Oval. 'Hail the Mighty Hawk Champs', read Lou Richards' headline in the Grand Final Souvenir in the *Sun*. 'I don't care what people are saying about cocky Hawthorn,' Richards wrote, 'it's been a long, long wait, so stick those chests out as far as they'll go, fellas.'
In 1961 Hawthorn won its first McClelland Trophy, which in those days was awarded to the club that accumulated the highest aggregate points in its Senior, Reserve Grade and Under-19 teams.

HAWTHORN

Falling away after Premiership glory

That Hawthorn was not immediately likely to follow on its 1961 success was apparent in the opening round of the 1962 season, when the Hawks lost the Grand Final 'rematch' to Footscray by 33 points. But perhaps no statistic better illustrates Hawthorn's post-Premiership let-down than the club's fall from first in 1961 to ninth in 1962. Hawthorn won only five games in 1962 (against 14 in 1961).

The debuts of Rod Olsson, Ken Beck, David Albiston and Des Dickson promised much in 1962, but Hawthorn prematurely lost the services of Premiership spearheads Brendan Edwards and John Winneke, who both left the club to concentrate on their non-football careers.

Dreams of a second flag were dashed in the 1963 Grand Final, when Geelong's Polly Farmer inspired a crushing win over the lacklustre Hawks, 15.19 (109) to 8.12 (60). There were high hopes again in 1964, but a controversial goal kicked by Melbourne's Hassa Mann in round 17 gave Melbourne a vital win which kept Hawthorn out of the final four.

In 1965 Graham Arthur switched from playing to non-playing coach, but poor results forced him to put the boots back on after two weeks on the sidelines. In a disastrous year, Arthur was later reported for the first time in his 11 seasons, suspended for four matches, and Hawthorn collected its eleventh (and last) wooden spoon after winning only four games for the year. Arthur was not reappointed coach.

Ninth in 1966 was scarcely an improvement under Peter O'Donohue and at the end of the season John Peck left, dissatisfied, to end his playing days with Port Melbourne in the VFA. Peck's goalkicking feats were often the only excuse Hawthorn had for holding its head high in the mid 1960s. But all was not lost. Across Bass Strait was a young Tasmanian forward who had just passed the 100-goal mark for his third season in a row. His name: Peter Hudson.

'Oh, Magoo! You've done it again.'

Two of the best

Rover Ian Law was Hawthorn's Best and Fairest in 1961, 1963 and 1964. Glasses worn off-field earned him the nickname 'Mr Magoo' after the bespectacled cartoon character whose bumbling antics were in stark contrast to Law's agility.

Full-forward John Peck led the League's goalkicking in 1963 (75 goals), 1964 (59) and 1965 (56). He topped Hawthorn's goalkicking eight times from 1956–66. At 6ft 2in and 14 st 5 lb, Peck was a handy extra ruckman in his early years with the Hawks.

John Peck: goalkicking was a highlight.

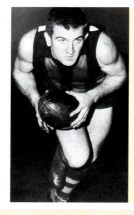

Rod Olsson was an outstanding ruck-rover during Hawthorn's 1963 finals campaign. He played 110 games for the Hawks between 1962 and 1969, and later coached Geelong to the finals in the late 1970s.

1962–1971 HONOUR ROLL

Year	Pos	Leading Goalkicker	No.	Best & Fairest	Captain	Coach
1962	9th	John Peck	38	Graham Arthur	Graham Arthur	John Kennedy
1963	2nd	John Peck	75	Ian Law	Graham Arthur	John Kennedy
1964	5th	John Peck	68	Ian Law	Graham Arthur	Graham Arthur
1965	12th	John Peck	56	David Parkin	Arthur/John Peck	Graham Arthur
1966	9th	John Peck	32	Ray Wilson	Graham Arthur	Peter O'Donohue
1967	10th	Peter Hudson	57	Bob Keddie	Graham Arthur	John Kennedy
1968	6th	Peter Hudson	125	Peter Hudson	Graham Arthur	John Kennedy
1969	5th	Peter Hudson	120	Bob Keddie	David Parkin	John Kennedy
1970	8th	Peter Hudson	146	Peter Hudson	David Parkin	John Kennedy
1971	1st	Peter Hudson	150	Leigh Matthews	David Parkin	John Kennedy

CLUB NEWS 1962–1971

'Delicate' Des Dickson weighed in at 17 stone in his debut year of 1962, but lost three stone in nine weeks under John Kennedy's commando training program.

Despite Hawthorn protests, Brendan Edwards retired after the 1961 Flag to develop his fitness business. When he came back in 1963, he finally ended his career with a serious knee injury.

In the first half of the Round 1, 1962 match against Collingwood, John Winneke was concussed by a collision with Barry Rist. Winneke had to be forcibly restrained and stripped of his guernsey to prevent him from returning to the field.

A sensational SA v Victoria game in 1963 resulted in a two-week suspension to John Peck for knocking out Brian Sawley, who Peck alleged had kicked him in the back.

Due to an employment transfer to the country, John Kennedy stepped down as Hawthorn's coach in 1964. Graham Arthur took over as captain–coach.

Former Hawthorn captain Peter O'Donohue replaced Graham Arthur as coach in 1966. John Kennedy, back in Melbourne, took the reins again in '67.

Before the Hawks faced Geelong in June 1966, the *Globe* commented Hawthorn had 11 university men in the side. Unfortunately, brawn beat brains. By 60 points.

After 1966, when Hawthorn became its own ground manager at Glenferrie, the club built a new grandstand at

1962 – 1971

'Peerless Pete': Hudson soars over the pack.

Ken Beck with a spent Don Scott.

Hawthorn underwent a tremendous upheaval during Hudson's first few seasons. He overshadowed the arrival of Don Scott, Ian Bremner and Geoff Angus in the side in 1967 and the passing of numerous older players who were eased out over the next year or two to make way for future champions like Kelvin Moore, Leigh Matthews and Peter Knights.

In April 1969 Hawthorn suffered the humiliation of losing to Carlton, 12.10 (82) to 30.30 (210), but a few weeks later Hudson revived Hawthorn's confidence with 16 goals against Melbourne. Signs of future success were the Hawks winning back-to-back Night Premierships in 1968–69 and the Under 19s making the finals for the first time in 1969.

Hudson amassed huge personal goal hauls between 1969 and 1971. Hawthorn was not a one-man side, but with a freak full-forward it was sensible to revolve team strategies around his skills. Forwards have to be 'fed', and statistics do not show, for example, the number of times that half-back flanker Bob Keddie passed the ball into the grasp of Peter Hudson.

After finishing eighth in 1970, Hawthorn rose to the top of the ladder in 1971. Ten years after their first Premiership, the Hawks rediscovered that old brown and gold spirit to win 11 games on end during the season, but nowhere did they find it more than in the Grand Final against St Kilda. From 20 points down at three-quarter time, the Hawks came back to win by seven points. Bob Keddie played the game of his life, kicking four goals. During the match Hudson equalled Bob Pratt's all-time VFL record of 150 goals in a season and Hawthorn fans have little doubt he would have broken the record but for the head injury he sustained courtesy of a 'clash' with St Kilda's Kevin 'Cowboy' Neale, who flattened him early in the game. Pratt's record remained, but Hawthorn had the Flag.

Hawks back on track in 1970

When the young Tasmanian full-forward made his debut with Hawthorn in April 1967 he had to face the intimidating Carlton full-back Wes Lofts. Four goals wasn't a bad effort for the most talked-about full-forward debut since John Coleman's in 1949.

Hawthorn soon discovered Peter Hudson wasn't a keen trainer. He didn't care much for Kennedy's commando course, and even when the players did their warm-up laps, Hudson would be yards behind the pack. Within a month some suggested Hawthorn should try him in the Reserves.

He kicked 57 goals in his first season, but really made his mark in 1968. He booted 10 goals in the first round against Essendon and had 26 goals by Round 3. In June and July he kicked 10 goals against Fitzroy and 12 against Footscray. Hudson became the first Hawthorn player to kick 100 goals in a season on 3 August 1968. He passed that milestone five times in his career: 1968 (125), 1969 (120), 1970 (146), 1971 (150) and 1977 (110).

Hudson pulled down screamers, but John Kennedy valued his reliable 'snapshot' even more. He had an uncanny ability to read the play and position himself to advantage. His flat punts rarely missed the goals.

Glenferrie, named in honour of Dr A.S. Ferguson.

Phil Ryan replaced Dr Ferguson as club president in 1968. Ryan gained a reputation for reliability in his 52 games for Hawthorn in the early 1940s.

Barbecues became synonymous with the 'happy team', but in April 1973 thirteen players heard they had been given the chop at a pre-season barbecue.

17-year-old Drouin High School student Peter Knights debuted with Hawthorn against St Kilda in May 1968. A taxi usually took him after school for training in Melbourne.

In 1967 Hawthorn gave Rod Olsson an open clearance, but he stayed and kept his place. The club denied his request to transfer to Sandy Bay (Tas.) in 1970.

Centreman Robert Day, Hawthorn's expensive 1971 recruit from West Adelaide, failed to live up to expectations and ended his VFL career in 1972 with 38 games and 12 goals.

Unable to accept paid employment because of his appointment to the Victorian Teachers' Tribunal, John Kennedy began coaching Hawthorn on a voluntary basis in 1971.

After Hawthorn's 1971 Premiership win, the Hawks defeated SA premiers North Adelaide by 24 points in a 'Championship of Australia' confrontation at the Adelaide Oval.

Peter Hudson's right ear required eight stitches after the 1971 Grand Final. He was also suffering from foggy vision, which affected his aim for goal. Ruckman Don Scott collapsed of exhaustion during the victory lap.

HAWTHORN

Hawthorn fans watched with hearts in their mouths – Peter Hudson was down.

Tragedy and triumph for Hudson

A tragic moment in Hawthorn's history. Champion full-forward Peter Hudson lay on the ground in the 1972 opening-round match against Melbourne. He had kicked eight goals before half-time that day and sustained a severe knee injury that prematurely ended his brilliant career, but not before three comeback attempts.

Hawthorn found a temporary full-forward in 18-year-old Michael Tuck, but Michael Moncrieff proved the eventual replacement, kicking 628 goals from 1971 to 1983 and averaging around three goals per game against Hudson's 5.59.

After undergoing medial cartilage surgery in June 1972, Hudson returned to Tasmania. On 25 August 1973 he arrived at VFL Park by helicopter to kick eight goals for Hawthorn in a crucial game against Collingwood. He was unfit and on one leg, but still brilliant. Knee problems dogged his comeback in early 1974 and it seemed as though his career was over, but Hudson returned in 1977. He kicked his 100th goal in the Qualifying Final and became the leading VFL goalkicker with 110 for the season. But that was it. Flying in from Tasmania for games had taken its toll. Hudson then kicked 209 goals playing for Glenorchy in 1978. He kicked 727 goals in VFL football and by the time his playing days ended at the age of 35 in Tasmania he had amassed the incredible total of 2191 goals in senior football.

In the mid-1970s a local church produced a sign saying: 'What would you do if God came to Hawthorn?' Someone scribbled the answer underneath: 'Shift Peter Hudson to centre half-forward'.

Don Scott beats North for the knock-out.

Bitter rivals with North

There was fierce rivalry between Hawthorn and North in the mid-70s. They thrashed Hawthorn in the 1975 Grand Final, but the Hawks had their revenge in 1976. Despite poor kicking to three-quarter time, they went on to trounce North 13.22 (100) to 10.10 (70). Among many Hawk heroes, John Hendrie was best on ground and Peter Knights took some magnificent high marks.

The end of an era

Glenferrie Oval died as a VFL football venue in 1974, when Hawthorn moved its home games to the larger Princes Park ground in Carlton after a report by Hawthorn committeeman Harry McCurry in 1973 finally convinced the club there was no future at Glenferrie. Supporters were naturally sentimental about leaving Glenferrie, but the fact that Hawthorn won eight of its ten Princes Park matches in 1974 helped overcome the grief.

CLUB NEWS 1972–1976

Following the 1971 flag, Hawthorn won both the Reserve Grade and Under 19 Premierships in 1972, but the seniors were disappointing, finishing sixth with 13 wins.

After Peter Hudson's knee injury, 18-year-old Michael Tuck debuted at full-forward on 20 May 1972. He goaled with his first three kicks in League football and went on to play a record 426 games in a career that lasted until 1991.

Rover Leigh Matthews played his best-ever game in April 1973, when he earned 38 kicks and scored 11 goals in Hawthorn's record-breaking 27.8 (170) win over Essendon 15.12 (102) at VFL Park. Hawthorn kicked 9 goals in the final quarter.

A crowd of 48,000 went to VFL Park in August 1973 to see Peter Hudson play his first game in 18 months.

David Parkin resigned as Hawthorn captain in 1974 to become assistant-coach to John Kennedy. He left at the end of the year to undertake higher studies in Physical Education in WA, but returned as Kennedy's assistant in 1976 and took over from Kennedy as coach in 1977.

When colour television began in Australia in 1975, Hawthorn modified its uniform to adopt brown shorts with gold stripes and all-gold backs on guernseys.

The 17-year-old who debuted for Hawthorn against Fitzroy in August 1975 had the biggest name in League

1972 – 1976

Peter Crimmins – 'the little feller'

Peter Crimmins: a fearless leader.

For a little bloke, Peter Crimmins had a huge heart. When he came to Hawthorn from Assumption College, Kilmore in 1966, he immediately earned a place in the senior side as a rover. Crimmins was a terrier, extraordinarily agile and confident, fearless in the face of bigger players, a white-haired sprite of football muscle and skill that always seemed to be dashing from packs with the ball. He formed an exceptional roving combination with young Leigh Matthews in the early 1970s and starred in Hawthorn's 1971 Premiership team before taking over from David Parkin as Hawthorn captain in 1974.

Rumours of Crimmins' illness circulated in September that year, when it was announced that Hawthorn would be without its captain for a few weeks due to a 'serious injury'. Crimmins resumed in early 1975, but before Hawthorn met Fitzroy in May the players were told it would be his last game 'for a while' because he would be undergoing cancer treatment at the Peter MacCallum Clinic. 'Captain Courageous' had 20 kicks and Hawthorn won easily.

Later in 1975 Crimmins resumed with the Reserves, but he was not fit enough to return to the seniors and John Kennedy made an agonising decision to omit him from Hawthorn's Grand Final side.

In January 1976 Crimmins underwent major surgery. He still dreamed of returning to football, but his condition deteriorated. By the time Hawthorn faced North Melbourne in the Grand Final, the captain was clinging to life. 'There are lots of reasons why you have to win today,' Kennedy told the players. 'Most of all, though, win it for the little feller.' And after they did, Peter Crimmins died.

The man in the raincoat

He looks like one of a thousand Hawthorn supporters, right down to the worried look on his face. But underneath the raincoat and the frown, the man who played 165 games for Hawthorn and coached the club to Premierships in 1961, 1971 and 1976 was no ordinary mortal. He was a leader of men.

Kennedy was a teacher who taught by example. Cocky young footballers had something think about when the old, balding coach beat them home on 10-mile runs. They wondered why he never gave them much sympathy when they were injured, but then they learned that Kennedy had played with a broken arm back in 1956.

Coaching feats tend to overshadow Kennedy's playing days as an inspirational Hawthorn captain in the 1950s. Some said he didn't have much style. But there was no doubt about substance. Kennedy was tough, a clever spoiler and tagger, and a fine ruckman with great determination and leadership skills. Above all, he liked winning, and perhaps Kennedy's greatest legacy is that he taught Hawthorn how to win.

Kennedy: taught Hawthorn winning ways.

1972 – 1976 HONOUR ROLL

Year	Pos	Leading Goalkicker	No.	Best & Fairest	Captain	Coach
1972	6th	Peter Knights	46	Leigh Matthews	David Parkin	John Kennedy
1973	7th	Leigh Matthews	51	Don Scott	David Parkin	John Kennedy
1974	3rd	Michael Moncrieff	67	Leigh Matthews	Peter Crimmins	John Kennedy
1975	2nd	Leigh Matthews	68	Peter Knights	Peter Crimmins	John Kennedy
1976	1st	Michael Moncrieff	97	Leigh Matthews	Don Scott	John Kennedy

history: DiPierdomenico. Just call me 'Dipper', said the man with the 14-letter surname. The young Dipper was recruited from North Kew.

Leigh Matthews was the VFL's leading goalkicker with 68 goals in 1975. During his 332-game football career Matthews kicked 915 goals, a remarkable record for a rover. His best season was 91 goals in 1977.

In May 1976 Hawthorn became the seventh VFL club to announce a sponsorship arrangement when a $45,000 deal was clinched with Wynn Winegrowers.

Barrackers were highly amused at the sight of Don Scott soaring for a high mark against Geelong in June 1976, minus his guernsey, which had been ripped off earlier. The bare-chested Scotty was preoccupied with the play for some time and proved more slippery than usual.

Hawthorn beat SA club Norwood to win the inaugural NFL Wills Cup competition in August 1976. All Hawthorn's prizemoney went to the players.

Peter Knights, Hawthorn's high-flying centre half-back, missed out on winning the 1976 Brownlow Medal by only three votes, despite missing seven games during the season due to injury.

At quarter-time during the 1976 Grand Final, Hawthorn coach John Kennedy was punched in the face by a man wearing an MCC membership badge! Kennedy, of course, had been punched by experts in his time. He merely told the offender to sit down and behave himself.

HAWTHORN

Defender Peter Knights once confessed that he was terrified of heights. He fooled us.

Kelvin Moore: a man of character.

Peter Perfect – high-flyer

Champion centre half-back Peter Knights thrilled the crowds with his high marking aerial athletics over 17 seasons and 267 games with the Hawks from 1969 to 1985. But the price was high. Leg, back and collarbone injuries dogged his brilliant career. When out for seven games in 1976, he was runner-up by just three votes to Graham Moss in the Brownlow Medal. He was only one vote behind Malcolm Blight in 1978.

Injury caused Knights to miss Hawthorn's 1971 Premiership, but he was best on the ground for the 1976 Flag and played again in the 1978 and 1983 victories. Not a strongman, Knights was as fair as his long blond hair, a ball assassin with wonderful natural skills, who could pull down a 'screamer', then drive deep into the forward zone with finely balanced dropkicks and huge torpedo punts. And when called upon, he could also excel in attack.

Knights coached Hawthorn in 1994 and 1995. After the Hawks lost their last seven games in 1995 and the team finished fifteenth, he was not re-appointed. In an 'un-Hawthorn-like' episode, the media received the news before Knights did.

Knights coached a most inexperienced young Hawthorn side. His success in developing a number of talented, but raw, young players such as Shane Crawford, Daniel Harford and Nick Holland suggests that football history may treat him better than the club's administration did in 1995.

A stalwart defender

Full-back Kelvin Moore was Hawthorn's Best and Fairest in 1979. Like his successor, Chris Langford, Moore was a rock-solid, ice-cold defender who played more than 300 games and was always reliable. He joined Hawthorn from Frankston Peninsula as a centre half-forward but quickly found his true role in defence.

Moore represented Victoria 13 times between 1970 and 1984. He had 18 kicks in the 1971 Grand Final and was one of Hawthorn's best players in the 1978 Premiership. In 1983, he was among the players whose character Allan Jeans paid tribute to for making his job easier when Hawthorn defeated Essendon by a record 83 points in the Grand Final.

The Matthews boys: Kelvin (left) and Leigh.

CLUB NEWS 1977–1980

Alf Ablett, father of Hawthorn players Geoff and Kevin, walked into the dressing rooms in 1977 and presented his 16-year-old son Gary to match committee chairman Ken Herbert. 'This one could be the best of the lot,' he said.

Round 1, 1977 saw Hawthorn unfurl the 1976 Flag and celebrate the opening of their own grandstand at Princes Park. But the Hawks lost to North Melbourne, 13.14 (92) to 23.14 (152).

Accuracy was never more of a problem for Hawthorn than against St Kilda in May 1977. Hawthorn scored 41 behinds, to win 25.41 (191) to 16.7 (103).

Hawthorn 14.11 (95) defeated Carlton 11.5 (71) to claim the VFL Night Series Premiership (Amco-Herald Cup) in August 1977, but the Hawks lost to Collingwood in the 1979 Night Grand Final.

In 1978 Hawthorn were runners-up in the Reserve Grade Grand Final. Alan Goad won the Gardiner Medal.

Michael Moncrieff's eight goals in the 1978 Qualifying Final against Collingwood was a VFL record.

For some reason, Hawthorn never seemed to win on the day it unfurled a Premiership Flag. The omens were not good on Doomsday in 1979 when iron-man Don Scott was stopped in his tracks by the cheer squad's paper banner. The Hawks lost to St Kilda, 14.19 (103) to 19.14 (128).

Hawthorn kicked 16 straight

1977–1980

Parkin: let down

David Parkin emerged from the tough Kennedy school of football and played 211 games for Hawthorn between 1961 and 1974, mainly in the back pocket position where his tenacity earned him a reputation as one of the most courageous players in the game. He was Hawthorn's Best and Fairest in 1965 and captain from 1969 to 1973.

A qualified physical education teacher and academic, Parkin not unexpectedly proved to be a 'scientific' coach who emphasised skills development. His match preparation techniques included comprehensive analysis of performance to help players better understand their game and what was expected of them. He was an excellent communicator who formed a good rapport with the team.

In four seasons under Parkin, Hawthorn lost the Preliminary Final in 1977 and were Premiers in 1978, but failed to reach the finals in 1979 and 1980. He resigned at the end of 1980 when it was clear he no longer enjoyed adequate support from the club's administration. Many club stalwarts were disenchanted that one of Hawthorn's finest sons could be allowed to leave in such a way. But it had happened before, and would happen again. Parkin's subsequent success at Carlton in the early 1980s and mid-1990s confirmed his place as one of the great coaches of the modern era.

Coach Parkin explains the plot in May 1977.

Coach David Parkin (right) and captain Don Scott celebrate after winning the 1978 Flag.

Great in '78 with win over North

The Hawks defeated North Melbourne by 18 points in a wonderful display of discipline and teamwork in the 1978 Grand Final.

The pundits had tipped North Melbourne to win, though Hawthorn finished second on the ladder to North at the end of the home-and-away rounds, with both teams on 16 wins. Perhaps they should have taken more notice of the Qualifying Final in which Hawthorn thrashed Collingwood, kicking 23.16 to 14.14.

At half time, North Melbourne was leading by four points, but centre half-forward Alan Martello turned the match Hawthorn's way with an over-the-shoulder snapshot for goal early in the third quarter. Leigh Matthews took up the challenge and a third quarter burst saw him gather seven kicks and three goals. In the space of 12 minutes, Hawthorn kicked 6.3 to North's one behind and the Hawks went into the final quarter 22 points ahead. From there it was just a beautiful ride home.

It was a sweet victory for the Hawks, in the light of their humiliating loss to North Melbourne in the 1977 Preliminary Final.

1977–1980 HONOUR ROLL

Year	Pos	Leading Goalkicker	No.	Best & Fairest	Captain	Coach
1977	3rd	Peter Hudson	110	Leigh Matthews	Don Scott	David Parkin
1978	1st	Michael Moncrieff	90	Leigh Matthews	Don Scott	David Parkin
1979	7th	Michael Moncrieff	45	Kelvin Moore	Don Scott	David Parkin
1980	8th	Michael Moncrieff	86	Leigh Matthews	Don Scott	David Parkin

behinds against Fitzroy in May 1979. At half-time the Hawks' score was 0.14. Peter Russo kicked Hawthorn's first goal in the third-quarter.

Don Scott was unlucky when it came to umpires. In June 1979 he was suspended for abusive language after he disputed being penalised for crossing the centre square line. The tribunal didn't listen to the League's smallest man, Paul Callery, who confessed: 'I pushed Scotty.'

Nor was the tribunal enlightened by Scott's explanation that it was the dazzle of VFL Park's lights during the 1979 Night Premiership Grand Final that caused him to elbow Collingwood's Peter Moore. The tribunal's remedy? Four weeks in the dark for Don.

The end of 1979 saw the passing of several members of the Hawthorn old guard. Phil Ryan, Max Elmer and Dr A. S. Ferguson left the committee. New president Ron Cook had a simple philosophy: 'First you go and get footballers, and the rest comes easy.'

John Kennedy became chairman of selectors at Hawthorn in 1980. He coached North Melbourne from 1985 to 1989 and was appointed chairman of the AFL Commission in 1993.

Hawthorn suffered internal strife in late 1980 after the departure of coach David Parkin. Don Scott resented Parkin's treatment and stepped down as captain. Ken Herbert refused to accept life membership because of disillusionment with the club's administration.

HAWTHORN

Leigh Matthews slips the snare of South Melbourne centreman Greg Smith in 1981.

'Lethal' Leigh – the Matthews magic

What kind of a record is this? Leigh Matthews played 340 games for Hawthorn as a rover and forward from 1969 to 1985. He kicked 915 goals. He was Hawthorn's leading goalkicker over six seasons and the VFL's in 1975. He captained Hawthorn from 1981 to 1985 and was club Best and Fairest eight times. He polled over 200 Brownlow Medal votes, but never won. And he represented Victoria 14 times from 1971 to 1982, captained his State against Western Australia in 1980, and played in seven Grand Finals, four of them Premierships.

It is the record of a champion, one of just twelve 'legends of the game' who were named in the AFL's Hall of Fame in 1996. By these standards, Matthews must be regarded as Hawthorn's greatest player. Many would argue he was the finest footballer ever to put on a boot.

He was built like a tank – solid, armour-plated, with a low centre of gravity and extreme manoeuvrability. Matthews sometimes seemed like a tree stump on legs, but for all his brawn, he had a wonderful football brain with the champion's knack of reading the play. He was so strong he could escape most tackles. So athletic he could outmark most big-men. So reliable that you always knew the ball would find its mark when Matthews had control.

He was that rare kind of footballer who could lift his game when the rest of a side was down, and bang on a 10-minute burst that would turn a match around. And of course he could use the hip and the shoulder, and sometimes players got in the way when he was running for the ball, and mostly, he did run for the ball, despite that fearsome reputation. Yet people forget that Matthews copped plenty in his time. So many opponents tried to 'stop' him, but so few did. And Matthews never squealed.

Many Hawk fans will never forget the day in 1973 when he had 38 kicks and booted 11 goals against Essendon, or his 24 kicks and four goals in the 1978 Grand Final and his six goals in the 1983 Grand Final. And what about that Essendon match in 1984 when he snapped a behind post off its base at Windy Hill?

Matthews was prosecuted by police for an alleged assault on Geelong's Neville Bruns during the course of play at Princes Park in June 1985. He pleaded guilty and was convicted. Almost a year later the conviction was overturned in the County Court.

The event took a heavy toll on Matthews, who decided to make Hawthorn's 1985 Grand Final his final game after 17 seasons. Unfortunately, the Hawks lost the game. Shouldered high by his team-mates, the old, battle-scarred warrior was carried from the ground by his faithful comrades. He could barely see the final steps of his football journey, for the tough guy had tears in his eyes that day. And he wasn't the only one.

CLUB NEWS 1981–1985

New Hawthorn coach Allan Jeans had a dream start in 1981, when the Hawks won eight of their first eleven matches, but the rest of the season proved less satisfactory. Hawthorn won 13 games and finished sixth.

A VFL Park match attendance record of 92,935 was set in the 1981 Hawthorn/Collingwood clash, won by Hawthorn 18.19 (127) to 12.9 (81).

In April 1982 the future Geelong champion Gary Ablett played the first of six senior games at Hawthorn. But city life didn't suit the country lad, who once skipped a Reserves game to go rabbit shooting. Hawthorn reluctantly let him go in 1983, after he failed to attend pre-season training.

When 18-year-old Dermott Brereton made his debut with five goals at full-forward in Hawthorn's 1982 First Semi-final against North Melbourne, everyone knew a potential champion had emerged. The philosophical Allan Jeans described him as 'just a boy with a lot to learn'.

In 1983 centreman Terry Wallace became the first Hawthorn player since the commencement of statistics to gain over 500 kicks in a season.

Due to injuries to Leigh Matthews, Peter Knights and Michael Tuck, full-back Kelvin Moore became acting captain for his 300th game in 1984. After Hawthorn narrowly defeated Collingwood, Moore laughed: 'I think the boys must have responded to my leadership.'

1981 – 1985

See you in September!

Leigh Matthews composed his victory speech in the last quarter of Hawthorn's huge Grand Final Win over Essendon in 1983. There wasn't much else to do. The Hawks were 14.3 up at three-quarter time and Matthews had never heard of a side kicking 15 goals in the last term. Hawthorn's 20.20 (140) to 8.9 (57) massacre set a record Grand Final winning margin of 83 points. At one stage during the final quarter, the difference was 102 points.

Although the score shows that Essendon never got into the game, there was a major worry to Hawthorn in the opening minutes of the match when key forward Gary Buckenara collapsed with a serious knee injury. 'That's it, we're gone,' cried the pessimists in brown and gold ranks, but Jeans had Ken Judge on the bench, who capably stepped into Bucky's boots and reeled in a long series of six-point verdicts.

Leigh Matthews inspired the whole team with his six magnificent goals. Michael Byrne snared three and Richard Loveridge, Russell Greene and Judge each kicked two goals, but the whole side contributed. Best of all were John Kennedy Jnr and Colin Robertson, the Norm Smith Medallist. Robertson superbly checked Essendon's potential matchwinner, Tim Watson, who was unusually subdued after a heavy first-quarter clash.

Essendon did not easily forget the bitterness of September defeat. In the 1984 Grand Final the Bombers scored a narrow victory over Hawthorn, and continued to wreak revenge the following year with a crushing humiliation, 26.14 (170) to 14.8 (72). Some newspapers declared Essendon's 11-goal last quarter in 1985 heralded football's greatest-ever team. They scarcely noticed Hawthorn's young Dermott Brereton, who goaled in the opening minutes of the game, added seven more to his tally and was reported three times. He, too, had arrived.

The 1983 Hawks kicked a record Grand Final-winning margin against Essendon.

Umpires break up an all-in brawl in the opening minutes of the 1985 Grand Final.

1981–1985 HONOUR ROLL

Year	Pos	Leading Goalkicker	No.	Best & Fairest	Captain	Coach
1981	6th	Leigh Matthews	48	Terry Wallace	Leigh Matthews	Allan Jeans
1982	3rd	Leigh Matthews	74	Leigh Matthews	Leigh Matthews	Allan Jeans
1983	1st	Leigh Matthews	79	Terry Wallace	Leigh Matthews	Allan Jeans
1984	2nd	Leigh Matthews	77	Russell Greene	Leigh Matthews	Allan Jeans
1985	2nd	Dermott Brereton	58	Dermott Brereton	Leigh Matthews	Allan Jeans

An Essendon spyforce led the Drug Squad to investigate Hawthorn players taking a 'mysterious substance' during quarter-time breaks in late 1984. Evidence that a Hawthorn chemist had been supplying a sinus mixture cleared the air.

'Nothing is sacred,' the critics said when John Kennedy emerged from retirement in 1985 to coach Hawthorn's old rival, North Melbourne. But Kennedy came back, as he had left, 'for a good family reason'.

Hawthorn lost the 1984 Grand Final to Essendon after leading all day then letting the Bombers fly away in a 9.6 last-quarter burst.

On 10 June 1985 the master coaches, Kennedy and Jeans, met in a Queen's Birthday clash between Hawthorn and North Melbourne. Fittingly, the match ended in a draw.

Hawk running man Russell Greene captained Victoria at the peak of his football career in July 1985, but a high price was paid when he suffered a serious knee injury during the match.

Robert DiPierdomenico was Man of the Match (3 goals) in the 1985 Night Premiership, where Hawthorn 11.11 (77) narrowly defeated Essendon 10.8 (68). The Hawks won pre-season/night flags in 1968, 1969, 1977, 1985, 1986, 1988, 1991 and 1992.

The 1985 Reserves Grand Final, which Hawthorn won from Geelong, included three Hawk champions who would become League coaches: Peter Knights, Rodney Eade and Gary Buckenara.

HAWTHORN

The pride of the club in 1987. 'You'll be better people for wearing this guernsey'.

When the family club met the million-dollar team

In the mid 1980s Carlton followed Essendon as Hawthorn's major rival. Under John Elliott and other leading business figures, the Blues epitomised the modern, professional football club. They were thought to have spent over a million dollars buying talent. The Hawks had bought a few key players along the way, too, but mostly Hawthorn had cultivated the League's zoned recruitment areas and developed the most promising youngsters in the Reserves and Under 19s.

Michael Tuck played 50 Reserve Grade games before another 426 in the Seniors. In 1986, 14 seasons after his senior debut, he was appointed Hawthorn captain at the age of 32. It was around then that people started thinking that the Hawks were getting old, but how wrong they were. Tucky, like his team, defied the odds. He went on to captain the side in four Premierships over the next six years, but perhaps his most memorable was that first one in 1986, when Hawthorn defeated Carlton, 16.14 (110) to 9.14 (68).

Carlton was beaten by a team which preached old-fashioned ideas like playing for the guernsey and family values. The inspirational Norm Smith Medallist, Gary Ayres, kept Carlton's danger man David Rhys-Jones at bay and sent the ball up forward time after time where Jason Dunstall (6 goals), Gary Buckenara (4), Dermott Brereton (3) and a host of others finished the job. Most of all, it was the way Hawthorn suppressed the Blues' attack that won them the game. Rodney Eade held Craig Bradley to six kicks and Peter Schwab dominated Wayne Johnston as Hawthorn stamped their authority all over the ground.

But Johnston avenged that humiliation in the 1987 Grand Final, where he set up Carlton's win by kicking two vital goals and laying out the Hawk strongman Robert DiPierdomenico in the opening minutes of the game.

The day was unusually hot and Hawthorn were tired following a hard Preliminary Final contest with Melbourne the previous week, which saw them just sneak into the Grand Final courtesy of a 15-metre penalty to Buckenara, who goaled and sealed the match in the dying minutes.

In 1986–87 Hawthorn met Carlton nine times. The Hawks won six of these encounters. That's when the Blues learned that money doesn't always buy success.

Hawthorn won this Aussie Bowl medal and trophy with a 53-point win over Carlton in Yokohama, Japan in November 1986.

Ruck-rover Michael Tuck: built to last.

CLUB NEWS 1986–1987

After Hawthorn lost Premierships to Essendon in 1984 and 1985, the Bombers were paraded as a team likely to dominate the competition for many years. But it was Hawthorn that kept turning up in September.

The 1986 season was the 25th anniversary of Hawthorn's first Premiership in 1961. As part of various efforts to 'recapture the spirit' of that year, the '61 Premiership veterans came together before the Round 6 game against Essendon, which Hawthorn won by 24 points.

Another coach graduated from the Hawthorn school in April 1986, when Leigh Matthews was appointed coach of Collingwood mid-season.

A black dog took to the field in the final quarter of Hawthorn's game against Richmond at Princes Park in Round 3, 1986. According to Garrie Hutchinson in the *Age*, 'The Black Dog did a lap of honour and was cheered by each section of the crowd as he passed it … the most entertaining thing that happened on the field all afternoon.'.

The VFL commission changed the venue for the Hawthorn v Essendon clash on 3 May 1986 to VFL Park and did not notify Hawthorn of the change until the Friday night. Nevertheless, Hawthorn won the fixture 19.12 (126) to 15.12 (102).

In July 1986 Hawthorn won its fifth Night Premiership (and back-to-back night Flags) with a 30-point victory

1986–1987

Hawthorn's favourite strongman, Robert DiPierdomenico, after a big win.

Dipper wins a Brownlow Medal

Hawthorn received a tremendous morale boost when tough wingman Robert DiPierdomenico shared the 1986 Brownlow Medal.

He played 240 games for Hawthorn between 1975 and 1991. Dipper's enthusiastic, never-say-die attitude won many matches, but two that live long in Hawthorn memories are the 1978 Grand Final when he was best-on-ground, and the 1989 Premiership where he played with a broken rib and punctured lung.

The Dipper earned his football success more than many players with greater skills. He worked hard to rescue his career from an ordinary life in the Reserves and amazed team-mates with flamboyant behaviour. Jason Dunstall said he didn't know what to make of Dipper until he realised the swaggering strongman was basically normal, only louder.

Allan Jeans had a profound influence on Dipper's playing performance, and he knew a few tricks to keep that extroverted personality in check. Dipper never quite got over the day that Jeans challenged him to a wrestle in the Hawthorn gym, where they grappled for about 20 minutes or so before Dipper found himself pinned to the floor. 'Say I'm the best, son,' urged Jeans. 'Say I'm the best.' But Dipper refused, of course, so Jeans tightened his grip: 'Tell me who's best. Come on, tell me.' The Dipper screamed abuse. And a minute went by, then out came the muffled cry, 'Okay, okay, you're the best', and the wily old coach released his hold.

Two on trot

Rover John Platten followed Robert DiPierdomenico's 1986 success by taking out the award in 1987 (in a tie with St Kilda's Tony Lockett). Platten came to Hawthorn from South Australia in 1986. He had already won the Magarey Medal and had actually signed up with Carlton, but Hawthorn had prior claims. Allan Jeans says in Platten's autobiography, *The Rat* (1997): 'From day one, Platts was a sensational player and pound for pound is as good as anyone I've coached.'

You begin to understand Platten's drive to succeed when you realise he was the seventh of nine children in a sports-mad family of six boys and three girls. He had to try hard to be noticed. Platten made up for his lack of size on the football field with incredible determination, dynamic pace and superb ball skills. At the bottom of almost every pack in a Hawthorn match, the Rat was usually down there somewhere, burrowing away before scampering off into open space with the ball. He was a wonderful team player, and as fair as any footballer comes. In a dozen seasons with the Hawks, Platten put in a bad game about as often as he had a haircut – and nobody remembers when that last was.

Platten rules.

He averaged 25 possessions per match in his Brownlow year. In 1988 his stats for the last four matches were 35, 47, 43 and 32 possessions. The 43, which was against St Kilda at Waverley, did not merit a single Brownlow vote, so either the umpires were blind that day or they were starting to take the Rat for granted. And that's something no one should ever do.

1986–1987 HONOUR ROLL

Year	Pos	Leading Goalkicker	No.	Best & Fairest	Captain	Coach
1986	1st	Jason Dunstall	77	Gary Ayres	Michael Tuck	Allan Jeans
1987	2nd	Jason Dunstall	94	John Platten	Michael Tuck	Allan Jeans

over Carlton.
Rover John Platten had 18 handballs against Melbourne on 12 July 1986.
Hawthorn kicked its highest-ever score, 35.15 (225) against Geelong 13.12 (90) in August 1986. Jason Dunstall kicked nine goals.
During 1986 Hawthorn sought the advice of sports psychologist Rob Kirkby. Jason Dunstall benefited from taking his techniques seriously. The 'Dipper' didn't.
Hawthorn won the Dr W. C. McClelland Trophy for the third year in a row in 1986.
'A good driver in heavy traffic' was how Allan Jeans described 1986 Norm Smith Medallist Gary Ayres.
Dermott Brereton caught the eye with his lime-green boots in 1987. His 64 goals that season were even more spectacular.
'Let's do it for Yabby,' said Michael Tuck before Allan Jeans' 500th game as coach, when the Hawks met Carlton in Round 14, 1987. They did, by a point.
In May 1987 the Hawthorn Reserves kicked a record VFL score of 45.20 (290) to the Sydney Swans 6.12 (48).
Jason Dunstall kicked 11 goals when Hawthorn defeated the Brisbane Bears, 24.21 (165) to 11.4 (70) on 14 June 1987.
In the final minutes of the 1987 Preliminary Final, Melbourne's Jim Stynes inadvertently stepped over the mark when Hawthorn's Gary Buckenara was kicking toward goal. A 15-metre penalty put 'Bucky' within range and his goal secured the Grand Final berth.

HAWTHORN

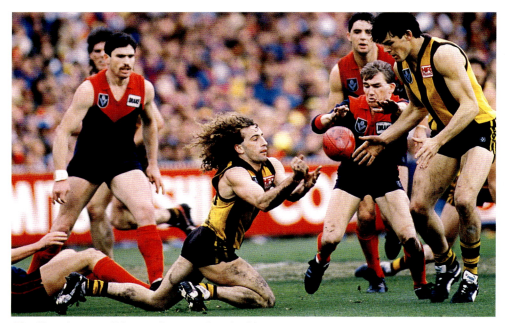

The Hawthorn wall leaves Demons just looking on.

Allan Jeans: 'Pay the price.'

The running wall

Midway through the 1988 Grand Final between Hawthorn and Melbourne, around a dozen Hawthorn players formed a chain across the half-back line and charged down the ground in a human wall. Onward they ran, drilling the ball left, then right, from one to another with flawless precision. Every man knew his job, every man his place. And as the movement gathered speed and strength and numbers with almost every step, it surged forth over 50 metres to the forward line.

Again and again it swelled that day, and in the spray of goals Jason Dunstall kicked seven, Paul Abbott six, and Dermott Brereton five. Hawthorn was three goals up at quarter time, eight goals at half-time, nine at the final change and in the end it was 16, as Hawthorn 22.20 (152) crushed Melbourne 6.20 (56). Was this the greatest win in Grand Final history? It was the greatest winning margin, but some people were bored. The wise ones knew that a running wall of gold and brown had just taken football to a new dimension.

The philosopher coach

Allan Jeans liked to tell Hawthorn players simple stories to convey basic truths. At half-time in the 1989 Grand Final he talked about buying shoes. A person had the choice between buying a cheap pair that didn't fit well, or a dearer pair that would last longer and fit much better. Would the person who settled for the lesser option be saying later, 'I wish I had paid the price'? That was every Hawthorn player's choice, Jeans explained, pay the price today or regret forever. And as they left the rooms, his voice rose to a crescendo. 'Pay the price,' he screamed, 'Pay the price.'

Some other 'Jeanspeak' football wisdom:

• 'Umpires make mistakes, but they don't make as many as players make.'

• 'Savour the moment, but remember there are losers in the next room.'

• 'No one has ever died on me yet, son. Go harder. It won't kill you.'

• 'Success needs no explanation. Failure will not accept any alibis.'

• 'Good players don't need any gimmicks.' (to Jason Dunstall after he appeared sporting a goatee beard in 1995)

• 'Get yourself fit and you'll be part of the ride.'

The caretaker coach

Alan Joyce stepped into the Hawthorn coaching role in 1988 when Allan Jeans took time off for health reasons. Joyce played 49 games for Hawthorn in the early 1960s and was the club's director of football when he accepted the coaching handpass, which he smoothly returned to Jeans a season and a Premiership later.

Joyce went on to coach Hawthorn again from 1991–93. He was sacked three days after Hawthorn failed in the finals, and coached Footscray from 1994–96.

CLUB NEWS 1988–1989

Hawthorn 10.10 (70) defeated Geelong 9.13 (67) to win its sixth Night Premiership (Panasonic Cup) in March 1988.

Following a push-and-shove incident with Essendon's Billy Duckworth, Dermott Brereton decided to run through Essendon's three-quarter-time huddle. The Bombers were so bewildered Brereton emerged unscathed.

John Kennedy Jnr showed his father's kind of character when he missed most of 1988 with a heart problem, but came back to be one of Hawthorn's best players in the finals series.

Jason Dunstall won the Coleman Medal in 1988 with 132 goals and again in 1989 (138). Hawthorn won 19 games and a Premiership in both seasons.

At a club function in 1988 Alan Joyce was introduced by Hawk president Trevor Coote as 'a man who makes Allan Jeans look extroverted'.

Gary Ayres was best on the ground in the 1988 Grand Final, winning his second Norm Smith Medal. Alan Joyce said he couldn't imagine a tougher or stronger footballer than Ayres, who played the match with a cheekbone fractured in a first-quarter clash with Melbourne's Jim Stynes.

The McClelland Trophy was won by Hawthorn in 1988. After the season, Hawthorn defeated Carlton at The Oval in London, then Collingwood at Varsity Stadium, Toronto.

1988 – 1989

Brereton: fierce in the 1989 Grand Final.

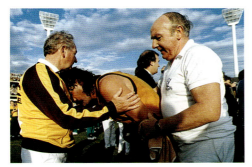
Dipper comes off second best and plays on.

Paying the price

The 1989 Grand Final saw Hawthorn defeat Geelong in a classic Premiership confrontation. Geelong hadn't won a Flag since 1963 and it was obvious from the outset that rules were not going to get in their way. In the first 20 seconds Geelong's Mark Yeates charged the unsuspecting Dermott Brereton, leaving him flat on the ground with a bruised kidney, damaged ribs and internal bleeding. Brereton couldn't breathe for nearly a minute, but he got up to kick three goals for the match, two in Hawthorn's opening quarter onslaught of 8.4 to Geelong's 2.0.

The Hawks held that six-goal break going into the last quarter, when Geelong desperately fought within reach, aided by Gary Ablett's nine goals. For Hawthorn, Jason Dunstall, Dean Anderson and Gary Buckenara each kicked four goals. Hawthorn had 47 tackles to Geelong's 25, but the injury toll was frightening.

Soon after Brereton was shirt-fronted, John Platten, best on the ground to the 20-minute mark, was knocked out in a clash with Gary Hocking. Robert DiPierdomenico returned the compliment to Hocking, later earning himself a five-match suspension. Dipper was collected by Ablett and suffered a broken rib and a punctured lung. He continued playing until the final siren, when he collapsed and was rushed to hospital. Platten, who was stretchered off in the first quarter, was so badly concussed that to this day he cannot remember the game.

Hawthorn fought the last quarter with barely a dozen fit players. Gary Ayres had suffered a torn hamstring. Darrin Pritchard, a corked thigh. Michael Tuck had split the webbing in his hand, but he still beat Geelong's Mark Bairstow. John Kennedy and Jamie Morrissey could hardly walk. Tuck was limping too. Peter Curran's ankle was gone, and Scott Maginess had come off second-best after a collision with a behind post.

Geelong kicked 8.5 in the last quarter to Hawthorn's 3.5, but when the siren rang the Hawks were still standing, six points up. Days later, the Dipper was flat on his back at St Vincent's Hospital, still mumbling away something about 'paying the price'.

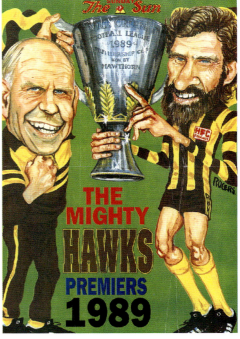
Something to smile about for Hawks leaders Allan Jeans and Michael Tuck.

The 'Kid' became a man

Dermott Brereton is helped to his feet after being flattened in the first minutes of the 1989 Grand Final. Moments later, he marked and goaled.

His performance inspired the Hawks and his determination to overcome the pain and keep playing were captured by the cameras, and will be replayed for years to come.

The 'Kid' grows up.

1988 – 1989 HONOUR ROLL

Year	Pos	Leading Goalkicker	No.	Best & Fairest	Captain	Coach
1988	1st	Jason Dunstall	132	Jason Dunstall	Michael Tuck	Alan Joyce
1989	1st	Jason Dunstall	138	Jason Dunstall	Michael Tuck	Allan Jeans

At the Hawthorn Annual Meeting late in 1988, Allan Jeans announced that he would be returning as coach in 1989, despite calls for him to resign. Alan Joyce returned the coaching handpass with characteristic Hawthorn dignity.

Hawthorn made a minor change to its uniform in 1989, adopting gold socks instead of gold and brown hoops.

A fine judge of form, Allan Jeans predicted in May 1989 that Geelong would make the Grand Final that year.

Against Geelong on 6 May 1989, Hawthorn came back from nearly nine goals down at half-time to win by eight points. Gary Ayres drove the Hawks home in the second half, which included a 10-goal last quarter.

In a bad season for injuries, Paul Abbott broke his leg in 1989 and talented half-forward flanker Tony Hall suffered a severe knee injury playing for SA in a State of Origin game. He had been tackled by fellow Hawk Andy Collins.

Dunstall v Collingwood on 22 July 1989: the Hawthorn forward kicked 11.2. Collingwood managed 11.9.

Among eight retrospective Brownlow Medals awarded in 1989 because of a rule change, the former Hawthorn star Col Austen received the medal for his 1949 season.

Dermott Brereton shirtfronted Essendon's Paul Van der Haar in Hawthorn's 36-point Second Semi-final win in 1989. Peter Schwab was later suspended for striking Andrew Manning, and missed the Grand Final.

HAWTHORN

The family club

Paul Hudson with father Peter.

Above right: How time flies. Peter Hudson's son Paul, the bouncing baby who brightened up Hudson's knee injury woes in 1972, was a fully fledged Hawk by 1990. Michael Tuck played alongside both the father and the son.

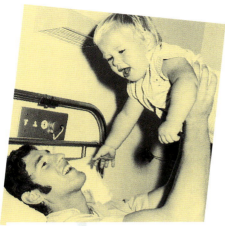

Michael Tuck celebrates 1991 with his kids.

Bucky celebrates with son Andrew, 1989.

Tucky calls it quits

There was no sign that Michael Tuck intended retiring as he relaxed after the 1991 Grand Final with (from left) daughter Renee, 11, and sons Shane, 9, and Travis, 4. Then a few weeks later came the announcement, 'I don't think I will ever play again.' He had 'a long talk' with Hawthorn's match committee, he said. 'They helped me make up my mind.' They wanted him to leave on a high note, and Tuck appreciated their honesty. We will never know whether their advice was right, but if Tuck's record proved anything, he was a footballer who defied history. People had almost written him off several times, as far back as 1984, in fact, and they were wrong then. Were they right in 1991?

From 1972 to 1991, Michael Tuck played a League record 426 senior games. He appeared in 39 finals, which included 17 Grand Finals and 13 Premierships: 1976, 1978, 1983, 1986, 1988, 1989, 1991 (day); 1977, 1985, 1986, 1988 (night); 1972 (Reserves); and 1976 (NFL). He was Hawthorn captain from 1986 to 1991, captain of Victoria in 1984 and a State representative 11 times. It wasn't a bad record for a kid from Berwick who arrived at Hawthorn in 1970 to be told he was too skinny to play football. But that was Tucky. An enigma.

Buckenara retires

Gary Buckenara was forced to retire in mid 1990 due to knee problems. The brilliant all-rounder from Subiaco had been one of Hawthorn's most expensive recruits, but proved a wonderful investment. He played in four Premierships and five Grand Finals, kicked the winning goal in the 1987 Preliminary Final, and set up countless opportunities with his superb long-kicking and marking skills. 'Bucky' coached the Sydney Swans in 1992.

CLUB NEWS 1990–1991

The publication in 1990 of Hawthorn's first club history, *The Hard Way* by journalist Harry Gordon, was dedicated to Peter Crimmins.

During 1990 Hawthorn shared its home games between Princes Park and VFL Park, Waverley. A full move was made to Waverley in 1991.

Jason Dunstall's 12 goals in the opening round against Geelong on 31 March 1990 silenced the traditional pre-season media comment that Hawthorn was getting too old and slow.

In May 1990 Hawk officials were bemused at the sight of Leigh Matthews trying to get into the Hawthorn coaching box at VFL Park, momentarily forgetting he was coach of the other side, Collingwood.

Jason Dunstall fractured his skull in the Hawthorn v Melbourne match in May 1990. He courageously returned in the first week of July, sporting a short haircut and helmet.

In August 1990 Michael Tuck became the second player to pass the 400-game mark. A few weeks later he broke Kevin Bartlett's all-time League record of 403 games.

Allan Jeans finally stepped down as Hawthorn coach in September 1990 and was replaced by Alan Joyce in 1991.

Hawthorn became victims of the League debut of the Adelaide Crows in March 1991. Before 44,902 fans at Football Park, the Crows led by 51

1990 – 1991

Johnny Platten and the team savour the moment at training before the 1991 Grand Final.

How sweet it is! The Hawks win in 1991.

The sweetest victory of all?

This was the one they said Hawthorn couldn't win. The Hawks were supposedly too old and too slow in 1991 to beat those young glamour boys from the West. But they did. The champion side that AFL Chief Ross Oakley inadvertently introduced as the West Coast Egos went down to the well-worn, but ever so efficient Hawthorn machine.

In a magnificent Grand Final at AFL Park, Hawthorn 20.19 (139) crushed the West Coast Eagles 13.8 (86). It was a day for Hawthorn's young, and old, as Paul Dear inspired the side on the forward line. Anthony Condon claimed the midfield. The

Moment of truth. Tuck leads the team down the race towards the 1991 Grand Final and destiny.

'freak', Jamie Morrisey, held the backline firm and Steve Lawrence dominated in the ruck. But what a sight it was to see that vintage model, Ayresy, still able to steer in the Waverley traffic. And Tucky, an old dog at 38, but with more than enough tricks to overcome the brilliant young ball-getter, Craig Turley, who had finished second in the Brownlow Medal. There was Chris Mew in his eleventh season and Dermott Brereton in his ninth. They were all there playing the game of their lives. And as the Hawks slammed on eight goals in the final quarter, the experts remembered that nobody knew more about finals football than this team. Flag number nine was theirs.

1990 – 1991 HONOUR ROLL

Year	Pos	Leading Goalkicker	No.	Best & Fairest	Captain	Coach
1990	5th	Jason Dunstall	83	Andy Collins	Michael Tuck	Allan Jeans
1991	1st	Jason Dunstall	82	Ben Allan	Michael Tuck	Alan Joyce

points at half-time and crushed Hawthorn, 24.11 (155) to 9.15 (69).
The Hawks threatened legal action unless a tribunal case was reopened involving Dermott Brereton being suspended for five matches for allegedly striking Adelaide's Chris McDermott. The League agreed, but Brereton lost the appeal.
In a huge win for Hawthorn, but a sorry day for one of the League's grand old clubs, the Hawks thrashed battling Fitzroy in Hobart, 36.15 (231) to 11.8 (74).
John Kennedy Jnr bowed out with Michael Tuck at the end of 1991. He played in 241 games and four Premierships, and was one of Hawthorn's best players in the 1983 Grand Final.
Two other Hawk greats to hang up their boots in late 1991 were Peter Schwab (who played 171 games, three Premierships) and DiPierdomenico (240 games, five Premierships).
After Michael Tuck retired in 1991, Hawthorn named the renovated Glenferrie Oval grandstand in his honour. The AFL struck the Michael Tuck Medal for the best and fairest player in the summer competition Grand Final. And Tuck was awarded an Order of Australia Medal for 'services to football'.
Richmond announced that Allan Jeans would replace coach Kevin Bartlett in 1992.
'Too old. Too slow. Too Good.' This was the message on Hawthorn's 1992 summer T-shirt.

HAWTHORN

The Demolition Dermie show

Dermott Brereton played in eight Grand Finals and five Hawthorn Premierships. As Hawthorn's champion centre half-forward from 1982 to 1993, he kicked more than 400 goals and was one of the most colourful players of the modern era. Big, brash and aggressive, Brereton's legendary toughness and natural exuberance sometimes overshadowed his superb marking and long-kicking skills.

Brereton first arrived at the club as a wide-eyed 14-year-old in 1979, after being invited to train with the Hawks' junior squad. He went into the rooms on that first Sunday morning to take a look at the big boys, who were playing cricket in the gym. Michael Tuck was at the crease. Suddenly there was a colossal bang and glass sprayed everywhere as Tucky smashed the ball into the window just above Dermie's head. The kid was impressed.

Right from the start, demolition and Dermie seemed to go together. They don't keep stats on how many players he 'dermolished' over the years, but let's just say his contribution was considerable. Mostly he used the old-fashioned hip and shoulder. Perfectly legal. But employed with an element of surprise and a dash of scientific strategy.

There was a famous day in 1988 when Brereton had his Irish up and ran right through the Essendon three-quarter time huddle. He emerged unscathed. Of course, his eyesight wasn't good. How else do you explain him planting a kiss on Billy Duckworth's lips earlier in the same game?

That was Dermie. Never short of confidence or cheek. Flashy like the lime-green boots he used to wear after half time. The man driving the red Ferrari in football's fast lane. But there was plenty of substance too. Many of his 189 games with the club were played with chronic back, hip and ankle problems. There was nothing wrong with his heart. He could always be counted on to play his part, like the eight goals he kicked in the 1985 Grand Final. Or his courage in 1989 when Geelong's Mark Yeates returned an old compliment. Or when he filled in at full-forward against Richmond in 1990 wearing a buoyancy vest to protect his broken ribs. He could hardly move and looked like the Michelin man, but he still booted 11 goals.

That was Dermie. Inspirational.

Dermott Brereton: makes it look easy.

Hawthorn's gold and brown age

Between 1982 and 1994 Hawthorn won five Flags, reached eight Grand Finals (including seven in a row) and made 13 successive finals campaign appearances. On this record, Hawthorn is the leading football club of the modern era.

Year	Stage	Result
1982	Prelim Final	Lost to Carlton (31 points)
1983	Grand Final	Defeated Essendon (83 points)
1984	Grand Final	Lost to Essendon (24 points)
1985	Grand Final	Lost to Essendon (78 points)
1986	Grand Final	Defeated Carlton (42 points)
1987	Grand Final	Lost to Carlton (33 points)
1988	Grand Final	Defeated Melbourne (96 points)
1989	Grand Final	Defeated Geelong (6 points)
1990	Elim. Final	Lost to Melbourne (9 points)
1991	Grand Final	Defeated West Coast (53 points)
1992	Elim. Final (1)	Lost to West Coast (13 points)
1993	Elim. Final (1)	Lost to Adelaide (15 points)
1994	Qual. Final (2)	Lost to North Melbourne (23 points)

CLUB NEWS 1992-1995

Hawthorn began playing all home games at AFL Park in 1992.

Paul Hudson became the first winner of the Michael Tuck Medal when he was best on the ground in the 1992 pre-season competition Grand Final, which the Hawks won by 62 points against Fitzroy.

Michael Tuck and his wife Fay were chosen to unfurl Hawthorn's Premiership pennant before the Round 1 match against Geelong at Waverley.

In August 1992 Hawthorn scored its greatest-ever winning margin, 160 points, in a 32.24 (216) win over Essendon 8.8 (56).

Veteran Chris Mews snapped an achilles tendon in the first round of the Reserves in 1993, which brought the 31-year-old's career to a sorry end. Mews played 230 games from 1980–92, including eight Grand Finals for five Premierships.

'Somebody's going to have his head kicked, so it might as well be mine,' said John Kennedy when taking over the chairmanship of the AFL Commission in 1993.

Hawthorn didn't renew Alan Joyce's coaching contract at the end of 1993. His record: five Premierships in four seasons (three pre-season, two AFL).

Angry members denounced Hawthorn's Board and administration at the annual meeting in 1993, when it was revealed the club had accrued losses of up to $2m. despite its on-field success.

1992–1995

A paltry $7000

Dermott Brereton hung up his brown and gold boots in 1993, a year that also saw the retirement of Gary Ayres, club captain in 1992–93. Ayres began coaching Geelong in 1995, while Brereton played on with the Sydney Swans and later Collingwood. Ayres and Brereton were the last players at Hawthorn who had participated in the 13 Grand Finals between 1983 and 1992. Other veterans to leave at the end of 1993 included James Morrisey, Tony Hall and Greg Dear. Certainly these players were in the twilight of their careers in 1993, but the best that Hawthorn's administration could offer the ageing heroes was a paltry $7000 per year base, according to Brereton, and their subsequent departures deprived the club of vital leadership skills. For some of those who paid the price in 1989, it was a shock that Hawthorn would not in 1993.

Full-forward Jason Dunstall takes a grab on the way to 12 goals against Geelong in 1990.

The goal king leaps

Jason Dunstall kicked 17.5 on 2 May 1992 against Richmond, just one goal fewer than Fred Fanning's 1947 League record. From 1985–96 Dunstall kicked bags of 10 or more goals in a match 16 times, and he has kicked over 100 goals in a season six times: 1988 (132), 1989 (138), 1992 (145), 1993 (123), 1994 (101) and 1996 (102). He kicked his 1000th goal on 28 August 1994 against the Brisbane Bears in his home State of Queensland, and his 1200th goal in the seventh round of 1997. Knee injuries in late 1996 and mid–1997 threatened to halt his magnificent scoring, which approaches the all-time great Gordon Coventry, who kicked 1299 goals for Collingwood in 1920–37.

Gary Ayres: contract not renewed.

Oops! This ad appeared on 29 July 1992.

1992–1995 HONOUR ROLL

Year	Pos	Leading Goalkicker	No.	Best & Fairest	Captain	Coach
1992	6th	Jason Dunstall	145	Jason Dunstall	Gary Ayres	Alan Joyce
1993	6th	Jason Dunstall	123	Jason Dunstall	Gary Ayres	Alan Joyce
1994	7th	Jason Dunstall	101	John Platten	Chris Langford	Peter Knight
1995	15th	Jason Dunstall	66	Darren Jarman	Jason Dunstall	Peter Knights

A loss to Carlton in April 1994 took Hawthorn to the bottom of the ladder for the first time since 1979.

Jason Dunstall kicked 10 goals straight before he managed his only point when Hawthorn defeated Footscray 20.5 (125) to 8.13 (61) in Round 11, 1994.

During the 1994 Qualifying Final against North Melbourne, Hawthorn became the first victim of the extra-time rule. North kicked 3.5 (23) to Hawthorn's nil in the tie-breaking period.

Peter Hudson replaced John Lauritz as Hawthorn Chief Executive in January 1995.

Andy Collins played his 150th consecutive senior game in Round 5, 1995. The team didn't let him down, beating Collingwood by 59 points.

In a turning-point game at Brisbane in July 1995, the Hawks sensibly sought shade at three-quarter time before being sunstruck by Brisbane's nine-goal last quarter, which recovered their 45-point deficit to win them the game.

On 27 August 1995 North Melbourne destroyed Hawthorn's chances of reaching the finals for the fourteenth time in succession. Peter Knights accepted the 'end of an era' verdict.

Darren Jarman was runner-up by three votes to Paul Kelly in the 1995 Brownlow Medal. His subsequent return to South Australia added to Hawthorn's woes.

When Hawthorn president Geoff Lord retired from the Board in 1995, Dermott Brereton accused him of 'ripping the heart and soul out of the club.'

HAWTHORN

Merger madness 1996

6 Aug 1994. Hawthorn president Geoff Lord reveals that Melbourne and Fitzroy are engaged in merger talks. Melbourne president Ian Ridley demands an apology for the 'lie'.

9 Aug 1994. The *Age* claims six clubs are engaged in merger talks.

3 Jun 1995. Rumours of a Hawthorn/Melbourne merger are 'a load of bulldust' says former Hawthorn president Ron Cook. Melbourne's Hassa Mann agrees.

12 Jun 1995. The AFL offers a $4m. inducement for the first two clubs to merge (later increased to $6m.).

19 Jul 1995. Geoff Lord says Hawthorn is open to offers, but the club is not making any commitment to merge.

1 Aug 1995. Hawthorn and Footscray question the AFL's motives in backing huge player payment increases which may send poor clubs broke or force mergers.

Jun 1996. The *Sunday Age* and other newspapers report Hawthorn and Melbourne are 'well down the track' towards a merged club to be known as the Melbourne Hawks.

29 Jul 1996. Official announcement that Melbourne and Hawthorn are entering merger discussions. Hawthorn president Brian Coleman says Hawthorn faces losses of up to $700,000 this season.

11 Aug 1996. Melbourne anti-merger forces led by Brian Dixon form the 'Demon Alternative'. Millionaire mining magnate Joe Gutnick promises Melbourne $3m. if the merger vote fails.

13 Aug 1996. Hawthorn anti-merger forces led by Don Scott form 'Operation Payback' to raise up to $1.7m. to eradicate Hawthorn's estimated debt.

Aug 1996. The AFL sponsors a massive public relations campaign endorsing the proposed merger. Former Hawthorn presidents Ron Cook, Phil Ryan and Dr A. S. Ferguson seek a Supreme Court injunction to halt the merger moves.

16 Sept 1996. Merger meetings. Angry scenes at the Camberwell Civic Centre as Don Scott pulls apart the proposed Melbourne Hawks guernsey to expose a Melbourne guernsey underneath. Hawthorn members vote against the merger 5241 to 2841. At another meeting, Melbourne members narrowly approve the merger (4679 to 4220), but it cannot proceed without the approval of members of both clubs.

Anti-merger: Don Scott (centre), flanked by Dermott Brereton (left) and Ian Dicker.

Merger, or takeover? – many believed that is what the proposed merger really was.

1996–1997 HONOUR ROLL

Year	Pos	Leading Goalkicker	No.	Best & Fairest	Captain	Coach
1996	8th	Jason Dunstall	102	Paul Salmon	Jason Dunstall	Ken Judge
1997	15th	Nick Holland	29	Paul Salmon	Jason Dunstall	Ken Judge

1996-1997

Pride shows the way

After more than doubling club membership to 27,400, the Hawks won eight games and finished second-last in 1997. Melbourne finished last. If the two clubs had merged, there might have been a Melbourne Hawks in the 1997 finals, but history had determined otherwise. The season was perhaps the most even in AFL history, and in a mid-year purple patch Hawthorn won five games in a row and leapt into the top eight.

Their run began with an overwhelming 53-point victory over Collingwood in Round 10, where at quarter-time the scores were Hawthorn 7.6 to Collingwood 0.1, and there was plenty of evidence that coach Ken Judge had the old Hawthorn machine up and running again. It rolled on to fine wins over Essendon, Geelong and Melbourne before showing signs of stalling against Port, when the Hawks enjoyed a big early lead but only just got home. They did not the next week against Richmond at the MCG, where most of the side stood still in the final term.

Morale fell as Hawthorn lost the last eight games of the season, but there were clear signs the team had recovered its endeavour before the final rounds. The problem was skills, especially in attack, where the absence of Jason Dunstall was compounded by the loss of big-marking forward Nick Holland, out with a knee injury for six games from Round 14.

The Hawks went down bravely to the Bulldogs in Round 22, bitterly disappointed at being unable to salvage a win for the retiring veterans Chris Langford and Darrin Pritchard. Hawthorn people should never forget Langford's last gesture, when he partly removed his guernsey and showed it to the crowd like he had done so dramatically a year earlier to signify his opposition to the merger. For old Langers' sign said footballers come and go, and seasons rise and fall, but the brown and gold lives on.

A fine catch

In 1997 Paul Salmon took out Hawthorn's club champion award for the second year running. The big 'fish' was hooked from Essendon early in 1996 and became the AFL's leading ruckman with his 352 hit-outs last season. Salmon's goalkicking and experience also proved major gains for Hawthorn as the club continued to lose old heroes like Andy Collins in 1996 and John Platten, Chris Langford, Darrin Pritchard and Ray Jenke, who each said farewell at the end of 1997.

Paul Salmon: good years left in 'the Fish'.

Looking forward

Seven-year-old James Mustey of Camberwell, Victoria has been barracking for the Hawks ever since he was a little kid. His hero is Jason Dunstall (of course), but he thought Peter Crimmins was fantastic when he saw him on the AFL video. James drives his Mum crazy by pretending to commentate while kicking balloons and socks around the house. On Saturday mornings he goes to Auskick, where his Dad takes the boys through their warm-up routine. The first AFL game he went to see was at Waverley, but Hawthorn lost. They lost the day he went to the MCG, too, and he cried all through the last quarter when the Tigers kicked 10 goals in a row and the Hawks got nothing. But in true Hawthorn style, James isn't giving up hope. Next year they'll be better. And after that? Well, he can already kick with both feet …

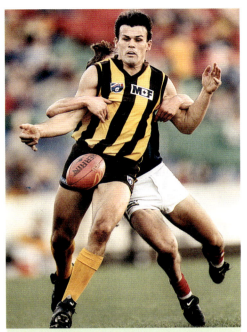

Defender Chris Langford breaks free.

Langford leaves

After 15 years and over 300 games, champion full-back Chris Langford called it a day in 1997. Superb physical strength and fitness enabled him to keep playing at a high level in his final seasons despite living in Sydney and flying in for matches. 'Langers' was Hawthorn captain in 1994 before handing over the reins to Jason Dunstall.

James Mustey

MELBOURNE

MELBOURNE

Year Established	1858
Joined VFL/AFL	1897
Home Ground	MCG
Premierships	1900, 1926, 1939, 1940, 1941, 1948, 1955, 1956, 1957, 1959, 1960, 1964
Brownlow Medals	Ivor Warne-Smith 1926, 1928; Don Cordner 1946; Brian Wilson 1982; Peter Moore 1984; Jimmy Stynes 1991
Record home crowd	99,346 v Collingwood, 15/6/58
Most games	Robert Flower, 272
Most goals	Norm Smith, 546
Notable supporters	Past: Sir Billy Snedden, Hugh Trumble; Present: Steve Moneghetti, Kylie Minogue, Neil Mitchell, Ian Henderson, Alan Stockdale, James Reyne, Rosemary Margan

MY CLUB
by John Ross

It was always going to be Melbourne. To hear Mum talk she was on first-name terms with Bobby McKenzie, Lance Rule and Shane McGrath, and may even have had a nodding acquaintance with the great Dr Don. My father, like so many dads whose names do not appear in the *Encyclopaedia of League Footballers*, had 'had a run' with Melbourne.

My first game was the replay of the 1948 Grand Final, and I peered through the elbows to see the play of men like Maxie Spittle and Alby Rodda, Norm Smith and Jack Mueller. I have been starry-eyed since, apart from my 'objective' period, when I was writing games for the *Age*. It so happened this stern professionalism coincided with the end of Melbourne's glory years, so I could not get caught up in the euphoria. I was first up the race as a reporter in 1964 and caught Ron Barassi, Don Williams and Co. still steaming from their exertion and seemingly unable to grasp the fact that they had won it. (As a Collingwood hater, I also concede that the most sportsmanlike and dignified man I met that day was Ray Gabelich.)

Soon after that I became a football follower again and renewed my vows with Melbourne, with the pure enthusiasm of my childhood, when my mates and I used to walk though the Botanic Gardens and on to the 'G' to sit in the Gods of the old Northern Stand. It wasn't much of a team then either, but our heroes were on the ground – men like Mike Woods, a solid teak backman, George Bickford, the stay-at-home centreman, Peter Marquis, the smiling Tasmanian. Our hopes rose when Noel Clarke, another Tasmanian, arrived on a sea of newsprint. His first touch was a swooping one-handed pick up and a drilled goal from the half-forward flank. It was probably the best thing he did as he became another of the imports who, over the years, have promised more than they have delivered.

I have been longing, since my renewal of pure faith, to bask in a Premiership like that one in '64, but I rejoined the Demons (there were no Dees then) at the start of long slide into mediocrity and worse. We watched though, always in hope, sometimes going away with a win to make the weekend shine. We revelled in the red and the blue, and in the skills of Stan Alves, Hassa Mann, Greg Wells, Gary Hardeman and Robbie Flower. We appreciated the toughness of men like Stephen Icke and Shane Zantuck and, yes, we even loved Crackers Keenan and Rod Grinter. There's something about that red and blue – the people wearing it

Robbie Flower, abundant skill.

Jim Stynes, lion-hearted ruckman.   **Ron Barassi, born to the club.**

can't be even half bad. We know the 'secret society' of the window sticker, that says there are good people on the road. We know the players in other colours are low down and mean, but when they come to us they are baptised with a new manliness and character. Take Carl Ditterich and Peter Moore, for instance.

After all those years it came as a surprise in 1987 to have that finals feeling again. The run-up to the finals, that game at Footscray when we all cried like fools, and the first two Semis brought the best football feelings I've ever had, followed by the worst in the tragedy at Waverley.

Sure, '88 was great, but we had got used to it by then. We are not used to it now, but the faithful are ever waiting, and the sea of red and blue that waves and quivers every winter weekend is getting ready for the full anemone when we start that climb to the top again.

A gentlemen's club? Well of course we are all nice people, and we have had some players from the silver-tail side of town over the years – say, one in every 100. Our heartland is everywhere, and the club has the demographics to prove it. There's a solid red and blue stripe running through the south-east, from South Yarra to Dandenong, and peaking in places like Ormond, Bentleigh and McKinnon. There are Demons in Ivanhoe (including the famous Ivan) and in Werribee and many places in between. Melbourne seems to have accrued its supporters through the same mystical attraction that has always bound the team – not place perhaps, but just a drop of passion mixed in with tradition.

Don Cordner, 1946 Brownlow.   **Garry Lyon, a fine leader.**

MELBOURNE

An early match in Yarra Park, outside the MCG. Note the on-ball scrum.

Tom Wills as a Melbourne cricketer.

Tom Wills invents a football game

Tommy Wills' return to Australia from his boarding at Rugby School, England, and his love of the new football game of England, prompted him to try out another new type of football game, suited to the Australian conditions.

Wills captained the football XI at Rugby and was a noted cricketer. It was natural the Victorian cricketers would turn to him for advice, particularly after the loss of two games to New South Wales.

Wills' advice was as blunt as his character, and his renowned blows with the cricket bat. The Victorian men were not fit enough for cricket, and ought to find a winter pastime to toughen them up.

Wills thought about rugby, but he also looked at the rough ground of the open spaces around Melbourne, a far cry from the gentle turf of England, and saw visions of torn and grazed bodies. Something different was needed, and something that steered a course away from the opposing camps in England, the Rugby men who ran with the ball and the Etonians, who liked to kick it.

He had the idea, but not the formula, when he wrote to *Bell's Life* on 10 July 1858.

Soon after Wills, then the secretary of the Melbourne Cricket Club and a smart young man around town, was asked to referee an impromptu football match between Melbourne Grammar School and Scotch College at Jolimont. Like many of the rough-and-ready games that were played in Melbourne in the 1840s onwards it had few rules, with 80 men all hugger-mugger on the ball and trying to run with it, kick it, push it and maul it towards the team's goal.

In this game the goals were set about 500 metres apart, and three afternoons of tussle resulted in only one goal, to Scotch. Because of the unsatisfactory nature of the game it was called a draw.

But it had given Wills some ideas for his cricketers. He thought a new game could be built from the scramble of rugby, one that was new to Australia and had some new elements – something to make it more airborne, and less of a struggle on the ground.

Rules had to be formulated, rather than the vague rules agreed upon by opposing captains whenever a football game was got up.

CLUB NEWS 1858–1899

The beginning. Melbourne Cricket Club was formed in 1838.

At Jolimont. The Jolimont Oval, the MCG's present site, became the home ground for the MCC.

Paddock games. The Melbourne Football Club was formed in 1858 after members played scratch matches of football in the paddock outside the cricket ground under the direction of the MCC secretary Mr Tom Wills.

All white. The 'Invincible Whites', as Melbourne was known at the time due to their all-white outfits, beat all comers in 1864, including the new clubs of Carlton, South Melbourne and Royal Park.

Team limit. A new orderliness came into the game in 1869 with the introduction of a rule that teams be limited to 20 players per side.

Harrison retires. H. C. A. Harrison retired as captain and player of the MFC in 1872. He remained as an administrator of the club.

Now the Redlegs. The Redlegs were born in 1872 when a member of the club, Larry Bell, returned from a trip to England with four pairs of stockings, two red and two blue. He gave the red pairs to Melbourne, and the blue to Carlton. Melbourne added blue knickerbockers and sweater and a red cap. The red cap gave birth to the nickname 'The Fuchsias'.

On the outer. Due to the damage to the turf caused by football, the Melbourne Football Club was barred

1858 – 1899

Henry Harrison, as seen by Spooner.

A Redlegs leader

Henry Harrison had a big hand in formulating the refined rules for the game in 1860, first as captain of the Richmond Club and then in the same role at Melbourne.

Harrison also went to Geelong as captain for a year in 1862 and then returned to Melbourne, to skipper the Redlegs until his retirement from the game in 1872.

He brooked no nonsense, and his attitude finally cemented the bouncing the ball rule into the game, and thus prevented it from reverting to a rugby-style game.

Harrison's natural leadership took him into football administration with the Melbourne team and to vice-presidency of the Victorian Football Association when it was formed in 1877. When Melbourne became part of the newly formed Victorian Football League in 1897 Harrison switched with the club. He was the inaugural VFL chairman of Melbourne and stayed in the post for 10 years. A new stand was named after him in 1906, although it was more often referred to as the Smokers Stand.

Although Harrison was only falsely credited with having established the original rules of the game, he became widely known as 'the father of Australian Football'.

Melbourne plays Essendon, 2 July 1881.

First Premiership

The Melbourne team was the first official Premier team of the colony of Victoria, in the 1870 season, playing 12 matches, winning seven of them and drawing five. Melbourne kicked 21 goals for the season and had only one goal kicked against it. Other teams in the senior competition at the time were South Yarra, Richmond, Carlton, South Melbourne, Royal Park and Geelong.

Melbourne continued its dominant form, and won again in 1872 and 1876. It was a solidly performing team in 20 years as part of the Victorian Football Association, with two seconds against the all-conquering Essendon. Key players in Melbourne's VFA years were rover Fred McGinis, forward Dave Christie, ruckman Herb Fry and centreman A. W. 'Goosey' Lewis.

The Rules meeting

It was not until 17 May 1859 that a meeting to draw up rules for a new game was held, at a hotel in Wellington Parade. Wills was not the instigator, but an invited participant. William Hammersley of *Bell's Life*, James Boyne Thomson of the *Argus*, Thomas Smith of Scotch College and Wills were all members of the Melbourne Cricket Club, and now of the Melbourne Football Club, which was formed on May 14.

The first five rules set out the measurements of the ground, the distances between the four goal posts, defined a goal, and gave the captains the toss for ends, the losing side to kick off.

Rule 6 was the defining rule, from which the modern game of Australian Rules Football has evolved. It allowed for catching the ball directly from the foot, calling 'Mark' and being entitled to a free kick. Rule 7 banned hacking (kicking in the shins).

Rule 8 added another new twist to the varying rules of running that had applied to the old games. It allowed running with the ball if it was taken from a mark or on the hop (bounce), but that it could not be picked up from the ground. This was the origin of the bouncing rule that was later brought in and refined.

Rule 9 allowed the captain of either team to claim an infringement and a free kick, with the captains to be the sole judges of an infringement. Central umpires were not introduced until 1872.

1897 – 1899 HONOUR ROLL

Year	Pos	Leading Goalkicker	No.	Best & Fairest	Captain	Coach
1897	4th	Jack Leith	26		E. H. Sutton	
1898	6th	Chas. Young	21		E. H. Sutton	
1899	6th	Jack Leith	21		E. Sholl	

from using the MCG in 1873, and played outside the ground in the park at Jolimont.
On the G. The first match was played on the cricket ground proper in 1876, between the Melbourne Football Club and the Metropolitan Police Force.
Under lights. The first night match was at the MCG when Melbourne and Carlton met under lights on 13 August 1879. Gate takings were £500, but the match was marred by the bursting of the white ball, and the substitution of a brown one which was difficult to see.
Fire! Fire! The reversible stand, which allowed cricket to be watched at the Melbourne Cricket Ground, or football to be seen in the park at Jolimont and held 3000 people, was destroyed by fire in 1884. The loss was disastrous to the MFC's finances.
Cricketers help. Melbourne finished bottom of the ladder in 1889 and approached the MCC for help. The two clubs were merged with the MCC as the controlling body.
Going up. Melbourne finished fourth in 1892, with 10 wins.
Runners-up. The strong Melbourne side played in successive Grand Finals in 1893 and '94, but in both cases was beaten by Essendon, which boasted a brilliant player in Albert Thurgood.
VFL founder. Dissatisfaction with VFA resulted in the formation of the VFL in 1896, with Melbourne one of the founding clubs.
Stalwart. Follower Vic Cumberland made his debut for Melbourne in 1898 and went on to play 50 games.

MELBOURNE

Lowly Melbourne lifts Flag from Fitzroy in 1900

Melbourne finished the 1900 home-and-away season with only six wins, yet it won the Premiership Flag. Fitzroy had won the last two Premierships and finished the pre-final season at the top of the ladder.

The peculiar system under which the finals were played helped Melbourne to stay in the race. In the round robin of matches, Melbourne won its section, beat the other winner, Essendon, and earned the right to challenge the ladder leader Fitzroy.

Melbourne had won two of the three sectional matches, but lost to Collingwood. However, because Collingwood had lost to Geelong, Melbourne scraped in at the head of the section. The next big surprise was the win over the highly fancied Essendon combination, 7.3 (45) to 5.13 (43). And now they were up against the mighty Fitzroy, which was two games clear in the home-and-away series.

So confident was the Fitzroy club that it had arranged for maroon and blue decorated coaches, with the words 'Fitzroy Premiers 1900' emblazoned on the sides, to carry its team from the ground on a victory tour of Melbourne's streets.

There were 20,000 at the East Melbourne ground for the match. Melbourne, two points down at half-time, threw themselves into the game with renewed energy, and led by 13 points at the last change. The last quarter was desperate, but Melbourne's backline stood firm.

The team of 1900, captained by Dick Wardill, is photographed at the MCG.

Captains Wardill and Sloan toss.

1900–1918 HONOUR ROLL

Year	Pos	Leading Goalkicker	No.	Best & Fairest	Captain	Coach
1900	1st	Tom Ryan	24		Dick Wardill	
1901	5th	Frank Langley	17		Bill McClelland	
1902	4th	Jack Leith	26		Bill McClelland	
1903	7th	Vince Coutie	19		Bill McClelland	
1904	6th	Vince Coutie	39		Bill McClelland	
1905	8th	Harry Cordner	16		Frank Langley	
1906	8th	Basil Onyons	16		Arthur Sowden	
1907	7th	Jack Leith	21		Vince Coutie	Alec 'Joker' Hall
1908	8th	Vince Coutie	37		Hugh Purse	Alec 'Joker' Hall
1909	5th	Harry Brereton	34		Bernard Nolan	Alec 'Joker' Hall
1910	9th	S.J. Fairbairn	24		Vince Coutie	
1911	7th	Harry Brereton	46		Vince Coutie	
1912	6th	Harry Brereton	56		Alf George	Alec 'Joker' Hall
1913	9th	Mickey Maguire	13		Alf George	Alec 'Joker' Hall
1914	9th	Arthur Best	30		Len Incigneri	Alec 'Joker' Hall
1915	4th	Roy Park	35		Jack McKenzie	Jack McKenzie
1916–1918		Club in recess due to World War One				

CLUB NEWS 1900–1918

Loss to Saints. Melbourne is the first team to be beaten by St Kilda in 48 matches of VFL football. The teams actually drew, but St Kilda successfully claimed that Melbourne had scored a point well after the three-quarter time bell.

100 Games. C. H. Young was the first player to play 100 games for Melbourne, in Round 6, 1903. Young, who played in the 1900 Premiership side, made his debut with Melbourne in the League's opening year. He went on to play 128 games before he retired in 1904.

Over the border. Sydney got its first taste of VFL in 1904 when Melbourne played Essendon in a match at the Sydney Cricket Ground for Premiership points. Melbourne won 9.17 to 6.3.

Carnival for Jubilee. Joe Pearce and Hugh Purse were the Melbourne representatives in the Victorian team which celebrated the Jubilee Year of Australian football.

Theme song. 'It's a Grand Old Flag' had its first airing in 1912 when the team travelled to Tasmania on June 12 on a mid-season trip.

Players protest. Melbourne players decided to stage a protest at the committee's lack of support for a player who had been charged by the police for striking a Carlton player during a match (he was eventually fined five pounds) on 17 May 1913. They refused to strip for the game against Fitzroy. Fifteen minutes before the game the

1900–1918

The great rover Fred McGinis: poor eyesight forced his retirement.

Fred McGinis is the best player in the colony

Fred McGinis from Tasmania was named the finest player in the colony for the 1897 season. McGinis, a rover, was described as being determined in getting the ball, and cool and quick in passing it on to a team-mate. He was renowned for his splendid drop kicking and his half-distance passing.

In one game in 1895 McGinis was so outstanding that he was regarded as having won the game off his own boot, inflicting Essendon's fourth loss in five seasons. Melbourne won that match 5.9 to 1.1.

When McGinis first came to Melbourne, he intended to join fellow Tasmanians George Vautin and Colin Campbell at Essendon. The Dons did not think him good enough, but Melbourne had no hesitation in signing him.

Failing eyesight then forced his retirement and return to Tasmania in 1902 after 84 games. His eyesight continued to deteriorate and a benefit match was held to raise funds for him.

McGinis' personal calibre can be seen from an incident that took place in 1901. McGinis was injured by a kick to the ankle which laid bare the bone in a match. After the game Collingwood's Robert Rush went to the Melbourne rooms and apologised to McGinis for unwittingly causing the injury.

McGinis replied: 'That's all right, old chap. I know it was an accident.' As Rush was leaving McGinis remarked to his team-mates that Rush was 'one of the fairest men in football.'

Melbourne and the 'Doc'

W.C. McClelland, or 'Doc', as he was widely known, was a Melbourne supporter who fulfilled a childhood ambition when he made his debut with the Redlegs in 1897.

He was made captain in 1901 and on July 13, with the team undermanned due to injury, took on Essendon, with the words: 'We're a sorry lot of cripples, but we'll make them play.' Melbourne defeated Essendon 6.6 (42) to 4.9 (33).

At the end of 1904, he retired having played 75 games, to concentrate on medicine. In 1909 he was elected to the committee and in 1913 he became president of the Melbourne Football Club.

In 1926, he was elected president of the Victorian Football League, a position he held for the next 30 years.

Some things don't change

Noted in the *Argus* of 20 July 1908, by the sportswriter, Observer:

'There is one respect, however, in which Melbourne is consistent from year to year – it always gives more free kicks than it receives. On Saturday it gave South Melbourne 40 as against 32, and it had been noted that this goes on from year to year, though in a long experience of football it has never struck me that Melbourne is at all a rough team, or has less respect for the rules than other people.

'On starting Saturday's game, Hiskins, of South Melbourne, got two free kicks within two minutes, and from the second of them, scored a goal.'

---

club president, Dr McClelland, gave them an ultimatum that if they didn't play, they would never play League football again. They played.

Melbourne's gain. On 19 September 1914, after 51 consecutive defeats, University disbanded. There was pressure for the club to merge with the Melbourne Football Club, but officially the merger failed. Nevertheless, most of the University's best players, including Roy Park, Jack Brake, Claude Bryan, Jack Doubleday, R.H.M. Gibbs and Percy Rodriguez joined Melbourne.

Long wait. Melbourne beat Essendon, 10.12 (72) to 6.17 (53), for the first time in five years, on 12 June 1915, under new coach 'Dookie' McKenzie, formerly of Essendon. Melbourne players wore black armbands out of respect for Joe Pearce, the first Melbourne player to die in World War One.

Out of control. An all-out brawl broke out in the final quarter when Melbourne met St Kilda on 31 July 1915. The umpire, given to awarding technical free kicks (108 frees for the match) lost control and Melbourne's Park, Baquie and Brereton were all stretchered from the ground. Roy Park finished his fine career with a four-week suspension.

Honoured dead. Melbourne footballers who died in World War One were: Lieut. Clifford Burge, killed in France 1918; L/Cpl Frank Lugton, killed in France 1916; Lieut. Jack Doubleday, died on voyage 1918; Lieut. Percy Rodriguez, killed in France 1917; Cpl Joe Pearce, killed at Gallipoli 1915.

MELBOURNE

Bert Chadwick takes up the challenge

In 1919 Albert Chadwick, returned from war service in the Flying Corps, wandered across to Toorak Park to watch an Association match. He thought the standard of play was poor and said so, out loud.

'Do you think you could do better?', a bystander enquired.

'Well, possibly,' he replied quietly.

'Good,' his interrogator said, to the amusement of those around him. 'You're the very man we want. Come and have a run on Tuesday. See me, I'm the Prahran secretary.'

Thus challenged, he turned up on the following Tuesday, and one year later, after a successful season with Prahran as a ruckman and forward, joined Melbourne at the age of 22. He played with them until 1929.

In 1924, Chadwick was second in the inaugural Brownlow Medal. He became the club captain that year and in 1925, he took over as captain–coach.

Bert Chadwick played in 22 interstate matches, 10 as captain and coach of the Victorian team. In 1929, he was persuaded to join Hawthorn as captain–coach, but he returned to Melbourne the following year, as a member of the MCC committee. From 1951–62, he was chairman of the Melbourne Football Club.

When Bob Corbett was unable to take his place in the Grand Final of 1926 Brownlow Medallist Ivor Warne-Smith took over in the centre. The selectors then took a gamble and selected a new boy, F. S. 'Pop Vine, in the forward pocket. Vine went on to play 105 games for Melbourne and captained the team in 1932–33.

Bert Chadwick.

Big Bob Johnson: a great mark.

Another new boy in 1926 was Bob Johnson, who was described by Bert Chadwick as the best mark of all time. He starred in the Grand Final, winning best on the ground for his 6 goals 7 from centre half-forward.

Stan 'Bunny' Wittman, the great half-forward flanker, was another among the best on the ground. 'Bunny' took some persuading before he joined Melbourne in 1924. 'I'm satisfied I can hold my own in League company,' he said, 'and now I'm going back to Rosedale.' He made a sensational debut in the second match of 1924, combining brilliantly with Dick Taylor on the wing.

Bunny Wittman on the run.

1919 – 1926 HONOUR ROLL

Year	Pos	Leading Goalkicker	No.	Best & Fairest	Captain	Coach
1919	9th	George Haines	15		George Haines	George Haines
1920	8th	Harold Harker	23		George Haines	George Haines
1921	6th	Harold Harker	47		Percy Wilson	Percy Wilson
1922	6th	Harold Harker	47		Percy Wilson	Percy Wilson
1923	9th	Arthur Tulloh	31		Percy Wilson	Percy Wilson
1924	8th	Arthur Tulloh	24		Bert Chadwick	Gordon Rattray
1925	3rd	Harold Davie	56		Bert Chadwick	Bert Chadwick
1926	1st	Harold Moyes	55		Bert Chadwick	Bert Chadwick

CLUB NEWS 1919–1926

No wins. Melbourne returned to the League after a three-year break due to World War One. Although a young recruit, Ivor Warne-Smith, played a outstanding game mid-season in his debut, the club failed to win a game for the season.

Recruits. Percy Williams transferred from Collingwood in 1920 to become the new captain–coach and the new recruits included Bob Corbett, from Ballarat, Albert Chadwick, from Prahran Football Club and 'Brum' Streeter.

McGinis benefit. A match was played in Hobart on 30 April 1923 as a benefit for Fred McGinis, the former Melbourne champion, who was blind.

Good start. Melbourne finished second last in 1923, after starting the season with three great wins out of four. Meanwhile, over at Richmond, a player by the name of Frank 'Checker' Hughes retired.

Three Big V's. Melbourne's Bob Corbett, Bert Chadwick and George Haines represented Victoria in the 1923 game against South Australia.

Career starts. Jim Abernathy, a hardy half-back flanker, who went on to play 130 games, was one of the 1923 recruits, along with Jack Collins (125 games) whose son Geoff captained Melbourne in 1954.

Second bests. The 1924 inaugural Brownlow Medal went to Geelong's Edward 'Carji' Greeves, with Albert Chadwick just one vote behind.

1919–1926

The 1926 Melbourne team under the leadership of Chadwick and Warne-Smith.

Spirit of '26 brings a huge victory

The Redlegs took the Flag in 1926 in a 57-point win against Collingwood. The club song 'It's a Grand Old Flag' was revived in the celebration of the win and the great team spirit and courage in a tough season.

For Melbourne supporters the Premiership was a relief after a long drought since the club's only Flag in 1900. Seasons of team building finally paid off in 1925 when they finished the season in third place.

In the Grand Final Melbourne had two goals on the board in the first five minutes. Collingwood soon scored, but Melbourne continued to break away. At the first change the score was 4.5 to 1.1 in Melbourne's favour.

Collingwood fought back in the second quarter. The game was at its fiercest, and Bob Johnson was laid out, much to the anger of the Melbourne supporters. At half-time Melbourne's lead had been reduced to nine points.

In the third quarter, Melbourne took possession of the game and played brilliant football as Collingwood ran out of legs. Only poor kicking stopped Melbourne's winning margin reaching record proportions. The final score was 17.17 (119) to 9.8 (62).

The boys celebrated by cruising through the city in open cars, singing the almost forgotten song, 'It's a Grand Old Flag'. The evening finished with a victory toast at ruckman Hughie Dunbar's milk bar in Bentleigh.

> **It's a Grand Old Flag**
> It's a grand old flag, it's a high flying flag,
> It's the emblem for me and for you.
> It's the emblem of the team we love,
> The team of the Red and the Blue.
> Every heart beats true, for the Red and the Blue,
> and we sing this song to you.
> Should old acquaintance be forgot,
> Keep your eye on the Red and the Blue.

Veneration for the Flag: Melbourne officials at the raising by H. C. A. Harrison.

The spirit of Bob Corbett

No one displayed the spirit of '26 more than the champion centreman, Bob Corbett. In the Preliminary Final against Essendon he was king hit from behind while leaving the ground at half-time and his jaw was broken. This meant that Melbourne, who were in control of the game up to this point, had to continue the game with 17 men.

The second half of the game was a gruelling effort on the part of the Redlegs and the lead dwindled to a few points. Then in the final minutes of the game Corbett, his head swathed in bandages, defied the club doctor's instructions and ran down the race and onto the field to an enormous roar of support from the crowd. 'I just sneaked out to help my side,' he said later.

His team-mates rallied. Although Corbett was in no condition to contribute to the game, his presence and the spirit he showed contributed to Melbourne holding on for a three-point win. Melbourne had won the right to contest the Grand Final.

The 'Corbett incident', as it quickly became known, was influential in bringing about the VFL's introduction of a substitute player (19th man) into the game in 1930.

Corbett was recruited from Ballarat in 1920 and made the State side in his first year. He wanted to go home in 1921 but Melbourne persuaded him to stay, and he played 161 games in 10 seasons.

Chadwick leads. Albert Chadwick was appointed captain and coach in 1925 and Melbourne recorded 13 wins for the season, finishing third. The club benefited from the return of champion Ivor Warne-Smith who went on to play 146 games and win two Brownlows – the first in 1926.

Partisans. MCC members were criticised in the press on 13 June 1925, for going beyond the bounds of decency in their support for the Redlegs. The members assumed the Melbourne champion Dick Taylor had been unfairly dealt with by a Fitzroy player, and cheered later in the game when the Fitzroy player was felled – fairly, of course. Their behaviour was described by an onlooker as being 'of 'a deplorably low level'.

Wrong club. Melbourne and Victorian wingman Gerald Donnelly had his playing permit cancelled for the rest of the season on 6 August 1925 when the League Investigations Committee ruled that he was residentially bound to North Melbourne.

A big haul. Full-forward Harry Davie kicked 13 goals, eight of them in the final quarter, when Melbourne 18.14 (122) thrashed Carlton 6.9 (45) on 22 August 1925.

Old supporter. Melbourne's Grand Final win in 1926 was watched by 96-year-old H. C. A. Harrison.

Triple-pronged. Three Melbourne players kicked 50 goals in the season of 1926: Harold Moyes, 55, Harry Davie, 50 and Bob Johnson, 50. It was Johnson's first season.

MELBOURNE

'Checker' Hughes; invented Demons.

The Demons are born

Frank 'Checker' Hughes joined the Demons as coach in 1933. He had played in two Premierships with Richmond, coached Tasmania and coached Richmond to a Flag in 1932. At his first Melbourne training session, he wore his Richmond guernsey: 'I wanted to stand out, and subconsciously, I wanted them to remember that I, too, had done the things that I was going to ask them to do.' He had done the things, on the field and off, with 87 games as a rover of great skill and with a lighting stab pass, as a soldier who won the DCM and as a Flag-winning coach.

Hughes axed 13 players from the Melbourne list. He set about training the players harder than they'd ever been trained before. He told the players after a poor period of play. 'You are playing like a lot of flowers. Lift your heads and play like Demons.' So the mighty Demons were born.

Hughes employed simple and workable team tactics and showed he could make a great team out of good players, rather then champion individuals. He ruled with a rod of iron in his coaching stints from 1933 to 1941 and from 1945 to 1948.

One man is balanced and has his eye on the ball – Ivor Warne-Smith.

One of Melbourne's finest – Ivor Warne-Smith

Dual Brownlow Medallist Ivor Warne-Smith was described by the Victorian selector George Cathie in 1949 as the most perfect footballer to play between the wars. Tall, strong and wiry, he was a superb mark and a long kick and had the knack of breaking through packs and into damaging space. He had an air of maturity and quiet confidence, and did everything with polish, handballing with precision and kicking equally well with both feet.

Originally from Sydney, he was a fine schoolboy footballer, cricketer and athlete at Wesley College before he enlisted with the army at the age of 17 and served in Gallipoli and France.

He played a season with Melbourne in 1919 before going to Latrobe, on the north-coast of Tasmania, to become an apple farmer. After a successful stint in Tasmanian football, he was approached to play with Richmond, but Melbourne refused to clear him and he returned to the team in 1925 at the age of 27.

Usually a defender, Warne-Smith was also a formidable ruckman and played plenty of games from the centre and as a forward in his 146-game career.

He was the first player to win the Brownlow Medal twice: first in Melbourne's Premiership year in 1926, when he received a record nine first votes, and again in 1928. He was captain–coach from 1928–31, and in 1932 came out of retirement to play a few games while coaching the team.

The veteran umpire Bob Scott said of Warne-Smith in 1936: 'He had brains, ability and temperament to a degree found in few footballers.'

Warne-Smith went on to serve on the MCC and Melbourne Football Club committees, and worked with coach Norm Smith in the 1950s as Chairman of Selectors, building the winning sides of Melbourne's finest era.

CLUB NEWS 1927–1938

A heart-stopper. Melbourne narrowly missed out against Collingwood at the MCG on 10 July 1927. The Redlegs fought back after trailing by three goals, but a kick from Collingwood rover Bill Libbis put the final score at 11.13 (79) to Melbourne's 10.12 (72). Melbourne went on to narrowly miss the 1927 finals – illness and injuries to key players had dogged the team all season.

Cumberland killed. Harry (Vic) Cumberland, the football great who began his career with Melbourne, was killed in a car accident in 1927.

Dangerous dogs. Bert Chadwick and Jack Collins were both seriously injured and other players received minor injuries when they were struck by an aluminium knee shield worn by a Footscray player on 30 June 1928. The club was told no rules existed to deal with the situation and thus the shield was legal.

Hero to villain. In 1928 Melbourne finished third and met Collingwood in the Semi-final. Collingwood was leading 9.8 to 4.8 at the beginning of the final quarter and Melbourne kept them scoreless. Rover Eddie McConville scored with only seconds to go and the game ended in a draw. In the replay McConville broke away in front of goal with only seconds to go, but this time he scored a behind and Melbourne was defeated by four points.

Long service. Wingman Dick Taylor was presented with a canteen of cut-

1927–1938

Norm Smith. Alan La Fontaine. Percy Beames. Colin Niven. Lewis, Reiffel and Chandler.

The new boys

Alan La Fontaine. A champion full-forward with University when he was recruited to Melbourne in 1934, he played three games as full-forward before he found his natural position in the centre. He retired in 1943 to go to war and played again in 1945, taking his games total to 171. He was club champion in 1935 and '36, and again in 1941 and '42. He captained Melbourne from 1936–41 and coached from 1949–51.

Norm Smith was the heart and soul of Melbourne for over 30 years. The slender, undemonstrative redhead joined Melbourne's forward line in 1935. Smith played 210 games for Melbourne and kicked 546 goals. He was leading VFL goalkicker in 1941 with 89 goals and club captain from 1945–47. He later coached the team to six Premierships.

Percy Beames arrived at Melbourne in 1931, a successful schoolboy sportsman from Ballarat, and went on to play 213 games, including three Grand Finals, before his retirement in 1944. He was a valuable rover and a prolific goalkicker and he was captain–coach from 1942–44. He also played Sheffield Shield cricket, and later was the *Age*'s senior football and cricket writer. Rucking to Beames was former Fitzroy star **Colin Niven**, who made such an impression he captained the side in 1934–35. Another ruck combination was headed by the giant John Lewis, with Bert Chandler and rover Lou Reiffel.

Jack Mueller, (left), one of Melbourne's finest players, was recruited from Echuca in 1934 at the age of 18. His career was almost finished in his first year when he lost the two middle fingers on his right hand in a carton-making machine at work, but he came back in 1935 wearing a protective glove, and his marking was as reliable as ever. Mueller was a solid, dependable, unflashy player, noted for his marking ability under all conditions. The *Herald*'s Alf Brown described him as 'one of the greatest all-rounders ever'. He also declared him 'the greatest big occasion player of all time.' He played in six Melbourne Premiership teams, helping to win four VFL Grand Finals and two Seconds Flags.

Maurie Gibb. A Rosedale boy, like 'Bunny' Wittman, Gibb was rejected by Carlton before Melbourne took him up in 1934. He was an old-fashioned half-forward, skilled and elusive and capable of turning a game with a purple patch of football. In 1935 he twice kicked nine goals in a game. He played in the Melbourne Premiership teams of 1940 and 1941.

1927–1938 HONOUR ROLL

Year	Pos	Leading Goalkicker	No.	Best & Fairest	Captain	Coach
1927	5th	Harold Davie	40		Bert Chadwick	Bert Chadwick
1928	3rd	Bob Johnson	55		Ivor Warne-Smith	Ivor Warne-Smith
1929	5th	Dick Taylor	30		Ivor Warne-Smith	Ivor Warne-Smith
1930	5th	George Margitich	73		Ivor Warne-Smith	Ivor Warne-Smith
1931	8th	George Margitich	66		Ivor Warne-Smith	Ivor Warne-Smith
1932	9th	George Margitich	60		F.S. 'Pop' Vine	Ivor Warne-Smith
1933	10th	Bob Johnson	62		F.S. 'Pop' Vine	'Checker' Hughes
1934	6th	Jack Mueller	52		Colin Niven	'Checker' Hughes
1935	6th	Maurie Gibb	59	Alan La Fontaine	Colin Niven	'Checker' Hughes
1936	3rd	Ted Glass	56	Alan La Fontaine	Alan La Fontaine	'Checker' Hughes
1937	3rd	Norm Smith	45	Jack Mueller	Alan La Fontaine	'Checker' Hughes
1938	5th	Norm Smith	80	Norm Smith	Alan La Fontaine	'Checker' Hughes

lery in 1928 in recognition of his playing 100 games in succession. He played another 27 before missing a game due to injury.

New secretary. Percy Page left the Richmond club to become the new MFC secretary. The previous incumbent, Andrew Manzie, had a lengthy term – from 1912 until 1931. Page was instrumental in the appointment of another former Richmondite, coach Frank 'Checker' Hughes.

Great start. Melbourne won the first six games in 1937, snatching three time-on goals to win against St Kilda, 12.23 (95) to 12.18 (90) in round four, despite being a man short. They finished second but fell in the finals, first to Geelong in the highest scoring match in League history, 16.17 (113) to 19.11 (125), and then to Collingwood.

Reshuffle. Ivor Warne-Smith replaced Bert Chadwick as captain–coach in 1928, but Chadwick remains as vice-captain. Melbourne reaches the Four only to finish third, but has Warne-Smith's Brownlow to celebrate.

New Chairman. Joe Blair takes over as Chairman of the Melbourne Football Club in 1929.

New coach. Ivor Warne-Smith retires in 1932 but is retained as coach. His efforts fail to arrest the slide and Melbourne finishes ninth.

On the rise. Melbourne showed significant improvement in 1934 to finish in sixth position. Colin Niven performed strongly in the ruck, and replaced the popular F.S. 'Pop' Vine as captain.

MELBOURNE

The talented 1939 team, captained by Alan La Fontaine and coached by 'Checker' Hughes.

Rover Ron Barassi Snr gets his kick.

A hat-trick of Premierships

1939 – success at last

A great year, with Melbourne finishing on top of the ladder, on percentage from Collingwood. Records were broken during the season, with the team winning 15 of the 18 games and kicking 100 points or more in each win, thus breaking Collingwood's record of 13 games in a season of 100 points. Nine successive 100-point wins beat Geelong's record of seven 100-point scores in a row. On September 30, Frank 'Checker' Hughes and the club secretary Percy Page's years of team-building and recruiting finally paid off with Melbourne's first Premiership since 1926.

The Red Demons (as they were called that year) met Collingwood twice in the finals, first in the Second Semi when they defeated them by 14 points, and then again in the Grand Final, when they won in the new Grand Final record score of 21.22 (148) to 14.11 (95) in front of a crowd of 78,110.

Melbourne made a fine comeback in the third quarter of the Second Semi-final, when they returned from being down 13 points and kicked 5.1 to 2.4. In the final quarter Melbourne kicked another five goals and they were easing up on the siren.

In the Grand Final the Demons were again trailing at half-time, by four points this time, but within the first 10 minutes of the third term they kicked three goals. In the first half a Melbourne goal was disallowed after umpire Coward went down in a pack. He was unable to give the all-clear to a goal kicked by Percy Beames and left the ground with a dislocated elbow.

Melbourne left Collingwood standing still in the second half of the game. Among the best on the ground for the Demons were 'Bluey' Truscott, who was declared by the *Age* as unbeatable at half-forward, half-back Frank Roberts, rover Percy Beames, wingman Sid Anderson and Ray Wartman, Norm Smith and Jack Mueller.

1940 – tactics pay off

The shrewd 'Checker' Hughes managed to snatch the 1940 Premiership Flag from his old team, Richmond, who were favourites to win. He identified the danger players in the Tigers' team and virtually tagged them out of the game. Richmond's Jack Dyer had wiped out Norm Smith in the Semi-final and Jack O'Keefe was given the job of 'shadowing' him. Consequently, Dyer had a quiet day, Norm Smith kicked seven goals in the wet and Melbourne defeated Richmond, 15.7 (107) to 10.8 (68). The nineteenth man, Ron Barassi, who had enlisted on July 15 and was due to embark with the 7th Division on October 18, replaced Ray Wartman who was injured in the first quarter. New boy Fred Fanning played in the forward pocket.

1939–1941 HONOUR ROLL

Year	Pos	Leading Goalkicker	No.	Best & Fairest	Captain	Coach
1939	1st	Norm Smith	54	Jack Mueller	Alan La Fontaine	'Checker' Hughes
1940	1st	Norm Smith	86	Ron Baggott	Alan La Fontaine	'Checker' Hughes
1941	1st	Norm Smith	88	Alan La Fontaine	Alan La Fontaine	'Checker' Hughes

CLUB NEWS 1939–1941

Thirty-niners. New boys in 1939 included rover Alby Rodda, Sid Anderson and Harold Ball. Ball won the club's Best First-Year Player trophy.

A new name. The Demons had another temporary name change in 1939 when they were known as the 'Red Demons' for a while.

Speed up. The abolition of the drop-ping-the-ball rule, which forced players to kick or handpass when tackled, was credited with speeding up the game In 1939 and was considered responsible for the huge aggregate scores recorded. On May 1 Melbourne kicked 21.15 (141) to defeat Essendon 19.21 (135) by one kick.

Magpies downed. Melbourne easily defeated Collingwood in Round 10 of 1939, 22.22 (154) to 8.12 (60).

Rained out. All VFL matches were postponed on 26 August 1939 because the grounds were under water, and played on September 2, the day World War Two was declared.

Big drop. Fred Fanning kicked a 105.50 metre drop kick in the 1939 Reserves Grand Final when Melbourne defeated Richmond.

Bentleigh connection. The Demons celebrated the 1939 Grand Final win with a quiet victory celebration drink at Dunbar's milk bar in Bentleigh.

A good crop. New boys for 1940 included John Atkins, Adrian Dullard, Fred Fanning and Colin McLean, who won the Best First-Year Player trophy.

Shameful score. Melbourne kicked a

1939 – 1941

New forward champion Fred Fanning.

The importance of Jack Mueller to Melbourne is very evident in this cartoon.

1941 - makeshift team

The Premiership hat-trick was completed on September 27 when Melbourne defeated Essendon in the 1941 Grand Final, 19.13 (127) to 13.20 (98) before a crowd of 79,687. The day was cloudy and humid with a gusty north wind which the Demons handled better than their opponents.

The team had finished second on the ladder to Carlton, whom they defeated convincingly in the Second Semi-final. Melbourne's Grand Final win was all the more remarkable because 12 of the team's senior-list players were unavailable on the day, due to military duties or injury. W. S. 'Pop' Heal, on leave from the Navy, played for Melbourne and then for Perth, which won the WA Grand Final the following week.

Best for Melbourne were backman Wally Lock, rover Percy Beames, wingman Stan Heal, forward Jack Mueller, ruckman Ted Cordner, defender Garry Daly, wingman Sid Anderson and centreman Alan La Fontaine. Norm Smith kicked four goals, which took his total for the season to 89 and put him at the head of the 1941 goalkicking list.

Smith & Mueller lead the Melbourne band

The success of the Melbourne teams from 1939–41 and again in 1948 was due in no small part to the revolutionary - and match-winning - forward system devised by the coach, Frank 'Checker' Hughes. It revolved around Smith – of whom team-mate Jim Abernethy said: 'I have never seen a more unselfish player' – and the remarkable Jack Mueller.

In Hughes' own words: 'When Smithy led out, Ron Baggott, centre half-forward, one of those loosely put together players who was always hard to beat, ran in. Smithy sometimes took the pass, but a quick hand pass to the running Baggott created more trouble for the defenders.

'Then we played a trump card by keeping Jack Mueller hanging around the goal square. One of the best marks in the game, he was a problem child in himself. No defender could leave him for a second.

'Two brilliant rovers in Beames and Rodda were always on the move, and if that was not sufficient we had that amazing fellow Maurie Gibb doing the cleverest things on the half-forward flank. On the other half-forward wing was that red-headed bullet, 'Bluey' Truscott. Smith, who was football brains from his thatch to his toes, was in clover.

'La Fontaine, our centre, diverted play to Gibb's flank or to Truscott, or maybe he drove direct to the fast-moving Smith, or again he might ignore the Smith lead and pass to Baggott, who would have doubled around just behind centre half-forward.

'Smith became a genius at handball. He flipped the ball like a flash to the man running in, and then never forgot to block. The things that fellow did amazed me. He was different from the others; he made a team work around him. Others made the team work for them. He was a real master at creating play.'

record of 34 behinds when they defeated North Melbourne on 8 June 1940, 12.34 (106) to 8.1 (49). Later in the year in Round 17, Melbourne kicked a record score on Hawthorn, 26.20 (176) to 8.14 (62).

Vital decision. On the King's Birthday game between Melbourne and Fitzroy Keith Forbes of Fitzroy ran into an open goal to put Fitzroy a goal up. The umpire ruled he had run too far without bouncing the ball, and gave a free kick to Melbourne. The Demons managed to get the ball into their forward line and rush two points. Fitzroy supporters were outraged.

Cordner on deck. New boys for 1941 included the first of the Cordner brothers, Edward 'Ted' Cordner, who was awarded the Best First-Year Player trophy, and George 'Pop' Heal, a wingman from Western Australia who was serving in the Forces and made a fine debut in a July game v Essendon.

War years. The MFC social committee had a nominal function only in 1941, as it was considered 'inadvisable to undertake the usual social program'.

Red and blue rules, OK? In 1941, the Premiers of all five major Australian rules competitions wore the red and the blue: Melbourne, Port Melbourne (captained by Tommy Lahiff), Norwood, West Perth and North Hobart.

Death at Tobruk. Ronald James Barassi died in hospital in Tobruk on 31 July 1941. The Last Post was played and black armbands were worn as a mark of respect at the August 16 game against Collingwood.

MELBOURNE

'Bluey' Truscott makes an appearance for Melbourne while on leave from the RAAF.

Squadron Leader Keith 'Bluey' Truscott DFC and Bar, the ace Australian fighter pilot.

helped Mrs Blair, the wife of the chairman of the MCC football club, unfurl the 1941 Premiership Flag before the game. It was Truscott's first game since the 1940 Grand Final. Melbourne, with a weakened team, made a fight of it for three quarters but went down 18.9 (117) to 30.16 (196). More importantly though, was the crowd's reaction to 'Bluey' Truscott. Most of the crowd of 20,000 at the ground stood to honour him and they cheered with delight when Truscott, although far from fit, swooped on a mark dropped (on purpose perhaps) by Richmond captain Jack Dyer and put it through for a goal.

Not long after the game, Truscott was asked by his old Melbourne High School headmaster, the Test cricketer Bill Woodfull, how he liked playing League football again. 'Not for me,' he replied. 'Too dangerous.'

In March the following year, Australia was shocked to hear the news that 'Bluey' Truscott had died in a target practice accident at Exmouth, Western Australia. He was killed instantly when his propeller clipped the water as he flew his fighter underneath an incoming 'target' Catalina.

In 1943, 'Checker' Hughes donated the Keith 'Bluey' Truscott Memorial Trophy in honour of the dead hero. The Truscott shield is awarded to the club champion each season. The first, in 1943, was awarded to Don Cordner.

The Legacy of 'Bluey' Truscott

The name and deeds of Squadron Leader Keith 'Bluey' Truscott, DFC and Bar, are remembered every year with the awarding of Melbourne's Best and Fairest trophy, the Truscott Shield. Truscott was a World War Two flying ace, but he had also been a hero on the football field, playing on the half-forward flank in 1939 and 1940 Premiership teams. He was best afield in '39, using his speed, bulk and strength in gathering a string of possessions. Truscott, who had learned to fly before the war, joined the RAAF in 1940 and served first in Britain where he took part in the Battle of Britain, and later in the Battle of Milne Bay. His exploits included having to 'ditch' his plane in the English Channel after an encounter with a German Messerschmidt fighter. His mascot, painted on his planes, was a small 'Red Demon'.

In 1942 on a visit home en route to the Pacific, he accepted an invitation to captain the Demons in a match against Richmond on May 16. He wore the No. 1 jersey for the occasion. The game was played at Punt Road (the Melbourne home ground for the season, as the forces had taken over the MCG) and Mrs Truscott, 'Bluey's' mother,

CLUB NEWS 1942–1944

Beames takes over. Percy Beames took on the role of captain–coach from Alan La Fontaine and 'Checker Hughes' who retired. Beames retired at the end of the 1944 season.

Uncle Sam takes over. Melbourne lost the MCG on 7 April 1942 and moved to Punt Road to play for the duration of the war. The club trained at the Albert Ground. The MCG became Camp Murphy, accommodating 14,000, when the United States Airforce pitched tents on the ground and moved into the grandstands.

A Demon in disguise. Seen among the Tigers at training in May 1942 was Demon Jack Mueller (wearing his Victorian jumper), who was training 'away' by agreement.

A win and a loss to the services. Alan La Fontaine and Jack Mueller played in the Combined Services League team which lost to Fitzroy/Richmond, 20.13 (133) to 19.11 (125) on 12 July 1942 in front of 25,000, raising 850 pounds for Patriotic Funds. Norm Smith was part of a League side chosen by the Lord Mayor of Melbourne, Sir Frank Beaurepaire, which played a Combined Services team, which again included Mueller and La Fontaine, in September. This time the Services team won, 15.7 (107) to 14.18 (102).

No Brownlow for the duration. The awarding of the Brownlow Medal was suspended from 1942–45.

And then there were three. A third

1942 – 1944

Melbourne at war

VFL football continued throughout the war though many of the members of pre-war teams were scattered to the far corners of the globe. Players whose military training was based within Victoria were allowed to continue to play, though last-minute changes to teams were frequent, due to players being unable to obtain leave from the camps.

The Melbourne 1939 and 1940 Premiership teams were virtually broken up. Many entered the armed services, and six Melbourne players – Keith Truscott, Noel Ellis, Sydney Anderson, John Atkins, Ronald James Barassi and Harold Ball – were killed.

The Truscott Trophy for Best and Fairest player, donated by 'Checker' Hughes.

'The Last Post' sounds at the MCG as the Demons remember fallen comrade, Ron Barassi.

1942 – 1944 HONOUR ROLL

Year	Pos	Leading Goalkicker	No.	Best & Fairest	Captain	Coach
1942	8th	Fred Fanning	37	Alan La Fontaine	Percy Beames	Percy Beams
1943	7th	Fred Fanning	62	Don Cordner	Percy Beames	Percy Beames
1944	8th	Fred Fanning	87	Norm Smith	Percy Beames	Percy Beames

Lest we forget

Ronald James Barassi

The first of Melbourne players killed in World War Two was the rover Ronald James Barassi, only 27 years old, who died on 31 July 1941, from wounds sustained while fighting for the AIF in Tobruk.

Barassi played 55 games and kicked 84 goals with Melbourne. He was recruited from Castlemaine in 1936 and he came on at quarter time to be a part of the 1940 Premiership team.

Harold Ball

Harold Ball, who played in the ruck in Melbourne's 1939 and 1940 Premiership teams, was posted missing after the Fall of Singapore, and was later reported to have been killed in battle in Malaya. Ball won the club's Best First-Year Player trophy in 1939 and Melbourne's annual trophy for their best first-year player is now named the Harold Ball Trophy.

Noel Ellis

Ellis made his debut with Melbourne in 1940 and played only two games in 1941 before joining the AIF. He was killed in a shooting accident on 6 July 1942 while undergoing officers' training in Queensland.

Sydney Anderson

Syd Anderson joined the Club in 1939 and quickly became a regular on the wing. He played in the Premiership teams of 1939, 1940 and 1941 and joined the RAAF in 1941. He became an officer and a navigator and was shot down in Wewak in May 1944.

John Atkins

John Atkins played four promising games in 1940, and left the club to enlist in the Navy. He saw service on the *Hobart* in the Mediterranean in 1941, and was killed when the *Perth* was torpedoed on 1 March 1942.

Cordner was cleared to Melbourne on 20 May 1943. Nineteen-year-old Denis, who had been in the Navy, played with the Melbourne Grammar team in 1941. **Another new boy for 1943.** Doug Heywood, former Scotch College and University half-forward, was rushed into the side for the 1943 Preliminary Final, while on leave from the Air Force. **La Fontaine spills the beans.** Alan La Fontaine spoke of retiring when he was interviewed in April by Hec de Lacy of the *Sporting Globe*, 'up north' in April 1943. He also told him what he thought of the Melbourne side he joined in 1934. 'When I went to Melbourne – I think our coach 'Checker' Hughes would agree – we had a shocking side. In fact in my first game at Richmond I was all set to gather a 'sitter', when one of my own men crashed into me and – well, there you are.' (Melbourne persuaded him not to retire and he played 14 games in 1945.) **Just one of those years!** At the beginning of the 1944 season, 22 of the 1943 season's players were unavailable. The 1944 Annual Report spelt it out: 'Notably amongst these were Ted and Denis Cordner and Bob Stone (all with the RAN), Jack Dalton, Adrian Dullard, Maurie Gibb, Don Hooper, Jack Mueller and Ron White (all AIF), Tom Ferguson, Alby Rodda and Ralph Shalless (with the RAAF), and Rich Emselle, Don Hewson and Keith Molloy (knee injuries).' **Fred's on target.** Fred Fanning won 1944 VFL Goalkicker of the Year with 87 goals.

MELBOURNE

The Cordner dynasty

When 18-year-old Denis Cordner ran on to the ground in June 1943 and won the first kick of the game, he joined his two brothers, Ted, 24 and Don, 21, as members of the Demons. Later in the game, in which Melbourne was soundly beaten by Richmond, he was cleaned up by Richmond's Jack Dyer. A long and worthy career had truly begun.

There were four Cordner brothers. Don, Denis, Ted and John were the sons of Edward Cordner (who had played with University) and nephews of Harry, who had played for Melbourne and University.

The young Cordners were in the same mould as their father and uncle. Tall, strong, handsome and fair-haired, they played the game with fairness and decency. Ted joined Melbourne in 1941. His football career was interrupted when he joined the Navy as a doctor in 1943, but he is remembered as a fine defender. Don, who played his first game of senior football in a 1941 Semi-final against Carlton, was a spectacular mark. He won the Brownlow Medal in 1946.

Denis served in the Navy and played three years in the amateurs before he reappeared as centre half-back for Melbourne, in the 1948 Grand Final. He went on to play 152 games. He captained the team from 1951–53 and retired in 1956. Courage, stamina and teamwork characterised his game, and he was one of the finest wet-weather players among the big-men of his era. Ted and Don followed their father and uncle into medicine.

Cordner family (clockwise) Denis, father Edward Cordner, Ted, John and Don.

Above: Ted Cordner congratulated brother Don on his Brownlow Medal win.
Left: Denis rucks while Ted waits down.

Denis and the youngest brother, John, studied science. John played six games for the club in 1951, and chose to go to England to further his career in nuclear science.

Ted Cordner's son David continued the family tradition and played 53 games for Melbourne between 1983–87, mainly as a forward. He had the Cordner looks and athleticism, but his career was dogged by injury.

Ted Cordner, star centre half-back.

CLUB NEWS 1945–1951

Checker's back. 'Checker' Hughes returned to the team as coach after a three-year absence, and Norm Smith took on the position of captain, with Don Cordner as vice-captain.

Fanning tops goalkickers. Fred Fanning won the VFL 1945 goalkicking award with 67 goals, along with the Bluey Truscott Memorial Cup and the MCC Trophy for the Best and Fairest Player. Norm Smith won the trophy for the most unselfish player.

Down to the Dons. Melbourne made it to the four from ninth position mid-season by winning 10 of their last 11 games. They made it through to the Grand Final, losing to Essendon, 22.18 (150) to 13.9 (87). The game was won in the third quarter when Essendon kicked a devastating 11.8 to 1.1.

Brownlow to Cordner. Don Cordner won the 1946 Brownlow Medal. In his six seasons from his debut in the Semi-final game of 1941, he had only missed three games. Though Cordner won the club's trophy for the Most Brilliant Player in 1946, he missed out on the Keith 'Bluey' Truscott Memorial Trophy for the Best and Fairest – that went to Jack Mueller in his 13th year with the club.

Experience pays. Norm Smith, in his 13th year with the Demons, was appointed captain for 1947, with Jack Mueller (in his 14th) as vice-captain.

Fanning kicks on. A VFL record was broken when Fred Fanning kicked 18 goals against St Kilda in the final

1945–1951

Elation: Noel McMahen and team-mates after the victory.

Don Cordner leads the team out.

1948 win after drawn Grand Final

A crowd of 85,658 saw Melbourne and Essendon make history in the VFL's first drawn Grand Final on 2 October 1948, with the score of Essendon 7.27 (69) to Melbourne, 10.9 (69).

Both teams threw away opportunities, Essendon with its atrocious scoring, and Melbourne when they narrowly failed to score in the last 60 seconds of the game.

Melbourne clearly missed half-forward flanker, Bob McKenzie, who withdrew on the morning of the game due to injury.

There were a few surprises in Melbourne's finals team. The selectors had brought back Jack Mueller, the 34-year-old captain–coach of the Melbourne Seconds, for the Preliminary Final against Collingwood. He combined superbly with his old partner Norm Smith, and kicked 8 goals. He lined up in the forward pocket in the Grand Final team, while at centre half-back was captain Don Cordner's brother, Denis, who had one Melbourne game to his name back in 1943.

The rematch the following week saw Melbourne easily eclipse Essendon. In a brilliant first term, the Demons scored 6.2 to 3 behinds. It was inspired football and a remarkable victory, which, Percy Beames wrote in the *Age*, 'will go down in history as the 'Checker' Hughes Premiership.'

It was a fitting tribute to Hughes that the dynamic duo of Mueller and Smith played a huge part in the finals' victories, being responsible for 28 goals in the three games.

But there were many other fine players for Melbourne. Shane McGrath was solid as usual at full-back, restricting the Essendon star Bill Brittingham. The blond wingman Max Spittle continually flashed into the play, while George Bickford was poised and creative in the centre. As well as Mueller and Smith, Melbourne had the high-marking Lance Arnold at centre half-forward and a champion flanker in Bobby McKenzie.

That last Grand Final game marked the end of an era. It was the last game for the coach, Hughes, and for Norm Smith, who took up a position as captain–coach with Fitzroy in 1949.

1945–1951 HONOUR ROLL

Year	Pos	Leading Goalkicker	No.	Best & Fairest	Captain	Coach
1945	9th	Fred Fanning	67	Fred Fanning	Norm Smith	'Checker' Hughes
1946	2nd	Jack Mueller	58	Jack Mueller	Norm Smith	'Checker' Hughes
1947	6th	Fred Fanning	97	Wally Lock	Norm Smith	'Checker' Hughes
1948	1st	Lance Arnold	41	Alby Rodda	Don Cordner	'Checker' Hughes
1949	5th	Bob McKenzie	46	Len Dockett	Don Cordner	Alan La Fontaine
1950	4th	Denis Cordner	36	Denis Cordner	Shane McGrath	Alan La Fontaine
1951	12th	Bob McKenzie	40	Noel McMahen	Denis Cordner	Alan La Fontaine

game of the 1947 season. It brought his annual total to 97, 20 goals clear of his nearest rival, and for the third year in a row he took out the VFL goalkicking award. Though only 25, he chose to retire and coach Hamilton.

Smith out. Norm Smith was suspended for four weeks on 1 June 1948 in his 200th game for abusing an umpire. He told the tribunal he said: 'Don't be silly.'

Record win. In the 1948 Preliminary Final against Collingwood, Melbourne kicked an all-time record score for finals matches, 25.16 (166) to Collingwood, 15.11 (101).

Following in the footsteps. Alan La Fontaine took over as non-playing coach in 1949.

Beyond the call of duty. Norm Smith and Jack Mueller were awarded a Trophy for Special Service in the Final Series in 1948.

One game out of the four. Melbourne played Essendon for a position in the four on 20 August 1949 and missed out. Essendon went on to win the 1949 Premiership. Melbourne's Second 18 won the VFL Seconds' Premiership.

Jack plays on. Jack Mueller played his 216th game, passing Percy Beames' club record of 213 and Norm Smith's 210. He retired in 1950.

Another Cordner win. Denis Cordner won the 1950 Keith 'Bluey' Truscott Memorial Trophy and Noel McMahen won the Most Improved Player Trophy.

Checker and the Vics. 'Checker' Hughes coached the 1950 Victorian side.

MELBOURNE

The Demons' glory years

Denis Cordner in the ruck.

1955 Demon dashers

Melbourne went into 1955 as runners-up in the previous year, determined to go one better. Ten successive wins at the start of the season gave the supporters reason to hope and Melbourne finished on top with 15 wins. In the Second Semi-final against Collingwood, the rover Stuart Spencer made light of the wet and boggy conditions, scoring five of Melbourne's eight goals to be the best on the ground. Melbourne won the tight encounter 8.8 (56) to 6.9 (43).

The weather was kinder for the Grand Final, when Melbourne faced Collingwood once again. The Demons won, 8.16 (64) to 5.6 (36) before a crowd of 88,053. Melbourne could have had the game won in the second term, but for poor kicking. Ten shots for goal resulted in 1.7. At the start of the final quarter, Collingwood kicked a goal to reduce the deficit to 1 point, but it was their last scoring shot for the day. The Demons took control and added 4.3 to win the 1955 Flag.

1956 – a crushing win

A record crowd of 115,802 watched Melbourne thrash Collingwood in the 1956 Grand Final, 17.19 (121) to 6.12 (48). It was a fitting finale to a year in which the Demons finished at the top of the ladder with 16 wins. 1956 was the Olympic year and it was May before the team played at the MCG and Mrs Bert Chadwick was able to unfurl the 1955 pennant. The ground had been closed for Olympic Games refurbishing. Only 15 hours after the Grand Final, the ground was closed again, and workmen began tearing up the MCG turf in preparation for the Games.

In the Second Semi-final, Melbourne met Collingwood and both teams struggled with the swirling wind. The game was tight for the first three-quarters, then Melbourne went away to win by 16 points.

The record crowd at the Grand Final against Collingwood caused chaos, with about 25,000 people turned away from the gates which closed 90 minutes before the start. Many broke into the ground and went uncounted. They saw a game dominated for three quarters by Melbourne. Denis Cordner and Bob Johnson were in control in the ruck, Ron Barassi and Laurie Mithen were both in fine form and rover Stuart Spencer, with five goals, was again the best on the ground.

Ron Barassi: among the best.

Big Bob Johnson; a menace up forward.

1957 – a triple crown

Melbourne was 'back to the field', the newspapers said, after Melbourne was beaten by Fitzroy in the first round in 1957. And it was generally agreed that 1957 would be a year of team building, given that the players lost included Noel McMahen, Denis Cordner, Stuart Spencer, Geoff McGivern, Ken Melville, Clyde Laidlaw and Ralph Lane. Nevertheless, the Demons finished on top of the ladder for the fourth year in succession. And although they reached the Grand Final – the fourth in a row, a club record – the hard way, losing to Essendon in the Second Semi-final, 8.19 (67) to 12.11 (83), and having to beat Hawthorn 22.12 (144) to 11.10 (76), in the Preliminary Final, they showed their true colours on Grand Final day, defeating Essendon 17.14 (116) to 7.13 (55).

Their ability to create the loose man as they swept the ball forward (and often that man was Barassi) contributed to their one-sided win. The game was seen as a tactical triumph for Norm Smith, as he had Essendon wrong-footed all day.

CLUB NEWS 1952–1958

Smith takes over. Former captain Norm Smith took over as coach from Alan Fontaine and took the team to sixth position in his first year, from last position in 1951. The Dees managed to inflict Collingwood's first defeat for the season in front of a record home-and-away crowd of 58,543 at the MCG, 12.10 (82) to 6.14 (50).

Barassi on the bench. Ron Barassi warmed the bench for his first game in 1953, against Footscray. He finally made it on to the ground, only to be flattened by Charlie Sutton. Other new boys in 1953 included 'Bluey' Adams, Peter Marquis, Ken Melville, Don Williams, Terry Gleeson and Geoff Case.

1954 Grand Final. Melbourne made it to the 1954 Grand Final but were defeated by Footscray by 52 points.
New captain. Noel McMahen was appointed captain in 1955 and Stuart Spencer won the Keith 'Bluey' Truscott Memorial Trophy for Best and Fairest in 1955 and 1956.
Lost. Laurie Mithen, Peter Marquis and their girlfriends were rescued in June 1956 after being lost for 18 hours one mile from the top of Mt Buller in a blizzard. They suffered frostbite to hands and feet and shock and exposure and were hospitalised on rescue.
Frank 'Bluey' Adams made a catastrophic debut appearance when, as 19th man, he came on to the ground as Collingwood wingman, Des Healey, was tearing down the wing with the

1952–1958

Explosive Ron Barassi

Ron Barassi came to Melbourne young and eager. He had a special relationship with the club, as a legatee and because he lived with Norm Smith, and also had the eagerness for football and the cheery personality that stamped him as a future star. Perhaps he tried too hard. His first years did not bear the fruit he or the club hoped for, but his determination was noted.

Norm Smith needed a strong, hard-working, mobile player around the packs – a ruck-rover, as he described him. Barassi was tried and a champion footballer was born. He had purple passages of play in which he could do not wrong. The whole team lifted around him and Melbourne became the complete fighting unit that was to go on and win seven Premierships.

The statistics are known – 204 games, six Premiership teams (one Grand Final missed through suspension), captain from 1960 to 1964, two club Best and Fairests.

But the statistics cannot capture the image of Barassi. with the slight limp and hands on hips, walking into the fray, Barassi bursting through the pack, Barassi outmarking bigger men or Barassi marauding into the forward line with the Demons supporters going wild.

The high-rolling Demons are seldom beaten.

Cruel fate in '58

Melbourne was looking to emulate Collingwood's four-in-a-row in 1958, but Collingwood had other ideas. The weather gave some indication of the kind of day it was going to be – bleak and black, with early heavy rain. The ground was wet and sloppy, but Melbourne began well, kicking 5.1 to 2.2 in the first quarter.

Collingwood set about roughing up Barassi and Mithen. Melbourne finished the first half two points down. In the third term, the game degenerated. Collingwood's Weideman and Harrison, in particular, instigated incidents all over the ground, leaving Melbourne players worrying more about evening up that score than winning the game. It was a fairly basic strategy, but it worked and Collingwood won 12.10 (82) to 9.10 (64), with Barassi reported.

Master coach

The name Norm Smith is synonymous with the glory years. The man described by 'Checker' Hughes as 'Football brains from his thatch to his toes' made the Demons the power team in the competition. After the 1948 Grand Final, Smith went to Fitzroy as coach. He returned to Melbourne in 1952. In 1953, the team was eleventh – or second bottom – on the ladder; the following year they were runners-up and in 1955 they were Premiers.

With original thinking, and the right clay in Ron Barassi, he invented the position of ruck-rover. The idea took Barassi from a promising player to a dominant force. The Melbourne teams under Smith were distinguished by their teamwork, and by the aggression with which they moved the ball forward from the backline. Norm Smith took the Demons to 13 successive finals appearances, and six Flags.

Coaching brothers, Norm (left) and Len.

1952–1958 HONOUR ROLL

Year	Pos	Leading Goalkicker	No.	Best & Fairest	Captain	Coach
1952	6th	Noel Clarke	49	Geoff McGivern	Denis Cordner	Norm Smith
1953	11th	Bob McKenzie	38	Ken Melville	Denis Cordner	Norm Smith
1954	2nd	Noel Clarke	51	Denis Cordner	Geoff Collins	Norm Smith
1955	1st	Stuart Spencer	42	Stuart Spencer	Noel McMahen	Norm Smith
1956	1st	Stuart Spencer	42	Stuart Spencer	Noel McMahen	Norm Smith
1957	1st	Athol Webb	56	John Beckwith	John Beckwith	Norm Smith
1958	2nd	Ron Barassi/Athol Webb	44	Laurie Mithen	John Beckwith	Norm Smith

ball. Adams was intent on getting to his position and Healey didn't see him. They collided head on, and were carried from the field with severe head injuries.

The end of a great career. Denis Cordner retired in 1956 after 152 games and 82 goals.

Nineteen in a row. Melbourne's 19-win sequence (over two seasons) came to an end on 21 July 1956 with a defeat to Footscray.

New boys for 1957. Neil Crompton, John Lord, Dick Fenton-Smith, Ian Thorogood and Geoff Tunbridge.

A first-round shocker. Melbourne was beaten by Fitzroy on 22 April 1957.

Tiger saves the day. Ian Ridley snapped a miraculous goal on the siren to enable Melbourne to draw with Collingwood on 13 July 1957.

He was right. Umpire Frank Schwab was pelted with bottles and rubbish after a controversial free kick enabled Melbourne full-forward Athol Webb to kick a match-winning point against Essendon, with the final score 11.7 (73) to 9.18 (72) on 27 July 1957.

Melbourne's birthday. The 100th year of football was remembered when Melbourne defeated Carlton by 24 points at the MCG on 12 April 1958. The coin used at the toss was donated to the team as a memento of the game.

Left standing. The Collingwood Committee stood amidst a crowd of 99,346 to see the Demons defeat the Magpies, 12.12 (84) to 10.13 (73) on 16 June 1958. A country football team had been given their seats.

MELBOURNE

Five out of seven

Norm Smith and his men.

The years from 1954 to 1960 were wonderful years for Melbourne supporters, with the club participating in every Grand Final and winning five out of seven Premierships. In those seven seasons, Melbourne played 141 games, won 108 of them and tied two.

Sensational recruiting in the early 50s saw an awe-inspiring list of newcomers to the Melbourne Football Club. In 1953 and 1954, new players included Ron Barassi, Geoff Case, 'Bluey' Adams, Terry Gleeson, Bob Johnson, Laurie Mithen, Brian Dixon, Ian Ridley, Clyde Laidlaw, Ken Melville, Peter Marquis and Don Williams. Already on the books were greats like Noel McMahen, John Beckworth, Denis Cordner and Stuart Spencer. Add to that a coach of the standard of Norm Smith – one of the League's great coaches over the years – and success follows. The team went from second-last in Smith's second year in 1953 to first in 1955!

Demons on a roll.

The team of the fifties played hard at the ball, and they played as a team, rather than as a team of individual champions. Bluey Adams said: 'I know people thought we were elitists or smart arses but I don't think we were, purely because Smithy wouldn't let us be. He wanted us to be modest winners, gracious losers.'

1959, 1960 Premierships

Melbourne was the team to beat in 1959, finishing on top of the ladder with 13 wins and a draw. The Demons won the Flag in a thriller against Essendon, 17.13 (115) to 11.12 (78), in front of a crowd of 103,506, the largest since seat booking was introduced in 1957.

Ron Barassi, in his sixth Grand Final, kicked four goals and was the undisputed best on ground. His spirit and determination lifted the Demons when the Dons were looking like a real threat.

One year later, in the 1960 Grand Final, Collingwood tried the tactics which had won them the Flag in 1958 and were thrashed by a cool-headed Melbourne. Rain on Friday night had raised the Magpies' hopes, but the Demons avenged the ignominy of 1958 and won easily, 8.14 (62) to 2.2 (14).

Smith sacked and back

In July, 1965, Norm Smith was sacked by the Melbourne committee, only to be reinstated four days later.

Smith was notified of his sacking by a letter after he had criticised the committee for their lack of support in a libel case brought against him by umpire Don Blew. On the Tony Charlton Football Show, Smith asked Melbourne supporters to make a public protest and said: 'Get rid of these blokes – that is the only way the club will progress.'

He said he had told the committee: 'You went to a public school, I went to a state school, but we still spelt principle the same way. If you haven't got principle, you haven't got anything, and I've got principles and I'll fight for that principle till the day I die.'

'Checker' Hughes was appointed replacement coach but after a loss to North, 11.5 (81) to 9.6 (60), and a threatened revolt from players and staff, the committee bent to popular opinion and reappointed Smith.

1959—1967 HONOUR ROLL

Year	Pos	Leading Goalkicker	No.	Best & Fairest	Captain	Coach
1959	1st	Ron Barassi	46	Laurie Mithen	John Beckwith	Norm Smith
1960	1st	Ian Ridley	38	Brian Dixon	Ron Barassi	Norm Smith
1961	3rd	Bob Johnson Jnr	36	Ron Barassi	Ron Barassi	Norm Smith
1962	4th	Laurie Mithen	37	Hassa Mann	Ron Barassi	Norm Smith
1963	3rd	Barry Bourke	48	Hassa Mann	Ron Barassi	Norm Smith
1964	1st	John Townsend	35	Ron Barassi	Ron Barassi	Norm Smith
1965	7th	John Townsend	35	John Townsend	Hassa Mann	Norm Smith
1966	11th	Barry Vagg	23	Terry Leahy	Hassa Mann	Norm Smith
1967	7th	Hassa Mann	38	Hassa Mann	Hassa Mann	Norm Smith

CLUB NEWS 1959–1967

New boys for 1959. Included Tassie Johnson, who went on to play 202 games and captain the side in 1969, the year he retired; and 'Hassa' Mann, who was discovered playing for Merbein by George Ball, the father of the Melbourne ruckman Harold Ball who was killed in Malaya in WW2.

Revenge! Melbourne defeated Collingwood by 13 points in what the papers termed a 'blood match' to avenge the Grand Final loss of 1958 on 2 May 1959. Former VFL umpire, Warwick Road, described the game as 'the most vicious on the MCG for years'.

Jetsetters. The 1959 season finished in October with a match against Port Adelaide, the South Australian Premiers in Adelaide, followed by nine days holiday at Coolangatta.

Captain Ron. Barassi became captain on 5 April 1960 when John Beckwith stood down for him. John Beckwith remained his deputy, and played his 175th and final game with the Demons in the 1960 Grand Final. Wingman Ian McLean also retired in 1960.

A harbinger of the 1960 finals. Melbourne defeated Collingwood by 46 points in front of a crowd of 81,089 on 6 August 1960.

Ivor Warne-Smith. Dual Brownlow Medallist, club champion and former chairman of selectors, Ivor Warne-Smith died in 1960.

A disappointment. In 1961 Melbourne failed to make the Grand

1959–1967

The men who made the Premierships

Stuart Spencer

An outstanding rover, Spencer was recruited from Portland in 1950, and played 122 games from 1950 to 1956, kicking 146 goals. He was the Melbourne Football Club president from 1986–91.

Frank 'Bluey' Adams

A talented rover and forward, Adams was one of the fastest men to play Aussie Rules. He played in six Melbourne Premierships from 1953–64, and later joined the Melbourne committee.

Laurie Mithen

Mithen, from the Ormond Amateurs, played on the half-forward flank in the 1955 and 1956 Grand Finals. After Ken Melville's retirement he took over in the centre and was brilliant until he retired in 1962. He won the Keith 'Bluey' Truscott Memorial Trophy in 1958 and 1959.

John Beckwith

A back-pocket specialist who captained the Demons from 1957–59. He was a master at kicking the ball along the boundary line, and out. He played 177 games.

Bob Johnson

The son of the 1926 Premiership team's Bob Johnson, he was one of the first of the very tall League ruckmen at 6'5". He also played in the pocket as a principal forward.

Brian Dixon

He was recruited from Melbourne High in 1954 as a 16-year-old with a mighty leap. Set a club record of 238 games in 1967 and went on to play 258 games before retiring in 1968.

Neil Crompton's kick seals 1964 Premiership

The last quarter of the 1964 Grand Final was an intolerably tense affair, with Melbourne and Collingwood locked in mortal combat. The ultimate move seemed to be Ray Gabelich's run, and the Collingwood skipper was entitled to think he had won the game after his 70-yard burst, punctuated by wobbling bounces and ending with a goal.

By contrast Neil Crompton's match-winning kick was the simplest of plays. The Melbourne back-pocket had followed his rover downfield to Melbourne's half-forward line. A huge pack rose to contest a kick from wingman Brian Dixon. The ball spilled clear, and Crompton picked it up, took a couple of steps and booted for goal. Melbourne won by four points, 12.16 to 12.12.

Bob McKenzie

A fast half-forward who could kick accurately both on the run and from a standing start. After being suspended before the 1954 Grand Final, he played his 125th and last game with the Demons in their 1955 Premiership triumph.

Noel McMahen

Captain of the Flag-winning teams of 1955 and '56, McMahen was a star defender who made his debut in 1946 and was a member of the 1948 Grand Final side. He played 175 games.

Final for the first time since 1954, finishing third.

Retirements in 1962. The time was up for Laurie Mithen, Terry Gleeson, Clyde Laidlaw, Geoff Tunbridge, Geoff Case and Trevor Johnson. Bert Chadwick retired as club chairman.

New boys for 1963. Included Ray Groom – a future Premier of Tasmania, and Tony Anderson.

Barassi outed. A suspension in the last game of the 1963 season saw Ron Barassi out for four weeks.

One goal puts the team on top. 'Hassa' Mann kicked a goal from an impossible angle in time-on for Melbourne to win the game against Hawthorn in the second-last game of the season, enabling the Demons to finish on top of the ladder in 1964.

Barassi to coach Carlton. Melbourne's favourite son swapped jumpers in January 1965 and announced he would taken up the position of captain–coach with Carlton. It was a sign of the times, with the initial offer to Barassi being £18,000. In going to the Blues, Barassi became the highest paid footballer in Australia.

A costly year. 1965 saw a financial deficit of £5,733, Melbourne's first in years.

Son of Smith. Peter Smith played 23 games with Melbourne in 1966 and 1967 and then went on to Carlton, where he played 15 games.

The end of an era. Coach Norm Smith, with six Premierships from 11 finals as coach, retired following the 1967 season.

MELBOURNE

The wilderness years

Gary Hardemans's big mark.

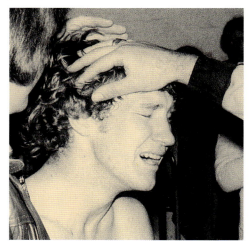

Hardeman – a miss in '76.

Melbourne's long drought began in 1965, when the Premiership team, missing only Barassi and Adams, suddenly lost momentum after winning the first eight games of the season. The team limped to seventh, and the slump became official in 1966 with only three wins out of fifteen games. From then on Melbourne had 20 years as non-contenders, with seasons in the cellar in 1969, 1974, 1978 and 1981. These disasters were at least shared around among the coaches, with John Beckwith, Bob Skilton, Denis Jones and Ron Barassi all tasting the ashes of failure. Skilton raised all hopes in 1976 as Melbourne zeroed in on the finals. They beat Collingwood at Victoria Park and were home if Carlton beat Footscray. Carlton, the top side, couldn't do it, and the resultant draw had Demon tears dropping on the alien turf at Collingwood.

The winter weeks dragged drearily on for the supporters, with the occasional win being greeted with the euphoria that the successful clubs saved up for September. The ranks of the fellow travellers thinned, but the true red-and-blues stuck and cheered the boys on. They may not have been good enough, but it wasn't their fault.

Why did such a proud club go into this long recess? With hindsight it is evident that Melbourne just plugged along with its recruiting and its players, splurging occasionally and inappropriately on a fading star and never having enough good players in the team to gain a winning momentum. Other clubs, notably Richmond, North Melbourne, Hawthorn and Essendon, had the players, the momentum and the will that Melbourne lost in the late 60s. Melbourne's efforts were more fitful and hopeful, while the others were driving and dedicated.

The supporters were comforted by the efforts of some wonderful players – like Hassa Mann, Stan Alves, Greg Wells, Gary Hardeman, Gerard Healy, Garry Baker and the incomparable Robbie Flower. But these players deserved better rewards for their skills and their effort, deserved to carry the colours into the finals.

It took a discarded coach in John Northey to gather up the more representative side that Melbourne fielded in the late-80s, and to bring some excitement into the Demons lives. The same momentum seems to be building again in the late 1990s as the Demons build a team.

The Irish experiment

An internationalist to his fingertips, Barassi saw in Gaelic football and its similarities to the local game an opportunity to find new talent. Along with Melbourne Football Club executive Dick Seddon, he hatched a plan to import Irish footballers.

The idea was laughed at back home, but Sean Wight, who began playing in 1985, went on to become a key defender, and Jimmy Stynes, the 1991 Brownlow Medallist, holds the record for the most consecutive League games played. The experiment was a success.

Barassi the Messiah fails to fire

It was the return of the prodigal son. Ron Barassi returned to Melbourne to coach in 1981, after coaching Carlton and North Melbourne to two Premierships each. The former Melbourne champion of 204 games brought with him the Brownlow Medallists Peter Moore from Collingwood and Kelvin Templeton from Footscray. Another player to join the team along with Barassi was former Demon Peter 'Crackers' Keenan.

No dreams came true during his five-year stint as coach – Melbourne finished 12, 8, 8, 9 and 11th. The fire and the desire was there, but the players were not, and 'Brasso' skinned his knuckles on the coaches' box roof and other rough surfaces a few times.

CLUB NEWS 1968–1986

Beckwith coach. John Beckwith was appointed coach for 1968. Dixon retired with 252 games.
'Tassie' captain. 'Tassie' Johnson was captain in 1969. The team won the wooden spoon with three wins for the season.
Bananas. Blair Campbell, the inventor of the banana kick, retired in 1969 after only 12 games with Melbourne. Campbell played cricket for Victoria and Tasmania.
Reserves Premiership. The Reserves won the 1970 Premiership with coach Ian Ridley.
New boys for 1970. Included Paul Callery and Peter Keenan.
New coach Ridley. 1971 began spectacularly with eight wins out of the first nine games, under new coach Ian Ridley and captain Barry Davis. The team won only three more games for the season and finished seventh.
Max chooses cricket. Melbourne ruckman Max Walker returned from the West Indies in 1973, having collected 26 wickets, and announced he was retiring from football.
Team colours tampered with. The 1974 advent of colour television in Australia sent the VFL into a spin and prompted a change from Melbourne's traditional red and blue to a blue and red that the powers that be deemed would look better on TV.
Brownlow set-up. In 1975, for the third time in four years, a Demon was the victim of a staged Brownlow count

1968 – 1986

Coaches and characters abound

There were plenty of comings and goings at Melbourne as it struggled to lift itself out of the football doldrums. Coaches were hailed as the men with the answer, but went away with empty hands.

Big Carl.

John Beckwith, a doughty captain, is best remembered for his playing days; Ian Ridley conjured eight wins in his first nine games before the players came back to earth; Bobby Skilton, keen and busy, nearly gained a finals appearance; Dennis Jones, a hard man in the ruck, had one abysmal year; Carl Ditterich dominated the field, dispensing pain and protection in equal amounts, but the team still hovered somewhere close to the bottom; Ron Barassi proved that desire, record and method are as nothing in the face of mediocrity.

Hassa Mann.

Some success.

There were some fine players in the ranks, a lot of ordinary workers and some rich oddities as well. Some big-time imports arrived in a shower of dollars and headlines. Diamond Jim Tilbrook could kick goals from the centre-line in South Australia, but he couldn't get much ball in Melbourne; Graham Molloy had a big reputation at Norwood, but couldn't get going for the Demons; Kelvin Templeton came from Footscray with a Brownlow Medal, but injury had left him vulnerable; Brent Crosswell crossed from North, more showman than champion in these later years.

Gerard Healy.

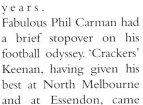
Wacko Jacko.

Greg Wells.

Fabulous Phil Carman had a brief stopover on his football odyssey. 'Crackers' Keenan, having given his best at North Melbourne and at Essendon, came back to finish his career.

The most memorable player was Mark Jackson, ugly and intimidating in the full-forward role, sometimes arguing with the umpire, the full-back, the crowd and the coach at the same time.

Diamond Jim.

Moore, Wilson Brownlows

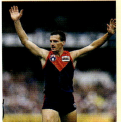

Imported players Brian Wilson and Peter Moore brought some light into the gloomy Melbourne camp with their Brownlow Medal wins. Wilson, discarded by Footscray and North Melbourne, had a great year in the centre in 1982 and, at the age of 20, won Melbourne's third Brownlow Medal. Moore, who had won the medal at Collingwood in 1979, took it again in 1984 with his towering ruck play.

1968 – 1986 HONOUR ROLL

Year	Pos	Leading Goalkicker	No.	Best & Fairest	Captain	Coach
1968	8th	Hassa Mann	31	Ray Groom	Hassa Mann	John Beckwith
1969	12th	Ross Dillon	53	John Townsend	Bob Johnson Jnr	John Beckwith
1970	10th	Ross Dillon	47	Frank Davis	Frank Davis	John Beckwith
1971	7th	Paul Callery	44	Greg Wells	Frank Davis	Ian Ridley
1972	8th	Greg Parke	63	Stan Alves	Frank Davis	Ian Ridley
1973	10th	Ross Brewer	32	Carl Ditterich	Stan Alves	Ian Ridley
1974	12th	Ross Brewer	40	Stan Alves	Stan Alves	Bob Skilton
1975	10th	Greg Wells	32	Laurie Fowler	Stan Alves	Bob Skilton
1976	6th	Ray Biffin	47	Greg Wells	Stan Alves	Bob Skilton
1977	11th	Robbie Flower	26	Robbie Flower	Greg Wells	Bob Skilton
1978	12th	Henry Coles	33	Gary Baker	Greg Wells	Dennis Jones
1979	11th	Robbie Flower	33	Laurie Fowler	Carl Ditterich	Carl Ditterich
1980	9th	Brent Crosswell	31	Laurie Fowler	Carl Ditterich	Carl Ditterich
1981	12th	Mark Jackson	76	Steven Smith	Robbie Flower	Ron Barassi
1982	8th	Gerard Healy	77	Stephen Icke	Robbie Flower	Ron Barassi
1983	8th	Robbie Flower	40	Alan Johnson	Robbie Flower	Ron Barassi
1984	9th	Kelvin Templeton	51	Gerard Healy	Robbie Flower	Ron Barassi
1985	11th	Brian Wilson	40	Danny Hughes	Robbie Flower	Ron Barassi
1986	11th	Greg Healy	35	Greg Healy	Robbie Flower	John Northey

finish. In this case, captain Stan Alves lost the medal by one vote to Gary Dempsey. In 1974, Gary Hardeman was defeated in the last call of the night when Keith Grieg defeated him by two votes, and in 1972, Melbourne rover Greg Wells was leading when Len Thompson won on the last vote. The Melbourne Football Club committee complained to the VFL.

Nearly made it. Only the last home-and-away game saw Melbourne fail to make a finals berth in 1976.

An amazing fightback. On 28 May 1977, St Kilda led Melbourne by 35 points at the beginning of the final quarter, then kicked two goals to make the margin 47 points. Melbourne fought back and kicked the final eight goals to win the match by five points.

Big Carl's a Demon. Carl Ditterich joined Melbourne in 1979 as captain–coach and immediately dumped 18 players. The new players included Gerard Healy.

Bye to the MCC. The Melbourne Football Club chose to go it alone again in 1980 for the first time in 91 years, and became Melbourne Football Club Limited, a company limited by guarantee. Mr Richard Seddon was appointed executive director as the club set out to rebuild.

Another new coach. After a coaching reign that brought little on-field success, Ron Barassi resigned at the end of the 1985 season. John Northey, a little-known coach rejected by the Sydney Swans ownership for a perceived 'lack of charisma', took over.

MELBOURNE

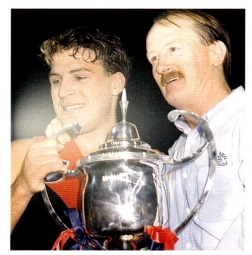

Greg Healy and Northey savour the win.

Night Final win

The Demons won their first Premiership in 16 years by defeating Essendon in the National Panasonic Cup Grand Final on 29 April 1987.

Rank outsiders and depleted by injury, the young Demons won by four points in the last minute of the game, when Brett Bailey kicked a miraculous goal from the forward pocket.

They went into the game only three days after a humiliating defeat by Brisbane at Carrara, missing their champion and captain, Robbie Flower, rovers Greg Healy and Ricky Jackson, ruckman Peter Moore, ruck-rover Chris Connelly and new boy Todd Viney.

Alan Johnson and Dudley Phillips.

Melbourne led at every change, but when Essendon hit the front eight minutes into the final quarter, it looked as if superior skills and experience would win out. But the young Demons fought it out to take the game. 'It was a magnificent effort by the players,' coach John Northey said afterwards. 'I told them that they would have to give 100 per cent. They gave 150 per cent.'

Robbie Flower gathers the ball, with a score for Melbourne looming.

A tilt at glory with a run to finals

After games in 1987 with only six wins, few had their hopes too high – which made what followed all the more glorious. A 40-point win against Geelong the next week was the beginning of an unbeaten run that took the Demons to within one game of the Grand Final.

A finals spot depended not only on their own ability to beat fifth-position contender Footscray at the notorious Western Oval, but also on Hawthorn defeating Geelong at Kardinia Park.

Melbourne went into the game minus O'Dwyer and Grinter, due to suspension, and lost Garry Lyon early in the game with a broken leg. During the third quarter, Footscray was four goals in front, while down at Kardinia Park, Geelong was leading by six.

That was not what the players heard though – they were reassured that Hawthorn had the game well in hand. Then, one goal up going into the last quarter, Melbourne finally kicked away and when the final siren blew the Demons had won, 12.11 (83) to 10.8 (68).

The Melbourne supporters sat paralysed. Radios all around the ground were tuned to the game at Kardinia Park. Whether to feel deliriously happy or tragically thwarted – an explosion of red and blue gave the answer as scarves and beanies were tossed high in the air and the cheers went up. Hawthorn had done the impossible and stolen the game in time-on by three points. Grown men and women stood on the seats and roared the club song, tears streaming down their cheeks. It was indeed a grand old Flag.

1987–1988 HONOUR ROLL

Year	Pos	Leading Goalkicker	No.	Best & Fairest	Captain	Coach
1987	3rd	Robbie Flower	47	Steven Stretch	Robbie Flower	John Northey
1988	2nd	Ricky Jackson	43	Steven O'Dwyer	Greg Healy	John Northey

CLUB NEWS 1987–1988

Old Colours. After wearing the 'TV colours' of Royal Blue and Red, Melbourne reverted to its traditional navy blue and red strip at the start of the 1987 season – and, coincidentally, started winning again.

New boys in 1987. Included West Australians Warren Dean and Earl Spalding, South Australian Todd Viney, Irishman Jim Stynes and Victorians Steve O'Dwyer and Glenn Lovett.

Roos by two points. North Melbourne first-gamer Alistair Clarkson sealed the fate of the Demons in Round 15, 1987, when he took a diving mark 40 metres from goal as the siren sounded, and goaled.

Behinds galore. Melbourne kicked 24 behinds in their defeat of Collingwood in Round 20.

1987 World Champions. Melbourne defeated the Sydney Swans and North Melbourne in Canada to become the 1987 World Champions.

New record for Robbie. Robert Flower played his 274th game to break the club record.

Retirements. 1987 saw the retirement of some of Melbourne's great contributors over the years, including Robbie Flower, Peter Giles, Brownlow medallist Peter Moore and Stephen Icke.

1987 AFL Team of the Year. Steven Stretch, Sean Wight.

Captain Healy. Greg Healy took over as captain in 1988 on the retirement of Robbie Flower.

1988 recruits. Steven Febey, Andy

1987 – 1988

Jimmy Stynes: tragic mistake.

Gaelic tragedy

In the 1987 finals, the Demons were the talk of the town for the first time in years, and the city was awash with red and blue. Then came the Preliminary Final against Hawthorn at Waverley.

The *Age* journalist Martin Flanagan put it better than most: 'It wasn't just that Melbourne lost, it was that they fell from the mountain top.'

In fact many Melbourne supporters believed that the young Demons didn't lose, that instead the game was snatched away in its final seconds.

It was a gruelling slog of a game in a tense last quarter. Robbie Flower was felled by Robert DiPierdomenico and Chris Mew by Rod Grinter. Graeme Yeats missed from 35 metres, Simon Eishold from 10 metres. Still Melbourne was in front.

Then Buckenara was given a free and the rest is history. Young Jimmy Stynes ran between Buckenara and Rod Grinter and a 15-metre penalty was given. Of course, Buckenara goaled and Hawthorn won the game.

As Demon supporters will tell you still, it wasn't *that* they won, it was *how* they won. Children sobbed, their parents cried too. The end of a dream.

The team trains in Grand Final week watched by thousands of excited supporters.

A game too far for gallant team of '88

1988 started gloriously, with Melbourne winning the first five games. It was a different story toward the end of the season when after a season in which the team had not been beaten twice in a row, five shock losses in succession saw only a win against Carlton in the final game securing fifth place.

Melbourne defeated the West Coast by two points in a heart-stopping Elimination Final, with the brilliant Alan Johnson in defence the best on the ground. The lead changed five times in the final quarter. They then won by 13 points over Collingwood in the First Semi-final, and then against Carlton, when they slipped away in the first quarter, only to have Carlton come back to two points in front at half-time. In the driving rain in the second half of the game, Melbourne escaped again and went on to win convincingly by 22 points.

They had earned their first Grand Final in 24 years. Thousands watched the boys train at the Junction Oval and fans lined the streets for the Grand Final parade down Bourke Street. The roar of pride that enveloped the team as they ran onto the

Yeats, Grinter exhausted.

ground on the Saturday was deafening.

The Grand Final saw Melbourne lose to Hawthorn by 96 points. Hawthorn had finished on top of the ladder with 19 wins for the season and the game was lost amidst a deluge of rain during a crushing first half.

One of the few bright spots for Melbourne on the day was the winning performance of fledgling ruckman Jim Stynes against Hawthorn's Greg Dear. The bright spot for the season was that Melbourne made it to the Grand Final, having valiantly fought through from fifth on the ladder to the final game – a great achievement.

Lovell, Jamie Duursma.

Trial by media. After media demands, the VFL called in VFL investigations officer Max Croxford on 12 April 1988 to investigate an incident arising from Melbourne's Round 2 match against Footscray three days earlier. Rodney Grinter was not reported by umpires for the incident involving Terry Wallace which resulted in Wallace receiving a broken jaw and Grinter a gashed hand. Melbourne general manager Tony King declared the VFL's response 'a massive knee-jerk reaction'.

Umpire banished. The umpire who chose not to report Grinter was banished to the bush for failing to lay a report.

Six weeks to Grinter. Rodney Grinter was suspended for six matches for striking Footscray's Terry Wallace, 11 days after the incident took place. Grinter was found guilty of bringing the game of football into disrepute.

O'Dwyer out. Steve O'Dwyer was suspended for three matches for striking Carlton's Steve Da Rui in the third quarter of the Preliminary Final on 19 September 1988. After the hearing, club president Stuart Spencer said: 'He has been greatly responsible for the rebirth of the Melbourne Football Club and it is a dramatic blow to our prospects for Saturday.'

A tough task for Robbie. The winning Hawthorn players were presented with their 1988 Premiership medals by the recently retired Melbourne champion Robbie Flower. He performed with his usual grace.

MELBOURNE

Robbie Flower – the ultimate Demon

Robbie Flower was a beautiful player to watch. Few players have given supporters more pleasure or wreaked more havoc. He was graceful and elusive, with a long and penetrating kick and he could mark high above the pack.

A slight, unassuming man with glasses, the young Robert Flower would have hardly bred fear in the opposition had they seen him enter the dressing rooms. He began playing in the Seniors as a 17-year-old schoolboy in 1973, scoring a goal in his first game, and he stayed there, a fixture for next 15 years and 272 games. During those years, Melbourne had six coaches and frequently finished in the doldrums, but when all else was bleak, it was always worth going to watch Robbie in action.

To the delight of the supporters, he would take off for a run in front of the Members' Stand, leaving his opponent in his wake as he turned, baulked and skilfully evaded all comers. Then he would pass, hitting his team-mate square on the chest. He was a champion who made the game look easy. And always he played the ball. He won the admiration of those he played against as well as his team-mates though his skill and fair play.

Robbie Flower was the definitive wingman, though Ron Barassi was one coach who liked to move him around. He played him on a half-back flank and was booed by the supporters who had come, after all, partly to watch Robbie fire. But fire he did, in whatever position he was played. He captained the team from 1981 and in his final years, played mostly on the half-forward flank, a position in which he was deadly.

A fine sight for Demon fans – Robbie Flower stretches for a mark.

To the bewilderment of Melbourne supporters, Flower never won the Brownlow Medal. Few players have fitted so aptly the description of 'fairest and best'.

His career ended in 1987, when Melbourne came within a kick of a Grand Final. His fragile build made him injury prone in his later years, but always he was an inspiration to the team. He is still very much a part of Melbourne and its plans for a bright future.

Jimmy is congratulated by his father.

Brownlow to Jimmy

When Jimmy Stynes stepped up to accept the 1991 Brownlow Medal, it was something beyond imagining when he arrived from Dublin in 1985. But the skinny boy who arrived in Australia with the promise of his teaching college fees, accommodation and $50 a week spending money, had turned out to be an extraordinary individual.

Stynes was plunged into football at the deep end in his first year, playing under Ray 'Slug' Jordan in the Melbourne Under 19s. The following year he was told he was to be leased to the VFA Club Prahran.

'I looked on it as a challenge,' he said. 'I thought "I've got to stick it up these fellas and show them that I can play senior footy."'

A challenge is something Stynes likes. After having run over Buckenara's mark in the 1987 Preliminary Final, he used the awful incident to spur himself on to better, more determined football the following year. He was the best Demon player in the 1988 Grand Final. Each year he set himself goals and each year – indeed, each game – he got better and better.

He won the Bluey Truscott Memorial Trophy in 1991, 1995, 1996 and 1997. In May, 1996, he played his 205th consecutive AFL game, and broke the record held by Richmond's Jack Titus for 53 years.

CLUB NEWS 1989–1996

1989 Night Premiership. Melbourne wins, making it two out of three.

God says sorry. Gary Ablett is believed to have apologised to Garry Lyon for a behind-the-play incident which resulted in Lyon requiring 12 stitches to three cuts around his mouth and chin in the Melbourne v Geelong game on 17 June 1989. A spokesperson for Channel 7 said there was no video of the incident: 'It shows Lyon lying on the ground and another Melbourne player biffing Ablett.'

Melbourne eliminates the Magpies. Melbourne defeated Collingwood in the 1989 Elimination Final but went on to lose to Geelong in the Second Semi-final.

Fourth again. Melbourne finished 1990 in fourth position for the second year in a row after defeating Hawthorn in the Elimination Final, then losing to the West Coast Eagles in the First Semi-final.

AFL Team of the Year 1990. Brett Lovett and Garry Lyon are selected in the year's best.

Jako on fire. In Round 20, 1991 a game in which Melbourne defeated Hawthorn, new boy Allen Jakovich kicked 11.7.

West Coast again. Melbourne went down to the West Coast Eagles in the 1991 First Semi-final and again finished fourth.

All-Australian. Jimmy Stynes was chosen in the 1991 All-Australian team.

1989 – 1996

The wonder of Jakovich

At his best, full-forward Allen Jakovich had every football fan shaking their head in disbelief. He was one of Melbourne's most exhilarating players and he carried his supporters with him as he punched the air with rapture and gave high fives to a member of the crowd. A game with Jako on fire was never dull, but injury ended his career all too soon. He kicked 71 goals in 14 games in 1991.

Garry Lyon, even when he was plagued by a recurring back injury, managed to lift the Melbourne team both on and off the field. He showed his strength as a captain during the merger debate, ensuring that there was still a team at the end of it all. The Demons and supporters alike look forward to him resuming his place on the field.

Shaun Smith took the mark of the year – if not the mark of the century – in the final game of the round in 1995 against Brisbane. Smith, who played for Werribee and North Melbourne before joining the Demons in 1992, knows how to fly – but not always how to land.

Merger drama

Passion flowed and tempers flared at the meeting held to vote on the Melbourne Football Club's potential merger with the Hawthorn Football Club on 16 September 1996. Club members had to queue around the block to gain entry to the Dallas Brooks Hall and once inside, spilled from the auditorium out into the foyers. The MFC committee had recommended that members vote in favour of the

Ridley takes a stance.

merger, which would have seen the birth of the Melbourne Hawks.

It was a tumultuous night. The decision to recommend the merger had obviously been a difficult one for president Ian Ridley and the committee, and they faced a noisy and hostile crowd at the meeting. Those who agreed with them sat quietly. Those who didn't angrily railed against them.

Most forceful in putting the anti-merger case were the Demon Alternative, a group put together by former winger and State politician Brian Dixon. The mining magnate and a member of the Alternative, Joseph Gutnick, concluded his emotional speech: 'I won't finish on a negative note. No merger!'

And no merger it was, despite the Melbourne Football Club narrowly voting 4679 to 4229 in favour. The merger was rejected by the Hawthorn Football Club, and thus the Demons (and for that matter the Hawks) live on.

1989 – 1996 HONOUR ROLL

Year	Pos	Leading Goalkicker	No.	Best & Fairest	Captain	Coach
1989	4th	Darren Bennett	34	Alan Johnson	Greg Healy	John Northey
1990	4th	Darren Bennett	87	Garry Lyon	Greg Healy	John Northey
1991	4th	Allen Jakovich	71	Jim Stynes	Garry Lyon	John Northey
1992	11th	Allen Jakovich	40	Glenn Lovett	Garry Lyon	John Northey
1993	10th	Allen Jakovich	39	Todd Viney	Garry Lyon	Neil Balme
1994	4th	Garry Lyon	79	Garry Lyon	Garry Lyon	Neil Balme
1995	9th	Garry Lyon	77	Jim Stynes	Garry Lyon	Neil Balme
1996	14th	David Neitz	56	Jim Stynes	Garry Lyon	Neil Balme

Northey resigns. John Northey announced his resignation as senior coach after a disappointing season in 1992 when Melbourne failed to make the finals. Ian Ridley replaced Stuart Spencer as chairman of the club and Hassa Mann was appointed chief executive.

Balme on board. Neil Balme, former tough man with Richmond and successful SA coach, was appointed senior coach in 1993. The Melbourne Reserves win the Premiership, the Seniors finish tenth.

All-Australian. In 1993, included Jimmy Stynes and Garry Lyon.

Billy Bennett kicks on. Darren Bennett, who played 74 games and kicked 215 goals for Melbourne from 1989–93, won a place in the US gridiron team, the San Diego Chargers and set about revolutionising kicking in the NFL.

AFL 1994 All Australian. Neil Balme chosen coach along with players Garry Lyon and Stephen Tingay.

Enter the eight. In the first year of the final eight in 1994, Melbourne finished seventh and was defeated in the Preliminary Final which, for the first time, was held in Perth. Beaten by those West Coast Eagles again.

At the Junction. Football operations were moved to the Junction Oval in 1994.

Leighoak opens. Melbourne's first gaming and social venue opened at Oakleigh in May 1995. While the club reported the best profit result in a decade, the team finished ninth.

MELBOURNE

Year of turmoil finishes on high

New chairman

The new president of the MFC Joseph Gutnick said he hoped he would contribute 'spirit and devotion' and be able to rally supporters. He has made a major financial commitment to the club.

A win at last!

You'd have thought Melbourne had won the Grand Final, had you heard the rendition of 'The Grand Old Flag' on the night of Saturday, May 31. Melbourne had at last won, downing Richmond by 25 points in their first victory since Round 1.

Victory over Blues

All gloom and doom was forgotten on Saturday, July 12 at the MCG when the true Demons stepped up and defeated Carlton in fine style, 18.11 (119) to 15.10 (100). From the first bounce, Melbourne looked to be in control.

First-round win

Melbourne kicked off the season in fine style with a win against reigning Premiers North Melbourne. While the rain tumbled down the Demons took North by surprise, winning by 15 points.

Neitz comes back

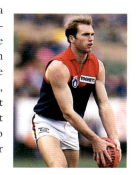

David Neitz signed a new three-year contract at the end of the '97 season. Although his contract had one year left to run, Melbourne made it clear that they want the 22-year-old to play out his career with the team.

Last-game win

The demons outplayed Fremantle in the final round. The boisterous team spirit as the retiring Andrew Obst was chaired from the ground may have bemused the media, but it made sense to every supporter.

Slump outs Balme

By Round 10, coach Neil Balme had been sacked in the wake of eight consecutive losses. The sacking was revealed by Joseph Gutnick, Cameron Schwab and David Schwarz during a live television cross to the Bentleigh Club.

Warrior Todd Viney

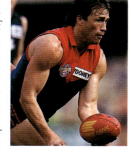

Todd Viney showed he had lost none of his toughness in his 11th year with the club in 1997, a season that saw him poll second to Jim Stynes in the Bluey Truscott award. If anything, Viney's workload seems to increase with the years.

Youngsters do well

Jeff Farmer.

A band of young players emerged in 1997 that left supporters with smiles on their faces, much to the mystification of the media commentators who dismissed the team en masse. But those who watched the Demons play game after game saw new boys Shane Woewodin, Anthony McDonald, Brent Grgic and Leigh Newton putting up their hands, alongside fine performances by young players of longer standing, such as Jeff Farmer, Andrew Leoncelli and Adem Yze.

The 1997 team was a team in transition, already showing signs of the better things.

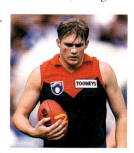

Leigh Newton.

A new coach

Melbourne was the first AFL team to start their 1998 pre-season training, under coach Neale Daniher. The appointment of Daniher, formerly assistant coach with Fremantle, was announced at the end of the 1997 season.

White big signing

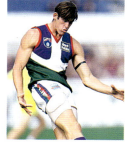

Jeff White, fresh from three years with Fremantle, signed with the Melbourne Football Club for a record three-year, $950,000 deal in October 1997. The 20-year-old 194cm player was keen to return to play in Melbourne.

1997

A day out with the Dees

June 8. Melbourne v Adelaide. There is excitement at the prospect of Melbourne, with a new coach and flush with a win over Richmond, preparing for battle at the MCG against Adelaide.

Lyon out and Schwarz in. A big emotional day for the Demons to see Schwarz back. We go down to the cavernous concourse at the back of the Northern stand – a place of perpetual half light – to see the people starting to turn up, Demon fans swathed in the beloved red and blue. It's wonderful to see so many families – mum and dad and the kids – all coloured up and eager for the fray.

We hear on the PA of the Demons special effort and of events at Leighoak and the Bentleigh Club. There is the feeling that the club is growing, despite the momentous week of Neil Balme's sacking.

In truth many supporters feel that Balmy – nice guy – had to go. His possession style was not working, as players seemed to be fiddling around and looking bewildered.

The cheer squad is out with the banner. On one side: 'Schwarz is back, the Dees are hot/ now let's make it two on the trot.' The other: 'The wooden spoon was on our plate/ now our sights are on the eight.'

The teams run out. Melbourne gets a big banner wave and a roar, while the Adelaidians raise a small but respectable flutter. The game is on, and Melbourne is all endeavour, sweeping the ball forward. Farmer and Charles create the chances and then can't finish. Then the ball is down the other end with Adelaide goaling twice. Viney goals, but it's all Adelaide's smoothness to Melbourne's fits and starts.

Marcus Seecamp starts a tremendous move down the outer wing, and all are in a position to receive when the umpire finds an infringement behind play. Umpires 6 and 36 are like twins, small and dark and giving bad decisions against Melbourne. Suddenly Adelaide is 6.4 to Melbourne's 1.1 and the game is gone before its properly begun.

All seems lost, but Schwarz lumbers on at the 13-minute mark of the second quarter to an enormous cheer from the Melbourne supporters, and a bit of clapping from Adelaide too. He looks huge and has a massive knee support. Soon he gets a chance on the goal square, removes an Adelaide obstacle and marks in front. Free kick. The

David Schwarz back in play.

Schwarz grabs a mark.

Demon fans howl against the savage injustice, the insensitivity of an umpire denying Schwarz his first kick in years.

The game continues its downward spiral as the Demons show more cohesion, but kick 1.7 for the quarter, while Adelaide is contained to 2.2. Seecamp is displaying rare dash, Leoncelli and Woewodin are solid in defence, Yze is smooth on the wing and Jimmy Stynes and Todd Viney are, as usual, playing strongly. But its all a bit late, and obvious in the third quarter that we are never going to catch up.

But Schwarz is there and kicks two goals, the only multiple scorer in the whole team. The game limps to an end, but the Demons come off as a team and, surprisingly, are given a rousing, flag-waving send off by the faithful red and blue wedge in the Northern Stand.

And in the rooms the spirit is buoyant. Schwarz, the man of the moment, is surrounded by microphones and cameras and officials are players are looking relaxed, if not beaming with delight. Perhaps they know something we don't.

1997 HONOUR ROLL

Year	Pos	Leading Goalkicker	No.	Best & Fairest	Captain	Coach
1997	16th	David Neitz/Jeff Farmer	30	Jim Stynes	Garry Lyon	N. Balme/Greg Hutchison

NORTH MELBOURNE

MY CLUB
by Gerard Dowling

'I barrack for North' were probably among the first words that I ever learned to pronounce. I imagine that I pretty well absorbed them with my mother's milk.

My father's parents lived in Lothian Street, North Melbourne, and my father was born in their home there, just one long Martin Pike dash and a few bounces from the Arden Street ground. So, even though I came into the world in the heart of Essendon territory, my dad saw to it that I, along with my twin sister, and our older brother were brought up in the spirit that is North.

I can't remember the first game that I watched, but I remember Dad and I taking our stand on a mound of earth at the northern end of the outer, close to where a giant scoreboard was erected in the 1960s. Originally I was too small to take in all the action down on the oval (my main interest was collecting bottles and claiming the deposit) but through those regular attendances I gradually acquired the North spirit.

All this was in the early 40s, as the 'Shinboners' (a term that I strongly disliked at the time) with a depleted player list, fought it out on the often soggy turf and our nation fought it out with the enemy in the war zones of Europe and the Pacific.

My first hero in the royal blue and white stripes was Syd Dyer (above), a courageous little rover who was one of our best players at the time.

Having finally made it into the League in 1925, after some real glory days in the Association, North Melbourne's first two decades in those elevated ranks were for the most part a dour struggle. Victories were always hard won, and defeat on a regular basis was a reality that had to be contended with and overcome.

As with all other clubs, this one that was centred in North Melbourne, and was among the last of the present AFL clubs to come into existence, had steadily fashioned a character all of its own. Various other factors contributed to this, such as its inner-city location, its lower to middle-class background, the doggedness of its successive administrations and the abiding vision of all associated with the club. These things enabled it to survive and eventually to get to the top, despite the odds against such achievement.

Two other qualities have pervaded the club in the 125 seasons since it first took the field as the North Melbourne Football Club, and have seen it through recurrent adversity and ensured it waves of spectacular success. One has been its enterprising sense of initiative and the other has been its perseverance in working at assembling the requisite ingredients for each phase of success on the field.

Pulling off the coup of signing four Carlton stars paved the way for its glory days in the VFA, when it won four Pennants between 1910 and 1918. And North's masterly, lightning use of the VFL's '10-year rule' gave its coach, Ron Barassi, the leadership and the type of specific talent to capture the 1975 and 1977 League Pennants.

With a small membership base, and

NORTH MELBOURNE	
Year Established	1869
Joined VFL/AFL	1925
Home Grounds	Arden St, Coburg City Oval, MCG
Premierships	1975, 1977, 1996
Brownlow Medals	Noel Teasdale 1965; Keith Greig 1973, 1974; Malcolm Blight 1978; Ross Glendinning 1983
Record home crowd	72,216 v Collingwood, 1994
Most games	Wayne Schimmelbusch, 306
Most goals	John Longmire, 504
Notable supporters	Past: Arthur Calwell Present: Sir John Gorton, Sigrid Thornton, Simon Crean, John Farnham, Ralph Willis, Ivan Deveson

Fans, Round 20, 1994.

enormous financial and other obstacles to contend with, this spirit that is North triumphed again when Denis Pagan coached and Wayne Carey captained the side that won the coveted AFL Centenary Premiership Cup in 1996.

Les Foote leads the team out in 1950.

Left: Yes, our first Grand Final! 1950. Above: Carna Roos, 1992 vintage.

North's 125th anniversary, 1994.

Arden Street, 1993: the old stand still standing.

Carey sinks the slipper to sink the Cats.

261

NORTH MELBOURNE

Football's champions in 1880. W. Johnston of North Melbourne stands on the right.

James Gardiner.

Another tradition holds that a certain Tom Jacks sold some roofing iron to cover the cost of the original team's first football. The venue for the club's home matches in those far-off days was 'the Royal Park' as it was for rivals from the other side, Carlton.

If any individual can be accorded the title of 'founder' of North, it was James Henty Gardiner, who is believed to have been the club's inaugural secretary. J. McIndoe appears to have been the club's first president and R. Collie its first treasurer.

The man who had the challenge of leading the team in its initial endeavours on the playing field was W. Marshall, who also played cricket with the North Melbourne Cricket Club. Harry Fuhrhop took over the captaincy in 1870 and continued in that capacity for a further five years.

At this time, Australian football had no controlling organisation. Club secretaries used to meet before the season to hammer out a schedule of contests for the ensuing season, and for the first five years of its existence the North side was rated as a junior club.

However for the 1874 season North Melbourne became a 'senior' club. This meant that it was now accorded much more publicity, and the general public was more interested in its exploits.

The North players appeared in the club's first uniform this year It consisted of narrow blue and white hoops, and this accorded them a much needed distinctiveness that allowed spectators to distinguish them from their well-established competitors.

From obscure beginnings in 1869

Unlike more recently founded League clubs, the events that brought North into being are long forgotten, and never written down. No record has survived of any meeting to launch its activities, if such a formal meeting ever took place.

All we have today, so far removed from the circumstances of the club's birth, is a tradition that 1869 was the inaugural year of North Melbourne, and some sketchy details of its concluding game for that season. An entry in the *Australasian* for 2 October 1869 informs its readers that 'The North Melbourne Club closed their season on Saturday by a match with the Northcote Club, in which they were victorious, a well-kicked goal being obtained for them by D. Cook.'

CLUB NEWS 1869–1887

On 25 September 1869 North Melbourne defeated Northcote at Royal Park in the final match of its first season. The first recorded mention of the club was published in the *Australasian* on 2 October 1869. A player named D. Cook kicked the club's first recorded goal.

Carlton United went down to North on 16 July 1870. Captain Harry Fuhrhop scored the only goal in the same week that a club named Hotham played Hobson's Railway Club. There were separate clubs in existence in 1870 – although some interchange of players appears to have occurred between them, common in the fluid days of early football.

In 1871 T. P. Power's *The Footballer* annual described North as 'in the spring of life'.

Playing as a 'junior' club, North played 14 games in 1873 and won seven, drew six and lost one. The one loss was to a senior club, Albert Park. In this season junior clubs apparently fielded 20 players, and senior clubs 18.

North became a Senior club in 1874, and finished behind Carlton, Melbourne and Albert Park in the season's tally of matches, after defeating Albert Park along the way.

In 1875 the North Melbourne Football Club had 120 members.

North Melbourne used 'the Royal Park' for all its home engagements from 1869–75.

On 12 April 1877 at Sutcliffe's Turf

1869 – 1887

Early players

While little is known of North's earliest players, T. P. Power's *The Footballer*, first published in the mid-1870s, offers some detailed information. Harry Fuhrhop, who captained the side during the 1870s, is described as 'commanding his team with judgment,' while his deputy, Billy Maclean was seen as 'a fine all-round player, steady and persevering.' And James Robertson, who led North in its second season in the new Association, was 'invested with a roving commission, being one of the fleetest runners in the colony [who] dodges and kicks splendidly,' while one R. Sutcliffe was a 'very effective goal-sneak', a point he proved by leading North's goalscoring in 1875, with eight for the season.

Harry Fuhrhop, captain.

The first known photograph of a North Melbourne team. Fuhrhop holds the ball, Gardiner wears a bowler hat and the stripes are horizontal.

Early amalgamation

One of the club's earliest setbacks came a mere seven years after its founding. Before the start the 1876 season, North Melbourne ceased to function and amalgamated with Albert Park. However despite a name change to 'Albert Park cum North Melbourne', it was predominantly a North side, captained by Fuhrhop and dominated by other former North players. A successful combination, the team finished its first season third behind Carlton and Melbourne, having beaten both sides during the regular season. The merger was short-lived however, and North was to begin the very next season as an independent club.

Hotham helps establish the VFA in 1877

The preparations for the 1877 season were to prove a watershed in the development of the game that became Australian Football. The major competing clubs came together and formed the first controlling body, which they called the Victorian Football Association.

The remnants of the club that had been founded by Gardiner and his companions, and that had survived the amalgamation with Albert Park, met at the Turf Club Hotel in Flemington Road, and re-established the club. However, as the municipality was then known as Hotham, it was decided to adopt that name and to operate under it.

While Melbourne's senior clubs had competed in an organised fashion since the 1860s, the competition was now better organised and run more effectively on a collective basis. Along with Hotham, seven other clubs were accorded first-class status: Melbourne, Geelong, Carlton, Albert Park, St. Kilda and East Melbourne.

While the team from North Melbourne territory did not achieve the ultimate success in the first decade of the Association, those seasons as Hotham turned out to be a time of considerable consolidation. After playing its home engagements at Royal Park, it moved temporarily to a site adjacent the University of Melbourne, before settling at its present home in Arden Street.

The club played its first match there on Saturday, 29 April 1882. Its opponent was Royal Park, and it triumphed by scoring 2.9 to 0.2 The following year, an admission charge was made for the first time, amounting to the princely sum of sixpence.

At the inception of the VFA, Hotham had appeared in the colours now traditional to North Melbourne, but wore guernseys with horizontal stripes. This had caused a good deal of confusion when the club clashed with Geelong, whose jumper was practically the same. The Association directed the change to the now familiar blue and white vertical stripes, and from 1886 the men from Arden Street went into battle in the new rig.

Another aspect of consolidation at this time was the decision of the club's executive to revert to the original name of North Melbourne. In August 1887 the Town of Hotham was officially renamed the Town of North Melbourne, and, appropriately, its football team followed suit.

While the club still lacked a Premiership, it had proved to be quite competitive, and had given indications that the prize was within its grasp.

Club Hotel (which is opposite the Dental Hospital where the Haymarket once stood), the club that Gardiner and his companions had formed back in 1869 was re-established, after its amalgamation with Albert Park, as Hotham Football Club. For a President, it turned to the licensee of the pub, R. Sutcliffe, who had occupied that position prior to the amalgamation. Harry Fuhrhop was again its skipper, and the indefatigable James Henry Gardiner once again became treasurer, after an absence from that position of four years.

Season 1878 saw the arrival of a new Senior captain Jimmy Robertson, who was regarded as 'the fastest man that plays'. North had four State representatives in 1879 – Billy McLean, Jimmy Robertson, Arthur Ley and F. Lording.

On 15 September 1883, A. Todd achieved a record 78-yard drop kick which also gave his club a goal against Carlton on 15 September. He and his brother H. Todd were joint leading goalkickers for the club with 10 goals apiece. The following year he led the club's goalscoring with 13 for the season.

In 1885 Hotham's G. Houston became its first team member to be the leading goalscorer in the Association, with 38.

In 1885 the Arden Street Reserve became permanently reserved to the Crown.

Playing for the first time in vertical blue and white stripes on 1 May 1886, Hotham defeated Melbourne on the MCG 4.13 to 2.8. Prior to the game the club decided to insure its players against injury.

NORTH MELBOURNE

The North Melbourne Football Club Coat of Arms.
A translation of the club's Latin motto is: 'Victory demands dedication'.

A view of the 'umpire of the future' prompted by the vicious game of 25 July 1896.

No VFL for North

In late 1896, the radical plan for a breakaway Victorian competition, which had been rumoured for years, finally reached fruition. Geelong Essendon, Melbourne, South Melbourne, Collingwood, Fitzroy, Carlton and St Kilda formed their own league, the VFL. It was a split that posed the immediate question; why was North Melbourne not invited to join?

There are several possibilities. Firstly, North was not a powerful club. They had yet to win a Flag in 20 years of competition, and had only finished in the top four once since 1877. The suburb had become industrialised, but the club was financially weak and lacked big backers. More importantly however, if both Essendon and North were to be in the same league, then Essendon stood to lose some of their most valuable recruiting ground in the area of Kensington and Flemington.

And then there was the trouble with hooligans at Arden Street earlier in 1896.

The Arden Street Affair

On 6 August 1896 a special meeting of the VFA was held at Young and Jackson's Hotel to consider the threat by umpires to refuse to officiate at North Melbourne games in the future. The umpires were furious over alleged cowardly treatment meted out to umpire Roberts by the mob at the match between North and Collingwood a fortnight earlier.

According to one report: 'Magpie Bill Proudfoot, while coming to Roberts' defence, had almost been knocked unconscious by a mob of ruffians intent on invading the ground and was later trampled on by the rioting mob. Knives, a metal rod and other weapons were produced as rowdies set upon the goal umpires. Goal umpire Wallace said that a North barracker had threatened to put a knife in him while another barracker had a bar of iron in a brown paper bag, known to the "push" as a "Ben Bolt".'

The match, which ended in a narrow Collingwood victory, was a thriller and in a fiery last quarter, Roberts elected to keep the game flowing, thus earning the enmity of North barrackers. 'Were it not for the efforts of Proudfoot and a few like-minded men, Roberts could have been torn to pieces,' claimed the same report.

The VFA decided to close the ground to football for the remaining four matches, and to insist on better protection of umpires by the club in the future. The umpires then withdrew their strike threat.

Joey Tankard: 1880s North champion.

CLUB NEWS 1888–1903

In June 1889 North defeated a visiting Port Adelaide side after winning four out of five games in Adelaide, losing to Norwood. Outstanding players for the club at this time were G. and R. Houston, Harry and Arthur Todd and the folk hero, Joey Tankard.

During 1891 L. Carroll was North's interstate representative.

North's W. R. Mullens was the driving force behind the VFA's first-ever subcommittee to draw up next season's fixture of matches in 1891, a time when the VFA adopted the rule banning payment of players.

Alf J. Woodham, one of North's greatest administrators, took up office in 1893. He had been recruited from the North Park Junior Football Club.

For season 1894 North's match against South Melbourne on June 16 and again on July 14 were named by the press of the day as being among the five best games for the year. North rose to sixth, winning eight games, with six draws and four defeats.

Following the breakaway formation of the Victorian Football League at the end of 1896, partly over the question of 'amateurism', North Melbourne continued as a member of the Association.

The Arden Street ground was under reconstruction in 1897, and North, who were runners-up that year, had to play all its home games away, winning 14, and finishing second behind Port Melbourne.

1888 – 1903

'At last!! The Secretary has visions of North's First Premiership' was the caption of this shot of three-quarter time in the 1903 Grand Final.

North's first VFA Flag: 1903

1903 saw the introduction of a finals system in the VFA for the first time. Richmond finished on top of the ladder and were minor Premiers, while North came in second, followed by Footscray and West Melbourne. In the following series, North defeated West, while Richmond went down to Footscray. North won the final staged between the victors, but as minor Premiers Richmond exercised its right to challenge North to a Grand Final. This was played at the old East Melbourne Cricket Ground on September 19, before a crowd of 20,000 fans.

Led by their rover Paddy Noonan, North Melbourne got off to a good start, kicking 3 goals 4 and holding Richmond scoreless in the first quarter. Almost the end of the second quarter Richmond registered a score, having been continually repelled by good defence from North's Barnes. A late rally saw a goal from Johnston, but due to poor kicking Richmond could add only four more points for the half. At half-time, North led 3.4 (22) to Richmond's 1.4 (10).

Early in the third quarter, Considine added another goal to North's tally – his third for the match – and after three more, North seemed home. As they enjoyed 'lemon time' before the final quarter, North officials joined their players on the field in anticipation of victory.

It was a vision that would hold for the final quarter, although Richmond managed to add a further two goals, giving their score a hint of respectability. The final score was North Melbourne 7.6 (48) to Richmond's 3.9 (27). The three finest players of the season, P. Noonan, L. Morrison and J. Stewart were later awarded a prize of a guinea each by the club, while the entire team and the head trainer were awarded a gold commemorative medal by the club

After 34 years, victory had finally come to North. As 'Markwell' (John Healy) put it in the newspaper 'Everything comes to him who waits, though the waiting be sometimes of mighty long duration.'

The 1903 Premiers: Captain Paddy Noonan is in the in the centre of the second row.

North Melbourne FC president, Cr D. Wadick died in 1898 only a few months after being elected to the office. The team did not regain its home ground until late July that year.
North Melbourne was unable to celebrate the first year of the twentieth century, or their 25th year in the VFA with a first Flag – finishing third with 11 wins from 16 matches.
In 1902 Cr George Michael Prendergast began his nine-year stint as one of the club's most successful presidents. During his term of office, North Melbourne would win three Association Premierships. He later became Premier of Victoria.
In the first finals series ever staged by the VFA, North went on to take out its first Flag. The men and the blue and white stripes were the toast of 1903, having won their first ever semi-final over West Melbourne, a final against Footscray and a Grand Final play-off against the minor Premiers, Richmond.
Paddy Noonan had the distinction of being the first North Captain to lead his team to its inaugural Premiership. He was a relentless and dedicated rover who played superbly to the following division of Graham and Morrison.
At the Club's annual general meeting at the North Melbourne Town Hall, North's President, G.M. Prendergast MLA, presented 26 players and the head trainer with a gold medal to commemorate the glory that they had brought to the Club by winning its first ever Premiership in its 34th competitive season.

NORTH MELBOURNE

The 1909 North Melbourne team in variegated uniforms.

Knocking on the VFL door, 1907, 1921

In 1907 North made its first attempt at admission to the VFL. North caused a sensation by deciding, subject to member's approval, to amalgamate with the West Melbourne Football Club (which at that time had found itself without a ground) with a view to seeking admission to the VFL. However the attempt failed, and Richmond and University were admitted instead; all that North and West got for their troubles was expulsion from the VFA. Fortunately, North was readmitted the following year after forming a new club under a new committee.

In 1921, North made another VFL attempt. The committee believed the club was strong enough, based on recent performance, and wanted admittance to the more powerful football body. With that in mind, they embarked on a considerable gamble. Several games into the season the North players were called together and informed that the North Melbourne Football Club had decided to disband.

The North Melbourne committee had been anxious for years to join the League, and thought that the side's record of achievement, as well as the location and quality of its arena warranted its admission. However it had come to believe that the only way in was an amalgamation with Essendon's League side. The Essendon League club was to play at North Melbourne the following season because Essendon's current home ground was being reclaimed by the council. What was envisaged was a virtual amalgamation of the Essendon League club and the North Association club.

As in 1907 however, the plan backfired. Due to legal difficulties, Essendon could not play at North Melbourne and North was left (again) without a team and (again) without a place in the VFL. The Essendon League team was given the ground previously belonging to the Essendon Association side, and North found itself forced to amalgamate not with Essendon's League team, but with its Association sister, after which it was forced to rejoin the VFA.

Syd Barker

Standing an even six feet and sporting a fine physique, Sydney Quinton Barker made his debut for North Melbourne in 1909. A fireman by trade, he had all the attributes required of a follower, including exceptional reach as well as an undeniable talent for leadership. As the key man in North's ruck he was a prominent figure in Melbourne football before and after World War One.

He played with North from 1909 to 1921, participating in four of their Premierships, and captained the side in 1912, 1913, 1915–19, and 1921. He moved to Essendon in 1921 when it was thought that North would finally join the VFL, but returned in 1927 as North's captain and coach. Johnny Lewis called him 'A great general who would never ask a player to do something he was not prepared to do himself.'

He died in 1930, still a comparatively young man. In the club's annual report Australian football to the same extent as the late Syd Barker. As a captain, he was an outstanding genius, and … led several Premiership teams.'

CLUB NEWS 1904–1924

In 1905 North Melbourne were minor Premiers with 15 wins from 19 games, but lost the Preliminary Final and Grand Final to Richmond.

For season 1906 North's home games were played in front of the wooden stand which had formerly stood at the Maribyrnong Racecourse. It was moved and erected at a cost of £850.

Early in 1908 North Melbourne reformed and gained admission to the Victorian Football Association 'under new management'. A new committee was formed after the old one deserted its task, as a result of a public meeting chaired by G. M. Prendergast MLA. In the 1908 season the new North won just four of 18 matches, but recruited the great Charlie Hardy.

The whole playing staff except for Charlie Hardy and Perc Speakman were sacked before the 1909 season.

On 27 August 1910 North amassed the highest-ever score in the Association, 23.21 to Preston's 1.1. That year Frank Caine became the VFA's leading goalkicker with 75 goals.

With the addition of George Rawle to its ranks in 1911, North's famous ruck combination of Barker, Rawle and Hardy was now as its disposal.

The finals series of 1912 created a sensation. On August 24 North drew with Brunswick, 9.6 each. Two weeks later they drew again, scoring 6.12 each. Finally, on September 19 North won through, 12.11 to 9.14. Strangely, these two teams staged yet another

1904 – 1924

Crowds watch North win the 1910 Flag from Brunswick.

16 years, five Flags

From being an underdog that had won only one Premiership in its first 35 years, North would rise to establish itself as a power during the next two decades. Over this period it recorded five Pennants, two of them being undefeated championships.

North were Premiers in 1903 and 1904, but achieved the second in unusual circumstances. While North had won its two final encounters, Richmond, who had dropped one of their games, still had the right to challenge North to a Grand Final. However, the Tiger administration declared that they would not play if umpire Allan was selected. The VFA defied them, named him for the job, and North won outright without having to play the Grand Final – the only time in VFL or VFA history that a team has won on forfeit.

Six years later, they reclaimed the Premiership, and again the circumstances were somewhat unusual. Prior to the 1910 season, North's secretary, Andy Curran, pulled off a coup; he signed Carlton's 'big four', 'Mallee' Johnson, Fred Jinks, Charlie Hammond and 'Silver' Caine. North won the Grand Final over Brunswick 9.14 (68) to 5.9 (39), and Caine kicked five goals before a record crowd for the North Melbourne Recreation Reserve of 28,000.

Then came an unlikely hat-trick of Flags, across five years during which the first World War interrupted football. No Premiership games were played in the VFA in 1916 and 1917. North teams therefore put together three successive Premierships in 1914, 1915 and 1918.

In 1915 it was the first time that an Association team had not lost a single game in a season since 1893. Indeed they were not defeated in 1915 or 1918, marking a period between 25 July 1914 and 30 August 1919, when North Melbourne won a national record of 49 consecutive competition matches, and 56 games in all. Its successive Premiership victims were Footscray (12.14 to 7.9), Brunswick (11.10 to 3.10) and Prahran (18.13 to 3.10). The *Sporting Globe* wrote on Saturday, 15 July 1939 that 'It is doubtful if North ever fielded a better side than the winners of the 1914 Pennant.'

Above: North's great ruck combination – Charles Hardy, Syd Barker, and George Rawle.
Left: Charlie Hammond: former Carlton champ, now at North.

North had obviously been well served by a strong administration over this period through C. Davidson as president and J. E. Heffernan as secretary, but it was on the field that all these successes were chalked up. The key to this longstanding dominance was its immortal ruck combination of Syd Barker (knock), George Rawle (shepherd) and Charlie Hardy (rover).

North's final season in the Association saw the club finish fifth, but in its last game it was the only team to beat the eventual VFA Premiers Footscray.

draw the first time that they met during the home-and-away series of 1913. Before the Final, played at Arden Street, in which North defeated Brunswick, the Lord Mayor unveiled a plaque honouring the players and officials who had volunteered to fight in World War One.
To raise money for the war effort, during 1915 North of the VFA. agreed to play St. Kilda of the VFL. The match took place at the Junction Oval and North defeated the Saints by 26 points.
Due to the wartime circumstances, the VFA competition was suspended during seasons 1916 and 1917.
In 1918 North's T. Stevens was the leading VFA. goalkicker for the season with 54.
North was 'robbed' of the 1920 Flag in the Preliminary Final against Footscray when forward Bill Considine took a mark on the siren in the goal square, but was denied his kick by a crowd invasion with 'Scray four points ahead. The game was abandoned when police could not clear a path. In the replay the next week North lost, ironically by four points, under bizarre circumstances when a North defender missed saving a bouncing shot at goal – twice.
After the re-forming of the North Melbourne club by merger with Essendon (Association) in the wake of the unsuccessful attempt to join the VFL in 1921, the team consolidated around captain–coach George Rawle, who, unlike Charlie Hardy and Syd Barker, was available. North made the finals by winning 13 of 18 games, but lost to Port Melbourne.

NORTH MELBOURNE

North joins the VFL at last

After the two unsuccessful attempts to join the VFL, North Melbourne, along with Hawthorn and Footscray, was finally invited to join in 1925. Even after 27 years the transition was not smooth, with the League delegates debating into the early hours of the morning on the choice of clubs to be invited in.

North's inaugural VFL jumper.

A supporter interviewed by Tom Kelynack ('Kickero' of the Herald) before the season began was confident – 'You can take it from me that we will be the best of the three teams making their first bid for League honours this season, and already several of our supporters have declared their readiness to back that in the usual manner.'

In the first match, against a Geelong side which would be that season's eventual Premiers, North was not given much chance of victory. At quarter time, already trailing 3.5 (23) to 0.1 (1), North was hoping at least to turn in a creditable performance in front of the 10,000-strong crowd, but a terrific second quarter saw them leading by 8 points at half-time. In a close second half, victory was finally sealed for North by a goal from Johnny Lewis. The final scores were 9.13 to 8.11.

Charlie Gaudion in the Big V.

After such a good start – the other debutants, Hawthorn and Footscray, both suffered defeats – North turned in a solid performance for its first season in the VFL. It won five games of its 17 and finished tenth, above both companions from the Association.

1925–1965 HONOUR ROLL

Year	Pos	Leading Goalkicker	No.	Best & Fairest	Captain	Coach
1925	10th	J. L. Wood	27		Welles Eicke	Welles Eicke
1926	12th	Frank Metcalf	26		Gerard Donnelly	Gerard Donnelly
1927	11th	Charles Tyson	23		Syd Barker/Charles Tyson	Barker/Tyson
1928	11th	Chris Nolan	24		Charles Tyson	Charles Tyson
1929	12th	John Dowling	28		Tyson/A. (Tim) Trevaskis	Tyson/Paddy Noonan
1930	12th	R. Matthews	29		Johnny Lewis	Johnny Lewis
1931	12th	Johnny Lewis	25		Johnny Lewis	Norman Clark
1932	8th	Tom Fitzmaurice	62		Dick Taylor	Dick Taylor
1933	8th	Tom Fitzmaurice	60		Dick Taylor	Dick Taylor
1934	12th	Tom Fitzmaurice	63		Taylor/Tom Fitzmaurice	Taylor/Fitzmaurice
1935	12th	Johnny Lewis	23		Fitzmaurice/Ted Llewellyn	Fitzmaurice/P. Scanlon
1936	11th	D. Cassidy	48		Charlie Gaudion	Paddy Scanlon
1937	12th	Stewart Anderson	18	Wally Carter	Charlie Gaudion	Paddy Scanlon
1938	9th	Sel Murray	56	Jock Cordner	Keith Forbes	Keith Forbes
1939	9th	Sel Murray	78	Syd Dyer	Keith Forbes	Keith Forbes
1940	12th	Sel Murray	58	R. 'Jimmy' Adamson	Len Thomas/Adamson	Thomas/Adamson
1941	9th	Sel Murray	88	George Kennedy	Bill Findlay	Bob McCaskill
1942	9th	Sel Murray	42	J. 'Jimmy' Allister	Bill Findlay	Bob McCaskill/Findlay
1943	9th	Bill Findlay	43	Danny Kemp	Bill Findlay	Bill Findlay
1944	6th	Bill Findlay	56	Alan Crawford	'Dally' O'Brien	Bob McCaskill
1945	4th	Bill Findlay	48	Les Foote	'Dally' O'Brien	Bob McCaskill
1946	9th	Syd Dyer	56	Don Condon	Fred Fairweather	Bob McCaskill
1947	10th	Syd Dyer	47	Keith McKenzie	Kevin Dynon	Bob McCaskill
1948	8th	Don Condon	38	'Dally' O'Brien	Les Foote	Wally Carter
1949	3rd	Jock Spencer	64	Les Foote	Les Foote	Wally Carter
1950	2nd	Jock Spencer	86	Les Foote	Les Foote	Wally Carter
1951	9th	Jock Spencer	57	Jock Spencer	Les Foote	Wally Carter
1952	7th	Jock Spencer	51	Jock McCorkell	Kevin Dynon	Wally Carter
1953	7th	Gerald Marchesi	49	Jack O'Halloran	Kevin Dynon	Wally Carter
1954	4th	Jock Spencer	38	John Brady	Gerald Marchesi	Jock McCorkell
1955	11th	Jock Spencer	68	Bob Brooker	Vic Lawrence	Jock McCorkell
1956	12th	Jock Spencer	40	Jack Edwards	Bob Brooker	Charlie Gaudion
1957	8th	John Dugdale	37	Brian Martyn	John Brady	Charlie Gaudion
1958	3rd	John Dugdale	57	Allen Aylett	John Brady	Wally Carter
1959	6th	Peter Schofield	46	Allen Aylett	John Brady	Wally Carter
1960	11th	John Dugdale	38	Allen Aylett	Albert Martello	Wally Carter
1961	12th	John Dugdale	47	Laurie Dwyer	Allen Aylett	Wally Carter
1962	11th	John Dugdale	44	Bill Serong	Allen Aylett	Wally Carter
1963	7th	John Dugdale	30	Noel Teasdale	Allen Aylett	Allan Killigrew
1964	8th	John Dugdale	46	Noel Teasdale	Aylett/Noel Teasdale	Allan Killigrew
1965	9th	Frank Goode	38	Noel Teasdale	Noel Teasdale	Allan Killigrew

CLUB NEWS 1925–1965

North had three coaches in 1926 – Welles Eicke, Charlie Thomas and Gerald Donnelly. Charlie Thomas held the reins for just one match.

In 1926 the former 'Shinboners' were known as 'Blue Birds'. Not surprisingly, the label did not stick.

For the national carnival in 1927, three North players were nominated – Bill Russ, Leo Dwyer and Dave Walsh. Unfortunately Walsh, a truly great fullback, got a severe knee injury and could not take his place in the side.

On 24 March 1928 the major brick grandstand that still dominates the Arden Street reserve was formally opened by Melbourne's Lord Mayor, Alderman Sir Stephen Morell.

Leo Dwyer was equal third in the Brownlow Medal count for 1928. This was the best performance by a North player until his son Laurie was also third in 1960.

Jack Adams, who would later be club secretary and eventually president, became a member of the committee for the first time in 1928.

On 20 December 1928 the battle between the 'Progressives' and the 'Welfare Party' for control of the Committee was resolved by club elections. The latter were swept into office.

The legendary Syd Barker died on 23 March 1930.

After adopting a royal blue guernsey with a white V for 1925 season, the North reappeared in vertical stripes of these colours once again in 1933.

1925 – 1965

Above: Les Foote; Centre: North's 1949 team. Right: John Dugdale hits the heights.

1945: first finals spot

After 20 slow years lodged in the bottom half of the VFL table, North finally found its way into a VFL finals series in 1945. Finishing the season in third spot, it had its first shot at a VFL crown since leaving the Association. Because the MCG was unavailable, the finals series was played at Princes Park, and a record crowd of 54,846 saw North's hopes of a Flag dashed. An in-form Carlton demolished North, despite a last-quarter comeback, by 26 points. Final scores were North 8.20 (68) to Carlton 14.10 (94).

1950: a Grand Final

North Melbourne's first Grand Final appearance in 1950 came after a brilliant win over Geelong in the Preliminary Final, and a stirring battle with Essendon in the Second Semi-final, going down by just three points. In the Grand Final a fresher Essendon jumped North in the first quarter kicking 7.3 to 4.0, and were never headed. The final score: North Melbourne 7.12 (54) lost to Essendon 13.14 (92) before a crowd of 85,876. More than half were disappointed in the result – an army of friends, as Hec de Lacy wrote in the *Sporting Globe*, won over by North's 'unbeatable spirit'. They would have to wait another generation.

1965 VFL night victory

Since the VFL's night competition's began in 1956, North had played in every season with the exception of 1958. In 1961, they played Geelong in the final without success. A VFL Premiership still eluded the Kangaroos. But in 1965, the year the club made the disastrous move to play home games at the Coburg City Oval, there was one bright note. The team made it to the Grand Final of the night competition after good wins over Hawthorn and Footscray. North was still rated an underdog, but played like winners in the final against Carlton. After a slow start saw North down by two goals at quarter time, they began to wear down the boys in blue, thanks mainly to the efforts of ruckman Bob Pascoe, who was unquestionably best on ground. In the end, they won comfortably by 40 points, and jubilant supporters poured over the fence. They streamed to the middle to help North celebrate its first Senior VFL Pennant by chairing coach Alan Killigrew and champions Noel Teasdale and John Dugdale from the ground. North won 14.13 (97) to Carlton's 9.3 (57).

Above: Roos fans of the 1950s. Right: Wells' view of North's night eclipse of the Blues.

On 5 December 1934 Arthur Calwell (later Labor leader) and Johnny Meere were made life members of the club.
The VFL lent North £500 in 1935 against a debt of £1200, provided the committee raised another £500, which they did by guaranteeing a bank loan. North, through stringent economies, repaid the other £200 before the season began and reduced it by £120 during the season – thereby saving the club.
During season 1936 Charlie Gaudion became North's first player to captain Victoria.
Season 1937 witnessed the creation of the Syd Barker Trophy for the team's best and fairest player. Wally Carter was the first recipient of this award.
Frank Trainor took over as club president in 1938 to begin a distinguished term in that office.
In 1945 the North side concluded the home-and-away rounds in third place, qualifying for a berth in the VFL Finals series for the first time.
Despite being VFL minor Premiers in 1949 for the first time, North lost both finals encounters.
North Melbourne took the sobriquet 'The Kangaroos' in 1950.
Les Foote won his third Syd Barker award in 1950.
During the 1950 finals series North won its first League finals match, over Geelong, 14.16 to 12.11.
On 16 August 1958 Essendon's captain Jack Clarke called for a count at Windy Hill in front of 27,500. The count found 18 North players, who went on to win 11.14 to 8.14.

NORTH MELBOURNE

Aylett's five-year plan

A new president of the club, Allen Aylett, led the club into 1971 – the first season of a five-year plan, strategically directed toward bringing home the club's first League Premiership. The club's entire structure and mode of operation were subjected to scrutiny, a plan designed to make the club more efficient. As an external sign of this change, their traditional royal blue socks were replaced by blue and white hoops, while any experienced player who failed to perform was removed – replaced by such young faces as Phil Baker, Ross Henshaw and Keith Greig.

Procedures from the old Association days, such as the election of captains and vice-captains were reinstated, and the club aimed to experiment with new, young players and to recruit wisely and swiftly, with the aim of building a team for the future. The plan got off to a flying start under new coach Brian Dixon. The first game of the new 1971 season, against the previous year's Premiers Carlton, resulted in a crushing victory to North. However this success was short-lived, and North would have to spend the next few years building the nucleus of a winning team before the plan could reach fruition.

The handball wizard, Barry Cable.

Left: Mick Nolan, the galloping gasometer.
Above: 'Slammin' Sammy Kekovich.

> 🏉 In 1972 the VFL, wanting to avoid restraint of trade litigation, introduced the '10-year Rule'. A player with 10 years service could transfer to the club of his choice. North delegate Albert Mantello saw immediately what this could mean, and North drew up a shortlist of players. 'The Great Persuader' Ron Joseph went after Barry Davis of Essendon, John Rantall of South Melbourne and Doug Wade of Geelong (pictured, left), and Carl Ditterich of St Kilda. He got three out of four, for $10,000 to sign, plus $5000 a year. Big Carl went to Melbourne.

CLUB NEWS 1966–1974

Back home at Arden Street in 1966, North had seven wins and a draw for the season. The draw was against Richmond on the Queen's Birthday – and kept them out of the Finals. North recorded its then-highest score – 22.8 (140) against Fitzroy.

Alan Killigrew coached Victoria to success at the Carnival series in Hobart in 1966. His team included Noel Teasdale (named All-Australian, as well as winning a record fourth Syd Dyer Trophy) and Mick Gaudion, who emulated his famous father Charlie who played in the Big V in the 1930s.

North made it back-to-back Night Flags by defeating Hawthorn 20.12 to 12.7 in 1966.

The Melbourne City Council granted the North Melbourne Football Club 21-year tenure of the Arden Street ground during 1967.

North staged the first Grand Final Breakfast as a valuable fundraising event for the first time in 1967 at the Southern Cross. The first guest speaker was the VFL's Eric McCutchan.

For season 1968 North coach Keith McKenzie persuaded his former RAAF mate and now Prime Minister John Gorton to accept the club's No. 1 ticket.

In 1968 Lou Richards hailed new star recruit, Sam Kekovich, as 'Slamming Sam' as he burst brilliantly onto the football scene.

North celebrated its centenary year 1969 by officially opening its own social club. This took place on August

1966 – 1974

Keith Greig's double

Between 1971 and 1985, Keith Greig became North's most honoured player. A dashing wingman and half-back, he played 297 games for North and was eventually bestowed with the club's highest honour – life membership. From his debut he displayed uncanny ball-handling skills and a technical brilliance which won him a place as one of the most revered players ever to don a blue and white jersey.

He won two Brownlow medals in succession, including North's first in 1973, and in both years he tallied an astounding 27 votes. As well as captaining North from 1976 until he resigned from the post in 1979, he represented his state 13 times and was named captain of Victoria in 1978. He was also a member of North's first Premiership side in 1975 and won the Syd Barker medal in 1980. He was even decreed a Member of the British Empire in the Queen's Birthday Honours List in 1975 for his services to sport.

After his retirement he kept a keen eye on North, and returned in 1992 as chairman of selectors. In 1996 he was also named on the wing in the AFL's team of the century, and was inducted into its Hall of Fame.

Left: To the victor, the rest. Ron Barassi pretends to sleep while guarding the 1975 Premiership Cup. His mind was wide awake plotting 1976.

The Barassi record

When Ron Barassi signed on as coach of North Melbourne in 1972, he did so on the back of a serviette. However, from such innocuous beginnings, a powerful partnership would grow. Barassi would coach North for eight seasons, during which he led them to seven finals series which included six consecutive Grand Finals, two Premierships and one Night Flag.

Born in Castlemaine on 27 February 1936, Barassi was North's 23rd coach, and coached them to 188 wins in 176 games. Barassi was not only a central figure at North, but as Malcolm Blight said 'I suppose for the past 25 years, if there has been one name synonymous with Australian Football it's been Barassi.'

He arrived at the club as part of Aylett's five-year plan which included luring Barry Davis, Doug Wade and John Rantall. The climax of this plan saw North win its first Flag in 1975. His tenure also saw the club notch up three Brownlow Medallists and one leading goalkicker.

When he left the club in 1980, after losing their first Elimination Final to Collingwood, he said 'The coach always feels lonely after a loss, but yes, there is a special sadness. When you understand it is your last game after eight years – a long time. People don't realise coaches love their players a lot more than it appears. North has been wonderful to me. I am a better person, a better coach.'

Alf Brown wrote after the 1977 Flag 'North won the Premiership in one of the greatest football performances of all times to stamp Barassi as the best coach the game has produced.'

During the AFL's Centenary Season, Barassi was named as a member of its Hall of Fame, a member of its Team of the Century and one of the AFL 'Legends'.

1966 – 1974 HONOUR ROLL

Year	Pos	Leading Goalkicker	No.	Best & Fairest	Captain	Coach
1966	7th	Frank Goode	49	Noel Teasdale	Noel Teasdale	Allan Killigrew
1967	8th	Gary Farrant	26	Laurie Dwyer	Noel Teasdale	Keith McKenzie
1968	12th	Doug Farrant	35	John Dugdale	John Dugdale	Keith McKenzie
1969	8th	Sam Kekovich	56	Sam Kekovich	John Dugdale	Keith McKenzie
1970	12th	Gary Farrant	32	Barry Cable	John Dugdale	Keith McKenzie
1971	9th	Sam Kekovich	35	David Dench	Barry Goodingham	Brian Dixon
1972	12th	Kekovich/Vin Doolan	19	Ken Montgomery	David Dench	Brian Dixon
1973	6th	Doug Wade	73	Barry Davis	Barry Davis	Ron Barassi
1974	2nd	Doug Wade	103	John Rantall	Barry Davis	Ron Barassi

5, and the honour went to Lord Mayor Rt. Hon. Cr. R. T. Talbot.
During 1970, the Roos downed the Bombers in their first-ever appearance at the VFL's new stadium at Waverley.
Ron Joseph gained the services of much sought after Western Australian star, Barry Cable, just for the 1970 season. Captain John Dugdale was injured pre-season and only played two of 22 possible matches.
On 14 November 1970 North announced that it had signed parliamentarian, Brian Dixon MLA to coach for the next two seasons.
With the advent of season 1971 North's new President, former club champion Allan Aylett, spearheaded the club's five year plan to win its first League Premiership.

In 1972 David Dench became the youngest captain in AFL history.
Ron Barassi, taking a year off from football coaching, was lured back to North in September 1972 by Albert Mantello. He signed a contract on a serviette worth $15,000 a year for three years, at the Old Melbourne Motel in Kangaroo territory. The super-coach also was backed by North businessmen (including Alan Aylett and Ron Joseph) for a loan of $50,000. Barassi also had the services of the trio snapped up by North under the short-lived 10-year rule, and North were set for a bright future.
Under Barassi's coaching North dramatically improved in 1973. It missed a finals berth by two points and a few percentage points.

NORTH MELBOURNE

Now or never – 1975

After a horror start to the year – losing six of its first nine games – and coming hot on the heels of their 1974 Grand Final defeat, 1975 was not looking good for North Melbourne. North Melbourne president Allen Aylett and coach Ron Barassi must have wondered whether the estimated $1 million and buckets of blood, sweat and tears expended had been worth it.

It was the final year in the much-lauded five-year plan, and high-priced recruits such as Doug Wade did not seem to be fulfilling their promise.

Barassi was unperturbed, and his confidence in the ability of his players was rewarded when North began to find its feet in the middle of the season. From late June to early August, they strung together an impressive seven consecutive victories, a feat which helped boost them to third on the ladder at the end of the home-and-away season – a good position but one from which no VFL team had ever won a Premiership in modern times.

In the finals series, their first opponents were Carlton, who did not really seem up to the task. It was only their accuracy, and North's inaccuracy, in front of goal which kept them in the game up to the final quarter, after which North kicked away to win 14.12 (96) to Carlton's 12.4 (76).

Their second final, the Preliminary Final, was against a Richmond side in search of its third consecutive Premiership. It wasn't to be however, with North looking the better side from the first whistle. Strong defence was North's greatest asset, with players such as Croswell and Rantall showing them the way to the Grand Final, North's second in two years.

It was a team of champions that got them there, the result of good recruiting by Joseph. The team that was to contest the final would include such greats as David Dench, John Rantall, Brent Croswell, Keith

Ron Barassi lays down the law in season 1975.

Greig, Wayne Schimmelbusch, Sam Kekovich, Doug Wade, Malcolm Blight, Barry Davis, Barry Goodingham and Gary Cowton.

Only Hawthorn stood between them and the crowning of their five year plan – or its utter failure.

Winners are grinners: the immortal 1975 team

1975 HONOUR ROLL

Year	Pos	Leading Goalkicker	No.	Best & Fairest	Captain	Coach
1975	1st	Doug Wade	47	Barry Davis	Barry Davis	Ron Barassi

CLUB NEWS 1975

An extraordinary brawl erupted at Princes Park in the opening-round clash between Hawthorn and North Melbourne, involving 34 of the 36 players on the ground – but not Hawk strongman Don Scott and North's Brad Smith. Former North coach (1971–72) and then Minister for Youth, Sport and Recreation Brian Dixon called for the order-off rule to be introduced. Hawthorn won the game by 29 points.

Swap soap opera – Brent 'Tiger' Croswell finally crosses from Carlton to North Melbourne (and his former coach Ron Barassi) and trains on May 8. He had threatened to play without a clearance for the Geelong West Roosters after being dropped by Carlton for disciplinary reasons. North then offered Sam Kekovich as a swap, which was refused.

Phil 'Snake' Baker took one of his patented huge leaps on April 26, and slotted a 70-metre goal. But it failed to ignite North, who fizzled to a 11.19 (85) loss to Fitzroy 17.13 (115).

Doug Wade had a long slow walk off the ground when dragged by coach Barassi in the third quarter, after kicking just three behinds against Essendon. He showered, changed and left the ground before the end of the game. Barassi was reported for abusing umpire Mike Henry, and later slams North players for throwing the game away – losing by 15 points. Barassi was fined $100 by the Tribunal.

1975

Barry Davis Best and Fairest and Premiership captain.

Above: Malcolm Blight – Kangaroo flies with Hawks.

Left: Three-quarter time – keeping a lid on it. Inset: A first for WEG as well.

North Melbourne's first VFL Flag

If any one day can be regarded as the most important day in the history of the North Melbourne Football Club, it must surely have to be Saturday, 27 September 1975. On that day the club that had begun in obscurity 106 years before achieved the pinnacle of success; it won its first League Premiership. The plan to win it may have begun in earnest in 1971, when Joseph began recruiting a galaxy of stars and supercoach Ron Barassi, but the plan to win the 1975 Grand Final began with a suggestion by Chairman of Selectors Max Ritchie to play veteran Barry 'Lurch' Goodingham. This was designed to induce Hawthorn into playing gangling Bernie Jones, and it worked a treat.

Goodingham trotted onto the field and then went straight to the bench while Jones played the whole match, accumulating only a few more possessions than Lurch in the last quarter. Doug Wade said the game passed like a fantastic 120-minute dream, but when it was all over he pinched himself, kissed the ball, and then knew it was real.

In truth, North never looked likely to be beaten, despite the nervous energy – the result of little finals experience on either side – that infected both teams. After John Burns bounced one through early in the first quarter, to the cheers of a crowd of 110,551, North never looked back.

In the North rooms at the break was a mixture of excited anticipation at the real prospect of victory, and nervous anxiety that something might go wrong. Their lead was good, but by no means unbridgeable, and while Hawthorn had some good players in defence, North was overall the stronger side.

After the break North went up a notch, and fine performances from such players as Brent Crosswell, Keith Greig, John Burns, David Dench, Mick Nolan, Sam Kekovich and Doug Wade made victory a certainty. John Rantall was best on ground.

As champion coach Ron Barassi said, 'It was magic, it really was. The first [Premiership] is something special; not many people in the modern era can claim that joy. My greatest pleasure that night was watching the older supporters, you know, 50-, 60-, 70-year-olds. They were saying, 'If I die now, it doesn't matter,' that sort of thing. It was absolutely magnificent.'

The final scoreboard read North 19.8 (122) defeated Hawthorn 9.13 (67).

North dumped star full-forward Doug Wade to the Reserves for the game against Fitzroy on July 6, choosing Brent Crosswell instead. Wade's revenge was to be chosen as one of the two sets of 'old bones' in the Grand Final team with Barry Goodingham. Wade finished the season with 47, less than half his return the year before (103 – North's first century-maker in front of goal) – but he also had a Premiership medal.

After the slow start, North entered the final five in Round 14 with a win over Fitzroy, following it up with a slogging win at a heavy VFL Park over Carlton the next week.

North beat the Blues in the Qualifying Final – 14.12 (96) to 12.4 (76). 26 shots to 16 was a more accurate reflection of the state of play. 74,015 fans watched at the MCG as Graeme Melrose, Barry Cable and Barry Davis carved Carlton up – and David Dench, John Rantall and Frank Gumbleton repelled all boarders.

In the 1975 Preliminary Final, North had to beat Richmond for the right to come up against minor Premiers Hawthorn in the big one. It rained for the whole week before the game, played at VFL Park. North were in front all day, and the tired Tigers could not bridge the gap – which was 26 points in the third quarter. Scores at the end saw North 10.16 (76) defeat Richmond 8.11 (59) with Arnold Briedis kicking three goals and Paul Feltham two. The defence, particularly Brent Croswell and John Rantall, played well. The whole team had the scent.

NORTH MELBOURNE

Phil Baker's leap in the '78 Grand Final.   *Schimmelbusch.*   *Kerry Goode takes a characteristic screamer.*

Heroes of the 70s

Not all North's finest in the 70s were from other League clubs – North was growing its own talent as well. Foremost among these were players of the calibre of Wayne Schimmelbusch from Brunswick and David Dench from West Coburg.

Wayne 'Schimma' Schimmelbusch, although a versatile player, spent most of his career between 1973 and 1987 on the wing or the half-forward flank. The prolific goal-kicker amassed a goal aggregate of 355 across his 306 games. An integral part of North's Premierships in 1975 and 1977, he was acting vice-captain in '77 and was appointed captain in 1979, a position he held until his retirement. In 1980, he captained North to a Night Premiership, but sadly ended his career with a serious knee injury against the Swans a few weeks after captaining Victoria in 1987.

One of the greatest full-backs ever to play the game, Dench was an equally popular member of the side in the '70s, spending his entire career, from 1969 to 1984, at Arden street. Throughout his 276 games he was the springboard for many a North attack, and in 1972, at the age of 20, he was appointed captain of North Melbourne – the youngest in League history. Although the honour was short-lived, with Barry Davis taking over the next year, he was vice-captain in North's historic first Premiership in 1975, and acting captain (with Keith Greig out injured) in their second Flag in 1977. He was North's Syd Barker Medallist a club-record four times, in 1971, 1976, 1977 and 1981, and represented Victoria four times.

1976–1978 HONOUR ROLL

Year	Pos	Leading Goalkicker	No.	Best & Fairest	Captain	Coach
1976	2nd	Wayne Schimmelbusch	43	David Dench	Keith Greig	Ron Barassi
1977	1st	Brent Crosswell	42	David Dench	Keith Greig	Ron Barassi
1978	2nd	Malcolm Blight	77	Malcolm Blight	Keith Greig	Ron Barassi

CLUB NEWS 1976–1978

In Round 10, 1976 North's Malcolm Blight made one of the most sensational finishes in League history. With North trailing Carlton by 27 points at half-time, he was told by coach Barassi that he was 'playing like a goose'. Still behind in time-on, Blight kicked three goals to snatch victory over the Blues at Princes Park. His last one, put through after the final siren, must have travelled at least 90 metres and his second goal was achieved with a boomerang kick, the first time he had attempted it.
North was fined $2000 by the VFL for wearing the wrong shorts – blue – instead of the approved white nicks in the match against South Melbourne on 12 June 1976.

Though North defeated Port Adelaide by 50 points in the NFL-Wills Cup in Adelaide, Malcolm Blight suffered. He appears to have developed an allergy to Adelaide grass, which President Allen Aylett believed might be damaging to his health if he ever returned.
For the first time, North in 1976 became the recipient of the Dr McClelland trophy for the best aggregate in all three divisions, Senior, Reserves and Under 19.
North presents a plan to the VFL by Melbourne restaurateur Robin Smith to cut the competition to eight teams after 15 rounds.
Ron Barassi underwent an emergency operation after a 12.35 a.m. car crash near Lismore, south west of Melbourne, on 18 August 1976. Neil

1976-1978

David Dench triumphantly holds the 1977 Premiership Cup.

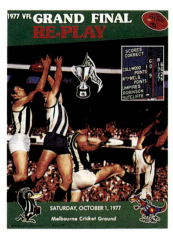

The *Football Record's* replay edition – note the scoreboard.

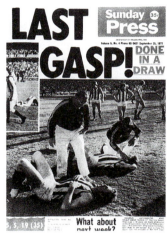

The *Sunday press* records the drawn Grand Final.

Two Grand Finals, one Flag: 1977

Coming off their first Flag in 1975, and second place in 1976, some around the club were afraid that North would slip, as had St Kilda and Footscray into the territory of the 'one-timer'. They were determined to build on their success however, and win another Flag. As with their completed five-year plan, such determination would be only part of the equation. Dynamic club president Allen Aylett had moved on to become president of the League, to be replaced by Lloyd Holyoak, already a member of the board himself. The club received a boost from the return of Ron Joseph to the administration, and things were looking good early in the season.

By Round 5 they were unbeaten, and comfortable at the top of the table, but in Round 6, tragedy struck. Not only did they lose to Richmond, but champion captain Keith Greig suffered a severe injury to his cruciate ligament, and although he would return for two matches in June, he would eventually miss the remainder of the season. At the close of the regular season, things were still looking positive for North, and third position on the ladder was no worse than it had been in 1975. They could not know it at the time, but North was about to embark on the longest finals campaign in League history.

The First Qualifying Final, against Hawthorn, was a disaster. Beaten soundly by 38 points, North fans were stunned to see North coach Ron Barassi slam his players the next day on Channel 7's 'World of Sport'. If it was a ploy to fire North up for the cut-throat First Semi-final, it worked, and North stunned Richmond by 47 points. The next week, again playing Hawthorn, but this time for a spot in the Grand Final, North dominated the Hawks to win 16.16 (112) to 5.13 (43).

The stage was set for a huge Grand Final. Already a sell-out, it would be the first Grand Final to be televised live in Victoria. A good first quarter saw North take the advantage, but a fightback by the Pies gave them a lead of 27 points. However, a strong last term saw North take the lead. With moments to go, Collingwood's Ross Dunne took a mark in the goal square. Seconds later, with the goal umpire signalling six points, the incredible had happened: the 1977 Grand Final had been drawn. It was only the second time in VFL history, the previous being in 1948.

The replay the next week promised an equally enthralling match. Inaccuracy cost North early in the game, but at three-quarter time they still led by 30 points, 15.19 (109) to 12.7 (79). Barassi urged his players on: 'We have to put the kibosh on them this quarter. I want everyone to marshal every fibre of force and energy within you, and pump it out … for bloody North Melbourne and yourselves.' And pump it they did, North holding on to win by 27 points, 21.25 (151) to Collingwood 19.10 (124).

Roberts, St Kilda Brownlow Medallist was also injured. Barassi conducted training the next week in a golf buggy, which broke down, forcing the great man onto crutches.

Hawthorn defeated North in the 1976 Qualifying final, 14.19 (103) to 12.11 (83), after an all-in brawl at the opening bounce.

The Galloping Gasometer Mick Nolan played a slashing game in the 1976 First Semi against Geelong. Schimma kicked six goals in the wet, North 14.9 (93) to Geelong 8.12 (60).

North went on to play in its third successive Grand Final in 1976 to consolidate itself as a League power but was not able to win 'back-to-back'. Only 10 points separated the teams at three-quarter time, but Hawthorn kept North goalless in the last stanza, with Peter Knights a titan in defence. They were going to do it for their mortally ill comrade Peter Crimmins, and did. Final scores 13.22 (100) to North 10.10 (70).

In 1977 North had a new president, Lloyd Holyoak, and had gained the services of Stan Alves from Melbourne and John Cassin from Essendon.

By season's end in 1977, John Cassin had established himself as the record holder for the most games played by a league player in one season. His tally was 25, made possible by the Grand Final replay.

Premiership Medallions were officially presented for the first time after the 1977 Grand Final, and Wayne Schimmelbusch was the first player to receive this honour.

NORTH MELBOURNE

Two great Kangaroos: Malcolm Blight and Allen Aylett.

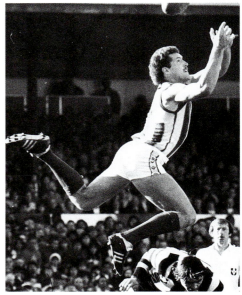

Ross Glendinning flies in 1983.

Brownlow boys: Blight and Glendinning

Only the second North player to take home the coveted Brownlow, Malcolm Blight was the toast of both his native State, South Australia, and his adopted State, Victoria. While at Woodville in the SANFL he won the Magarey medal, and came to North with high expectations in 1974. His aerial work was spectacular and effective, and he capped it all off with phenomenal kicking ability.

His Brownlow victory in 1978 was a much deserved honour, but quite possibly the worst-kept secret in the game. He played 178 matches for North between 1974 and 1982 and kicked 444 goals. He also coached them for 16 games in 1981, and holds a life membership with the club. In 1996 he was named a member of the AFL's inaugural Hall of Fame.

Another illustrious member of North's Brownlow brigade is Ross Glendinning, who had already established himself as a player to be reckoned with in Western Australia prior to being recruited by North. He missed the chance to play in the 1977 Grand Final because his previous club, East Perth, would not grant him a clearance. A tall, strong player, he had sure-marking hands and could achieve distance and accuracy with his kicking, making him perfect for centre half-back or centre half-forward.

While with North from 1978 to 1986, he played 190 games and booted 215 goals, winning the Syd Barker medal in 1982 and 1983. During that period he also won regular interstate selection, having this honour in successive years from 1981 to 1984.

The magic Krakouer brothers

Jim and Phil Krakouer were recruited to North together, and made their debut together in 1982, where they both remained until 1989. Jim appeared in 134 games and kicked 229 goals, while Phil played 141 games and tallied 224 majors. Their similarities extend beyond their names, however. In 1982 they were joint leading club goalkickers with 44 each, an honour which from 1985 to 1988 alternated between them. One honour which Jim received that Phil did not match was the Syd Barker Medal in 1986.

Throughout their joint careers they exhibited an extraordinary ability to find each other on the field, often with Jim roving and Phil on the forward or half-forward line. 'Krakouer Magic', as it was dubbed, saw the brothers work the ball forward between themselves.

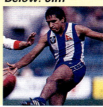

Above: Phil.
Below: Jim

CLUB NEWS 1979–1989

North players wore the emblem of the Tooth Breweries – a horse's head – in 1979 on their guernseys after that company became the club's new major sponsor.

For the first time since entering the League in 1925 the North Melbourne players defeated all other 11 teams in the competition during season 1979.

In the finals series of 1979, the North side defeated Collingwood in the Qualifying Final and lost to Carlton in the Second Semi-Final. North met Collingwood again the Preliminary Final. That occasion witnessed the rucking phenomenon of North's Gary Dempsey and Collingwood's Peter Moore holding onto each other at each bounce of the ball. It is hotly disputed as to who caused this but, whatever the answer, the League acted to prevent a recurrence. It decided on a line across the centre circle, requiring each follower to approach the hit-out from his side of that line.

North won its third Night Premiership in 1980, Barassi's final year as Senior coach. It created a sensation when North's Kerry Goode put through the winning goal after the final siren having received a pass from the astute Malcolm Blight. This occurred on July 15 at VFL Park in front of 50,478 screaming fans who drowned out the sound of the siren.

In July 1981, the Saturday after he stepped down as coach, Malcolm Blight equalled Jock Spencer's club

1979 – 1989

New blood – Wayne Schwass holds the 1990 Under 19s Premiership Cup.

Coaches between Flags

In the wake of the Ron Barassi, North would search long and hard for a coach in the 1980s. After Malcolm Blight filled in for 16 games, their first choice was Barry Cable. Cable would lead them to the finals in 1982 and 1983, but in both instances their form was disappointing, and after a disastrous year in 1984, Cable called it a day. North had missed the finals for the first time since 1974 and plummeted to second last on the table, avoiding the wooden spoon only by percentage.

His replacement amazed many observers; John Kennedy, who had already coached Hawthorn to three Premierships and who was thought to be untouchable, made the switch to the blue and white. His input was immediate, and North bounced back to finish fifth in 1985, although they would later be eliminated from the finals race by Footscray. North missed the finals in 1986 on percentage. Kennedy stayed with the club until 1989, and after five seasons his record stood at 55 wins, 55 losses, 3 draws.

He was replaced by Wayne Schimmelbusch, whose record was darkened by bad luck. In 1990 they missed the finals and finished sixth only a year before the final five became the final six, and in 1991 they were in sixth spot before a bout of food poisoning struck while the club returned from Sydney. They dropped their last three games and fell out of contention.

John Kennedy: coach of few words.

Matt Larkin

Matt Larkin was a born North player. The talented rover came up the ranks from the Under 19s and played his first Senior game in 1984. He remained at Arden street until 1993, during which time he chalked up a remarkable record. He played a total of 172 games, scored 143 goals and won the Syd Barker Medal three times. In 1990 he was appointed captain, a position he held until 1992. An extremely conscientious player, he chose to step down from the captaincy in 1993 following a downturn in his form, and then retired before the following season got underway. He is a life member of North Melbourne.

Matty Larkin: North's favourite.

Noel Teasdale

 In 1989, 24 years after he had tied for the 1965 Brownlow Medal, North's Noel Teasdale received the honour retrospectively. The club's four-times Barker Medallist, All-Australian and 1965–67 captain richly deserved the recognition for outstanding achievement as a follower and as a loose man on the backline. His superb skill as an overhead mark thrilled the crowds and frustrated many an enemy attack.

He led the Kangaroos to back-to-back Night Flags in 1965 and 1966, and he was gratefully voted life membership by the North committee. From 1956–67 at Arden St he chalked up 178 games and 71 goals.

1979 – 1989 HONOUR ROLL

Year	Pos	Leading Goalkicker	No.	Best & Fairest	Captain	Coach
1979	3rd	Malcolm Blight	60	Gary Dempsey	Wayne Schimmelbusch	Ron Barassi
1980	5th	Arnold Briedis	53	Keith Greig	Wayne Schimmelbusch	Ron Barassi
1981	8th	Malcolm Blight	70	David Dench	Schimmelbusch	Blight/Barry Cable
1982	4th	Malcolm Blight	103	Ross Glendinning	Wayne Schimmelbusch	Barry Cable
1983	3rd	Jim Krakouer/Phil Krakouer	44	Ross Glendinning	Wayne Schimmelbusch	Barry Cable
1984	11th	Donald McDonald	38	Kym Hodgeman	Wayne Schimmelbusch	Barry Cable
1985	4th	Phil Krakouer	35	Matthew Larkin	Wayne Schimmelbusch	John Kennedy
1986	7th	Jim Krakouer	32	Jim Krakouer	Wayne Schimmelbusch	John Kennedy
1987	5th	Phil Krakouer	43	Matthew Larkin	Wayne Schimmelbusch	John Kennedy
1988	11th	Jim Krakouer	35	Matthew Larkin	John Law	John Kennedy
1989	9th	Ian Fairley	28	Mick Martyn	John Law	John Kennedy

record of 11 goals in a Match. That was against Footscray at the Western Oval.
With 103 goals for the 1982 season, Malcolm Blight had become North's first Coleman Medallist at the close of the home-and-away fixture. (This award did not exist when Doug Wade won the League goalkicking in 1974).
Season 1983 boded well for a third Flag. North were minor Premiers and McClellan Trophy winners, but unfortunately lost both finals engagements. However, Ross Glendinning won the Brownlow that year. It was North's third.
North played its first home game at MCG on 28 April 1984, defeating Melbourne 16.17 to 14.14.
On 20 August 1985 the Kangaroos downed the Tigers in the last home match they ever played at Arden Street. The final scores were 16.20 (116) to 9.12 (66).
North's 1985 Elimination Final victory over Carlton was one of the great last-quarter efforts under the coaching of John Kennedy and the relentless captaincy of Wayne Schimmelbusch. Down by 17 points at three-quarter time, the Roos kicked 8.1 to the Blues' 2.1 in the last quarter to run out winners by 19 points, 20.6 to 16.11.
During 1986, the North Melbourne Football Club became a public company with a share issue of 3 million shares.
In 1987 Wayne Schimmelbusch broke Keith Greig's day game record with the club, finishing with 306 games.
During 1989 Noel Teasdale received a retrospective Brownlow Medal for his tied result in 1965.

NORTH MELBOURNE

Above: Big and little Roos, 1991.
Left: The North Melbourne State of Origin representatives 1994.

Building the strength

Season 1990 ushered in a new era for football, with the Victorian Football League becoming the Australian Football League. This change of identity reflected a new national character to the competition, as well as the ever-increasing travel demands that were being made on the players. The North Board launched 'Operation Kangaroo' in an attempt to improve the team's financial situation, and signed the players to performance-based contracts. In a minor victory, North's Under 19s won the first AFL Pennant.

1991 began with some controversy, as Carlton officials launched an effort to buy a controlling interest in the club through acquisition of Bob Ansett's shares. They hadn't done their homework, however, because North's float had been so structured that no one person could ever gain full control of a majority of the shares. Disaster had been avoided off the field, but it still got to them on it. North narrowly missed the finals again, although their Under-19s made a record ninth consecutive appearance in the Grand Final, and won their fifth Flag.

After the close misses of 1990 and 1991, North must have hoped that 1992 would turn the tide and push them back into the finals. It didn't. They recorded their worst result in 20 years, finishing second last. And as 1993 began, it looked as though the rot would continue. North dropped the opening night game to Adelaide by 147 points – their worst beginning to a season in the history of the club – and coach Wayne Schimmelbusch resigned. Thankfully, former player Denis Pagan was there to assume the coaching duties for North's Senior side. He had already coached the Under 19s at North to five Premierships, followed by a Reserves Premiership with Essendon in 1992. His return to the Arden Street change rooms witnessed a total transformation in the Senior side's performance.

The Kangaroos bounced back into the finals in 1993, ending the home and away season with the League's highest percentage, only half a game off top spot. They were defeated in the Second Elimination Final, but the evidence was there that a return to the top was imminent. One highlight worth noting was the club's highest ever score, 35.19 to the Swans 16.9.

Stung by its poor showing in the previous year's finals, the North side was committed to making amends in 1994. It was the club's 125th Anniversary, and it chose its match against Collingwood on Friday night, May 20, to celebrate that landmark. Before 72,216 people North triumphed, with final scores 17.19 to 13.10. They also reached the Preliminary Final for the first time since 1978, and only missed out on a place in the Grand Final by one solitary goal kicked after the final siren.

North faltered once more at the Preliminary Final in 1995. Carlton demolished the Roos in the final quarter to win 18.10 (118) to North 8.8 (56).

1990–1995 HONOUR ROLL

Year	Pos	Leading Goalkicker	No.	Best & Fairest	Captain	Coach
1990	6th	John Longmire	98	John Longmire	Matthew Larkin	Schimmelbusch
1991	8th	John Longmire	91	Craig Sholl/Mick Martyn	Matthew Larkin	Schimmelbusch
1992	12th	John Longmire	64	Wayne Carey	Matthew Larkin	Schimmelbusch
1993	5th	John Longmire	75	Wayne Carey	Wayne Carey	Denis Pagan
1994	3rd	John Longmire	78	Wayne Schwass	Wayne Carey	Denis Pagan
1995	3rd	Wayne Carey	65	Wayne Schwass	Wayne Carey	Denis Pagan

CLUB NEWS 1990–1995

John Longmire kicked a club-record 12.5 in Round 2, 1990 against Richmond, in North's second-highest score of 32.17 (209), and greatest winning margin over any rival, 141 points. The Tigers totalled just 9.14 (68).

The club record didn't last long. 'Horse' Longmire broke his own club goalkicking record with 14 goals (and two behinds) against Melbourne in Round 14, 1990. North kicked 31.14 (200) to the Demons 10.13 (73).

The AFL Under 19 competition concluded with season 1991. North had won seven in total (from nine Grand Final appearances) 1946, 1976, 1984, 1987, 1988, 1990 and 1991, the last five under the brilliant coaching of Denis Pagan.

In 1992 North negotiated a 21-year lease of the North Melbourne Recreation Reserve and launched its Kanga Kasino with 105 poker machines.

Denis Pagan turned North's fortunes around and the Kangaroos were on top of the ladder in Round Five.

North kicked its highest score in history, kicking 35.19 (229) to the Swans 16.9 (105) in Round 6, 1993, including 10 from Adrian McAdam, at Princes Park. Denis Pagan looked at the result realistically: 'The Swans haven't got a coach.' (Barassi took over the next week.)

Adrian McAdam kicked 23 goals in his first three games of AFL football, in 1993.

1990 – 1995

Wayne Carey leads them in after the win against Essendon, Round 10, 1995.

Above: Corey McKernan flies over Brisbane's Matthew Clarke.
Left: Matthew Capuano and Mick Martyn in 1995.

The king Kangaroos of the 90s

There are many players who deserve mention in any discussion of North's rise to victory in the 90s, but four stand out as deserving special praise: Wayne Carey, John Longmire, Michael Martyn and Corey McKernan.

Quite possibly the best player in the competition at present, in the eyes of North fans anyway, Wayne Carey played his first game for North in 1989. Possessing almost the perfect build for a modern footballer, his on-field achievements, generally from centre half-forward, speak volumes. He was appointed captain of North by Pagan in 1993, and he led New South Wales in the same season. In 1995 he was chosen as the inaugural captain of the Allies, although injury prevented him from playing. He has been chosen as a member of the All-Australian side for four consecutive years, and led North to victory in the 1996 Grand Final. At the end of the 1997 season, he had played 163 matches and kicked 411 goals.

Another player deserving of mention in any discussion of North's rise to power, John Longmire, began his career at North in 1988 at the age of just 17. In only his third season of League football, he had what has probably been his best year so far. He won the Coleman medal, kicking 98 goals, kicked an MCG record of 14 goals and won the Syd Barker Medal. He also became an All-Australian player. He lead the goalkicking at North from 1990 to 1994, and in 1995 he became North's all-time leading goalscorer, eclipsing Jock Spencer's record of 475. Sidelined for all of 1996 by injury, he has so far played 180 games for North and kicked 504 goals.

Recruited from Newport Central in 1988, Michael Martyn has been one of North's shining lights at full-back throughout the 90s. With 201 matches, two Syd Barker Medals, a Night Premiership, the Michael Tuck medal and the 1996 Flag under his belt, he is already a cult figure among North supporters. Capable of handling the best of AFL full-forwards, he played every game in 1996 and was a star performer in the finals. Although only 29, he is viewed around the club as one of the veterans whose experience and influence in the rooms and on the field provide so much for younger players.

Perhaps the 'unluckiest player in the AFL' Corey McKernan had a sensational season in North's triumphant march toward the Flag in 1996, and would have had a Brownlow had it not been for a dubious one-match suspension. It was a recurring feature of his football. In 1994 he had been favourite to take out the Norwich Rising Star award but was ineligible due to a one-week suspension for tripping – a charge which is no longer reportable. In 1996, North's spring-heeled ruckman gained interstate and All-Australian selection, and took home a Premiership medal. By the end of 1997 he had played 93 Senior games and kicked 96 goals.

The locker room, 1993.

During 1993 Brett Allison played his 100th game with the Kangaroos and along with his father, Tom, he became North's first father/son combination to play 100 games for the club.
Having failed to defeat the Hawks since 1980, the Kangaroos did it twice in 1994. On April 8 at the MCG they kicked 25.33 to 6.10. And on 23rd July at Waverley they kicked 15.9 to 9.5.

North captain Wayne Carey was described by Martin Flanagan as 'Elle McPherson with biceps' in the Age on 31 March 1994.
Criticism is levelled at the AFL's Ian Collins for pre-tribunal hearing comments, after Wayne Carey is suspended for three matches for striking Adelaide's Ben Hart, on a video charge laid by Collins.

In the Second Qualifying Final for 1994 at Waverley, North Melbourne became the first club to win a game involving extra time, because the scores were tied at the final siren, North 12.19 (91) and Hawthorn 13.13 (91). During that extension of play against Hawthorn, North kicked 3.5 to the Hawks' 0.0.
North was perhaps unlucky to lose the first 1994 Preliminary Final to Geelong by a single Ablett kick – 14.19 (103) to 16.13 (109) – but the team was back in the top echelon again.
In the 1995 Ansett Cup North Melbourne defeated Adelaide, 14.9 (93) to 8.15 (63). Mick Martyn was named Michael Tuck Medallist as Best and fairest in the Grand Final. Wayne Carey kicked 18 goals in the series.

NORTH MELBOURNE

Anthony Rock's speccie.

18 with a bullet: Wayne Carey.

**Above: Ansett Cup win.
Left: Corey McKernan can fly.**

The Season

No season in the entire history of the VFL/AFL seemed to carry as much weight as that of 1996, its centenary year. Amidst the hype (and hyperbole) this was to be the League's year of years, and to celebrate the Premiership trophy was to be a special gold Premiership cup, and its Premiership players and coach were to receive gold medallions. Prize enough for any finals contender.

During its course AFL Legends were named, and former North coach, Ron Barassi was included among them. A VFL Hall of Fame was also created and 10 former players with the Kangaroos were given this honour: Allen Aylett, Malcolm Blight, Barry Cable, Russel Ebert, Welles Eicke, Tom Fitzmaurice, Les Foote, Keith Greig, John Rantall and Doug Wade. Chairman Ron Casey was similarly honoured as a representative of those who have covered football within the Media. Dual Brownlow Medallist, Syd Barker Medallist and former captain of Victoria, Keith Greig was also elevated to a very exalted position; he was named in the VFL/AFL Team of the Century as a wingman.

Early setbacks such as Longmire's knee injury and Carey's broken thumb were forgotten as North won their first three games. Once started, the North machine would not be stopped on its quest for a finals berth. Along the way they notched up a few milestones, such as their highest winning margins over Footscray (131 points) and Fitzroy (105 points). Their total of 16 wins for the season was only one shy of North's 17 in 1979.

Indeed, their victory against Fitzroy would be their best, and their last. Had the boards of both clubs had their way, the two would have merged prior to the commencement of the 1997 season, with North hungry for the influx of cash and membership. In the end, however, the AFL had other ideas, and North withdrew its offer. Fitzroy would eventually merge with Brisbane.

In the pre-season North had set themselves two goals: first, to finish in the top two, and second, never to lose two games in a row. By the conclusion of the season, North had achieved both.

To get them in the right frame of mind, Denis Pagan and Ron Joseph arranged a visit to the hallowed turf of the MCG after a club dinner. Joseph had previously hidden the 1975 Premiership trophy on the ground and as the players walked out into the darkness he challenged them to hold it aloft, to get a feel for it, in the hope that they would be able to repeat the performance come Grand Final day.

1996 HONOUR ROLL

Year	Pos	Leading Goalkicker	No.	Best & Fairest	Captain	Coach
1996	1st	Wayne Carey	82	Wayne Carey	Wayne Carey	Denis Pagan

CLUB NEWS 1996

Round 1. North 15.19 (109) defeated St. Kilda 12.13 (85), Peter Bell four goals on debut, Corey McKernan best.
Round 2. North 26.12 (168) defeated Footscray 5.7 (37) McKernan again best on ground. Wayne Carey six goals.
Round 3. North Melbourne 22.21 (153) defeated Hawthorn 12.8 (80). North had 14 goal kickers.
Round 4. Brisbane 18.17 (125) defeated North 14.11 (95) in the heat of the Gabba.
Round 5. North Melbourne defeated Adelaide 23.14 (152) to 17.11 (113) Carey five, McKernan four.
Round 6. North Melbourne 15.14 (104) defeated Geelong 13.15 (93). McKernan suspended for one match.
Round 7. West Coast defeated North Melbourne 19.11 (125) to 7.16 (58) at Subiaco.
Round 8. North Melbourne 20.24 (144) defeated Richmond 14.5 (89). McKernan back in injury-depleted side.
Round 9. North Melbourne demolished Fitzroy 25.20 (170) to 9.11 (65). Mark Roberts 150, merger talks had been revealed.
Round 10. North Melbourne 12.17 (89) defeated Footscray 10.9 (69) Jason Danilchenko booted six goals.
Round 11. Sydney 24.8 (152) defeated North Melbourne 10.13 (73). Thrashed in Wayne Schwass' 150th.
Round 12. North Melbourne 16.11 (107) defeated Essendon 14.11 (95) in very wet and slippery conditions. Glen Archer best in last quarter.

1996

The coach and the captain show fans the prize.

Glen Archer: Norm Smith Medallist.

The Grand Final – the favourites storm home

Football observers felt before the Grand Final that Sydney would need an early break to hold back their more talented opposition, and for a brief moment it looked like they might have grabbed that opportunity.

A crowd of 93,102 watched in surprise as the Swans shot away to a three-goal break at the end of the first quarter. Lockett was looking dangerous and had already notched four, but if Sydney were to win, he would have to kick 10 or more.

North had been clear pre-match favourites, but another quick goal to the Swans early in the second quarter had many biting their nails. Then, a turning point. Paul Kelly drove the ball forward, low and hard, toward Lockett's outstretched arms, but the big man fumbled, and in moments the ball was up the other end of the ground and North had clawed six points closer.

McKernan was beginning to assert himself in the ruck and North began to steady. A goal to Freeborn followed by another narrowed the gap to 10 points and North was looking the better side. At half-time, North had squeezed two points in front.

The third quarter was North's. They added 4.7 to Sydney's 1.2, with McKernan doing most of the damage. Leading by 25 points at three-quarter time, and then 38 early in the last, it may have looked as though yet another Grand Final was to slip away into boilover territory, but Sydney had one shot left in them. Goals to Lockett and O'Loughlin gave them some hope, but goals to the brilliant Rock and McKernan put it beyond doubt. As the siren sounded and the familiar strains of North's club song wafted out onto the ground, North had taken their third Flag, 19.17 (131) to 13.10 (88).

The aerial skill of Glenn Archer won him the Norm Smith medal, but Corey McKernan and Anthony Rock were equally good. 'I was only after the gold one,' said Archer. 'The other one's just a bonus. I'll go down in history, I suppose. It's just fantastic.'

All the hard work put in by Ron Casey and his Board, Greg Miller as Chief Executive and Geoff Walsh as Football Manager paid off as Denis Pagan coached the North side to the Centenary Premiership. Tony Elshaug completed the double on the last Saturday in September, coaching the Reserves to a Premiership as well. North Melbourne, captained by the remarkable Wayne Carey with Wayne Schwass as his deputy, had overpowered the Sydney Swans to win the match of the century.

How did it feel? According to captain Carey it was 'the ultimate'.

A Grand Final spray.

Round 13. North Melbourne 9.20 (74) over Fremantle 8.10 (58) at the WACA.
Round 14. North Melbourne 21.18 (144) thrashed Carlton 13.11 (89) under lights at the MCG. Archer, Carey, Rock three goals each.
Round 15. Collingwood 22.12 (144) defeated North Melbourne 12.11 (83). Enough said.
Round 16. North Melbourne 17.16 (118) defeated St. Kilda 4.5 (29). McKernan again, Carey's five goals more than the Saints' total.
Round 17. North Melbourne 28.15 (183) defeated Melbourne 11.4 (70) Wayne Carey 11.
Round 18. North Melbourne 19.16 (130) defeated Hawthorn 15.9 (99). Carey slotted seven more goals.
Round 19. Brisbane 11.11 (77) defeated North Melbourne 8.11 (59) at Optus Oval.
Round 20. North Melbourne 10.16 (76) defeated Adelaide 9.10 (64). Carey (cleared of striking charge) kicks winning goal in tight last quarter.
Round 21. Geelong 16.13 (109) defeated North Melbourne 14.12 (96) A bad loss; North slipped from the top two.
Round 22. North Melbourne 21.15 (141) defeated Richmond 16.13 (109) and regained important second spot. Sholl five goals.
Qualifying Final. North Melbourne 19.17 (131) defeated Geelong 9.17 (71).
Second Preliminary Final. North Melbourne 17.12 (114) defeated Brisbane 11.10 (76).
Grand Final. North Melbourne 19.17 (131) defeated Sydney 13.10 (88).

NORTH MELBOURNE

Wayne Carey: down and out for 11 games.

Corey McKernan: the pain of a Preliminary Final loss. Right: Carey – too strong.

An injured season in '97

The 1997 got off to the worst possible start. Wayne Carey crashed to the MCG turf in a marking contest in the second quarter of the opening round against Melbourne, tearing shoulder ligaments. He had to undergo his third shoulder reconstruction – he had one in his first season at North, when he missed eight games. This time Carey would be out for 11 games, returning in Round 13.

North lost to Melbourne in an ominous sign of things to come. It wasn't simply a question of 'No Carey – No North' because Corey McKernan was also off the ground in the second half.

North did defeat Carlton in the wet in Round 2, but that was also a slightly devalued currency, as the season was to demonstrate. Glen Archer showed his thirst for the hard ball in defence, covering for Carey's absence.

Wayne Schwass reappeared in the Essendon game after his 1996 suspension, but the Roos were soundly beaten, and followed this game with a loss to Brisbane in Archer's 100th game at the Gabba.

Coach Denis Pagan had more luck as the team turned on a sparkling performance for his hundredth game as coach in the 95-point win over Richmond. Pagan has been a 64 per cent winner so far.

Another milestone in the season was reached by John 'Horse' Longmire, who kicked his 500th career goal in the first quarter of the game against Hawthorn. North also won the game and crept into eighth spot after six rounds.

A loss to Collingwood in Round seven was followed by a win in Round 8 over Port Adelaide. Rookie list player Julian Kirzner made his Senior debut and kicked four goals. Goalkicker Longmire was at centre half-back.

1997 clearly had a different flavour to it as Footscray defeated North in Round 9 to move to fourth spot while the reigning Premiers languished in tenth position.

John Blakey played his hundredth game in a North Melbourne jumper after his switch from Fitzroy in 1993 in the solid win over West Coast at Optus Oval. For this game Wayne Schwass was dropped to the Reserves after he gained only four possessions the previous week – the first time since 1988, and Robert Scott kicked four goals including his 200th career goal.

Wayne Carey made a welcome return to the team for the loss against Sydney in Round 13. It was the great man's 150th game, and one of his quietest. He still seemed to have trouble freely raising his arms over his head. Corey McKernan left the field with an ankle injury as the Grand Final replay had the 'wrong' result.

St Kilda's smokey at full forward Jason Heatley beat three opponents including the reported and suspended Glen Archer (for 'attempting' to strike), and kicked nine goals as the Saints outran and out-possessed North Melbourne. Wayne Carey showed a bit of form, but in his three games for the season thus far had played in three losses.

Geelong made it three losses in a row, in Mark 'Fridge' Roberts 100th game for North Melbourne. It was another undisciplined performance from the Kangaroos. North was now 11th.

John Longmire.

A win against Melbourne halted the slide, and catapulted North into the eight. Wins over Carlton, Essendon and Brisbane had the club back on track for the finals, and perhaps for a top-four finish, something which looked out of the question a month before. The win over Brisbane had some gloss taken from it by a strange injury to Corey McKernan – a tissue strain below his right knee. He missed two weeks.

In the interim North slipped to a one-point defeat by Richmond, when Glen Archer was also missing. Students of North noted that McKernan had missed six games in the past four seasons, and North had not won one of them. It seemed that it was actually 'No Corey – no North.' This theory went west in the next game, where North defeated Hawthorn.

The last game of the home-and-away round saw Wayne Carey notch his 400th career goal in a loss to Collingwood.

Seventh place was a disappointment after last year, but also better than might have been expected at stages during the season. Injuries to stars were crucial, but perhaps so too was the 'Premiership hangover'.

1997

Craig Sholl's gold-medal performance on the horizontal bars.

Carey and Corey's finals flings

Wayne Carey shrugged off an indifferent and injured season with one of the great individual finals games. Coach Denis Pagan, when asked whether Carey was a big occasion player after his exultant and exhilarating effort in the Qualifying Final win over Geelong, said 'A big-time player? That's an understatement.'

Ashley Browne in the *Age* wrote 'Carey was simply inspirational last night, his brilliance standing out like a beacon … when the damp and muddy conditions brought back memories of the MCG finals of yesteryear.'

Martin Blake noted in the same paper that the Carey that came back from injury was 'an efficient Carey and a worthy Carey. But it was not the old Carey.'

Then 'on a filthy, wet, slogger's night at the MCG, Carey kicked seven of North's 11 goals. He crumbed them. He bombed them from outside the 50 metre arc. He grubbed one through as he was slung to the ground. He had a hand in several others, gathering 20 disposals and taking 10 marks.'

Carey was down a bit in the win over West Coast, but Corey made up for it, as North advanced to the Preliminary final – and another shoulder injury – this time to Corey. Carey played a pretty good game, but in the end back-to-back dreams faded with the lights at the MCG on a disappointing Friday night in September.

Peter Bell: big season.

Michael Martyn: determined defender.

1997 HONOUR ROLL

Year	Pos	Leading Goalkicker	No.	Best & Fairest	Captain	Coach
1997	4th	Brett Allison	43	Anthony Stevens	Wayne Carey	Denis Pagan

Port Adelaide

MY CLUB
Tim Parker, as told by Ashley Porter

It didn't take much for the Parker kids to get excited when they lived on their family's wheat and sheep farm at Karkoo on the Eyre Peninsula.

One morning there was a commotion in the kitchen when Tim, who was then nine, had a fight with his older sister Cathie, over a free football sticker tucked in the Cornflakes packet.

Mum intervened and told Tim not to worry. 'It's only a Rooster sticker,' she said. 'The only club is Port.' Those words stuck in Tim's mind – 'Mum was always right' – and it was the start of an incredible passion for a club he had never seen.

When he was 14 his family moved to Glenelg and he regularly caught two buses to Alberton to see Port. His kid brother John got tired of Tim tossing him in the air when Port kicked a goal.

There are millions of fans like Tim, but what made him special was that Port became his lifeline while he was battling cancer. Shortly before he died in 1995 – three days before Port won another SANFL Premiership – he spoke of his love for Port. It was his personal tribute to His Club. No one had more right than Tim to stake this claim.

He spoke with pride and passion when he reflected on his long-time heroes.

'Bob Kingston – this bloke had plastic knees but he was still good enough to bring down the big marks and kick goals. They don't make 'em like him anymore.

'Bucky [now Port Power's chief executive Brian Cunningham] was a little bloke with a lot of guts. I can still hear the roars every time Brucey Light went near the ball. And Russell Ebert – well, he was the greatest of all.

'I remember the '71 Grand Final when I was sick as a dog with the flu but somehow I was still able to camp myself outside the Adelaide Oval gates at the crack of dawn to get the best spot. I can still see Fritzy Freeman, with blood pouring from his forehead, trying his heart out.

'Those guys, and everyone else who has put on a black and white guernsey, have inspired me. I was never good at sport. I was one of those asthma kids, but Port always made me feel like I was out there with them and being a real winner. Everyone who followed other clubs hated my guts because I barracked for Port, but I didn't mind because Port made me a winner.'

In his closing months what Port meant to him became much deeper.

'There have been times when I've gone through hell with the cancer treatment, and the only way I've coped has been thinking about Port,' Tim said. 'They'd be giving me this radiation stuff, and I'd lie there naming Port Premiership sides. I'm sure the staff thought I was mad.

'But this is what Port has done for me. It has been my inspiration; I've felt that the club has always been there for me, giving support when I've needed it most.

'The one Port game that sticks in my mind was the big one I couldn't go to, the 1990 Grand Final. I was just too sick, and my mate Rob Kelvin from Channel Nine came around to watch the final on TV with me. He was presenting the awards after the game and he could have had the best seat at Football Park, but he was there with me until midway through the last quarter.

'At first I found it incredible that someone would so something like that. That's the type of bloke he is. But then I thought, "No, this is merely typical of a Port supporter."

'Port is a club that puts hope in your heart and you always believe you can win no matter whether the odds be great or small. When I feel really down I put on the Port guernsey my sister gave me and say to myself: "Tim, you're a Port player now, you're six goals down at three-quarter time and kicking against the breeze, but you can still win."'

This was one big game Port and Tim didn't win, and he was denied watching the Power play its first game in the AFL. But he left behind thousands of people like him with his Port spirit, the love of a club, His Club.

PORT POWER	
Year Established	1870
Joined VFL/AFL	1997
Home Ground	Football Park
Record home crowd	47,256 v Crows, 1997
Most games	Shane Bond, Donald Dickie, Josh Francou, Adam Hueskes, Brendon Lade, Stephen Paxman, Michael Wilson 22
Most goals	Scott Cummings 70
Notable supporters	Jimmy Barnes, Allan Scott, Colin Hayes, Chris Dittmar, Darren Cahill, Kevin Crease

New name, new generation of devotees.

The new kids on the block – but with a wealth of tradition behind them.

Above: Port Power's cheer squad is ready to take on the AFL in 1997. Right: Port's mascot, Round 1.

PORT ADELAIDE

The 1888 Port Adelaide team finished second on the SANFL ladder.

Tough from the start

They've always been a tough lot down at Port Adelaide. Mostly wharfies, they used to play a few games at Buck's Flat before the 1870s, and folklore says that when they lost, juveniles threw cow dung at anyone in sight.

Mind you, it was said not much was done about it – the property was owned by South Australia's Premier of the day, Captain John Hart. His son, John Jnr, was elected as Port's first president, on Friday, 13 May 1870. Acknowledged as the real founders of the club, however, were carpenter/builder John Rann, businessman George Ireland, and timber mill manager R. W. J. Leicester.

They set the foundation for Australia's most successful football club, and a dynasty of champions.

Port's third guernsey: 1883–1902.

Changing times

SA's oldest continuous football club was referred to variously as the Port's, the Magentas, the Cockledivers and the Wharfies in the 19th century, and as the Magpies for most of the 20th century.

Port's colours were blue and white until 1878, pink and white until 1883, magenta and blue until 1902, and black and white thereafter. Now teal blue, said to represent the water of St Vincent Gulf, has been added to the club's striking new Power guernsey.

For all that, nicknames and colours seem very much side issues to the real business of the club – success. Port won three Premierships before 1900, five from 1900 to World War One, five from 1920 to the World War Two, and 21 since then – an incredible total of 34. Port was also crowned Champions of Australia in 1910 and 1914.

And since John Hart Jnr threw a 'few bob' into the club, Port has finished lower than fourth only 15 times!

Frank Knapman takes a strong mark for Port Adelaide in 1911.

CLUB NEWS 1870–1950

John Hart Jnr was elected as the first president of the Port Adelaide Football Club on 13 May 1870 and advertised, inviting players to attend practice.

Port moved from Glanville Park Oval in 1880 and played its first game at Alberton Oval. When the Port Adelaide Cricket Club, with whom they originally shared the ground, went out of existence the football club took it over. It has leased the ground, making improvements when they were required, for all but two years in the 1970s, since then.

Port won its first Premiership in 1884, and more followed in 1890 and 1897. By now the team was getting a taste for them.

Port won the Championship of Australia in 1890, beating South Melbourne.

Syd Malin won Port Adelaide's first Magarey Medal in 1899.

Port finished bottom in a six-team competition in 1900. It hasn't finished bottom since.

After being known as the 'Magentas', and having trouble finding the appropriate dye for its guernseys, Port changed its colours to black and white in 1902, and became known as the 'Magpies'.

Harold Oliver made his League debut in 1907, in a career spanning 14 seasons. He won the club's Best and Fairest award in 1911 and 1912 and was the club captain in his final year, 1921.

Port kicked its lowest winning score, 1.4 (10), against Norwood at Alberton in 1909.

1870-1950

Big Bob McLean

Bob McLean was an institution not only at Port Adelaide, but in South Australian League football, both on the playing field and at administration level. Affectionately known as 'Big Bob', he played for Norwood from 1934–38, and then teamed with Allan 'Bull' Reval and Bob Quinn at Port. Together they revolutionised the ruck-roving role, initiating the loose-man, play-on style of football.

McLean retired as a League player in 1948 after 231 senior games. He also represented SA in Sheffield Shield cricket and topped the Australian batting aggregate in 1949–50.

However, he is perhaps best recognised for his outstanding administrative contribution to Port and the SANFL.

At Port, McLean was honorary secretary from 1949–69, then secretary/general manager, and finally chairman from 1983 to 1989. Port's SANFL delegate for 29 years, he was awarded SANFL Life Membership in 1959. He was a selector at Port and for the State for many years.

Bob McLean was an incredible character; feared by Victorian clubs that sought to poach his players and dreaded by the players themselves when it came time to negotiate their match payments.

Captain–coach Bob Quinn is chaired from the ground by Lew Roberts.

Bob McLean with Fos Williams, 1954.

Courageous Quinn

Bob Quinn was the real 'Triple M', having won a Magarey Medal in 1938, going to war and being awarded a Military Medal, and returning to win another Magarey Medal in 1945.

Still rated as one of the finest rovers and exponents of the stab pass in the history of South Australian League football, Quinn was captain–coach of Port's great 1939 Premiership side, captain–coach of SA's 1947 Hobart carnival side and four-times winner of the club Best and Fairest award.

Sergeant-Major Quinn, of the AIF's 2nd/43rd Battalion, was awarded a Military Medal after being wounded in the knee while serving in the siege of Tobruk. He was later wounded in the arm while serving in the Pacific. To return to the game at the highest level, with his war injuries heavily strapped, was indeed remarkable.

After his retirement from League football in 1948, Quinn became a publican in Kadina. As a supposedly non-playing coach of the local Yorke Peninsula Association team against the Yorke Valley League, he found himself going onto the ground as 20th man in an emergency with only 10 minutes remaining. He was involved in a heavy collision and broke his pelvis, and never donned his football boots again. His courage was extraordinary, both on the football field and the battlefield.

Victory Dinner: November 1939.

By defeating Collingwood, Port again won the Champions of Australia title in 1910.

From 21 June 1913 to 31 July 1915, Port was unbeaten in a record 30 games (including a draw).

In a record-low Grand Final score in 1914 North Adelaide lost to Port 13.15 (93) to 1.8 (14) in the Grand Final. (It held North to 1.8 again in the 1989 Grand Final). Port also won the Champions of Australia title in 1914 by defeating Carlton by 34 points. That same year the South Australian League put a combined team together to take on Port and the Magpies won again.

Bob Quinn, one of four sons of Jack Quinn (Port's captain in 1904–05), made his League debut in 1933. His brothers, Tom, Bob and George also played for the Magpies.

The Obst football dynasty had its beginning in 1933 when Ken Obst began his 10-year career with Port. Later his sons Peter and Trevor played for Port, with Trevor 'Bubbles' Obst winning the Magarey Medal in 1967. Peter's son Andrew played with the 1988 and 1989 Port Premiership teams and finished his career with Melbourne in 1997.

Samson 'Shine' Hosking, who won the Magarey Medal in 1910, made a comeback to League football for one game in 1936 at the age of 48.

Port kicked its record number of behinds, scoring 15.36 against West Torrens at Adelaide Oval in 1939.

In the war years from 1942–44, Port combined with West Torrens, and won the Grand Final in 1942.

PORT ADELAIDE

Russell Ebert: four times a Magarey Medallist and one of Port's best players.

Ebert the Great

Russell Ebert is probably the greatest player South Australia has produced. His records are unsurpassed: a SANFL record four Magarey Medals (1971, '74, '76 and '80), a club-record six club Best and Fairest awards, a club-record 392 games (plus 29 State games and 22 for North Melbourne for a career tally of 443), plus he was club captain, 1974–78, captain–coach 1983–85 and non-playing coach in 1986–87.

From his debut in 1968, Ebert developed into one of the most skilful centremen and on-ball players the game has ever seen. He could control and win games with his masterly play, especially his skilful overhead handballs. Ebert went in hard for the ball and copped plenty of attention, but remarkably, in 18 years he missed only 6 games due to injury.

The dynasty Fos Williams founded

Fos Williams, during 33 emotional and action-packed years, made one of the greatest individual contributions to South Australian League football, and is as much of the Port Adelaide heritage as the famous black and white gate guernsey.

After serving in the navy in World War Two, Williams started his League career in 1946 at the comparatively late age of 24. His brothers were also playing League football; Alec with Sturt, and Frank with Port.

Fos, a stocky rover with a mop of jet-black curly hair, brought to the game a new level of tenacity, and was lured to Port from West Adelaide as captain–coach in 1950. In a rare football statistic, he virtually filled the year's honour rolls as he was also Port's Best and Fairest winner and leading goalkicker.

A Premiership came in his second year, but it was in 1954 that a remarkable era of Port dominance began — six straight Premierships.

Yet the Williams legend was only beginning. He played 239 games over 13 seasons (West 54, Port 151) and represented the State 34 times. In 21 years as coach, from 1950–58 and 1962–73, he took Port into 16 Grand Finals for nine Premierships.

Williams also led the State for five years as captain and a remarkable 13 years as coach. His 'fire and brimstone' addresses were notorious. To acknowledge his contribution to State football the SANFL struck a medal in his honour, which is presented to SA's best player in an interstate game.

The Williams and Port dynasty continued with sons Mark, Anthony and Stephen representing Port. Stephen took over as coach of Port Magpies in 1997, and Mark became assistant coach at Port Power.

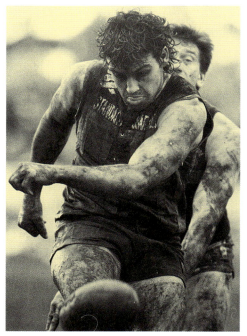

Port's Mark Williams, son of Fos.

CLUB NEWS 1951–1990

Port's Dave Boyd won the 1956 Magarey Medal.

After Port beat West Adelaide in the 1958 Grand Final by two points — West's third Grand Final loss to the Magpies in five years — with West hitting the post in the dying seconds, the goalpost was cut down and burnt during the night. Some 30 years later it was revealed that the culprit was Neil Kerley.

On 23 May 1959 Ted Whelan became the first to play 200 games for Port.

Port won its sixth successive Premiership in 1959, a feat equalled only by Norwood from 1878–83.

John Abley retired in September 1961 after 212 games over 14 seasons — all at full-back.

The Port Adelaide Footballers Club became the first football club in South Australia to obtain a liquor licence on 13 April 1962.

Geof Motley won the Magarey Medal in 1964 and Trevor 'Bubbles' Obst won it in 1967.

After playing its home games at Alberton Oval for 95 years, in 1975 Port had a dispute over a ground manager's fee with Port Adelaide Council and moved to Adelaide Oval. The Magpies returned to Alberton in 1977.

Port and Sturt drew a record attendance for a SANFL Grand Final — officially 66,897 — at Football Park in 1976. But 20 years later it was revealed the crowd was about 76,000, which contravened the then public entertainment laws.

1951–1990

1990 Magarey Medallist, Scott Hodges, kicked a record 153 goals in 1990.

Tumultuous times over AFL bid

It was described as the 'greatest act of treachery in football history'. It was an act that split the Port Adelaide Football Club, tore the heart out of the SANFL, and caused an unprecedented wave of football emotion.

Port shouldn't have expected anything else when it broke all the rules of trust and applied to join the Australian Football League in July 1990. But it did. Then president Bruce Weber said: 'Football in South Australia is Port Adelaide.' After pledging allegiance as one of 10 SANFL clubs to defer a combined entry into the AFL in order to gain better terms, Port chose to go it alone. And no doubt SA would not have had a side in the AFL – the Crows – in 1991 had Port not been so 'selfishly minded'.

When the SANFL was finally officially told of the bid on Tuesday, 31 July 1990, all hell broke loose. After numerous meetings, the AFL Commission and Port finalised a heads of agreement and Port publicly unveiled its ambitious plan at an emotionally charged meeting of 2500 club members.

The SANFL started defensive action, and Glenelg attacked from another front. It went to the Supreme Court of South Australia in Adelaide on August 10 and was granted a temporary injunction forbidding Port from dealing with the AFL. South Adelaide, Sturt and West Torrens joined Glenelg as plaintiffs, while Norwood took separate legal action. Port found itself battling against time as its heads of agreement with the AFL was to expire on August 31.

On August 13 in an effort to scuttle Port's plan, the SANFL produced a counter-bid to field a composite team in the AFL in 1992. The AFL Commission reacted coldly but the SANFL gained support from the AFL clubs, and slowly but surely the clubs swung against Port, believing it was jeopardising SA's domestic competition.

On 11 October 1990, the SANFL met the AFL Commission and the necessary documents were signed. Port had lost this battle, but the war was far from over.

Coaching turmoil

This era of the Port Adelaide Football Club also contained another dark chapter – when it sacked its greatest-ever player Russell Ebert as coach at the end of the 1987 season, and returned John Cahill to the helm.

After Cahill had coached Port from 1974–82 and brought four Premierships to the club – and left to coach Collingwood and West Adelaide – Ebert took Port to sixth, second, seventh, fourth and fourth. Until then Port had finished lower than fourth on only eight occasions this century, but what was so conveniently forgotten during Ebert's reign was the fact Port had lost a lot of champions to the VFL or through retirement, and because of financial restraints didn't replace them with players of anywhere near their quality. And when Cahill resumed a lot of brilliant youngsters were ready for League ranks.

Ebert's sacking brought a wave of protest from his fans and public demonstrations were held on the Port Adelaide docks, but obviously to no avail. Perhaps, more than anything else, it wasn't the fact that Port exercised the right of any club to replace its coach with someone previously highly successful, it was the manner in which it happened. There was an air of controversy, and claims of mistrust and a lack of loyalty. Sadly, Ebert has never been close to the club since.

Left: John Cahill: brought back as coach.

Tony Giles got into a fight with his mate, Woodville player Ian Rainbird, on 11 September 1980, outside a city hotel and cut his hand on Rainbird's teeth. A serious infection resulted, forcing him out of the finals series. Port won its second successive Premiership.

Russell Ebert became the first-ever player to win a fourth Magarey Medal in 1980.

Tim Evans kicked 16 goals against West Adelaide at Alberton in 1980, the most goals in a match by a Port player. He finished the season with a then SANFL-record 146 goals, making him the first Port player ever to kick 100 goals or more in a season.

Port Adelaide defeated Norwood by 43 points on 4 May 1981 in the first SANFL game ever played under lights at Football Park.

Port finished sixth in 1983 – missing the finals for the first time in 35 years.

Port captain Brian Cunningham announced his retirement after 256 games over 13 seasons in 1983, after a pay dispute with the club. He returned to the club in 1992 as general manager.

Greg Anderson won the Magarey Medal in 1986. He then transferred to Essendon for a highly successful 103-game stint, before going to the Crows.

Port made its very first approach to the AFL about 'going alone' and joining the national competition on 4 July 1990.

Port won its third successive, and 30th, Premiership in 1990, beating Glenelg by 15 points. This was the third time Port had won three or more Premierships in a row.

PORT ADELAIDE

Clive Waterhouse (left) and George Fiacchi hail Port's 1995 Premiership.

Greg Anderson, first to the ball in 1995.

Port tries again to join the biggest League

After its controversial and unsuccessful bid to join the AFL, Port Adelaide was left to pick up the pieces. The Crows were up and running, and for the first time ever Port Adelaide wasn't commanding most of the attention. In many ways instead, it was viewed as a loser. However, its aspirations to join the AFL had far from subsided.

The SANFL had the power. The Adelaide Football Club licence was given first option on a second licence should one become available, and the other clubs, especially Norwood, were determined to keep Port out in the cold.

Port knew that to have any chance it would need to prove that it was prepared to remain united with the SANFL. Its first step was to appoint a new chief executive, Brian Cunningham, a former champion State and Port rover who had an image of trust, professionalism and popularity.

Port officially launched its new AFL bid on 8 June 1992. But the League and the clubs seemed to have difficulty in reaccepting Port while Bruce Weber, the frontman of Port's first bid, was still president-chairman. At Port's 1992 Annual General Meeting, Weber wasn't even re-elected to the board. In many ways he became the scapegoat for Port's 1990 actions. The failed bid was a united club approach, yet he publicly carried the blame.

Greg Boulton replaced Weber, and Cunningham worked tirelessly – and very openly – for Port's AFL bid. Working in Port's favour was its continued on-field success with more Premierships in 1990, '92, '94 and '95, which led to a flood of donations.

Port versus Norwood

Norwood was working just as hard to win that second sub-licence, backed-up by a plan to amalgamate with Sturt. There were also bids from a cartel involving North Adelaide, Central District, West Adelaide and Woodville-West Torrens, plus a combined bid from Glenelg and South Adelaide.

It really got down to Port or Norwood, and Port basically won because it was the club interstate people knew about.

On Tuesday, 13 December 1994, SANFL president Max Basheer announced Port Adelaide would be SA's second side in the AFL when a second licence became available.

1992 Magarey winner, Nathan Buckley.

CLUB NEWS 1991–1996

With Scott Hodges playing for the Crows, Darryl Borlase won Port's goal-kicking award with only 25 goals in 1991 – the lowest tally by a Port leading goalkicker for 71 years. Port finished fifth.

Nathan Buckley, one of the many players Port lost to the AFL, won the Magarey Medal by 11 votes under a 3-2-1 voting system in September 1992, and later won Port's Best and Fairest award, the McLean Medal.

Port won the 1992 Grand Final against Glenelg in appalling conditions. Just before half-time it began to pour, but Port kicked 3 quick goals and never looked back.

Greg Phillips played his last game for the club on 26 September 1993, after 343 games – a tally second only to Russell Ebert.

Early in 1994, the Melbourne-based *Inside Football* magazine published its annual 'wish-list' which included the wish that Port Adelaide be accepted to the AFL. Describing Port as 'the most successful club' in Australian football history, the writer said: 'Port remains the logical choice as South Australia's second side.'

On 6 April 1994, Port submitted a business plan for its AFL team to the SANFL.

Port won the 1994 SANFL Grand Final on October 2 against the Eagles, who were the reigning Premiers. Port went into the game the underdogs and the Eagles opened up with six quick goals. The Magpies fought back but trailled

1991–1996

The Port Power strip is unveiled in front of 8000 Port Adelaide supporters.

Moving into gear

With the licence saga cast aside, it was full swing into action. There were the cosmetics to worry about. Port couldn't retain its Magpie name or wear solely black and white colours – rightfully so, they remained with Collingwood. And there were appointments to be made too: the coach and staff, including a recruiting manager who would lead a team to find a team.

John Cahill was the obvious choice as coach, and all everyone wanted to know was what the new team would be called, and see the new colours and guernsey.

It was always going to be Port Adelaide, but Port Adelaide what? Among the popular nicknames were the Pirates, Black Diamonds, Mariners and Sharks.

On 31 August 1995, all was revealed when 8000 fans packed the Adelaide Entertainment Centre. Enter Port Power in striking black, white and teal-blue guernseys. Port had revealed a slogan.

Now the Power was ready to be turned on (the clichés about Port's new name were spouted within hours of the announcement). But it still had nowhere to go. Fitzroy survived for another year; the AFL clubs didn't want a 17th club and the resultant bye situation.

In retrospect, Port was better off being forced to wait another year to enter the AFL. It was able to prepare better both on and off the field. And it ended its transitional SANFL existence in the way the famous club knows best – by winning another Premiership.

The dynasty rolls on

John Cahill stepped aside as coach of Port Adelaide after Round 13, 1996 to concentrate on planning for the AFL. He was replaced by Stephen Williams, son of the legendary Fos. Port also had new names for the sides to prevent confusion – Port Adelaide Magpies in the SANFL, and Port Adelaide or Port Power in the AFL. The pending AFL entry also forced a relocation for the local side to nearby Ethelton Oval, which was upgraded. The Magpies were to continue playing their home games at Alberton, but the historic ground was reserved for the Power come training nights.

Stephen Williams celebrates.

by two goals at three-quarter time. Then Scott Hodges appeared from nowhere and suddenly booted five goals. It was a fighting win – and pure Port Adelaide.
SANFL president Max Basheer announced that Port Adelaide would be South Australia's second side in the AFL on 13 December 1994.
John Cahill – then coach of the Port Adelaide Magpies – was announced as the team's new coach.
Port was notified on 27 October 1995 that it would have to wait another year before entering the AFL – something which was obvious to most observers already.
Robbie West, a Best and Fairest winner at Port, suffered a serious head injury following an incident at Victor Harbour in February 1996, and almost died. Remarkably, he resumed playing in 1997.
On 21 May 1996, Port Adelaide was given the okay by the AFL to start planning for the 1997 season.
John Cahill stepped aside as coach of Port Adelaide in the SANFL on 22 June 1996 to concentrate on the Power, and was replaced by Stephen Williams.
Scott Hodges, who played six quarters with the Crows in 1996, also led the SANFL goalkicking with 102 goals to clinch his third Ken Farmer Medal.
It was the goal of the season. On 29 September 1996, with seconds remaining, Scott Hodges did it again and kicked a goal from an incredibly tough angle to give Port a four-point win over Norwood in the Preliminary Final. A week later the Magpies beat Central District by six goals in the Grand Final.

PORT ADELAIDE

Port Power kick off the new year and their pre-season training.

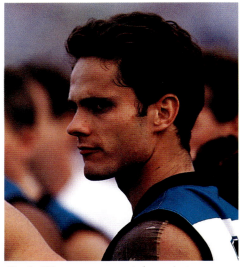
Gavin Wanganeen: captain and star.

A whole new football game

Finally, after six years of trauma, wasted nervous energy, pain and jubilation, Port Adelaide embarked on its greatest mission, in the AFL.

Brownlow Medallist Gavin Wanganeen was the best of the few 'stars' in this new 46-man squad, made up of four uncontracted players, eight who were traded from other AFL clubs, 29 from the SANFL competition, and four who were picked up from the national draft.

Given the circumstances – hardly generous player concessions – the Power did well in assembling its first squad, but few observers gave it much chance of winning more than four games.

Guiding them was John Cahill, who had an amazing record at Port – playing 296 games including 29 State games, and coaching a SANFL-record 10 Premierships at a winning rate of 73.6 per cent. He'd tasted the 'big time' before, at Collingwood (sixth and third) and West Adelaide.

With these impeccable credentials and strong Port ethos, he was the right man for the job, but still there were doubts whether even he could turn the Power into a competitive unit. For so long Port had won against all odds in the SANFL, often through sheer courage and stimulated by tradition, but obviously this was to be a completely new ball game where clubs play 'finals' every week.

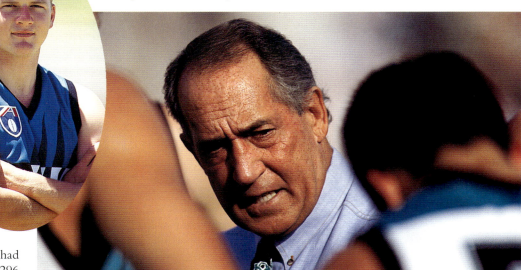
Above: Coach John Cahill – a wealth of AFL experience to offer. Inset: Port's full-forward Scott Cummings ready to go for season 1997.

CLUB NEWS 1997

Coach John Cahill went on record at the start of the season with his sights for the club: 'Who knows? It's an unknown quantity how we'll come up, but you don't want to lose every game. Between six and eight, similar to the Dockers, I think people around the club will be happy.'

Port's No. 1 ticket-holder, Fos Williams, was asked about Port's new colours: 'I say no good. I would have liked Port to ask the AFL whether we could still play in black and white and change the jumper only for Collingwood games.'

The Western Bulldog's Chris Grant – out of contract – refused Port's offer and chose to stay with the Bulldogs. The figure of $2 million over three years was mentioned in the Port bid.

In May, coach John Cahill walked out on the team for a couple of days after a slanging match with the club's football operations manager Mick Moylan, who was recruited from the West Coast Eagles. The incident captured a huge amount of media attention. Cahill said to Moylan: 'You've burnt me. You're claiming I'm not training the players hard enough. I've had it.' The disagreement was patched up but Moylan resigned at the end of the season.

Melbourne went down at Football Park under lights in Round 9. The Power kept Melbourne to only 3 goals, their lowest score since Round 1, 1991.

Port Adelaide became the first newly admitted League club to record four successive wins in its first season

1997

A historic moment: Port's first team hit the ground running at the MCG for their first AFL game.

The first team

Port Adelaide's first captain, Gavin Wanganeen, missed the Power's first match because of a one–match suspension. The first team, which played against Collingwood at the MCG on Saturday, 29 March 1997, was: Shane Bond, Shayne Breuer, David Brown, Peter Burgoyne, Stephen Carter, Scott Cummings, Donald Dickie, Ian Downsborough, Fabian Francis, Josh Francou, Brent Heaver, Adam Heuskes, Adam Kingsley, Brendon Lade, Brayden Lyle, Darren Mead, Stephen Paxman, Darryl Poole, Matthew Primus, Damian Squire, Michael Wilson.

The other squad members were: Paul Geister, Scott Hodges, Warren Tredrea, Nigel Fiegert, Tom Carr, Paul Evans, Scott Bassett, Stephen Daniels, Tom Harley, Roger James, Jonathon Yerbury, Mark Conway, Jarrod Cotton, Stuart Dew, Nathan Steinberner, Rhett Biglands, Scott Freeborn, Jake Lynch, Scott Mathews, Andrew Osborn, Nathan Eagleton, John Rombotis, Bowen Lockwood, Mark Harwood.

Above: David Brown – 69 games with Adelaide.
Right: Fresh from the SANFL – Donald Dickie.
Pre-season: hard work to get ready.
Shane Bond: with Port after 39 games for West Coast.

when it defeated Richmond at Football Park in Round 7.

Scott Cummings played his 50th game in June, having played 40 games for Essendon before he arrived at Port for 1997.

Port Adelaide's $1.2 million extension to the upstairs members' area at Alberton Oval began in June.

Port's David Brown, who turned 28 in June, played six games with the Crows in 1993 before returning to Port Adelaide, and compared the two clubs: 'I think the main difference is that Port Adelaide is a club-based side with a tradition and a culture that's been there for 120 years and is now moving into a new era, whereas the Crows are building their tradition and club.'

By Round 13, Port Adelaide had rethought their ambitions for the 1997 season: 'We have set our sights on winning enough games to make the finals,' Brayden Lyle said.

Port Power players to represent SA in the State of Origin Match against the Vics included: Shane Bond, Donald Dickie, Adam Heuskes, Brendon Lade, Brayden Lyle, Darren Mead, Gavin Wanganeen and Michael Wilson.

Port's Michael Wilson took out the 1997 Norwich Rising Star award. Wilson started at Alberton in the Under 8s and played in Port's 1995 and 1996 Premiership teams.

Other Port Power players to be nominated were 19-year-old Bowen Lockwood and 18-year-old Nathan Eagleton. Port scored the most nominations of any of the AFL clubs.

PORT ADELAIDE

The umpire begins Port Power's first game.

Fabian Francis in the action.

Historic first bounce

When the first day finally arrived – Saturday, 29 March 1997 – the assessments were even less favourable as the Power was thumped by Collingwood by 79 points at the MCG.

But there has always been something special about Port Adelaide. Call it self-belief, a never-say-die attitude, it has had a proven track record of proving its most ardent critics horribly wrong.

As the work rate intensified both on and off the track, and the newcomers adapted to the Port style of football, the hopes of thousands of fans began to rise. After losing to Essendon at home by 33 points, rival coach Kevin Sheedy said he was grateful to have played Port so early in the season and it reminded him of young Essendon sides of the past which went on to win Premierships.

When Port won its first game in the AFL, beating Geelong 18.21 (129) to 14.6 (90), there seemed no doubt Port was not there just to make up the numbers. And a week later it stunned the city of Adelaide when it beat the Crows by 11 points.

Mark Williams: assistant coach.

Another Williams

The Williams dynasty continued with the Power. Former Port champion Mark Williams became the assistant coach to John Cahill. Williams played 135 games for Collingwood from 1981–86 and won the club Best and Fairest in his first year. He was made captain in his third year and in 1985 won his second Copeland trophy. He moved to Brisbane in 1987 and played 66 games with the Bears before returning to Port Adelaide.

Port Power's first home game, and the banner says it all.

1997 HONOUR ROLL

Year	Pos	Leading Goalkicker	No.	Best & Fairest	Captain	Coach
1997	9th	Scott Cummings	70	Darren Mead	Gavin Wanganeen	John Cahill

1997

Port Adelaide achieves a historic victory against the Crows in Round 4.

Josh Francou: beats the Dogs.

David Brown: one step ahead.

Season one, 1997

Port won eight of its first 13 games and was being touted as a genuine finals contender. At all times it fought to the end, and its most outstanding performance was against the Western Bulldogs at Optus Oval when it came from seven goals down at quarter time to win by 12 points.

But like the other recent clubs in their debut season, as the weeks progressed it got tougher, not so much because of a lack of ability or desire, but because of a lack of that solid fitness preparation that can make finalists sustain a long, hard season.

Port finished ninth with 10 wins, 11 losses and a draw, and missed the finals on percentage. It was a magnificent achievement, and a warning that it would continue to make a strong impact on the AFL.

New stars become national figures

They were 'unknown' outside of South Australia until they played for the Power. Michael Wilson, who won the Norwich Rising Star Award, and Darren Mead, who clinched the John Cahill Medal as Port's Best and Fairest.

Port also had Adam Heuskes, a former Norwood player recruited from Sydney, in the AFL's All-Australian Team of the Year.

Norwich winner Michael Wilson.

Port's Best and Fairest, Darren Mead.

Adam Heuskes: 1997 All-Australian.

RICHMOND

MY CLUB
by David Austin

Heroes have never been in short supply at Punt Road. In the summer of 1946–47, a trip to the big smoke from home town Hamilton included an afternoon at a district cricket match at Punt Road. The ground, with its backdrop of eucalypts and elms seemingly as old as the colony itself, had the air of Hamilton's well-manicured Melville Oval, complete with picket fence. There, that day, was Big Bill Johnston, standing 6ft 2 in and bowling off 10 paces, dipping his head in a curious fashion just before delivery and swinging the ball this way and that. His cap was black and yellow. The Tigers went on to win the Pennant. The ground, and those blessed to uphold its colours in combat, had cast their spell. Bugger the MCG and the big-end-of-town next door.

When that summer had run its course, the turf once more felt the thud of a thousand leather boot-stops. Out of the wee cottages and grand homes on 'The Hill' flowed Tiger fans warmed by the coals of optimism against the Antarctic winds blowing up Punt Road.

Stars were in plentiful supply for Round 1 (against North Melbourne at Punt Road) in 1947. The overdue rent and leaking roof were of no account as Jack Dyer, Captain Blood himself, led Richmond on to the ground for his 17th season. He was captain, coach and mentor, a five-star warhorse. He was all of 34 but to us young folk looked older, an avuncular Achilles with strong heels and crook knees, bandaged for battle. He had a frame that might have been chiselled out of granite.

Following him on to the ground came a tall young man with a fluent gait and film-star looks – Bill 'Paleface' Morris, the fairest of the following division who palmed the ball with easy grace to his rover. Ah, the rover. Billy Wilson, neat, tough and fleet of foot as top rovers usually are. A Richmond lad, through and through!

Combining skill and aggression came Max Oppy and Don 'Mopsy' Fraser (known as Mopsy because his short back and sides gave his lustrous crop of red hair the appearance of a mop). Mopsy loved a scrap and the races. He could drop kick a ball over the Yarra, so to speak, and floor an opponent on his follow through. After that, he would peruse the race results on the tiny scoreboard.

In the wings, waiting to win two Brownlows (1952 and 1954), was the gentle giant, Roy Wright. At centre half-forward was Ray 'Joe' Poulter, known for big marks and long, raking drop kicks. Downwind, Joe's longest kicks would land in Punt Road and, like a fan flushed with success, bounce in the direction of the Cricketers' Arms.

Oppy, the original ruck-rover, solid as an oak and with forearms like pylons, played algebraic football – in a straight line. Defender Des Rowe gave the word 'dependable' new meaning. Wingman Leo Merrett was slicker than the Stawell Gift winner. Midfielder Ray Stokes loved the mud, the gooier the better. Even if Richmond had lost that day in 1947, it would not have mattered a tinker's cuss. Happily, the Tigers romped home 18.27 (135) to 15.14 (104), with Dyer kicking six goals.

Big Bill Johnston: Test star.

RICHMOND	
Year Established	1860
Joined VFL/AFL	1908
Home Ground	Punt Road Oval, MCG
Premierships	1920, 1921, 1932, 1934, 1943, 1967, 1969, 1973, 1974, 1980
Brownlow Medals	Stan Judkins 1930; Bill Morris 1948; Roy Wright 1952, 1954; Ian Stewart 1971
Record home crowd	90,564 v Essendon, 1982
Most games	Kevin Bartlett, 403
Most goals	Jack Titus, 970
Notable supporters	Past: Sir Dallas Brooks, Ray Dunn, Professor Ian Turner Present:: Archbishop George Pell, Lindsay Thompson, James Campbell, Robin Delves

It was all irresistible. Family loyalties to Geelong were out. It was Richmond for me. Dyer's well-chronicled notion that if you lived in Richmond you had two obligations – vote Labor and barrack for the Tigers – still held firm, but the barracking bit was beginning to spread outside Richmond.

Boys have no need of politics; heroes, too right! Back in Hamilton, the school bully was reminded that if he didn't pull his head in Captain Blood would come to town and rearrange it for him. The bully looked for other targets. Every picture of a Tiger player in the *Age*, *Argus*, *Herald* or *Sun News Pictorial* was cut out and pasted in a scrap book. The *Sporting Globe* became the Wisden of winter, the crackling mantel radio the lifeline between country and Punt Road. Mel Morris, a former Tiger, called the action in mellifluous tones.

With the urban sprawl travelling ever eastward, young folk in the suburbs looked around for heroes. There were no League teams in North Balwyn, Deepdene, Knox and Glen Waverley. Richmond began playing

1948 team – Back row: R. Poulter, R. Wiggins, R. Wright, W. Morris, D. Rowe, D. Fraser. Middle row: K. Roberts, F. Burge, J. Dyer (captain–coach), R. Stokes, W. Perkins, K. Sier. Front row: K. Albiston, J. Stokes, G. Spring, L. Merrett, W. Wilson, M. Oppy.

Matthew Knights: classy centreman.

Bill Morris: graceful.

Matthew Richardson: 'up there, Richo'.

at the MCG in 1965 and the club began to flourish again. Suddenly, little Richmond barrackers sprang up like daffodils in the spring. No. 4, Royce Hart, was number one. Black and yellow jumpers with a hand-sewn No. 4 on the back dotted the parks and side streets. Would-be wingman/backmen and rovers wore 30 (Francis Bourke) and 29 (Kevin Bartlett). The fearless sported 10 (Kevin Sheedy).

When Hart and company had put the Tigers back on the map with four Premierships, new heroes took their place – Geoff Raines (4), Michael Roach (12) and Jim Jess (20), who could have put a torp over a wheat silo if Punt Road had boasted such a rural appendage. Giant ruckman Mark Lee (1) needed a rover, so along came Dale Weightman (3). Then there was quicksilver centreman Maurice Rioli, sporting the famous No 17 – Captain Blood's number.

Today it's Matthew Knights (33), Wayne Campbell (9), Matthew Richardson (12), Duncan Kellaway (3), Benny Gale (25) and more. The vibes are good. Eat 'em alive!

Jim Jess: the Ghost that flies.

Royce Hart: a champion.

Jack Dyer: alias Captain Blood.

RICHMOND

The opening of the cricket season at Punt Road in the 1860s.

The birth of the Punt Road Oval

The Punt Road oval had its beginnings in October 1855, the year Richmond was declared a municipality. The committee and members of the newly formed Richmond Cricket Club met at Howe's Royal Hotel in Punt Road and, over a lager or two, voted to ask the Colonial Governor for permission to select and improve a site in the Richmond Paddock 'for the playing of cricket'.

On 27 December 1856 the Richmond Cricket Club played its first fully fledged match, against Melbourne. It attracted a large number of the elite of the neighbourhood. Members of the Richmond team took the field in white shirts and trousers and, draped around their necks in the English tradition, black and yellow scarves. Since then black and yellow – symbolic of strength and vibrancy – have prevailed at Punt Road.

Before long, Punt Road boasted a fair wicket. Indeed, when Stephenson's XI visited Australia in 1861–62, it practised at Punt Road rather than at the nearby MCG. The proximity of the oval to local inns, however, caused consternation one evening when a member of Stephenson's side cracked a ball into the bar of the Royal Hotel. Drinking continued unabated.

In the beginning

In the early days of Melbourne, a country walk much favoured by the townspeople was to Richmond Hill, a pleasant expanse of well-timbered bushland with fine views. Running off the dirt road to Richmond was a track down to the Yarra River. Later on, a punt took people to and fro across the river to the distant land of South Yarra and beyond – hence the name Punt Road.

An auctioneer of the time forecast that Melbourne would shortly go out of town because 'fashion now seems to fix her abode in Richmond, and the talent of Confucius is not required to foretell that ere six months the locality will be studded with the dwellings of the wealthy and respectable.'

Indeed, a flourishing village soon sprang up in Richmond. It was rich in human spirit, a blend of penury and prosperity. The toffs, merchants and businessmen lived on the Hill and the working classes on the river flats, many in dwellings that were prone to flooding.

Left: Swan Street in the early 20th century.

On the Richmond side, punts on the Yarra in the 1840s.

CLUB NEWS 1885–1907

The pioneers: The following personnel played in the first game under George Smith (captain) and Jack Baker (ex-Carlton, vice captain) – Searle, Wookey, Stephens, Graham, Stewart, Layton, Crohan, Lyle, Sells, Adams, Mullaly, Howarth, Owen, Watkin, Soutar, Rushton and Conlon.

First win: This came against University in Round 2 of 1885 – 3.12 to 1.9. The Age predicted that 'Richmond would soon take a high place in the ranks of the senior clubs.' It had to wait a while.

Rough element: At Prahran one day in 1887, hooligans tore pickets from the fence and threw them at the Richmond players. After a particularly torrid game against Port Melbourne, rapidly becoming a hated rival, the newspapers called for play to be 'cleaned up'.

New colours: The all-blue guernsey was discarded in 1888. The new colours were black and yellow horizontal stripes. With them came success – 11 wins from 19 matches and fifth place, the club's highest to date. After thumping Carlton 6.5 to 2.9, president Bennett exclaimed: 'We used to be treated with contempt: now look at what we have accomplished today.'

Fashion-setters: In the early 1890s, Punt Road became known as 'The Jungle' and the team 'The Tigers'. Officials clamped down on 'bad language and misconduct.' The team wore boaters, blazers and white shoes.

Betting scourge: Bookmakers began to invade the rooms in 1890, goading

1885 – 1907

Henry Harrison: a Tiger to begin with.

1889 Richmond team sporting assorted livery. Its record: nine wins, 14 losses, two draws.

A stuttering start

The first Richmond Football Club was formed in 1860. The men behind it were the game's founders – Tom Wills, a star Richmond cricketer and son of a prosperous grazier, and his cousin Henry Harrison. Wills and Harrison played for Richmond in three games in 1860, all against Melbourne.

Sadly for Richmond, the two men soon left the club and enthusiasm for the new game of football dwindled in the suburb. The club went into recess for 20 years.

Cricket and other sports flourished as the somnolent football club awaited rebirth. The grand day came in 1885 when a motley gathering of individuals assembled at Byrne's Royal Hotel on February 20. Despite a constant flow of lager, they managed to resolve to form a club and seek admission to the VFA.

It was decided the club would play in an all-blue guernsey with a black and yellow cap. The first game, a practice run, was against Cremorne juniors on 25 April 1885. Richmond had a resounding win, though in the excitement the scores were not recorded. Importantly, 'The Tigers' were on the prowl. They joined the VFA, playing their first match a week later at Williamstown.

Finally a Flag

Third in 1900. Second in 1901. First in 1902. Richmond's arrival at the pinnacle of the VFA, at the expense of the hated Port Melbourne, 'filled every heart in Richmond with joy,' reported the local paper, the *Guardian*.

Richmond began 1902 with a resounding win over Port, 6.13 to 4.6, before a large crowd, some of whom disgraced themselves by interfering with the players and causing disorder on the field.

At season's end (there were no finals), Richmond had 15 wins and one loss (to Port). Port ended with 14 wins, a shock 18-point defeat by fourth-placed Williamstown in the last round costing it a play-off with the Punt Road brigade for first place. This would have been a sell-out. Richmond so dominated the 1902 season that it kicked 103 goals and had only 44 scored against it. Membership swelled to 800 and, in celebration of the Premiership a bazaar at the Town Hall continued for fully a week.

Wrote Follower: 'The team's splendid record speaks eloquently of the form shown by the players. Much of the credit to the excellent manner in which training has been conducted must go to trainers Joe McCormick, Whittaker and Watson.'

The 1902 Premiership team. Skipper Alex Edmonds holds the ball.

players into backing themselves.
Big wet: The year 1891 was the wettest on record. On July 11, water flowed down Punt Road and the oval was under water.
Low ebb: A count of heads against Essendon in 1896 revealed that Richmond had 21 players on the field. Its score to that point was erased.
Flying start to 20th century: Richmond attained its highest VFA place to date, third in 1900, after thrashing North in the last round. 'Our finest moment,' was the enthusiastic appraisal of secretary George Beechcroft (giving Churchill a line) after the team's 10th win in 16 games. 'By dint of dogged and scientific play, our great team will long be remembered as the founder of the future.' The club returned a profit of £162 and the players got new dressing rooms.
Mounted police: The rivalry with Port Melbourne continued with its usual ferocity into the 1900s. After humbling newcomer Essendon Town in the first round of 1900, Richmond demolished Port, though at a cost. Two officials were bashed. At their next match, mounted police were in evidence.
'Miss Tabulo': In 1900, in an example of administrative overkill, Richmond President George Bennett had no fewer than 36 vice-presidents, including a 'Miss Tabulo'. Supporters included the Minister for Railways, Mr Trenwith.
Skipper hurt: Captain Alex Edmonds was struck on the head by a rock on leaving the Brunswick ground in May 1903. Not long after, louts attacked Richmond players and the umpire at Footscray.

RICHMOND

Eat 'em alive

Richmond and generations of supporters should be grateful to an ordinary bloke called Miles, who was down on his luck around 1918 and could not afford the price of a ticket (sixpence) to see Richmond play at Punt Road. So he used to climb a big gum tree outside the ground to watch. All day, Miles would yell in a big booming voice: 'Eat 'em alive, Tigers.'

Len Incigneri with the colours.

The nickname had been around since the 1890s. For a time, another popular moniker was 'The Wasps' but it soon ran out of sting. Before that the unimaginative tag 'Richmonites' reigned.

After various uniform designs, the diagonal yellow sash on a black background surfaced in 1915. By 1924 it had become the norm.

In 1911, Tiger skipper Len Incigneri represented Victoria. In 1915, by then at Melbourne, he copped eight weeks for flattening a South player.

Two killed in action

Two Richmond players were killed in World War One – a big, likeable athletic youngster by the name of Leslie Edward 'Leggo' Lee and Billy Nolan. Lee, born and bred in Richmond, had only two games, in 1913, before joining up. He lost his life serving in Belgium in 1917. The year before he had starred in a services match in London. Nolan, who joined Richmond from Brighton juniors, played 30 games in 1914–15.

Another Richmond hero at the front was Hugh James, a former club captain. He rose to the rank of Lieutenant in the AIF and won the Military Cross for gallantry. He repaired a bridge under heavy fire 'thereby setting a fine example to his men'.

James returned to Richmond after the war and played until 1923. This wonderful ruckman/defender eventually clocked up 188 games and 119 goals.

In total, 43 past or present Richmond players served in World War One.

Punt Road, 1920. James taps, Minogue waits.

The 1919 team: Tigers' first to reach a VFL Grand Final.

Hugh James, MC: war hero and ruckman.

1908–1921 HONOUR ROLL

Year	Pos	Leading Goalkicker	No.	Best & Fairest	Captain	Coach
1908	9th	Bill Bourke	24		Charlie Pannam	Dick Condon
1909	8th	Bill Bourke	20		Condon/John 'Ivo' Lawson	Dick Condon
1910	7th	Mickey Maguire	20		Billy Schmidt	Alec 'Joker' Hall
1911	8th	Mickey Maguire	29		Len Incigneri	Len Incigneri
1912	9th	Edward Keggin	24		Ted Ohlsen	Charlie Pannam
1913	7th	Percy Martyn	32		Hugh James	Ern Jenkins
1914	8th	Clarrie Hall	32		Bill Thomas	Charlie Ricketts
1915	6th	Clarrie Hall	25		Bill Thomas	Charlie Ricketts
1916	4th	Percy Martini	22		Bill Thomas	Charlie Ricketts
1917	6th	Charles Fehring	14		Percy Maybury	Percy Maybury
1918	6th	Donald Don	19		Clarrie Hall	Bernie Nolan
1919	2nd	Donald Don	31		Bill Thomas	Norman Clark
1920	1st	George Bayliss	63		Dan Minogue	Dan Minogue
1921	1st	George Bayliss	53	Hugh James	Dan Minogue	Dan Minogue

CLUB NEWS 1908–1921

Ex-Magpies in control: Under captain Charlie Pannam, a flying wingman, and coach Dick Condon, a fiery character – both former Collingwood players – Richmond won its first VFL match in 1908, defeating Melbourne 8.14 (62) to 7.9 (51). The season yielded only six wins, the club finishing second last.

Locals please: Early in 1910, the *Guardian* urged that more home town boys play for Richmond, saying: 'One young Richmondite with his heart and soul in the club is worth a dozen hirelings from distant parts.' Club climbed to seventh and membership rose to 2000.

Thorp joins: In 1910 dashing defender Vic Thorp, first of the Richmond legends, had his first season with the club. His career lasted until 1925.

First 1000: For the first time, Richmond topped the 1000-point mark in 1913, kicking 1034.

Good news: Despite only 35 wins to 72 losses from 1908–13, the *Argus* had some cheerful news in 1914, saying that since joining the VFL, Richmond had 'grown up in a football sense, since suffering a series of drubbings conscientiously administered by more experienced opponents.' In 1914, with new rover Frank 'Checker' Hughes prominent, Richmond twice pushed Premiers-to-be Carlton, losing by two points and a goal. Hughes joined up in 1915, winning the DCM with the army. He returned to Punt Road in 1919.

1908 – 1921

Dan Minogue and his men: the Richmond champions of 1921.

The Minogue/Thorp show

Dan Minogue joined Richmond in 1920 after a falling-out with his former club, Collingwood. In 12 seasons, Richmond had not won a VFL Premiership. Minogue soon rectified that, leading the Tigers to their first two Flags in 1920 and 1921.

Minogue, a strongly built fellow standing 6ft 1 in, was a powerful ruckman-forward. He made up for his lack of pace with shrewd judgment, good handball and strong marking. Minogue left Punt Road at the end of 1925, having played 94 games and won six out of eight finals. He went on to coach Hawthorn, Carlton, St Kilda and Fitzroy.

Dan Minogue: a marvel.

Vic Thorp, the first Richmond player to break the double century (260 games) was described by Collingwood's great spearhead Dick Lee as the best full-back he played against. At 5ft 10 in and 13 stone, Thorp was a rugged, yet fair player, and liked to back his judgment with aggressive play. His long drop kicks were superb. Flippa, as he was known, played at full-back in the 1920–21 Premiership teams and was Champion of the Colony, the equivalent of the Brownlow, in 1916 and 1919. He was inducted into the Hall of Fame in 1996.

Back-to-back Flags

Richmond players and supporters, in a joyful repeat of the previous year, were entertained at dinner on the night of 15 October 1921, after the club's second successive VFL Premiership. Dinner over, 11 motor cars, the leading car bearing a Tiger skin with its head set defiantly, carried the victorious team through the streets of Richmond to the town hall where the Tigers' Flag was flown from the mast.

The 1921 match against Carlton was played in appalling, wet conditions. The *Age* writer Pivot reported that though the game was not great from the viewpoint of excellence it was so because of 'brilliant individual efforts, the closeness of the scorers and a fine finish.' When Richmond had won, 5.6 (36) to 4.8 (32), even the Carlton fans applauded. Excited Tiger supporters among the crowd of 43,122 invaded the MCG.

The shocking weather was in contrast to 1920, when Richmond beat Collingwood 7.10 (52) to 5.5 (35) in perfect conditions before 53,908 fans. Although without top goalkicker George Bayliss (injured), Richmond always had Collingwood's measure, leading by nine points at half time and by the same margin at three-quarter time in a tight, low-scoring game.

Willy Schmidt: 1910 skipper.

Essendon knifed

When Richmond kicked a behind against Essendon in 1921, the ball was knifed before being returned from the outer. Instead of kicking out, the Essendon full-back aimed a soft pass at the umpire for inspection. Tiger forward George Bayliss (right) intercepted it and kicked a soft goal. The umpire had to let it stand.

The first Premiership team, 1920: too tough for Collingwood.

Wartime four: Richmond finished third of four in 1916 — its first appearance in the finals, even if it was by default, after six clubs pulled out for the duration of World War One.
Costly miss: In the Second-Semi against Carlton in 1916, full-forward George Bayliss, normally a sharpshooter, had the chance to seal victory in the closing minutes. He missed from 30 yards out, Carlton winning by three points — 10.15 (75) to 10.12 (72) — and advancing to the Grand Final.
Ranks dwindled: With so many top players in the armed forces, Richmond finished last of the six teams in 1917 with only three wins.
At last: In May 1918, Richmond beat Carlton for the first time, after 24 losses since 1908 — 7.16 (58) to 8.5 (53).
Here we come: After narrowly making the finals, by two points from Fitzroy, the Tigers signalled their arrival as a force by finishing runner-up to Collingwood in 1919, losing the Grand Final by 25 points, 11.12 (78) to 7.11 (53).
Not a drop in sight: Heavy rain turned the MCG into a quagmire on 18 September 1920 for the Second Semi-final between minor Premiers Richmond and Carlton. Carlton won 7.11 (53) to 4.6 (30).
Premiership line-up in 1920: Backs: Hede, Thorp, Taylor. Half-backs: Parkinson, Hislop, Smith. Centres: Morris, Hughes, Carew. Half-forwards: Don, Weatherill, Harley. Forwards: Hugh James, Minogue, Bill James. Rucks: Herbert, Moffat. Rov: Hall. Captain–coach: Dan Minogue.

RICHMOND

Checker checkmates the opposition

In the six years that Frank 'Checker' Hughes was coach at Punt Road, Richmond was never out of the finals, and his greatest reward came with the Premiership in 1932.

Discipline laced with sarcasm was Hughes' main weapon to lift flagging teams. Wrote Dyer: 'Many a time I've sat among dejected players at half-time wondering how we could come back and win. Then Checker would rise quietly and you wouldn't dare drop a pin while he had the floor.

Checker Hughes: sardonic.

'He'd open with, "It's a very pleasant afternoon. I can imagine being out in that sunshine, getting plenty of fresh air and playing a nice friendly game in nice clean togs.

"I won't spoil it for you. We'll lay out the white linen at three-quarter time. The ladies will supply the cream cakes and tea. And we'll have a jolly pleasant afternoon.

"But I'm blowed if any of you will ever play for Richmond again. Get out there and play like men, even if you're not."'

Jack Dyer in 1931.

It mostly worked. Before crossing to Melbourne in 1933 for bigger pickings, Hughes coached Richmond in 120 games, winning 87, drawing two and losing 31.

Rocks of Gibraltar – Bolger, Sheahan and O'Neill.

The Three Musketeers of the Tiger defence

They called them the 'Three Musketeers': the last line of the Tiger defence that launched attacks like Aramis, Athos and Porthos. The D'Artagnan, or mentor, of the unit was coach Frank 'Checker' Hughes.

The names of the Musketeers were Martin Bolger, Maurie Sheahan and Kevin O'Neill. As the line-up implies, Sheahan was the full-back: a dashing, long-kicking, safe-marking one at that. Sheahan, at 5ft 11in, was the tallest. His trusty back-pocket players both stood 5ft 9in. All three weighed in at around 12 stone.

Bolger was the steady type, whereas O'Neill and Sheahan were dashers who backed their judgment. The three played 90 games together from 1930–36 and were members of the 1932 and 1934 Premiership teams. Between them, the Musketeers played 434 games – Bolger 185, Sheahan 123 and O'Neill 126. Still revered in Richmond circles, they made life intolerable for champion South Melbourne full-forward Bob Pratt at finals time, restricting him to two goals in the 1934 Grand Final and to three in South's 1933 Premiership.

1922 – 1934 HONOUR ROLL

Year	Pos	Leading Goalkicker	No.	Best & Fairest	Captain	Coach
1922	5th	George Bayliss	32	Mel Morris	Dan Minogue	Dan Minogue
1923	8th	Don Fraser	18	Hugh James	Dan Minogue	Dan Minogue
1924	2nd	Mel Morris	44	Vic Thorp	Dan Minogue	Dan Minogue
1925	7th	Mel Morris	25	Tom O'halloran	Dan Minogue	Dan Minogue
1926	7th	Dave Lynch	31	Alan Geddes	Mel Morris	Mel Morris
1927	2nd	Jack Baggott	37	Basil McCormack	Alan Geddes	'Checker' Hughes
1928	2nd	Jack Baggott	61	Basil McCormack	Alan Geddes	'Checker' Hughes
1929	2nd	Jack Titus	54	Jack Titus	Charles Lilburne	'Checker' Hughes
1930	3rd	Jack Titus	50	No Award	Alan Geddes	'Checker' Hughes
1931	2nd	Doug Strang	68	No Award	Maurie Hunter	'Checker' Hughes
1932	1st	Doug Strang	49	Jack Dyer	Perc Bentley	'Checker' Hughes
1933	2nd	Doug Strang	51	Maurie Hunter	Perc Bentley	Billy Schmidt
1934	1st	Jack Titus	80	Ray Martin	Perc Bentley	Perc Bentley

CLUB NEWS 1922–1934

Heads roll: Aiming for its third Flag in a row, Richmond lost four of its first five games in 1922 and wound up in fifth place.

Big slide: In 1923, Richmond crashed to second last place with only 4 wins. More than 40 players were tried. Clearly, new blood was needed.

Enter Percy Page: With only 11 wins in two seasons, it was revolution time and, in 1924, Percy Page was elected secretary and Jack Archer president. Things immediately looked up, the team finishing second to Essendon.

Sharp-shooters: Doug Hayes kicked eight goals and Mel Morris seven in Richmond's three 1924 finals.

New talent: 1925 brought mixed blessings. George Rudolph was suspended and injuries to Dan Minogue and Percy Bentley saw the side slip to seventh with only six wins. But newcomers included stars-to-be Basil McCormack, Alan Geddes and Tom O'Halloran.

Thanks for the memory: On a sad note, 1925 was Vic Thorpe's last season. The magnificent full-back bowed out having played a record 261 games in a career that began in 1910.

Short and sharp: In 1926, Mel Morris, who played in the centre in the 1921 Premiership side, took over as coach from Dan Minogue. He lasted only one year. His replacement, in 1927, was the shrewd Checker Hughes.

Lean and lively: A skinny larrikin kid called Jack Titus turned out for the Tigers for the first time in 1926.

1922 – 1934

Back at the top

Richmond put five frustrating years behind it with a hard-fought win over bitter rival Carlton in the 1932 Grand Final. Runners-up in 1927–29 and 1931, the Tigers finished second to the Blues on the ladder in 1932 then ran all over them in the Second Semi-final, 18.16 (124) to 14.15 (99). Doug Strang kicked seven goals and Maurie Hunter six.

The Grand Final against the Blues at the MCG before 69,724 was torrid, Richmond leading by only seven points at orange time.

The lead changed several times in the last quarter, bringing the crowd to a frenzy. Finally Jack Anderson (Richmond's 19th man) and Jack Titus goaled to give the Tigers their first Flag since 1921 – 13.14 (92) to 12.11 (83). Young Jack Dyer missed the match because of a knee injury.

The next year, in the Grand Final, the Tigers ran into 'The Foreign Legion' – as South Melbourne was known – and were humbled 9.17 (71) to a miserable 4.5 (29).

The Tigers had their revenge in 1934 under new playing coach Percy Bentley, and were fortunate that Sheahan contained Bob Pratt. A blistering third quarter on a sunny day saw Richmond kick 6.3 to 0.6 to seal South's fate. With Jack Titus (six goals) starring, the Punt Road boys romped home 19.14 (128) to 12.17 (89). Young Jack Dyer was reported to be 'vigorous in the packs'.

The 1934 team: romped home after a third-quarter burst.

Tigers' first Brownlow

Stan Judkins – small and nippy as wingmen were in his era – was the first Richmond player to win the Brownlow Medal, in 1930. He tied with Harry Collier (Collingwood) and Albert Hopkins (Footscray) but won on a countback having played in fewer games (12). A fine ball handler, Judkins played in the 1932 and 1934 Premiership sides.

In those days, there was little ceremony over the Brownlow. Winners were notified by mail to attend VFL House to collect their medal.

Doug Strang.

Basil McCormack: tough.

Skinny Titus: six goals in Grand Final.

1932 Premiership team

B: Bolger, Sheahan, O'Neill
HB: Baggot, Murdoch, McCormack
C: Judkins, Zschech, Geddes
HF: Twyford, G. Strang, Titus
F: Heifner, D. Strang, Hunter
Foll: Bentley (c), O'Halloran
Rov: Martin
19th: Anderson   Coach: Hughes

1934 Premiership team

B: Bolger, Sheahan, O'Neill
HB: Baggot, G. Strang, McCormack
C: Judkins, Zschech, Geddes
HF: O'Halloran, Baxter, Murdoch
F: Foster, Titus, Harris
Foll: Bentley (c), Dyer
Rov: Martin
19th: Edmonds   Coach: P. Bentley

Thrashing: Checker Hughes was unfazed by a horror start to his coaching career in 1927, a 50-point hiding by Premiers Melbourne, 16.19 (115) to 9.11 (65). The Tigers went on to win 14 of their next 17 games and finish runner-up to Collingwood.

That's entertainment, '27 style! Secretary Percy Page had his jaw broken at a dance after the July 2 game. That day Richmond ended Geelong's winning streak of eight wins, 9.15 (69) to 7.11 (53), on the swampy Punt Road ground.

Big Vs galore: Seven Tigers played for Victoria in 1927 – Jack Baggott, Percy Bentley, George Rudolph, Tom O'Halloran, Donald Don, Alan Geddes and Basil McCormack.

In the goals: Jack Baggott kicked 61 goals in 1928, including a club-record 12 against South at Punt Road. Doug Strang beat the record with 14 goals v North in 1931.

Cricket scores: Richmond kicked a century in three consecutive games midway through 1928, a VFL record. Scores were 19.6 (120) v Fitzroy, 21.16 (142) v South Melbourne and 13.24 (102) v Hawthorn.

Captain kid: A raw-boned 17 year-old called Jack Dyer, earmarked by Checker Hughes as a star in the making, played six Senior games in 1931, including two finals. He kicked three goals in the Tigers' 33-point win over Geelong in the Second Semi-final but did not bother the scorer from the forward-pocket in the Grand Final, won by Geelong by 20 points.

RICHMOND

Captain Blood on warpath

Jack Dyer: a Richmond legend.

Jack Dyer was a riot on the field – and off it. As a player he took no prisoners but he was suspended only once (for four weeks in 1944) in his 312 games with Richmond from 1931–49.

Dyer was dubbed Captain Blood in 1935 after a particularly torrid game against Fitzroy, in which he flattened three opponents. After the game, the *Age* football writer John Ludlow followed Dyer into the rooms. 'Golly, Jack,' said Ludlow, 'I haven't seen bodies piled up like that since I saw Errol Flynn in that Captain Blood movie.'

Monday's *Herald* carried a cartoon of Dyer dressed as a pirate, a skull and crossbones on his cap and a cutlass between his teeth. The name stuck. Dyer didn't like it but grew into it. Opposition fans loathed and abused him. Tiger supporters worshipped him.

As a player, Captain Blood, master of the crunching hip-and-shoulder, had more polish than his name suggested. He was quick for a ruckman, a fine mark and kick and the ultimate protector of his small-men. Dyer kicked 443 goals (he played at full-forward in his last few seasons), won Richmond's Best and Fairest award six times, played in two Premiership teams (1934 and 1943) and captained the Tigers in 160 games. He was coach for 12 years and played for Victoria in 1941 and 1949.

Dyer was always good company. Yarning

Captain Blood's last game, against Geelong.

one day, he recalled an 'unbelievable' mark he took just before three-quarter time in an interstate match. 'I went up so high that I was just kind of hovering there when the bell went,' he said, smiling. 'They had to throw my orange up to me.'

In 1944, Melbourne skipper and rover Percy Beames said that if he had all the players in the VFL to choose from 'I'd pick Jack Dyer before I considered any other player in the game.'

Hero remembered

In 1943 Max Oppy won the inaugural Bill Cosgrove/Harry Jenkins Trophy for the best first-year player. The trophy was struck in memory of young Tiger defender Bill Cosgrove, who played three games for Richmond in 1940. All Tigers mourned when Flight-Sergeant Cosgrove was killed when his Beaufighter bomber was shot down in 1943. Cosgrove had Jack Dyer's name and the Tiger emblem painted on the planes he flew. Four other Tigers lost their lives in World War Two – Bill Garvie, Ossie Jennings, Frank Stamford and M. Wheeler.

Flight Sergeant Bill Cosgrove at Punt Road.

1935 – 1949 HONOUR ROLL

Year	Pos	Leading Goalkicker	No.	Best & Fairest	Captain	Coach
1935	3rd	Jack Titus	83	Ray Martin	Perc Bentley	Perc Bentley
1936	6th	Jack Titus	83	Martin Bolger	Perc Bentley	Perc Bentley
1937	4th	Jack Titus	65	Jack Dyer	Perc Bentley	Perc Bentley
1938	6th	Jack Titus	72	Jack Dyer	Perc Bentley	Perc Bentley
1939	4th	Jack Titus	48	Jack Dyer	Perc Bentley	Perc Bentley
1940	2nd	Jack Titus	100	Jack Dyer	Perc Bentley	Perc Bentley
1941	4th	Jack Titus	87	Jack Titus	Jack Dyer	Jack Dyer
1942	2nd	Jack Titus	67	Leo Merrett	Jack Dyer	Jack Dyer
1943	1st	Dick Harris	62	Ron Durham	Jack Dyer	Jack Dyer
1944	2nd	Dick Harris	66	Leo Merrett	Jack Dyer	Jack Dyer
1945	7th	Fred Burge	55	Bill Morris	Jack Dyer	Jack Dyer
1946	5th	Arthur Mooney	48	Jack Dyer	Jack Dyer	Jack Dyer
1947	4th	Jack Dyer	46	Billy Wilson	Jack Dyer	Jack Dyer
1948	5th	Jack Dyer	64	Bill Morris	Jack Dyer	Jack Dyer
1949	6th	Ray Poulter	51	Geoff Spring	Jack Dyer	Jack Dyer

CLUB NEWS 1935–1949

On target: Young Skinny Titus kicked 83 goals in 1936, including 10 in one match against Footscray, while cries of 'too old' convinced stalwarts Doug Strang and Basil McCormack that it was time to move to Tasmania, and Joe Murdoch to go to the bush.

Sponsors!: In its 1937 Annual Report, Richmond thanked powerful sponsors Carlton & United Brewery and Bryant & May (matches), which both contributed the decimal equivalent of $10.50. Rosella, Marchants and Fred Hesse Menswear also chipped in. A record $107.25 was donated.

Incorruptible: Skinny Titus reported that he had refused a $50 bribe from a betting syndicate to 'play dead' against South Melbourne on 22 June 1938. The Tigers won 20.15 (135) to 8.14 (62).

Smith KO'd: Melbourne star Norm Smith was carried semi-conscious from the ground after clashing heavily with Jack Dyer during the 1940 Second Semi-final, which Richmond won by a goal, 16.11 (107) to 14.17 (101). The Demons won the Grand Final.

Percy retires: At the end of 1940, great ruckman Percy Bentley retired after 16 years with the club and a record 263 games. He was captain for nine years and coach for seven (1934–40).

Austerity crowd: World War Two saw attendances dwindle dramatically. Only 3000 fans attended the hate-match between Richmond and Collingwood in Round 14, 1942. Richmond won 16.21 (117) to 12.11 (83)

1935–1949

The 1943 Premiership team: triumphant over Essendon.

Bill Morris: Brownlow winner.

Operation Oppy wins day

The Richmond tactic going into the 1943 Grand Final against old rival Essendon was simple: stop Dick Reynolds.

But how? Jack Dyer hatched a plot. He entrusted the job of keeping Reynolds quiet to tough newcomer Max Oppy, who happened to be a cousin of Reynolds.

By quarter-time, Reynolds had a cut over his eye and the Tigers led 4.2 (26) to 2.4 (16) At half-time, with Richmond eight points up, Dyer pleaded with his players to 'Give me just one more hour of your lives.'

They did. When the giant bell rang to end the game the Tigers had won by five points – 12.14 (86) to 11.15 (81). Reynolds had been held goalless by his young cousin.

Much-loved badman

Dashing centre-half back Don 'Mopsy' Fraser was the wild boy of Punt Road from 1945–52. Few of his 124 games after being discharged from the army were without incident. In his own words, 'Trouble seemed to follow me.' Numerous visits to the tribunal resulted in a total of 84 weeks suspension for his career.

When he applied himself, there was no better player than Fraser. He was fast, a great mark and a long kick. Jack Dyer said Mopsy would have won a Brownlow but for his incurable habit of 'going off the planet'.

Two masters to serve

Private Jack Broadstock, a rugged 6-footer who, in Jack Dyer's words could 'charm the pitchfork off the devil', was wanted on two fronts on Grand Final day, 1943 – at army camp in South Australia and by Dyer to play for Richmond.

Broadstock went AWOL, only to find the military police waiting for him at Princes Park. Dyer pleaded and the Army decreed that Broadstock must return to camp straight after the game.

As anticipated by Dyer, Broadstock was one of Richmond's best players, at half-forward. After the victory, Broadstock, who enjoyed a beer, won another reprieve to join in the victory celebrations.

Mopsy Fraser: fiery.

Jack 'Skinny' Titus.

Paleface wins Brownlow

One of the game's grandest ruckmen, Bill Morris, brought glory to Richmond in the lean years after World War Two. Morris, known as 'Paleface' because of his pallid complexion, won the Brownlow Medal in 1948 with 24 votes.

Morris could palm the ball to his rover (Bill Wilson) with either hand, seemed to glide through the air to take fine high marks and kicked accurately with the left foot. His coach, Jack Dyer, described him as the greatest ruckman he had seen. Not surprisingly, he wasn't Dyer's style, being 'the ultimate gentleman', with a habit of helping opposition players to their feet after he had knocked them over.

Skinny quits on 970

A gentleman off the field, a wisecracking larrikin and genius on it. That was Jack 'Skinny' Titus, who quit football at the end of 1943, only 30 goals short of the magic 1000.

His 970 goals were kicked in 294 games (a VFL record 204 in succession) over 18 seasons. He was the first Tiger to kick 100 goals in a season (1940), played in the 1932 and 1934 Premiership sides (kicking six goals in the 1934 Grand Final) and represented Victoria 14 times. Three times he kicked 10 in a match – against Footscray in 1936, Hawthorn in 1941 and Collingwood in 1942.

---

to grab top spot on the ladder. It finished second to Essendon after losing to Carlton, by 53 points, in the last round.

Dyer smoulders: Jack Dyer, stung by defeat, reluctantly went to the Essendon rooms to congratulate the Dons after they had won the 1942 Grand Final by 53 points. He promised the merry Dons merry hell in 1943!

Red Cross benefits: Richmond raised $13,000 for the Red Cross in 1943.

Titanic struggle: Without injured stars Harris, Broadstock and Durham, and Dyer and Morris not completely fit, the Tigers were valiant in defeat in the 1944 Grand Final, losing to Fitzroy 9.12 (66) to 7.9 (51) before 43,000 at the Junction Oval.

At the front: In 1944, Richmond had 62 players in uniform, mostly in the Army. Highest rank was obtained by Lieutenant Ray Steele, a member of the 1943 Premiership team.

'Mugs to backline': With these words, captain–coach Jack Dyer ordered ex-Private Mopsy Fraser to play in defence after Fraser had kicked 1.13 against St Kilda. Fraser's opponent was subsequent Test cricketer Keith Miller.

300 up: Jack Dyer played his 300th game, against St Kilda, on 7 May 1949. He kicked four goals. In Round 11, he played his 307th game, beating Gordon Coventry's VFL record of 306.

Big finish: In his last game (against Geelong at Punt Road in 1949) Jack Dyer kicked six goals in a winning score of 22.12 to 10.15. Dyer ended the season with 46 goals.

RICHMOND

Captain Blood stirs the troops pre-season.

Max Oppy: on warpath.

Dyer sacked as coach

Getting the sack is one thing. Losing your job to someone from Collingwood is tantamount to treachery.

That's how Jack Dyer felt at the end of 1952 when he was replaced as coach by former Magpie Alby Pannam. Dyer, who joined Richmond in 1931 and became its most famous son, had taken over as playing coach in 1940 from Percy Bentley, and led the Tigers to the 1943 Flag. He retired as a player at the end of 1949, having played a VFL record number of games – 312.

He became non-playing coach in 1950 and was given only three years before the axe fell – harsh treatment for one who had given so much to the club.

But Dyer never lost his love of Richmond. When the club was in financial trouble in the early 1990s, Dyer was in the forefront of the move to save the club. And help save it, Captain Blood did.

Captain Blood: 'old softie'

So Jack Dyer was tough! On the football field, yes, very hard. But as coach of Richmond for 12 years (1941–52) he was an old softie, too easy on his players, recalled one of his charges of yesteryear, 71-year-old Des Rowe.

Rowe's eyes light up with affection when he talks about Dyer. 'Jack is a wonderful fellow,' he says. 'As a coach, Jack was too nice. Players took advantage of him.'

And what of the legendary Dyerisms on training nights? No, Rowe cannot recall Jack saying to 'pair off in threes'. On training nights, 'Jack was pretty serious out in the middle as we did circle work, kicking, marking and handballing, and a few sprints.' Training started at 4.30 p.m. because most players worked (Rowe for stock agent Goldsborough Mort) and ended before dark. There were no lights. There was no gym for toning up rippling biceps, but a lot of players had manual jobs so were pretty fit.

In Rowe's time Richmond had more characters than a comedy festival. The toughest player Rowe has ever seen is team-mate Max Oppy, a human tank. Oppy was a great inspiration, and on occasions unforgiving. Rowe recalls the day Roy Wright flew for a mark, crashed over Carlton's Jack Howell and fell heavily. There was blood everywhere. Oppy rushed up from the back-pocket and said 'Get up you weak so and so.' When he saw the blood, Oppy relented. 'Oh, you poor bastard, stay there.'

Captain Blood: Gladstone bag and fan club.

Gentle Giant's Brownlows

Ruckman Roy Wright, known as the 'Gentle Giant', won the Brownlow Medal in 1952 and again in 1954. The plucky Wright overcame great difficulties to become a star. Until he was 10, his knees were so weak that his legs had to be kept in splints. He did not play football until he was 16 but soon showed outstanding ability. He had to compete with Bill Morris, the senior ruckman, when Wright first joined the Tigers in 1946. When Morris retired in 1951, Wright came into his own, clocking up a total of 195 games and going on to captain Richmond in his last two seasons. He was renowned for his clean play, although he suffered numerous injuries.

Nine broken noses.

CLUB NEWS 1950–1966

New skipper: Brownlow Medallist Bill Morris replaced Jack Dyer (retired) as skipper at the start of 1950. Don Fraser was vice-captain.

Missed: Jack Dyer's presence on field was missed in 1950 and the team finished sixth with 10 wins. Centre half-forward Ray Poulter was the club's top goalkicker with 56.

MCG talk: 42,000 fans packed Punt Road for the fifth-round match against Collingwood in 1951, breaking down fences and spilling on to the ground. It sparked talk of Richmond moving to the MCG. The Tigers won 16.20 (116) to 9.11 (65), their fourth win in five matches. Mid-season, the team lost six on the trot, infuriating coach Dyer.

Governor dies: Richmond's No. 1 member, the Governor, Baron Dugan, died in 1951. The new Governor, Sir Dallas Brooks, accepted the No. 1 ticket.

New skipper: Des Rowe was appointed skipper at the start of 1952. Despite high hopes, the team once again slipped to ninth place with only eight wins.

Sydney loss: In 1952, a crowd of 24,000 turned out for the June 14 Richmond v Collingwood game at the SCG, the first VFL game for points outside Victoria. The Magpies won 10.12 (72) to 5.6 (36).

Mopsy 3, Twomeys 0, In Round 11, 1952, Mopsy Fraser cleaned up the three Twomey brothers, Bill, Pat and Mick, at Victoria Park. All three were

1950 – 1966

Graeme Richmond: passionate club man.

Joy in 1966: acting joint coaches Dick Harris and Jack Titus (left) help celebrate a win.

The Godfather

In the 1950s, Geelong Grammar boys weren't supposed to be Tigers. But Graeme Richmond, a handy footballer and amateur boxer, and his mate Ian 'Octa' Wilson, top oarsman and rugged ruckman in the 1951 GGS Thirds (unbeaten), had black and yellow blood in their veins.

As club secretary from 1962 to 1968, Richmond (and president Ray Dunn) orchestrated the club's return to power – recruiting vigorously, overseeing the welfare of players, and ruthlessly pruning dead wood.

Wilson, a raconteur and character, was Tiger President from 1974 until 1985, presiding over two Premierships.

27 wins on end

The 1966 Reserve Grade team went through the season unbeaten, though it got a fright in the Grand Final, winning by only five points from Collingwood, 14.11 (95) to 13.12 (90). Barry Richardson (3) and Royce Hart (2) were among the chief goal kickers. Other notable players to turn out for the Reserves in 1966 were Kevin Bartlett, Mike Patterson, Billy Brown, Dick Clay, Francis Bourke and Mike Green.

The Reserves extended their winning streak to 27 with three wins at the start of 1967.

On the move to the MCG

The 19 years from 1948 to 1966 were the leanest to date in Richmond's long history. In that time, its highest spot was fifth – in 1948, 1954, 1965 and 1966.

The years 1965 and 1966 heralded a Tiger revival. In 1965 the Tigers moved to the MCG and, under shrewd tactician Len Smith, developed a more attacking game. Big scores flowed. Although the Tigers finished eight points out of the four, they kicked the second highest number of points, 1561 to St Kilda's 1573, for a percentage of 125.

The trend continued in 1966, when the Tigers missed out on the finals by only two points, winning 13 games, losing four and drawing one. Again, big scores were evident. tally, 1626. Clearly good times were ahead.

1950 – 1966 HONOUR ROLL

Year	Pos	Leading Goalkicker	No.	Best & Fairest	Captain	Coach
1950	6th	Ray Poulter	56	Bill Morris/Roy Wright	Bill Morris	Jack Dyer
1951	6th	Jack O'Rourke	58	Des Rowe	Bill Morris	Jack Dyer
1952	9th	Jack O'Rourke	43	Roy Wright	Des Rowe	Jack Dyer
1953	10th	Ron Branton	22	Havel Rowe	Des Rowe	Alby Pannam
1954	5th	Ron Branton	33	Roy Wright	Des Rowe	Alby Pannam
1955	6th	Ray Poulter	49	Des Rowe	Des Rowe	Alby Pannam
1956	10th	Rob Dummett	32	Laurie Sharp	Des Rowe	Max Oppy
1957	7th	Rob Dummett	41	Roy Wright	Des Rowe	Alan McDonald
1958	10th	Ted Langridge	28	Dave Cuzens	Roy Wright	Alan McDonald
1959	11th	Rob Dummett	45	Dave Cuzens	Roy Wright	Alan McDonald
1960	12th	Graeme Wilkinson	21	Ron Branton	Ron Branton	Alan McDonald
1961	10th	Ted Langridge	29	Ron Branton	Ron Branton	Des Rowe
1962	8th	Ted Langridge	42	Ron Branton	Ron Branton	Des Rowe
1963	10th	Ian Hayden	25	Neville Crowe	Neville Crowe	Des Rowe
1964	8th	Roger Dean	23	Neville Crowe	Neville Crowe	Len Smith
1965	5th	Mick Erwin	32	Bill Barrot	Neville Crowe	Len Smith/Jack Titus
1966	5th	Paddy Guinane	50	Neville Crowe	Neville Crowe	Tom Hafey

carried off. With Magpie supporters throwing more than insults, Dyer and Fraser were escorted by police when they left the ground. The Magpies won 10.19 (79) to 8.8 (56).

Mopsy goes: After a row over John Coleman's 100th goal for season (against Richmond), Don Fraser left at the end of 1952 to play in the VFA. New recruits in 1953 included Tom Hafey.

Please return: In 1953, Richmond lost four of first five games and fans pleaded with publican Jack Dyer to return as coach. He declined. The team sank to 10th with three wins. Things looked up in 1954, with the team missing the finals by only one game.

Stars quit: The club lost rugged Max Oppy (176 games) and top rover Billy Wilson (185 games, 226 goals) at the end of 1954. Dyer returned to club as vice-president.

No gold medals: In Melbourne's Olympic year (1956), Richmond, under new coach Max Oppy, won only two of its first 10 games, defeating Collingwood by 36 points and North by 10 points on the way to 10th place with six wins. Oppy resigned at the end of the season.

Not so gentle: In 1958, a spectator attacked dual Brownlow winner Roy Wright in the race after Tigers had lost to Carlton, 2.9 (21) to 6.15 (51).

Fresh approach: Coach Des Rowe established a fitness program at the start of 1961, which also saw the arrival of the 17-year-old Bill Barrot. In Round 16, the Tigers were goalless, kicking 0.8 to St Kilda's 12.19 (91).

RICHMOND

Eat 'em alive, Tigers!

Above: Skipper Fred Swift delights in being 'drowned' after Richmond sealed top place. Inset: Royce Hart soars in Grand Final.

At last a Flag

Played before a capacity crowd of 109,396 on a sunny day at the MCG, the 1967 Grand Final between Richmond and Geelong was hailed as a classic encounter.

It had all the essential ingredients – pace, skill, fine drop-kicking, high marking and high drama. The result was in doubt until the final few minutes. Richmond led at every change but Geelong levelled the scores early in the last quarter then went ahead by a goal. The turning point came at the 18-minute mark of the last term when Barry Richardson passed the ball to ruckman John Ronaldson on the members' wing.

'You couldn't see him kicking it,' cried Mike Williamson into the Channel 7 microphone. 'I tell you what, this is a ripper …' Yes, Ronaldson's drop kick, as casual as they come, rifled through the uprights from 60 yards out.

The action reached a crescendo, with Royce Hart taking the mark of the season, Billy Barrot running wild and Ronaldson kicking another goal from a free kick. The fitness of the Tigers under new coach Tom Hafey was a telling factor.

Geelong attacks too often resulted in behinds and when Kevin Bartlett sharked a boundary throw-in and backed out of a pack to goal, the Flag was Richmond's. It only required skipper Fred Swift to take a saving mark on the goal line in the final seconds for Richmond to start celebrating. Richmond had prevailed, but only by nine points – 16.18 (114) to 15.15 (105).

Barrot was unanimously best on the ground with 26 kicks and seven marks. Hart had 13 kicks, Brown 17, Bartlett 16 and Barry Richardson 15. Sadly the match was Fred Swift's last. He retired immediately, having played 146 games from 1958–67. He was made Richmond mayor for a day after the Tigers' Grand Final win.

So, to the delight of the multitudes in the inns in Swan Street and Bridge Road and beyond, the Tigers were on top again after the longest drought in the club's history – 24 years.

Charlie Callander + Cup.

1967 Premiership Team (with ages) –
B: Dean (27), Swift (29), Jewell (23)
HB: Burgin (19), M. Perry (23), Strang (23)
C; Clay (22), Barrot (23), Bourke (20)
HF: Northey (24), Guinane (26), B. Richardson (21)
F: Ronaldson (20), Hart (19), Brown (24)
Foll: Patterson (26), A. Richardson (25)
Rov: Bartlett (20)
Out suspended: N. Crowe
Reserves: Green (19), J. Perry (22)
Coach: Tom Hafey

CLUB NEWS 1967

A new star: Royce Hart, playing at full-forward, made an impressive debut in the Round 1 win over Essendon, 15.20 (110) to 11.9 (75), He took 10 marks, though his kicking (3.7) was astray. Centreman Bill Barrot was best afield and Dick Clay starred on a wing. Fred Swift replaced Neville Crowe as captain.

No clearance: Kevin Sheedy, having crossed from Prahran without a clearance, was picked in the centre for the Round 3 match against Fitzroy. Barrot was on a wing and Francis Bourke was playing in defence in the Reserves.

Rift healed: Secretary Graeme Richmond announced that Barrot and the club had healed their rift. Barrot said some people at the club had 'rubbished him'. He played in the Reserves against North.

First game: After four matches in the Reserves, Francis Bourke was named as a reserve against Hawthorn. Rover Kevin Bartlett kicked six goals as the Tigers recorded their fourth win in five games.

On the up: Richmond jumped to second place on the ladder with a 38-point win over Geelong 18.11 (119) to 12.9 (81) at MCG in Round 7. Eight goals in the third quarter sealed it. Hart kicked 4 goals and an experiment of playing Bourke on a wing was deemed a success. Geelong coach Peter Pianto said the Tigers played 'some of the best football I've seen'.

Fred the dasher: Veteran Fred Swift

1967

Dick Clay: a great mark.

Francis Bourke: never beaten.

Bill Barrott: energy and mischief.

BBC provided rare entertainment

The centreline of Bourke, Barrot and Clay, the BBC of the VFL, provided Richmond supporters with grand entertainment.

Midfielder Billy Barrot, late of the Glen Iris under 16s, enjoyed the spacious MCG. A well-muscled, predatory roamer with a full tank of energy and mischief, his drop kicks ripped through opposing defences. The showman in him surfaced with his clever use of the baulk. Having wrong-footed an opponent, he would bound away and thump a torp into attack.

On the wings, Barrot had the ultimate support in Francis Bourke and Dick Clay, both 6ft 1in. Bourke, from Nathalia, had Tiger blood, corpuscles of courage, in his veins. His father was the amiable Frank Bourke, a tall, classy full-forward who had kicked 50 goals in 16 games for the Tigers. Francis Bourke once played out a game with a broken bone in his leg and with blood pouring from a face wound. He always made good ground when a match-saving spoil or mark was called for. If he ever played a poor game, no one can remember it. His son David make his debut for the Tigers in 1995.

Kyabram-born Richard (Dick) Clay glided over the ground. Good hands, superior judgment and balance yielded a high tally of strong marks. He had 'flair' but was never flamboyant. He was so versatile that he ended his days at full-back.

Len Smith dies

Len Smith, the architect of Richmond's modern, long-kicking game, died on 24 July 1967 – just two months before the Tigers won their first Flag for 24 years. He was 55.

Smith, a brother of Melbourne's most successful coach Norm Smith, coached Richmond in 1964 and for part of 1965. A heart attack forced him to stand down. He was a selector from 1966 until his death in Sacred Heart Hospital, Moreland. He left a wife and three children.

A quietly spoken man, Len Smith was regarded as one of the shrewdest coaches in the business. He played with Melbourne in 1934–35 then with Northcote and Fitzroy from 1937–43. He coached Fitzroy, training them to bamboozle opponents with slick handball, into the finals in 1960.

1967 HONOUR ROLL

Year	Pos	Leading Goalkicker	No.	Best & Fairest	Captain	Coach
1967	1st	Royce Hart	55	Kevin Bartlett	Fred Swift	Tom Hafey

lived up to his name with a 50-metre solo run against Collingwood, outpacing two pursuers.
On target: Royce Hart kicked 7 goals in Victoria's big 20.15 (135) to 11.16 (82) win over WA at the MCG. Bill Barrot was best on ground in middle.
Last loss: Richmond's defeat by Essendon in Round 12, 10.12 (72) to 13.15 (93), was its last that season.
Hart moved: Royce Hart played at centre half-forward for the first time in the Round 15 match against North. The Tigers won by 20 points, with new spearhead Paddy Guinane kicking four goals.
Premiership look: Fred Swift, formerly a midfielder/forward, was moved to full-back and Bourke, Barrot and Clay formed the centreline for the first time in a big win over Hawthorn 23.30 (168) to 7.12 (54) in Round 15. Clay and Bourke both starred.
Top of heap: Richmond displaced Carlton in top place with a 32-point win over St Kilda in Round 17.
Cats beaten: Richmond ended its home-and-away games in top place (15 wins, 3 losses, percentage of 145.9) with a last round win over Geelong at Kardinia Park, 18.9 (117) to 15.15 (105). Flanker John Northey ended the home-and-away games with 47 goals.
In tears: Richmond's top ruckman Neville Crowe was in tears after being suspended for four weeks on September 14 for striking Carlton's John Nicholls during the Second Semi-final. He missed the Grand Final, but was first onto the ground when the Tigers won the Flag.

RICHMOND

Tom Hafey and pooch: fitness first.

Royce Hart attacks as Northey supports.

Bull Richardson.

Kevin Sheedy.

Mike Green.

Barry Richardson.

Hafey's heroes go to the top

Tiger fans called them Hafey's heroes: Hart, Bartlett, Northey, Sheedy, Barrot, Bourke, Clay and lots more.

Richmond got Royce Hart from Tasmanian club Clarence for a bargain – a new suit, six shirts and a pair of shoes. In 1967, aged 19, he played like a veteran as Richmond won its first Premiership for 24 years, and drew on rich reserves of judgment, balance and courage. His marking was uncanny. He would float in from the side of a pack, twist his solid 6ft 2in frame and clasp the ball.

Hart played in four Premierships: 1967, 1969 and as captain of the 1973 and 1974 teams. He played for Victoria in his first year and on 10 other occasions, once as captain.

Lightly-built half forward flanker John Northey would go unnoticed until opportunity knocked. Then he would swoop on the ball and goal before you could say 'Punt Road'. The MCG was his favourite hunting ground. He played 117 games from 1963-70.

The impish Kevin Bartlett was well blessed in speed, alertness and sure ball-handling. He was the club's leading goalkicker three times, kicking 778 overall, was Best and Fairest five times and skipper in 1979. He played for Victoria 20 times, being captain in 1980. He played in five Premiership teams and coached the side from 1988 to 1991.

Roger Dean.

Kevin Sheedy was tough and professional. He crossed from Prahran to Richmond in 1967 and stayed with the Tigers until 1979, playing in four Premiership teams. He was captain in 1978 and played 251 games.

Roger Dean was described as a gentleman off the field and a terrier on it. He joined the club in 1957, playing in the 1967 Grand Final, and captaining the 1969 Premiership team. He played in the back-pocket after stints as a half-forward and rover. He kicked 204 goals in his 244 games.

Ruckman Mike Green was Richmond's best player in each of its three 1969 finals wins. Recruited from Old Xaverians, Green, 6ft 4in tall, had a good spring and was a fine mark. He played 145 games from 1966–75.

The Richardsons, Barry and Alan (Bull) are unrelated. Barry, 6ft 3in tall and slender, was known as 'Bones'. He was a most versatile member of the 1967 and 1969 Premiership sides, playing on a forward flank in 1967 and at full-back two years later. Bull Richardson, father of present-day player Matthew, came from Casterton and played 103 games. A six-footer, he bullocked his way through packs and used handball effectively.

Early in the career of Paddy Guinane, coach Des Rowe tried to get him to play in front. It was a lost cause. Paddy preferred to take screamers from behind, and did so often.

1968—1969 HONOUR ROLL

Year	Pos	Leading Goalkicker	No.	Best & Fairest	Captain	Coach
1968	5th	Paddy Guinane	41	Kevin Bartlett	Roger Dean	Tom Hafey
1969	1st	Rex Hunt	55	Royce Hart	Roger Dean	Tom Hafey

CLUB NEWS 1968–1969

Crowe calls it a day: After 151 games and the disappointment of missing the 1967 Grand Final because of suspension, Neville Crowe, captain from 1963–66, retired at start of 1968. A fine follower, he played for Victoria seven times.

Dean skipper: Tough defender Roger Dean, who joined the club in 1957 and was a stalwart through the bad times, was made captain in 1968.

More members: Fans jumped on to the Tiger bandwagon in 1968, club membership swelling from 6592 to 10,994. The club bought a 16-acre holiday training camp at Torquay.

Fast start: As reigning premiers, Richmond made a bright start to 1968, though inaccurate kicking (11.22) led to only a 16-point win over Collingwood in the first round. The team was on target in second round, thrashing Carlton 17.16 (118) to 10.12 (72).

What goal?: A dicey goal-umpiring decision cost the Tigers victory over Essendon in Round 7. The Bombers' second last goal in the gloom at Windy Hill seemed to miss but the goal umpire raised two flags. The Tigers lost 10.18 (78) to 11.14 (80) after kicking 1.9 in the final term.

It's close: After Round 11 in 1968, only four points separated the top five teams, with Richmond fifth. Carlton was leading from Essendon, Geelong and St Kilda.

Paddy fires: Despite 8 goals from Paddy Guinane, Richmond lost a

1968 – 1969

Skipper Roger Dean with cup.

Coach Tom Hafey: victory ride.

Captain Dean with team-mates and club mascot, a Bengal Tiger.

From fourth to first for 1969 Flag

Like a well-prepared Bart Cummings stayer, Richmond came with a powerful run to win the 1969 Premiership.

Having squeezed into the four, the Tigers shaped up to Geelong in the First Semi-final. No one could have anticipated the outcome. In the most one-sided final on record, Richmond crushed Geelong by 118 points, 25.17 (167) to 7.7 (49). Top goalkickers were Eric Moore 6, Francis Bourke 4 and Kevin Bartlett 3. Eleven players kicked goals.

In the Preliminary Final against Collingwood, Richmond began quietly, the scores being level at half-time, 48 points apiece. Goals to Barrot, Bartlett and Moore (2) early in the third term set up the 26-point win, 15.17 (107) to 12.9 (81). The next big question was: could Richmond topple the hot favourite Carlton in the Grand Final and become only the third club, after Carlton and Essendon, to win the Flag from fourth place?

The Grand Final, before a crowd of 119,165 at the MCG was a dour, close struggle up to three-quarter time, when the Blues led 8.10 to 8.6. Critics had predicted that a seemingly fitter Carlton would run away from Richmond, which had had a hectic few weeks, but the opposite happened. It was the Tigers who finished full of running, kicking four goals to nil in the last quarter to win comfortably, 12.13 (85) to 8.12 (60). It was the Tigers' seventh win on end.

1969 Premiership team

B: Sheedy, B. Richardson, Beard
HB: Strang, Burgin, Owen
C: Clay, Barrot, Bourke
HF: Northey, Hart, Dean (c)
F: Ronaldson, Moore, Brown
Foll: Green, Bowden
Rov: Bartlett
Res: Hunt, Bond   Coach: Hafey

Barrot bags eight

The irrepressible Billy Barrot came to Richmond's rescue when all seemed lost in 1969. To stay in the fight for the final four, Richmond had to beat highly-rated Carlton in the second last round.

At three-quarter time, the Tigers trailed by 23 points. Was it '68 all over again? No. The Tigers hit Carlton hard in the last quarter. Barrot, who had been switched to full-forward at half-time, kicked four goals of a total of eight for the match. The Tigers stormed home with 9.1 to 1.3 in the final term, and won 24.12 (156) to 20.7 (127).

Geelong's defeat of Hawthorn in the second-last round helped Richmond's cause. In the last round Richmond buried Footscray by 90 points to claim fourth place on percentage from the Hawks (124.6 to 98.8). The Tigers were into the finals.

---

thriller to Collingwood in Round 12 at MCG – 17.12 (114) to 17.15 (117).
Run ends: Richmond's run of six straight wins over Carlton ended at Princes Park in Round 13, 1968. Carlton kicked 11.14 (80) to 10.14 (74).
Too late: Despite a win over top side Essendon in third-last round, Richmond had left its run too late and missed out on the 1968 finals by two points.

Admin. change: Secretary Graeme Richmond stepped down at the end of 1968 (handing over to Alan Schwab) but stayed on as chief recruiting officer.
Paddy retires: Paddy Guinane, a colourful character who loved taking big marks from behind, left the club at the end of 1968 after 145 games and 213 goals. He was the club's top goal-kicker in 1968 with 41 goals.

Fired up: The Tigers, still smarting after their failure to make the finals in 1968, started the 1969 season with a bang, thrashing Essendon 15.12 (111) to 12.10 (82) in the first round.
Three poll well: Kevin Bartlett (14) and Mike Green and Kevin Sheedy (11 apiece) were the Tigers' top vote getters in 1969 Brownlow Medal, won by Kevin Murray (19).

Ruckman retires: Mike Patterson, known as 'The Swamp Fox', retired after the 1969 Grand Final. A tough, strong ruckman from Mirboo North, he played 152 games and kicked 74 goals. In the 1967 Grand Final, he was thrust into the No. 1 ruck spot due to the suspension of Neville Crowe. He acquitted himself well and played for two more seasons. He coached Richmond in 1984.

RICHMOND

All hell breaks loose at Windy Hill as players and officials tangle.

War breaks out at Windy Hill

The wild brawl between Richmond and Essendon players and officials at Windy Hill on 18 May 1973 lasted most of the half-time interval. The repercussions dragged on even longer – until December, in fact – as the VFL tribunal hearings and various legal proceedings were played out.

It began when Richmond's Mal Brown tangled with Essendon big-man Graeme Jenkin as the players were about to leave the field. An Essendon runner confronted Brown and it was on. Spectators and officials invaded the field, punches flew and the boot went in. Police were forced to move in to break up the combatants.

The Tribunal handed out six-week suspensions to two Essendon staff and one Essendon player, Ron Andrews. Tiger Steve Parsons was outed for one match and the VFL fined Graeme Richmond $2000 and suspended him until 31 December. He took out a Supreme Court writ over the fine, which was subsequently dropped. Graeme Richmond and Steve Parsons were also charged by police over incidents during the brawl, but the charges were later withdrawn.

Richmond won the match 16.19 (115) to 15.15 (105) on its way to the Flag.

One to forget

Richmond was a warm favourite going into the 1972 Grand Final against Carlton. It had thrashed Collingwood by 44 points in the Qualifying Final, and had beaten the Blues by 41 points in the replay of the Second Semi-final (following a 61-point draw).

In the Grand Final, Carlton stationed out-of-form John Nicholls in a forward pocket. Nicholls kicked three goals in the first term as the Blues raced to an 18-point lead. They never looked back, slamming on goals at will to lead the stunned Tigers 25.9 (159) to 15.15 (105) at three-quarter time.

Richmond had a good last quarter but Carlton coasted home with a record 28.9 (177) to 22.18 (150). Richmond's score was the second highest in a Grand Final. That was no consolation!

Barrot goes, Stewart wins Brownlow

The stormy relationship between Bill Barrot and the club came to a head when he was swapped with St Kilda's Ian Stewart in 1971. The loss of the strong-willed Barrot, a great character and footballer, saddened Richmond, but Stewart soon settled in. He won his third Brownlow on debut for Richmond, combining brilliantly with Royce Hart and the rest of the attack. Stewart, one of the game's finest midfielders with his strong marking and penetrating left-foot kicks, polled 21 votes in the Brownlow.

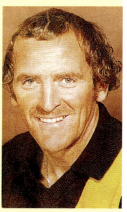

Ian Stewart.

1970–1974 HONOUR ROLL

Year	Pos	Leading Goalkicker	No.	Best & Fairest	Captain	Coach
1970	6th	Rex Hunt	36	Francis Bourke	Roger Dean	Tom Hafey
1971	3rd	Royce Hart	59	Ian Stewart	Roger Dean	Tom Hafey
1972	2nd	Ricky McLean/Neil Balme	55	Royce Hart	Royce Hart	Tom Hafey
1973	1st	Neil Balme	34	Kevin Bartlett	Royce Hart	Tom Hafey
1974	1st	Kevin Bartlett	47	Kevin Bartlett	Royce Hart	Tom Hafey

CLUB NEWS 1970–1974

Billy Barrot and Royalty: At the Royal Tour game between Premiers Richmond and Fitzroy on Sunday, 23 April 1970, Princess Anne said to Billy Barrot: 'I understand there were a couple of punch-ups before we got here. Do you think there'll be any more?' Barrot's reply was not recorded. Fitzroy won 16.20 (116) to 14.12 (96).

Another hangover: In 1970, as in 1968, Richmond suffered a Premiership hangover, finishing sixth (two games out of four) with 12 wins. In a topsy-turvy season marred by injuries to Hart, Green and Clay, the Tigers beat all the teams above them on the ladder.

Swooper moves on: John Northey retired at the end of 1970, having played 117 games and kicked 192 goals.

War Talks: The pressure was on coach Tom Hafey at the start of 1971 after the disappointments of 1970. Dunn, Richmond and Hafey declared that a ruthless approach was the only answer. As a result, Richmond blitzed Fitzroy in the opening round 22.18 (150) to 14.15 (99), only to lose to the Magpies by 37 points in Round 2. Stirred into action, Richmond won seven of its next nine games.

Rain falls: After finishing third on ladder with 16 wins, Richmond thrashed Collingwood 18.13 (121) to 11.11 (71) in the 1971 First Semi-final. But despite five goals by Barry Richardson, a lacklustre Richmond played poorly in the wet Preliminary

1970-1974

Royce Hart and the Cup on Mike Green's shoulders as the Tigers do a lap of honour. Inset: Hart receives cup from the Governor, Sir Henry Winneke.

Fourth Flag for Bourke and Sheedy.

Back-to-back Tigers Flags – first since the 20s

In contrast to 1972, Richmond was the underdog and Carlton the hot favourite in the 1973 Grand Final. In keeping with the hot, blustery weather, the opening was fiery.

Richmond put its stamp on affairs in the third minute when back-pocket Laurie Fowler crashed into an unguarded John Nicholls, who was juggling a mark. Nicholls went down heavily and, though he goaled from a free kick, he and Carlton never quite recovered. Kevin Sheedy kicked Richmond's three goals in the first quarter and continued to star in the second quarter in which the Tigers piled on 8.3 to 5.4 to lead by 26 points. Carlton full-back Geoff Southby came off second best in the second quarter, after a clash with rugged Neil Balme. A revved-up Richmond went on with the job, winning 16.20 (116) to 12.14 (86), sweet revenge for the happenings of the previous year. Stewart, Hart and Sheedy, with three apiece, were the chief goalkickers and Bartlett was best afield.

It was Richmond all the way in 1974. The Grand Final, before a pro-North crowd of 113,839 at the MCG, was a tight affair until three-quarter time, with the inaccurate Tigers ahead by 19 points, 12.17 (89) to 11.4 (70).

Richmond broke away quickly in the last quarter, Barry Richardson goaling at the 51-second mark. He kicked two more as the Tigers, now on target, ran away to win 18.20 (128) to 13.9 (87).

A creative passage of play by Kevin Sheedy exemplified Richmond's last-quarter dominance. After marking in the forward-pocket, he turned to walk back and have a shot. But Mike Green had drifted alone into the goal square. Sheedy casually handballed over the man on the mark and Green goaled. It was too easy. The Tigers were the first team to win back-to-back Flags since Melbourne in 1959–60.

The Fowler/Nicholls incident.

Neil Balme barges through.

Final, succumbing to a polished St Kilda 16.12 (108) to 12.6 (78) before a crowd of 102,494. Maurice Carr wrote in the Age that the rain only seemed to fall on Richmond.

It's Captain Hart: Royce Hart was named skipper in place of Roger Dean at the start of 1972.

Captain Blood speaks: Long locks replaced short back and sides in the early 70s but Jack Dyer didn't mind so long as the players 'don't play like sheilas'.

Sharp-shooters: Barry Richardson kicked nine goals against Essendon in Round 3, 1972, but the team lost 19.17 (131) to 16.15 (111). Royce Hart kicked his highest tally, seven goals, against South in the last round in 1972.

Second on ladder: Richmond ended the 1973 home-and-away season with 17 wins and 5 losses, but lost the Qualifying Final to Carlton, 13.13 (91) to 10.11 (71).

Revenge: Beaten by St Kilda in the 1971 Preliminary Final, Richmond squared the ledger with a 40-point win over the Saints in the 1973 First Semi-final, 15.18 (108) to 9.14 (68). After losing the 1973 Qualifying Final to Carlton, 13.13 (91) to 10.11 (71), the Tigers then beat Collingwood to have another crack at Carlton in Grand Final.

Almost 200! In Round 13, 1974, Richmond blitzed Fitzroy by 129 points, kicking 29.21 (195) to 9.12 (66) and went on to top the ladder with 17 wins. The Tigers kicked 2558 points in the 22 rounds, the highest on record. They kicked 15 goals or more 16 times.

313

RICHMOND

Hungry's halcyon day at 1980 Premiership

Kevin 'Hungry' Bartlett came close to bringing the house down at the MCG in the 1980 Grand Final against Tom Hafey's Collingwood.

For Richmond, Grand Final day 1980 was a day of stunning highlights – a 6.5 blitz in the first quarter, a lead of 59 points at three-quarter time and, at the final siren, a record winning margin of 81 points – 23.21 (159) to 9.24 (78).

The *piece de resistance* came at the 26-minute mark of the last term when Bartlett and Magpie Stan Magro flew for a mark deep in Richmond's forward pocket. Bartlett spilled the mark, recovered quickly, grabbed the ball, and danced around a bewildered Magro. With his wispy hair blowing in the wind, Bartlett dashed towards goal and drilled the ball through a gap. For the seventh time that warm afternoon, Bartlett punched the air with both hands and Richmond fans rejoiced with him.

Bartlett, his few strands of hair plastered down with sweat, received a mighty roar when it was announced he had won the Norm Smith Medal for best afield. No one argued. He had had 20 kicks and, would you believe, had fired out one hand-pass to a startled team-mate. Another star was midfielder Geoff Raines, who had 19 kicks and 17 handpasses!

A Kevin Bartlett goal buries Collingwood.

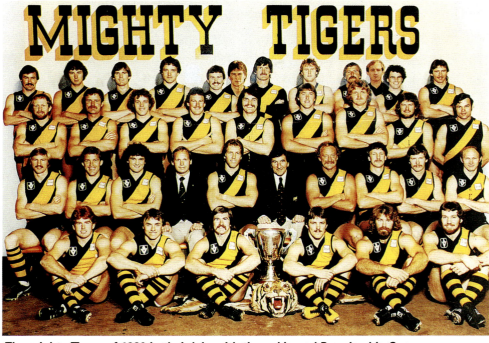

The mighty Tigers of 1980 in their lair, with tiger skin and Premiership Cup.

More coaches than the Orient Express

The Richmond knives were out for Tom Hafey at the end of the 1976 season. Aware that the club was hell-bent on change, he retired, and moved to Collingwood.

So began a sorry saga at Punt Road in which 11 coaches came and went in the space of 22 years until 1996. Barry Richardson, who replaced Hafey, had two years (1977–78). He was followed by Tony Jewell (1979–81), Francis Bourke (1982–83), Mike Patterson (1984), Paul Sproule (1985), Jewell again (1986–87), Kevin Bartlett (1988–91), Allan Jeans (1992), John Northey (1993–95) and Robert Walls (1996).

Under John Northey the Tigers slipped to second last in 1993 but rose to ninth in 1994 and, joy of joys, third in 1995. Just when it seemed some stability had emerged, Northey upped and left for the Brisbane Bears a few days after the 1995 Grand Final, swapping places with Robert Walls.

Michael Roach: a mark to remember.

CLUB NEWS 1975–1996

Out in final: Chasing its first hat-trick of Premierships, Richmond bowed out of the 1975 finals race when downed by eventual Premiers North in the Preliminary Final, 10.16 (76) to 8.11 (59).

Poor finish: Only six wins in the last 15 rounds in 1976 spelt the death knell for coach Tom Hafey. The team finished sixth with 10 wins and 12 losses.

Star goes: Royce Hart retired at the end of 1977, having played 187 games and kicked 363 goals. At 22, Hart had written a book naming himself at centre half-forward in a best-ever team. It was probably the only slip of his great career.

Back in finals: In his first season as coach, Richardson lifted the Tigers to fourth in 1977 only to lose to North (by 47 points) in the First Semi-final. Dale Weightman, a lively rover from Mildura Imperial, joined the club.

Roach 90: The Tigers' topsy-turvy form continued in 1979 under new coach Tony Jewell. Michael Roach kicked 90 goals. His best bag was 10.4 against St Kilda.

Captain Blood honoured: The City of Melbourne was thrown open to Jack Dyer for a day in April, 1981, to celebrate his 50th year in football. The Tigers had a poor year, finishing a dismal seventh with 13 wins.

Bourke coach: Francis Bourke replaced Tony Jewell as coach in 1982. The Tigers re-emerged as force, finishing top of the ladder with 18 wins and only four losses.

1975–1996

Tigers saved in dark debt days

Jack Dyer was hopping mad with the VFL in the spring of 1990 over moves to have the Tigers merge with St Kilda because of the club's $1 million debt.

'Why are they after Richmond?' cried Captain Blood. 'Richmond players like Bill Cosgrove lived for the club and died for their country. The VFL has more staff than Myer's. Could you imagine the VFL having a go at Collingwood if it was $10 million in debt?'

A 'Save Our Skins' rally, led by president Neville Crowe, raised $150,000 at the MCG on 22 October 1990. More than 10,000 supporters turned up, and dug deep.

A loan of $400,000 from coterie member Gary Krauss put the Tigers back on the road financially. One seven-year-old donated the proceeds of his money box – $50.40.

Captain Blood could rest. Or could he? 'I don't sleep for a week if we get beat. I should be over that now, shouldn't I?'

Saviours: Jack Dyer and small fan.

No biff: The ball was Captain Blood's target, not Tom Meeham.

If you don't mind, ump!

If you don't mind, umpire! Jack Dyer's famous radio expression, trotted out vigorously when he believed the man in white had lost his marbles and wrongly penalised a player in black and yellow, dated back to his playing days in the early 1930s.

Impeded on the field one afternoon, Dyer pushed the palm of his hand into the face of an opponent and, ball in hand, headed for goal. Suddenly, the whistle blew. 'Rough play,' cried umpire Scott. 'Rough play,' screamed Dyer in protest. 'If you don't mind, umpire, where's that in the rule book?'

Replied Scott, sternly: 'I am the rule book. Shut up and get on with the game.'

When he was replaced as coach of Richmond at the end of 1952, Dyer simply switched stages to the media, newspapers and radio. And, of course, television – 'World of Sport', and 'League Teams'.

Dyer's sayings were legendary. Geelong, given a hiding one day, didn't capitulate. It 'copulated'. Paul Salmon's long arms reached up like testicles, not tentacles. Dyer once said of Lou Richards: 'Lou hasn't got any enemies but his friends don't like him.' As Captain Blood modestly said of himself, he was truly 'a legion in his own lifetime'.

1975–1996 HONOUR ROLL

Year	Pos	Leading Goalkicker	No.	Best & Fairest	Captain	Coach
1975	3rd	Kevin Bartlett	42	Kevin Morris	Royce Hart	Tom Hafey
1976	7th	Robert Lamb	38	Kevin Sheedy	Francis Bourke	Tom Hafey
1977	4th	Kevin Bartlett	55	Kevin Bartlett	Francis Bourke	Barry Richardson
1978	7th	Bruce Monteath	55	Geoff Raines	Kevin Sheedy	Barry Richardson
1979	8th	Michael Roach	90	Barry Rowlings	Kevin Bartlett	Tony Jewell
1980	1st	Michael Roach	112	Geoff Raines	Bruce Monteath	Tony Jewell
1981	7th	Michael Roach	86	Geoff Raines	Bryan Wood	Tony Jewell
1982	2nd	Brian Taylor	71	Maurice Rioli	David Cloke	Francis Bourke
1983	10th	Bartlett/Michael Roach	37	Maurice Rioli	Barry Rowlings	Francis Bourke
1984	8th	Brian Taylor	61	Mark Lee	Barry Rowlings	Mike Patterson
1985	8th	Michael Roach	80	Trevor Poole	Mark Lee	Paul Sproule
1986	10th	Michael Roach	62	Dale Weightman	Mark Lee	Tony Jewell
1987	14th	Michael Roach	43	Dale Weightman	Mark Lee	Tony Jewell
1988	10th	Jeff Hogg	57	Michael Pickering	Dale Weightman	Kevin Bartlett
1989	14th	Jeff Hogg	34	Tony Free	Dale Weightman	Kevin Bartlett
1990	11th	Stephen Ryan	28	Matthew Knights	Dale Weightman	Kevin Bartlett
1991	13th	Jeff Hogg	68	Craig Lambert	Dale Weightman	Kevin Bartlett
1992	13th	Jeff Hogg	45	Matthew Knights	Dale Weightman	Allan Jeans
1993	14th	Jeff Hogg	57	Tony Free	Jeff Hogg	John Northey
1994	9th	Matthew Richardson	56	Chris Bond	Tony Free	John Northey
1995	4th	Nick Daffy	45	Wayne Campbell	Tony Free	John Northey
1996	9th	Matthew Richardson	91	Paul Broderick	Tony Free	Robert Walls

Resentment: The Tigers self-destructed in 1983. The team crashed to third last and Bourke was relieved of his post. Bartlett hung up boots after a record 403 games and 778 goals.
Tragedy: 1967 Premiership skipper Fred Swift was shot and killed by intruders at his property near Bendigo in 1983.
Unhappy century: Richmond's 100th year in 1984 was not a happy one under coach Mike Patterson. It finished 10th.
Personal best: Michael Roach kicked 11.3 in its Round-5 win over Hawthorn in 1985 – 29.14 to 21.23.
Down the bottom: From 1986 to 1993, Richmond never rose above 10th on the ladder. In 1989 it was saddled with the wooden spoon.
Cloke returns: David Cloke, a member of the 1980 Premiership team, was picked up in the draft in 1990. In 1991, in his last game, he kicked eight goals against Carlton. He played 219 games for Richmond and kicked 272 goals.
Richo arrives: Matthew Richardson, son of Bull Richardson, joined the club in 1993. Very tall and very talented, Richo soon made his mark, kicking 31 goals in 14 games.
Revival at last: After finishing 12th in 1992 and 14th out of 15 in 1993 with only four wins, things looked up in 1994 with 12 wins. The team missed out on final eight by 6.1 per cent.
Sad end: A great season in 1995 came to an end when the Tigers were drubbed by Geelong, 20.9 (129) to 6.4 (40).
The last word: Jack Dyer hung up his quill (as *Truth* columnist) in October 1993, after 53 years in the media.

RICHMOND

Stops and starts

In racing parlance, Richmond leapt out of the stalls in 1997 like an Oakleigh Plater, only to lose ground dramatically mid-race and drop out to near-last. It then finished-on stoutly but 13th in a field of 16 (10 wins, 12 losses) was disappointing after such a merry beginning.

So what went wrong after such an encouraging start in 1997? Was it just the weekly grind that led to five losses in six games from Round 5? Possibly. Gone are the days when there were easy-beat sides in the league. Nowadays every game is a mini-final.

Leon Daphne.

Just when supporters were becoming churlish, the Tigers bounced back with a crushing win over the West Coast Eagles in Round 8, 18.11 (119) to 9.13 (67). The Tigers kicked 12 goals to one in the first half!

Then the pendulum swung once more. The dismissal of coach Robert Walls after the horrendous 137-point loss to Adelaide at Football Park was front page news, as was Justin Charles' 16-match suspension for taking steroids.

But out of all this drama emerged a sounder unit, which in August alone accounted for North Melbourne (by a point), Port Power (by a crushing 85 points) and, best of all, Carlton (by two points).

Fast start: Tigers roar after their first-round win over Geelong by nine points.

Axe falls on master coach Walls

Coach Robert Walls' spell at Punt Road was short – 39 games. The axe fell after Richmond had lost to Adelaide by 137 points on July 26. The former Carlton great expressed his disappointment, writing in the *Age*: 'Even though my time at Punt Road was brief, there will be many fond memories ... I liked the players. Maybe liked them too much. Kellaway's courage, Gaspar's professionalism, Prescott's selflessness, Butch and Benny Gale's loyalty, Campbell's integrity and so it goes, each one leaving an impression.'

Walls had some advice for future coaches. They would need their own off-field support team – assistant/specialist coaches, fitness personnel, video guru, psychologist etc.

Victorian clubs, he said, faced tough times. 'Alarmingly, the six interstate clubs are poised to make up the bulk of the final eight positions. Sixteen teams is too many.'

Benny Mr Popularity

The Tiger cheer squad, led by Gerard Egan, had 710 members in 1997. The cheer squad is justifiably proud of its innovative and cleverly worded banners, such as 'Unleash the Giesch in 98', which greeted the Carlton crowd in the last round.

The cheer squad conducted a 'Most Popular Player' award in 1997. It cost $1 a vote and Benny Gale won from Richo.

Mr Popular: Benny (left) pips Richo.

Duncan's day

Popular backman Duncan Kellaway will not forget Sunday, 24 August 1997 in a hurry. It was the day he kicked a goal at the MCG, his first for Richmond. With the Tigers well in control against Port Power, Kellaway was moved to attack to give it some marking power. His first mark resulted in a near goal. His second, after a pass from Richo, bisected the big sticks. In Kellaway's own words: 'The whole team mobbed me. The crowd was going stupid. It was a great feeling.' Richmond won 22.14 to 8.13.

Duncan Kellaway.

1997

Coach Jeff Gieschen and triumphant Tigers after win over Carlton.

Last-round comeback beats the Blues!

Richmond KO'd Carlton's hopes of playing in the finals with a thrilling two-point win over the Blues at Princes Park in the last round. The Tigers won 13.13 (91) to 13.11 (89) before a full house of 34,922 enthusiastic, and at times boisterous, fans.

Carlton seemed set to sail into the finals when it led 7.1 to 2.3 at quarter-time and 10.5 to 6.7 at the long break. But the Tigers, desperate to finish the season on a high after so many lows, gave notice of a revival with a spirited third quarter, to trail by only 14 points at three-quarter time.

To the disbelief of Blues' supporters, their team was held goalless in the last term as Richmond added 3.3. Fourteen minutes into the final term, a lovely left-foot goal by Joel Bowden put the Tigers within one goal of Carlton. Five minutes later the rampant visitors hit the front when Ben Harrison, groggy from a third-term collision, kicked a long goal with his left foot. In the closing minutes, the Tigers lived up to their name, vigorously defending their lead until the siren.

Stars for Richmond were Rogers, Knights and Benny Gale. Rogers kicked three goals, while two each were recorded by Harrison, Powell and Benny Gale.

So Carlton, instead of finishing seventh with 44 points, ended up with 40 and 11th spot. Richmond also won 10 games for 13th place.

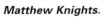
Matthew Knights.

Charles takes it on chin

In September 1997, ruckman Justin Charles became the first AFL player to be suspended for taking a banned performance-enhancing drug. He was outed for 16 matches.

Charles admitted his guilt and apologised to everyone – Tiger team-mates, the club, supporters, family and friends. 'I made a mistake trying to cheat. I was overcome by injuries and my intention was to get back to playing,' he said.

Charles and Richmond accepted the decision of the Tribunal. Club President Leon Daphne said the Tigers would stick by Charles.

Justin Charles.

Charles would not reveal who had offered, sold or even advised him to take the anabolic steroid, boldenone.

Richmond had picked up Charles, formerly of Footscray, in the 1994 National draft. In 1996 he finished equal third with 17 votes in the Brownlow, did not miss a game and was third in the club's Best and Fairest.

A big finish

Jeff Gieschen, appointed coach of the Tigers for seasons 1998–99 after the team had beaten Carlton in the last round, capped a remarkable season by directing the Reserves to a 44-point win over Hawthorn in the Grand Final. The Tigers led at every stage and won 17.12 (114) to 10.10 (70).

Gieschen acknowledges the power of the fans. Before the MCG game against Port Power in round 21, he invited 350 members of the cheer squad into the rooms for a rousing mix of togetherness. The pumped up Tigers took to heart the words on the banner – 'It's time we taught this mob some respect'. Indeed. The Tigers had their biggest win of the season – 22.14 (146) to 8.13 (61). Said Gieschen: 'Football isn't just about players and coaches. It's about the people who watch and barrack.'

After his appointment as coach, Gieschen said: 'Richmond has promised a lot and delivered little in recent years. We aim to change that.' Duncan Kellaway echoed this attitude: 'We know what we're capable of. Under Giesch, everyone's determined that next year we won't miss out.'

Eat 'em alive.

1997 HONOUR ROLL

Year	Pos	Leading Goalkicker	No.	Best & Fairest	Captain	Coach
1997	13th	Matthew Richardson	47	Wayne Campbell	Matthew Knights	Walls/Jeff Gieschen

ST KILDA

MY CLUB
by Russell Holmesby

Barracking for St Kilda is like taking the same Lotto numbers each week. On a balanced analysis it can often seem to be a pointless exercise, but you would never be game to give up for a week because that might just be the week when something special happens that goes against all logical odds.

How, then, can the enduring fascination with this club be explained? The Saints have gone through the most barren, depressing sequences of any League club – periods when the very existence and worth of St Kilda has come into question.

Certainly the question of survival has confronted other clubs down through the years, but what do the tribes that follow Carlton, Essendon or Collingwood know of the feeling that your club might not even be around to see the light of day next season.

St Kilda has often plumbed the depths, and the dark days started early. In the 1880s the club all but disappeared from view as it slid from senior to junior level. The early years of VFL football were nothing short of terrible, with not a single win coming in the first three seasons. The early 1950s teams were just chopping blocks, and in the early 1980s St Kilda sailed perilously close to extinction at a time when unsuccessful teams were constantly placed under the microscope.

Yet, through it all, the Saints have been able to bob up and shock higher-placed exponents. There has also been a long line of absolute champion individuals and their presence may go some of the way toward explaining St Kilda's continuing attraction.

The artistry of players like Darrel Baldock and Robert Harvey has enthralled St Kilda fans, but other champions have often been strong-willed individuals who have been hard to control. Dave McNamara was an early superstar who clashed with committees, and Welles Eicke, Bill Cubbins and Colin Watson were all strong-minded types.

The line extends down to Tony Lockett in the modern era, and begs an interesting question. Was it just a coincidence that so many stars had a mind to go their own way with their individualism, because they were lionised at a success-starved club?

Another important factor is St Kilda's abysmal record of administration. For every champion player there have been 10 committeemen who have been duds. Meddlesome individuals, with more interest in their own status than in the club's stability, have bedevilled the club at every turn and resulted in an endless procession of coaches. It is no coincidence that the Saints' three Grand Final appearances in the 1965–71 era, and the reappearance in 1997, have been at times when the administration has been at its most stable and the respective coaches – Allan Jeans and Stan Alves (as of 1998) – have been the two longest-serving in St Kilda's history.

The players-versus-committee scenario has had bizarre and often comical outcomes. A players' strike in 1911 was the ultimate confrontation and there have been other skirmishes, such as the well publicised punch-up between Tony Lockett and chief executive Ricky Watt.

Often the players' commitment to each other has brought temporary success, despite the lack of off-field organisation. Trevor Barker believed that battling teams in the 1980s often lifted off the canvas to win games at Moorabbin which they should really not have pulled off. Only the closeness to each other managed to mesh under-resourced teams together for glimpses of success. Barker himself was an icon in terms of loyalty and long service, although he admitted that he was once close to accepting a lucrative offer from Melbourne. When President Lindsay Fox invited him on stage before a huge crowd at an annual general meeting to reaffirm his commitment to St Kilda, Barker had no choice but to do so.

In the end Barker was glad to have remained, as he termed it, a 'one club player'. He reminded his good friend Stewart Loewe of that when Loewe was being wooed by huge financial offers from Fremantle.

Retaining star players has been a recurring problem for the Saints. McNamara, Lockett, Carl Ditterich and Ian Stewart all

ST KILDA	
Year established	1873
Joined VFL/AFL	1897
Home Grounds	Junction Oval; Moorabbin; Waverley Park
Premierships	1966
Brownlow Medals	Colin Watson 1925; Brian Gleeson 1957; Neil Roberts 1958; Verdun Howell 1959; Ian Stewart 1965, 1966; Ross Smith 1967; Tony Lockett 1987; Robert Harvey 1997
Record home crowd	51,370 v Collingwood, 1965
Most games	Barry Breen, 300
Most goals	Tony Lockett, 898
Notable supporters	Molly Meldrum, Shane Warne, Sir Zelman Cowen, Ronnie Burns, Graham Kennedy

The famous 'animal enclosure' salutes its heroes at Moorabbin. Right: Tony Lockett: adored by fans.

left for a variety of reasons. The departures of Lockett and Ditterich struck to the core of the St Kilda psyche because their whole demeanour on the field showed that they weren't prepared to take any rubbish from anyone.

The fiercely parochial Moorabbin grandstand always knew that they walked a tightrope when watching these short-fused powerhouses, but they also knew that Ditterich and Lockett would never be cowed by anything the opposition could throw at them.

So often, St Kilda has been made to feel inferior by its fellow League members. Curly Jones, a rover in the 1890s and later a president of the club, told Alan Killigrew that whenever others queried St Kilda's existence they should be reminded that the Saints were there at the very start and had a right to be there.

From Curly Jones to Aussie Jones, St Kilda people have refused to buckle under, and it is that quality that makes the club special.

Brownlow winner Robert Harvey.

Nicky Winmar and Trevor Barker.

ST KILDA

St Kilda's team of 1888 takes time out for a photo. Famous trainer Billy Plummer (top left) prepared Saints teams for many years. Back Row: W. Plummer (trainer) F. Burton (secretary), A. Moorhouse, A. Stooke, Keogh. Second Row: Snowy Griffiths, M. Fox, W. 'Toby' Stiffe, E. Dunn, A. Rusden, Doug Robertson. Third Row: Carbine Simpson, W. Newlands, J. Blake, W. Lockett (Capt), G. Wilson, J. Jackson. Front Row: R. Speary, T. Farley, S. Harding, H. McCoy, A. Smith, J. Moorhouse, Frank McDonald, W. Layton.

A Saintly start for the seasiders

St Kilda had a colourful and exciting history in colonial times. Bushrangers roamed the track known today as St Kilda Road that linked the affluent seaside area with the main town of Melbourne. Before long, St Kilda had established itself as a recreational centre featuring bowls, archery and cricket, and even a racecourse, to add to the physical attractions of the seaside. The football team that represented the district inherited the exhilarating characteristics of the suburb.

As early as July 1858, there was a scratch team from St Kilda playing football against a Melbourne Grammar School outfit. The name of St Kilda appears sporadically throughout the football notes in newspapers of the mid-19th century, and there is evidence that a St Kilda team took part in the Junior Premiership battle in 1862.

Alf Rusden in the colours.

The origins of the present club lie more with the South Yarra Football Club. The gentlemen of South Yarra won the Challenge Cup in 1867 and played a historic challenge match against Albert Park on the St Kilda Cricket Ground in 1870, but plummeted quickly into hard times and had disbanded by 1872.

A strong core of the South Yarra team was present at the meeting on 4 April 1873 that formed St Kilda Football Club. The newcomers emphatically stated that St Kilda wanted to play as a senior club.

Early games were played on the 'Alpaca Paddock' – a patch of turf which had been used for an ill-starred attempt to breed the South American animals in the 1860s – now the site of the St Kilda Park School.

Slipping away

It was not long before the St Kilda club found itself teetering on the edge of extinction.

Things hit an all-time low late in 1879 when none of the team turned up for the game with Essendon and a newspaper asked plaintively: 'Where were they this time?'

From 1880 to 1885 St Kilda fell into the murky, disorganised world of junior football. References to the club in newspapers were rare, but by 1884 the team began to gather strength – men like Alf Smith and Jimmy Stiffe were footballers who could hold their own in any company.

Readmission to the senior ranks of the Victorian Football Association came in 1886, and the club was allowed for the first time to play matches on the St Kilda Cricket Ground. By building a fence around the ground the St Kilda football and cricket clubs could charge admission. The nickname 'Saints' gained currency in this season for the first time.

Many observers pushed hard for the Saints to amalgamate with neighbouring Senior club Prahran, and after initial resistance the marriage was consummated in March 1888. St Kilda retained its name, colours and ground in addition to gaining tremendous players, including star full-back William Lockett.

Adventure to Adelaide

While the game of Australian Rules may have been nurtured in Melbourne, the seeds were also blown west and in 1877 St Kilda took up a challenge to travel to South Australia and meet the Adelaide Football Club.

The St Kilda boys had been thrashed a week earlier in Melbourne, but rose to the occasion before a big crowd that was graced by the attendance of the acting governor, the mayor of Adelaide and the Anglican archbishop. Led by the long-kicking Tommy Riddell, St Kilda won by seven goals to two and dazzled the locals. A day later they recorded an equally triumphant win over a combined team of South Australians.

CLUB NEWS 1873–1903

The first-ever Saints team was announced in the *Age* of 31 May 1873. The squad was Footie, Curr, Shew, Grace, Hughes, Fulford (2), Skinner (3), Lush, Moore, Rankin, Dwyer, Anderson, Turner, Wright, McDonald, McKenzie, Lempriere. St Kilda won the game three goals to nil.

Absence of a ball delayed the start of the St Kilda v Albert Park game in 1874. The only ball in the vicinity of the ground had burst while it was being blown up and the game did not start until 3.40 p.m.

A St Kilda player settled an old score when his team met Melbourne in 1876. Synott was not playing in the game, but at half-time he advanced on a Melbourne player and struck him. It was made worse by the fact that a few of the St Kilda players knew what was going to happen beforehand.

St Kilda was not mentioned in newspaper reports from 1880 to 1884, but in 1885 was reported to have played against teams such as Hawksburn, Southern Cross, Evandale, Caulfield, Moonee Ponds, Southern Cross, South Yarra and Brighton.

St Kilda's match with neighbouring Prahran in 1886 was said to have attracted a large crowd of 600 people. Obviously the clubs expected big attendances in 1887, as the Prahran v St Kilda game was played at the bigger South Melbourne ground.

11 July 1891 was one of the wettest Saturdays on record and many games

1873 – 1903

Ending an association

St Kilda had varying degrees of success in the 1890s. There were occasional dips to the lower reaches of the ladder, but there were also short-lived periods when everything came together.

Under the clever training methods of Billy Plummer, St Kilda had a storming finish to the 1890 season, winning five and drawing three of its last nine games.

St Kilda had true stars of the game and one of the brightest was Alf Smith – a rover who was part of the Victorian side that took part in the first intercolonial match in 1890.

Smith was one of the most respected men in the game, but was not immune to controversy In an 1890 game he and the Saints' skipper Alf Rusden were accused of wearing 'illegal metallic projections in their boots' and had to change footwear at half-time. This precursor to 'stops' was considered illegal.

When the great split in the game occurred in 1896 St Kilda was one of the last clubs invited to join the VFL.

It is a popular misconception that the Saints were only included because of their excellent ground at the Junction which was well served by public transport and represented, with South Melbourne, a presence on the on the south side of the Yarra.

Certainly the venue was a major consideration, but in 1896 St Kilda finished ninth on the 13-team VFA ladder. Geelong and Carlton shared bottom place.

The Saints in action against Essendon in 1903 at the East Melbourne ground.

The poor relations go into the VFL

The opening stages of 1897 did not bode well. St Kilda struggled to muster a full team when assembling at the Junction to board the dray headed to Victoria Park and arrived late, earning the VFL's first ever fine – five guineas. In the first game they met premier team Collingwood and were beaten 5.11 to 2.4.

Joe Hogan was the star of the team and was a defender who could have stepped into any team in the League. At the end of 1898 he was described as 'the grandest high marker of the year'.

St Kilda did not win a game in its first three seasons of League football. Probably the most damning indictment was in September 1899 when the red, white and blacks could score just a solitary point against Geelong's 23.24 (162) at Corio Oval.

St Kilda's 48 defeats on the trot has only once been surpassed (by University), and it was not easy to maintain enthusiasm. In one 1898 game against Fitzroy it was reported that St Kilda turned up without half a dozen of their best players and after hunting around for substitutes they took the field with 18 players pitted against Fitzroy's 20.

The Saints had their first VFL win in the opening round of 1900 … but had to wait six days to confirm that the match was theirs. Melbourne captain Wardill took a mark right at the end of the third quarter and kicked a behind. St Kilda protested that umpire Freame had paid the mark after the bell. The VFL upheld the St Kilda protest.

1897 – 1903 HONOUR ROLL

Year	Pos	Leading Goalkicker	No.	Best & Fairest	Captain	Coach
1897	8th	W. Ahern/R. Stewart	6		William Shaw	
1898	8th	A. Stewart	21		William Shaw	
1899	8th	A. Stewart	14		William Shaw	
1900	8th	E. Sutherland	13		Cecil Sandford	
1901	8th	Cecil Sandford	9		Richard McKay/James Smith	
1902	8th	Chas Baker	30		Joseph Hogan	
1903	5th	Chas Baker	22		W. C. Jackson/James Smith	

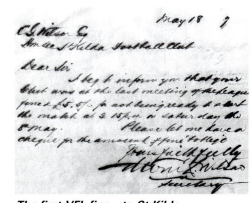

The first VFL fine – to St Kilda.

were abandoned. The St Kilda v Footscray game at St Kilda went ahead in farcical circumstances. The Footscray captain did not want to play the game and began with just 12 players whom they did not put into places. St Kilda kicked 10 goals five behinds to nothing.

St Kilda's backline was under constant bombardment in 1897 and it was only the talent of the defenders that prevented bigger scores. Joe Hogan, Harry Aylwin and Stan Phillips were all quality players. Philips had not missed a game for four years.

The return match between St Kilda and Collingwood did not start until 3.20 p.m. due to players from both sides coming late because the weather looked bad.

St Kilda's first League Captain Billy Shaw copped plenty of criticism from the press – 'With Shaw, the capacity to command is not too prominent and as a consequence the discipline of his team is lax.'

St Kilda scored just 0.2 (2) against Geelong's 16.23 (119) on 12 August 1899, but sank to an all-time low on September 9 when they could only manage a single behind while Geelong piled on 23.24 (162).

By the end of 1902 St Kilda had played 99 games in six seasons of VFL football and won just two games. One shining light in 1902 was young forward Charlie Baker who booted 30 of his team's 64 goals. His tally was just three short of the competition's equal top scorers.

ST KILDA

Finals at last

It took 10 years for St Kilda to reach its first finals series. From the first bounce in 1907 the Saints showed that they meant business by beating reigning Premiers Carlton at Princes Park.

The Saints won the first six games in a row. The mighty Dave McNamara was a dominant forward and was supported by deadly flanker Jim Stewart, who put on a virtuoso display with seven goals against Geelong. In 10 seasons no Saint had scored more than four goals in a game.

Cracks began to appear when injuries hit the team in mid-season. Morale would not have been helped when a letter from Renfrey to his old Perth mates was published in the *Melbourne Herald*. He wrote: 'The fault with us is that every man thinks he is a champion and reckons when he gets the ball that he can beat everything near him.'

Despite the late season stumbles St Kilda scraped into the finals. *Punch* magazine gave an insight to the pre-game lead-up with a peep into the rooms of the Saints and their opponents Carlton. Not surprisingly there was a contrast between the finals-hardened Blues and the new boys.

'St Kilda's dressing room is the reverse of

Horrie Bant, Vic Cumberland and Jack Wells.

Carlton. Everything is bustle and excitement. Barrackers, trainers, boots, togs and a stray dog are all tangled up together. One celebrated player puts his trousers on the wrong side around. The whole team is one babble.' Carlton players formed a guard of honour to acknowledge the Saints' first final. After that they showed no mercy and proceeded to hand out a 56-point thrashing.

A young Saint at the game.

Flying into action in 1907.

For 1915 St Kilda changed from their traditional red, white and black colours (those of the enemy Germany) to Belgian colours – red, yellow and black.

Committee troubles

St Kilda's propensity for pushing the self-destruct button was never more evident than in 1908 and 1909. Things began well enough with the appointment of former Fitzroy and Carlton star Mick Grace as coach.

He must have wondered what he had walked into, when just a few weeks into the season the Saints plunged into controversy. There were accusations that players had been paid to 'play dead' in the loss to League novice club University.

A St Kilda vice-president was accused of having bet money on the opposition and the committee started an inquiry into the form of star players Vic Cumberland, Dave McNamara, George Morrisey and Jim Stewart. Cumberland and Morrisey were stood down for the next match, but another motion to dump McNamara was defeated. His departure was averted for the time being, but within 12 months he was given the shove by the Saints and walked out in disgust.

Amazingly the team settled down after the uproar and proceeded to win six out of the next seven games. The team made the finals to again be overpowered by Carlton.

CLUB NEWS 1904–1917

A youngster from Wangaratta named David McNamara made his debut late in 1905. He originally intended to join South Melbourne, but they had decided not to change the side for the rest of the year. The Saints had trouble finding a uniform big enough to fit him.

St Kilda attracted a huge crowd when they met South Melbourne in mid-1907 and won a vicious bruising game. The following week the Saints captain Jack Wells approached his opposite number from Carlton before the game, and the two agreed that the match should be played in the right spirit.

The Saints' first finals appearance came in 1907, but Carlton thrashed them 13.13 (91) to 4.11 (35). St Kilda's team for that game was Backs: D. Feehan, P. O'Connor, C. Bant. Half-Backs: E. L. Renfrey, H. Bant, J. Julian. Centres: W. Scott, J. Wells, H. Brain. Half-Forwards: V. Cumberland, J. Cowell, W. Williams. Forwards: C. Clymo, J. Stewart, T.J. Jackson. Followers: D. McNamara, G. Morissey. Rover: V. Barwick.

St Kilda struck the hurdle of Carlton again in the 1908 finals when the Blues delivered another hiding, 12.12 (84) to 3.8 (26).

One of the few positives to emerge late in 1909 was the debut of the teenage Welles Eicke. At 15 years and 315 days old he remains the youngest player in the club's history.

A protest by Geelong overturned St Kilda's one-point win against the

1904–1917

1911 strike

Antagonism between St Kilda's committee and its players reached an all-time low in 1911 and culminated in a players' strike. Barrackers began to speculate when Melbourne took the field some minutes before St Kilda.

St Kilda players had been reluctant to take the field because passes issued to family and friends had been withdrawn. The committee refused to budge and the players ran onto the field, albeit reluctantly.

They could just as easily have stayed in the grandstand, as they played abysmally and the side was thrashed. During the following week, when the players fronted the committee they were ordered to hand in their uniforms.

The club trawled the local district for players to fill the side for the following match and the team was effectively made up of juniors. Not surprisingly it was walloped by 19 goals. In the end the six players who persisted in the strike – Plowman, Lever, Dangerfield, McKenzie, Thomas and Eicke – were reinstated, but St Kilda lost the final match of the year by 57 points to Collingwood.

The Saints before the 1913 Grand Final. Back row: Mons Baird, Henry Hattam, Pat Lynch, Bill Woodcock, Vic Cumberland, Percie Jory, Ernie Sellars. Middle row: Welles Eicke, Billy Schmidt, Harry Lever, Algy Millhouse, Dick Harris. Front row: Reg Ellis, Bob Bowden, Ted Collins, Roy Cazaly, Gordon Dangerfield, George Morrisey.

Saints miss in the big one

St Kilda made a storming run to the 1913 finals and played Fitzroy for the Premiership for the first time in the club's history.

The match became a nightmare for the Saints when they hadn't scored a goal by half-time. At the last change they trailed by 25 points. Suddenly St Kilda sparked to life and four goals brought them within a point.

St Kilda charged forward again and landed the ball with Baird who marked within scoring range, yet amazingly tried to handpass to Morissey who hurriedly shot for goal, scoring just a point. Fitzroy then scored two more goals to win by 13 points. St Kilda would have to wait another half a century.

Harry Lever: Saints leader.

1904–1917 HONOUR ROLL

Year	Pos	Leading Goalkicker	No.	Best & Fairest	Captain	Coach
1904	8th	Chas Baker	28		James Smith	
1905	7th	Chas Baker	19		Victor Barwick	
1906	6th	Dave McNamara	23		James Smith	
1907	3rd	D. McNamara/J. Stewart	21		Jack Wells	
1908	3rd	James Finley Stewart	28		Jack Wells	
1909	10th	Victor Barwick	15		Victor Barwick	
1910	10th	Arthur Thomas	15		Samuel Gravenall	
1911	9th	Ernie Sellars	22		Gordon Dangerfield	
1912	8th	Ernie Sellars	44		George Morrisey	
1913	2nd	Ernie Sellars	53		Harry Lever	George Sparrow
1914	7th	Dave McNamara	48		H. Lever/D. McNamara	George Sparrow
1915	8th	Harold Moyes/A. Boyd	32		Gordon Dangerfield	James Smith
1916–17		Club in recess due to World War One				

Pivotonians in 1909. St Kilda initially won the game, 6.13 (49) to 6.12 (48), but the Premiership points were awarded to Geelong because the Saints had played Bill Stewart who was under suspension by the Bendigo League where he had been playing early in the season.
St Kilda used 62 Senior players in its side in 1911 – a number that has never been surpassed in League history. The player strike late in the year resulted in a huge turnover of players.
Diminutive goalkicker Ernie Sellars came from local club Grosvenor and booted seven goals in his debut against University in 1911.
St Kilda captain George Morissey was suspended for 10 weeks for abusive language to field umpire Norden during a match in 1912.
By Round 15 of 1913 St Kilda was in fifth place on the League ladder, half a game behind fourth-placed Carlton. The two teams met in a showdown at St Kilda and the Saints led all day until Carlton hit the front with just three minutes remaining. Saint Billy Schmidt marked the ball just before the final bell sounded. He launched a long drop-kick that went straight through the centre and gave St Kilda a win, 10.10 (70) to 11.3 (69).
The Saints beat Fitzroy 10.10 (70) to 6.9 (45) in the Final, but because Fitzroy had finished on top they had the right of challenge and the teams met in a Grand Final the following week. Fitzroy won the Premiership with a scoreline of 7.14 (56) to 5.13 (43).

ST KILDA

Gordon Dangerfield: plays on.

The magnificent kicking style of the master Dave McNamara.

Back in action

The Saints emerged from their wartime exile in 1918 with an excellent core of players such as Dave McNamara, Gordon Dangerfield, Ted Collins, Welles Eicke, Bob Bowden, Roy Cazaly, Billy Schmidt, and Jack James.

Beating South Melbourne was an outstanding achievement, as the Bloods lost just one game for the home-and-away series.

Selectors made an extraordinary move just before the finals when they rested McNamara, Collins and three others for the last home-and-away game and were duly thrashed by Geelong. The First Semi-final against Collingwood drew a crowd of 30,000 – the biggest since pre-war days. McNamara was pivotal to the St Kilda cause and Collingwood hammered him early in the game.

It was a tight game all day and the teams were locked together on the scoreboard late in the final term, before Collingwood pulled away to a nine-point win.

The ultimate superboot

Dave McNamara's physical stature was enough on its own to ensure that he would stand out on a football field. Towering at 6'4", he was a giant in days when the average height of the population was much shorter than today. McNamara was blessed with the ability to kick the ball enormous distances. Over the years it has been said that he kicked the ball further than 100 yards, but he denied that, saying 'No man that ever lived could kick a ball 100 yards ... my longest kick ever measured was one of 93 yards made at St Kilda in 1923.'

What McNamara neglected to mention was the fact that he was 36 years old at the time of that monster kick.

A full house for South v Saints.

In 1922, a full 17 seasons after his debut with the Saints, McNamara kicked an astonishing 10 goals in a game against Geelong. Nine of the goals were from his beloved place-kicks and many were shots taken from near the centre of the ground.

As captain–coach he was the driving force behind the Saints' push up the ladder in 1923. The Saints had to beat neighbours South Melbourne in the final game and the showdown drew a huge crowd of over 50,000 to the Lake Oval. They pushed down fences, perched atop grandstands and grabbed any position they could.

Sadly the team lost and missed a place in the finals. That famous match was McNamara's last game for the Saints, but he would eventually return as president.

CLUB NEWS 1918–1929

St Kilda celebrated its return to competition with a mighty win over South Melbourne in the fourth round of 1918. The Saints won 6.13 (49) to 6.8 (44) and it turned out to be South's only loss for the year.

St Kilda was rated one of the most skilful sides in the League in 1918, but went down to Collingwood 7.7 (49) to 7.16 (58) in the First Semi-final.

A miserable performance against South Melbourne in July 1919 reflected the disharmony within the St Kilda side. The Saints managed just 2.6 (18) to South's 29.15 (189). This was the biggest losing margin in League history and would stand as a record for the next 60 years.

Vic Cumberland resumed with St Kilda in 1920. Twenty-nine of the 36 players on the field had not been born when he played his first game in 1898.

Champion defender Bill Cubbins was dropped for disciplinary reasons in 1920. He responded by kicking 22 goals in the reserves.

Within a couple of seasons St Kilda was on both ends of abysmal kicking days. The Saints held Geelong to 0.18 (18) and kicked 6.10 (46) in 1919. Two years later it was St Kilda who kicked 0.18 (18) against Fitzroy's 6.18 (54).

Ted Collins kicked a goal in the dying moments of the 1921 clash with Melbourne that put the Saints one point ahead on the scoreboard, but when the goal umpires tallied their cards the scores were equal. St Kilda

1918-1929

Internal squabbles

Why fight the opposition when you can fight at home?

St Kilda's internal squabbles have become legendary, but in the years immediately after World War One they became the laughing stock of the League with some of their shenanigans. In one game it was said that a St Kilda player reeled off a punch that felled a team-mate!

Then there was an unseemly and very public dispute between star players Welles Eicke and Billy Schmidt. A week after Schmidt had represented his State, he withdrew from the strife-torn St Kilda side and helped throw the club into deeper turmoil. At three-quarter time the team retreated into the dressing rooms and onlookers wondered whether they would come out again.

In 1920 the old hatreds continued to fester and late in June, Eicke, Bill Cubbins, Percy Jory and Ted Collins threatened to go on strike rather than play alongside Schmidt. In the end they relented, but the feeling around the club sank deeper by the minute.

Wind and injuries bring down the Saints

St Kilda's 1929 team, under the preparation methods of coach George 'Sugar' Sparrow, rose to a place in the finals.

Bill Roberts recalled years later that Sparrow had been a master of bringing his players to the peak of fitness. Tactically, it seems, Sparrow was no wizard, and Roberts recalls that he would often not attend the Saturday games because of his commitments as a racehorse trainer.

On-field moves were the domain of skipper Bill Cubbins. The Saints had a colourful and eventful year. In one game Cubbins was struck by stones thrown from the crowd and the following week there was a near riot when a former St Kilda player named Reynolds crucified the Saints in his role as umpire.

Reynolds had been kicked out of the club a few years earlier and took a savage revenge as his umpiring led to the Saints losing to Geelong by three points. Hundreds of St Kilda fans milled around the rooms for ages after the match as troopers protected the umpire's rooms.

St Kilda recruited extensively with mixed results. Plenty of hype surrounded the huge South Australian Les 'Tiny' Mills who at 6'7" was the tallest man to play League football at that time. 'Tiny' lasted two games.

St Kilda prepared for the Semi-final by being rubbed down with whisky – a George Sparrow idea designed 'to keep the muscles warm'. By early in the last quarter Carlton had skipped to a 20-point lead, but the Saints battled on gamely despite kicking into a wind that had changed direction at three-quarter time. In the end they fell eight points short of the Blues in a game remembered for the heroic marking of Fred 'Flops' Phillips, who turned out the Blues time and time again.

Bill Cubbins tosses, Ray Brew watches.

Colin Watson was a footballer of exciting, precocious talent. It was no surprise when he won the 1925 Brownlow Medal.

When a business opportunity arose in Stawell in 1926 he moved there.

In 1927 he coached Maryborough without receiving a clearance and the VFL disqualified both Watson and the Ballarat League.

At 33, he returned to the Saints after a gap of seven years, and made the Victorian team in his first season back.

1918-1929 HONOUR ROLL

Year	Pos	Leading Goalkicker	No.	Best & Fairest	Captain	Coach
1918	4th	Dave McNamara	17		Harry Lever	James Smith
1919	7th	Jack James	12		Welles Eicke	Welles Eicke
1920	9th	Jack James	13		Roy Cazaly	Percy Wilson
1921	8th	Harold Moyes	22		C. Ricketts/D. Williams	Charlie Ricketts
1922	7th	Harold Moyes	22		Bill Cubbins	Dave McNamara
1923	6th	Harold Moyes	29		Dave Mcnamara	Dave McNamara
1924	9th	Jack James	28		Welles Eicke	Welles Eicke
1925	6th	Jack Shelton	42		Cubbins/C. O. Carr	Norman Clark
1926	9th	Jack Shelton	47		Bill Cubbins	Norman Clark
1927	7th	Jack Shelton	24		Angus 'Horrie' Mason	George Haines
1928	6th	Bert Smedley	51		'Horrie' Mason/Cubbins	George Sparrow
1929	4th	Bill Mohr	38		Bill Cubbins	George Sparrow

protested, but the scores went into the book as St Kilda 12.18 (90) and Melbourne 13.12 (90).

In 1923 St Kilda reverted to its original colours of red, white and black - eight years after changing due to World War One, and five years after the war had finished!

St Kilda took on the highly fancied Collingwood in the third game of 1923 and scored a mighty 21-point win, but all talk centred on Dave McNamara's stupendous kicking. He booted one goal in the second quarter that soared over the heads of defenders. An official measured the kick at half-time and measured it at 72 yards. It had gone another 20 yards back into the crowd. In the last quarter he booted a behind that was measured at 93 yards.

Saint skipper Welles Eicke called for a count of the Carlton team in 1924. He revealed later that he had called the count because one of his players was losing his temper and he feared that he would be reported. When the umpire decreed that there were only 18 Carlton players, a St Kilda player quipped: 'But you didn't count yourself.'

A wild game at Geelong in 1926 ended with St Kilda's Jack Shelton being attacked by a spectator. As Shelton confronted his aggressor another man pulled a picket off the fence and threatened him. Shelton grabbed the picket to ward off further blows and then a mounted trooper rode up the race and grabbed the picket before herding Shelton and team-mate Stan Hepburn into the rooms.

ST KILDA

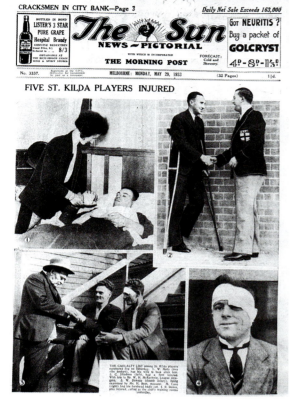

Heroes of the battle against North.

Shield of honour

Of all the matches in St Kilda's history, the 1933 Round 5 match against North would have to rank as one of the most incredible.

With nine players injured and reduced to just 15 men on the field, St Kilda scored a stunning win against all odds. Defender Stuart King ran down the field in the final term, but had nobody to kick to!

Cave (gashed eye), Bence (gashed head), Hindson (broken leg), Mohr (broken ribs), and George (ankle) were all on the injured list. Yet despite all of that, the Saints stood tall for a 14-point win.

A medal was struck in honour of the effort, with replicas going to each member of the side. The shield on that medallion was incorporated on the guernsey for the following season and has remained part of the St Kilda uniform ever since.

Bill Mohr stars

Bill Mohr, the goalkicking machine from Wagga Wagga, was an ornament to the game from the moment he arrived.

Every week he was up against the odds as St Kilda struggled to get the ball to his end of the ground. A demonstration of his brilliance came in 1931 when he booted 11 goals against the Collingwood side regarded as one of the all-time greatest, to spearhead an unlikely St Kilda victory. In the previous year Mohr kicked 10 goals against Collingwood, and his effort so impressed the Collingwood Club that at the return match at the Junction Oval they presented him with a commemorative trophy.

Mohr was a champion in every sense and year after year he continued to amass goals for the Saints. His greatest year came in 1936 when, after a slow start of only two goals in two games, he consistently starred. Mohr's eight goals in the final home-and-away round took him to the top of the VFL goal-kicking list with 101 — a mighty effort in a struggling team.

1930–1944 HONOUR ROLL

Year	Pos	Leading Goalkicker	No.	Best & Fairest	Captain	Coach
1930	8th	Bill Mohr	83	Fred Phillips	Bill Cubbins	Bill Cubbins
1931	9th	Bill Mohr	57	Harold Neill	Harold Matthews	Charlie Hardy
1932	11th	Bill Mohr	68	Bill Mohr	Stuart King	C. Hardy/S. King
1933	9th	Bill Mohr	74	Harold Comte	Colin Watson	Colin Deane
1934	7th	Bill Mohr	66	Jack Davis	Colin Watson	Colin Watson
1935	5th	Bill Mohr	83	Jack Davis	Colin Watson	Dan Minogue
1936	7th	Bill Mohr	101	Bill Mohr	Jack Perkins	Dan Minogue
1937	6th	Bill Mohr	58	Jack Davis	Bill Mohr	Dan Minogue
1938	8th	Bill Mohr	34	Stan Lloyd	E. Ansell Clarke	E. Ansell Clarke
1939	3rd	Bill Mohr	47	Roy Fountain	E. Ansell Clarke	E. Ansell Clarke
1940	11th	Bill Mohr	25	Allan Killigrew	Stan Lloyd	E. Ansell Clarke
1941	11th	Ron Flegg	47	Reg Garvin	Jack Knight	Jack Knight
1942	7th	Jack Kelly	21	Ken Walker	Reg Garvin	Reg Garvin
1943	11th	Jack Connelly	27	Ken Walker	Reg Garvin	Reg Garvin
1944	9th	Sam Loxton	52	Reg Garvin	Jack Kelly/C. Vontom	Hughie Thomas

Bill Mohr takes a clean mark.

CLUB NEWS 1930–1944

The St Kilda v Collingwood game of 5 September 1931 was a goal-fest with St Kilda winning 21.16 (142) to 20.8 (128). The combined total of 270 points set a new record for overall scoring in a game.

St Kilda celebrated the opening of the new cricket club grandstand at the Junction Oval in 1934 by kicking a new club record score of 22.23 (155).

The Saints had a fine year in 1935, just missing a place in the final four. St Kilda was one win behind fourth-placed Richmond, in the club's best season since 1929.

Tough-man Jack Perkins was a St Kilda ruckman on weekends and a Collingwood policeman during the week. The locals weren't pleased when he flattened Magpie hero Gordon Coventry at Victoria Park in a 1935 game and a metal object whizzed past his head as he left the field.

A pre-season practice match between St Kilda and and Association club Prahran in 1937 ended with an all-in brawl between the smaller players from both teams.

Wingman Doug Rayment was the target of plenty of anger after he flattened Melbourne winger Dick Emselle behind play in 1937 at the Junction Oval. Melbourne hung on to win by five points – 12.23 (95) to 12.18 (90).

St Kilda's 80-point hiding of North Melbourne late in 1937 came on a day with a carnival air. A man giving an exhibition of boomerang throwing at

1930 – 1944

Trouble and strife

For St Kilda the 1930s meant agony off the field due to constant wrangling.

The committee's attitude was epitomised when the players were hauled up before them in 1930 and told that they had 'entered into a contract with the committee and they are in the position of servants whose services may be dispensed with at any time.'

When the committeemen weren't handing down stentorian advice to players they were usually arguing among themselves or targeting the coach. In mid-1932 coach Charlie Hardy was handed £6 and his notice.

A meeting of football club members was issued a questionnaire asking whether supporters had confidence in the committee, 'No confidence' registered 492 votes to 136.

Late in 1932 the committee was voted out of office, but the acrimony continued with the installation of the new group. Discontent simmered throughout the decade and the manoeuvring was endless. Typical was the upset in 1938 when president Bill McKechnie was voted off the selection committee by his fellow selectors. Later in the year he was overthrown as president by yet another reform group headed by former star Dave McNamara, and things settled down temporarily.

Alan Killigrew under siege by Magpies in this game at the Junction Oval.

Thirty-niners fall short of a Flag

St Kilda's 1939 combination was one of the most talented teams ever to don the club's famous red, white and black guernsey.

Big, powerful and bristling with skill in every department, it was a side that had the capacity to beat any opposition on its day.

The backline featured dashing men like Sam Snell, Stan Lloyd and the powerful Arthur Robertson. Doug Rayment and Jack Kelly were electrifying wingers and the veteran Bill Mohr, a former captain, headed up a fine attack.

In field play, tenacious rovers Clarrie Vontom and Alan Killigrew scouted to strong rucks Roy Fountain, Reg Garvin and Col Williamson.

The Fountain-Garvin-Killigrew first ruck took on and beat Richmond's feared ruck headed by Jack Dyer in the 1939 First Semi-final, and set up a sensational victory.

St Kilda's dream hit the rocks against Collingwood in the Preliminary Final when the brilliant Ron Todd took advantage of the absence of St Kilda's top defenders Robertson and Lloyd who were both missing through injury.

The Magpies skipped away at the end of the match to win by 30 points in a high-scoring affair.

It would be almost a quarter of a century before St Kilda made it to another final.

Keith Miller in Saints defence.

Jack Davis in desperate defence.

half-time could not get out of the way when it returned and hit him in the shins. The session ended with a policeman having a throw, as did the players when they returned to the field.

St Kilda had a fluctuating start to the 1939 season with two wins out of the first four games, but then hit their straps from Round 6 and had a record-breaking run of eight wins in a row. By the 13th round St Kilda was on top of the ladder, but then lost three games in a row and slipped out of the four.

St Kilda made the finals with two wins in the last two rounds. World War Two broke out a few days before the First Semi-final and there was speculation that St Kilda might change their colours as they had done in World War One, but when they entered the field there was no objection to the colours matching those of Germany.

Reserves Flags. Under former Magpie Reserves coach Hughie Thomas, the Saints won successive flags in the Reserve Grade competition in 1942 and 1943. In 1940 the Saints won the Lightning Premiership conducted among all clubs to raise funds for the war effort.

With Geelong already out of action due to the war, the VFL decided that after the 11th round of 1943 the bottom team would drop out of the competition. In what turned out to be a true 'elimination' match, the lowest teams, South and St Kilda, played each other in that round. St Kilda lost the crucial decider 11.14 (80) to 16.19 (115) and went into mothballs.

ST KILDA

Lemon time, and the Saints are in trouble again.

Nervy star Harold Bray.

Panthers plummet to bottom of pile

It is a sure sign of despair when a club changes its guernsey design, logo or name, and in 1945 St Kilda fitted that description well.

Thus came the birth of 'The Panthers' nickname at the start of 1945. Not surprisingly, it made no difference to performances on-field, and in time the players' locker-room humour turned to jokes about 'Panther Pee'.

This was the start of one of the club's most barren periods in which a succession of coaches held football's most thankless job.

The committees of those times blamed everyone except themselves. As Keith Drinan commented in later years, 'They were small businessmen who just didn't know how to run a club,' so St Kilda had trouble hanging on to the few good players it had.

Late in 1947 the local newspaper, the *St Kilda News* posed the question 'Are our St Kilda footballers an asset?' and no doubt there were few readers who would have answered 'Yes'. St Kilda's wooden spoons of 1945, 1947 and 1948 were interrupted only by a second-last placing in 1946.

Lone star Bray

Harold Bray could have easily been part of that select band of men who have won three Brownlow Medals. Bray missed out by two votes in 1947, three votes in 1949 and by two votes in 1952 – his final year.

His fragile nerves were legendary and he reckoned that he seldom heard a coach's pre-match address because he was being physically ill somewhere.

Bray came from VFA club Prahran. Speed, anticipation and the ability to read a game were attributes that made him a thorn in the side of opposition teams.

Drinan hangs on

Defender Keith Drinan almost went to Collingwood after he was criticised by committeemen for being a malingerer after missing most of the 1948 season with knee problems. It was then discovered that he had cracked a bone in his knee.

Fortunately for the Saints, Drinan stayed and became a fine defender for the next decade, to be club Best and Fairest twice, most consistent twice, captain for five years and a committeeman.

1945 – 1955 HONOUR ROLL

Year	Pos	Leading Goalkicker	No.	Best & Fairest	Captain	Coach
1945	12th	Jim Hall/Sam Snell	20	Harold Bray	Clarrie Vontom	Hughie Thomas
1946	11th	Sam Loxton	40	Keith Rosewarne	Alan Hird	Alan Hird
1947	12th	Peter Bennett	37	Harold Bray	Alan Hird	Alan Hird
1948	12th	Peter Bennett	33	Robert Hancock	Harold Bray	Fred Froude
1949	11th	John McDonald	33	Jim Ross	Fred Green	Fred Froude
1950	9th	Peter Bennett	59	Bruce Phillips	Fred Green	Fred Froude
1951	10th	Peter Bennett	47	Jim Ross	Keith Drinan	Fred Green
1952	12th	John McDonald	31	Jim Ross	Keith Drinan	Colin Williamson
1953	9th	Peter Bennett	36	Keith Drinan	Keith Drinan	Colin Williamson
1954	12th	Jim Ross	34	Les Foote	Les Foote	Les Foote
1955	12th	Jim McDonald	24	Neil Roberts	Les Foote	Les Foote

CLUB NEWS 1945 – 1955

In a rather pointed action, the St Kilda committee had an actual wooden spoon made to hang in the committee room as a reminder of their disastrous 1945 season.

St Kilda finished 1947 in dismal and embarrassing style against Melbourne. The Demon full-forward Fred Fanning booted a League record 18 goals and propelled his side to win 27.9 (171) to 10.18 (78). Fanning's 18 goals came from 19 shots and ensured that St Kilda finished rock bottom with just six Premiership points – 10 below the second-last side.

In the 1949 final-round game against Collingwood, St Kilda scored a direct hit on an enemy that had inflicted plenty of pain over the years. St Kilda robbed the Magpies of the double chance with a nine-point win.

St Kilda fell away after its blazing start to 1950, yet still had a chance of making the four as late as Round 15. But they were thrashed by North by 57 points. Secretary Sam Ramsay addressed the players after the post-match speech by coach Fred Froude.

The two clashed angrily during the following week and at the end of the year Froude retired from the position.

Life was tough in the early 1950s for the struggling Saints and some players wondered whether it was all worthwhile. Mark Langdon's application for a clearance to Melbourne was rejected in May 1952. It was his 22nd clearance application in three years. John Coffey,

1945–1955

Meteor flies in 1950 skies

For one dazzling spell in 1950 St Kilda shook clear of the mire and dazzled the football world. Harold Bray and Jim Ross led the way in a talented goal-to-goal line including Peter Bennett at full-forward and Bruce Phillips and Keith Drinan as key defenders. Then there was the tenacious rover Keith Rosewarne and brilliant youngsters such as Jack Coffey and Jack McDonald.

The Saints entered the fifth round of 1950 undefeated and the Cinderella team was the League's new glamour side. Somehow 46,973 people crammed into the Junction Oval to watch the Saints do battle with Carlton, and Saint supporters left the ground ecstatic with an impressive victory.

Sadly the fairytale was about to end. Bray, so pivotal to the upsurge, was first to go with a hamstring, then Bruce Phillips and McDonald were injured. The dream was over. St Kilda won just two more games and had a draw to finish ninth.

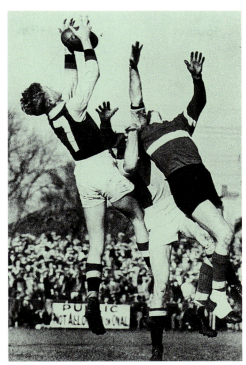

Bruce Phillips: champion full-back.

Jim Ross flies high to punch.

Jim Ross is class

No St Kilda player has yet won four Best and Fairest club awards, but Jim Ross could claim to be the most unfortunate of the three triple award winners.

His story reflects the committee pettiness that cost St Kilda so dearly down through the years and in his case meant that one of the Saints' greatest-ever footballers played his last game in the colours at the age of just 26.

Ross was a grand mark, had great dash and superb anticipation. There is little doubt that he would have won his fourth Best and Fairest in 1954 if the chairman of selectors had not been angry at him over a pre-season request for financial assistance.

As one of a family of eight, Ross craved financial independence and wanted the club to help him out with the purchase of a house. Chairman of selectors Bert Day told him he could have a clearance on the spot if that was what he wanted.

He had another fine season in 1954, but at the end of the year he decided to accept a coaching offer from Tasmanian club North Launceston.

The Saints of 1954 are all smiles, but they had only four wins for the season. Back row: Bob Watts, Neil Roberts, Mike Giblet, Jim Ross, Dave Bland, Ray Houston, Bruce Phillips. Centre: Max Mollar, Alan Callow, Jack McDonald, Les Foots (captain–coach), Keith Drinan, Nev Linney, Ron Derrick, Peter Bennett. Front: Harold Davies, Graham Minihan, Geoff Jones, Bruce McLennan, Brian Milnes.

meanwhile, had his fourth application for a clearance to Moe knocked back, and was reported to be playing soccer.

The Saints wished they could have played all their games in Yallourn. They met Footscray there for the VFL's promotional round in 1952 and won 7.7 (49) to 5.4 (34). It was the only win for the season until they pipped Fitzroy by a goal in the last round.

Young defender Neville Linney was chosen for the Victorian team after just 10 games in his first season in 1953. He had been an Under 19s player in 1952.

St Kilda rolled Footscray in the opening round of 1954, but it was no indicator of what lay ahead. St Kilda finished last and Footscray won the Premiership.

Harold Davies was so disappointed with his 1954 form that he asked selectors to omit him from the senior team.

St Kilda plumbed the depths in 1954, winning just four games. With a black sense of humour one fan sent his kelpie dog out on the field to 'lead' the team. The kelpie wore a St Kilda rug and a dunce's cap!

St Kilda's game against Carlton in 1955 was a spiteful, mean-spirited affair. Carlton won easily 11.21 (87) to 3.13 (31) and the Saints committed every sin in the book. Five players were reported and an angry crowd gathered at the dressing rooms, threatening players. Saints coach Les Foote tried to calm the waters by taking his team en masse to the after-match get-together, only to discover a chalked notice saying that the entertainment had been cancelled.

ST KILDA

Killa sees a big win coming.

Killa spirit

If ever there was a man for a moment in time, it was Alan Killigrew at St Kilda in 1956. The hot-gospelling tongue of the little man with the hunched walk lifted St Kilda from oblivion and set the club on the road to power. Killigrew was a courageous little rover in the 1939 finals side. When he was stricken with tuberculosis at the end of World War Two the Saints fans raised £1000 in a testimonial.

Killigrew got the St Kilda job by a whisker. The committee swung his way when they heard his oratory in a Ballarat League final.

Killigrew scoured the countryside for potential players. 'The only way we could get players was by inducements. We were the first to do it. We would put 200 ten-bob notes on the table because it looked more impressive than 100 one pound notes,' he said.

He declared that nobody would laugh at St Kilda again. Neil Roberts observed later that Killigrew convinced them to think that they were not second-class citizens in the football world.

Killigrew engineered the biggest clear-out of players in League history – only 16 players from the 1955 list retained their places in 1956. Ten of the St Kilda players for the opening game against North Melbourne were wearing the colours for the first time.

Champ after champ

Team success was Alan Killigrew's aim, but the St Kilda advance up the ladder in the late 1950s had a by-product on an individual basis.

Bill Young was a late starter from the bush. There was no doubt he could kick goals – in a few short years he bagged 563 for Stratford – but Young's light build of 75kg did not fit the stereotype of a VFL full-forward.

Despite missing the first two games and then starting slowly, Young came good in a big way and by season's end he had booted 56 goals and sat atop the VFL goalkicking list. He booted the same tally in each of his next two seasons.

Brian Gleeson, Neil Roberts and Verdun Howell are all Brownlow Medallists. Howell had to wait many years to receive his honour retrospectively, but the listings for 1957, 1958 and 1959 now show three Brownlow medals to St Kilda.

A Brownlow Medal for Gleeson had looked out of the question when he made his entrance to the game in 1953. The fumbling youngster copped a blast from the St Kilda Cricket Club reserve of: 'Get back to Berrigan, you mug Gleeson!' and the 18-year-old thought that sounded like a good idea.

A savage 1956 night game between St Kilda and South Melbourne saw a battered Gleeson contemplating at half-time whether he even wanted to continue in VFL football. It produced an eerie piece of prophecy from Killigrew who told him that he had enough ability to win a Brownlow.

Brian Gleeson.

The seed had been planted and 12 months later the medal hung around Gleeson's neck.

Neil Roberts had started his football life as a forward, but errant kicking had caused his coaches to tear out their hair in frustration. In mid-1954 he was moved to centre half-back where his high marking and natural athleticism were ideally suited.

Neil Roberts: pin-up.

Roberts took over as captain in Gleeson's absence through injury in 1958 and scored the Brownlow triumph to top off a memorable year.

Verdun Howell was pursued by St Kilda from the time he was 15. On his eventual arrival in 1958 Howell was thrust into the troublesome full-back position. It was a master-stroke by coach Killigrew and after playing just six games in 1958, Howell dominated the 1959 season.

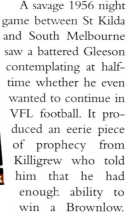

Verdun Howell.

Brian Moloney cheers the Saints on.

CLUB NEWS 1956–1960

Boom recruit full-forward Bill Young had his problems kicking for goal in his early games. Against Essendon he had seven shots for goal – one went out of bounds and six were behinds. But he came good later in 1956, and with 56 goals became only the second St Kilda man to head the goalkicking list.

Moody half-forward Jack McDonald landed in hot water when he failed to turn up for a Seconds match after being dropped, and went to the horseraces instead. He was dumped as vice-captain and replaced by Ken Mulhall.

St Kilda's sudden improvement in 1956 caused an unusual casualty. In the cliffhanger one-point win over Footscray captain Keith Drinan lost his voice when urging his team on in the last term.

The Saints claimed a little piece of history when they took part on the first night series game on 23 August 1956. They met old foes South Melbourne in the competition which featured the eight teams that had not made the finals. South won a vicious game 13.15 (93) to 10.13 (73) and five players were reported.

St Kilda entered the 1957 season with a new guernsey design. The old white sleeves were replaced by black sleeves.

Brian Gleeson was sadly injured in the opening pre-season practice match of 1958. Ironically, coach Killigrew had placed him at centre half-forward to protect him. He never played again for the Saints.

Atrocious goal umpiring left St Kilda back-pocket Brian Walsh 'cred-

1956-1960

Alan Killigrew exhorts.

Killa forced out

The Saints finished eighth in 1958, recorded wins against quality opposition and also took out the Night Premiership contested by the eight teams that did not make the day finals. To the outsider it was inconceivable that St Kilda could even consider parting with coach Alan Killigrew.

But there was unrest behind the scenes. Part of it was rooted in sectarian division, part was old-fashioned committee meddling.

Killigrew announced in his newspaper column that an unharmonious 10 per cent of the club wanted him out of the job. On the eve of the club elections he said that he would knock back an offer from SA club Norwood if there were changes on the St Kilda committee. Initially the players kept out of the battle, but then they decided on a petition supporting Killigrew. The coach added to the drama by nominating for a committee position.

It was no surprise that the annual meeting was a heated and torrid affair and fist fights broke out among the crowd. The election solved nothing, with members of both factions being elected and Killigrew refusing to serve under a committee that included Reilly and Laurie Hallam. Even Reilly's subsequent resignation did not sway the coach. The self-destruct button was pushed again.

New coach, team prospers

Killigrew's replacement Jim Francis was appointed just a couple of months before the 1959 season. A principled individual, Francis had left Carlton after a savage internal battle. He served St Kilda with honour for two years and helped the healing process.

The Saints improved marginally, but many believed that they should have gone further and reached the finals under Francis. Where Killigrew had used handball as an attacking weapon, Francis favoured a more traditional mark-and-kick game.

Eric Guy.

Each year St Kilda had built its player stocks bit by bit and by the end of the 1950s had the tightest defence in the competition, i.e. Backs: Walsh, Howell, Annand. Half-backs: Guy, Roberts, Guyatt. Neil Roberts rated back-pocket Brian Walsh as the best defender of the lot – high praise indeed as all six played State football and two won Brownlow Medals.

Bill Young.

Walsh officially kicked a goal for the opposition in 1958. More than any other St Kilda defender, he hated conceding anything to an opponent. Ironically, he went into the record books for that one, but never kicked a goal for the Saints in his nine seasons with the club.

Neil Roberts flies high.

A mighty grab by Verdun Howell.

1956-1960 HONOUR ROLL

Year	Pos	Leading Goalkicker	No.	Best & Fairest	Captain	Coach
1956	11th	Bill Young	56	Keith Drinan	Keith Drinan	Allan Killigrew
1957	9th	Bill Young	56	Brian Gleeson	Keith Drinan	Allan Killigrew
1958	8th	Bill Young	45	Neil Roberts	Neil Roberts	Allan Killigrew
1959	8th	Bill Young	45	Verdun Howell	Neil Roberts	Jim Francis
1960	6th	Bill Young	37	Lance Oswald	Neil Roberts	Jim Francis

ited' as a goalkicker for Carlton. Walsh kicked the ball off the ground through the Carlton goals, but despite no Carlton player being near the ball, the goal was awarded. St Kilda lodged a protest, the goal umpire was suspended, but the scoreline stood.

South's Ian Tampion scored an unusual goal when he was awarded a free kick on the half-time siren a long way out from goal. St Kilda defenders began walking off the ground and the long kick bounced and bounced through for a goal 20 yards clear of the nearest backman.

The Saints won the 1958 Night Series Grand Final with a great victory over Carlton. Full-forward Bill Young booted six goals in the 16.13 (109) to 15.11 (101) victory. The Saints led most of the night and held off a late Carlton rally. Young, Eric Guy and Graeme Minihan were the stars.

Bill Young would prove to be one of the deadliest kicks in the game. Among his bag of tricks was the 'banana kick' or 'check-side' shot, later used by Blair Campbell who at that stage was just another St Kilda follower in the crowd. Although credited with inventing the kick, Campbell gave the credit to Young.

Ex-Maryborough defender George Deller was all set to play his first game when he got the tap on the shoulder. 'Verdun Howell isn't tied up with National Service duties after all, so you can go out and play the last quarter of the Seconds curtain-raiser.' It was a bitter and demeaning blow for Deller, who went back to the country.

ST KILDA

Allan Jeans in playing days.

Young Saint Ditterich: a powerhouse.

A common sight – Smith to Baldock.

Bob Murray.

Stevo's injured.

New coach in '61

Changing coaches was nothing new to St Kilda Football Club and in mid-September 1960 the committee placed its faith in Allan Jeans, who at 27 had just retired as a player.

Jeans tackled the task with typical grit. Killigrew wished him the best in a letter, saying he was 'the solid one among the jellies'.

Allan Jeans was offered a £100 bonus if the Saints made the finals, but after 21 unsuccessful years, it didn't seem likely that he'd collect. Nothing in the first two games of 1961 suggested that he'd be able to lift the club. Then, after those early losses, the pendulum began to swing St Kilda's way.

The team comes out for the 1961 Semi.

New champions on scene

In the early 60s St Kilda began to gather strength on the field. Veterans such as Neil Roberts, Eric Guy and Bill Young were supported by players in the 22 to 25-year age bracket who had been brought into the club by Killigrew and the ever-active recruiters secretary Ian Drake and president Graham Huggins.

Alan Morrow and Bill Stephenson gave the team tremendous marking power around the field, and free-roaming Lance Oswald was the best centreman in Victoria. Unfortunately, full-forward Bill Stephenson wrecked his knee in 1962 and became a hobbling headline for the rest of his career.

After 22 years St Kilda was once more a finalist, but it fell at the first hurdle, losing to Footscray.

In 1962 the club had secured one of Australia's most brilliant footballers in Tasmanian Darrel Baldock, who once deployed at centre half-forward used his ball-playing skills to devastating effect.

The crop of 1963, East Brighton youngster Carl Ditterich, Tasmanian Ian Stewart and ex-VFA star Bob Murray, all became champions for the Saints. A fourth new boy, Jim Wallis, could have reached those stellar levels too had a knee injury not cut him down in his prime.

The side scraped into the finals and played Melbourne in the First Semi-final. St Kilda started badly, but spurred on by Ditterich, Howell and Kevin Roberts, surged back at the end and just went down by seven points.

1961–1965 HONOUR ROLL

Year	Pos	Leading Goalkicker	No.	Best & Fairest	Captain	Coach
1961	4th	Ian Rowland	26	Lance Oswald	Neil Roberts	Allan Jeans
1962	6th	Darrel Baldock	33	Darrel Baldock	Neil Roberts	Allan Jeans
1963	4th	Darrel Baldock	35	Darrel Baldock	Darrel Baldock	Allan Jeans
1964	6th	Darrel Baldock	29	Ian Stewart	Darrel Baldock	Allan Jeans
1965	2nd	Darrel Baldock	44	Darrel Baldock	Darrel Baldock	Allan Jeans

CLUB NEWS 1961–1965

In 1961 St Kilda started a six-week winning run from Round 3 that was the club's best winning sequence since the record of eight in 1939.
St Kilda held Richmond to 0.8 (8) in their 1961 Round 16 match at St Kilda. It was only the third instance since World War One of a League side failing to score a goal in a game. St Kilda had also been involved in the other two games – as the scoreless team in 1921 – and as the team that held the opposition scoreless in 1919.
The St Kilda Reserves won the 1961 Premiership in unusual circumstances by 10 points over Geelong. The Grand Final was played a week after the senior Grand Final as there had been a draw during the Reserves finals series. A crowd of more than 15,000 attended the MCG on a hot afternoon. The Saints pulled clear in the last quarter when Lindsay Fox and Kevin Hassett kicked the only goals of the final term.
One of football's longest-running hoodoos was broken when St Kilda knocked off Collingwood at Victoria Park in the opening round of 1962. The 9.9 (63) to 5.8 (38) win was only their second Victoria Park win in 65 years. The previous occasion was in 1919.
St Kilda scored an amazing victory over South Melbourne in the 1962 Lake Oval clash, after looking dead and gone at three-quarter time. They trailed the Swans 3.9 (27) to 9.9 (63), but stormed home to win 11.14 (80) to 9.9 (63), thanks to an eight-goal last quarter.

1961 – 1965

The Saints run out at their new home at Moorabbin.

In March 1964 St Kilda dropped a bombshell by announcing that it would move to the Moorabbin ground in the 1965 season. The club had long chafed under the tenancy control of the cricket club. At first it was agreed that the club would amalgamate with VFA side Moorabbin and be known as St Kilda-Moorabbin for 10 years before becoming Moorabbin. However a long-forgotten rule in the club's constitution stated that the name could not be changed unless three quarters of the members voted for it.

As the Moorabbin debate swirled and eventually settled, the club struggled through a patchy year on the field, finishing sixth. A postal vote among members saw 2862 vote in favour of the move and 697 against. In the final round St Kilda bowed out of their last game at the Junction in grand style, beating highly placed Geelong by 12 points.

Ian Stewart.

The honours kept coming St Kilda's way in 1965 when its midfield maestro Ian Stewart won the Brownlow Medal. Stewart tied with Noel Teasdale on 20 votes, but was awarded the medal on a countback (Teasdale later received a retrospective medal).

Saints' Grand Final agony

In hindsight Allan Jeans would look back on the preparation for the 1965 Grand Final against Essendon and liken it to a circus.

One error was holding a team meeting at Allan Jeans' house the night before the game. The Friday meeting pumped up the team so much that they were mentally 'gone' before the game.

St Kilda suffered a crippling blow in the match when Alan Morrow limped off. They could not get their game going and when Essendon started to kick straight the issue was settled. The Dons ran away to a 35-point win and the St Kilda dream was shattered.

Ditterich at work in 1965 Grand Final.

Darrel Baldock had the chance to win the game against Hawthorn in 1963 when he ran into an open goal only moments from the finish, but he mistook the point post for a goal post and slammed through a behind. St Kilda lost 8.13 (61) to Hawthorn 9.11 (65).

Youngster Daryl Griffiths goaled with his first kick against the Bombers in 1963. St Kilda achieved their first win at Windy Hill for 27 years.

Bill Stephenson's troublesome knee finally gave up in a 1964 practice match, when he snapped a cruciate ligament. His career was over at the age of 27, after playing 88 games over seven seasons.

Victoria Park's reputation as a nightmare venue for the Saints returned in 1964, when Collingwood won by 14 points. The turning point was umpire Brophy's decision to give Magpie Bert Chapman a free kick after Carl Ditterich pushed him as he kicked a goal. Chapman scored another goal from the second kick.

Essendon inflicted St Kilda's first loss at their new home ground, Moorabbin, in Round 5, 1965. The Bombers won 14.9 (93) to 7.14 (56). Happily, the Saints did not lose another game at Moorabbin for two years.

The upset of the season was averted in the last round of 1965. Bottom-placed Fitzroy kicked away to a lead of 27 points at half-time, thanks to eight goals in the second quarter. Inspired by forward Bob Morton, the Saints came back, kicking nine goals in the third quarter and going on to win 19.13 (127) to 16.6 (102).

ST KILDA

The Flag – at last. Saints be praised!

Baldock and Co. – hands on the prize as they run a lap of the MCG.

To the victor the spoils.

Paddy plays blind

It all sounded like a bad Irish joke. Kid named Paddy Murphy gets picked for a big game/loses a contact lens before the game/plays in match without lens/gets dropped and never plays again.

That bizarre scenario unfolded in the showdown Round 10 game between St Kilda and Collingwood.

Paddy Murphy.

On what should have been his big day, Murphy lost his lens in the dressing rooms at Victoria Park. For half an hour officials and players pulled up mats and searched for the tiny piece of glass with torches and matches.

Murphy played the game, but could not even see his fellow rover Ross Smith signalling to him. Murphy was taken off the ground in the third quarter. Sadly, Murphy was never given another senior game.

Shaking the stand

A mid-season slump put St Kilda's place in the finals under threat. Despite the fact that the Saints had been in the top four all year, there was still a possibility that they could miss the finals if they lost the final home-and-away game.

The latter part of the year had strained St Kilda's resources to breaking point with the most savage blow being Baldock's knee injury just three weeks before the finals.

By the third quarter St Kilda was in deep trouble against Hawthorn. With the home crowd chanting 'We want Baldock' the tubby spell-binder nervously rose to his feet and warmed up for the fray. The grandstand literally rocked that day as he ran onto the field to a thunderous reception.

His appearance knocked the legs from beneath Hawthorn.

Beaten in Semi

A flying start by Collingwood in the 1966 Semi-final rocked the Saints, but by half-time they had fought to the lead. St Kilda went into the final term still leading, but Collingwood skipper Des Tuddenham took over the game with a devastating burst. He kicked them from everywhere, destroying Daryl Griffith's day, taking Collingwood to a 10-point win.

Griffith's anguish.

The Saints had to wait to beat Essendon in a muddy Preliminary Final, before they could have a crack at the Flag.

There was drama in the Saints' last training session as Baldock injured his knee again. He recalled: 'I yelled out to Jeansie straight away and he told everyone training was finished. We all ran off so no one knew I had hurt it again.'

CLUB NEWS 1966

A great start to the season saw the Saints, bent on the Flag, effortlessly crushing Melbourne and Carlton in the first two rounds.

The rampaging Saints had a perfect record after seven games, and a capacity crowd of 50,458 went to the Grand Final replay against Essendon at Moorabbin in the eighth round. St Kilda won a low-scoring game in the wet 8.8 (56) to 7.7 (49). Their percentage was a phenomenal 177.4.

It seemed apparent early in the season that the dominant clubs would be St Kilda and Collingwood. After eight rounds Collingwood was only one game behind.

St Kilda collapsed against Richmond in Round 9 and was then thrashed by Collingwood in Round 10, to begin a mid-season slump that saw its ratio slump to 12–4 by Round 16.

Talented half-forward Kevin Roberts had his collarbone broken in the Round 12 match against Melbourne, and was unable to take to the field for the rest of the season.

In a horror day at Princes Park in Round 13, St Kilda lost Verdun Howell (broken jaw) and Carl Ditterich (strained shoulder). The Saints finished with only 17 men after Ross Smith was knocked unconscious in the last quarter, and went down 5.11 (41) to the Carlton's 7.15 (57).

The Saints' season seemed in the balance when Darrel Baldock crashed to the ground with a knee injury in

1966

The big game

In the opening minutes of the Grand Final Baldock marked 60 metres out from goal. He unwound a long shot that went straight through the centre, but his leg felt like it went all the way too.

The pro-St Kilda crowd was ecstatic with St Kilda booting two goals in the first five minutes, but on this day neither side would be able to break away.

There was just a point in it at half-time and when the final term began, St Kilda was four points to the good.

The sides tensed themselves for a big final term and St Kilda got away to a great start when Griffiths handballed to the speedster Moran, who goaled on the run.

Tuddenham revived thoughts of his destructive Semi-final when he sent a long shot downfield that bounced over the pack for a goal. Ian Graham booted another for the Pies, but St Kilda had the answer with a calm goal from 'Cowboy' Neale after he had marked in the midst of a swarming pack.

A point to Tuddenham at the 23-minute mark levelled scores and with both teams near exhaustion it became a desperate grind.

Ian Cooper's miskick was almost marked by Collingwood's Ted Potter who was swamped by a sea of players before another bounce was signalled.

Potter tried to handball clear, but Barry Breen intercepted and snapped hurriedly. The ball seemed to take an eternity to wobble, land and eventually dribble through for a point. It was his fifth behind for the day. He said later that he was happy just to get boot to ball.

After further desperate play the ball ended in the safe hands of Alan Morrow just as the siren sounded. The crowd erupted, Collingwood players slumped in despair and some of the St Kilda players seemed momentarily stunned.

Morrow recalled: 'When I marked it I wasn't even sure that the siren had gone.

The kick that made St Kilda history.

Scores level and all to play for.

Then Coop and Doc ran over and said that we had won.' It was a magical moment that has been relived thousands of times over in black and white replays. There are those who can recite the TV commentary of the last five minutes word for word.

In the end an emotional Jeans told his boys: 'Whatever you do, wherever you go, I'll always remember you for this wonderful moment you gave me today.'

The Premiership team. back row: Jim Read, Rodger Head, Allan Davis, Jeff Moran, Kevin Billing, Ross Smith. Middle: Daryl Griffiths, Travis Payze, Bob Murray, Brian Sierakowski, Ian Synman, John Bingley, Allan Morrow, Ian Stewart. Front: Kevin Neale, Barry Breen, Verdun Howell, Allan Jeans (coach), Darrel Baldock (captain), Brian Mynott, Ian Cooper.

1966 HONOUR ROLL

Year	Pos	Leading Goalkicker	No.	Best & Fairest	Captain	Coach
1966	1st	Kevin Neale	55	Ian Stewart	Darrel Baldock	Allan Jeans

Round 16 match against South Melbourne. He was diagnosed as having strained knee ligaments.

Darrel Baldock persuaded a specialist not to put his injured leg in plaster, as he knew he would be out for the season. He opted for a pressure bandage and, still 'carrying the leg', got himself right to play in the final series.

Carl Ditterich put himself out of the finals when in a meaningless last quarter against Fitzroy, he took it into his head to flatten Daryl Peoples. He was suspended for six weeks.

Verdun Howell battled to make the finals after suffering a broken jaw, and played with his jaw still wired up.

Ian Stewart made it back-to-back Brownlows after another fine season.

Brilliant wingman Ross Oakley was forced off with a knee injury in the Second Semi-final against Collingwood. Oakley had suffered the same injury in the same game 12 months earler.

Daryl Griffiths was in tears after the Second Semi-final, as Collingwood captain Des Tuddenham had kicked seven goals againt him in a match-winning effort. 'I had one of those days. It was like a nightmare,' Griffiths said.

'He even blind-turned on the boundary line and kicked a goal from there.'

St Kilda was confident that it would best Essendon in the wet conditions of the Preliminary Final, as it was well known the Dons did not like the wet. The Saints' two mudrunners from Tasmania, Darrel Baldock and Ian Stewart, were the two best on the ground in the easy win.

ST KILDA

After the bell – not over!

A crook set of wiring helped short-circuit St Kilda's bid for back-to-back Premierships in 1967. Just before half-time in the Round 5 clash with Carlton the siren failed to sound.

St Kilda's Fred Farrell endured the timekeeper's ultimate nightmare. Time was up in the second quarter and as he tried to press the button he could only watch helplessly as Carlton ran the ball downfield. Farrell was clanging an antiquated hand bell as the crowd yelled to umpire Crouch to stop the game and amid the chaos Blue John Gill booted a goal. Carlton went into the half-time break five points up – and that was also the margin at the end of the match.

Daryl Griffiths swims against a tide of black and white in the year of '70.

Cats tip out Saints in sour season '67

South Melbourne had always been a tough nut to crack for St Kilda sides and it was no different in the opening game of 1968 when the rank outsider rolled a cocksure St Kilda outfit. The dynamic Bobby Skilton amassed 36 kicks.

The loss jolted St Kilda into rebuilding its side. Champion Verdun Howell was dropped and Ian Synman's club-record sequence of 123 consecutive games ended abruptly when he was omitted along with Kevin Roberts and ruckman Brian Mynott. A seven-game winning streak was highlighted by some dazzling football from Carl Ditterich who hit the best form of his career.

The Saints had a mid-season slump, but gathered momentum late in the year. They went into the final game against Geelong needing a win to stay in the final four.

It was a day when St Kilda turned on its brilliant best and Barry Breen started the ball rolling with a sensational 40-metre run which he capped off with a 40-metre snap from the boundary line. The Saints won by 51 points. St Kilda was virtually unbackable as they were due to meet Geelong again just seven days after the demolition at Moorabbin. Geelong had other ideas and, showing its liking for the open spaces of the MCG, proceeded to dismantle St Kilda. When the dust had settled on the game, Geelong emerged with a 44-point win.

Rover **Ross Smith** had an emphatic Brownlow Medal win in 1969. Smith believes his transition into the top bracket was gradual.

'In 1965 Allan Jeans changed my role and that was the turning point.' He was given the job of running with the opposition's number one rover. It wasn't a straight tagging role, but it meant that he was on the ball for 75 to 80 per cent of the game. Smith's long and honourable career included captaincy of the club.

1967–1973 HONOUR ROLL

Year	Pos	Leading Goalkicker	No.	Best & Fairest	Captain	Coach
1967	5th	Kevin Neale	37	Ross Smith	Darrel Baldock	Allan Jeans
1968	4th	Kevin Neale	33	Carl Ditterich	Darrel Baldock	Allan Jeans
1969	7th	Kevin Neale	50	Bob Murray	Ian Stewart	Allan Jeans
1970	3rd	Barry Breen	35	Daryl Griffiths	Ross Smith	Allan Jeans
1971	2nd	Alan Davis	70	Ross Smith	Ross Smith	Allan Jeans
1972	3rd	John Stephens	53	Stuart Trott	Ross Smith	Allan Jeans
1973	4th	Alan Davis	48	Kevin Neale	Stuart Trott	Allan Jeans

CLUB NEWS 1967–1973

Saints coach Allan Jeans was reported for abusing a boundary umpire during a game against Fitzroy in 1967. The Saints won by 48 points.

Against Essendon in mid-1967 'Cowboy' Neale was thrown into the forward line at the start of the third quarter with St Kilda 23 points down. He booted six goals in the term and then bagged two more in the final quarter. St Kilda won 18.6 (114) to 13.13 (91).

St Kilda lost to lowly Fitzroy in Round 14, 1969. The Lions won 11.8 (74) to 9.4 (58), their first win at the Moorabbin ground. Fitzroy had not beaten St Kilda on the Saints' home ground (either Junction Oval or Moorabbin) since 1956.

Carl Ditterich had a series of scrapes with the tribunal in 1970. By the 14th round he had been reported three times and suspended twice.

South Melbourne was the crowd favourite in the 1970 First Semi-final against St Kilda as it was the Swans' first finals appearance since 1945. St Kilda ran over the top of South and won 22.11 (143) to 13.12 (90). Two weeks later the Saints bowed out when they managed just 7.19 (61) to Carlton's 17.21 (123) in the Preliminary Final.

Elusive forward Allan Davis had a day out against Collingwood at Moorabbin in 1971, bagging 10 goals.

In the 1971 Second Semi-final St Kilda played as if in a daze. By three-quarter time Hawthorn led by 33 points and looked to be doing it comfortably. But

1967 – 1973

Guess who did it? The Hawks' Peter Hudson is the victim of a mauling in the Grand Final.

Another Flag chance is blown away

St Kilda had regained its place in the finals in 1970 and by late 1971 were the only team that threatened Hawthorn's runaway train. The teams met head-on in the Second Semi-final.

The Saints went into the last term 33 points in arrears. Then suddenly they shook clear of the lethargy and stormed the goals to get within five points. St Kilda bombarded the goal, but could not find the target and a bewildered Hawthorn fell over the line by two points.

St Kilda knocked off Richmond in the Preliminary Final. As had been expected, the Grand Final was a bruising, physical affair. In the opening term 'Cowboy' Neale crunched Peter Hudson, but the Saints' 19-point lead at three-quarter time was overcome by Bob Keddie, who kicked four goals for the Hawks.

The Greening incident

Minutes into the match-of-the-day clash with Collingwood, the Moorabbin crowd was stunned when Collingwood's John Greening went down behind play. Saint half-back Jim O'Dea was subsequently outed for 10 weeks. The following week when Kevin Neale accidentally collected Footscray's Stephen Boyle, the player lost the sight in one eye.

The endless controversy rocked St Kilda, but the club rallied to make the 1972 finals, rolling Essendon and Collingwood. Another Flag beckoned, but injuries and a number of players down with flu left the Saints unable to resist Carlton, who kicked away after three-quarter time in the Preliminary Final.

The end of the party

The exodus of senior players started after the 1972 finals with Ditterich being snapped up by Melbourne under the 10-year rule and Smith crossing to WA.

St Kilda's season ended in the Semi-final against Richmond when the Tigers exposed the deficiencies around the packs that had been papered over. Kevin Bartlett and Paul Sproule exploited the gap left by Smith's departure and Richmond won by 50 points.

It had been St Kilda's fourth year in a row in the finals, but now the club was to embark upon another long drought. This barren period would at times see St Kilda drift perilously close to total extinction.

Left behind

From the start of the 1969 season St Kilda found itself out of step and off-balance.

New captain Ian Stewart and vice-captain Carl Ditterich missed the first game through injury and it was a sign of things to come. Each man endured an injury-riddled, struggling season and the side was never able to gather any steam.

Barry Lawrence.

A big hope was Tasmanian recruit Barry Lawrence, but the boom centre half-forward took two seasons to find his feet, becoming a fine defender in the back pocket.

The big swap

When St Kilda champion Ian Stewart traded places with Richmond's Billy Barrot it was the biggest football story in years.

It was revealed later that Stewart's departure was part of a plan designed by Stewart, Richmond official Alan Schwab and Tiger strongman Graeme Richmond.

Bustling Billy Barrot.

A story was circulated that Stewart wanted to go to WA, while Richmond was telling St Kilda what a good catch Barrot would be. When Schwab said Stewart could be part of a possible swap, St Kilda jumped at the idea.

After just seven quarters, the temperamental Barrot walked out on St Kilda, but Stewart resurrected his career at Richmond and won the 1971 Brownlow Medal.

---

by the 23-minute mark of the last term the Saints were five points down. Wasted chances saw the Saints go down by 12.16 (88) to 12.18 (90).

St Kilda selectors took only 90 minutes to pick the side for the 1971 Preliminary Final and changed every line. In wet conditions the Saints held all the aces and rolled Richmond 16.12 (108) to 12.6 (78).

The Saints went within a point of setting a new club record for scoring in the one quarter with an 11.3 third-quarter effort against Footscray in their 1972 clash at Moorabbin. The best by a Saints side had been 11.4 in 1956. This was subsequently bettered by the 1978 side.

St Kilda gained some small revenge on Hawthorn for the 1971 Grand Final result by knocking the Hawks out of the final five in the last round of 1972. The Saints made history by winning the first ever final at Waverley with an 18.16 (124) to 10.11 (71) Elimination Final victory over Essendon.

After the controversial O'Dea-Greening incident earlier in the year, the 1972 First Semi-final clash between St Kilda and Collingwood was expected to be a fiery affair. The spite never eventuated, and St Kilda won 11.17 (83) to 8.17 (65).

George Young's silky brilliance fuelled St Kilda's 1973 Elimination Final win over Essendon at VFL Park. Young kicked six goals in St Kilda's 24.14 (158) to 13.13 (91) win. The Saints' run ended in the First Semi-final at the hands of eventual Premiers Richmond.

ST KILDA

On and off-field battles

After a marathon coaching stint of 16 years, Allan Jeans announced that he would retire at the end of 1976, saying simply: 'A coach gets tired of it. It is very demanding.'

In the midst of a depressing era there was one golden year. Mike Patterson came to the coaching job in 1978, and his reinvigorated Saints were a talented and tough unit. After a roller-coaster season, St Kilda had to win the last game against Carlton and hope that Geelong would go down to Fitzroy.

Fuelled by the power of Ditterich and Sidebottom, St Kilda simply blew Carlton off the park with an awesome display from men like Geoff Cunningham and Graeme Gellie. Sadly Geelong held off Fitzroy and the Saints missed the finals.

After the dizzying highs of the previous year, 1979 was an unmitigated disaster as St Kilda sunk to the bottom of the ladder. Trucking magnate Lindsay Fox was installed as president. He injected money by attracting sponsors, revamped everything in the club, and turned the tide around. Without Fox's efforts the Saints would have died.

A big grab by Steve Theodore.

Garry Sidebottom on the mark.

Money troubles

Disunity between the social and football clubs wasn't the main reason that St Kilda endured such hard times from 1974, but it was a key factor in hobbling progress.

The social club's intention of putting profits back into its own club infuriated the financially strapped football club and relations between the two entities plummeted to an all-time low. The situation reached farcical proportions in the 1974–75 summer when football club president Graham Huggins issued eviction notices on the social club, which retaliated with legal action.

By 1978 the trading loss had blown out to an ominous $124,000. By 1984 the club saw a scheme of arrangement as the only way out. The scheme offered reduced payments to creditors and hinged on the past players accepting the offer of 22.5 cents in the dollar.

Former coach Allan Jeans and players Gary Colling, Barry Breen, Alex Jesaulenko, Bruce Duperouzel, Kevin Neale and Jeff Sarau met privately and announced that they did not wish to destroy the club.

The Saints members responded magnificently and raised $150,000 to keep the wolves from the door.

1974–1989 HONOUR ROLL

Year	Pos	Leading Goalkicker	No.	Best & Fairest	Captain	Coach
1974	10th	Bruce Duperouzel	26	Glenn Elliott	Barry Lawrence	Allan Jeans
1975	6th	George Young	53	Jeff Sarau	Barry Lawrence	Allan Jeans
1976	9th	George Young	52	Trevor Barker	Carl Ditterich	Allan Jeans
1977	12th	George Young	58	Jeff Sarau	Carl Ditterich	Ross Smith
1978	6th	George Young	70	Graeme Gellie	Gary Colling	Mike Patterson
1979	12th	Gary Sidebottom	56	Jeff Dunne	Barry Breen	Mike Patterson
1980	11th	Mark Scott	48	Jeff Dunne	Garry Sidebottom	Mike Patterson
1981	10th	Con Gorozidis	34	Trevor Barker	Bruce Duperouzel	Alex Jesaulenko
1982	11th	Mark Scott	45	Peter Kiel	Bruce Duperouzel	Alex Jesaulenko
1983	12th	Mark Jackson	41	Max Crow	Trevor Barker	Tony Jewell
1984	12th	Tony Lockett	77	Greg Burns	Trevor Barker	T. Jewell/G. Gellie
1985	12th	Tony Lockett	79	Paul Morwood	Trevor Barker	Graeme Gellie
1986	12th	Tony Lockett	61	Greg Burns	Trevor Barker	Graeme Gellie
1987	10th	Tony Lockett	117	Tony Lockett	Danny Frawley	Darrel Baldock
1988	14th	Nicky Winmar	43	Danny Frawley	Danny Frawley	Darrel Baldock
1989	12th	Tony Lockett	78	Nicky Winmar	Danny Frawley	Darrel Baldock

CLUB NEWS 1974–1989

The Saints' fortunes plummeted in 1974 and at one stage they lost eight out of nine games. It was the worst losing run since 1958.

Ross Smith took over in 1977 as coach, but the club finished last for the first time in 21 years. St Kilda set a club record with a score of 31.18 (204) against Melbourne's 21.15 (141). It was also the first time a League team had scored 31 goals in a game and the 11.5 burst in the second term was the club's best-ever quarter.

Less than a year after the record score St Kilda was on the end of a humiliating debacle at Collingwood when the Magpies won 31.21 (207) to 3.11 (29). After a mass exodus of players St Kilda was at rock-bottom.

At the end of 1979 St Kilda announced that it had a total debt of $750,000. Trucking magnate and former player Lindsay Fox took over as President and immediately revamped the club from top to bottom.

Former Richmond coach Tony Jewell took over the Saints job in 1983 and introduced youngsters such as Tony Lockett and Rod Owen.

St Kilda's scheme of arrangement in 1984 placed a moratorium on all debts, with players and coaches owed $470,497. Barry Breen headed the list as he was owed $64,000. The creditors agreed to the scheme and the club was saved.

After a particularly dismal effort against Footscray late in 1984, Tony

1974–1989

Trevor Barker

Trevor Barker was the golden-haired boy of the St Kilda side – good looking and slim with blond hair and a perennially boyish look. He took spectacular marks and so gained a reputation as a bit of show pony, totally undeserved for a man who was always putting his body on the line and was one of the best tacklers in the St Kilda side.

It was his fate to be in a succession of mediocre sides, never to play in a finals match and never to receive his just financial rewards as a star footballer. But he stuck to St Kilda through all its turmoil, playing 231 games and captaining the side with distinction for four years.

He seemed a natural forward, but was moved to the backline by coach Allan Jeans early in his career and thrived on the challenge of playing many games at full-back. But in weak teams he was required to move his skills around the ground, and played in most positions. He became a successful coach of the VFA club Sandringham, ideal for a local boy, and was back at his beloved St Kilda as Assistant Coach before his brave and untimely death in 1996.

The on-field fate of St Kilda in the late 1980s and early 1990s depended solely on one man – Tony Lockett. The beefy spearhead from Ballarat was a controversial figure, but no matter what anyone said, he was an absolute champion. He powered St Kilda to finals appearances in 1991 and 1992 with a combination of unmatchable strength, razor sharp anticipation and deadly kicking. Along the way in his 12 drama-charged seasons there were suspensions, injuries, fines imposed by the club and clashes with the media, yet he gave St Kilda fans hope in even the darkest times. In the end the big fellow simply could not ignore the huge money offer from the Sydney Swans.

Trevor Barker gets some on-field praise.

Skid row Saints down to the bare boards

Coaches came and went at St Kilda in the mid-80s as the club turned over players at a bewildering speed.

The inescapable truth, however, was the fact that St Kilda was landed with its fourth successive wooden spoon in 1986. No side had experienced such abject failure since University finished last from 1910 to 1913.

When coach Graeme Gellie sought reasons for the endless losses at a team meeting, the ever-blunt centreman Greg Burns said: 'Have you ever thought that we just may not be good enough?'

Darrel Baldock was stunned by the lack of skill when he took over in 1987, but there were some things that could be built upon.

Powerhouse full-forward Tony Lockett showed his wares by kicking 12 out of 14 goals in a losing side against Melbourne and the addition of West Australian Nicky Winmar and youngsters like Nathan Burke gave the side a better look.

St Kilda started to string wins together and there was talk the statistical possibility of St Kilda making the finals. Then came a body blow. Baldock was admitted to hospital suffering from a mild stroke.

The year wound down, and St Kilda was back on skid row again with a last in 1988 and second last in 1989.

Jewell said he would not coach the side in 1985. General Manager Ian Stewart and Chairman Lindsay Fox sacked Jewell and appointed Graeme Gellie as caretaker coach for the last couple of rounds. The side responded with a win over Richmond in Gellie's first game in charge.
St Kilda's opening to the 1985 season was abysmal. Beaten by the Swans by 110 points, they were then thrashed by Carlton by 140 points and Richmond by 113 points. They had a percentage of 34.1 after three games.
A late season burst in 1987 suddenly put St Kilda in the unthinkable position of having a chance for the finals. Five wins in a row was the club's best sequence for 15 years. In the midst of it all Tony Lockett booted his 100th goal.
Tony Lockett created history by becoming the first full-forward to win the Brownlow Medal, capping a landmark 1987 for the Saints.
Of all Tony Lockett's memorable performances for St Kilda the last-gasp goal against Carlton in 1989 ranks near the top. With less than a minute to play, Nicky Winmar shot a bullet-like pass to Lockett who booted his 10th goal for the day to give the Saints a win, 13.18 (96) to 13.14 (92).
In 1989, St Kilda's wheels began to fall off against West Coast when Tony Lockett swung wildly at Guy McKenna and flattened the Eagle defender. Lockett bagged 12 goals to equal his own club record and move to 70 goals in nine games – but was rubbed out for four weeks.

ST KILDA

Sheldon fires up rebounding Saints

Ken Sheldon had a couple of distinct advantages when he took over the St Kilda coaching position for 1990.

For starters he had been at a successful club, Carlton, in a successful era. He also knew the 'lie of the land' at St Kilda as he had spent three seasons at the club as a player immediately before his coaching appointment.

The Saints' growing popularity drew 67,893 people to a nail-biter at the MCG against Collingwood. St Kilda went down by a point, but then scored a heroic three-point win against Hawthorn in Round 6.

It was a psychological triumph as 12 seasons had passed since the previous win over the Hawks. In those dozen years the Saints had been on the end of some fearful batterings at the hands of the League's dominant team of the era.

Above: Danny Frawley: great skipper and full-back.
Left: Ken Sheldon delivers a message.

Nathan Burke: all heart and St Kilda spirit.

Stewart Loewe: powerhouse up forward.

St Kilda could not sustain the level of performance, and a knee injury to Lockett and a hefty 10-week suspension of Winmar (who erupted after a taunt from Dermott Brereton) threw their finals hopes aside The season's dreams ended in a shambles at Collingwood with Sheldon so bitterly hurt by the effort that he hurriedly left the ground, giving his press conference on a footpath.

Back in the finals

When Gilbert McAdam straightened on the outer wing at Waverley and fired home a running goal in the September sunshine, it was as if all the hurt and trauma of the previous 18 years welled up and overflowed.

McAdam's was the opening goal of the 1991 Elimination Final against Geelong – St Kilda's first finals appearance in 18 years.

Early in 1991 the Saints had struggled in the absence of Winmar and Lockett. The pair became available for the seventh round. A Robert Harvey pass found Lockett in the opening seconds and from that moment St Kilda's progress to the finals began.

Nicky Winmar's stand

When Nicky Winmar lifted his jumper to point to the colour of his skin to mindless Collingwood fans in 1993, he began a chain of far-reaching events.

The affair prompted the AFL to initiate action against racial abuse, but this matter would prove to be a hot potato.

There was a damaging spin-off for the Saints when Essendon's Gavin Wanganeen visited Winmar to congratulate him.

The talk turned to money – and then St Kilda was served with a demand for a package worth $650,000 per year. Winmar was stood down from the side and in the following three weeks the Saints totally lost their way.

CLUB NEWS 1990–1996

St Kilda's defeat of Hawthorn early in 1990 was the Saints' first win over the Hawks since 1979. St Kilda won 15.14 (104) to 14.17 (101).

The Saints dished out a 131-point hiding to AFL new chums Adelaide, 24.18 (162) to 4.7 (31) at Moorabbin in Round 7, 1991.

Lockett's 12-goal haul in that victory was followed by 10- and 12-goal tallies in the next two rounds – the most prolific three-week spell in League history.

Tony Lockett set a new club record with 13 goals against Carlton in the Round 21 game of 1991. St Kilda charged to a 23.17 (155) to 15.11 (101) win that began the charge to the club's first finals appearance in 18 years.

St Kilda's Second Elimination Final against Geelong in 1991 was regarded as a classic match. Injuries to Nathan Burke and David Grant told heavily on the Saints, and Geelong prevailed 15.14 (104) to 14.13 (97).

In a day out in Round 13, 1992 Tony Lockett kicked 15.4 – a new club individual goals record. Between quarters, sections of the crowd moved from one end of the Moorabbin outer to the other to watch Lockett more closely.

The Saints were led from the front by Tony Lockett in a crucial win over Melbourne in the second last round of 1992. They had a bye in the last game and had to rely upon Hawthorn or Carlton being beaten. Carlton lost to West Coast. Sixth-placed St Kilda pulled off a shock by rolling third-

1990–1996

Moorabbin was the Saints' spiritual home and the push from the AFL to shunt the Saints off to Waverley was seen as an attack on the very heart of the club. The club's annual meeting degenerated into farce when one of the pro-Moorabbin group leaders used a loud hailer to drown out the on-stage speakers. It was a divisive issue, but St Kilda played its last game at Moorabbin in Round 20, 1992. For much of the dour game it seemed that Fitzroy might upset the party. In the closing stages the Saints cleared away to win by 17 points. Jubilant fans spilled over the fence at the end of the game, with many claiming sections of the sacred turf.

The Animal Enclosure

The patch of dirt between the St Kilda race and the umpires' race at Moorabbin became known as 'The Animal Enclosure' and in subsequent years the regular occupants have been surprised as the number of people who also claimed that they were 'Animal Enclosure' regulars. Another group, 40 metres towards the South Road end, titled themselves the 'Terrace Rats'. But there was only one real batch of animals, and they came to represent the fierce, unrelenting, backs-to-the-wall type of bias that Saints fans loved to espouse.

The air was usually thick with epithets and cynicism and during one particularly woeful St Kilda performance in 1984 a section of the 'enclosure' staged a sit down protest during the second quarter. 'We're not putting up with this crap any more,' they said, and lowered themselves to the concrete with no other view than the backsides of those in front.

But when the Saints were on a roll there was no better place to be.

Stan Alves and the boys celebrate St Kilda's win over Carlton in the 1996 Ansett Cup Final.

1990–1996 HONOUR ROLL

Year	Pos	Leading Goalkicker	No.	Best & Fairest	Captain	Coach
1990	9th	Tony Lockett	65	Stewart Loewe	Danny Frawley	Ken Sheldon
1991	5th	Tony Lockett	127	Tony Lockett	Danny Frawley	Ken Sheldon
1992	4th	Tony Lockett	132	Robert Harvey	Danny Frawley	Ken Sheldon
1993	12th	Tony Lockett	53	Nathan Burke	Danny Frawley	Ken Sheldon
1994	13th	Tony Lockett	56	Robert Harvey	Danny Frawley	Stan Alves
1995	14th	Stewart Loewe	76	Nicky Winmar	Danny Frawley	Stan Alves
1996	10th	Stewart Loewe	90	Nathan Burke	Stewart Loewe	Stan Alves

placed Collingwood in the first week of the 1992 finals, 13.13 (91) to 12.11 (83).

Footscray ended St Kilda's 1992 finals campaign by winning 19.5 (119) to the Saints' 14.6 (90). On a blustery afternoon every St Kilda player was outpointed, apart from Tony Lockett (four goals).

The 1993 season was a disappointing one overall for the Saints, but they managed to emerge triumphant at the two venues that had caused them the most trouble over the years. They beat Collingwood 18.18 (126) to 15.14 (104) – the first St Kilda win at Victoria Park since 1976 – and Carlton 11.18 (74) to 10.17 (77), the first win at Princes Park since 1964.

Tony Lockett kicked his 898th and last goal for St Kilda to stitch up a two-point victory over Collingwood in the second-last round of 1994. It continued the immediate history of close encounters between the two sides. St Kilda lost by a point in 1990, won by a point in 1992 and had a draw in 1991.

St Kilda gave stalwart skipper Danny Frawley a mighty send-off in the last round of 1995 with a convincing win over Footscray. He had captained the Saints in a club-record 177 games since taking over the position at the start of 1987.

St Kilda confounded the odds and won the Ansett Australia Cup Grand Final, 20.10 (130) to Carlton's 10.12 (72). The win was St Kilda's first Premiership of any sort since the 1966 win. St Kilda had won only one previous night series Flag – in 1958.

ST KILDA

The Saints bust onto the arena, ready to do battle in the finals series.

Magical run takes Saints from depths

Four games into 1997 St Kilda sat at the bottom of the ladder with just one win on the board. It looked like yet another wasted year.

Coach Stan Alves called the players together for a special 'cards-on-the-table' meeting after losing to Fremantle in the fifth game. At one point he offered to resign, but players said that they didn't want him to go.

Looking at their first five games the Saints recognised that they had lacked decisive aggression at the ball – a strong point when they were playing well.

Coming into the clash with Melbourne, another team which had won just a single game, there was speculation that the coach of the losing team would face the axe. Alves was no stranger to such conjecture and it seemed that his post had been forever under threat.

St Kilda's turnaround started on that bleak, wet day at Waverley Park in a display that was hard and decisive from the outset. The 86-point win also helped rectify the club's woeful percentage. Critics opined that it was only Melbourne, but in the context of the year this proved to be a turning point. It was never doubted that St Kilda had a handful of some of the best players in the competition.

'The Big Four' title applied to Robert Harvey, Nathan Burke, Stewart Loewe and Nicky Winmar gained momentum with the club's win in the 1996 night series. Fullback Jamie Shanahan was on the periphery of that group, not so much in terms of individual brilliance, but more as a team leader.

St Kilda's biggest need was for the next group of players to step up – a theme often expressed by Stan Alves. Six weeks into the 1997 season, the youngsters began to blossom.

Peter Everitt, having requested and being given the No.1 ruck post, began to show the talent that he really possessed. The blandly named triumvirate of Jones, Smith and Brown also began to make their mark on a more regular basis.

The form of Austinn Jones and Everitt lifted so sharply that they were picked in the Victorian team in mid-season.

St Kilda was a young, enthusiastic side that had the propensity to run over teams in last quarters. 'Waverley Legs', they called it.

Week by week the momentum built, aided by a dream run with injuries. Deep into the season there was a week in which 41 of the 42-man list were available, with only the suspended Barry Hall excluded. A nine-goal runaway win over reigning Premier North Melbourne in Round 14 had even the sceptics sitting up to take notice, and although the Saints went down in Adelaide it was an honourable loss. It would also prove to be the club's last defeat in the home-and-away series. Seven wins in a row took the club to the top of the ladder after the completion of 22 games.

Winmar: one of the big four.

1997

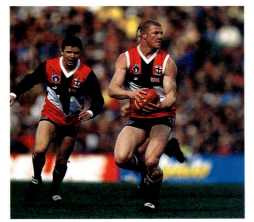

Above: Barry Hall: great burst.
Below: Aussie Jones a dasher.

Above: The Saints' Grand Final is over, but the glamour team of the year is ready to rise again.
Below: Coach Stan Alves is strong in defeat as he rallies the team around him.

An hour away from glory

In the end, St Kilda fell just an hour short of completing a modern-day football fairytale. The Saints could not hold out a flying Adelaide finish in the 1997 Grand Final.

St Kilda's fantastic journey for 1997 continued with thrills and setbacks in September. Losing Peter Everitt with a shoulder injury in the Qualifying Final was a severe blow as the dreadlocked ruckman had been a pivotal figure in the rise to the top.

Full-forward Jason Heatley was also injured in the Qualifying Final, but the two-week break gave him the chance to recover. St Kilda's nine-goal win over Brisbane was a highly creditable one.

With Everitt and Lazar Vidovic gone it meant there was a huge burden on third-string follower Brett Cook. Like all of his team-mates, Cook rose to the occasion in sensational fashion, and St Kilda managed to end North Melbourne's defence of its Premiership title. With the prolific midfielders Robert Harvey and Nathan Burke in command the Saints were irresistible. Heatley's deadly accuracy at full-forward produced seven goals and the Saints charged into the Grand Final.

The whole of Victoria threw its weight behind the team of crusaders taking on the dreaded new boys from across the border. 'Go Sainters' became a greeting not just in the streets around the spiritual home of Moorabbin, but, it seemed, around the whole state. The Saints' 'Haka' (really an American routine called the Quarter Eagle) had a Thursday night training crowd of 12,000 people chanting along with the team.

In the big game the Saints took a while to settle, but Barry Hall's second quarter burst of three goals in four minutes gave a bit of hope. Sadly the Saint engine never really kicked. At half-time St Kilda was ahead despite not playing well, but on this day of days the young team would never break clear of Adelaide. Even the recently anointed Brownlow Medallist Robert Harvey and the industrious Nathan Burke could not get the clear-cut disposals that could set up victory.

Darren Jarman was swung to full-forward for a devastating last quarter that produced five goals and sank the battling Saints.

1997 HONOUR ROLL

Year	Pos	Leading Goalkicker	No.	Best & Fairest	Captain	Coach
1997	2nd	Jason Heatley	73	Robert Harvey	S. Loewe/N. Burke	Stan Alves

SOUTH MELBOURNE

MY CLUB
by Kevin Taylor

To follow the South Melbourne club required a deep sense of passion. In the 100-plus seasons the club was a feature of its birthplace, a feeling of hope was ever-present for most supporters.

During the early days the South Melbourne team was known as the Bloods, even the Angels, then from the 30s as the Swans. The name was derived from a comment made by Hec de Lacy, a popular journalist for the pink-coloured *Sporting Globe*, which like the Swans has now disappeared from the Melbourne scene. De Lacy wrote in 1932 that there were so many Western Australians playing with South the club should be known as the Swans.

The name stuck, as did the hopes for success through the dark days of the 1930s Depression. It's curious that the club seemed to enjoy success in hard times. During the crash of the 1890s, South Melbourne won three successive Premierships with the VFA. Two other Premierships arrived with long stretches between them – in 1909, then nine years later in 1918. In 1933, when Australia was in the grip of the Depression, South again achieved the ultimate football prize.

There have been lengthy passages of time where hopes for the team and the club were always present, yet success proved elusive. Men in fur-felt hats, women with their umbrellas, kids in short pants arriving on foot or in the crush and frantic movement from the endless stream of trams disgorging their passengers on Albert Road – all moving with only one focus: toward the Lake Oval.

It was a ground of great character and history. The tall palms on the lake side of the ground that had been there longer than most could remember. And the cramped, turn-of-the-century press and score box at the south-eastern corner. The grandstand of (for its day) considerable proportions. There was no greater joy than to be at the Lake Oval on a Saturday, when for two bob, even in the rain, you would forget the pressures and worries as the South side of the day moved tirelessly to defeat their visiting adversaries.

The turf of the Lake Oval had seen many champions stride, jump, mark and kick – Peter Burns and 'Sonny' Elms, Bruce Sloss and Charlie Ricketts, Vic Belcher, Roy Cazaly, the great Bob Pratt, the talented Laurie Nash, Herbie Matthews, Jack Graham, Jim Taylor, Fred Goldsmith and Bobby Skilton.

The 1930s were exciting times. Pratt was always likely to produce a sensational mark and have the crowd gasping. He led a long way out, but was such a good kick that many of his goals were from long range. Nash was a great mark, and could have held the full-forward post (as he did for his State once, kicking 18 goals), but had to be content with being impassable at centre half-forward.

In the 1930s South was recognised as a team of champions, with stars gathered from near and far. They proved their abilities by playing in four successive Grand Finals – they were indeed champions, yet not a champion team.

Perhaps it is Bobby Skilton who best embodies all that was South Melbourne – courageous, often brilliant, a winner of three Brownlow Medals, yet a player who was given the opportunity to play in just one final.

Or was it Jack 'Twister' Marshall? He can be seen in photographs from the late 1880s, or in the team groups for the Premiership years of 1909 and 1918. Jack was there at the Melbourne Cricket Ground on 30 September 1933, still a trainer. Through his hands had passed the tissue and muscles which had brought every major trophy to South for almost half a century.

Four Premierships with the VFA before the Victorian Football League was born and another three for the next 90 years may seem a scant return. The measure however should be the hopes, dreams and aspirations of the countless battlers who were proud to be supporters of the South Melbourne club.

You lived and died as a 'Blood', yet when the cheering died away following their last victory at the Lake Oval on 30 August 1981, South Melbourne were no more. Only the precious memories remained.

SOUTH MELBOURNE	
Year Established	1874
Joined VFL/AFL	1897
Home Grounds	Lake Oval, Princes Pk, Junction Oval, SCG
Premierships	1909, 1918, 1933
Brownlow Medals	Herbie Matthews Snr 1940; Ron Clegg 1949; Fred Goldsmith 1955; Bob Skilton 1959, 1963, 1968; Peter Bedford 1970; Graham Teasdale 1977; Barry Round 1981
Record home crowd	44,047 v Geelong, 1996
Most games	John Rantall, 260
Most goals	Bob Pratt, 681
Notable supporters	Archie Crofts, Lindsay Hassett, Lloyd O'Neil, Ian Johnson

Proud players for a proud suburban club: the South Melbourne team of 1930.

Bob Skilton: South's finest.

Stars down the years: Bill Ghent, Vic Belcher, Fred Fleiter and Brighton Diggins.

South do battle with Geelong in the early VFL days.

SOUTH MELBOURNE

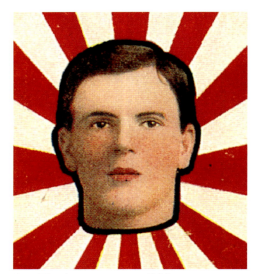

Len Mortimer: great goalkicker.

Ruckman Vic Belcher flies high in the 1909 Grand Final, the year VFA great Charlie Ricketts became South Melbourne's first official coach. His thorough team preparation and cool captaincy led South to its first League Premiership. Ricketts was well supported by vice-captain Bill Dolphin and key performers Hughie Callan, Vic Belcher, 'Joker' Cameron and Bert Franks. South won nine of its first 10 games in 1909, but in Round 11 went down to Carlton at Princes Park. On Saturday October 22 the Grand Final against Carlton was a battle to the final siren. South held on to win by two points, 4.14 (38) to 4.12 (36).

The colours of the club

The name of South Melbourne first appeared in football circles around 1868 when one of the clubs was referred to as 'Albert Park or South Melbourne'. The formation of the club which became South Melbourne is clearly documented. In 1879 the *Follower*, a paper devoted exclusively to football, published the minutes of the inaugural meeting held on 19 June 1874. The minutes were later republished in the SMFC Annual Report of 1924 when the club celebrated its jubilee.

Following the amalgamation with Albert Park on 22 January 1880, the club played in red and white hooped jerseys in the VFA and the VFL until 1903. For the three following seasons, a white jersey with vertical red panels was adopted. In 1907, the uniform became a white jersey with a red sash from the left shoulder, which was worn until 1921.

For the 1921 season the club appeared in a red jersey with a white SMFC monogram, but the red sash on a white guernsey returned in 1922. This strip lasted until 1932 when the white jersey with a red 'V' was introduced. Red and white hooped socks were replaced with all-red socks in the late 1970s.

1897–1918 HONOUR ROLL

Year	Pos	Leading Goalkicker	No.	Best & Fairest	Captain	Coach
1897	5th	Dinny Mckay	13		William Fraser	
1898	5th	Charlie Colgan	13		William Fraser	
1899	2nd	Charlie Colgan	27		D. Adamson	
1900	6th	Harold Lampe	16		William Windley	
1901	6th	Harold Lampe	20		Albert Trimm	
1902	5th	Harry Goding	19		William Windley	
1903	8th	Harry Goding	10		Thomas Fogarty	
1904	5th	Charles Clements	37		William McGee	
1905	5th	Charles Clements	31		William McGee	
1906	5th	Len Mortimer	24		Herb Howson	
1907	2nd	Len Mortimer	37		Bill Dolphin	
1908	5th	Len Mortimer	40		Bill Dolphin	
1909	1st	Len Mortimer	50		Charlie Ricketts	Charlie Ricketts
1910	3rd	Len Mortimer	28		William Thomas	William Thomas
1911	4th	Len Mortimer	44		William Thomas	William Thomas
1912	2nd	Len Mortimer	40		Charlie Ricketts	Charlie Ricketts
1913	4th	Bill Strang	29		Harvey Kelly	Vic Belcher
1914	2nd	Jack Freeman	36		Vic Belcher	Vic Belcher
1915	5th	Harry Morgan	48		Vic Belcher	Vic Belcher
1916		Club in recess due to World War One				
1917	3rd	Harry Morgan	23		Vic Belcher	Vic Belcher
1918	1st	Gerald Ryan	32		Jim Caldwell	Herb Howson/'Sonny' Elms

CLUB NEWS 1874–1918

Cecil FC formed: Twelve people attended a meeting on 19 June 1874 at the Temperance Hall, Napier Street, Emerald Hill, for the formation of the Cecil Football Club.

Change of name: At a Cecil FC meeting held at Mr Evers' house on 15 July 1874, it was moved the club be called The South Melbourne Football Club.

VFA's first season: Clubs participating in the inaugural VFA season of 1877 included: South Melbourne, St Kilda, Victorian Railways, Ballarat, Standard, Essendon, Williamstown, Albert Park, West Melbourne, Northcote, Hawthorn, Melbourne and Victoria United.

Behinds recorded: Behinds were recorded for the first time in 1878, but not counted in the score.

Home games: The SMFC commenced playing its home games at the South Melbourne Cricket Ground in 1878.

First Premiership: In 1881 the SMFC finished ahead of Geelong, Carlton and Melbourne to win its first Premiership.

Best in Victoria: Leading football writers of the metropolitan press voted South Melbourne vice-captain Peter Burns Champion of the Colony, as most outstanding player of the 1885 season. Dinny McKay was similarly recognised in 1888 and Burns again in 1891.

Agitation: The Geelong FC proposed in 1889 that the better-class clubs of Melbourne join them to form a new competition.

Three Premierships: Of 57 matches played, South Melbourne lost on only

1874–1918

Early players

Peter Burns commenced his Senior career aged 17 with Ballarat. He was capable of playing any position and became known at 'Peter the Great' while vice-captain of South during its triple Association Premierships of 1889–90–91. The captaincy was the unshakeable province of 'Sonny' Elms, known as the Prince of Captains. Burns transferred to Geelong where he continued to play brilliantly.

Recounting his lifetime in football for the *Sporting Globe* in 1940, Burns said of the game: 'I think the players of today are spoon-fed – too much so. They want everything done for them. They squabble over money. They won't even buy a bootlace for themselves.'

Sonny Elms.

Peter Burns

Vic Belcher is the only player to have played in two Premiership sides for South (1909 and 1918), after joining in 1907. Belcher was a reliable key position player and could ruck all day. The brother of Essendon captain Alan, Belcher was South's captain in 1913, captain–coach during 1914–17 and a vital player in the South team that took the 1918 title from Collingwood.

He retired at the end of 1920 with 226 matches to his credit, and later coached Fitzroy to the 1922 VFL Premiership.

Of the 78 goals that South kicked in their first VFL season, 'Dinny' McKay kicked 13 to lead the club tally. Only 10 days after South's closing game of 1897, McKay was buried. The funeral following his sudden death was notable: it was reported that it took the funeral cortege half an hour to pass.

The proud team of 1918, South's second Premiership combination.

'The Bloods' back on top in 1918

South enjoyed one of their most brilliant seasons in 1918, winning 13 of the 14 matches. The only failure occurred on the King's Birthday Monday on 3 June 1918 at the Junction Oval. The Saints battled desperately in a last-half fightback to win 6.13 (49) to 6.8 (44). However, South recovered form and in the Second Semi-final accounted for traditional rivals Carlton 8.10 (58) to 7.11 (53).

With the War in its final stages, the biggest crowd for five years (39,168) assembled at the MCG on September 7. The umpiring legend Jack Elder had charge of his 27th VFL finals game (he went on to umpire 12 more). The crowd saw Collingwood hold South scoreless in the second term as the Magpies went to a 16-point lead, 4.9 to 2.5. An even third term still had the Pies holding a 12-point margin.

Against the wind in the last quarter, Belcher went into the ruck and got the Southerners moving. Gerald Ryan goaled, 'Chook' Howell added a behind and another goal to Ryan levelled the scores. The Magpies attacked to recover the lead with a behind. Collingwood kept possession but Dick Lee's shot fell short and was marked by Vic Belcher. Belcher's kick found Mark Tandy on the wing who, after dodging three opponents, had a ping at the goals. From the resulting scrimmage Chris Laird's kick off the ground went through with less than a minute to go. South had won their second VFL Premiership, again by less than a goal, 9.8 (62) to 7.15 (57).

South in Sydney – nearly 100 years ago.

---

six occasions to capture the successive Premierships of 1888–89–90.
Gate takings to London: Gate takings from a South Melbourne v Carlton match were donated to help striking dock workers in London.
33,000 at MCG: In 1890, 33,000 supporters packed the MCG to watch a match between South and Carlton. The SMFC won three goals to two.

Record VFA crowd: A record crowd of 36,188 saw South (7.8) and Essendon (7.9) draw at the East Melbourne Cricket Ground in 1891. The *Argus* described the contest as 'a magnificent one, full of fast play and team work with brilliant marking and hard ruck clashes'.
First Grand Final: South Melbourne and Collingwood finished level at the end of the 1896 season, each winning 14, losing three and drawing one (when they played each other), both kicking 86 goals and having 55 scored against them. It resulted in the first Association Grand Final played at the East Melbourne Cricket Ground on Saturday 3 October 1896. Collingwood won six goals to five (6.9 to 5.10).
One-point Premiership loss: Three finals following the 14-round home-and-away season of 1899 saw South and Fitzroy deciding the Premiership at the Junction Oval on September 16. Playing with three obviously unfit members, South lost 3.8 (26) to Fitzroy 3.9 (27).
South in Sydney: South played Fitzroy at the Sydney Cricket Ground on Saturday, 24 June 1905. Fitzroy won 9.10 (64) to South Melbourne's 8.9 (57).

SOUTH MELBOURNE

Bob Pratt: a classic mark.

Laurie Nash: devastating.

Cazaly: the game's big name.

The great forward

Born on 31 August 1912, Pratt graduated from Mitcham to play with South in 1930. Between 1932 and 1936 he became a legend of League football, possibly the most brilliant high-flyer the game has produced.

Pratt was a polished forward, who will long be remembered for his 1934 season, when he accumulated 150 goals, the highest tally recorded in the VFL. Pratt had already made it to his 100th goal by the 13th round of 1934. His rivalry with team-mate Laurie Nash, with whom Pratt competed for a place in the record books, obtained 199 goals for South in 1934. When asked years later how they played together, Pratt recalled that Nash had passed to him once, 'but it was a mistake.'

In 1940, Pratt transferred to Association club Coburg. In the opening match of 1946, Pratt attempted a VFL comeback against Carlton at the Junction Oval. He kicked two goals, injured his ankle and retired.

He registered 681 goals in 158 League matches at an average of 4.8 goals per game.

Fearsome Laurie Nash

Laurie Nash was born in Fitzroy on 2 May 1910, the son of former Collingwood captain Robert Nash. He was raised in Tasmania, and joined the City (Launceston) club in 1930 where he was coached by Cazaly.

An all-round sportsman, Nash played cricket for Tasmania, scoring a century against Victoria. He took 4 wickets for 18 runs against South Africa in his 1932 Test debut.

Nash, who signed for South in 1933 at £3 a week, was a devastating footballer in either defence or attack. He was a hero of the 1933 Grand Final, during which he took 13 marks. He captained South in 1937 but transferred the following year without a clearance to Camberwell in the VFA, where he won a Best and Fairest award in 1939.

He returned to South in 1945, playing in 17 of the Swans' 22 matches, including the 'Bloodbath' Grand Final, kicking a total of 56 goals. He then retired after 99 VFL games and 246 goals. He later coached South in 1953.

When named in the AFL's Hall of Fame, the summary commented: 'One of the most gifted players ever, his career was half as long as many but it shone twice as brightly as most. Considered by many judges (himself included) the best player in the land ...' He died in Melbourne on 24 July 1986.

Up there Cazaly

Roy Cazaly is the best-known name the game has produced. Born at Albert Park in 1893 he stood just 5 feet 11 inches (180cm) tall, and weighed 12 and a half stone. He did not smoke, drink or eat fried food; a fitness fanatic before his time. His career spanned five decades, during which he played 425 Senior matches and 32 State matches for Victoria and Tasmania.

His first League games were played with St Kilda in 1911. After 99 games with the Saints, Cazaly transferred to South in 1921 after being refused a clearance to Carlton. He became coach of the Swans in 1922, and played with the Swans until 1927, with a year's break in 1925.

Cazaly added to his natural leap by controlling his breath. He could take a fingertip mark, turn a complete circle, land and keep running without missing a step. His aerobatic performances inspired the term 'Up There Cazaly', a phrase that would be shouted by team-mate Fred 'Skeeter' Fleiter when he wanted Cazaly to go for the mark.

CLUB NEWS 1919–1936

South's revenge: Taking revenge for their single defeat the previous year, the Bloods beat St Kilda at the Junction Oval by 171 points, 29.15 (189) to 2.6 (18). Harold Robertson kicked a new VFL record of 14 goals in the game. The winning margin remained a League record for 60 years.

Cazaly traded to South: Though voted Champion of the 1920 season with St Kilda, captain Roy Cazaly, now 27, applied for a clearance to Carlton after 99 games. The Saints refused the transfer but agreed to trade him to South in 1921.

Greatest-ever 'Lake Premiership': There was a huge crush when South and their neighbouring rivals St Kilda drew an estimated 50,000 to Albert Park in the last round of 1923. Sections of the boundary fence broke under the crush of the crowd, and spectators were perched in trees and along the roof of the stand. Both teams were playing for a place in the finals. South broke away for a 20-point victory 8.20 (68) to 7.6 (48), rising from wooden-spooners to third place.

A very even season: In 1930, the Swans lost their first six games, then won eight of their last nine, ending with nine wins, nine losses. They scored 1553 points for the season, with the same kicked against them, to finish seventh with a modern-day percentage of 100.

New forward from Mitcham: Fifteen new faces were tried in the

1919–1936

1933 captain–coach Jack Bissett and secretary Dick Mullally welcome the newcomers.

Austin Robertson: speedy forward.

Depression brings the Foreign Legion

The midnight oil burned brightly at South Melbourne after the 1931 season, as Jack Rohan and Archie Crofts set out to rebuild the Bloods. With hands tied locally, they turned their eyes to the rich talent available from Western Australia. Good footy and a job with Crofts' Stores were the carrots to lure players over to the east.

The classy rover Johnny Leonard from Subiaco was their first valuable signing. Leonard, now 30, gathered fellow westerners Brighton Diggins, Billy Faul and Bert Beard, plus centreman James 'Brum' O'Meara from Perth and speedy flanker Austin Robertson from Subiaco. The Bloods also gained Jack Bissett from Richmond.

Season 1932 saw South reborn, the transformation confirmed as the distinctive and modern blood-red 'V' replaced the old uniform. The new South Melbourne were dubbed 'The Foreign Legion' and they took the new season by storm, winning their first 10 matches.

This became the most exciting period of South's modern history. When Jack Bissett took over as coach from Leonard in 1933, four successive Grand Final appearances resulted, with records galore – but only one Premiership.

South took the 1933 Flag in front of a record crowd of 75,754. With terrific speed, accurate passing, and leading out into position, 'The Foreign Legion' out-classed the reigning Premiers, Richmond, with a convincing score of 9.17 (71) to the Tigers' 4.5 (29). Thousands of fans greeted the victorious team at the Lake Oval.

'Brum' O'Meara.

1919–1936 HONOUR ROLL

Year	Pos	Leading Goalkicker	No.	Best & Fairest	Captain	Coach
1919	4th	Harold Robertson	38		Jim Caldwell	Herb Howson/'Sonny' Elms
1920	5th	Stan Wootton	28		Vic Belcher	Albert Hiskins
1921	7th	Roy Cazaly	19		Carl Willis	Arthur Wood
1922	9th	Roy Cazaly	28		Mark Tandy	Roy Cazaly
1923	3rd	Ted Johnson	45		Paddy Scanlan	Charlie Pannam
1924	4th	Ted Johnson	60		Paddy Scanlan	Charlie Pannam
1925	8th	Ted Johnson	59		Paddy Scanlan	Charlie Pannam
1926	5th	Ted Johnson	44	Roy Cazaly	Charlie Pannam	Charlie Pannam
1927	6th	Ted Johnson	50	Hec McKay	Charlie Pannam	Charlie Pannam
1928	10th	Ted Johnson	60	Claude Stanbridge	Joe Scanlan	Charlie Pannam
1929	8th	Austin Robertson	52	Danny Wheelahan	Chas Stanbridge	Fred Fleiter
1930	7th	Austin Robertson	54	Ron Hillis	Joe Scanlan	Paddy Scanlan
1931	7th	Austin Robertson	38	Len Thomas	Joe Scanlan	Paddy Scanlan
1932	4th	Bob Pratt	71	Bill Faul	Johnny Leonard	Johnny Leonard
1933	1st	Bob Pratt	109	Hec Clarke	Jack Bissett	Jack Bissett
1934	2nd	Bob Pratt	150	Terry Brain	Jack Bissett	Jack Bissett
1935	2nd	Bob Pratt	103	Ron Hillis	Jack Bissett	Jack Bissett
1936	2nd	Bob Pratt	64	Herbie Matthews	Jack Bissett	Jack Bissett

colours in 1930, including a youth with good credentials from Mitcham: Bob Pratt, who had kicked 43 goals from 18 games at the age of 17.

Crofts resigns: Archie Crofts' concerns about the amount of liquor being consumed at after-match functions reached flashpoint after a Geelong game. He called a halt to late-night proceedings and promptly resigned, then left for a four-week holiday in Queensland. He returned on July 8, 1933 and reclaimed the presidency.

24 wins at the Lake: From Round 8 on 30 June 1934, when the Swans beat Fitzroy 13.19 (97) to 13.10 (88), South won 24 consecutive games at the Lake Oval through to 29 August 1936, when they beat Hawthorn by five points in the 17th round. At their next home game on 2 May 1937, the Magpies broke the chain. In the same era, Richmond also won 24 consecutive games at Punt Road, from 1932 until South defeated them there on 8 June 1935. Their 24-home-game winning streak remains the record.

Pratt hit by a truck: In 1935 Bob Pratt had kicked 103 goals, recently turned 23, and got married. In High Street Prahran on Thursday, October 3, Pratt was about to board a tram when he was hit by a lorry laden with five tons of bricks and thrown onto the footpath. Bruised and shaken, with lacerations to both legs and an injury to an ankle and thumb, Pratt withdrew from the Grand Final side. South lost to Collingwood by 20 points. All at South agreed that Pratt would have made the difference.

SOUTH MELBOURNE

Brownlow win to rover Herb Matthews

Sturdily built, Matthews was a gifted player. He started as wingman when he joined South from the metropolitan club Fairfield in 1932. In the following five seasons he developed into one of the finest footballers to wear the red and white of South, playing in the 1933 Premiership and the three subsequent Grand Finals when the Swans were runners-up.

Herb Matthews.

Herbie Matthews was a tough player when required, a brilliant mark for his size, and his stab-passing was a delight. He is best remembered for his sportsmanship, winning the 1940 Brownlow Medal (South Melbourne's first) and coming second in 1937 and 1941. He won the club Best and Fairest award on five occasions; in 1936, 1937, 1939, 1940 and 1945.

Matthews, with nine other players, was reported during the notorious 1945 Grand Final. The charge of 'throwing the ball away after a free kick had been given against him' was sustained and he received a severe reprimand. He withdrew as a protest, after 191 matches over 14 seasons.

He transferred to the VFA club Oakleigh as coach where his coaching skills were acknowledged, coming runner-up in the Association's J.J. Liston Trophy of 1946. He had coached South in the 1939 season, and later returned to the Lake as Seniors non-playing coach from 1954 to 1957.

Golden era over

The Swans continued with successful seasons in 1934–36, gaining three Grand Final berths in a row, but without managing to again grasp the greatest prize. Sadly, South Melbourne's success had reached its zenith. Between 1932 and 1936, South played 101 matches, winning 78 and losing 23.

Gradually, the 'Foreign Legion' disbanded. Ron Hillis retired after 138 games, as did Jack Bissett after 90. Smarting at the appointment of Laurie Nash as captain in 1937, Brighton Diggins walked out. Bob Pratt crossed to Coburg without a clearance in 1938. Archie Crofts announced in 1937 that he would not stand for re-election as president. The golden era was over.

It was the beginning of a long, dark period for the Swans. 1938 saw the worst slide from the top by a VFL club. The club finished in ninth position and the crowds and support disappeared. A berth in the 1942 First Semi-final was to be the next finals appearance, and not until the 1945 'Bloodbath' Grand Final were the Swans to look anything like the champions they had been in the early 30s.

Jack Graham: captain and ruck.

1937–1956 HONOUR ROLL

Year	Pos	Leading Goalkicker	No.	Best & Fairest	Captain	Coach
1937	9th	Laurie Nash	37	Herbie Matthews	Laurie Nash	Roy Cazaly
1938	12th	Bob Moore	34	Len Thomas	Herbie Matthews	Roy Cazaly
1939	12th	Bob Pratt	72	Herbie Matthews	Herbie Matthews	Herbie Matthews
1940	10th	Len Reiffel	33	Herbie Matthews	Herbie Matthews	Herbie Matthews
1941	8th	Jack Graham	33	Reg Ritchie	Herbie Matthews	Joe Kelly
1942	3rd	Lindsay White	80	Jim Cleary	Herbie Matthews	Joe Kelly
1943	8th	Claude Culph	35	Herbie Matthews	Herbie Matthews	Joe Kelly
1944	7th	Ron Hartridge	31	Jim Cleary	Herbie Matthews	Joe Kelly
1945	2nd	Laurie Nash	56	Jack Graham	Herbie Matthews	William 'Bull' Adams
1946	7th	Henry Mears	32	Billy Williams	Jack Graham	William 'Bull' Adams
1947	8th	Billy Williams	38	Billy Williams	Jack Graham	William 'Bull' Adams
1948	10th	Jack Graham	32	Ron Clegg	Jack Graham	Adams/Jack Hale
1949	10th	Ray Jones	27	Ron Clegg	Bert Lucas	Jack Hale
1950	11th	Gordon Lane	47	Billy Williams	Gordon Lane	Gordon Lane
1951	8th	Billy Williams	41	Ron Clegg	Gordon Lane	Gordon Lane
1952	5th	Gordon Lane	33	Keith Schaefer	Gordon Lane	Gordon Lane
1953	8th	Ian Gillett	34	Jim Taylor	Ron Clegg	Laurie Nash
1954	10th	Eddie Lane	28	Eddie Lane	Ron Clegg	Herbie Matthews
1955	10th	Eddie Lane	36	Ian Gillett	Bill Gunn	Herbie Matthews
1956	9th	Bill Gunn	28	Jim Dorgan	Ian Gillett	Herbie Matthews

CLUB NEWS 1937–1956

Another Test: After a five-year absence from Test cricket, Laurie Nash was recalled for the fifth and deciding Test in 1937 – reputedly at the behest of Don Bradman. At the MCG, Nash took 4/70 and 1/34 against England for a victory and the Ashes, three–two.

South thrashed: The 1937 opening game at Princes Park under coach Roy Cazaly brought the Swans' heaviest defeat of 90 contests with Carlton since 1897. The 70-point humiliation was the heaviest South had suffered to any team since 1929.

Third wooden spoon: South finished bottom of the ladder in 1938, their first wooden spoon since 1922. The Swans would finish in last place again in 1939.

South to Carlton: Several VFL grounds were acquired for military purposes as the war with Germany and Japan reached crisis level. South played their 'home' games at Princes Park in seasons 1942–43, moving to the Junction Oval for 1944–46. The Swans returned to Albert Park in 1947.

Back to the finals: South finished second in 1942 and won its way to the Preliminary Final, where it lost to Essendon. With Geelong in recess, Lindsay White was playing with the Swans, finishing with 80 goals (an outstanding nine in the Preliminary Final) to head the VFL goalscorers list.

Minor Premiers: Losing only four of the 20 rounds of 1945, South, led by Herbie Matthews in his eighth season as captain, finished with the minor

1937–1956

Suggested attire for future Grand Final matches.

The Bloodbath makes livid news

War broke out again when South Melbourne played the 1945 Grand Final on the battlefield of Princes Park. An amazing attendance of 62,986 squeezed into the venue before the gates were closed at 2.45 p.m.

In fierce first-quarter clashes which flared every few minutes, three Carlton players, Ken Hands, Jim Mooring and skipper Bob Chitty were dropped with punches and two South players, Ron Clegg and Don Grossman, were felled with equal violence. The *Argus* recounted the game: 'Bottles, thrown by the crowd, just missed players and six policemen had to help the umpires to restore order after one bitter all-in fight.

Clegg

'Fast, clever open football gave South six quick goals in the second quarter. But Carlton quickly proved it was the better-balanced side, and led at the last change, 12.9 (81) to 8.10 (58).

'In further brawling in the last quarter, Carlton captain Bob Chitty was knocked out. A donnybrook lasted for several minutes and the Blues centreman Clinton Wines took advantage of the confusion by breaking away for a long-range goal. When tempers calmed down Carlton was never seriously challenged and won the flag, 15.13 (103) to 10.15 (75).'

The match received the condemnation of all commentators. Umpires, under heavy police escort after the game, retired to the rooms for two hours of writing reports. Ten players were reported and appeared before the tribunal; nine were found guilty.

South lost the fight and the match on points. A quarter of a century would elapse before South next played in a final, and it was another 51 years until the red and white next played in a Grand Final.

The victims shown by Truth *newspaper.*

A Goldsmith grab.

Brownlow boys

The hearts of South's long-suffering supporters were gladdened during the dark days of the 50s with the awarding of Brownlow Medals to Ron 'Smokey' Clegg in 1949 and Fred Goldsmith in 1955.

Clegg was a natural to win the medal. The rangy centre half-forward with the film star looks was a regular Victorian representative. He was a fine mark and a long kick, and could star at either centre half-forward or centre half-back. Over the years he held all the honours at South, including the captaincy and captain–coach.

Goldsmith was a dark-horse Brownlow winner. A failed forward turned defender, he played with tight concentration, but could mark brilliantly when he had the opportunity. He was a booming kick.

Premiership. Under coach 'Bull' Adams they defeated Collingwood in the Second Semi-final to enter their first Grand Final since 1936, where Carlton defeated them 15.13 (103) to 10.15 (75).
Coach replaced: Internal problems brought the replacement of coach 'Bull' Adams in 1948. Former Carlton player Jack Hale took over from Round 11.
Clegg's Brownlow: In his fifth season, Ron Clegg won South's second Brownlow Medal in 1949, on a count-back from Col Austen of Hawthorn.
Clegg stars: On 23 June 1951, at Brunswick Street Oval against Fitzroy, Ron 'Smokey' Clegg took 32 marks. The match was drawn. Clegg's 32 was one short of the record tally taken by Carlton's Alec Duncan against Collingwood in 1927.
Fireman Fred: Fred Goldsmith learned of his Brownlow victory when on duty at Eastern Hill Fire Station in 1955. The full-forward turned classy full-back became the third South Melbourne player to win the coveted honour.
Thirds Premiership: South won the Third 18 Flag in 1956. It was the only VFL Premiership other than the Senior pennants of 1909, 1918 and 1933 ever won by the SMFC.
First night Flag: Night football was introduced at the Lake Oval after the minor series in 1956, featuring the clubs who failed to make it into the final four. South 13.16 (94) defeated Carlton 13.10 (88) before a crowd of 32,450: it was South's first Senior title since 1933. The Swans followed it up by beating Geelong for the Night Flag in 1957.

SOUTH MELBOURNE

Ken Boyd: one of the toughest.

Ken Boyd's greatest hits

The Swans' season of 1961 was highlighted by two spiteful encounters against Carlton. In the fourth round at the Lake, South's aggressive ruckman Ken Boyd was reported twice – first for striking the Blues' John Nicholls on the jaw, and seconds later for flattening rover John Heathcote with a punch to the face. The tribunal suspended Boyd for eight weeks, and he was back in time for the return meeting in Round 15 at Princes Park.

Boyd and Nicholls again tangled and slugged it out, but no reports were laid. However, the following day John Nicholls gave a television account which according to Boyd was a 'very one-sided account'. Boyd contacted the newspapers and claimed that Nicholls had threatened that if Boyd bothered him in the match, Nicholls would kick him in the groin. Boyd had replied in the exchange, that if Nicholls did, he would get his head knocked off. Boyd continued: 'We went for a throw-in. He went up and drove his boots right in the middle of my stomach. I was in excruciating agony – when I got up I went straight back and hit him as hard as I could. That was behind the play.'

Ken Boyd was later suspended for 12 weeks: he never played League football again.

South's greatest son

Of all the 1279 players to have worn the colours across the 101 seasons of League competition, the greatest son of South Melbourne is Robert John Skilton.

Born 8 November 1938 – the season of a South wooden spoon – he was raised in Port Melbourne, where his father Bob Snr captain–coached the Borough. Skilton graduated through the ranks until he played his first Senior game on 12 May 1956 at the Western Oval against Footscray.

The 'Chimp' played during 'the desperate years', an era when the club enjoyed little success. Across the 16 seasons he wore the red and white, the Swans played in 301 matches, winning 100, losing 198, and drawing three times. Skilton wore the Swans colours on 237 occasions, but only once in a final – the 1970 First Semi-final, which was lost. Apart from the outstanding 1970 season, in all of Skilton's years the Swans were never higher than eighth place. In his farewell season, they finished 12th for a wooden spoon.

Robert Skilton was the most highly decorated player of any era. He was winner of the Brownlow Medal in 1959, 1963 and 1968. He won the Swans Best and Fairest award on nine occasions; led the goalkicking with 60 in 1959 and topped the club tally in 1962 and 1963 with 36 in both years. In total he kicked 412 VFL goals. His goalscoring peak was at Albert Park on 11 July 1959 when he kicked eight goals in the Swans' 17.16 (118) win over Geelong 12.12 (84).

He captained South from 1961 to 1971 (expect 1969 which he missed due

Skilts gets his third Brownlow Medal.

to injury), and led as both captain and coach in the seasons of 1965 and 1966. His great pace and remarkable skills made him a target, and he was frequently 'ironed out' by fierce bumps from opponents.

He represented Victoria on 25 occasions – acknowledgment of his status as the nation's first-ranked rover – and captained his State in 1963 and 1965.

His last appearance for the Swans was on Saturday, 28 August 1971. Only 9307 were at the Lakeside Oval the day Skilton farewelled League football. Though the Bloods were destined for their sixth wooden spoon, the whole side rose to the occasion. The Bloodstained Angels gave Bob Skilton a thorough victory note to depart on – they defeated North Melbourne, 19.17(131) to 8.11 (59).

CLUB NEWS 1957–1971

Television arrives: Footy's love affair with television began in 1957 when the last quarters of three home-and-away games were broadcast live on all three channels, GTV-9, HSV-7 and ABV-2.

Goldsmith's nine: Fred Goldsmith, the full-back Brownlow winner of 1955, kicked nine goals (a personal VFL best) against Richmond at the Lake Oval on 12 April 1958.

Earliest start: In the Centenary year of the game, the earliest calendar opening to a season, 12 April 1958 was enjoyed. March opening seasons did not arrive until 1979.

Frank Johnson recruited: Already retired as a Senior player, Frank Johnson, at 27, became one of the oldest League recruits when he joined South in 1960. The VFA Liston Trophy winner of 1952 had played in eight successive Association Grand Finals with Port Melbourne then became coach of South Warrnambool. He won the SMFC Best and Fairest in his first year. The talented, great marking ruckman gave the Swans 64 quality games until the end of 1964.

Long run of outs: South suffered 13 consecutive losses in 1962: their worst run of defeats since 1938, when they lost 14 games in a row. The 13 losses equalled their lack of success across 1903 and 1904.

One goal: South at Kardinia Park scored 1.9 (15) against Geelong 8.9 (57) in the match on 8 August 1964. The score was South's lowest since

1957 – 1971

Bill Faul: no luck.

Above: Fathers and sons – three Herb Matthews, two Fauls, two Pratts, two Brains and two McLaughlins. Inset: Norm Smith.

Coaches come, coaches go

Bill Faul was retained as coach for 1960 and 1961. He was replaced by Noel McMahen in 1962, who coached South for three lack-lustre seasons. Bob Skilton was captain–coach for 1965–66, and in 1967 South appointed Allan Miller as senior coach, allowing Skilton to concentrate on playing. Miller was a rarity in League ranks, as he had never played a Senior game.

Norm Smith accepted the task to coach South Melbourne in 1969. He came as a package with his own support staff. The taskmaster was swift with the new broom: down came the cobwebs; the rooms were repainted, and even carpeted!

Bob Skilton was absent through injury for all of 1969 and the side was led by his deputy John Rantall. The year at South produced a greater spirit and coordination, though the lack of depth was evident. The Swans gained seven wins for ninth place.

The pace quickened in 1970. The Swans were sentimental favourites for the First Semi-final, but were easily beaten by St Kilda, 22.11 (143) to 13.12 (90). The crowd of 104,239 is likely to remain the largest crowd ever to see the red and white play.

The end of South

The writing was on the wall for the Bloods. The Swans squeaked into the 1975 final series at the bottom of the five, only to be outclassed in the First Semi-final by the finals-hardened Richmond, 13.10 (88) to 7.12 (54).

Two Brownlow Medallists for the decade – Peter Bedford in 1970 and Graham Teasdale in 1977 – were bright spots in an otherwise dark time. Mounting debts, dwindling membership and lack of on-field success made the club's future at South look bleak. On 29 August 1981, the South Melbourne club colours were carried onto the Lake Oval by a Senior team for the 1570th and final occasion. North Melbourne led at every change to inflict the Swan's 839th League defeat.

1957 – 1971 HONOUR ROLL

Year	Pos	Leading Goalkicker	No.	Best & Fairest	Captain	Coach
1957	10th	Fred Goldsmith	43	Jim Taylor	Ron Clegg	Herbie Matthews
1958	9th	Max Oaten	34	Bob Skilton	Ron Clegg	Ron Clegg
1959	9th	Bob Skilton	60	Bob Skilton	Ron Clegg	Ron Clegg
1960	8th	Max Oaten	39	Frank Johnson	Ron Clegg	Bill Faul
1961	11th	Brian McGowan	38	Bob Skilton	Bob Skilton	Bill Faul
1962	12th	Bob Skilton	36	Bob Skilton	Bob Skilton	Noel McMahen
1963	11th	Bob Skilton	36	Bob Skilton	Bob Skilton	Noel McMahen
1964	11th	Max Papley	25	Bob Skilton	Bob Skilton	Noel McMahen
1965	8th	Ron Kingston	48	Bob Skilton	Bob Skilton	Bob Skilton
1966	8th	Austin Robertson	60	Max Papley	Bob Skilton	Bob Skilton
1967	9th	John Sudholz	35	Bob Skilton	Bob Skilton	Allan Miller
1968	9th	John Sudholz	36	Bob Skilton	Bob Skilton	Allan Miller
1969	9th	John Sudholz	35	Peter Bedford	Bob Skilton	Norm Smith
1970	4th	John Sudholz	62	Peter Bedford	Bob Skilton	Norm Smith
1971	12th	Peter Bedford	44	Peter Bedford	Bob Skilton	Norm Smith

1902. The year brought only two wins, equalling the worst seasons of 1903 and 1938 for South.

13 newcomers: New players for South in 1968 numbered 13 and included a 'useful ruckman' from Richmond, Neil Busse. He would later become the chairman of the AFL tribunal.

Bedford joins: The classy 20-year-old VFA centreman Peter Bedford from Port Melbourne played his first game for the Bloods at Glenferrie Oval on 20 April 1968, when they drew with Hawthorn.

Chimp's third Brownlow: Skilton equalled the feats of Bunton and Reynolds when he won his third Brownlow in 1968. At his presentation his battle-won black-eyes still shone – one shiner collected against Footscray on August 24, the other a week later against Collingwood. Earlier in the season, Skilton was knocked unconscious at Glenferrie; recovered, and then kicked five goals for the Bloods. Skilton also won the SMFC Best and Fairest in 1968, for a record ninth time.

Skilton misses season: Skilton tore an Achilles tendon in a pre-season practice match in 1969. The injury sidelined the triple-Brownlow winner for all of Norm Smith's first season as coach. His next game was 11 April 1970 versus North.

South slump back: From their 1970 finals appearance, the Swans slumped to lose their opening six 1971 matches. Wooden spooners with only three wins, their 2.6 (18) versus Melbourne at VFL Park remains the lowest at Waverley – equalled by Collingwood in 1987.

SYDNEY

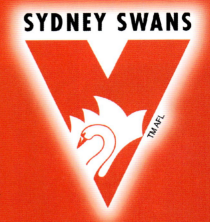

SYDNEY SWANS

MY CLUB
by Kevin Taylor

There are still charges made that the Sydney club have been given an 'armchair ride'; that too many concessions, too many sweetheart deals, too many digressions have been allowed, to the disadvantage of other League member clubs.

The others should show more gratitude, as the Swans are the trailblazers who have led to the AFL becoming the most powerful sporting institution in the nation. The Sydney club of today has generated a cash flow (derived chiefly from television) into football that has kept many other clubs alive.

South Melbourne was 'the club that refused to die'. The red and white move from Melbourne to Sydney in 1982 began the process that, five years later, gave the VFL confidence to expand their horizons to embrace a national competition. Before any other VFL club flew, the Swans had more frequent flyer points on the board, and the rest began in catch-up mode.

While the 'Victorian game' first sprouted competitive roots in Sydney in 1880, it is the success of South Melbourne in its Sydney form that will ensure a blossoming of the Australian code throughout the 21st century. It will not become a 'quaint little game played in the corner …' as Ron Barassi warned in 1993.

The Sydney club is a vibrant and competitive force in a city of well over three million, though in many areas it still struggles to be recognised as part of the culture.

The Sydney Cricket Ground has become a unique feature of AFL competition. It has been elevated (by Kevin Sheedy) to 'Colosseum' status with a force of 40,000 fans cheering the red and white colours with as much fervour as the 40,000-strong crowd cheering their champions at Albert Park more than a century ago.

Turmoil, traumas, a handful of different owners, and endless rescue packages have been necessary to keep the red and white blood flowing in Sydney. As recently as October 1992, an AFL vote was taken in Melbourne of 11–nil (Carlton and North Melbourne abstained, Sydney and Brisbane refrained from voting) approving a $1.985 million licence fee be waived, to provide working capital for the following three years.

Then came the desperate seasons of 1993 and 1994 where games regularly failed to attract SCG attendances of more than four digits. When Sydney made the Grand Final of 1996, it attracted SCG crowds (13 matches and two finals) averaging 26,850, reporting a membership base of 9525 and a rare profit of some $75,000. By 1997, average crowds zoomed to 35,818 (11 games) and produced a 136 per cent membership increase to 22,500.

The claims that games in Sydney chiefly draw 'the chardonnay set' or 'theatregoers' is nonsense, yet it is articulated in authoritative journals. While super-boxes at any sporting contest have their freeloaders and many who are present only to be 'seen', the crowds of the late 1990s show greater passion and understanding than those that bloated the figures in the Powerplay-Edelsten days of the mid-1980s. The thrills and excitement are now delivered to a wide range of fans well versed in the rules and nuances of the game.

SYDNEY

Year Established	1874
Joined VFL/AFL	1897
Home Grounds	Lake Oval, Princes Pk, Junction Oval, SCG
Premierships	1909, 1918, 1933
Brownlow Medals	Herbie Matthews Snr 1940; Ron Clegg 1949; Fred Goldsmith 1955; Bob Skilton 1959, 1963, 1968; Peter Bedford 1970; Graham Teasdale 1977; Barry Round 1981; Greg Williams 1986; Gerard Healy 1988; Paul Kelly 1995
Record home crowd	44,047 v Geelong, 1996
Most games	John Rantall, 260
Most goals	Bob Pratt, 681
Notable supporters	Bob Carr, Gary Wilkinson, Nick Greiner, Anne Fulwood, Barry Crocker, Ross Symonds, Tim Fischer, Neil Brooks

The day of days: Swans fans at the MCG for the Grand Final.

Television, as a nationwide vehicle of information, delivers. Local radio and newspapers in Sydney still have a narrow-minded view of the Australian game. It is often dealt with as a 'curiosity': to put it succinctly, how could anyone be attracted to something which doesn't interest Sydney? The newspaper culture of the 1960s and 1970s, when it was prescribed that the word 'Rules' had to appear in every headline so that uninterested readers could ignore the item, has only in part disappeared from the minds of Sydney people who organise what is to be read or heard.

After 16 seasons of competition at the SCG, there are those who seek worlds beyond the confines of their city, who look to the broader aspects of the AFL, and want to be dealt with as thinking supporters of the national code. The *Sydney Morning Herald* is the first local newspaper to have two journalists, Gerard Wright and Richard Hinds, to report on AFL games. Other media, including radio, may broaden their vision with the game's continued success and with the increasing demands of their readers and listeners.

The Sydney club, to the end of 1997, has shown an amazing resilience. Should their present administration remain in place, there is hope that the Swans will at last gain a meaningful and respected presence in their own city.

Barry Round: two-city hero.

Greg Williams: dominating Diesel.

Paul Kelly: inspirational.

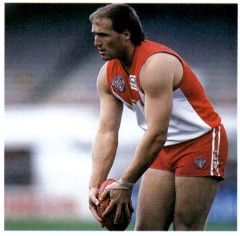
Tony Lockett: trump card.

The old Sydney–Melbourne rivalry is given a new impetus on the football field.

SYDNEY

The old days at South, with palm trees around the Lake Oval.

Graeme John: brought the news.

The storm clouds gather

Through the dark period of the 1970s it was clear that South Melbourne were haemorrhaging and a fatal collapse was imminent. The culture of football had changed with the population movement away from inner-city suburbs, resulting in a drop in grass-roots support. The Swans would be the first casualty unless dramatic changes were made. Revived expectations after an appearance in the 1970 First Semi-final soon faded as the club proved uncompetitive throughout 1972 and 1973.

After 98 years of existence, with a near to empty financial kitty, the Swans were sinking. The Club limped along until new president Craig Kimberley kicked in with a $100,000 sponsorship from his Just Jeans company in 1976. Football at South began to direct its destiny as a new group which included Kimberley, George Camakaris, Keith Hooker and Barry Rogers spearheaded a thrust for redevelopment.

Though cash-strapped, Ian Stewart as coach managed to take them to one final in 1977. The operating loss was $150,000. Kimberley stepped aside, as South received offers from St Kilda to play at Moorabbin, or to share with Fitzroy at the Junction Oval.

Members of the South Melbourne executive breathed a sigh of relief when Fitzroy announced in August 1978 it had abandoned a plan to play games in Sydney: privately, the Swans had harboured the idea of moving to Sydney long before Fitzroy.

The VFL power-brokers of the day pushed forward with 'The Sydney Experiment' in 1979 by again playing matches at the SCG, after a long break. The VFL was intent on creating an opening for the code, as it had detailed in its confidential report titled 'The Sydney Solution: VFL at the Crossroads', tabled on 13 August 1979.

South lacked success, debts continued to mount and the death rattles became audible, as their new president Graeme John noted in the *Age* in April 1979. An independent survey by the club concluded that South Melbourne would cease to exist within three to five years. The club accepted the inevitable – long considered secretly, but rejected as suicidal – that survival would only be found in Sydney.

South had played exhibition games in the early part of the century and in the 1930s in Sydney, but their first formal competition game was against Geelong at the SCG on Sunday, 15 June 1980. They lost heavily.

> 🏈 The first VFL game since 1952 was played in Sydney when Hawthorn met North for match points at the SCG on Sunday, 10 June 1979 in front of a crowd of 31,391. Richmond and Fitzroy played on 15 July 1979. These games were followed in 1980 by matches on April 27, May 25, June 15 and July 20. In 1981, two more matches were played, on May 3 and July 26. Two of these eight matches were played by the Swans, at what was eventually to become their home ground.

CLUB NEWS 1972–1981

29 successive defeats: South experienced its worst period with 29 consecutive losses. Having lost the previous four games, the Swans beat North. Then, starting with a loss against Hawthorn on 13 May 1972, they lost all contests until beating Geelong on 7 July 1973. The losing streak more than doubled their previous worst of 14 consecutive losses in 1938.

Smith retires: Failing in health, the spirited Norm Smith decided to step down as coach in 1973. His 87-game coaching career brought 26 wins for the Swans and their 1970 First Semi-final appearance. Graeme John, a Swan of 77 games (1964–69), took over. Smith passed away on 29 July 1973.

Rantall defects: South veteran John Rantall (174 games) was lured to North in 1973 by a $15,000 deal and a $10,000 signing-on fee.

Only 31 players used: Three new players won a senior guernsey in 1974: Alf Beus, Tony Franklin (a ruckman from Penguin) and Graeme Wilson. Only 31 players were used for the season, the least to wear the colours since 1952. For his achievement with the available talent, one newspaper voted Graeme John Coach of the Year.

Pitura cleared: John Pitura (99 games) was cleared by South to Punt Road in exchange for Francis Jackson, Brian 'Whale' Roberts and Graham Teasdale.

Board changes: Incumbent president Keith Hooker (of the Hooker group of companies) marshalled the forces of

1972 – 1981

Veteran Swan John Rantall leads a players' meeting.

Barry Rogers: influential.

South to go north – Sydney or bust!

Graham Huggins, who guided the Saints to their first Flag in 1966, resigned as a VFL vice-president on 29 January 1981, and in the following month arrived in Sydney to begin talking to 'interested parties'.

During this period SMFC's Graeme John and Jack Marks, president of the SM Club Limited and a Swans supporter all of his days, met at VFL House with Allen Aylett (League president) and Jack Hamilton (VFL general manager).

Huggins presented a detailed study to the VFL Board on 17 June recommending a three-year trial for a Sydney-based team.

The following Saturday, the *Australian* reported: 'South Melbourne is considering making a bid to become the VFL's Sydney-based club next year.' Tensions ran high, with abusive phone calls, threatening mail and death-threats requiring police protection for Marks and Rogers.

After their July 26 win over Collingwood at the SCG, South Melbourne supporters learned on the following Wednesday that the VFL 'Board of Directors voted in favour of an application from the South Melbourne Committee to play 11 Sydney matches in 1982.'

Opposition fails

Spirited opposition to a move resulted in numerous meetings and rallies. At one meeting, the elected representatives were deposed amid claims by a 'Keep South at South' group that they would overturn the Sydney move.

Though Rick Quade had been selected by the SMFC Board as the 1982 coach, the rival action group voted in John Rantall as coach. Players took sides and a large group went on strike early in December. By December 23, unable to deliver their promised 'million-dollar sponsorships' and with overwhelming financial difficulties, the KSAS group capitulated. With phone calls at 2 a.m. by Alan Schwab and an early morning meeting at headquarters, the VFL imposed its will by reappointing Barry Rogers (football manager), Dean Moore (administration) and Rick Quade (coach).

The Swans had well and truly left their nest at the Lake.

Rick Quade.

1972 – 1981 HONOUR ROLL

Year	Pos	Leading Goalkicker	No.	Best & Fairest	Captain	Coach
1972	11th	Peter Bedford	28	Russell Cook	John Rantall	Norm Smith
1973	12th	Peter Bedford	52	Peter Bedford	Peter Bedford	Graeme John
1974	9th	Norm Goss	37	Norm Goss	Peter Bedford	Graeme John
1975	12th	Graham Teasdale	38	Peter Bedford	Peter Bedford	Graeme John
1976	8th	Robert Dean	37	Rick Quade	Peter Bedford	Ian Stewart
1977	5th	Graham Teasdale	38	Graham Teasdale	Rick Quade	Ian Stewart
1978	8th	John Murphy	31	John Murphy	Rick Quade	Des Tuddenham
1979	10th	Tony Morwood	56	Barry Round	Rick Quade	Ian Stewart
1980	6th	John Roberts	67	David Ackerley	Barry Round	Ian Stewart
1981	9th	John Roberts	51	Barry Round	Barry Round	Ian Stewart

Craig Kimberley (head of Just Jeans), George Camakaris, John Burton (a local publican) and Barry Rogers (publicity officer), to restore the credibility of the SMFC in 1975. Kimberley would later contribute a $100,000 Just Jeans sponsorship deal.

The untried Stewart: It was a surprise to the football world when recently retired Ian Stewart came in as South coach for 1976. He had won three Brownlows in his 205 VFL games with St Kilda and Richmond, but was untried as a coach. Stewart proved innovative, helped by the leadership of Peter Bedford and the returning John Rantall.

Push for Sydney: The *Melbourne Truth* on 4 December 1976 reported moves to add a Sydney team to the VFL competition.

Tuddenham is chosen: Des Tuddenham, the former Collingwood player, was chosen to coach South in 1978. 'Tuddy's' different style gained early success yet the Swans slumped to end in eighth place.

Rantall passes Skilton: John Rantall played his 238th game for South on 26 August 1978, passing Bob Skilton as the longest-serving Swan.

Sydney support: *Melbourne Truth* on 31 December 1978 revealed support from Ron Barassi and Allen Aylett of the VFL's plans to expand to Sydney.

Fitzroy eye Sydney: In the red by $400,000, Fitzroy president Frank Bibby in 1978 revealed his push for the Lions to move to Sydney. The ensuing uproar by Fitzroy members resulted in Bibby abandoning the plan on August 30.

SYDNEY

Graham Huggins: spearhead.

And here they are. The Swans on parade at the Opera House launch.

The vision splendid

The case for the existence of a VFL side based in Sydney wasn't exactly watertight; there were holes. If all the true facts had been provided, it's doubtful VFL directors would have given the green light. However, the vision splendid proceeded.

From a distance most Melbournians in the early 1980s viewed the prospective Sydney scene as an 'untapped mountain of gold'. A number of VFL clubs feared that Sydney would be unfairly advantaged through these new-found riches, which they believed would come from the rivers of coins streaming from the pokies. In reality, the stream had run out years before, and even the rugby league clubs were not in good shape.

Knowing only that South Melbourne would be playing 11 matches in 1982, Graham Huggins established temporary offices at North Sydney late in January. In 'let's get it done' mode, most of the costs came from Huggin's pockets. He found some difficulties getting repaid later, as would others.

Gala launch at Opera House

'The Swans' were launched at the Sydney Opera House on 22 February 1982 when coach Rick Quade introduced his players to the 200 invited guests and the media. The bash cost some $20,000, but no one cared: someone had to be paying.

In his Opera House address, president Aylett stated the VFL saw no conflict with rugby league and welcomed guests from that code who cheerfully wore red and white rosettes proclaiming 'I'm a Sydney Swan'.

One man not wearing a rosette was VFL general manager Jack Hamilton, who may have been thinking: how do we get the $400,000 loan back from the SMFC, and how much more will it cost before it works?

It had been envisaged that all players would be relocated to Sydney by mid-1981. The delays caused by the KSAS group threw a large spanner in the works, but former player Rod Carter remembers that two-thirds of First 18 players, and key administration, were in Sydney by the start of the season. It became a nightmare for the two coaches (Ron Thomas was Quade's assistant) as 'The Swans' had to field three teams – Firsts, Reserves and Thirds – with the bulk of players still living and training in Melbourne.

With senior preparation so disrupted, it was amazing the Swans ever made it, but they did. The on-field leadership of captain Barry Round and his deputy Mark Browning was intact for their first home game at the SCG on Sunday, 28 March 1981 against Melbourne. The home side won 20.17 (137) to 16.12 (108).

Their 'arrival' was celebrated by a spectacular party at 'Fairwater', the Point Piper home of Lady Mary Fairfax, where there was no shortage of spotlights, live music, microphones, cameras, oysters, caviar and champagne. It was a far cry from the beer, pies and an accordion at a Lake Oval after-match celebration.

CLUB NEWS 1982

Shared grounds? A study commissioned by the VFL in 1982 considered St Kilda sharing the SCG and Moorabbin with the Swans, as dual home grounds. The proposal was never taken up.

New players: New players attracted to the colours in 1982 were: Craig Braddy (from Fitzroy), Gerard Neesham (Swan Districts), John Reid (ex-Melbourne and Footscray) and the big-hearted ruckman Steve Taubert. Neesham played only nine games with the Swans, but following a successful WAFL career was the first AFL coach of Fremantle in 1995.

A master round: On 16 May 1982 a crowd of 20,905, the biggest SCG crowd to that date, watched Collingwood kick 8.4 (52) to 1.5 (11) in the last quarter. The Swans, however, held on to win by 18 points. Barry Round gave an outstanding performance, kicking seven goals in a ruck and high-marking display which captured the plaudits.

Seven straight wins: Starting with a win over St Kilda at the SCG on June 20, the Swans then defeated Fitzroy (Junction Oval), Geelong (SCG), Essendon (Windy Hill), Footscray (SCG), Collingwood (Victoria Park) and Carlton (SCG). The seven consecutive victories was the Bloods' best run since 1936.

Name change: The team that started the year as South Melbourne officially changed its name mid-season to reflect its new home, becoming the Sydney Swans.

1982

Bernie Evans in a tight spot against Hawthorn at the SCG.

Round a Sydney star

Round was recruited by Footscray from Warragul in 1969, and played 135 games for the Bulldogs before moving to South Melbourne in 1976. Of big proportions at 105kg and 193cm, his transfer to the Swans was opportune after new coach Ian Stewart had dispensed with 'Whale' Roberts. The number one ruckman for South, Round was equally adaptable at centre half-forward, and with a great pair of hands he delivered many telling goals when needed by the Swans.

At the end of the 1981 season, Round capped off his career at the age of 31, coming equal first for the Brownlow Medal with former Footscray team-mate, Bernie Quinlan of Fitzroy.

The move by the club to Sydney in 1982 saw Round develop into their first major star. He captained the Swans for five seasons, represented Victoria and in a 1981 game against Tasmania took an amazing 22 marks. He retired from the League in 1985 at the age of 35, having clocked up 328 VFL games (193 with the Swans).

From 1986 he played six VFA seasons with Williamstown, leading them to the 1986 Premiership, and winning the Liston Trophy. In all, he played nearly 500 senior matches.

New team makes a decent start

The Seniors achieved 12 wins for the year, which meant seventh placing, in what seemed to be a satisfactory start for their transfer to Coathanger City. Featuring in their 22 matches were: David Ackerley (who was judged Best and Fairest), Mark Browning, Dennis Carroll, Rod Carter, Max Kruse and Stevie Wright. Others to play at least 20 matches were: Silvio Foschini, Tony Morwood, Paul Morwood, David Rhys-Jones, Barry Round and Greg Smith.

David Rhys-Jones in contemplation.

The Swans also won the Australian Football Championships Escort Cup night competition in July and collected $105,000 in prize money. However, in the same month, the SMFC were already asking for deferment of the first $150,000 payment due on their $400,000 loan. The gates for home games in Sydney had lifted only marginally above the Albert Park average in 1981, from 14,647 to 15,993, which failed to compensate for the burden of additional expenditure. With the Swans netting less than $8000 a game, director Kevin Campbell resigned following his authorisation of a report warning of the Swans facing bankruptcy.

There were still those who believed South would return to Albert Park. The threat did not begin to evaporate until September 21 when six members from Sydney and four from Melbourne were elected to the new Board.

1982 HONOUR ROLL

Year	Pos	Leading Goalkicker	No.	Best & Fairest	Captain	Coach
1982	7th	Tony Morwood	45	David Ackerley	Barry Round	Rick Quade

Expectations fall short: Administration and team costs reached over $2.5 million, $900,000 greater than had they been when the club was based in Melbourne. Match receipts were $100,000 lower than expected with an average of only $7202 taken for SCG games.

Dixon appointed: Former Victorian Liberal politician Brian Dixon, dubbed 'The Minister for Getting His Picture in the Paper', was appointed as executive director of the Club in October 1982. His services were terminated by the Board on 7 May 1983. Dixon sued days later; but the matter was never resolved.

The lost cheque: The cash-strapped Sydney operation raised a $500,000 loan in December 1982 through Westpac under a VFL guarantee. The Swans' accountant, Barry Lyon, passed the cheque to the office boy for banking – who lost it. An embarrassed Lyon obtained a replacement from the bank.

Dearly departed: Garrie Hutchinson writes in the *Age* that 'To have your football team taken out of town is like a death in the family.'

The new strip: *Cleo* magazine editor Sue Wendt reveals that the new glamour boys of the VFL, the Sydney Swans, will pose for a magazine photo spread – wearing somewhat less than their guernseys.

Leading goalkicker: Tony Morwood was the Swans leading goalkicker in 1982 with a total of 45 goals. Brothers Shane and Paul Morwood also kicked nine and 12 goals respectively, bringing the family's total for the year to 66.

SYDNEY

A turning point

Friday, 14 May 1983 was a turning point in the history of the club.

The VFL agreed to subsidise the SMFC with an additional $900,000 and appointed a new eight-man board to run the club. The SMFC representatives were John Keogh and Michael Edgley.

The two and a half hour League meeting placed the SMFC into a scheme of arrangement to settle the club's outstanding debts. In all, past and present players were owed a total of $334,385, including $36,500 to senior coach Rick Quade, $17,500 to captain Barry Round and $15,900 to vice-captain Mark Browning. There were 300 unsecured creditors and the club had a deficit of $1,679,789, with assets of only $16,364. The largest creditor was the Westpac Banking Corporation.

Michael Edgley.

The name of the club was changed to the Sydney Swans Limited. Barry Lyons, a man with a sharp pencil, was named Sydney manager to control expenditure; Barry Rogers would stay as general manager until the end of the year.

More than one year later, the VFL's Annual Report for the period to 31 October 1984 bore an explanatory note: 'An unsecured loan to the Sydney Swans Ltd has been made by the League to fund the company's Scheme of Arrangement and ongoing operations in accordance with the Scheme. Further advances subsequent to 31 October 1984 have increased the loan to $1,432,000'.

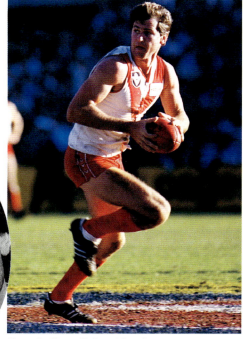
Dennis Carroll: loyal leader.

Stevie Wright: hard worker.

Bernie Evans: full of fight.

Trailblazers of the north

The Sydney-based Swans had their problems. The critical shortage of money was causing a morale problem. This was compounded by living in a city where the only way to get real 'news' was to drive to the airport and buy a Melbourne paper or *Inside Football*. There was no media hype, no mention of the game by any radio station.

Some players were still flying in: some even had to be introduced on match days to their new team-mates. The distance from friends and relatives in Melbourne was a vital factor. Its impact was most noticeable among the wives and companions of the players, with disagreements, extra-marital relationships, break-ups and a yearning to return to Melbourne. These pressures caused several players to quit and continue their careers at other clubs.

Successive losses in 1984 to Carlton, Essendon, Melbourne and St Kilda were not the ideal preparation for the much-awaited July 1 match against Collingwood at the SCG. Much had gone on behind the scenes – outside of football and in private lives. Following a punch-up in the car park which left coach Rick Quade with a blackened eye, the selectors produced a bombshell: they dropped Barry Round to the Reserves. He announced his retirement. Rick Quade was hospitalised with a recurrence of a bleeding ulcer and Tony Franklin became caretaker coach as Collingwood swept to a 31-point victory. Rick Quade, under pressure, resigned.

Bob Hammond, a SANFL-Norwood legend and recent SA coach was enticed to resurrect the Swans. Hammond only coached Sydney for eight games but his straight-talking maturity and common sense got the players back into believing in themselves. Barry Round returned to the side on August 26 and the Swans handed out a blistering 56-point defeat to the top side Essendon, 23.17 (155) to 14.15 (99).

CLUB NEWS 1983–1985

Edgley replaces Sir James: Sir James Hardy resigned as President on 23 January 1983. Dixon, without Board authority, appointed Michael Edgley for a period of three years.

13 fit men: The Swans first game of the season on 27 March 1983 at the SCG left them with only 13 fit players, yet the team managed to grind out a heart-thumping one-point win over Essendon.

Board meeting: Far from an April Fools joke, a 'secret' meeting on 1 April 1983 realised if the club continued to trade, Board members would be liable. After discussions with the Board, the VFL offered to assume full management control of the SMFC.

Foschini wins, VFL loses: On 15 April 1983 Swans player Silvio Foschini won a Supreme Court judgement and his clearance to St Kilda. The Supreme Court ruled the VFL Permit rules and regulations were in restraint of trade and therefore invalid.

Dixon decision: A board meeting of the South Melbourne Club Limited on 7 May 1983 unanimously resolved to terminate the services of Mr Brian Dixon, the executive director.

One away win: Visits to Victoria in the entire 1983 season ended in defeat, with only one exception. On May 14 the Swans beat Geelong at Kardinia Park.

11th position: Finishing just two games ahead of St Kilda, the Swans with five wins escaped the wooden spoon to finish 11th in 1983.

Tough opener: Sydney lost to reigning

1983 – 1985

NSW Premier Neville Wran meets the Edelstens – the good doctor and Leanne.

John Northey: had to go.

Extraordinary Edelsten

One of the messiest deals in football occured in 1985 when the VFL sold the Sydney Swans to the Powerplay-Edelsten consortium. Edelsten, Bob Pritchard and their Powerplay operation were to become major players for an extraordinary three years.

On 31 July 1985, 'The Victorian Football League took only two hours to sell the Sydney Swans to football-mad Sydney doctor Geoffrey Edelsten, for an estimated $6 million,' according to the *Australian*. The agreement between Edelsten and the VFL for buying the Swans in reality was $2.932 million – this included paying the club's debts of $1.432 million. An independent review of Edelsten's finances commissioned by the VFL had concluded that 'Dr Edelsten has the capacity to fund the proposed financial commitments.' On the night of the announcement Edelsten at his Dural home revealed to Bob Pritchard that the funds required were not available.

By early 1986, it was clear a rift had developed between Pritchard and Edelsten when the doctor was not invited to the media launch. On July 1, less than a year after taking the helm, Dr Edelsten resigned as chairman of the Sydney Swans.

On 7 May 1988, three years after Edelsten had bought the Swans for almost $3 million, the Sydney club licence was sold back to the VFL for ten dollars. At that time, the merchant bank Hambros alone was owed some $3.2 million from the Powerplay disaster.

Dr Edelsten was struck off the NSW medical roll in 1988. In 1990 he was convicted and jailed for six months for conspiring to pervert the course of justice and for soliciting a killer to assault a former patient. Dr Edelsten was also struck off the Victorian medical roll in 1992.

The football romp of Dr Edelsten had lasted two seasons – seasons in which glamour and marketing hype were a substitute for on-field performance.

Northey too quiet

There was no way that John Northey and Dr Edelsten were going to sit comfortably together, and as Edelsten had the upper hand the coach had to go. Northey had great credentials as a player at Richmond and as a coach at Ballarat, but Edelsten wanted someone more flamboyant, a headline grabber who fitted the new glittering image. It mattered little to him that the deeply thoughtful, quiet and determined Northey was respected by the players. His record of six wins and 16 losses in 1985 did not read well, but he was building some teamwork, tactics and spirit in the disrupted club. Northey went on to Melbourne, and two years later had them in the finals.

Hidden partners

Published revelations in November 1985 showed Dr Edelsten was not the sole owner. He had obtained joint venture partners in Powerplay. Westeq, a Perth company had obtained an interest in the Swans by investing $400,000 in Powerplay. Westeq also lent $1 million to Sydney Swans Limited, a $2 company owned by Powerplay. Westeq, whose chairman was former Perth Lord Mayor Michael Michaels, had provided most of the $3 million to buy the Swans. Each of the 11 VFL clubs received $255,697 from the purchase of the Swans: only three clubs, Geelong, Essendon and Carlton, were able to show a 1985 surplus without the cash from the Swans.

1983 – 1985 HONOUR ROLL

Year	Pos	Leading Goalkicker	No.	Best & Fairest	Captain	Coach
1983	11th	Craig Braddy	48	Mark Browning	Barry Round	Rick Quade
1984	10th	Warwick Capper	39	Bernie Evans	Round/Browning	Quade/Bob Hammond
1985	10th	Warwick Capper	45	Stephen Wright	Mark Browning	John Northey

Premiers Hawthorn at Princes Park in the opener on 31 March 1984. After nine rounds, Sydney was in fourth place with six wins. However, with five successive losses and the instability following the resignation of coach Rick Quade, the side tumbled to finish 10th.

Roach new CEO: SANFL general manager Don Roach was appointed new CEO of Sydney on 15 October 1984.

Introducing Geoffrey Edelsten: The Melbourne *Herald* reported on 9 January 1985 that Sydney doctor Geoffrey Edelsten had offered to pay off debts and finance operations of the Sydney club. Within days, 'a Sydney businessman, living in Melbourne' (Richard Pratt) becomes another interested party. At the end of January, the Basil Sellers syndicate was a third bidder.

Northey becomes coach: Former Richmond Premiership player John Northey returned to the VFL as coach of Sydney in 1985. Carlton poached the exciting David Rhys-Jones from the Swans – another factor to destabilise confidence within the club.

Bids all round: In March 1985 the VFL announced that it was delighted that it had three soundly based bids for private ownership of the Sydney Swans.

What happened? On 14 April 1985 HSV-7 'pulled the plug' on a Sydney v Fitzroy match with only seven minutes to go. The switchboard at the station went into overdrive as irate fans voiced their objections.

Hafey appointed: Sydney appoints Tom Hafey to replace John Northey on 3 September 1985.

SYDNEY

The spirit of Sydney: showbiz at the Sydney Cricket Ground.

Hafey's impact

Almost before the ink was dry on their deal, Pritchard and the doctor cast their net wide for a new coach. Top of the list in coaching circles was Tom Hafey, a vibrant man and a fitness fanatic.

Ever in the spotlight, Geoffrey Edelsten was cheered by 600 Swans members on October 2 when three voted against him buying the club. That night it was announced Melbourne's highly-rated Gerard Healy was a signing for 1986.

A host of others started to join the throng as training began, among them Merv Neagle (Essendon), Stephen James and Tim Barling (Richmond), Greg Williams, David Bolton and Bernard Toohey (Geelong) and Jim Edmond (Footscray). These players soon received the revived tag of 'The Foreign Legion'. Questions were raised about the Swan's salary cap of $1.2 million, and investigations resulted in penalties and fines. But who cared – it was only money.

The 'footy-wise' Hafey possessed the ability to insulate his charges from events outside the playing arena. Both Rod Carter and Craig Davis recall that everything in 1986 was smooth; players happy, bills paid.

1986 produced SCG crowds of 284,312 (11 games) with an average attendance of 25,847; not until 1997 would these records be surpassed. However, Bob Pritchard's marketing strategies had required an outlay of $2.8 million: $400,000 greater than raised by the company's public listing. The 'Doc' was history by the end of the season. By mid-1987, Pritchard had overstayed his welcome and was sent packing: paid out with $100,000 plus shares. The 1987 on-field success brought a $600,000 operating profit, but the drain of a satellite television company called Sportsplay was horrendous. After losses of some $14 million, Sportsplay was unloaded to Alan Bond for one dollar in October 1987.

A great opening

By the time the season began, Sydney was buzzing. The paparazzi switched on, and brought out the free-loaders and 'flash-trash' to the SCG matches. The food, the wine and the stories flowed.

Six straight victories in 1986 provided the Swans with their best opening in 50 years. Sydney held second place for most of the year, but soon exited the finals, losing by 16 points to Carlton in the Qualifying Final, and to Fitzroy 13.16 (94) to 13.11 (89) in the First Semi-final. Blond bombshell Warwick Capper kicked 92 goals.

1986–1988 HONOUR ROLL

Year	Pos	Leading Goalkicker	No.	Best & Fairest	Captain	Coach
1986	4th	Warwick Capper	92	Gerard Healy	Dennis Carroll	Tom Hafey
1987	4th	Warwick Capper	103	Gerard Healy	Dennis Carroll	Tom Hafey
1988	7th	Barry Mitchell	35	Gerard Healy	Dennis Carroll	Tom Hafey

 Greg Williams, an amazing winner of the ball at centre bounces and a master of the creative handpass, won the club's sixth Brownlow Medal in 1986. He polled 17 votes to share the medal with Hawthorn's Robert DiPierdomenico. Williams played in all 24 matches and was the Swans' highest possession winner, but he could not beat Gerard Healy for the club's Best and Fairest that year.

Williams: handball master.

CLUB NEWS 1986–1988

Queen's Birthday shock: In a vicious game, Sydney overwhelmed the Bombers in muddy Windy Hill conditions to win by 20 points on 9 June 1986. David Bolton (Swans) became the first man to be charged and suspended (for eye-gouging) on video evidence.

Capper zooms: Warwick Capper kicked 10.1 against Richmond at the SCG on 18 May 1986, the first time a Swan had kicked 10 in a game since Jack Graham in 1948. In four successive wins, Capper was prominent, kicking six goals against Geelong, three against Footscray, eight against Essendon and five versus Melbourne.

Carroll injured: After a top season, captain Dennis Carroll suffered an untimely injury in the game against Fitzroy at Victoria Park in the last round. The absence of his defensive skills (honed in 107 games) largely contributed to the Swans sustaining two consecutive defeats in the finals.

Awesome display: At the SCG on 4 April 1987, only 15,268 spectators were witness to an awesome display against Footscray. The Swans had over 390 disposals, including 186 handpasses. Williams, Healy, Browning and Murphy all had in excess of 30 possessions.

Close calls: Against front-runners Carlton on May 1 under SCG lights, 33,659 watched the Blues take the lead with seven minutes remaining. In a barnstorming finish, the Swans scraped home by seven points. The fol-

1986 – 1988

Warrick Capper uses Hawthorn's Chris Langford as a recliner as he takes a big grab.

Huge wins, a shattering finish

The West Coast Eagles and the Brisbane Bears were born on 1 October 1986 with licenses worth $4 million each. New players attracted to Sydney for the 14-team season of 1987 were, Michael Byrne (Hawthorn), the Cordy brothers, Neil and Graeme (Footscray) and Wayne Henwood, a good ruckman in Glenelg's twin SANFL Premierships of 1985 and 1986.

In their new guernseys with a Sydney Opera House silhouette on the chest, the Swans started in great style, recording their greatest win over Collingwood (91 points), followed by a 102-point victory over Footscray. After eight rounds, only one and a half games separated nine clubs, with Carlton and Sydney leading.

Losing three in a row mid-season dropped Sydney to third, but then came eight wins (the best run since 1936), capped by three successive weeks of kicking 30 goals or more. More losses then shook them from top spot. They then played three of the last four games at the dreaded Princes Park. They lost heavily to both Carlton and Hawthorn (and to Geelong in Sydney). In the last round, the Swans wrapped up a double chance with Capper kicking his 99th goal for the year to seal a nail-biting eight-point win over 11th placed Fitzroy: the Swans' first win after 34 consecutive failures at Princes Park.

Sydney was embarrassingly overwhelmed in both their finals: a 99-point loss to Hawthorn and 76-point loss to Melbourne. The funereal silence in the rooms after the game was shattered only by the violent outbursts of criticism from several officials. Their words had a devastating impact on the players.

The big sell-off

By February 1988, Capper was gone: sold to Brisbane, and his transfer fee of some $400,000 disappeared swiftly into the gaping holes of the Powerplay operation.

There were stories of lack of basic medical supplies; of wingman David Murphy receiving a cut at training and having to drive to his own doctor to have stitches; of phones disconnected, cars repossessed. The end of Powerplay was nigh. On May 7, the Swans' licence was sold back to the VFL for 10 dollars.

Sydney failed by one game in 1988 to reach the final five, with a game record of 12 wins, 10 losses. However figures often lie: while the Swans suffered some fearful defeats, they also produced displays worthy of Premiership contenders.

As the crowds fell away, so did the morale. Many players rebelled against the training regimen of coach Tom Hafey. His contract was terminated on September 7.

On 12 December 1988, the VFL chief commissioner Ross Oakley announced that a new group had taken over the affairs of the Swans for a period of five years. A total of 16 owners invested $250,000 each to meet outstanding player contracts of some $800,000, as well as settling many other debts of the club.

Healy: linkman.

Gerard Healy capped his first three brilliant years in Sydney with the 1988 Brownlow Medal. Healy was one of the experienced players at the club who responded to Tom Hafey's positive coaching and the new club spirit in Sydney. His game was characterised by great ball-getting skills, fine marking and brilliant linking work in the forward zones. After 81 games for the Swans, he retired due to chronic wrist problems at the age of 29.

lowing week against the equally dangerous Hawthorn, a late surge for Sydney sealed another close one by eight points.
Largest SCG crowd: A record VFL crowd of 39,763 saw Hawthorn and Sydney face each other for top spot on 10 August 1986. The Hawks whipped the Swans – by 98 points.
Finally, a win in Carlton: In Round 22, an out-of-form Sydney met Fitzroy at Princes Park where the Swans had lost 34 consecutive games against Carlton, Fitzroy and Hawthorn. The 22-year hoodoo ended when Sydney won by eight points. The victory secured third place for the Swans in the finals.
Hafey's 500th: Sydney coach Tom Hafey joined coaching legends Jock McHale and Allan Jeans when he coached his 500th senior game in the Qualifying Final on 6 September 1987 His previous coaching stints had been at Richmond from 1966 to 1976 and at Collingwood and Geelong.
Capper's century: Warwick Capper kicked four goals when Sydney suffered a 99-point thrashing by Hawthorn in the Qualifying Final. This took him to 103 goals for the year, the best haul of goals by a Swan since Bob Pratt's 103 in 1935.
The stylish Healy: Gerard Healy was universally acknowledged as the best footballer of the 1988 season. Skilful and stylish as ruck-rover, he won his third consecutive club Best and Fairest award that season. In 1984 Healy also had won a club Best and Fairest award at his former club, Melbourne, and he topped their goalkicking in 1982.

SYDNEY

Bernard Toohey: sterling service.

Captain Dennis Carroll, Willesee and coach Col Kinnear.

A new deal

The new consortium led by Mike Willesee faced the future beyond 1988 boldly. Willesee held a 20% interest, John Gerahty 20%, Basil Sellers 20%, Jack and Peter Weinert 10%, Craig Kimberley 10%, Glenn Wheatley 5%, with several others holding one per cent each or less.

The merchant bank Hambros hit the League and the Swans' new owners with the facts of their deal with Powerplay, in which the club's licence had been used as security. It had been pivotal to the deal between the new owners and the VFL that they would not be responsible for debts of the previous owners. The matter of the $3.2 million owed to Hambros was pursued through the courts for another year, with a confidential settlement being reached.

From another traumatic season, the new owners in 1989 would lose near to $1.4 million, in addition to the required payment of $1,050,000 for the VFL licence.

Support dwindles as failure mounts

Col Kinnear, a former Coburg VFA and North Melbourne Reserves coach, was appointed as head coach in 1989. Kinnear had early success with four wins from the first five games. Then came a succession of critical injuries, including a wrist injury to Healy which put him out of the game. The minor round ended with Sydney short of the five in seventh place, with a win/loss record of 11:11, with eight of the defeats by three goals or less.

The 1990 season was a disaster for Sydney. The side managed only five century scores and finished second last in 13th place. Home support was wiped out – the best attendance was 12,551, with many of the SCG matches attendances below five figures. Morale was at its lowest point since the movement from Melbourne in 1982. On May 14, with the club facing a $1.5 million loss, executive director Geoff Slade announced a 20 per cent salary cut for players and staff, to produce savings of $600,000. Slade resigned on July 27, and shortly afterwards Barry Breen left, after less than two years as CEO. Breen was replaced by Barry Rogers who had long been part of the club, both at South and Sydney.

Goal! The Swanettes shake it about as Sydney celebrates another score.

CLUB NEWS 1989–1992

Thirds return: The Third 18s returned to the VFL competition in 1989 coached by Greg Harris. They had been ditched by Powerplay in 1986. During the season, 59 Sydney-based players participated, 16 earned promotion to the Reserves and two players (Glenn Page and Sandford Wheeler) reached the Seniors. The Thirds remained until the end of 1991, when they were overtaken by the creation of the Victorian State Football League Under 18 competition.

Kinnear a rare coach: Col Kinnear coached the Sydney side for three seasons, from 1989 to 1991. He is one of only three men who coached in League ranks without having ever played VFL football. The others were Hugh Thomas (St Kilda) and Alan Miller (South Melbourne).

Williams cops eight weeks: The 9 June 1989 game against Carlton was spiteful. David Rhys-Jones (Carlton) was reported three times for striking Greg Williams. On viewing video, the VFL Commission cited Williams who was suspended for eight games. Rhys-Jones was found guilty on only one charge and was given a further suspended sentence, added to three carried over from the year before!

First at Carlton for 25 years: The single success of a disappointing season came on opening day, 31 March 1990. Barry Mitchell goaled inside the last minute giving the Swans victory by five points – their first win over the Blues at Princes Park since 1965.

1989 – 1992

Capper pulls down one with snow on it.

Capper back in town

Back for 1991 was Warwick Capper, but his glamour, magic and confidence never shone again. In August, Col Kinnear announced he would not coach the following season. Of the 15 clubs, the Harboursiders finished in 12th place, one place higher than 1990. The Reserves finished on the bottom, while the Thirds missed the finals by one game.

When Kinnear stepped down, media speculation centred on Kevin Sheedy, but he re-signed with Essendon for another three years. On October 14, Gary Buckenara, the former Hawthorn forward flanker, became coach of Sydney. His would be a tough initiation: of the first eight rounds, the Swans beat West Coast (SCG), Carlton (Princes Park), drew with Melbourne (MCG) and thrashed Brisbane (SCG). The victory over the Bears would the last Sydney would enjoy for a long time: they lost their last 15 games to finish on the bottom at 15th place.

The club that won't die

At the end of 1991, key players were departing, and rumours about threats to the very existence of the club pushed morale close to desperation level. Media and newspaper support in Sydney was close to nil, with the club forced to spend $2000 weekly for a regular sports page with the *Daily Telegraph*. SCG crowds for 1992 totalled 109,590 for 11 games.

In the days before a meeting at AFL headquarters, pages of text were devoted to the issue, even in Sydney newspapers. The *Sydney Morning Herald* on the Monday before blazed a front-page story: 'The Sydney Swans are dead.'

The AFL meeting on 14 October 1991 heard an impassioned plea from Peter Weinert. Sydney were given five days to produce a guaranteed plan for their survival, with $2 million required in sponsorships.

It was revealed the AFL had not only sought Carlton for a merger with the Swans, but mid-season had proposed a merger option to North Melbourne. With Sydney toiling to meet their tight deadline, AFL chief commissioner Ross Oakley telephoned on October 19, proposing a merger with the Bears to become the Brisbane Swans.

The momentous two and a half hour meeting that followed had only one speaker in favour of meeting Sydney's requests: Collingwood president Allan McAlister. At 7.33 p.m., an 11–nil vote waived the Swans $1.985 million outstanding licence fee, providing working capital for the club for three years.

The Swans were to survive – the club refused to die.

1989 – 1992 HONOUR ROLL

Year	Pos	Leading Goalkicker	No.	Best & Fairest	Captain	Coach
1989	7th	Bernard Toohey	27	Mark Bayes	Dennis Carroll	Col Kinnear
1990	13th	Jim West	34	Stephen Wright	Dennis Carroll	Col Kinnear
1991	12th	Jason Love	52	Barry Mitchell	Dennis Carroll	Col Kinnear
1992	15th	Simon Minton-Connell	60	Paul Kelly	Dennis Carroll	Gary Buckenara

Life-threatening injury: Gareth John, Swans' ruckman, suffered a 'one-in-a-million' injury in an accidental collision with Essendon's ruckman Simon Madden. Madden's knee caught John in the throat, inflicting a crushed larynx. Operations repaired the damage at St Vincent's Hospital Sydney. Gareth returned to running in July, and played again with Sydney in 1992 and 1993.

Anzac Day blitz: At the MCG, Sydney led North by 30 points midway through the third quarter on 19 April 1991. Sydney failed to score for the rest of the match while North kicked 12.12 to win by nine goals. In the last quarter, 10 Swans failed to get a kick, and eight of them didn't have a possession!

Dennis Carroll: Carroll, captain of the Swans for seven seasons, became the first player to complete 200 League games as a Sydney player on 19 July 1992. Carroll had started with Sydney as a winger, but became one of the great all-rounders, his time at Sydney even including a stint at half-back.

Last at the Lake Oval: On 27 July 1991, the Sydney Under 19s carried the red and white colours for the last time at Albert Park, defeating Fitzroy.

Williams cleared to Carlton: In a three-way deal involving Carlton, Fitzroy and Sydney, Greg Williams was cleared to the Blues in 1992. The Swans gained Simon Minton-Connell (Carlton) and Darren Kappler (Fitzroy). Sydney were later fined $50,000 and Williams $25,000 for not making 'full disclosure of football payments in 1990'. Williams was also deregistered until May 3.

SYDNEY

Kelly: young captain.

Ron Barassi: brought his winning ways.

The strong and the silent

Through all the administration problems, the coaching changes and negative headlines that beset the Swans, the steady servants of the club kept their heads down and kept going. They were off the field – the training and support staff – and they were on the field, playing with pride of performance. Typical was Dennis Carroll, captain for six years and loyal to the club through 217 games. His grace, high marking and long kicking from centre half-back were a delight to watch. Rod 'the tilt' Carter put in 10 hard years as one of the tightest full-backs in the game. David Murphy was a champion on his wing and played 156 games, displaying his pace, fine ball handling and an ability to absorb punishment. Rover Barry Mitchell faded at Collingwood and Carlton, but he had proved his mettle in Sydney through 170 games for the club he loved and had to leave. Mark Bayes' long career, distinguished by his brilliant marking and raking left-footers, was highlighted by a Best and Fairest in 1989. Stevie Wright played 246 games for South and the Swans, and was always hard at the ball. He won Best and Fairests in 1985 and 1990. These players were leaders among those who kept the Swans afloat.

Rod Carter.

Barry Mitchell.

The recovery

As the Swans approached their 120th season, it was announced the former North Melbourne administrator Ron Joseph would become supremo of footy in NSW in an AFL-funded position. It would take time before Joseph found himself accepted by the established Swans management.

In 1993 Paul Kelly became captain at age 23. By week four the Swans had suffered three losses. The sacking of Buckenara followed, and on May 4 Ron Barassi was appointed coach. His coming was only the tip of the iceberg, as the AFL Commission launched a Sydney rescue mission.

Mike Willesee announced that the key to restructuring was: (1) the Swans would become a traditional membership-based club, (2) Barassi would coach until the end of 1995 and (3) Alan Schwab would be appointed to Sydney, heading a rescue task force. This mission was seriously damaged when Alan Schwab was found dead in a Sydney hotel room on 18 June 1993, but the AFL's committment was secured when Ken Gannon replaced him.

Barassi's effect was immediate, despite seven further losses. On June 27, Sydney broke its 26-game losing drought with a 40-point victory over Melbourne.

The two Ronnies

Even though Sydney brought home another wooden spoon in 1994, there was a new feeling about the Swans. Morale was up with the improvement of SCG facilities, and as 'the two Ronnies' (Barassi and Joseph) and new chairman Richard Colless got to work.

The jigsaw slowly was coming together with the Swans maintaining their accent on youth, and also gaining former Fitzroy captain Paul Roos, a 269 game veteran. Joseph battled to obtain the services of Tony Lockett from St Kilda, with negotiations taking several months. The announcement of Lockett's move to Sydney came on October 21.

A hiccup occured at the February 21 draft when it was confirmed Sydney had exceeded the $2.3 million salary cap. This drew a $10,000 AFL fine and the resignation of Ron Joseph, who carried the can.

The Swans won only eight of 22 games in 1995, yet the improvement was noticeable. The value of Lockett was clear: he contributed 33 per cent of the Sydney score in his first season, kicking 110 goals and 44 behinds.

Ron Barassi stepped down at the end of 1995 (he became a Sydney director), and Rodney Eade, an innovative man from the modern school, was named coach for 1996.

CLUB NEWS 1993–1996

Mitchell defects: Barry Mitchell, the Swans Best and Fairest of 1991 (170 games) was drafted by Collingwood for $1,025,000 over five years.

Carroll retires: The last playing link with South Melbourne was severed when Dennis Carroll made his final appearance on 24 April 1993. He called it a day after 219 games dating back to the Lake Oval in 1981. Carroll was captain of Sydney for seven seasons (1986–92) and played under eight coaches, six general managers and five owners.

Barassi's first game: Only 9214 were at the SCG to see Barassi's first game as coach on 9 May 1993. Sydney suffered their 24th consecutive loss. Carlton coach David Parkin commented: 'I saw them in the last couple of weeks and they were a rabble. They'd have to be pleased with the way they committed themselves …'

Sickening collision: In the last quarter at the SCG on 23 May 1993, Sydney's top forward Richard Osborne was knocked unconscious in a sickening collision with team-mate Dale Lewis. Though concussed, a brain-scan and examinations cleared Osborne, who returned to the Senior line-up after only four weeks.

Brereton recruited: While their primary accent was on youth in recruiting, the Swans also gained the experience of Hawthorn's Dermott Brereton. Following a pre-season practice game at Glenferrie, new Swan Brereton was found guilty of standing on the head of

1993-1996

Hullabaloo at the scoreboard end as the Swans' cheer squad moves into top gear.

Kevin Dyson collects the ball.

The Swans in Grand Final

Despite the vitriol poured on them by some sections of the media, the Swans received a warm reception from the people who counted when they took part in the street parade through Melbourne. The roar when they ran onto the MCG was overwhelming.

The AFL Cinderfellas in the early stages took it all before them, leading by 25 points midway in the second term. Then North Melbourne lifted their work rate, and errors by the Harboursiders gave North a two-point lead at half-time, 8.7 (55) to 8.5 (53).

Ruckman Greg Stafford, who had been so dominant early for the Swans, tired. The game swung to North in the third term and they soon had a strong grip with a 25-point break at the last change, at 12.14 (86) to 9.7 (61).

Eade did everything to lift the dropping heads, but the difference was that North, after Preliminary Finals for two successive years, was ready, and Sydney was not.

Though losing, the Swans had turned the corner. Gerard Wright in the *Sun Herald* summed up the Sydney view: 'Sydneysiders have flocked to the Swans not just because they're winners, but for the pluck and style they have displayed ... Thanks, Swans, for a wonderful year.'

Drive to finals

In the AFL Centenary Year, after two matches (a loss in Adelaide by 90 points, and an SCG defeat by Fremantle) the Swans were 100–1 to make the finals. Driven by Paul Kelly, Tony Lockett, Andrew Dunkley, Paul Roos, Greg Stafford and a host of others, Sydney began to produce exciting Lazarus-like performances the likes of which the red and white had not experienced in years. From 12th place in 1995 to minor Premiers was a breathtaking advance. Lockett captured the Coleman Medal, kicking 114 goals before the finals. However, his most memorable score was against Essendon in the Preliminary Final, when he kicked a behind from outside the 50 metre mark after the siren, to put the Swans into their first Grand Final since 1945.

The build-up to Sydney's biggest ever game was fuelled by the drama of a tribunal charge against full-back Andrew Dunkley. This reached Supreme Court level on the eve of the Grand Final, when the Swans succeeded in obtaining an injunction allowing him to play in the Premiership decider.

1993–1996 HONOUR ROLL

Year	Pos	Leading Goalkicker	No.	Best & Fairest	Captain	Coach
1993	15th	Simon Minton-Connell	41	Paul Kelly	Paul Kelly	Gary Buckenara/Barassi
1994	15th	Simon Minton-Connell	68	Daryn Cresswell	Paul Kelly	Ron Barassi
1995	12th	Tony Lockett	110	Tony Lockett	Paul Kelly	Ron Barassi
1996	2nd	Tony Lockett	121	Paul Kelly	Paul Kelly	Rodney Eade

Rayden Tallis (Hawthorn) and suspended for seven weeks. Later in the season, Brereton was found guilty on two striking charges and suspended for another seven weeks. He played only seven games before moving to Collingwood.

1000th defeat: The Swans suffered their 1000th loss in League football when losing to Adelaide in Sydney on 10 April 1994.

Full force of Lockett: Sydney's Peter Caven suffered a compound fracture of the nose and required plastic surgery when hit by St Kilda's Tony Lockett in the first quarter on 8 May 1994. Lockett was suspended for eight matches. Sydney lost the match, giving the Swans the unwanted record of the longest span a club had played without a Premiership: 1204 games had elapsed since their Flag in 1933.

Rogers retires: After a 24-year association with South Melbourne and Sydney, life member and general manager Barry Rogers announced his retirement in May 1994.

Kelly's Brownlow: Swans captain Paul Kelly won Australian football's highest award in 1996. Kelly thanked coach Ron Barassi and former teammate Barry Mitchell at the ceremony for their contribution to his, and the Swans', success.

New SCG record: The SCG overflowed with 44,047 ($206,561.20) to see Sydney defeat Geelong by 51 points. The 11 home-and-away games drew 270,309. Two finals drew a further 78,741. Membership for the year climbed to 9525.

367

SYDNEY

Swan songs ...

'Ian Collins, AFL football operations manager, on the Swans: "What do they [the clubs] want them to be? Dead in the water? ... They don't want them to be successful – or not too successful. They like them there, as long as they are the easy-beats ..."'
Trevor Grant, *Herald Sun*, 16 November 1994

~

'The memories are still vivid; of fist-fights in the car park when one Swan found that another had been showing more than an inordinate amount of attention to his wife ... of comforting a tearful club official who was devastated the Swans were crumbling around him ... of the Swans losing over and again ... of realising one had to get out of here before everyone got hurt ...'
Greg Growden, *Sydney Morning Herald*, 21 September 1996

~

'Australian Rules is still a silly game. It has been around for 100 years. It always was a silly game and it always will be ... But spare me from all the superlatives. Save me from all the sales talk. Don't try telling me it's "the game". I've seen it before. It's not new and improved. And it's certainly not "the game". It's aerial ping pong, the same silly old game that's been around for 100 years ...'
Mike Gibson, *Daily Telegraph*, 2 September 1996

~

'...The Sydney sporting media, however, are clearly in need of a lot more match practice ... They miss the essential point – that Rules is only incidentally to do with football and everything to do with the tribe. The football games themselves are merely the way you keep score ... The essence of it is this: you are born into an Australian Rules tribe and it immediately becomes the central fact of your identity and purpose on the planet ...'
Bob Mills, *Australian Financial Review,*, 27 September 1996

The key players of today's Swans

Paul Kelly.

Tony Lockett.

Paul Roos.

Andrew Dunkley.

M. O'Loughlin.

Paul Kelly.
The captain's courage and his skilful running play is always an inspiration. Occasionally he does the impossible and the Swans go into overdrive. He is enemy No.1 to the opposition and is teamed-up, tagged and buffeted about.

Tony Lockett.
The key to the Swans hope, the big, enormously strong and fearsome forward is virtually unstoppable when he gets going and the team get the ball to him. Suffers a lot of attention, but can never be shut down.

Paul Roos.
The highly skilled and durable backman reads the play as well as anyone in the game, and is there to take the stopping mark and the relieving kick. He says the move from Fitzroy to Sydney gave him a couple of extra seasons, and he is making the most of them.

Andrew Dunkley.
Sydney say he is the best full-back in the League, in spite of the other claimants. He certainly has the build, the cool, the toughness and the skills to contain the best full-forwards in the land.

Michael O'Loughlin.
The best is probably yet to come, and its going to be mighty good. He is a slick and elusive forward, a brilliant mark and a beautiful kick, with an inbuilt radar when the goals are in the picture.

Mark Bayes.

Dale Lewis.

Daryn Cresswell.

Craig O'Brien.

Greg Stafford.

Mark Bayes.
Bayes has been at the Swans since 1985 and has seen the highs and the lows. He is a shrewd player now, adaptable to either defence or attack and is one of the best kicks in the League, particularly on his natural left foot.

Dale Lewis.
A most gifted player who was sometimes accused of being a bit casual, until people realised that was his way. The Swan's leading mark taker and third-highest kickgetter came third in Best and Fairest in 1997.

Daryn Cresswell.
Tough and undemonstrative, Cresswell is underrated by some outsiders, but showed his value again in 1997 with second in the club Best and Fairest. He is a strong mark and never shirks the hard stuff as he links up the play around the centre and half-forward.

Craig O'Brien.
A talented and courageous player, who provides an alternative route to goal when Tony Lockett has defenders hanging all over him. A tenacious mark and an excellent kick.

Greg Stafford.
A mobile ruckman who is approaching his full potential with his strong marking and accurate ruckwork. He has lifted his round-the-ground work-rate. Bound to play a key part in the future.

1997

No shortage of support for Sydney, as the fans turn the SCG into a riot of white and red.

At long last the game soars in Sydney

Expectations for 1997 following the Swans' Grand Final appearance were high, and the crowds flocked to the SCG as never before. Media coverage in Sydney became a daily feature for the first time in the Swans' emotion-charged Harbour City existence. However, there was something too relaxed in the performances of the two opening rounds; the Swans losing against the Eagles and the newly renamed Western Bulldogs.

Sydney (still without the injured Lockett) started to claw their way back with an SCG win over Melbourne then a thumping victory over the Saints at Waverley. However, the win at Waverley would be one of only three 'away' wins for the season: the others were at Football Park (Port Adelaide) and the MCG (Melbourne).

It was a different story at the SCG, where the Swans enjoyed an almost record run of successive wins. Attendances climbed with each SCG appearance, and totalled 393,999 by season's end: an average of 35,818 for 11 games. A 20-match winning run was ended by a loss to St Kilda on August 10.

The Swans membership climbed from 9,525 to 22,500. Most of the games in the latter half of 1997 were sold out well in advance of match days. In the match against the Cats on August 31, 46,168 packed the 42,000 capacity SCG.

By early August the Swans were at their highest, in third position. A two-week suspension to Tony Lockett about this time did not help matters. Unfortunately, Sydney fell away badly at the end, and were savaged by the Western Bulldogs in the Qualifying Final.

Headliners of the year were: Paul Kelly, who won a much-deserved accolade with his fourth club Best and Fairest, Daryn Cresswell, who dominated the possession department with 367 kicks; Dale Lewis, Paul Roos and Michael O'Loughlin.

The most immediate question for 1998 is: how much more can the Swans get from Tony Lockett? He will have passed his 32nd birthday as he begins his 16th League season in 1998, having kicked 1166 goals from his 236 matches.

In the broader view, the biggest changes are likely to lie in the ever-advancing presence of the game itself. In a city with a population approaching four million souls, the 21st century will bring Homebush Stadium, with a capacity of 80,000 people, to Australian Football.

Sydney, the footy club, is only the beginning. An abundant future lies ahead for the Australian code.

1997 HONOUR ROLL

Year	Pos	Leading Goalkicker	No.	Best & Fairest	Captain	Coach
1997	7th	Tony Lockett	37	Paul Kelly	Paul Kelly	Rodney Eade

UNIVERSITY

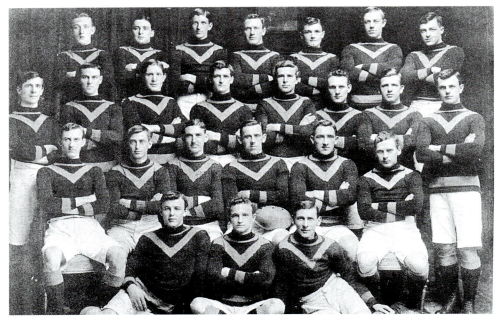

University's 1909 team won seven and drew two of 18 matches.

UNIVERSITY	
Joined VFL	1908
Home ground	East Melbourne Cricket Ground
	Melbourne Cricket Ground
Year retired	1914

Joining the VFL

The University Football Club, affectionately known as the 'Students' or 'Professors', joined the VFL ranks in 1908, registering their uniform and colours as black jersey with blue facing (collar, cuffs, waistband and V), white knickers, black stockings with blue tops, and optional black and blue cap.

Players were required to have completed the Matriculation Certificate or a higher degree as a condition for selection.

A cheering verse

With best of morals I embue
The lines of this, my closing stanza.
You in the outer ground, and you
Who look on from the member's stand, sir,
If you must barrack, then should be
Your war cry, 'University'.

From 'Observations of our National Game', published in *Melbourne University Magazine*.

A dismal record

University Football Club was represented by 112 players during its seven years in the VFL. Gifted centreman and 1913 captain Bert Hurrey had the distinction of being the only player to reach 100 games – he played 101.

During the VFL days, University maintained a team in the Metropolitan Football Association and won a keenly contested Inter-Collegiate Premiership.

In VFL games, University won 27, lost 97 and drew 2. The club defeated each competing side with the exception of Collingwood with whom they managed to draw.

The first season, 1908, was promising and the club finished sixth with eight wins and ten losses. The 1910 season was the most successful, but a loss to Melbourne in the final round ended finals hopes and the club finished sixth, with 10 wins and eight losses. In the next four seasons, from 1911–14, the club managed two wins and finished last on the ladder.

CLUB NEWS 1908–1914

1907 Premiers. The University Football Club was admitted to the Victorian Football League in October 1907 after winning the Metropolitan Football Association Premiership two years in a row.

University defeats Geelong. University recorded its highest score, 13.18 (96), in Round 17 in 1908 when it beat Geelong at the East Melbourne Cricket Ground. They kicked their biggest winning margin in any game in Round 6 when they defeated Melbourne by 60 points.

Is there a doctor in the team? When University played Collingwood in Round 16 in 1909, 13 of the selected 18 University players were medical students or doctors. The result was a draw, the best effort of the students against the Magpies.

On a roll. The students won five consecutive games from Round 9 in 1910 in the club's longest winning streak. After Round 12 they were third on the ladder and likely finalists. Former Carlton player Mick Grace was the club's first coach in 1910 and he took them to sixth on the ladder.

New coach. The former Fitzroy Premiership captain Gerald Brosnan became coach in 1911 and the team won just one game for the season.

Court sensation. University shocked the football world by pressing assault charges against a Carlton player they believed responsible for knocking the University player, Victor Trood, uncon-

Jack Brake – champion

Jack Brake studied Agricultural Science at the University of Melbourne.

A triple blue at University for athletics, football and rifle, he played with University Football Club from 1909–14, in all but one of the club's seasons in the VFL. Known as 'University's sterling follower', his absence from a game in 1914 prompted the newspaper report: 'University with Brake out – and he is practically half the team – gave Richmond a grand go.'

He represented Victoria in six games from 1912–14, was club vice-captain in 1913 and played the third-highest tally of University games with 81, kicking 21 goals. He went on to play for Melbourne in 1915 before enlisting, and again from 1919–21, playing a further 17 games in all. In later life Brake was a member of the VFL Tribunal.

Above: Jack Brake.
Right: Albert Hardkopf.

University plays Geelong (and wins) at the East Melbourne Cricket Ground, June 1909.

The players

Tom Ogilvie, Dave Greenham, George Elliott, Jack Brake, Bert Hurrey, Lester Kelly, Eric Wood and Roy Park all gained Victorian selection while playing with University. Roy Park was just 5 ft 5 in tall and weighed 8 st 10 lb, but was a fast-leading, nippy full-forward who kicked 111 goals in 44 games with the club.

Edgar Kneen was a fine wingman/forward who played in Fitzroy's 1904 Premiership side and, like half-back or forward-flanker Jack West, captained the students for one season.

Many excelled in other sports. Roy Park and Albert Hartkopf played Test cricket and Heinrich Schraeder played at Shield level. Simon Fraser was an Olympic oarsman and Jack Brake held the Australian pole vault title in 1911 and 1914.

The end

E. R. Cordner.

University Football Club left the VFL in 1914. It was termed a 'retirement' and club president Professor Baldwin Spencer explained, 'It was impossible to get the whole team up to League form.' He added 'the demands upon students at examination time precluded them giving that attention to training which was so essential.'

Several players volunteered and enlisted in late 1914, further disrupting the team, and sadly University suffered the VFL's highest number of casualties in World War One.

Melbourne Football Club actively sought the services of the student footballers and club officials. Brake, Little, Bryan, Rodriguez, Park and Doubleday went to Melbourne, while Barker went to Fitzroy, Willis to South Melbourne and McIntosh to Essendon.

1908–1914 HONOUR ROLL

Year	Pos	Leading Goalkicker	No.	Best & Fairest	Captain	Coach
1908	6th	Martin Ratz	25		Tom Fogarty/Edgar Kneen	
1909	7th	Albert Hartkopf	19		Tom Fogarty/Harry Cordner	
1910	6th	Albert Hartkopf	30		Edgar Kneen/Ted Cordner	Mick Grace
1911	10th	Albert Hartkopf	19		George Elliott/Dave Greenham	Gerald Brosnan
1912	10th	Roy Park	22		Elliott/Greenham/Lester Kelly	Gerald Brosnan
1913	10th	Roy Park	53		Bert Hurrey	Victor Upton-Brown
1914	10th	Roy Park	26		Jack West/Roy Park	Gerald Brosnan

scious in a 1911 match. Carlton's Martin Gotz was found guilty but the conviction was quashed on appeal.

Student suspended! In Round 4, 1912, Carl Willis was reported for striking Fred Hansen of St Kilda and became the only University player to be suspended, outed for four weeks.

The beginning of the end. University won its last VFL game in Round 3, 1912 when it beat Richmond at the MCG. The following sequence of 51 losses ended in the club's demise at the end of the 1914 season. University finished last in four out of seven seasons.

Goalkicking champion. Full-forward Roy Park finished equal second on the 1913 goalkicking list with 53 goals in 18 losing games.

For the love of the game. 1913 coach Victor Upton-Brown refused any payment, advocating involvement for the sake of the game.

Rest in peace. University Football Club had 14 known players who lost their lives in World War One, and a number who died soon after as a result of that war. Students who lost their lives included: Rupert Balfe, Arch Corbett, Jack Doubleday, George Elliott, Chris Fogarty, Richard Gibbs, Arthur Hinman, Fred McIntosh, Stan Martin, Stan Neale, James Nicholas, Percy Rodriguez, Robert Seelenmeyer and Maldwyn Williams.

New reserves. University competed in the newly established amateur Reserves competition from 1919, with A and B teams, but never returned to the VFL senior ranks.

WEST COAST

MY CLUB
by Gary Stocks

Any player who has been in a position to make a declaration says there is only one thing which compares to playing in a Premiership – being there at the moment he became a father.

There is no greater feeling than the arrival of a newborn, but a Flag comes closest. For me, being bedside when my three children entered the world was almost overwhelming. I was also fortunate enough to be at another birth which has been dear to my heart.

It was late October 1986 at the Merlin Hotel, just a couple of torpedo kicks away from the WACA Ground. Amid a sea of yellow and blue, in a Hollywood-style launch, the West Coast Eagles joined an expanded VFL competition.

It was a moment many West Australians had craved. An emotion spawned by the stream of stars from these parts who every year drifted east to join Melbourne clubs in the nation's elite competition.

Back then the only fix for footy heads came on Sunday night with the hour-long ABC program 'The Winners', our only chance to catch a glimpse of local heroes starring in the VFL. Players like Maurice Rioli, Robert Wiley, Ross Glendinning, Brad Hardie, the Krakouer brothers, Peter Bosustow and Kenny Hunter. All outstanding players in WA before heading to Melbourne where they achieved superstar status.

It was a source of great annoyance to hear commentators speak of a player's 'League debut' despite having carved out a strong reputation in the WAFL.

Before the Eagles were conceived the only chance West Australians had to compete against the Vics was State of Origin and that annual match became the showcase for football in WA. Now, with the arrival of this new outfit, came the chance to beat them every week.

With Glendinning, Phil Narkle, Wiley, John Annear and Dean Turner leading, the Eagles had managed to provide some experience to a squad that also boasted the youthful expertise of players like John Worsfold, Chris Mainwaring, Michael Brennan and Chris Lewis – players who developed into marque names for the club.

The Eagles' campaign began with a Panasonic Cup match against Footscray, and after being 38 points down at half-time they stormed home to win by 23 points.

While that was the first official game, it was at Subiaco Oval on Sunday, 29 March

The 1992 Premiership Flag is unveiled.

WEST COAST EAGLES	
Year Established	1987
Joined VFL/AFL	1987
Home Grounds	Subiaco, WACA Ground
Premierships	1992, 1994
Brownlow Medals	Nil
Record home crowd	42,209 v St Kilda, 1991
Most games	Guy McKenna, 213
Most goals	Peter Sumich, 514
Notable supporters	Ernie Dingo, Damien Oliver, Dennis Lillee, Tony Bonner

1987 that the club took its first positive steps. Richmond was its foe in the first game played for Premiership points and before a bumper crowd, the local boys recovered from a 33-point three-quarter-time deficit to win by 14 points.

Eleven wins and 11 losses in their first season was more than an adequate start for the fledgling club and since then it has blossomed into a genuine power of the 90s.

Under the direction of Mick Malthouse the Eagles have not missed out on the September action, and have won two Premierships and the hearts of many West Australians.

The plan when the Eagles were launched was to win a Premiership after five years. They made the Grand Final when in their fifth season, but after an enterprising start were overrun by Hawthorn.

That served merely to fire the desire within and a year later West Coast scored an emphatic victory over Geelong. It was a day no Eagles fan will ever forget – the genius of Peter Matera, who won the Norm Smith medal, timely goals from 'the money man' Tony Evans, the brilliance of Peter Sumich at full-forward.

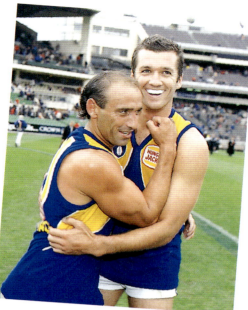

Above: An Eagle ready for battle with the Dockers. Right: Peter Matera and Mitchell White celebrate a win in 1995.

Ross Glendining and John Gastev in 1988.

Waverley, 1988: the Eagles burst through their first finals banner.

It was a remarkable day – and night. Indeed weeks. As weary players wandered in to Subiaco Oval the next morning, having whooped it up in Melbourne overnight, they were greeted by thousands of adoring fans only too willing to celebrate the first trip outside of Victoria for the Premiership Cup.

The players were feted for weeks, a ticker-tape parade a couple of days later evidence of the gratitude and adoration of the West Australian football public. Thousands lined the city streets, 10 to 15 deep in places, as fans tried to get a glimpse of the heroes who had brought the Premiership cup west.

The euphoria was no less evident two years later when again the Eagles eclipsed Geelong in the Grand Final, this time so much more ruthlessly than the first.

A club which had no place to call home in its first three years – shunted from training venue to training venue until moving in to Subiaco Oval in 1990 – had become the competition benchmark.

The Eagles detractors says that the club had a head start. That it was a virtual State side. They forget, though, that stars like Nicky Winmar, Mark Bairstow, Earl Spalding, Michael Christian, Richard Dennis, Craig Starcevich, Darren Bewick, Paul Harding, Mark Hepburn, Michael Mitchell and Peter Wilson were snared before the VFL directors agreed to admit West Coast into the competition.

The decision was not reached until 1 October 1986, making some of those players nervous and unwilling to simply wait another season before trying their hand at elite level. Things were not made easy, given the limited time frame in which to establish the club and its player list, which was merely 35-strong – considerably fewer than its opponents.

From those shaky foundations has been built a solid, stable outfit which has set the standard both on and off the field. Surely there will be more Premierships to come.

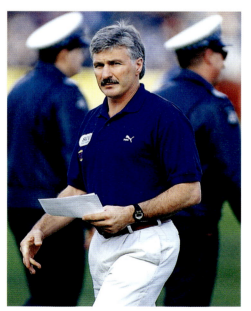

Michael Malthouse in charge, 1995.

WEST COAST

Dean Turner, Don Holmes, Ross Glendinning, Laurie Keene and John Annear: ready.

Polly Farmer and John Annear, 1989.

Giving the Eagles their wings

It was Chairman Mao who suggested that a journey of a thousand miles begins with one step. And WA football's entry into the big league began long before the first official fixture against Richmond on 29 March 1987.

Indeed, the first tottering advances for a West Australian-based VFL franchise were made three and a half years before that historic match when the eight WAFL clubs signed away their control of the game.

The first seeds in the shift of power were sown when the State government appointed a three-man task force on 8 August 1983 to examine the long-term viability of football. That task force, consisting of Bill Mitchell (chairman), John Horgan and Peter Collins, was initiated after a formal request from football for government aid.

Many of the WAFL clubs were struggling and the WAFL's funds were being eroded by repayments on the two-tier stand at Subiaco Oval. Football had fallen on hard times and there were serious doubts whether the game alone could generate the capital to escape the tightening financial noose.

The task force tabled its report to the government on 16 January 1984 and made the following recommendations: That an independent board of directors be appointed to take overall control of the game and that the State government assumes financial responsibility for Subiaco Oval.

Those recommendations were duly adopted when the WAFL's old board of directors voted in favour of an independent board, thus relinquishing its power. WAFL president Vincent Yovich continued as chairman of the new board, businessman Roy Annear resigned as president of South Fremantle to join the new controlling body and Mitchell was the government's representative. Other directors were Dwane Buckland, Tom Stannage, Peter Fogarty and Richard Colless.

To complete the overhaul, the new board, shortly after, appointed the deputy town clerk of the City of Perth, John Walker, as the League's chief executive.

Four of those men would later become key players in the evolution of the West Coast Eagles. Colless, who more recently piloted the Sydney resurgence, was the inaugural West Coast chairman, Mitchell an original board member, Buckland was chairman from 1993–96 and Walker was the club's first chief executive.

The appointment of the new board underlined the problems of club representatives running the game. It was impossible under the old system for directors to divorce themselves from their own club's needs to look at the broader picture.

That was the forerunner to further momentous decisions which would alter forever the structure of the game, right across the nation.

The next key date was 29 October 1985. It was the day that Yovich's four-year reign as chairman of the WAFL came to an end, with Annear taking control.

But more significantly it was the day that VFL commissioners released details of plans for a 14-team national competition, including one from Perth, for 1987.

Ron Alexander, Laurie Keene and Barry Cable, 1991.   Murray Wrensted, 1989.

EAGLES TO 1986

Four of the originals: Chris Mainwaring, John Worsfold, David Hart and Chris Lewis.

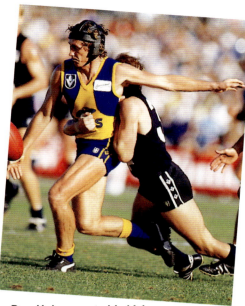

Don Holmes gets his kick.

A VFL team from the West is up and running in just 160 days

There was strong opposition to a Perth VFL team from WAFL loyalists, who considered that to jump in to bed with the VFL would be no less than sleeping with the enemy.

Those detractors considered it a betrayal to link forces with the Victorians who for so long had pillaged the domestic competition by signing local stars on lucrative contracts, deals that the WAFL clubs had no chance of matching.

The pro-VFL contingent lobbied fiercely until on 22 August 1986 the six WAFL directors and six of the eight WAFL clubs voted in favour of a composite team from Perth joining an expanded 14-team VFL competition.

All that was required for a WA side to join this exciting new entity was for approval of the concept to be given by the VFL commission at a meeting on October 1.

In anticipation of the scheme being rubber-stamped, East Fremantle coach Ron Alexander was appointed mentor of a club which as yet had no name, no players and no strip.

A two-thirds majority vote of the Victorian clubs was required to see the face of the game change forever, and there was strong opposition to the expansion. Indeed, had it not been for the fact that several clubs were facing financial ruin the vote would almost certainly have gone the other way.

The first vote was 7-5, one short of the requirement. There was a short adjournment and during that break one club changed its vote, creating an 8-4 result which was enough to grant entry to a WA team.

During the break VFL director Graeme Samuel rang Colless, then a WAFL director, and told him the $10 million licence fee would need to be paid up-front instead of a proposed 10-year instalment period.

The Eagles had 160 days to formulate a squad – a list which was restricted to just 35 players in their first two years and which swelled to 40 in 1989 before reaching parity in 1990 when all clubs had 52-man lists.

Between the time of that phone call from Samuel to Colless and the opening bounce of the 1987 season there was much to be done and little time in which to do it.

Securing the return of former East Perth utility player Ross Glendinning from North Melbourne was the most positive development on the player front. The Eagles also targeted former Subiaco champion Gary Buckenara and East Fremantle ruckman Paul Harding.

Buckenara had been integral in the powerful Hawthorn teams of that time and obviously was a prime target. He agreed to play with the Eagles, but it was not to be. Harding's path to the Eagles was also blocked by the Hawks.

The Victorian Supreme Court ruled that a 1984 agreement signed by Harding declaring his intention to join Hawthorn in 1987 was binding and that Buckenara remained a Hawthorn player because the club had an option agreement written into his contract – an option it wished to exercise.

To rub salt into the wound the Eagles were also fined $60,000 by the VFL after being deemed to have contravened poaching rules.

After dishing out $1 million in transfers the Eagles netted Glendinning, Robert Wiley, Phil Narkle, John Annear and Dean Turner from rival clubs and pinned its faith in speculative selections of young players like John Worsfold, Chris Lewis, Chris Mainwaring, Michael Brennan, Dean Laidley and David Hart.

Its squad in place, the Eagles were ready to play.

Mark Zanotti in the 1989 jumper.

WEST COAST

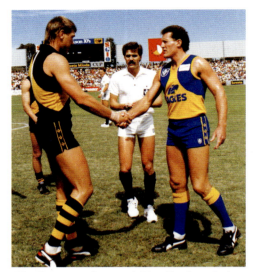
The first toss: Lee and Glendinning shake.

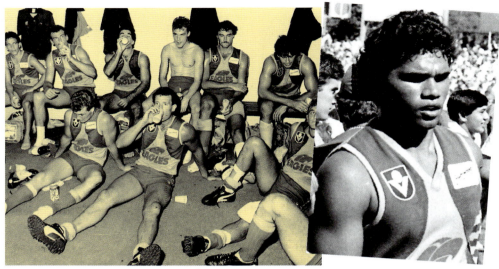
Debut win over Tigers: satisfaction in the dressing room.   Chris Lewis: played first game.

1987 – solid foundation

Eleven wins. Eleven losses. Eighth place on the Premiership table. Offer that result to any of the new franchises that have joined the AFL/VFL in the last decade and they would gratefully accept it as the perfect foundation.

Through the course of its initial season West Coast beat the eventual Premier Carlton (once), runner-up Hawthorn (twice) and finished above long-time League heavyweights like Essendon and Collingwood.

It was not enough to save the neck of Ron Alexander after making such an enterprising start with West Coast in 1987. After a season which even the most expectant of supporters would have considered better than satisfactory, Alexander was called in to the club's offices in Kings Park Road in early October and told his services were no longer required.

He had been sacked, and replaced by John Todd. The explanation to the media from chief executive Bill Kerr was simply that Todd was 'a better coach'.

A season in which so much was achieved was clouded by this decision just a week after the Grand Final, souring a start worthy of celebration.

Considering that Alexander achieved his coaching record when the team trained at a local college and that the property room was a mobile van, the actual worth of the club's debut season seems even greater.

Still, there was much to get enthused about during the season. The debut match against Richmond at Subiaco Oval on March 29 is a fair place to begin.

Down by 33 points at three-quarter time Alexander swung skipper Ross Glendinning from centre half-back to centre half-forward, a move which was the catalyst for a remarkable finishing burst. The Eagles kicked 9.4 to 1.5 in the final quarter to win by 14 points and give the club a dream start.

A week later, in losing by a mere five points to Essendon at Windy Hill, it was obvious the new kids on the block would cause some pain to those who had ruled the precinct for decades.

In the rematch against Carlton in Round 16 the Eagles clawed their way to victory after a see-sawing encounter at the WACA Ground, eventually winning by three points.

A fortnight later against Hawthorn the Eagles snuck home by a point, again Mainwaring's personal victory over DiPierdomenico pivotal in the success. So was the form of ruckman Laurie Keene.

There were also games which indicated that the Eagles had some work ahead of them. The most stinging reminder came against Sydney in Round 17 – sandwiched between those victories against Carlton and Hawthorn.

At the SCG the Eagles put up a pitiful performance and were thumped by 130 points – 30.21 (201) to 10.11 (71).

1987–1989 HONOUR ROLL

Year	Pos	Leading Goalkicker	No.	Best & Fairest	Captain	Coach
1987	8	Ross Glendinning	38	Steve Malaxos	Ross Glendinning	Ron Alexander
1988	5	Ross Glendinning	73	John Worsfold	Ross Glendinning	John Todd
1989	11	Peter Sumich	45	Guy McKenna	Murray Rance	John Todd

CLUB NEWS 1987–1989

1987, first round: West Australian fans learned a harsh lesson about VFL football when thousands were left milling outside Subiaco Oval when the ball was bounced to begin the Eagles' life in the big league. In the end gates were thrown open and the official crowd of 23,879 was well short of the number of fans who witnessed the debut.

Expertise: West Coast called upon the expertise of many people with previous VFL experience, including 1976 Brownlow Medallist Graham Moss. As the club's first football manager, Moss returned to Windy Hill for the Round 2 game against the Bombers and was labelled a traitor by one particularly animated female Essendon supporter.

First squad: Of the 35 original Eagles, only two did not play a game with the club before being de-listed. West Perth wingman Dean Warwick was the first serious knee injury at the club and Swan Districts ruck-rover Don Langsford did not earn an opportunity. West Perth half-back Paul Mifka and midfielder Sean King each played in the last game against St Kilda when it was obvious the team could not make the finals.

Milestones: During 1987 Ross Glendinning played his 200th VFL game, Robert Wiley his 100th and Phil Narkle and Geoff Miles their 50th.

Fans and wins: Best attendance of the inaugural season was 38,274 at Subiaco against Collingwood on June 1 – a win 19.23 (137) to 11.14 (80), Alex Ischenko best on ground. Lowest

1987 – 1989

Dean Turner (on shoulders): happy 100th.

Jubilant Eagles in 1987: Gastev, Holmes, Zanotti, Worsfold, MacNish, Lamb, Hart, Lewis.

1988 – finals success is just one kick away

The big development of 1988 came with the appointment of Todd. There were also some important changes in personnel and training facilities. Wiley retired to take over as captain–coach of Perth and eight others were dropped off the list.

Among the players the Eagles recruited were Guy McKenna, Chris Waterman, Karl Langdon and Murray Rance. McKenna and Waterman both played in WA's only Teal Cup victory in 1985 and joined Chris Lewis and John Worsfold who were team-mates in the side that beat Victoria in the final at Leederville Oval.

Finally the club had some sort of training facility worthy of a team playing in the VFL. McGillivray Oval was the ground that was used and its proximity to the Superdrome, which provided a pool and gymnasium of suitable standard, was a key factor. Players could walk from one facility to the other.

Todd had his first test as a VFL coach on 2 April 1988 against Geelong at Kardinia Park and it was a triumphant debut, with the Eagles charging to a 21-point victory.

That was the first of 13 victories which elevated the Eagles to their first finals appearance – a shot at Melbourne in the Elimination Final at the MCG.

It is a game no Eagles supporter – or Murray Wrensted for that matter – will ever forget. The Eagles were three points down with just seconds remaining when Wrensted, usually a reliable shot at goal, lined up from about 30 metres, but his shot at goal drifted away to the left, giving Melbourne victory.

It was a classic battle, the match-winning goal coming from a remarkable Garry Lyon snap just a few moments earlier.

It was doubtful the Eagles could have been competitive had they survived into the second week of the finals because ruckman Phil Scott, forward David O'Connell and McKenna were all injured and highly unlikely to play if required.

Sadly, there was another casualty. Wrensted was never again the same player. The man who won the 1985 Sandover Medal was devastated, and at Collingwood did not reach the levels expected of him.

Down but not out in '89

Having performed so creditably in its second season, much was expected of West Coast in its third. John Todd had done a remarkable job in taking the club to its first finals campaign and there was a sense of anticipation about the new season.

It started badly when skipper Glendinning decided after 230 games – 40 with the Eagles – that he should retire.

Thirteen losses from the first 15 games was indicative of a club in deep strife. And not just on the field. Indian Pacific Limited had accumulated losses of $13.5 million by October 1989 and the very fabric of football in WA was fraying.

Eventually IPL became an unlisted public company, the WA Football Commission gained a 75 per cent stakes in the Eagles and the debt was brought under control.

By the end of the season things were on the upward swing as the Eagles won five of the last seven games and there was new-found stability within the organisation

However, as soon as the season ended Todd was replaced by former Footscray mentor Michael Malthouse.

---

was against Brisbane at Carrara, 4,859 on August 16, when the Eagles won 21.14 (140) to 18.11 (119). Don Holmes was best with seven goals.
1987 Honours: At the end of the 1987 season the Eagles inaugural captain, Ross Glendinning, was named captain of an Australian team to tour Ireland. Others selected to play a composite Test series, using Gaelic and Australian football laws, were Steve Malaxos, Chris Mainwaring and Chris Lewis.
Todd debut: Newly appointed Eagles coach John Todd found himself in hot water when he struck West Perth president Rod Brown during a commercial radio panel show at Mandurah on the eve of the season. The next day Todd issued a public apology, just 24 hours before his debut against Geelong at Kardinia Park, a game the Eagles won.
All-Australians: Steve Malaxos and John Worsfold were named in the All-Australian side in 1988.
Plenty of VC's: Murray Rance was named 1989 captain of the Eagles at the Nedlands Park Hotel on March 28, and he had plenty of support. Steve Malaxos, Laurie Keene, John Annear and John Worsfold were vice-captains.
Cellar Dwellers: The Eagles were sitting on the bottom of the Premiership table with an 0–4 record in 1989 when they travelled to Carrara for a clash with Brisbane. The team broke VFL rules by backing themselves to open their account, at the odds of 9/4. They romped home by nine goals. The players won $9000, but were then fined that amount for placing the wager.

WEST COAST

Left to Right: Stevan Jackson against Melbourne; the blond bombshell Karl Langdon; an angry Peter Sumich; a happy Steve Malaxos.

Enter Mick Malthouse: the force is with him

In so many respects 1989 was a disaster. But the wreck was salvaged to a degree with the enterprising finish to the season.

Coupled with the appointment of Mick Malthouse as coach, Trevor Nisbett as football manager and Brian Cook as chief executive there was reason for optimism as 1990 approached.

It would be fair to say that the arrival of those three men, just a few months apart, was pivotal in the future success of a club which has not missed a finals campaign since their cumulative appointments. You would find it difficult to argue that there are better in their respective fields in the League. Perhaps some just as good, but none better.

Cook has an astute business mind and an ability to communicate with the average fan as well as corporate high fliers, while the relationship between Malthouse and Nisbett is built on mutual respect, values and judgments.

It would be difficult to forge a better union between the man who calls the on-field plays and he who makes the important off-field football decisions.

The other important factor at this time was that the Eagles were granted Subiaco Oval as a home base. Then came the draft, another important development in what would become the Eagles' dynasty.

Using the inside knowledge that five years as Subiaco football manager had given him, Nisbett threw up a couple of tyros by the names of Dean Kemp and Brett Heady as draft selections. Heady was snared at 72nd pick and Kemp was a selection the Eagles used to bolster their squad when all other clubs had completed the football lottery.

Also selected in this remarkably productive November draft were Peter Matera, Ashley McIntosh (under the father–son clause) and Tony Evans. They had also traded with Richmond to bring Peter Wilson home and secured Ryan Turnbull and Peter Mann as pre-draft concessions.

It is doubtful one club has netted so much talent in a single draft before or since.

So there was reason for optimism when the 1990 season began. It was quickly reflected in on-field performance as the Eagles won seven of their first nine games, the perfect platform for another finals assault.

Eventually the Eagles finished third, equal on 16 wins with Collingwood and Melbourne, but a game behind League leader Essendon. Percentage determined that the Eagles played the Pies in the Qualifying Final.

If the 1988 campaign was remembered by one kick, so would this assault on the Premiership. With a point the difference Peter Sumich had the ball deep on the Waverley boundary line as the siren sounded.

His ensuing shot missed, resulting in a tie and the need for a replay the following week. The rematch was a no match, with the Magpies romping to a 59-point victory. The Eagles then dispensed with Melbourne in the First Semi-final, but could not handle Essendon in the Preliminary Final.

CLUB NEWS 1990–1991

Jakovich feat: Champion defender Glen Jakovich earned a rare distinction in 1990, being captain of the WA Teal Cup team, playing for a state WAFL team against SA and then playing state-of-origin for WA against Victoria. Aged 17 years and 94 days, he became the third-youngest player to represent WA behind John Todd (17 years, 58 days in 1955) and Grant Campbell (17 and 91 days in 1979).

Arm of Lamb: The selection of Dwayne Lamb to play in the Round 22 game against Geelong in 1990 came out of the blue. An errant kick from Jim Stynes had broken Lamb's arm only two weeks earlier. He took the field wearing an arm guard which umpire Chris Mitchell demanded should be re-strapped before he could play any part in the game. Lamb missed the first five minutes of the contest as the bandage was adjusted.

Malaxos' exit: Captain Steve Malaxos played his last game for West Coast in the Qualifying Final against Collingwood on 15 September 1990. After drawing with Collingwood in the initial match, the Eagles were 10-goal losers in the replay and Malaxos was overlooked for selection in the First Semi-final against Melbourne.

Gallstones: Despite some evidence to the contrary, Mick Malthouse had his gallstones removed at the end of the 1990 season, preventing him from coaching the team in an exhibition game against Melbourne in Portland,

1990 – 1991

The worst feeling in football: Michael Brennan after the 1991 Grand Final.

The Eagles on the road in 1991.

A first shot at football's holy grail

The primary reason for the appointment of Malthouse was a perception that the Eagles needed a Victorian influence to adjust to a tougher, more direct style of football.

Then, it was reasoned, West Coast would come to terms with winning the required number of games away from the sanctuary of Subiaco Oval and the WACA Ground.

The Eagles won four and lost five qualifying games in Melbourne in 1990. The following season they won six and lost three, but also recorded victories at the SCG and Carrara. Those three defeats were the only losses from the 22 preliminary games.

They won their first 12 games before falling to a three-point loss to Carlton at Princes Park and audible groans of concern could be heard filtering across to Perth from Melbourne on a still night.

While the Eagles looked a supreme outfit, they chose a bad time for a hiccup, losing the last qualifying game to Fitzroy at Princes Park. It was hardly the tonic the team needed as the first interstate final loomed.

The Eagles tackled the might of Hawthorn at Subiaco Oval on September 8. In front of a sell-out crowd, however, the Hawks accepted the challenge.

With ruckman Stephen Lawrence in a dominant mood and Jason Dunstall finally breaking clear of Michael Brennan in the last quarter to kick four final-quarter goals – on the way to a 23-point victory – the party was spoiled for most of the 44,142 fans who crammed into Subiaco.

The Eagles rallied to destroy Melbourne in the First Semi-final and then accounted for Geelong in the Preliminary Final to earn a rematch with Hawthorn in the club's first Grand Final. It had taken just five years for the Eagles to earn a shot at football's holy grail.

Because the MCG was undergoing a facelift, with the construction of the Southern Stand, Waverley was the venue for the Grand Final – a ground which was deemed to suit the pace and skill of the Eagles.

After winning the toss and kicking with the breeze, West Coast posted the first four goals, but two late goals by Dermott Brereton put Hawthorn back on track and the day belonged to the Hawks thereafter. Again it was Lawrence and Paul Dear, two men the Eagles had difficulty in nullifying, who were pivotal as Hawthorn kicked eight last-quarter goals on the way to a 53-point victory.

Another of the big issues to consume the Eagles was a charge against Chris Lewis for biting Melbourne's Todd Viney in a spiteful Round 15 clash at the MCG. Despite no official complaint by Melbourne and no videotape evidence of the incident, Lewis was summoned to Melbourne for a tribunal hearing on the eve of the Round 16 Friday night clash against Collingwood.

Lewis was found guilty and suspended for three weeks. The Eagles were incensed by the process which led to his appearance before the tribunal.

1990 – 1991 HONOUR ROLL

Year	Pos	Leading Goalkicker	No.	Best & Fairest	Captain	Coach
1990	3	Peter Sumich	90	Chris Lewis	Steve Malaxos	Michael Malthouse
1991	2	Peter Sumich	111	Craig Turley	John Worsfold	Michael Malthouse

Oregon. The Eagles lost 10.13 (73) to 24.16 (160). Malthouse signed a three-year extension to his contract, til the end of 1994.

Pyke position: Rover Don Pyke announced his intention to quit the Eagles as the 1991 season loomed. Disgruntled at a lack of opportunity in 1990 he said he wanted to play with Claremont and look at changing clubs the following season. Eventually he was convinced to remain and became one of the keys in the 1992 and 1994 Flags.

Skipper Lewis: When the Eagles played Essendon in Round 7, 1991 they went into the game without captain John Worsfold, vice-captain Michael Brennan and deputy vice-captain Phil Scott. Chris Lewis was chosen to lead the team, the first time he had been charged with that responsibility since being captain of the Mirrabooka 15s in 1983. The Eagles won a tense battle by seven points.

Sumich surge: Peter Sumich will always remember the match against Footscray at the WACA Ground on 14 June 1991 when he kicked 13.3 as the Eagles coasted to an 118-point victory. Sumich kicked seven goals in the third quarter to have 12 at three-quarter time to be within sight of Fred Fanning's VFL record of 18 goals in a match, but was kept relatively quiet in the last quarter.

Mollydooker's first ton: Peter Sumich became the first left-footer in VFL/AFL history to kick over a hundred goals in a season, when he tallied 111 in the 1991 season.

WEST COAST

From left: Paul Peos – 50th game in 1992; Matt Clape on the ball; Trent Nichols gets a kick.

Soaring through to the ultimate test

The devastation of a Grand Final loss can work one of two ways.

Either it leaves the players and the club completely empty, a feeling which takes years to diminish, or it steels the personnel to such an extent that remedying the wrong is *the* most important motivational tool the following season.

Paul Harding handpasses.

Glen Jakovich will never forget Dermott Brereton giving his head a playful rub and saying to him that his time would come, before Dermie headed off to join his triumphant team-mates in the wild celebrations which marked the 1991 Grand Final.

But Jakovich and those around the Eagles' nest must have doubted that 1992 would be the year when the club made such a tardy start.

After sitting out with a bye in Round 1, the Eagles had a three-point loss to Sydney at the SCG to kick things off, then a victory against St Kilda at Subiaco Oval in Round 3 – when Daniel Metropolis made an auspicious start kicking goals with his first four kicks in the AFL – and then a loss to Geelong at Subiaco Oval. This was followed by a draw against the lowly Brisbane at Carrara, and there was cause for real concern.

A come-from-behind one-point victory against Richmond was hardly a tonic to instil confidence in the camp and then a loss to Fitzroy – fast becoming West Coast's nemesis – at North Hobart Oval and things were taking on a desperate appearance. The Eagles were 10th and looked anything but a Premiership fancy.

Although the situation was retrieved in winning the next four matches, the club's longest winning streak of the season – which was achieved another three times – the Eagles limped in to fourth place and looked vulnerable.

When they lost to Footscray in the second-last qualifying match by 30 points, confidence was at a low ebb, but the preliminary campaign was completed with an emphatic victory over Carlton, which was set up with a blistering seven-goal first quarter.

So, in a repeat of the draw a year earlier, West Coast hosted Hawthorn at Subiaco Oval on the first week of finals action.

There was a sense of deja vu about this return bout when Hawthorn kicked the first four goals, silencing the crowd of 40,000, but the Eagles were not about to lie down. They produced a supercharged recovery.

Eventually West Coast won a gripping final by 13 points and it seemed momentum was filtering through to the camp at the right time of the year. Because of the way other results fell, the Eagles were elevated to a Second Semi-final clash with Geelong and earned another Grand Final berth, courtesy of a solid 38-point victory.

In advancing to the Grand Final and earning a week's break – while Geelong and Footscray slugged it for the right to challenge – the Eagles had established another contrast to their failed 1991 bid.

1992 HONOUR ROLL

Year	Pos	Leading Goalkicker	No.	Best & Fairest	Captain	Coach
1992	1	Peter Sumich	82	Dean Kemp	John Worsfold	Michael Malthouse

CLUB NEWS 1992

Round 3, 1992: A sensational six-goal debut by Daniel Metropolis was the catalyst for victory against St Kilda. He kicked his first goal 40 seconds into the game and kicked three more for the quarter – four kicks for four goals.

Fitzroy flop: Fitzroy was fast becoming the Eagles' bogey team and a trip to Hobart served only to confirm that standing. At windswept North Hobart Oval on May 3, the Lions posted a 20-point victory, with Darren Wheildon in spectacular form.

Round 22, 1992: Volatile West Coast half-forward Karl Langdon was fingered on a charge of pushing boundary umpire Andrew Neale as the Eagles soared to victory over Carlton. Neale produced a muddy shirt at the tribunal to indicate where the alleged contact was made, but the charge was dismissed by Neil Busse, who was not convinced contact was deliberate.

Finals bonus: On the eve of the club's Second Elimination Final with Hawthorn, the Eagles received a bonus when St Kilda beat Collingwood. It meant that if the Eagles won they would qualify for a spot in the Second Semi-final against either Geelong or Footscray. The Eagles did win, by 13 points, in a memorable encounter and played Geelong the next week.

To the letter: As the Eagles prepared for their second Grand Final two important letters were penned. The first, by Adrian Barich and Phil Scott, outlined the pain they would feel at

1992

From left: The captain, John Worsfold, and coach Mick Malthouse; Peter Matera, Norm Smith Medallist; Peter Sumich in the Second Semi.

Matera's magic takes the prize

The contrast to 1991 was further emphasized in the Grand Final against the Cats. In a hectic start to the big game, rover Don Pyke was carried from the ground after only three minutes when collected by Gary Ablett, and Geelong started with the impetus running its way.

The Cats clawed to a 23-point lead in the middle of the second quarter before Tony 'the money man' Evans kicked two goals in a minute, which saw the margin reduced to just 12 points at half-time.

Those who were in the Eagles rooms at half-time have often since said that, after soaking up the atmosphere in the long break, they felt certain the Premiership Cup was about to leave Melbourne for the first time.

When the Eagles kicked five goals to one in the third quarter it was going to take something special to stop them. It was a charge built around the brilliance of Peter Matera and a resurgent Brett Heady who was relishing a run in the middle.

With history at their fingertips West Coast was not about to surrender the opportunity and they rammed home the advantage in the last quarter, a freakish snap over the head from Peter Wilson the clincher.

The Eagles went on to win by 28 points. The final siren sent 12,000 West Australian fans at the ground into a frenzy. One could only imagine the scenes right across their home State.

The players did not need to wait long to discover the mood. After a long night of celebrations in Melbourne, the players arrived in Perth mid-morning. They immediately boarded a bus for Subiaco Oval were thousands of fans revelled in the glory and rejoiced at the sight of the Premiership cup.

The following Tuesday many thousands more lined the city streets for a ticker-tape parade. In places they were 10 to 15 deep on both sides of major city arteries as supporters young and old struggled for a glimpse of the precious silverware and the men who had made it possible.

It had taken just six seasons to build a team, a club capable of winning football's ultimate prize.

Matera was rewarded for his sizzling display on the wing with the Norm Smith Medal as best afield and Dean Kemp won the club champion award a few weeks later. The evidence, if it were needed, again pointed to the amazing draft of 1989.

Karl Langdon in triumph.

missing out on the opportunity to create history, but urged their teammates to sieze the moment. The second from defender Andrew Lockyer spoke about the difficulties the team experienced, particularly on the east coast, in the early years and suggested Saturday, 22 September 1992 was the chance to put things right.
Grand message: When the Eagles ran onto the ground to play Geelong in the 1992 Grand Final, skipper John Worsfold hovered around the centre circle as self-appointed protector of Peter Matera. He remembered the '89 Grand Final when Mark Yeates picked off Dermott Brereton at the opening play, and warned the opposition that any similar tactic would be met with severe reprisals.
Matera Magic: Peter Matera achieved what greats like Graham 'Polly' Farmer, Barry Cable and Bill Walker could not when he won an award run jointly by local newspaper the *West Australian* and Caltex. The Sports Star of the Year award had run for over 30 years and Matera became the first footballer to win the title, courtesy of his Norm Smith Medal-winning Grand Final performance.
MCG hoodoo: Including the Grand Final, the Eagles won the last four games of the season at the MCG in a row – banishing the idea of a hoodoo.
And not just the Flag: West Coast not only won the Premiership in 1992, but membership topped 20,000 in the same season – 23,500 in total. Marketing income was over $5 million.

WEST COAST

Playing through hangover

The maxim decrees that to be forewarned is to be forearmed, but knowing the pitfalls does not guarantee that those traps will be avoided.

West Coast coach Mick Malthouse was aware of the dangers that awaited after the Eagles won their first Premiership. He had lived through it as a player with Richmond when he was part of the 1980 Grand Final team and then saw the Tigers plummet to seventh in the year of their title defence.

The Eagles started well enough, winning five of their first six games, and showing no signs of a Premiership hangover. But things turned. Quickly. Dramatically.

After the Round 6 victory against Geelong the Eagles were stunned by a loss to lowly Fitzroy. When things unravel they do so quickly. Three days after the Fitzroy defeat came another blow to the Eagles. Pin-up boy Craig Turley decided to turn his back on the game. He had had enough.

The season was then punctuated with losses. They came close to putting together a run of victories, but two matches probably summed up the season. Against Carlton on July 4, Chris Mainwaring took possession deep in the forward pocket with six seconds left on the clock.

An attempted banana kick looked like it would sail through, but banged into the top of the goal post, giving the Blues a one-point victory.

A week later against Essendon a two-point defeat at the MCG served merely to intensify the pain. That was the day Bomber coach Kevin Sheedy initiated a tradition which probably will last forever in clashes between the two clubs, twirling his jacket over his head in helicopter fashion to mark the triumph.

The Eagles finished 6th to take the last spot in the finals. They accounted for North Melbourne in the Second Elimination Final to earn another shot at Essendon, but faded to a 32-point First Semi-final defeat.

Chris Lewis in evasive mode.

Assault on second Flag

🏆 If there was one thing to be learned from the failed 1993 campaign it was the importance of a top-two finish and an automatic home final – so that was the emphasis of the 1994 assault.

The task of constantly travelling was too difficult from the western extreme of this vast country, so Malthouse and his team set about the task of giving themselves the best possible chance of winning another Flag.

The first stage of that plan, however, did not go according to the script.

Just as Essendon had ended the Eagles torment in 1993 so too did it ensure a miserable start to 1994. Up by 33 points in the middle of the third quarter, the Eagles could not resist an impressive final-quarter charge as the Bombers clawed their way to a thrilling three-point victory.

Again Paul Salmon, fast becoming the Eagles nemesis, was the man who denied them, taking a diving mark in the last 90 seconds to kick the winning goal.

A disastrous start was avoided in Round 2 as the Eagles recovered from a 20-point three-quarter time deficit against Adelaide to produce a 20-point victory – in a match most memorable for a collision between John Worsfold and Tony Modra which left the Adelaide forward concussed.

That was a start of a brilliant 10-round sequence, which produced only one more defeat, at the hands of Hawthorn in Round 5. Other than that it was a scintillating two and a half months of football.

With so much of the hard work done early the Eagles were on track for the pre-season goal they had set themselves.

And seven wins in the last 10 games meant they achieved that, securing top position with 16 wins and two losses. It would mean West Coast would play two of its finals at home, venturing to Melbourne only for the Grand Final.

The last of those matches, against Footscray at Subiaco Oval on September 4, was most notable for a half-time brawl. Players joined the fray from all directions and at the end of it all West Coast forward Peter Sumich lay unconscious.

AFL investigator Max Croxford spent two days looking into the incident but found no players had a case to answer. AFL football operations manager Ian Collins, in a behind-closed-doors deal with the respective presidents, fined each club $20,000.

The AFL commission overruled the deal and eight players, five from the Eagles and three from the Bulldogs, were cited to front the tribunal. Footscray went to the Supreme Court and successfully sought an injunction.

Eventually Daniel Southern was the only player penalised after the incident, fined $10,000 for his part in the melee while all others escaped penalty.

With that out of the way, the Eagles prepared for a Qualifying Final against Collingwood at the WACA Ground. Subiaco Oval had been ruled out because of work on the Southern Stand.

The Magpies showed tremendous spirit and stuck with the Eagles, who several times threatened to break away. Three goals from skipper Gavin Brown in the last quarter saw Collingwood twice edge to within two points, before the Eagles eventually prevailed.

Next the Eagles confronted Melbourne

CLUB NEWS 1993-1994

Brotherly love: The Round 8 game against Melbourne in 1993 would be best remembered for a kiss Allen Jakovich planted on his younger brother Glen. Playing for Melbourne, Allen had kicked a goal and decided to celebrate in that fashion to give his mother Mary, who had flown to Melbourne for the game, a special memory from the encounter. At the time Glen did not see the humorous side of things.

1993 honours: Don Pyke showed that his career had turned the full circle when he shared the club Best and Fairest award with Glen Jakovich. After contemplating leaving the club a couple of years earlier he had developed into one of the Eagles' midfield players while Jakovich continued to build an imposing record for a man so young. It was the first of three successive club champion awards for the star defender.

Turnbull win: Ryan Turnbull won the *West Australian* media award in 1993 for games played in the WAFL as well as the AFL. He won despite playing all games with East Perth and naturally the Eagles had him pencilled in for 1994.

Gerhig drafted: Remarkably the 17-year-old All-Australian schoolboy champion Fraser Gehrig was still available at pick 16 in the 1994 draft.

Winging it: The Eagles had revenge on their minds when they played Fitzroy at the WACA Ground in Round 4, 1994, having been embarrassed by the Lions a year earlier at the same

1993–1994

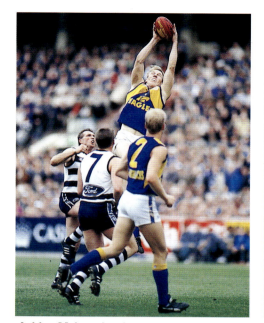
Ashley McIntosh takes a big grab.

The Eagles in celebration mode. Inset: Brett Spinks on the burst.

in the Second Preliminary Final – again at the WACA Ground – and this time they were far more convincing winners, by 65 points.

So it was on to their third Grand Final, against a familiar foe. Geelong had worked their way into the Premiership game after a six-point thriller against North Melbourne.

It was to be a comprehensive victory for the Eagles, the tone set when they kicked the first three goals of the game. Geelong fought back, but they always seemed to be in trouble.

The Eagles led by six goals at three-quarter time and when Chris Waterman extended the lead to seven goals inside the first minute of the final quarter the champagne corks were popping in the west.

The margin blew out to 80 points as the Eagles went on the rampage.

Dean Kemp was the architect of the victory, producing some dazzling football in the middle of the ground, while Guy McKenna, Chris Lewis, Don Pyke, Brett Heady, Michael Brennan, Jason Ball, Tony Evans, Glen Jakovich and Ryan Turnbull also played significant roles.

From left: Dean Kemp motors downfield. The Cup back home. Winners are grinners.

1993–1994 HONOUR ROLL

Year	Pos	Leading Goalkicker	No.	Best & Fairest	Captain	Coach
1993	4	Peter Sumich	76	Don Pyke/Glen Jakovich	John Worsfold	Michael Malthouse
1994	1	Peter Sumich	49	Glen Jakovich	John Worsfold	Michael Malthouse

ground. Wingmen Chris Mainwaring and Peter Matera set the standard, gathering more than 50 possessions between them as the team romped to a 76-point victory.

Waterlogged home advantage: Coach Mick Malthouse called reporters aside at Wednesday training at Subiaco and dug his heel into the soggy turf. 'We are now playing on a ground that is anything but a traditional West Australian surface. Something has to be done'. (It was – by next season.)

Milestone men: Rugged midfielder Dwayne Lamb became the first Eagle to reach the 150-game milestone, thus earning life membership through playing deeds, against Sydney in Round 10, 1994 at the WACA Ground. An original squad member, it was testimony to the durability of the man who was also the first Eagle to play 50 and then 100 games. Other 150-gamers in 1994 were Michael Brennan, Chris Mainwaring, John Worsfold, Chris Lewis and Peter Wilson (54 with Richmond).

Round 21: After the Eagles' loss to Carlton, coach Mick Malthouse sprang to the defence of maligned full-forward Peter Sumich, who had kicked just four goals in three games and 41 from 14 in the season. Malthouse said no other player had been under as much pressure nor analysed as brutally by the public as Sumich.

No hangover at the Oval. Despite the Premiership celebrations, the Eagles managed to defeat Adelaide at the Oval in London by 40 points.

WEST COAST

The old firm – Worsfold & Matera. Glen Jakovich: club champ. Guy McKenna: outstanding player of 1995. Jason Ball: 43 goals in 1995.

New challenges of 1995

The 1995 season was always going to be challenging. Not only was there the task of backing up after the club's second Premiership, but things had changed on the domestic front.

There was another kid on the football block. The Fremantle Dockers were born. After ruling the town for eight seasons there was now a challenger in every sense of the word. The Dockers were expected to hurt the Eagles, more in the commercial sense than on-field, but the new club's presence created an impact upon every aspect of the club. West Coast handled the presence of another contender for the corporate dollar with aplomb, but its on-field exploits were disappointing.

Membership actually grew from 23,000 to 27,000 and sponsorship levels were also lifted from $2.7 million to $5.1 million.

But on the field the Eagles never really struck any momentum. It was still good enough to finish fifth after the home-and-way rounds but significantly they had trouble beating other top-eight teams.

Two losses to Carlton and further defeats inflicted by North Melbourne, Essendon, Richmond, Geelong and Footscray hardly instilled confidence approaching the finals series. The only teams inside the eight the Eagles had beaten were North Melbourne in Round 3 and Brisbane on June 4.

With those statistics in mind the most meaningful qualifying-round matches of the season came against the Dockers. The first of these matches, dubbed the western derby, was played at Subiaco on May 14, Mother's Day.

It was a game where the Eagles flexed their muscle, with John Worsfold setting the physical tone in the opening minutes as West Coast stormed to an 85-point victory in front of 40,355, including the prime minister Paul Keating who had earlier opened the new Town and Country southern stand.

The second western derby marked the end of the qualifying rounds and the Eagles again dominated to win by 53 points, after staving off an early Fremantle challenge.

The Eagles looked good initially in the Third Qualifying Final against Essendon, controlling the first quarter and a half, but then lost momentum and slipped to a 19-point defeat.

The First Elimination final against North Melbourne started reasonably well for the Eagles, down by just two points early in the second term. But the Kangaroos then produced an irresistible surge and ran out 58-point winners. A season which spluttered along had finished in a similar manner.

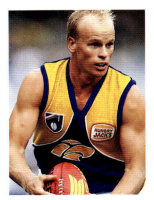

Dean Kemp: steely.

1995–1996 HONOUR ROLL

Year	Pos	Leading Goalkicker	No.	Best & Fairest	Captain	Coach
1995	6	Jason Ball	43	Glen Jakovich	John Worsfold	Michael Malthouse
1996	5	Mitchell White	37	Drew Banfield	John Worsfold	Michael Malthouse

CLUB NEWS 1995–1996

Stand up man: When the new Town and Country stand was opened at Subiaco Oval in May 1995, two of WA's great football achievers were honoured. One room in the stand was named after Barry Cable, another after tough Eagles skipper John Worsfold. It was a great honour for Worsfold, who still had many games ahead of him.

Cousins signs: Shortly after dispensing with Hawthorn in Round 14, 1995 at Waverley, the Eagles announced they had signed outstanding young midfield prospect Ben Cousins under the father–son law. Cousins, the son of former Geelong and Perth centreman, Bryan Cousins, had the choice of three clubs (West Coast, Geelong or Fremantle) but opted to play with the Eagles.

Seven-second delay: Eagles coach Mick Malthouse created something of a record when he gave a post-match press conference which lasted all of seven seconds, after losing 18.15 (123) to 9.9 (63) to Richmond on June 10. 'We totally embarrassed ourselves,' was his comment.

Young gun: Brilliant West Coast centre half-back Glen Jakovich played his 100th game when the Eagles played Geelong at Kardinia Park in Round 13, 1995. At 22 years and 98 days he became the seventh youngest player in AFL/VFL history to achieve the feat. Essendon champ Tim Watson remains the youngest at 20 years and 273 days.

Stone the Crows: The Eagles' 100th win for Mick Malthouse was also a

1995–1996

Drew Banfield: B & F 1996. Chris Mainwaring: runner-up. Fraser Gehrig: full of potential.

'Minimise the tumble, maximise the talent'

The blueprint for 1996 was drawn at the 1995 post mortem. West Coast football manager Trevor Nisbett, coach Mick Malthouse and members of the match committee recognised the need to rebuild. It needed to inject some youthful exuberance into its squad or face the prospect of an ageing list.

Senior players like Michael Brennan, Paul Harding, Peter Wilson and Karl Langdon retired. Paul Peos, who had returned after a stint with Brisbane, also called it a day while Craig Turley (Melbourne), David Hynes and Tony Godden (Fremantle) were traded.

Eventually players like David Wirrpunda, Brendan Fewster, Phil Matera, Ben Cousins, Andrew Donnelly and Chad Morrison would work their way into the team. There was no doubt the Eagles had replaced that slab of experienced campaigners with a batch of quality young players.

The season started well enough with a first-round victory against Fremantle, but the margin was just 22 points. The Dockers were starting to establish a pattern of halving their previous loss against their home town rivals.

Round 2 saw the Eagles lose for the first time to Brisbane at the WACA ground. A heavy defeat at the hands of Essendon at Waverley in Round 3 and Malthouse tried to convince non-believers in the post-match press conference that his club was in a rebuilding phase. The task, he said, was to minimise the tumble while introducing the new talent.

When the Eagles slumped to a 1-4 win–loss record after five rounds – the last of them a controversial defeat against Carlton – they were in serious strife. Against the Blues at Optus Oval Greg Williams was credited with a goal when replays showed that Eagles rover Tony Evans had soccered the ball through for a behind. Carlton won by a point.

From that moment, however, the Eagles won 11 successive games with Morrison and Cousins having tremendous impact. West Coast had emerged from barely final-eight material to serious contenders yet again.

In the middle of that run, however, the Eagles lost champion defender Glen Jakovich to a knee injury. Turning quite innocently in the Round 12 game against St Kilda, Jakovich's knee buckled underneath him.

Perhaps the most absorbing of the qualifying rounds was against Essendon at Subiaco Oval on August 4, when the Eagles clawed their way off the canvas to post a brilliant six-point victory.

West Coast led by 20 points at half-time but a nine-goal third quarter onslaught lifted the Bombers to a 17-point advantage. With freakish goals from Peter Sumich and Mitchell White, the Eagles eventually prevailed and the fans celebrated with the now traditional jacket wave.

The preliminary matches ended with a showdown with Sydney at the SCG. The Swans mastered a filthy night in the harbour city much the better, to win by 35 points.

Bombed out of finals

The Eagles finished fourth and hosted Carlton in the First Qualifying Final, jumped the Blues in the opening quarter and coasted to a 55-point win, 18.17 (125) to 10.10 (70).

Despite winning that match, the Eagles had to play the Bombers in the First Semi-final at the MCG. Kevin Sheedy stirred the emotions within the Melbourne public, urging all Victorians to support his side against the interstate challengers.

The result was a crowd of 85,656 which played a role in a blistering start by the Bombers, who kicked five early goals to put the visitors under pressure. The Eagles never recovered and slipped to a demoralising 71-point defeat.

While the team's season ended in disappointment, there was some compensation when Cousins won the Norwich Rising Star award.

Ben Cousins: a star on the rise.

---

record winning margin. West Coast won 26.21 (177) to Adelaide 5.12 (42). Fourteen players got among the goals at Subiaco on August 13.
Wirrpunda: The Eagles' reputation as the outstanding draft performers of their time was enhanced during the 1996 pre-season draft when they secured outstanding Victorian youngster David Wirrpunda as compensation for losing Tony Godden to Fremantle. Wirrpunda had been outstanding for Victoria Metropolitan in the 1995 Commonwealth Bank Cup.
Demons demolished: The Eagles kicked their highest score of 1996 before the smallest crowd of the season in the Round 6 clash with Melbourne. The win 24.12 (156) to 7.8 (50) at Optus Oval was before a miserable 8747 spectators.
Mick's mark: Mick Malthouse reached the 300-game milestone as a Senior coach in the Round 17 game against Brisbane in 1996. But as is so often the case, the achievement was soured by defeat. In a high-scoring encounter the Bears surged to a 47-point win, 25.13 (163) to 17.14 (116). Chris Mainwaring's thumb was broken that day too.
Youngest Eagle: Against Carlton on August 18, David Wirrpunda made his debut for the Eagles at 16 years and 268 days.
Banfield's reward: Drew Banfield was honoured for his contribution when he was judged the 1996 club champion. One of the best run-with players in the game, Banfield had also blossomed into a fine attacking player.

WEST COAST

An injured season

The 1997 season was almost over even before it had begun. West Coast had suffered badly enough in the AFL's centenary season with skipper John Worsfold and champion defender Glen Jakovich needing knee surgery.

After starting the 1997 quest for the Premiership with a solid victory over Sydney at Subiaco Oval – the first game at WA football headquarters played under lights – signs of things to come came in Round 2 against Geelong at Kardinia Park.

Barely halfway through the first quarter star wingman Chris Mainwaring backed into a pack and was off balance as he was hit by an avalanche of players descending from a marking contest. Mainwaring badly damaged a knee and became the third Eagle inside a year to require a reconstruction. Three weeks later Mitchell White – an All-Australian half-forward in 1996, joined Mainwaring as a casualty of the footballer's scourge of the 90s.

White delayed surgery for as long as he could, hoping that the internal damage was not serious enough to require a full reconstruction. It proved to be in vain, eventually having surgery 10 weeks after the initial injury against Melbourne. Other senior players to miss almost half the season included Worsfold (10 games) Jason Ball (10 games) David Hart (18 games) Chris Lewis (nine games), Chris Waterman (12 games), Andrew Donnelly (14 games), Daniel Metropolis (21 games) and Tony Evans (10 games). Even with the vein of new-found youth it was difficult to cover the heavy casualty list.

The Eagles limped in to the finals series although things looked encouraging when they won five of their last six qualifying

Fraser Gehrig in a mob of Roos.

The Eagles defeat Collingwood.

games, the only defeat coming against the reinvigorated Western Bulldogs at Whitten Oval in Round 21.

That game would best be remembered for the pre-game clash between rookie ruckman Michael Gardiner and a cluster of Bulldogs defenders who cannoned into him before the ball was bounced.

Jason Ball floated in to assist his young team-mate, but was reported and subsequently suspended for two games.

Having missed out on the right to host a final themselves, the Eagles travelled to Adelaide for the Fourth Qualifying Final. Gardiner was unable to play because of a knee problem. Ashley McIntosh was ruled out with a thigh strain and when Brett Heady (knee) and Guy McKenna (ankle) left the ground with three quarters to play, the Eagles' cause looked hopeless.

Neither Heady or McKenna, who in Round 7 against Richmond became the first Eagle to reach the 200 game milestone, was available to play the following Saturday against North Melbourne in the First Elimination Final. Remarkably, that was the first time the Eagles went into a finals battle in the absence of McKenna, who had racked up 22 finals matches, including two Premierships.

The casualty list did not end there, however, as the Eagles prepared for a game against North, who had been outstanding in miserable conditions under lights at the MCG against Geelong the previous week.

Fraser Gehrig was out suspended and Ilija Grgic finally succumbed to a back injury, the result of a bone-rattling confrontation with Tony Lockett at the SCG in Round 16.

To add to the problems, half-forward Andrew Donnelly came down with a severe dose of influenza on the eve of the game and as a result young forward Brendan

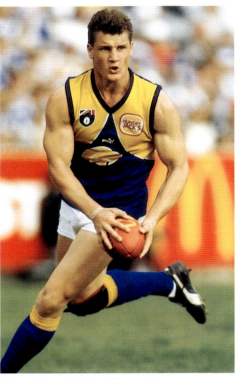

Glen Jakovich: back from injury.

Fewster was rushed into the team on the morning of the match.

Fewster, who had also undergone a knee reconstruction in 1996, had played just two games before the finals showdown with the Roos and all things considered the Eagles were given little chance of winning.

But with Jakovich supreme against Wayne Carey and Fewster giving them some life up forward the Eagles looked ominous until the middle of the third quarter. To that stage West Coast had dominated and led by 32 points, looking every bit like winners.

Although Carey was well held by Jakovich, Corey McKernan cut loose and kept his side in the contest. North Melbourne trailed by just eight points at three-quarter time thanks to the late rally inspired by

Ben Cousins.

1997

Chris Lewis: still full of running.

Peter Matera: a deserving club champion.

David Wirrpunda and Phillip Matera.

the versatile big-man.

The Eagles had early opportunities in the last quarter, but those opportunities were wasted and North produced a sizzling finish to advance to the third week of finals action. Considering West Coast's debilitating run of injuries it was a season of high achievement. Again its squadron of young players excelled with all six of its 1996 draftees playing a role in the club's season.

Josh Wooden, Michael Braun, Nick Stone, Grgic, Gardiner and Trent Cummings were all given an opportunity through the '97 campaign and that class measured up pretty well against that of the previous season.

Almost as important to the Eagles cause was the way Jakovich and Worsfold finished the season.

Jakovich made a triumphant return in the Round 6 match against the Western Bulldogs to be clearly his team's best player in a losing effort at the WACA Ground, but at times had looked a little cautious in his movement. That was quite understandable considering he had a second knee scare against Port Adelaide mid-season.

Worsfold, too, took time to regain form, fitness and confidence but he was another shining light in the loss to North Melbourne.

The season ended with Peter Matera finishing runner-up to St Kilda's Robert Harvey in the Brownlow Medal, the second time he had been the bridesmaid in Australian football's most cherished individual honour.

Just a couple of weeks after the season, however, Matera earned the distinction of his first club champion award.

Derby drama.

The rivalry between West Coast and Fremantle was intensifying and the lead-up to the first showdown of 1997 was packed with drama. Peter Matera did not train on the Eagles final training night, sparking speculation that he was injured. It was later discovered that Matera was actually in the maternity wing of a local hospital for the birth of his first child. The Dockers were not fooled by the training absence of Matera. Perth is a small town and the Dockers were more aware than most of Matera's movements.

A figurine of club icon Peter Matera.

Johnny come back ...

Much fuss was made about the return of three-time club champion Glen Jakovich when he resumed in Round 6 against the Western Bulldogs in 1997. But skipper John Worsfold came back amid much less fanfare, resuming against Fremantle in Round 2. His return was somewhat less spectacular as well, but Worsfold finished the season strongly.

Goal race

For the majority of his career with the Eagles, Peter Sumich had been the club's leading goalkicker and he earned that distinction again in 1997, though with considerably fewer goals than in other years and against considerably greater competition. The emergence of Phillip Matera as a sharpshooter and Sumich's alternation between Westar Rules and AFL made it a close contest. Fraser Gehrig was also a contender until late in the year. Eventually Sumich kicked 33 goals and Matera 30.

Fluctuating form

West Coast, a club which built its reputation on consistency over a decade, struggled to fulfil that ambition in 1997. It was probably best illustrated in two performances a week apart. The first was at the Gabba in Round 7 when it steamrolled the Brisbane Lions by 85 points. The next came against Richmond on a Monday night at the MCG when it suffered a humiliating 52-point defeat.

Young star

Most pundits would have predicted that Michael Gardiner would have been judged the Eagles' best first-year player of 1997. But that honour went to Josh Wooden, recruited from Lockhart in NSW. Under the Eagles' intricate voting system, Wooden won the award both on performance and the number of games (18) that he played. Gardiner played only 10 regular games during 1997.

1997 HONOUR ROLL

Year	Pos	Leading Goalkicker	No.	Best & Fairest	Captain	Coach
1997	5	Peter Sumich	33	Peter Matera	John Worsfold	Michael Malthouse

INDEX OF PLAYERS

Page numbers in italic type refer to illustrations.

Abbey, Angus 152
Abbey, Ross 152
Abbott, Gordon 112, 189, *189*, 190
Abbott, Paul 224, 225
Abernethy, Jim 238, 243
Ablett, Gary 124, 176, *177*, 198, *198*, 199, 200, 201, *201*, 202, 218, 220, 225, 256, 381
Abley, John 288
Abraham, Winston 162, 170, *171*, 173
Abrahams, Owen 135
Ackerley, David 357, 359
Acraman, John 12
Adams, Bill 132, 350, 351
Adams, Frank 90, 248, 250, 251, *251*, 252
Adamson, D. 346
Adamson, Jimmy 268
Adcock, Brenton 14
Ahern, Charlie 84
Ahern, W. 321
Ainsworth, Geoff 196
Aish, Michael 14
Aitken, Jimmy 49
Aitken, Michael 169
Albiston, Alec 208, 210, *210*
Albiston, David 214
Alessio, Stephen 126
Alexander, Ron 137, 169, *169*, *374*, 375, *376*
Allan, Ben 165, *165*, 170, *170*, 171, 173, 174, 227
Allen, Les 53
Allison, Brett 279, 283
Allison, Tom 279
Allister, Jimmy 268
Alves, Stan 232, 252, 253, 275, 318, 341, *341*, 342, 343, *343*
Alvin, Tom 66, 67
Anderson, Dean 225
Anderson, Gordon 211
Anderson, Greg 22, 24, 122, *122*, 289, *290*
Anderson, Jack 303
Anderson, Jim *101*, 105
Anderson, Stewart 268
Anderson, Syd 242, 243, 245
Anderson, Tony 251
Andrew, Bruce 85, *85*
Andrews, Gareth 196
Andrews, Ron 118, 121, 312
Angus, Geoff 215
Angus, George *78*, 79, 80, 81
Angwin, Andrew 208
Angwin, Stewart 102
Annand, 'Bud' 331
Annear, John 372, *374*, 375, 377
Arceri, Mark 68
Archer, Glen 280, 281, *281*, 282
Arklay, Tom 190, 191
Armour, David 197
Armstrong, 'Skeeter' 142
Armstrong, Albert 105, 107
Armstrong, Barry 60, 61
Armstrong, Les 182
Arnold, Lance 247
Arthur, Graham 205, 211, 212, *212*, 213, 214
Ashcroft, Marcus 32, 36, 37, 38, *38*, 43
Ashman, Rod 65
Atkins, John 242, 245
Atkins, Simon 139
Atkinson, Jim 132
Austen, Col 204, 208, 209, *209*, 210, 225
Austin, Rod 138
Aylett, Allen 268, 270, 271, 272, 274, 275, *276*, 280, 357, 358

Aylwin, Harry 321
Ayres, Gary 199, 200, 201, 202, 204, 222, 224, 225, 227, 229
Bacquie, Jack 79
Baggott, Jack 109, 110, 302, 303
Baggott, Ron 242, 243
Bagshaw, Paul 14
Bailes, Barclay 131
Bailey, Brett 254
Bain, David 32, 33, *33*, 37
Bairstow, Mark 161, 169, *177*, 200, 201, 225, 373
Baker, Charlie 323, 321
Baker, Garry 252, 253
Baker, Jack (Geel) 183
Baker, Jack (Carl) 47, 298
Baker, Jack (Jnr) (Geel) 183
Baker, Leon 100, 121, 122, 169
Baker, Phil 270, 272, *274*
Baker, Ted 187
Baldock, Darrel 318, 332, *332*, 333, 334, *334*, *335*, 336, 338, 339
Ball, Fred 103
Ball, Harold 242, 245, 250
Ball, Jason 383, 384, *384*, 386
Balme, Neil 257, 258, *258*, 259, 312, 313, *313*
Bamford, Scott 43, 139
Banbury, Vernon 144, *144*, 145
Bandy, Daniel 173
Banfield, Drew 384, 385, *385*
Banfield, Peter 30, 31
Banks, Denis 96
Banks, Tom 130, *130*
Barassi, Ronald Dale 44, 56, 57, *57*, 58, 59, 60, 61, 90, 115, *115*, 119, *233*, 248, *248*, 249, *249*, 250, 251, 252, 253, 256, 260, 271, *271*, 272, *272*, 273, 274, 275, 276, 277, 278, 280, 354, 357, 366, *366*, 367
Barassi, Ronald James 242, *242*, 243, 245
Barbary, Barry 13, *13*
Barich, Adrian 380
Baring, Fred 106, 107
Barker, George 105
Barker, Jack 208
Barker, Syd 109
Barker, Syd (Jnr) 266, *266*, 267, *267*, 268
Barker, Trevor 318, *319*, 338, 339, *339*
Barling, Tim 362
Barnard, Paul 125
Barrot, Bill 136, 307, 308, 309, *309*, 310, 311, 312, 337, *337*
Barry, Peter 56, 194
Bart, Horrie 322
Bartlett, Kevin 157, 226, 227, 296, 297, 307, 308, 309, 310, 311, 312, 313, 314, *314*, 315, 337
Bartlett, Trent 43
Barwick, Victor 323
Basheer, Max 12, *12*, 290, 291
Batchelor, Arthur 132
Batters, 'Dolly' 47
Baud, Alf 51
Baxter, Ken 53, 55, 56
Baxter, Ray 155, 162
Baxter, Tom 79, 81
Bayes, Mark 365, 366, 368, *368*
Bayliss, George 146, 302
Beames, Percy 241, *241*, 242, 243, 244, 247, 304
Beard, Bert 349
Beasley, Simon 140, 156, 158
Beasy, Doug 56
Beasy, Maurie 52
Beck, Ken 214, *215*

Beckett, Tony 30, *30*
Beckton, Norm 109, *109*
Beckwith, John 249, 250, 251, *251*, 252, 253
Bedford, Peter 155, 344, 353, 354, 357
Beecroft, Bob 137
Belcher, Alan 105, 106, 107, 3*47*
Belcher, Vic 132, 344, 345, 346, *346*, 347, 349
Bell, Peter 170, 171, 280, *283*
Bennett, Darren 257
Bennett, George 146
Bennett, Peter 328, 329, *329*
Bentley, Percy 55, 56, 86, 302, 303, 304, 306,
Benton, Ron 13
Best, Arthur 236
Betts, Gerald 169
Beus, Alf 356
Beveridge, Jack 82
Bewick, Darren 122, *122*, 124, 125, 126, 373
Bews, Andrew 33, 36, 37, 42, *43*, *177*, 201
Bickford, George 232, 247
Bickley, Mark 21, *22*, 24, 25, *26*, 27
Biffin, Ray 253
Bills, Fred 13
Birt, John 114, 115, 116, 117, 118
Bisset, George 140, 145, 155, 156, 157, *157*
Bissett, Jack 349, *349*, 350
Black, Heath 175
Blackman, Jack 208
Blackwell, Wayne 169
Blake, Rod 197, *197*, 198
Blakey, John 282
Blethyn, Geoff 58, 117, 118, 119
Blight, Malcolm 14, 20, 22, 23, 24, *24*, 25, 26, *27*, 62, 176, 200, *200*, 201, 218, 260, 271, 272, 273, 274, *276*, 277, 280
Bloomfield, Sam 47
Bohan, Jim 208, 209
Bolger, Martin 302, *302*, 303, 304
Bolton, David 199, 362
Bond, Chris 315
Bond, Shane 25, 284, 293, *293*
Bond, Troy 22, *25*
Bone, Randall 19
Borlase, Darryl 290
Bos, Mark 198
Bosustow, Peter 64, *64*, 65, 169, *169*, 372
Bourke, Barry 250
Bourke, Damian 198, 201
Bourke, David 309
Bourke, Francis 61, 297, 307, 308, 309, *309*, 310, 311, 312, *313*, 314, 315
Bourke, Frank 309
Bourke, Gerald 56
Bourke, John 95
Bowden, Bob *323*, 324
Bowden, Joel 317
Bowe, Len 105
Bowyer, Percy 85, *85*
Box, Peter 140, 149, 150, 152, 153, *153*
Boyd, A. 323
Boyd, Brad 42, 43, 138
Boyd, Dave 288
Boyd, Nev 352, *352*
Boyle, Harry 46
Bradbury, Peter 121, 127
Braddy, Craig 358, 361
Bradley, Craig 14, *14*, 66, *66*, 67, *67*, 68, 69, 70, 70, 71, 222
Bradshaw, Daniel 41, 43
Brady, John 268
Brain, Terry 349

Brake, Jack 237, 371, *371*
Branton, Ron 307
Braun, Michael 387
Bray, Harold 328, *328*, 329
Bray, Jess 13
Breen, Barry 318, 336, *336*, 338, 364
Bremner, Ian 215
Brennan, Michael 166, 372, 375, 379, *379*, 383, 385
Brereton, Dermott 67, 200, 220, 221, 222, 223, 224, 225, *225*, 227, 228, *228*, 229, *230*, 340, 366, 367, 379, 380, 381
Brereton, Harry 236, 237
Brereton, Leo 56
Breuer, Shane 293
Brew, Ray 53, *325*
Brewer, Ian 90
Brewer, Ross 94, 128, 253
Briedis, Arnold 273, 277
Briggs, Robert 131
Bright, Terry 198
Brittingham, Bill 110, 111, *111*, 247
Broadstock, Jack 305
Brockwell, Charlie 142
Broderick, Neville 135
Broderick, Paul 315
Bromage, Keith 90
Brooker, Bob 268
Brosnan, Gerald 77, 131, 370, 371
Brown, Billy 307
Brown, David 24, 293, *293*, 295
Brown, Fraser 69
Brown, Gavin 73, 94, 96, 97, 98, 99, 382
Brown, John 194
Brown, Mal 118, 168, *169*, 312
Brown, Nathan 163
Brown, Norm 135, 137
Browne, Morton 212
Browning, Mark 358, 359, 360, 361, 362
Brownless, Billy 163, *200*, 201, 202, 203
Brownless, Tom 182
Brownlow, Charles 176, 179, *179*, 183
Bruce, George 49, *49*
Bruns, Neville 198, 199, 220
Bryan, Claude 237
Bryce, Edward 109, 110
Bryden, Dave 149, *149*, 151, *153*
Buckenara, Gary 204, 221, 222, 223, 225, 226, *226*, 255, 365, 366, 367, 375
Buckley, Jim *63*, 64, 65
Buckley, Nathan 33, 37, 96, 97, 98, *98*, 99, *99*, 290, *290*
Buhagiar, Tony 121, 166
Bunton, Haydn 110, 111, 128, *128*, 132, 133, *133*, 134, 139, 209, 353
Bunton, Haydn (Jnr) 168, 169
Burge, Clifford 237
Burge, Fred *297*, 304
Burgess, Reg 114
Burgoyne, Peter 293
Burke, Nathan 339, 340, *340*, 341, 342, 343
Burke, Pat 208
Burleigh, Herb 50
Burns, Greg 338, 339
Burns, John 273
Burns, Peter 176, 178, *178*, 180, 344, 346, 347, *347*
Burns, Ronnie 176, 202, 203
Burrows, Craig 170, 171
Burton, Matthew 165, *170*, 171, 173, *174*

Busbridge, Bill 105, 106, 107, *107*
Bushby, Percy *110*, 112
Busse, Neil 353
Butcher, Jack 190, 191
Buttsworth, Wally 110, 111, *113*
Byrne, Michael 221, 363
Cable, Barry 167, *270*, 271, 273, 277, 280, *374*, 381, 384
Cahill, John 13, 14, 24, 94, 95, 289, *289*, 291, 292, *292*, 294
Cahill, Terry 119
Caine, Frank 49, *49*, 266, 267
Caldwell, Jim 53, 346, 349
Callaghan, Craig 165, 175
Callan, Hughie 346
Callan, Terry 194
Callery, Paul 219, 252, 253
Calthorpe, David 18, 101, 124, 125
Calverley, Bert 134
Cameron, 'Ducky' 142
Cameron, Charles 132, 135
Cameron, David 32, 200
Cameron, Ernie 106, *106*, 107
Cameron, Jim 346
Cameron, Leon 160, 161, 163
Campbell, Adrian 158
Campbell, Blair 252, 331
Campbell, Bruce 132
Campbell, Colin 103, 237
Campbell, Garnet 109
Campbell, Graham 135, 136, 137
Campbell, Grant 378
Campbell, Matthew 30, 31, 33
Campbell, Wayne 297, 315, 317
Camporeale, Scott 68, *68*, 69
Capper, Warwick 30, 31, 32, *32*, *120*, 361, 362, 363, *363*, 365, *365*
Capuano, Matthew 279
Caracella, Blake 101, 126, *126*
Card, Ray 198
Carey, Peter 14, *14*, 25
Carey, Wayne 260, *261*, 278, 279, 280, *280*, 281, *281*, 282, *282*, 283, 386
Carman, Phil 93, *93*, 94, 95, 119, 253
Carman, Syd 109
Carmody, Jack 208
Carney, Jack 187, *187*
Carol, Hughie 207
Carroll, Dennis 359, *360*, 362, *364*, 365, 366
Carroll, L. 264
Carroll, Tom 56
Carroll, Trent 172
Carter, Billy 199
Carter, Harold 53
Carter, Nick 138
Carter, Rod 358, 359, 362, 366, *366*
Carter, Stephen 293
Carter, Wally 268, 269
Case, Geoff 248, 250, 251
Cash, Pat 210, 211, 213
Cashman, Jack 132
Cassidy, D. 268
Cassidy, Jim 143, 146
Cassin, Jack 110, 111, 112, 118
Cassin, John 275
Caven, Peter 22, 367
Cazaly, Roy 133, 208, 209, *323*, 324, 325, 344, 348, *348*, 349, 350
Chadwick, Bert 208, 209, 238, *238*, 239, 240, 241, 251
Challis, George 51
Chalmers, Brett 19
Chambers, Jack 187
Champion, Richard 32, *35*, 36
Chandler, Bert 241, *241*
Chandler, Neil 61
Chandler, Newton 53

388

Chanter, Vic 134, 135
Chapman, Charles 132
Chapman, Nathan 33, 36
Chapple, Les 146
Charles, Justin 161, 316, 317, *317*
Chesswass, Harry 85, *85*
Chisholm, Scott 171
Chitty, Bob 54, 55, 148, 351
Christian, Michael 373
Christie, Dave (Melb) 235
Christie, David (Fre) 173
Christou, Ang 71
Clape, Matt 68, *380*
Clark, Jim 56
Clark, Michael 172
Clark, Norman 49, *49*, 50, 53, 268, 325
Clark, Wally 135
Clarke, David 176, 196, 197, 198, 199
Clarke, E. Ansell 53, 326
Clarke, Ern 93, *93*
Clarke, Hec 349
Clarke, Jack (Ess) 114, 115, *115*, 116, 117, 118, 269
Clarke, Jack (Fre) 166, *166*, 172
Clarke, Matthew 36, 37, 38, *38*, 43, *279*
Clarke, Noel 232, 249
Clarke, Tom 109
Clarkson, Alistair 254
Clay, Bert 134
Clay, Dick 307, 308, 309, *309*, 310, 311, 312
Clayden, George 82, *82*
Clayton, Scott 138
Cleary, Jim 350
Cleary, Phil 157
Cleary, William 131
Clegg, Ron 209, 344, 350, 351, *351*, 353, 354
Cleghorn, Arthur 105
Clement, James 172
Clements, Charles 346
Cleverdon, A. S. 207
Cloke, David 315
Close, Robin 117
Clover, Horrie 52, *52*, 53, 60
Clymo, Charlie 187
Cockatoo-Collins, Che *101*
Coffey, John 328, 329
Coghlan, Arthur 184, *184*, 187, 188
Coghlan, Kevin 210, 211
Colbert, Leigh 202
Coleman, John 44, 101, *101*, 112, *112*, 113, *113*, 114, 115, 116, *116*, 117, 118, 134, 215, 307
Coles, Charles 180
Coles, Henry 253
Colgan, Charlie 346
Collier, Albert 53, 72, 82, 84, *84*, 85, 86, 87, 88, 98, *98*
Collier, Harry 72, 82, 83, 84, *84*, 85, 86, 87, 88, 98, 303
Colling, Gary 338
Collins, Alan 148, 149
Collins, Andy 225, 227, 229
Collins, Denis 157
Collins, Geoff 249
Collins, Goldsmith 132
Collins, Jack (Melb) 238, 240
Collins, Jack (Foots) 148, 150, *150*, 151, 152, 154, 155, 187, *187*, 190, 192
Collins, Lance 55
Collins, Matthew 19
Collins, Ted *323*, 324, 325
Collins, Tod 105
Collis, Gordon 44, 56, 57, *57*
Comden, Bruce 56, *56*
Comte, Harold 326
Condon, Anthony 227
Condon, Dick 75, 76, *76*, 77, 78, 79
Condon, Don 268
Conlan, Micky 128, 137, 138
Connell, Matt 21, 23
Connelly, Chris 254
Connelly, Jack 326
Connor, Ryan *126*
Considine, Bill 145, 267
Conway, Jack 180

Cook, Brett 343
Cook, Russell 357
Cook, Tim 24
Cook, William 50
Cook, D. 262
Cooper, Ian 335, *335*
Cooper, Jack 132
Copeland, Ern 75, 83, *83*
Corbett, Bob 238, 239, *239*
Cordner, David 246
Cordner, Denis 211, 245, 246, *246*, 247, 248, *248*, 249, 250
Cordner, Don 149, 232, *233*, 244, 246, *246*, 247, *247*
Cordner, Edward 246, *246*, 371, *371*
Cordner, Harry 236, 246, 371
Cordner, Jock 268
Cordner, John 246, *246*
Cordner, Ted 243, 245, 246, *246*
Cordy, Graeme 363
Cordy, Neil 363
Cornes, Graham 14, *14*, 16, 17, 18, *18*, 19, 20, 22, 25
Cosgrove, Bill 304, *304*, 315
Cotton, Ray 143
Couch, Paul 176, *177*, 198, 200, *200*, 201, 202, 203
Coulthard, George 46, *46*, 47
Cousins, Ben 384, 385, *385*, *386*
Cousins, Bryan 197, 384
Coutie, Vince 236
Coventry, Gordon 12, 72, 81, 82, *82*, 83, 84, 85, 86, 87, *87*, 90, 96, 98, 229, 305, 326
Coventry, Syd 72, 81, 82, *82*, 83, 84, *84*, 85, 86, 87, 90, 91, 98, 146, 147
Cowton, Gary 272
Craddock, Johnny 144, *144*, 148
Craig, Neil 14, 15
Crane, Garry 58, *60*
Cransberg, Peter 122
Craven, Harry 184, 185
Crawford, Alan 268
Crawford, Shane 218
Crebbin, Bill 102, 104
Cresswell, Daryn 367, 368, *368*, 369
Crichton, Arthur 107
Crimmins, Peter 217, *217*, 226, 275
Crisp, Mick 53
Croft, Edgar 104
Crofts, Archie 349, 350
Crompton, Neil 91, 249, 251, *251*
Crosisca, Gavin 94, 99
Cross, Max 152, 194
Crosswell, Brent 44, 45, 58, *58*, 59, 253, 272, 273, 274
Crow, Max 118, 338
Crowe, Jim 148
Crowe, Neville 307, 308, 309, 310, 315
Crowley, Ern 50
Cubbins, Bill 146, 147, 318, 324, 325, *325*, 326
Culph, Claude 350
Culpitt, Wally 208, 209
Cumberland, Vic 235, 240, *322*, *323*, 324
Cummings, Scott 125, 284, *292*, 293, 294
Cummings, Trent 387
Cunningham, Brian 289, 290
Cunningham, Geoff 338
Curcio, Frank 132, 134
Curran, Kevin 208, 210, *210*, 211
Curran, Peter 32, 225
Curtin, Claude 132, 135
Curtis, Harry 81
Cuzens, Dave 307
Daffy, Nick 315
Daicos, Peter 73, 94, 95, *95*, 96, 97, *97*, 98, *98*
Daily, Lou 142, 188
Dalton, Jack 245
Daly, 'Bunny' 13
Daly, Gerry 243
Dangerfield, Gordon 324, *323*, *323*, *324*
Daniels, Allen 169

Daniher, Anthony 127
Daniher, Chris 122, 124, 127, *127*
Daniher, Neale 64, 120, 121, 127, *258*
Daniher, Terry 100, 118, 119, 121, 123, *123*, 127
Danilchenko, Jason 280
Dare, Norm 32, *32*, 33
Darley, Peter 14
Davey, Charley 53
Davie, Bert 183
Davie, Harry 238, 239, 241
Davie, Jack 183
Davies, Fred 57, 132
Davies, Harold 329, *329*
Davies, Rick 14, 15
Davis, Alan 335, 336
Davis, Barry 116, *116*, 117, *117*, 118, *118*, 119, 252, 270, *270*, 271, 272, 273, *273*, 274
Davis, Bob 191, 192, 193, *193*, 194, 195, 195, 196
Davis, Craig 61, 62, 94, 118, 362
Davis, Frank 253
Davis, Jack 326, *327*
Day, Albert 108
Day, Robert 13, 215
Daykin, Richard 79
Dayman, Les 146
De Coite, Dave 142, *142*, 179
Deacon, Bert 44, 54, 55, *55*, 70
Dean, Archie 207
Dean, Bill 74
Dean, Peter 69, *69*
Dean, Robert 357
Dean, Roger 307, 308, 310, *310*, 311, *311*, 312, 313
Dean, Warren 254
Deane, Colin 326
Deane, Jim 13, *13*
Dear, Greg 229, 255
Dear, Paul 227, 379
Delahunty, Joe 74
Delaney, Tony 170, *173*
Deller, George 331
Del-Re, Danny 161
Dempsey, Gary 140, 154, 155, 156, *156*, 157, 160, 253, 276, 277
Dench, David 271, 272, 273, 274, *275*, 277
Denham, Sean 125, 126, 127
Denning, Clendon 132
Dennis, Richard 373
Dent, Matthew 163
Devine, John 194, 198, 199, *199*
Dhurrkay, Gary 165, 171, 173
Dibbs, Charlie 82, *82*, 188, *188*
Dick, Alick 102
Dick, William 50, 51, 183
Dickfos, Danny 35, 36, 43
Dickie, Donald 284, 293, *293*
Dickson, Dale *30*, 31
Dickson, Des 214
Diggins, Brighton 53, 55, 190, *345*, 349, 350
Dillon, Ross 253
DiPierdomenico, Robert 67, 138, 158, 204, 217, 221, 222, 223, *223*, 225, *225*, 227, 255, 362, 376
Ditterich, Carl 118, 233, 253, *253*, 270, 318, 319, 332, *332*, *333*, 334, 335, 336, 337, 338
Dixon, Brian 230, 250, 251, *251*, 252, 257, 270, 271, 272, 359, 360
Dockendorff, Syd 146
Dockett, Len 247
Doig, 'Hooky' 166
Doig, Billy 166
Doig, Charlie 166
Doig, Charlie (Jnr) 166
Doig, Edgar 166
Doig, George 166
Doig, Norman 166
Doig, Ron 166
Doig, Scotty 166
Dolan, Jerry 167

Dolphin, Bill 346
Don, Donald 303
Donald, Wally 148, 149, *149*, 151, 152, 153
Donaldson, Graham 56, 137
Donnelly, Andrew 385, 386
Donnelly, Gerald 239, 268
Donohue, Larry 196, 198
Donovan, Jack 46, 47
Doolan, Vin 271
Dorgan, Jim 350
Dorotich, Jon 66, *66*
Doubleday, Jack 237
Douglass, Percy 178, 179
Doull, Bruce 44, 61, 62, *62*, 63, 64, 65, 66, 67, 70
Dowling, John 268
Downs, Lyle 52
Downsborough, Ian 293
Doyle, Peter 197
Drew, Davey 142
Drinan, Keith 328, *328*, 329, *329*, 330, 331
Drohan, Edward 79, 206
Drummond, Tom 81
Duckworth, Bill 127, 224, 228
Duffy, Roger 141, 148, 151
Dugdale, John 268, 269, *269*, 271
Dullard, Adrian 245
Dullard, Anthony 242
Dummett, Alfred 78
Dummett, Rob 307
Duncan, Alec 53, *53*, 351
Dunell, Frank 30, *30*
Dunkley, Andrew 367, 368, *368*
Dunn, Harvey 53
Dunne, Jeff 338
Dunne, Ross 94, 275
Dunnell, Frank 30, *30*
Dunstall, Jason 35, 67, 199, 204, 222, 223, 224, 225, 226, 227, 229, *229*, 230, 231, 379
Dunstan, Ian 156, 157
Dunstan, Maurie 89
Duperouzel, Bruce 338
Durham, Ron 304, 305
Duursma, Jamie *30*, 255
Dwyer, Laurie 268, 271
Dwyer, Leo 268
Dyer, Jack 113, 134, 208, 213, 242, 244, 246, 296, 297, *297*, 302, *302*, 303, 304, *304*, 305, 306, *306*, 307, 313, 314, 315, *315*, 327
Dyer, Syd 260, 261, 268
Dynon, Kevin 268
Dyson, Kevin 367
Eade, Rodney 31, 32, 204, 221, 222, 366, 367, 369
Eagleton, Nathan 293
Eakins, Peter 92
Eason, Alex 145, 146, 176, *177*, 182, 183, *183*
Eason, Bill 176, 180, 182
Ebert, Russell 14, 280, 288, *288*, 289, 290
Edmond, Jim 30, *30*, 31, 156, 157, 158, 362
Edmonds, Alex 299, *299*, 303
Edmonds, Travis 170
Edwards, Arthur 149, 151
Edwards, Brendan 211, *211*, 212, 213, 214
Edwards, Greg 14
Edwards, Jack 268
Edwards, Scott 170, 171
Eicke, Welles 53, 268, 280, 318, 322, *323*, 324, 325
Ellen, Shane 22, 26
Ellingsen, Percy 183
Elliott, Fred 48, 49, 50, 144
Elliott, George 371
Elliott, Glenn 338
Ellis, Edward 148
Ellis, Noel 245
Elms, Sonny 344, 346, 347, *347*, 349
Elshaug, Tony 281
Emselle, Dick 245, 326

English, Des 65, 67
Epis, Alec 116, 164
Equid, Harry 112
Erwin, Mick 94, 95, 307
Eustice, Ken 13
Evans, Bernie *359*, *360*, 361
Evans, Jack 188, *188*, 189, *189*, 190
Evans, Ron 114, 115
Evans, Roy 146, 147, 148, 155
Evans, Tim 14, 289
Evans, Tony 372, 378, 381, 383, 385, 386
Everett, Allan 188, 189, *189*, 190
Everitt, Peter 342, 343
Ezard, Alan 121, 123
Fairbairn, S.J. 236
Fairley, Ian 277
Fairweather, Fred 268
Fanning, Fred 229, 242, 243, *243*, 245, 246, 247, 328, 379
Farmer, Graham 56, 164, 166, 167, *169*, 176, *177*, 194, *194*, 195, 196, 197, 214, *374*, 381
Farmer, Jeff 258, *258*, 259
Farmer, Ken 12, *12*, 13
Farrant, Doug 271
Farrant, Gary 271
Faul, Bill 349, 353, *353*
Featherby, Peter 157, *157*, 198
Febey, Steven 254
Fellowes, Wes 94
Feltham, Paul 33, 273
Fenton-Smith, Dick 249
Ferguson, Tom 207, 245
Fewster, Brendan 385, 386
Fidge, John 30, *30*, 31
Fields, Neville 118, 119
Fielke, Grantley 16
Findlay, Bill 268
Fisher, Charlie 53
Fitzgerald, Jim 191, *191*
Fitzgerald, Len 13, 86, 89
Fitzgibbon, Fred 54
Fitzmaurice, Tom 107, 108, *108*, 109, 145, 166, 187, 268, 280
Fitzpatrick, Mike 61, 62, *62*, 63, 64, 65
Flacchi, George *290*
Flaherty, Danny 75
Flanagan, Fred 176, 191, 192, *192*, 193, *193*, 194
Flanigan, Robert 148
Flegg, Ron 326
Fleiter, Fred *345*, 348, 349
Fleming, Eric 184, *184*
Fletcher, C. 36
Fletcher, Dustin 101, 124, 125, *126*
Fletcher, Ken 117, 118, 119
Fletcher, Ted 211
Flood, David 124
Flower, Robert 232, *233*, 252, 253, 254, *254*, 255, 256, *256*
Flynn, Jim *49*, 49
Fogarty, Thomas 346, 371
Foote, Les *261*, 268, 269, *269*, 280, 328, 329, *329*
Forbes, Charles *101*, 102, 103, *103*, 104
Forbes, Keith 108, *108*, 109, 111, 242, 268
Ford, Norman 144, 145, 146
Fordham, Ted 117
Foreman, Wayne 157
Forsyth, Keith 111
Foschini, Silvio 359, 360
Fothergill, Des 72, 86, 88, *88*, 89, 93, 95, 98
Foulds, Garry 124
Fountain, Roy 326, 327
Fowler, Laurie 61, 253, 313, *313*
Fox, John 195
Fox, Lindsay 332, 338, 339
Francis, Fabian 293, *294*
Francis, Jim 53, 55, 56, 331
Francis, Tony 96, 99
Francou, Josh 284, 293, *295*
Franklin, Tony 356, 360
Franks, Bert 346
Fraser, Don 161, 296, *297*, 302, 305, *305*, 306, 307

389

Fraser, Ken 100, 116, *116*, 117
Fraser, Simon 371
Fraser, William 346
Frawley, Danny 338, *340*, 341
Freake, Jimmy 132, *132*
Free, Tony 315
Freeborn, Scott 281, 293
Freeman, Jack 346
Freyer, Ted 109, 110
Fricker, Pat 89
Froude, Fred 328
Fry, Herb 235
Fuhrhop, Harry 262, 263, *263*
Fulton, Terry 191
Furness, Don 135
Gabelich, Ray 90, 91, 93, 251
Gale, Alan 135, *135*
Gale, Benny 297, 316, *316*, 317
Gale, Mark 175
Gallagher, Adrian 44, 58
Gallagher, Fred 114, *114*
Gallagher, Jim 149, *149*, 151, 153
Galt, Rod 63
Gambetta, Cyril 208
Garby, Ray 56
Garden, Jack 107, 109
Gardiner, Alec 155
Gardiner, Jack 50, 51
Gardiner, Michael 386, 387
Gardiner, Vin 49, 50, *50*, 51
Garvie, Bill 304
Garvin, Reg 326, 327
Gastev, John 32, 33, *33*, 96, *373*, 377
Gaudion, Charlie 268, *268*, 269, 270
Gaudion, Mick 270
Gavin, Hugh 105
Geddes, Alan 302, 303
Geddes, Jack 207
Gehrig, Fraser 382, *385*, 386, *386*, 387
Gellie, Graeme 338, 339
George, Alf 236
Gerlach, Daryl 118, *118*
Ghent, Bill *345*
Gibb, Maurice 241, 243, 245
Gibbs, Richard 237
Gieshen, Jeff 316, 317, *317*
Giles, Peter 254
Giles, Tony 289
Gill, Frank 53, 55
Gill, John 58, 114, *114*
Gillett, Ian 350
Gilmore, Brian 151
Gilmour, Donald 153
Glascott, David 65, 66
Glass, Ted 241
Gleeson, Adrian 66
Gleeson, Brian 318, 330, *330*, 331
Gleeson, Terry 248, 250, 251
Glendinning, Ross 260, 276, *276*, 277, 372, *373*, *374*, 375, 376, *376*, 377
Glenister, Norm 191
Gniel, George 55, 190, 191
Goad, Alan 218
Godden, Tony 172, 385
Goggin, Bill 156, 176, 195, *195*, 196, 198, 199
Golding, Frank 12
Golding, Harry 346
Goldsmith, Fred 344, 351, *351*, 352, 353, 354
Goninon, George 191, 193, 194
Goode, Frank 268, 271
Goode, Kerry *274*, 276
Goodingham, Barry 271, 272, 273
Gorozidis, Con 338
Gosper, Geoff 117, 118, *118*
Goss, Norm 357
Gove, Cyril 107
Gowers, Andrew 36, 37, 43
Grace, Jim 130
Grace, Mick 48, *48*, 49, *49*, 130, 131, 322, 370, 371
Graham, Ben 202
Graham, Ian 93, 335
Graham, Jack 344, 350, *350*, 362
Graham, Michael 14
Grant, Chris 140, 160, 161, 163, *163*, 292

Grant, David 340
Grant, Jack 135, 190, 191
Gravenall, Samuel 323
Green, Brent 37
Green, Doug 166
Green, Fred 328
Green, Gordon 53
Green, Jack 208
Green, Mike 307, 308, 310, *310*, 311, 312, 313, *313*
Green, Ritchie 57
Greene, Russell 221
Greenham, Dave 371
Greenham, Jim 147
Greenhill, Jack 52
Greening, John 92, 337
Greeves, Edward 176, 184, *184*, 187, 238
Gregory, Art 143
Greig, Keith 253, 260, 270, 271, *271*, 272, 273, 274, 275, 277, 280
Grenvold, David 122, *122*
Grgic, Brent 258
Grgic, Ilija 386, 387
Grieg, Keith 119
Grierson, Piggy 144
Grieve, Ollie 54, 56, *56*, 57
Griffith, Bill 105
Griffiths, Daryl 333, 334, *334*, 335, *335*, 336, *336*
Grigg, Dick 180, 182, 183
Grinter, Rod 232, 254, 255, *255*
Groom, Ray 251, 253
Groome, Chris 19
Grossman, Don 351
Guinane, Paddy 307, 308, 309, 310, 310, 311
Gumbleton, Frank 273
Gunn, Bill 350
Guy, Eric 161, 213, 331, *331*, 332
Hacker, Harold 238
Hafey, Tom 94, *94*, 95, 198, 307, 308, 309, 310, *310*, 311, *311*, 312, 314, 315, 361, 362, 363
Hagger, Lloyd 184, 185, *185*, 187
Haines, George 238, 325
Halbert, John 13, 15
Hale, Jack 53, 54, 190, 210, 211, 350, 351
Hall, Alec 184, 208, 236
Hall, Barry 342, 343, *343*
Hall, Jim 328
Hall, Norm 107
Hall, Tony 19, 21, 225, 229
Hamilton, Jack 96
Hamilton, Kevin 56
Hamilton, Shane 32
Hammond, Bob 13, 360, 361
Hammond, Charlie 49, *49*, 267, *267*
Hampshire, Ian 156, 157, *157*, 197
Hancock, Robert 328
Hando, Arthur 184
Hands, Ken 54, *54*, 55, 56, 351
Hanna, Ian 15
Hanna, Mil 68, 71
Hannaford, Ian 15
Hardeman, Gary 232, 252, *252*, 253
Hardie, Brad 30, *30*, 31, 32, *32*, 33, *38*, *38*, 39, 140, 157, 158, *158*, 167, *167*, 372
Hardie, Charlie 109
Hardiman, Les 188, 189, *189*, 190
Hardiman, Peter 190
Hardiman, Tom 180
Harding, Greg 172, 175
Harding, Paul 166, 373, 375, *380*, 385
Hardwick, Damian 125, *126*
Hardy, Charlie 109, 266, 267, *267*, 326, 327
Harford, Daniel 231
Harmes, Wayne 63, *63*, 65
Harper, Bert 113
Harris, 'Ching' 142, 143, *143*
Harris, Bernie 30, 31, *33*, 138
Harris, Dick 304, 305, 307
Harris, John 208
Harris, Leon 138

Harrison, Barry 91, *91*
Harrison, Ben 317
Harrison, Henry 12, 178, 234, 235, *235*, 239, *239*, 299, *299*
Harrison, Joe 109
Hart, Ben 24
Hart, Darrell 16, 17, 21
Hart, David 375, *375*, *377*, 386
Hart, Eddie 135
Hart, Royce 61, 156, 157, 297, *297*, 307, 308, *308*, 309, 310, *310*, 311, 312, 313, *313*, 314, 315
Hart, Shaun 34, 36, 37, 42, 172
Hartford, Daniel 218, 231, *231*
Hartigan, Dean 118
Hartkopf, Albert 371, *371*
Hartridge, Ron 350
Harvey, Mark 121, 122, *123*, 124, 125, 127, *127*
Harvey, Robert 26, 318, *319*, 340, 341, 342, 343, 387
Harvey, Ron 135
Hassell, George 111, 112
Hassett, Kevin 332
Hawke, Neil 13
Hawker, Glenn 100, 119, 121, 122
Hawking, Fred 188
Hawking, Simon 43
Hawkins, Doug 138, 140, 141, 158, 160, *160*, 161
Hayden, Ian 307
Hayes, Doug 302
Hayes, John 135
Head, Lindsay 13
Heady, Brett 378, 381, 383, 386
Heal, George 243
Heal, Stan 243
Healey, Des 89, 90, 248
Healey, Greg 253, 254, *254*, 257
Healy, Gerard 252, 253, *253*, 354, 362, 363, *363*, 364
Heaney, Tom 132
Heard, Shane 100, 119
Hearn, Maurice 33
Heathcote, John 56, 352
Heatley, Jason 282, 343
Heaver, Brett 293
Heffernan, Chris 126
Hein, Neil *30*, 31
Heinz, George 182
Helmer, Clyde 190, *190*, 191
Henderson, Herbie 149, *149*, 151, 152
Henderson, J. 93
Hendrie, John 216
Henfry, Ern 55, *55*, 56, 57
Henshaw, Ross 270
Henwood, Wayne 363
Hepburn, Mark 373
Heuskes, Adam 284, 293, 295, *295*
Hewson, Don 245
Heywood, Doug 245
Hickey, Con *133*
Hickey, Harry 55, 141, 148
Hickey, Joe 135
Hickey, Pat 131
Hickey, Reg 176, 187, 188, *188*, 189, *189*, 190, 191, 192, 193, 194
Hickinbotham, Dave *179*, 180, 181, 182
Hickmott, Peter 100
Hicks, Daryl 15
Higgins, Brett 19, 21
Hillard, Norm 134, 208
Hillis, Ron 349, 350
Hinch, Paddy 142, 143
Hinkley, Ken *177*, 201
Hird, Alan 328
Hird, James 37, 100, 101, 124, 125, 126, 161
Hiskins, Albert 349
Hiskins, Fred 105
Hobbs, Merv 155, *155*, 212
Hocking, Eddie 16
Hocking, Gary 176, 201, 202, *202*, 203, 225
Hocking, Gordon 89
Hocking, Steve 176, 199
Hodgeman, Kym 277

Hodges, Scott 17, 19, 21, 24, *289*, 290, 291, 293
Hodgson, Arthur 56, 57
Hogan, Joe 321
Hogg, Jeff 315
Hoiles, John 155
Holden, George 132
Holland, Nick 218, 230, 231
Holmes, Don 169, *374*, *375*, *377*, 377
Hooper, Don 245
Hopkins, Albert 303
Hopkins, Allen 85, 140, 146, 147, *147*
Hopkins, Ted 59
Hosking, Samson 287
Houston, G. 263, 264
Houston, R. 264
Hovey, Ron 176, 194, 201, *201*
Howell, Jack 55, 56, *56*, 144, 145, 306, 347
Howell, Verdun 318, 330, *330*, 331, *331*, 332, 334, 335, *335*, 336
Howson, Herb 346, 349
Hudson, Paul 226, 228
Hudson, Peter 92, 93, 113, 196, 204, *205*, 214, 215, *215*, 216, *216*, 219, 226, 229, 337, *337*
Hughes, Alf 211
Hughes, Danny 253
Hughes, Frank 238, 240, *240*, 241, 242, 243, 244, 245, 246, 247, 249, 250, 302, *302*, 303
Hughes, Les 79, 80, *80*, 81
Hughson, Fred 132, 134, *134*, 135, 149
Hunt, Rex 310, 311, 312
Hunter, Ken 64, *64*, 65, *66*, 67, *168*, 372
Hunter, Kingsley 173, *173*, 174, 175
Hunter, Maurie 302, 303
Huppatz, Ray *14*, 157
Hurrey, Bert 371
Hutchinson, Jack 143
Hutchison, Bill 100, 110, 111, 112, 114, 115, *115*
Hutchison, Greg 259
Hutton, John 33
Hyde, Bert 208, 209, *209*
Hyde, John 191
Hyde, Robert 93
Hynes, David 172, *172*, 385
Icke, Stephen 232, 253, 254
Incigneri, Len 236, *236*
Ingerson, Anthony 21, *21*
Ingersoll, Terry 211
Ion, Graeme 155
Irwin, Vince 109
Irwin, Warwick 137
Ischenko, Alex 376
Jackman, Kevin 155
Jackson, Francis 356
Jackson, Jim 208
Jackson, Mark 198, *198*, 199, 253, *253*, 338
Jackson, Newhaven 104
Jackson, Ricky 254
Jackson, Stevan *378*
Jackson, Syd 59, 164
Jackson, W.C. 321
Jakovich, Allen 256, 257, *257*, 382
Jakovich, Glen 174, 378, 380, 382, 383, 384, *384*, 385, 386, *386*, 387
James, Brett 24
James, Eddy 180, 181
James, Hugh 183, 302
James, Jack 324, 325
James, John 44, 56, 57, *57*, 153, 194
James, Stephen 362
Jameson, Rod 16, 17, 22, 24
Jarman, Andrew 14, 16, 21, 22, 23, *23*, 24
Jarman, Darren 21, 22, 23, *23*, 25, 26, *26*, 229, 343
Jeans, Allan 204, 218, 220, 221, 223, 224, *224*, 225, 226, 227, 314, 315, 318, 332, *332*, 333, 335, *335*, 336, 338, 332, 361, 363
Jenkin, Graeme 118, 312
Jenkin, Horrie 132
Jenkins, Ernest 131

Jenkins, Tom 109
Jennings, Geoff 156
Jennings, Ossie 304
Jesaulenko, Alex 15, 44, 58, 59, *59*, 60, 61, *61*, 62, 63, *63*, 64, 66, 67, 68, 69, 70, 338
Jess, Jim 297, *297*
Jewell, Tony 308, 314, 315, 338, 339
Jillard, John 155
Jinks, Fred 49, *49*, 267
John, Gareth 365
John, Graeme 356, *356*, 357
Johns, Keith 185
Johnson, Alan 253, 255, 257
Johnson, Bob 238, *238*, 239, 241
Johnson, Bob (Jnr) 248, *248*, 250, 251, *251*, 253
Johnson, Brad 140
Johnson, Chris 43, 138
Johnson, Frank 352, 353
Johnson, George Sidney 48, 49, *49*, 267
Johnson, Joe 131
Johnson, Kane 23, 25, 163
Johnson, Len 109
Johnson, Maurie 53
Johnson, Tassie 250, 252
Johnson, Ted 349
Johnson, Trevor 251
Johnson, Wally 131, 132
Johnston, Bill 296, *296*
Johnston, Peter 199
Johnston, W. *262*
Johnston, Wayne 63, 64, *64*, 65, 66, 67, 70, 222
Johnstone, Norm 135
Jones, 'Curly' 319
Jones, Austinn 319, 342, *343*
Jones, Bernie 273
Jones, Dennis 252, 253
Jones, Jack 111
Jones, John 182
Jones, Percy 58, 60, 61, 63, 64
Jones, Ray 350
Jory, Percy *323*, 325
Joyce, Alan 161, 212, 224, *224*, 225, 226, 227, 228, 229
Judge, Ken *30*, 204, 221, 230
Judkins, Stan 35, 296, 303, *303*
Kappler, Darren 138, 365
Kearney, Dan ˙83, 199
Kearney, Jim 182, 183, 199
Keating, Aaron 24, *26*, 27
Keddie, Bob 214, 215, 337
Keenan, Peter 252, 253
Keene, Laurie *374*, 376, 377
Kekovich, Brian 58
Kekovich, Sam 270, *270*, 271, 272, 273
Kellaway, Duncan 297, 316, *316*, 317
Kelly, Craig 96
Kelly, Des 167
Kelly, Harvey 346
Kelly, Jack 326, 327
Kelly, Joe 146, 147, 148, 350
Kelly, Lester 371
Kelly, Paul 229, 281, 354, *355*, 365, 366, *366*, 367, 368, *368*, 369
Kemp, Danny 268
Kemp, Dean 378, 380, 381, 383, *383*, 384
Kendall, Tom 46
Kennedy, George 268
Kennedy, Greg 60, 61
Kennedy, John 204, 210, *210*, 211, 212, 213, 214, 215, 216, 217, *217*, 219, 221, 228, 277, *277*
Kennedy, John (Jnr) 221, 224, 225, 227
Kennedy, Matthew 36
Kennedy, Rick 140, 158, 162
Kennedy, Ted 51
Kennett, Toby 19, 21
Kennon, Bill 207
Kenny, Peter 66
Keogh, Trevor *60*, 61, 63
Kerley, Jack 179
Kerley, Neil 13, *13*, 15, 25, 161, 288

Kernahan, Harry 13, *13*
Kernahan, Stephen 14, *14*, 44, *45*, 52, 62, 66, 67, *67*, 68, *68*, 69, *69*, 70, *70*, 71, 124
Kerr, John 151, *151*
Kickett, Dale 164, 165, 171, *172*, 173, 175, *175*
Kickett, Derek 122, 124, 164
Kiel, Peter 338
Kiernan, Chris 131
Killigrew, Allan 196, 268, 269, 270, 271, 319, 326, 327, *327*, *330*, 331, *331*, 332
Kilpatrick, Glenn 202
King, Sean 376
King, Steven 202, 203
King, Stuart 326
Kingsley, Adam 293
Kingston, Ron 353
Kink, Rene 93
Kinnear, Col 364, *364*, 365
Kirby, Jack 107
Kirzner, Julian 282
Klug, John 16
Kluzek, Matthew 19, 24
Knapman, Frank 286, *286*
Kneen, Edgar 371
Knight, Jack 326
Knight, Jim 190, *190*, 191
Knights, Matthew 297, *297*, 315, 317, *317*
Knights, Peter 30, *30*, 31, 32, *32*, 33, 204, 215, 216, 217, 218, *218*, 220, 221, 229, 275
Kolyniuk, Steve 160
Koops, Steven 172
Koster, Kym 22, 25
Koutoufides, Anthony 68, 70, 71
Krakouer, Jim *168*, 169, 276, *276*, 277, 372
Krakouer, Phil *168*, 169, 276, *276*, 277, 372
Kruse, Max 359
Kuhlken, Bill 187
Kyne, Phonse 86, 87, 88, 89, 90, *90*, 98
La Fontaine, Alan 241, *241*, 242, 243, 244, 245, 247, 248
Lacey, William 47
Lade, Brendon 284, 293
Lahiff, Tommy 208, 243
Laidlaw, Clyde 248, 250, 251
Laidlaw, Nick 24
Laidley, Dean 375
Lake, Bruce 117
Lamb, Dwayne 377, 378, 383
Lamb, Robert 315
Lambert, Chris 111
Lambert, Craig 33, 36, 37, 38, *38*, 42, 43, 315
Lambert, Harold 111
Lampe, Harold 346
Lancaster, Ralph 190, *190*
Land, Chris 347
Landy, Graeme 197
Landy, William *182*
Lane, Eddie 350
Lane, Gordon 110, 111, 113, 350
Lane, Ralph 248
Langdon, Karl 377, *378*, 380, *381*, 385
Langdon, Mark 320
Langford, Chris 199, 218, 229, 231, *231*, 363, *363*
Langley, Frank 236
Langley, Gil 111
Langridge, Ted 307
Langsford, Don 376
Lappin, Nigel 36, 43
Larkin, Matthew 277, *277*, 278
Law, Ian *205*, 212, 214, *214*, 241
Law, John 277
Lawrence, Barry 337, *337*, 338
Lawrence, Steve 43, 227, 379
Lazarus, Gary 135, 137
Leach, Arthur 78, 79, 90
Leach, Fred 76, *76*, 77, 79, 90
Leach, Quentin 170, 171, 174, 175, *175*

Leahy, Terry 250
Leahy, Tom 13
Lee, Dick 78, 79, 80, *80*, 81, 86, 98, 347
Lee, Mark 297, 315, *376*
Lee, Scott 16
Leehane, Ted 110, 111, 112, 113
Leek, Geoff 114, *114*, 115, 116
Lehmann, Troy 33
Leith, Jack 235, 236
Leonard, Johnny 349
Leoncelli, Anthony 258
Leppitsch, Justin 33, 36, 37, 42, 43
Leslie, Martin 32, 33, 35, 38, *38*
Lester-Smith, Rod 31, 32
Lethbridge, Chris 132, 133
Lever, Harry 323, *323*, 325
Lewington, Clive 166, 167, 172
Lewis, A.W. 235
Lewis, Chris 372, 375, *375*, *376*, 377, *377*, 379, *382*, 383, 386, *387*
Lewis, Dale 366, 368, *368*, 369
Lewis, John 241, *241*, 268
Ley, Arthur 263
Leydin, Tommy 47
Libbis, Bill 82, *82*, 240
Liberatore, Tony 140, 160, *160*, 161, 163
Lilburne, Charles 302
Lindner, Bruce 16, 198
Lindner, Don 13
Lindsay, Bruce 16
Linney, Neville 329, *329*
Linton, Alby 148
Liptak, Matthew 17, 22, 23, *23*, 25, 26
Llewellyn, Ted 268
Lloyd, Matthew 101, 125, 126, *126*, 127
Lloyd, Stan 326, 327
Lock, Wally 243, 247
Lockett, Tony 173, 223, 281, 318, 319, *319*, 338, 339, *339*, 340, 341, *355*, 366, 367, 368, *368*, 369, 386
Lockett, William 320, *320*
Lockwood, Bowen 293
Lockwood, George 77
Lockwood, Ted 77, 86, 176, 180
Lockyer, Andrew 381
Loewe, Stewart 170, 318, *340*, 341, 342, 343
Lofts, Wes 117, 215
Long, Doug 13
Long, Michael 101, 122, *122*, 124, *124*, 125, *125*, 126
Longmire, John 260, 278, 279, 280, 282, *282*
Lord, Alistair 176, 194, 195, *195*
Lord, John 249
Lord, Stewart 194, 195
Lording, F. 263
Love, Jason 365
Loveless, Ernie 208
Loveless, Shane 156
Lovell, Andy 255
Loveridge, Richard 221
Lovett, Brett 256
Lovett, Glenn 254, 257
Low, Ian 157
Loxton, Sam 326, 328
Lucas, Bert 350
Lucas, Scott 101, 126
Luders, Roger 15
Lugton, Frank 237
Luke, Charlie 146
Lumsden, Ernie 107
Lyle, Brayden 293
Lynch, Alastair 29, 33, 35, 36, 37, 38, 41, 42, 138
Lynch, Dave 302
Lynch, Jack 190
Lynch, Marty 191
Lynch, Paul 203
Lynch, T. 36
Lyon, Garry *233*, 254, 256, 257, *257*, *259*; 377
Mackenzie, Tom 13
Maclean, Billy 263
Maclure, Mark 63, 64, 65, 66, 67
MacNish, Andrew 377

MacPherson, Steve 160, *160*
MacRae, Cliff 147
Madden, Justin 64, 66, 67, 68, 69, 70, 71, 173
Madden, Michael 105, *106*
Madden, Simon 100, 118, *118*, 119, *119*, 121, *121*, 122, *123*, 124, 365
Magee, Stuart 155
Maginess, Scott 225
Magro, Stan 61, 63, 94, 314
Maguire, Mickey 236
Maher, Frank 23, 109, 132
Mahon, Geoff 191
Mail, Josh 19
Main, Lindsay 207
Mainwaring, Chris 166, 372, 375, *375*, 376, 377, *382*, 383, 385, *385*, 386
Makeham, Bob 85
Malaxos, Steve 169, *169*, 376, 377, 378, *378*, 379
Malin, Syd 286
Malthouse, Mick 38, 156, 157, 158, 159, 160, 372, *373*, 377, 378, 379, 380, *381*, 382, 383, 384, 385, 387
Manassa, Phil 94
Mann, Hassa 214, 230, 232, 250, 251, 252, 253, *253*, 257
Mann, Neil 89, 90, 93
Mann, Peter 164, 171, 173, 174, 175, 378
Mansfield, Michael 202
Mantello, Albert 114, 270, 271
Marchbank, Jim 49, *49*, *50*
Marchesi, Gerald 268
Margitch, George 87, 241
Marker, Peter 14, 25
Marmo, Joe 142, 143, *143*
Marquis, Peter 232, 248, 250
Marsh, Steve 167, 172
Marshall, David 16
Marshall, Denis 196, 197
Marshall, Jack 344
Marshall, W. 262
Marsham, Alan 199
Marsham, Harry 182, 199
Martello, Albert 219, 268, 271
Martin, Alan 149, 151, 152
Martin, Jim 105
Martin, Johnny 144
Martin, Ray 302, 303, 304
Martin, Russell 207
Martini, Percy 180, 181, 182, 183
Martyn, Brian 114, 268
Martyn, Colin 53
Martyn, Mick 277, 278, 279, *279*, 283
Mason, Angus 325
Matera, Peter 170, 372, *373*, 378, 381, *381*, 383, *384*, 387, *387*
Matera, Phil 385, 387, *387*
Matthews, Harold 326
Matthews, Herb 54, 88, 109, 148, 344, 349, 350, *350*, 353, *353*, 354
Matthews, Kelvin *218*
Matthews, Leigh 94, 95, 96, 97, 158, 199, 204, 214, 215, 216, 217, *218*, 219, 220, *220*, 221, 222, 226
Matthews, R. 268
May, Charlie 109
Maylin, Phil 65, 158
Maynard, Rodney 16
McAdam, Adrian 278
McAdam, Gilbert 33, 35, 36, 340
McAlister, Daniel 126
McAlpine, Ivan 146, 208
McBean, Charlie 207
McCallum, Firth 180, 183
McCanckie, Len 149
McCarter, Billy 185
McCarthy, Billy 142, 143
McCarthy, Con 81, 145, 146, *146*, 151, 158
McCarthy, Mick 30, *30*, 31
McCartney, Jason 19
McCaskill, Bob 210, 211, 268
McClelland, Bob 236, 237, *237*
McClure, Bob 111, 112
McConnell, A. 138

McConville, Eddie 240
McConville, Peter 65
McCorkell, Jock 268
McCormack, Basil 302, 303, *303*, 304
McDermott, Chris 14, 16, 17, 18, 19, 20, *20*, 21, 22, 23, 24, 227
McDonald, Alan 307
McDonald, Anthony 258
McDonald, Donald 277
McDonald, Frank 107, 109
McDonald, Jack 328, 329, 330
McDonald, John 211
McDonald, Norm 112, 114
McDonnell, Marty 149
McEwin, Ron 113
McGee, William 346
McGhie, Robert 157
McGinis, Fred 235, 237, *237*, 238
McGivern, Geoff 248, 249
McGowan, Brian 353
McGrath, Shane 247
McGrath, Tim 202, *203*
McGregor, Rod 48, 49, *49*, 50, 51, 52
McGuane, Mick 94, 96, 97
McGuinness, Tony 16, 17, 19, 21, *21*, 22, 23, 24, 158
McHale, Jock 73, 77, 79, *80*, 81, 83, 84, 85, 86, 88, 89, 98, 363
McInerny, Jack 75
McIntosh, Ashley 378, *383*, 386
McIntosh, Garry 14
McIntyre, Don 53
McIntyre, Peter 16
McIvor, Scott 30, 31, 32, 35, 37, 38, *38*, 40, 138
McKay, Andrew *68*, 69
McKay, David 60
McKay, Dinny 346, 347
McKay, Hec 349
McKay, Richard 321
McKenna, Guy 339, 372, 376, 377, 383, *384*, 386
McKenna, Peter 59, 62, 92, *92*, 93, 94, 95, 118, 136
McKenzie, Bob 232, 247, 249, 251, *251*
McKenzie, Brian 95
McKenzie, Don 116, 117, 118, *118*, 156
McKenzie, Graham 135
McKenzie, Jack 105, 236, 237
McKenzie, Keith 268, 270, 271
McKernan, Corey 279, *279*, 280, *280*, 281, 282, *282*, 283, 386
McKinnon, Martin 19, 21
McLean, Bob 287, *287*
McLean, Colin 242
McLean, Hugh 179
McLean, Ian 250
McLean, Michael 32, 33, 36, 37, 38, *38*, 41, 43
McLean, Ricky 312
McLennan, Harold 132
McLeod, Andrew 11, 19, *19*, 20, 24, 26, *26*
McMahen, Noel 247, *247*, 248, 249, 250, 251, *251*, 353
McManus, Shaun 173, 174
McMaster, Bill 196, 197
McNamara, Dave 144, 318, 322, 323, 324, *324*, 325, 327
McPherson, Ken 74
McRae, C. 36
McShane, Henry 176, 179
McShane, Jack 176, 179
McShane, Jim 176, 179, 180
McShane, Joe 49, 176, 179, 180
McShane, Paddy 130, 176
McShane, Phil 176, 179
McShane, Tom 176, 179
McSpeerin, Bill 131, *131*
Mead, Darren 293, 294, *295*
Mears, Henry 350
Meeham, Tom 315
Melling, T. 132
Mellington, Anthony 138, 139
Melrose, Graeme *168*, 169, 273
Melville, Ken 248, 249, 250, 251
Mercuri, Mark 101, 124, 125, 126

McConville, Eddie 240
Merillo, Jamie 171
Merrett, Leo 297, 296, 304
Merrett, Roger 28, *29*, 30, 31, 32, 33, 34, 35, *35*, 36, 37, 38, *38*, 39, 120, 122
Merrett, Thorold 89, 90, 91, *91*, 98
Merrick, Bob 132
Merrigan, Harvey 128, 136, 137
Metcalf, Frank 268
Metherell, Jack 188, 190
Metherell, Len 187, 190, 191
Metropolis, Daniel 380, 386
Meuleman, Jack 144, 146
Mew, Chris 199, 227, 228, 255
Michael, Stephen 167, 172
Mickan, Mark 16, *17*, 30, *30*, 31, 32, 33, *33*
Middlemiss, Russell 191
Mifka, Paul 376
Miles, Geoff *376*
Millane, Darren 94, 96, 97, *97*, 98, *98*
Miller, Allan 353
Miller, Jim 147, 155
Miller, Keith 305, *327*
Mills, Bert 208, *209*
Mills, Les 131, *325*
Milne, Herbert 131
Milroy, Bill 56
Minihan, Graeme 331
Minogue, Dan 53, 81, *81*, 132, 135, 208, 209, 302, 326
Minton-Connell, Simon 163, 365, 367
Misiti, Joe 101, 124, 126
Mitchell, Barry 362, 364, 365, 366, *366*, 367
Mitchell, Gavin 172, 173
Mitchell, Hugh 114, 116, 117
Mitchell, Michael 373
Mithen, Laurie 56, 248, 249, 250, 251, *251*
Modra, Tony 10, 17, 18, *18*, 19, 20, 21, 22, 24, 25, *25*, 26, 27, 382
Mohr, Bill 87, 325, 326, *326*, 327
Molloy, Graham 253
Molloy, Jarrod 43
Molloy, Keith 245
Moloney, Basil 195
Moloney, Brian *330*
Moloney, George 87, *186*, 187, *187*, 188, *188*
Moncrieff, Michael 216, 217, 218, 219
Monkhorst, Damien 94, 125
Monohan, Jack 75, 78, *78*
Monteath, Bruce 315
Montgomery, Ken 271
Mooney, Arthur 304
Moorcroft, Gary 126
Moore, Bob 350
Moore, C. 105
Moore, Eric 311
Moore, Kelvin 215, 218, *218*, 219, 220
Moore, Peter 72, 94, *94*, 95, 219, 232, 233, 252, 253, *253*, 254, 276
Mooring, Jim 54, 55, 351
Moran, Jeff 335, *335*
Morey, Sony 14
Morgan, Harry 144, 149, 346
Morgan, Laurie 135
Moriarty, Dan 13
Moriarty, Geoff 132
Moriarty, Jack 109, 128, 132, 133
Morris, Bill 296, *297*, 304, *305*, 305, 306, 307
Morris, Kevin 315
Morris, Mel 302
Morrisey, George 322, 323, *323*
Morrisey, Jamie 225, 227, 229
Morrison, Alby 146, 147
Morrison, Bruce 191, 192, 199
Morrison, Chad 385
Morrison, L. 265
Morrow, Alan 332, 333, 335, *335*
Morrow, Tom 191, 193
Mort, Ian 212, 213
Mortimer, Len 346, *346*

391

Morton, Bob 333
Morwood, Paul 338, 359
Morwood, Shane 359
Morwood, Tony 357, 359
Moss, Graham 100, 118, 119, *119*, 169, 218, *376*
Mossop, John 198
Motley, Geoff 13, 15, 288
Motley, Peter 66, 67
Moyes, Harold 238, 239, 323, 325
Mueller, Jack 241, *241*, 242, 243, 244, 245, 246, 247
Muir, David 171
Mulhall, Ken 330
Munday, Jim 191, 199
Murdoch, Joe 87, 303, 304
Murphy, David 362, 363, 366
Murphy, Frank 82, *82*, 89
Murphy, John (Fitz) 137
Murphy, John (Sth) 357
Murphy, Len 85, *85*
Murphy, Leo 208
Murphy, Paddy 334, *334*
Murray, Bob 332, *332*, 335, 336
Murray, Kevin 128, 129, *129*, 135, *135*, 136, *136*, 137, 138, 140, 155, 311
Murray, Sel 268
Mynott, Brian *335*, 336
Naismith, Alby 208
Nankervis, Bruce 176, 196, 198
Nankervis, Ian 56, 176, 196, 198, 199, *199*
Nankervis, Vic 176, 191
Nardard, Paul 125
Narkle, Phil 169, 372, 375, 376
Nash, Alan 19, 21
Nash, Bob 79, 143
Nash, Laurie 86, 143, 344, 348, *348*, 350
Nash, Robert 348
Naylor, Bernie 167, *167*, 172
Neagle, Merv 100, 119, 362
Neale, Kevin 215, 335, *335*, 336, 337, 338, *338*
Neesham, Gerard 164, 169, 171, 172, 173, 175, 358
Negri, Romano 16
Neill, Harold 326
Neitz, David 257, 258, *258*, 259
Newland, Ken *196*
Newling, Ernest 181
Newman, John 176, 196, 197, *197*
Newton, Leigh 258, *258*
Nicholls, Doug 133
Nicholls, John 56, 58, *58*, 59, 60, *60*, 61, 62, 65, 70, *70*, *194*, 309, 312, 313, *313*, 352
Nichols, Trent *380*
Niven, Colin 132, 241, *241*
Nolan, Bernard 236
Nolan, Chris 268
Nolan, Mick *270*, 273, 275
Noonan, Alan 117, 118, 140
Noonan, Paddy 265, *265*, 268
Norman, Dave 93
Northey, John 35, 36, 37, *37*, 41, 42, 252, 253, 254, *254*, 257, 308, 310, *310*, 311, 312, 314, 315, 361, *361*
Nunan, Mike 15, 138
O'Brien, 'Dally' 268
O'Brien, Cameron *30*, 31
O'Brien, Craig 368, *368*
O'Brien, Jack 146
O'Brien, Noel 56, 59
O'Brien, Paddy 51, 52, *52*, 53
O'Cock, Wally 49
O'Connell, David 377
O'Connor, Ryan 125, *126*
O'Dea, Jim 92, 337
O'Dea, Tommy 49
O'Donnell, Gary 122, *122*, 124, 125, 127
O'Donohue, Peter 211, 214
O'Dwyer, Steven 254, 255
O'Halloran, Jack 268
O'Halloran, Tom 302, 303
O'Keefe, David *30*, 31
O'Keefe, Jack 242

O'Loughlin, Michael 281, 368, *368*, 369
O'Meara, James 349, *349*
O'Neill, John 194
O'Neill, Kevin 302, *302*, 303
O'Reilly, Stephen 165, 171, 173, *173*
O'Rourke, Jack 307
O'Shea, Fred 106, *106*
O'Sullivan, Peter 114
Oakley, Ross 159, 335, 363, 365
Oaten, Max 353
Oatey, Jack 15, *15*
Oatey, Robert 13
Obst, Andrew 287
Obst, Ken 287
Obst, Peter 287
Obst, Trevor 287, 288
Officer, Ned 102
Ogden, Percy 106, 107, 109
Ogilvie, Tom 371
Okey, Howard 109
Olarenshaw, Ricky 101, 124, 125
Oliver, Harold 13, 286
Olliver, Arthur 146, 148, 149, *149*, 155
Olsson, Rod 198, *198*, 214, *214*, 215
Ongarello, Tony 135
Onyons, Basil 236
Oppy, Max 296, *297*, 304, 305, 306, *306*, 307
Orchard, Bill 182
Ormond-Allen, Trent 24
Osborne, Richard 138, 161, 366
Oswald, Lance 331, 332
Outen, Albert 146
Pagan, Denis 260, 278, 279, 280, 281, *281*, 282, 283
Page, Charles 148
Page, Glenn 364
Palmer, Ambrose 148, *148*
Palmer, Doug 193
Pannam, Alby (Jnr) 79, 86, 88, 89, 306, 307
Pannam, Alby 79
Pannam, Charlie 75, 76, 78, 79, *79*, 86, 89, 349
Pannam, Charlie (Jnr) 79, 81, 89
Papley, Max 353
Park, Roy 145, 236, 237, 371
Parke, Greg 253
Parker, Daniel 172, 174
Parker, Shane 165, 175
Parkin, David 61, 62, 64, 65, 66, 68, 69, 71, 138, 154, 204, 212, 214, 216, 217, 219, *219*, 366
Parratt, Percy 53, 132, *132*, 133, 188, *188*
Parsons, Steve 312
Pascoe, Bob 269
Patterson, 'Tattles' 144
Patterson, Mike 15, 307, 308, 311, 314, 315, 338
Paxman, Stephen 284, 293
Pay, Kevin 90
Payne, Charles 117
Peake, Brian 166, *166*, 172, 198
Pearce, Brad 68, 69
Pearce, Joe 236, 237
Pearson, Bill 111
Pearson, Charles 103
Peck, John 211, 212, 213, 214, *214*
Pedler, Simon 21
Penberthy, Stan 146
Peos, Paul *380*, 385
Perkins, Jack 326
Pert, Gary 128, 138
Pesch, Nick 19
Phillips, Brenton *30*, 31
Phillips, Bruce 328, 329, *329*
Phillips, Fred *205*, 325, 326
Phillips, Greg 14, 290
Phillips, Stan 321
Pianto, Peter 194, 196, *196*, 308
Picken, Bill 94, *94*, 98
Pickering, Liam 202, *202*, 203
Pickering, Michael 315
Pike, Martin 138
Pilkington, Ernie 54, *54*
Pimm, Jack 89

Pincott, Arthur 180
Pink, Arthur 184
Pittman, David 24, 25, 27
Pitura, John 356
Platten, John 14, *14*, 204, 223, *223*, 225, 227, 229
Plummer, Billy *320*, 321
Plunkett, Jack 187
Polinelli, Tony 194
Pool, Ted *205*, 208, 209
Poole, Darryl 293
Poole, Trevor 315
Potter, Jess 13
Poulter, Ray 296, *297*, 304, 306, 307
Powell, Ray 110
Pratt, Bob 32, 86, 87, 215, 302, 303, 344, *348*, 348, 349, 350, 354, 363
Prevot, Ted *46*, 207
Price, Barry 93
Price, Mick 54
Primmer, Wayne 118, 119
Primus, Matthew 139, 293
Prince, George 166
Prior, Albert 208
Pritchard, Darren 225, 231
Proudfoot, Bill 74, 75, *75*, 77, 78, 264
Pryor, Geoff 118, *118*
Purse, Hugh 236
Purser, Andrew 156, 166
Pye, Len 132
Pyke, Don 379, 381, 382, 383
Quade, Rick 357, 358, 359, 360, 361
Quinlan, Bernie 128, *129*, 136 *136*, 137, 138, *138*, 156, 157, *157*, 359
Quinn, Bob 13, 287, *287*
Quinn, Jack 287
Quinn, Tommy 188, 190, 191
Quirk, Bryan 56, 58
Rademacher, Arthur 208
Rainbird, Ian 289
Raines, Geoff 30, *30*, 31, 38, *38*, 297, 314, 315
Rait, Alan 146, 147, *147*
Ralph, Warren 64, *168*, 169
Rance, Murray 169, 376, 377
Rankin, Bert 18, 182, 183, *184*, 185, *185*, 199
Rankin, Cliff 176, 182, 184, *185*, *185*, 186, 187, 199
Rankin, Doug 176, 199
Rankin, Teddy 176, 180, 181, *181*, 183, 199
Ransford, Vernon 207
Rantall, John 270, *270*, 271, 272, 273, 280, 344, 353, 354, 356, 357, *357*
Raper, Bill 107
Rasmussen, Gary 211
Ratten, Brett 68, 69, 71, *71*
Rattray, Gordon 132, 133, 238
Rawle, George 266, 267, *267*
Rawle, Keith 111
Rayment, Doug 326, 327
Rayson, Arthur 176
Rayson, Noel 153, 176, 194
Reedman, 'Dinny' 13
Rees, Evan 149
Reeves, Michael 138
Regan, Jack 53, 85, 86, *87*, 89, 98
Rehn, Shaun 19, *19*, 20, 22, 25, 26
Reid, John 358
Reiffel, Lou 241, *241*, 350
Rendell, Matthew 137, 138
Renfrey, Russ 191, 193, 194
Retz, Martin 371
Reval, Allan 287
Reynolds, Dick 100, *101*, 109, 110, *110*, 111, *111*, 112, 113, 114, 124, 127, 305, 353
Reynolds, Doug 151
Reynolds, Tom 110
Reynoldson, Steve 30, *30*, 31, 33
Rhys-Jones, David *66*, 67, 222, 359, *359*, 361, 364
Ricciutto, Mark 18, 19, *19*, 25, 26
Rice, Colin 194
Rice, Dean 69
Richards, Lou 79, 88, 89, *89*, 90

Richards, Ron 79, 89, 90
Richardson, Alan 308, 310, *310*, 315
Richardson, Barry 307, 308, 310, *310*, 311, 312, 313, 314, 315
Richardson, Matthew 297, *297*, 310, 315, *316*, 317
Richardson, Max 93, *93*, 94
Richardson, Michael 31, 94, 169
Richardson, Wayne 92, 93, 98
Richmond, Graeme 307, *307* *397*, 312, 337
Ricketts, Charles 325, 344, 346
Riddell, Tommy 320
Ridley, Ian 230, 249, 250, 252, 253, 257, *257*
Riley, John 14
Ringrose, Doug 132
Rioli, Maurice 167, 169, *169*, 297, 315, 372
Ritchie, Reg 350
Roach, Don 361
Roach, Michael 297, 314, *314*, 315
Robbins, Ben 43
Roberts, Brian 356, 359
Roberts, Frank 242
Roberts, John 357
Roberts, Keith 332
Roberts, Ken 119
Roberts, Kevin 334, 336
Roberts, Lew *287*
Roberts, Mark 30, 31, 280, 282
Roberts, Neil 275, 318, 328, *329*, 330, *330*, 331, *331*, 332
Robertson, Arthur 327
Robertson, Austin 349, *349*, 353
Robertson, Colin 221
Robertson, George 47
Robertson, Harold 348, 349
Robertson, Jimmy 263
Robinson, William 105, 142
Robran, Barrie 14, 15, *15*, 25
Robran, Matthew 22, 23, 25
Rocca, Anthony 90, 98, *98*, 99
Rocca, Saverio 90, 96, *97*, 98, 99, *99*
Rock, Anthony 280, 281
Rodda, Alby 242, 243, 245, 247
Rodriguez, Percy 237
Roebuck, Les 180
Rogers, Norm 166
Rogers, Terry 116
Rogerson, Roger 135
Romero, Jose 161, 163
Ronaldson, John 308, 311
Roos, Paul 128, *129*, 137, 138, *138*, 366, 367, 368, *368*, 369
Rose, Bill 90
Rose, Bob 89, 90, *90*, 92, 93, 94, 95, 98, 156
Rose, Colin 90
Rose, Kevin 90, 97, 137
Rose, Ralph 90
Rosenow, Geoff 196, *196*
Rosewarne, Keith 328, 329
Ross, Bob 84
Ross, Don 151, 152
Ross, Jim 328, 329, *329*
Ross, Jonathan 24
Round, Barry 118, 156, 157, 344, 354, 355, 356, 357, 358, 359, *359*, 360, 361
Rouvray, Paul 21
Rowan, Paddy 53, 80, 81, 83, 132
Rowe, Brad 172
Rowe, Des 296, 297, 306, 307, 310
Rowe, Havel 307
Rowe, Percy 53, 80, 81, 83, 132
Rowe, Stephen 21
Rowell, Ted 76, 77, *77*, 78, 79, 86
Rowland, Ian 332
Rowlings, Barry 315
Royal, Brian 140, 156, 158
Rudolph, George 208, 302, 303
Rumney, Harold 82, 86, 98, *98*
Ruscuklic, Alex 137
Rusden, A. *320*, 321
Rush, Robert 79, 237
Russ, Bill 268

Russ, William 146
Russell, Scott 96, 99
Russo, Peter 2˜9
Ruthven, Allan 128, *128*, 134, *134*, 135, 149
Ryan, Bill 196, 197
Ryan, Denis 128, 132, 133
Ryan, Gerald 346, 347
Ryan, Jack 208, *209*
Ryan, Joe 146, 148
Ryan, Lionel 151
Ryan, Stephen 315
Ryan, Tom 236
Sachse, Neil 156
Sadler, Jim *81*
Salmon, Paul *101*, 121, 122, 123, 124, 125, 230, 231, *231*, 382
Sampson, Alf 147
Sampson, Clay 24
Samson, Vic 144, 145, 145, 146
Sanderson, Brenton 202
Sandford, Cecil 51
Sandilands, Laurie 156, 157, *157*
Sankey, Maurie 56
Sarah, Paul 136
Sarau, Jeff 323
Saunders, Harry 81, 85
Saunders, S. 146
Savage, Ron 54, 55
Sawley, Brian 13
Scanlan, Bill 149
Scanlan, Joe 349
Scanlon, Paddy 53, 146, 268, 349
Schache, Laurence 33
Schaefer, Keith 350
Schimmelbusch, Wayne 260, 272, 274, *274*, 275, 277, 278
Schmidt, Billy 302, 323, *323*, 324, 325
Schmidt, Paul 54, 55
Schoff, Rick 14
Schofield, Peter 268
Schraeder, Heinrich 371
Schultz, John 140, *154*, 155, 157, 212
Schwab, Peter 222, 225, 227
Schwarz, David 258, 259, *259*
Schwass, Wayne 277, 278, 280, 281, 282
Schwerdt, Stephen 19
Scott, 'Wacka' 13
Scott, Chris 33, 36, 42, 43
Scott, Dion 36
Scott, Don 15, 157, 215, *215*, 216, *216*, 217, 218, 219, *219*, 230, *230*, 272
Scott, Lee 21
Scott, Mark 338
Scott, Phil 377, 379, 380
Scott, Robert 282
Searl, Doug 137
Seddon, Malcolm 80
Sellars, Ernie 323, *323*
Sellwood, Joe 189, *189*
Serafini, Laurie 137
Serafini, Renato 137
Serong, Bill 91, 268
Sevior, Tom 143
Sexton, Jack 132, 133
Sexton, Michael 71
Shalless, Ralph 245
Shanahan, Jamie 342
Shanahan, Pat 142
Sharland, Wally 185
Sharp, Jim 131
Sharp, Laurie 307
Sharp, Norm 193, 194
Sharrock, John 176, 196, 197
Shaw, Billy 321
Shaw, Gary 169
Shaw, George 132
Shaw, Ray 94
Shaw, Robert 18, 20, *20*, 21, 22, 24, 25, 138
Shaw, Tony 72, *73*, 82, 94, 96, *96*, 97, 98, *98*, 99
Shea, Keith 52, 208
Shea, Pat 105, 106
Sheahan, Maurie 302, *302*, 303
Shearman, Bob 13, 14, 115

392

Sheedy, Jack 166, 172
Sheedy, Kevin 41, 100, 119, 120, 121, 123, 124, 125, 127, *127*, 170, 172, 294, 297, 308, 310, *310*, 311, 313, *313*, 315, 354, 365, 382, 385
Sheehan, Percy 79
Sheldon, Ken 63, *63*, 65, 340, *340*, 341
Shelton, Ian 115, 116
Shelton, Jack 325
Sherry, Tom 180
Sholl, Brad 202
Sholl, Craig 278
Sholl, E. 235
Shorten, George 109
Shorten, John 79
Sidebottom, Alan 169
Sidebottom, Garry 199, 338, *338*
Sier, Ken 134, *297*
Sierakowski, Brian 335
Silvagni, Sergio 56, 58, *59*, 62
Silvagni, Stephen 64, *66*, 68, *68*, 69, 70, *71*, 136
Sime, Charles 79
Simmonds, Roy 210, *210*, 211
Sinclair, Jess 175
Skilton, Bob 252, 253, 336, 344, *345*, 352, *352*, 353, 354, 357
Slack, Laurie 190
Slater, Joe 182, *182*, 207
Sloan, Alex 131, *236*
Sloss, Bruce 344
Smale, Ken 90
Smallhorn, Wilfred 128, *129*, 133
Smart, Nigel 10, 16, 17, 22, 23, 24, *24*, 27
Smedley, Bert 325
Smith, Alf 320, *320*, 321
Smith, Archie 76, 77, 86
Smith, Bernie 176, *177*, 191, 192, *192*, 193, 194
Smith, Brad 272
Smith, Darren 16
Smith, Dave 105, 107
Smith, George 298
Smith, Greg 220, 359
Smith, James 321, 323, 325
Smith, Len 129, 134, 135, *135*, *249*, 307, 309
Smith, Noel 111
Smith, Norm *90*, 135, 232, 241, *241*, 242, 243, 244, 246, 247, 248, 249, *249*, 250, *250*, 251, 304, 309, 353, 356, 357
Smith, Peter (Melb) 251
Smith, Peter (Bris) 30, *30*
Smith, Rohan 163, *163*
Smith, Ross 169, 318, 332, 334, *335*, 336, *336*, 337, 338
Smith, Shaun 257, *257*
Smith, Steven 253
Smith, Syd 193
Snell, Sam 327, 328
Solin, Tony 169
Somerville, John 117, *117*
Sorrell, Ray 166
Southby, Geoff 60, 61, *63*, 313
Southern, Daniel 161, 382
Sowdon, Arthur 236
Spalding, Earl 69, 254, 373
Spargo, Bob 147
Sparrow, George 323, 325
Speakman, Perc 266
Spencer, Jack 56
Spencer, Jock 268, 276, 279
Spencer, Stuart 248, 249, 250, 251, *251*, 255, 257
Spinks, Brett *383*
Spinks, Stan 208, 209, *209*
Spittle, Max 247
Sporn, Kieran 122
Spring, Geoff *297*, 304
Sproule, Paul 314, 315, 337
Squire, Damian 293
Stackpole, Keith 134
Stafford, Fred 55, *55*, 57, 112
Stafford, Greg 367, 368, *368*
Stamford, Frank 304
Stanbridge, Claude 349

Standfield, Barry 24
Starcevich, Craig 33, 373
Steele, Ray 305
Steer, Trevor 93
Stephen, Bill 118, 119, 135, 137
Stephens, John 336
Stephens, Peter 181
Stephenson, Bill 332, *332*, 333
Stephenson, Ted 143
Stevens, Anthony 283
Stevens, Harvey 148, 150, 150, 151, 152
Stevens, Phil 197
Stevens, T. 267
Stevenson, Edward 184
Stewart, A. 321
Stewart, Bill 323
Stewart, Ian 58, 296, 312, *312*, 313, 318, 332, 333, *333*, 335, *335*, 337, 339, 356, 357, 359
Stewart, Jim 322, 323
Stewart, Stewart 205, *209*
Stiffe, Jimmy 320, *320*
Stockdale, Greg 108, 109
Stockman, Ron 151, 153
Stokes, Ray 296, *297*
Stone, Bob 245
Stone, Nick 387
Stoneham, Alan 157
Stoneham, Barry 177, 201, 202, *202*
Stooke, A. *320*
Strang, Bill 346
Strang, Doug 302, 303, *303*, 304, 308, 311
Streeter, Charles 238
Stretch, Steven 254
Strickland, Bill 47, 74, *74*, 75, 76, 77, 78, 79
Stuckey, George 102, 105
Stuckey, William 49
Stynes, Jimmy 80, 223, 224, 232, *233*, 252, *252*, 254, *254*, 255, *255*, 256, *256*, 257, 258, 259, 378
Sudholz, John 353
Sullivan, Jim 109
Sullivan, Joe 49
Sumich, Peter 372, 376, 378, *378*, 379, 380, *381*, 382, 383, 385, 387
Sutcliffe, R. 263
Suter, Bob 115, *115*
Sutherland, E. 321
Sutton, Bert 208, 209
Sutton, Charlie 141, 148, 149, *149*, 150, 151, *151*, 152, *152*, 153, 160, 248
Sutton, E.H. 235
Swift, Fred 196, 308, *308*, 309, 315
Synman, Ian *335*, 336
Tampion, Ian 331
Tandy, Mark 349
Tankard, Joey 264, *264*
Tassell, Doug 118
Tate, Sid 191
Taubert, Steve 358
Taylor, 'Fishy' 143
Taylor, Bert 185
Taylor, Brian 94, 95, *95*, 315
Taylor, Dick 238, 239, 240, 241, 268
Taylor, Jim 344, 350, 353
Taylor, Michael 14, 21
Taylor, Zane 198
Teasdale, Graham 344, 353, 354, 356, 357
Teasdale, Noel 260, 268, 269, 270, 271, 277, *277*, 333
Templeton, Kelvin 140, 156, 157, *157*, 252, 253
Thomas, Arthur 323
Thomas, Hughie 326, 327, 328
Thomas, Len 208, 268, 349, 350
Thomas, Stan 184
Thomas, William 346
Thompson, Clayton 211, *211*
Thompson, Henry 49
Thompson, Len 72, 92, *92*, 93, 94, 95, 98, 253
Thompson, Mark 121, 123, 124, 125
Thompson, Reginald 206, 297

Thompson, Robbie 16
Thoms, Jim 149
Thornton, Ross 137, 138
Thorogood, Ian 62, 63, 249
Thorp, Vic 302
Thorpe, David 155, 156, 157
Thurgood, Albert 77, 235, 100, *101*, 102, 103, 104, 105, *105*, 171, 173
Tilbrook, Jim 253, *253*
Tingay, Stephen 257
Titus, Jack 80, 87, 256, 296, 302, 303, *303*, 304, 305, *305*, 307, *307*
Todd, Arthur 263, 264
Todd, George 184, 186, *186*, 187
Todd, Harry 263, 264
Todd, John 167, *167*, 168, *168*, 169, 172, 376, 377, 378
Todd, Ron 53, 86, *86*, 88, *88*, 92, 327
Toia, Luke 165, 173
Toll, Alf 74
Tomlinson, Ern 153
Tongerie, Shane 19
Toohey, Bernard 199, 362, *364*, 365
Topping, George 49, *49*, 50
Torney, Hugh 110
Townsend, John 250, 253
Tredrea, Jack 13
Tregenza, Simon 16, 17, 25
Trevaskis, Tim 268
Trezise, Neil 191, 194
Trimm, Albert 346
Trood, Victor 370
Trott, Stuart 336
Trotter, Percy 131, *131*, *133*
Truscott, 'Nipper' *166*, 172
Truscott, Keith 242, 243, 244, *244*, 245
Tuck, Frank 90
Tuck, Michael 94, 204, 216, 220, *222*, 223, 225, *225*, 226, *226*, 227, *227*, 228
Tuddenham, Des 90, 91, 92, 98, 93, 118, 119, *119*, 334, 335, 357
Tulloch, Len 77, 79, 182
Tulloh, Arthur 238
Tunbridge, Geoff 56, 249, 251
Turley, Craig 227, 379, 382, 385
Turnbull, Ryan 378, 382, 383
Turner, Dean 372, *374*, 375, *377*
Turner, Leo 191, 199
Turner, Michael 198, 199, *199*
Turner, Peter 19
Twomey, Bill 81, *81*, 90, 208
Twomey, Bill (Jnr) 86, *89*, 90, 95, 306
Twomey, Mick 90, *90*, 306
Twomey, Pat 90, 306
Tyson, Charlie 81, 83, *83*, 268
Ukovic, Andrew 126
Upton-Brown, V. 371
Utting, Charlie 89
Utting, Ted 81, 209
Vagg, Barry 250
Valentine, Viv 50, *50*, 51, 53
Vallence, Harry 52, *52*, 53, 54, 70, 71, 84, 87, 147
Van Der Haar, Paul 100, 119, 121, 123, 225
Vardy, Peter 23, 25
Vautin, George 237
Vidovic, Lazar 343
Vine, F.S. 238, *238*, 241
Viney, Todd 254, 257, 258, *258*, 379
Voigt, Noel 205
Vontom, Clarrie 326, 327, 328
Voss, Brett 35
Voss, Michael 28, *29*, 33, 35, 36, *36*, 37, *37*, 38, *38*, 39, 41, 42, 43, 125, 161
Vosti, Jack 109
Waddington, John 114
Wade, Doug 56, 194, *194*, 195, 196, 197, *197*, 270, *270*, 271, 272, 273, 277, 280
Walker, Bill (Ess) 106, 107, 381
Walker, Bill (Fitz) 131, 132
Walker, Ken 326
Walker, Max 252
Walker, Peter 194, 196
Walker, Ray 155
Wall, David 137

Wallace, Terry 140, 158, 161, 162, *162*, 204, 220, 221, 255
Wallis, Dean 122, 125
Wallis, Jim 332
Wallis, Steve 158
Walls, Robert 28, 32, 33, 34, 35, *35*, 37, 39, 60, *60*, 61, 62, 63, 66, 67, 137, 314, 315, 316, *316*, 317
Walsh, Brian 61, 330, 331
Walsh, Dave 107, 268
Walsh, Paddy 109
Walsh, Philip 30, *30*, 31, *33*
Walters, Terry 196
Walton, Ernie 49
Wanganeen, Gavin 100, 123, 124, 125, *125*, 292, *292*, 293, 294, 340
Warburton, Keith 56, *56*, 57
Wardill, Dick 236, *236*, 321
Ware, Norm 140, 146, 147, 148, *148*, 149, 154, 155
Warhurst, Tom 16
Warne-Smith, Ivor 232, 238, 239, 240, *240*, 241, 250
Wartman, Ray 242
Warwick, Dean 376
Waterhouse, Clive 172, 174, 175, *290*
Waterman, Chris 377, 383, 386
Waters, Terry 90, 92, 93, 95
Waterson, Chris *30*, 31
Watson, Colin 318, 325, *325*, 326
Watson, Tim 100, 118, 119, *120*, 121, 122, 123, 124, 125, 221, 384
Watt, George 74
Watters, Scott 173
Watts, Jason 161
Watts, Ray 111
Waugh, Norman 104, 105
Webb, Athol 249
Webber, Fred 49
Webster, Len 110
Wedding, Bill 13
Weideman, Murray 90, 91, 93, *93*, 98, 249
Weidemann, Wayne 24
Weightman, Dale 297, 314, 315
Wellman, Sean 19, 21, *126*
Wells, Greg 232, 252, 253, *253*
Wells, Jack 50, 322, *322*, 323
Welsh, Peter 156
West, Jack 371
West, Jim 365
West, Mark 163
West, Robbie 291
West, Roy 194, 197, 199
West, Scott 141, 161, 163
Weston, Paul 127
Wheelahan, Danny 349
Wheeler, M. 304
Wheeler, Sandford 364
Wheeler, Terry 159, 160, *160*, 161
Wheildon, Darren 138, 380
Whelan, Marcus 72, 86, 87, *87*, 98
Whelan, Ted 288
White, Darryl 33, 36, 37
White, Jeff 173, 258, *258*
White, Les 106
White, Lindsay 191, *191*, 350
White, Mitchell 373, 384, 385, 386
White, Ron 245
Whitfield, Ted 54
Whitten, Ted 32, *57*, 140, 141, *141*, 149, *149*, 150, 151, 152, 153, *153*, 154, *154*, 155, 156, 157, 160, 161, *161*, 212, 213
Whittington, Bert 182
Wight, Sean 252, 254
Wigney, Stuart 19
Wigraft, Len 132, 133
Wiley, Robert 372, 375, 376, 377
Wilkinson, Alf 131
Wilkinson, Graeme 307
Willey, Graham 114
Williams, Alec 288
Williams, Anthony 288
Williams, Arthur 142, 143
Williams, Billy 350
Williams, Darren 121, 122

Williams, Don 248, 250
Williams, Fos 13, *13*, *287*, 288, 291, 292
Williams, Frank 288
Williams, Geoff 193, 194 199
Williams, Greg 44, 68, 69, *69*, 70, *70*, 71, *71*, 198, 199, 354, *355*, 362, *362*, 364, 365, 385
Williams, Jack (Geel) 191
Williams, Jack (Sth) 111
Williams, Mark 30, *30*, 31, 94, 288, *288*, 294, *294*
Williams, Paul *99*
Williams, Percy 238
Williams, Peter 48
Williams, Robert 208
Williams, Steve 30, *30*, 288, 291, *291*
Williamson, Col 327, 328
Willis, Carl 349, 371
Wills, Andrew 174, *174*, 175
Wills, Tom 12, 176, 178, *178*, 234, *234*, 235, 299
Wilson, Andrew 118
Wilson, Billy 296, *297*, 304, 305, 307
Wilson, Brian 157, 232, 253, *253*
Wilson, Garry 137, *137*
Wilson, Graeme 356
Wilson, Ian 307
Wilson, Jim 178, *178*, 179
Wilson, Michael 284, 293, 295, *295*
Wilson, Percy 80, 81, 238, 325
Wilson, Peter 166, 373, 378, 381, 383, 385
Wilson, Ray 214
Windley, William 346
Wines, Clinton 351
Winmar, Nicky 26, 96, 167, *167*, *319*, 338, 339, 340, *340*, 341, 342, *342*, 373
Winneke, John 211, 212, 213, 214
Winter, Bruce 14, 15
Wirrpunda, David 385, *387*
Withers, Mark 30, *30*, 31
Wittman, Stan 238, *238*
Woewodin, Shane 258
Wolf, Clinton 171
Wood, Arthur 349
Wood, Bill 148, 149
Wood, Bryan 315
Wood, Eric 371
Wood, J.L. 268
Wooden, Josh 387
Woodford, L. 208
Woodley, Allan 211
Woods, Bervin 88, *88*, 89
Woods, Ike 180
Wooller, Fred 194, 195, *195*, 196
Woolnough, Michael 197
Wootton, Stan 349
Worrall, Jack 47, 48, 49, 50, 51, 52, 106, *106*, 107, 130
Worsfold, John 372, 375, *375*, 377, *377*, 379, 380, 381, *381*, 382, 383, 384, *384*, 386, 387
Worthington, Kevin 94
Wraith, Tom 81
Wrensted, Murray *374*, 377
Wright, Duncan 117
Wright, Graham 96
Wright, Kevin 135, *135*
Wright, Roy 296, *297*, 306, *306*, 307
Wright, Stevie 359, *360*, 361, 365, 366
Wrout, Jack 53, 55
Wynd, Scott 140, 160, *160*, 161, 163
Yea, Norman 105
Yeates, John 194, 199
Yeates, Mark 199, 200, 225, 228, 381
Yeats, Graeme 255, *255*
Young, Barry 125
Young, Bill 330, 331, *331*, 332,
Young, Chas 235, 236
Young, Garry 211
Young, George 337, 338
Young, Henry 180, 181, *181*
Yze, Adam 258
Zanotti, Mark 375, *377*
Zantuck, Shane 232

BIBLIOGRAPHY

The *Age*, Melbourne, 1854–.

The *Argus*, Melbourne, 1846–1957.

Atkinson, Graeme, *Everything You've Ever Wanted to Know About Australian Rules Football*, The Five Mile Press, Canterbury, Vic., 1982.

Atkinson, Graeme, *The Book of VFL Finals*, The Five Mile Press, Canterbury, Vic., 1973 & 1981; revised as *The Book of Australian Rules Finals*, The Five Mile Press, Canterbury, Vic., 1983; and revised as *The Complete Book of VFL Finals*, The Five Mile Press, Canterbury, Vic., 1989; revised as *The Complete Book of AFL Finals, Centenary Year Edition*, The Five Mile Press, Canterbury, 1996.

Aylett, Allen, *My Game: A Life in Football as Told to Greg Hobbs*, Sun Books, South Melbourne, 1986.

Barassi, Ron, with Peter McFarline, *Barassi: The Man Behind the Legend*, Simon and Schuster, Sydney 1995.

Blainey, Geoffrey, *A Game of Our Own: The Origins of Australian Football*, National Australian Football Council, Information Australia, Melbourne, 1990.

Branagan, Mark and Lefebvre, Mike, *Bloodstained Angels: The rise and fall of the Foreign Legion*, self published, South Melbourne, 1995.

Buggy, Hugh, *The Carlton Story: A History of the Carlton Football Club*, Eric White Associates, Melbourne, 1958.

Butler, Mark and Stephen Mime, *Sons of the 'Scray: Footscray's Finest 50*, Williamstown, Melbourne, 1993.

Christison, Darren, (ed.), *Football Yearbook*, 1993. GMG Sport, Woollhara, NSW.

Christian, Geoff, *Soaring: The Official History of the West Coast Eagles Football Club's First 10 Years*, West Coast Eagles, Perth, 1997.

Craven, John, ed., *Football the Australian Way*, Lansdowne Press, Melbourne 1969.

Delbridge, Noel, ed., *The Bulldog Book, Sons of 'Scray (1883–1983)*, Footscray Football Club, West Footscray, Vic.

Denham, Greg, *Football Year*, Annual record of the AFL seasons 1991–1997, Pagemasters, Melbourne 1991–1997.

Dowling, Gerard P, *The North Story*, The Hawthorn Press, Melbourne, 1973; revised and enlarged as *The North Story: the History of the North Melbourne Football Club*, Playright Publishing, Sydney, 1997.

Dunn, John, with Jim Main, *Australian Rules Football: An illustrated History*, Lansdowne Press, Melbourne, 1974.

Dunstan, Keith, *The Paddock That Grew: The Story of the Melbourne Cricket Club*, Cassell, 1962, revised edn, Cassell, Melbourne, 1974.

Dyer, Jack as told to Brian Hansen, *'Captain Blood'*, Stanley Paul, London 1965.

Dyer, Jack, and Brian Hansen, *Captain Blood's Wild Men of Football*, Hansen, Cheltenham, 1993.

East, Alan, ed., *Eagles for the Flag*, Australian Sports Publications, North Perth, 1992, 1993.

Feldmann, Jules and Russell Holmesby, *The Point of It All: The Story of the St Kilda Football Club*, Playwright Publishing, Melbourne, 1992.

Fiddian, Marc, *Boilovers, Thrillers and Grand Eras*, Pakenham Gazette, Pakenham, 1994.

Fiddian Marc, *Goals, Goals, Goals: A study of League and Association Full-forwards*. South Eastern Independent Newspapers, Pakenham, 1996.

Fiddian, Marc, *The Pioneers*, Victorian Football Association, Melbourne, 1977.

Fiddian, Marc, *The Roar of the Crowd*, Victorian Football Association, Melbourne, 1987.

Fitzgerald, Ross and Ken Spillman, eds, *The Greatest Game*, William Heinemann Australia, Melbourne, 1988, repr. 1989, 1992.

Flanagan, Martin, *Southern Sky Western Oval*, McPhee Gribble, South Yarra, 1994.

The Footballer: An Annual Record of Football in Victoria and the Australian Colonies. Ed. Thomas Power, Henriques & Co, Melbourne, 1875–1882.

Flower, Robert with Ron Reed, *Robbie*, Caribou Publications, Melbourne, 1968.

Football Life, Melbourne, 1968–1972.

Football Record, Victorian/Australian Football League, Melbourne, 1912–.

Gordon, Harry, *The Hard Way: The Story of the Hawthorn Football Club*, Lester-Townsend Publishing, Sydney, 1990.

Gordon, Kerrie and Alan Dalton, *Too Tough to Die: Footscrays' Fightback 1989*, self-published, Melbourne, 1990.

Handley, George, *The Great Grand Finals*, Walshe, Geelong, 1989.

Hansen, Brian, with Jack Dyer, *Jack Dyer's the Greatest*, Brian Hansen Publications, Melbourne, 1996.

Hansen, Brian, *The Magpies: The History of the Collingwood Football Club, from 1892 to 1992*, Semis Carla, Cheltenham, Vic., 1992.

Hansen, Brian, *Tigerland: The History of the Richmond Football Club from 1885*. Richmond Former Players and Officials Association, Melbourne, 1989.

Hart, Royce, *The Royce Hart Story*, Thomas Nelson Melbourne, 1970.

Hawke, Steve, *Polly Farmer: A Biography*, Fremantle Arts Centre Press, South Fremantle, 1994.

The Herald, Melbourne, 1839–1991.

Hewat, T., *The Blues*, Carlton Football Club, Melbourne, 1982.

Hobbs, Greg, *125 Years of the Melbourne Demons*, Melbourne Football Club, Melbourne, 1984.

Holmesby, Russell, *Heroes with Haloes St Kilda's 100 Greatest*, Playright Publishing, 1995.

Hutchinson, Col, *Cats' Tales: Geelong Football Club, 1897–1983*, Geelong Advertiser, Geelong, 1984.

Hutchinson, Col (ed.), *1995 AFL Media Guide*, AFL Communications Dept., Melbourne.

Hutchinson, Garrie, *Australian Rules Football: The Watchers Guide*, William Heinemann Australia, Melbourne, 1988.

Hutchinson, Garrie and Rick Lang, John Ross, eds, *Roar of the Lions: Fitzroy Remembered*, Lothian, Melbourne, 1997.

Hutchinson, Garrie, *From the Outer: Watching Football in the 80s*, McPhee Gribble, Fitzroy, 1984.

Hutchinson, Garrie, *The Great Australian Book of Football Stories*, Currey O'Neil, Melbourne, 1983, repr. as *Great Australian Football Stories*, Viking, Melbourne, 1989.

Johnston, Wayne, with Ron Reed, *The Dominator*, Caribou Publications, Melbourne, 1991.

Lack, John, Chris McConville, Michael Small and Damien Wright, *Unleashed: A History of the Footscray Football Club*, Aus-Sport Enterprises, Melbourne, 1996.

Laurence, L., *History of South Melbourne Football Club*, South Melbourne Football Club, Melbourne 1963.

Linnell, Garry, *Football Ltd, The Inside Story of the AFL*, Ironbark, Sydney, 1993.

Lockett, Tony with Ken Piesse, *Plugger*, Sun Books, Melbourne, 1992.

Lovett, Michael, ed., *AFL '97: The Official Guide to Australia's Greatest Game*, Mandarin, Melbourne, 1997.

Mattkews, Leigh with Mike Sheahan, *Lethal*, Caribou Publications, 1986.

McHale, J. A. E. Chadwick and E. C. H. Taylor, *The Australian Game of Football*, C. C. Hartley & Co., Melbourne, 1931.

Main, Jim and Ken Piesse, *The A to Z of Football*, Wedneil Publications, Melbourne, 1982.

Main, Jim, ed., 1988 *Football Year: The Year in Review*, Century Magazines, Melbourne, 1988.

Main, Jim and Darren Christison, eds, 1989 *Football: The Year in Review*, Century Magazines, Melbourne, 1989.

Main, Jim and Russell Holmesby, *The Encyclopedia of League Footballers*, Wilkinson Books, Melbourne, 1992, rev. edn., 1994.

Mancini, A. and G. M. Hibbins, eds, *Running with the Ball: Football's Foster Father*, Lynedoch Publications, Melbourne, 1987.

Maplestone, Michael, *Flying Higher: The History of the Essendon Football Club 1872–1994*, Essendon Football Club, Melbourne, 1994.

Matthews, Leigh with Mike Sheahan, *Lethal*, Caribou Publications, 1986.

Nicholls, John, with Ian McDonald, *Big Nick*, Garry Sparke & Associates, Hawthorn, 1977.

Palmer, Scott and Greg Hobbs, *100 Great Marks*, Sun Books, Melbourne, 1974.

Pascoe, Robert, *The Winter Game: The Complete History of Australian Football*, Text Publishing, Melbourne, 1995.

Piesse, Ken, *The Complete Guide to Australian Football*, Pan Macmillan, Chippendale NSW 1993.

Piesse, Ken, *Ablett: The Gary Ablett Story*, Wilkinson Books, Melbourne, 1994.

Porter, Ashley, *Something To Crow About: A Celebration of the First 100 Games*, HarperCollins, Sydney, 1995.

Powers, John, *The Coach: A Season with Ron Barassi*, Thomas Nelson, West Melbourne, 1978.

Roberts, Michael, *A Century of the Best: The Stories of Collingwood's Favourite Sons*, Collingwood Football Club, Melbourne 1991.

Rodgers, Stephen, *Every Game Ever Played: VFL/AFL Results 1897–1989*, Viking O'Neil, Melbourne, 1983, rev. edn, 1990, 1992, 1994.

Rodgers, Stephen, *100 Years of AFL Players 1897–1996*, three volumes, self-published, Melbourne, 1995.

Ross, John and Hutchinson, Garrie, eds, *100 Years of Australian Football*, Viking, Ringwood, Vic., 1996.

Sandercock, Leonie and Ian Turner, *Up Where, Cazaly? The Great Australian Game*, Granada, London, 1981.

Stephens, Russell H. T., *The Road to Kardinia: the story of the Geelong Football Club*, Playright, Sydney, 1997.

Stremski, Richard, *Kill for Collingwood*, Allen & Unwin, Sydney, 1986.

Sutherland, Mike, Rod Nicholson and Stewart Murrihy, *The First One Hundred Seasons: Fitzroy Football Club, 1883–1983*, Fitzroy Football Club, Melbourne, 1983.

Taylor, E. C. H. *100 Years of Football: The Story of the Melbourne Football Club*, Melbourne Football Club, Melbourne, 1958.

Taylor, Kevin, *Footystats 1993: Australian Football League Statistics, 1897–1992*, Fast Books, Sydney, 1992 (and 1993, 1994, 1995, 1996, 1997 updates).

Taylor, Kevin, *The Sydney Swans, The Complete History 1874–1986*, Allen and Unwin, Sydney, 1987.

Victorian Football League, *League Football in Victoria*, VFL, Melbourne, 1972–1988.

Weightman, Dale with Bruce Eva, *Saving Our Skins, and Other Tiger Tales*, Floradale Productions, Kilmore, 1991.

Whimpress, Bernard, *The South Australian Football Story*, SANFL, West Lakes SA, 1983.

Williams, Greg, *Diesel The Greg Williams Story*, Ironbark, 1995.

PICTURE CREDITS

Special thanks to the following: title page painting by Ginger Riley. *Wul gori-yi-mar – football for all Aboriginal people,* 1996, Australian Football League collection by permission of Ginger Riley and by courtesy of Alcaston Gallery; at Sporting Pix: Kerryn Feder, Tony Feder, Hamish Blair, John Daniels, Sean Garnsworthy, Greg Ford, Stuart Milligan; at the *Age* Pictorial Library: Katherine Ryan, Paul Rovere; at the Australian Gallery of Sport: Gregor McCaskie; at the MCC Museum Kristin Thornton and Graeme Atkinson; and to Gregor McCaskie, Barbara Cullen and the Football Heritage Group.

Adelaide: *Adelaide Advertiser,* Football Plus, Ashley Porter, John Sherwell, Sport The Library, Sporting Pix, *Sunday Mail,* Mark Thomson.
Brisbane: Brisbane Lions, Peter Blucher, Just Photography – Brisbane, Sporting Pix.
Carlton: The *Age,* Australian Gallery of Sport, Carlton Football Club, Stephen Gough, Garrie Hutchinson, Lisa King, Michael Leunig, Michael Roberts, Grant Shallard, Sporting Pix, Times on Sunday.
Collingwood: Collingwood Football Club, Michael Roberts, Sporting Pix.
Essendon: Essendon Football Club, Essendon Football Club Hall of Fame – Barbara Cullen, Michael Maplestone – *Flying Higher,* Bruce Postle, Sporting Pix.
Fitzroy: Graeme Atkinson, Australian Gallery of Sport, Brisbane Lions, David Gale, Bette Hughson, Garrie Hutchinson, Rick Lang, Pauline Paton, Dave Scott and the Rose Hotel, Kevin Wright.
Footscray: Glenn Allen - Big Sky Photographics, Darren Arthur, John Lack et al. – *Unleashed,* Scharlaine Cairns, Sporting Pix, Ray Stevens, Western Bulldogs.
Fremantle: Bob Gordon, Sporting Pix.
Geelong: Geelong Football Club, Col Hutchinson, Private Collection, Russell H. T. Stephens – *The Road to Kardinia,* Sporting Pix.
Hawthorn: City of Boroondara Library, Peter Habey, Hawthorn Football Club, Bruce Postle, Sporting Pix.
Melbourne: The *Age,* Kerri Cuman, Lynda Carroll, Nicole Lovelock, Melbourne Football Club, Sporting Pix.
North Melbourne: Gerard Dowling, W.E.G., North Melbourne Football Club, Bruce Postle, Sporting Pix.
Richmond: The *Age,* David Austin, Private Collection, Richmond Football Club.
South Melbourne/Sydney: Sporting Pix, Sydney Football Club, Kevin Taylor.
St Kilda: Russell Holmesby, Sporting Pix, St Kilda Football Club.
University: David Allen, Australian Gallery of Sport, Private Collection.
West Coast: Les Everett, Bob Gordon, Sporting Pix.

'God' soaring above the Demons – Bruce Postle's classic image of Gary Ablett.

AUTOGRAPHS